D1577506

C

NO END
SAVE VICTORY

NO END
SAVE VICTORY

NEW SECOND WORLD WAR WRITING BY
Antony Beevor, John Keegan,
Stephen Ambrose, Alistair Horne,
Victor Davis Hanson and many more

EDITED BY
Robert Cowley

CASSELL&CO

Cassell & Co
The Orion Publishing Group
Wellington House
125 Strand
London WC2R 0BB

First published in the UK in 2002

All articles were previously published in *MHQ: The Quarterly Journal of Military History*.
The following essays are excerpts from books and are reprinted by permission of the
publishers: 'Patrolling Guadalcanal' from William H. Whyte, *A Time of War*, Fordham
University Press. 'The Airborne's Watery Triumphs' from T. Michael Booth and Duncan
Spencer, *Paratrooper, The Life of Gen James M. Gavin*, Simon & Schuster. 'Rommel's Last
Battle' from David Fraser, *Knight's Cross: A Life of Field Marshall Erwin Rommel*,
HarperCollins Publishers, Inc. 'Berlin' from John Keegan, *The Second World War*, Viking
Penguin. All other articles are reprinted by permission of the authors.

A catalogue record for this book is available from the British Library

ISBN 0-304-36109-7

All maps for this anthology were prepared by MapQuest.com
Book design by Deborah Kerner

Printed and bound in Great Britain by MPG Books Ltd, Bodmin, Cornwall

This nation has placed its destiny in the hands,
heads, and hearts of its millions
of free men and women, and its faith
in freedom under the guidance of God.
Freedom means the supremacy
of human rights everywhere.
Our support goes to those who struggle
to gain those rights and keep them.
Our strength is in our unity of purpose.

To that high concept there can be no end save victory.

†

- FRANKLIN D. ROOSEVELT,

The Four Freedoms Speech, The State of the Union
6 January 1941

CONTENTS

LIST OF MAPS

INTRODUCTION

SWEEPING GENERALIZATIONS ABOUT WORLD WAR II HAVE BE-
come largely superfluous. Most of what needs to be said has been said. The
event has long since been big-pictured to death. Occasionally a magisterial
work like Gerhard L. Weinberg's *A World of Arms* will come along to overwhelm us with insight; but we will probably have to wait for the settling of
more historical dust, and a generation or so, before we can expect a truly startling reevaluation, and one in keeping with events still to unfold. The consequences of World War II are that far-reaching.

Generalizations aside, the particulars of those 2,194 days, from September 1,
1939, to September 2, 1945, remain as appalling and fascinating as ever, and as
open to fresh examination, dispute, and reinterpretation. Some major
episodes, unbelievably, have been passed over or have only come to light recently. This is especially true of the Eastern Front, where vast battles, whose
outcomes defied the political necessities of the time, were simply forgotten
and remained buried in the Soviet archives. And how little has been written
about the war in the Pacific and Asia as the Japanese and the Chinese experienced it. Even American campaigns like our twenty-month slog through Italy
or the invasion of southern France in the summer of 1944 have not received
their due, perhaps because they were hardly triumphal passages of arms.

A thorough scrutiny of those particulars has always been a major concern
of *MHQ: The Quarterly Journal of Military History,* both in my decade-long
tenure as the magazine's founding editor and the current one of Rod Paschall,
who is also a distinguished soldier. Yet another account of a familiar battle or
campaign is all very well, but seeing it in a different perspective is far more
rewarding. In this anthology, you will find that those different perspectives
are not just plentiful but unexpected and, in cases, contrary to the prevailing
historical fashion. You may not agree with the novelist Caleb Carr (who is also
an able historian) that Dwight D. Eisenhower's "broadfront strategy" played
into the hands of the Germans and prolonged the war in Europe by half a
year—or with those writers in the final section of the book who feel that we
had no choice but to use the atomic bomb. As do I, for that matter.

You'll come on insights in this anthology that you are not likely to find elsewhere. Robert A. Doughty, who is head of the history department at West Point, describes how close the French came to containing the Germans at Sedan in May 1940—and how General Heinz Guderian's breakthrough at the Meuse River depended on a handful of company-sized actions. Bruce I. Gudmundsson tells a similarly unexpected story: the bravery with which large parts of the French army, including the Maginot Line garrisons, fought *after* Dunkirk. Eliot A. Cohen points out that if Pearl Harbor was a disaster for us, it was also a missed opportunity for the Japanese, who lost a chance to alter the balance in the Pacific not just for months but for years. Antony Beevor's examination of the German disaster at Stalingrad, based on newly discovered material, reveals suffering more terrible than anyone imagined. But at the same time that Marshal Georgy Zhukov was springing his famous Uranus trap on Stalingrad, a twin operation—Mars—was turning into a disaster in which the Soviets suffered 500,000 casualties. For the first time, a Western historian, David M. Glantz, reconstructs a battle that simply disappeared from the historical radar screen. Edward J. Drea reports a story that has been mostly unknown—how American intercepts of Japanese codes revealed a buildup on Kyushu, where the invasion of the home islands would have taken place, that made many of our military leaders question its chances of success. The dropping of the two atomic bombs has to be seen against this background.

History, as the old saw goes, is written by the victors, but *MHQ* has constantly tried to present the story of World War II as experienced by the other side. This is relatively easy for the German role in the war, especially with the opening of military archives formerly sequestered behind the Iron Curtain in the German Democratic Republic. A notable example is Sir David Fraser's splendid account of Field Marshal Erwin Rommel's brilliant defense of Normandy, even though he was convinced the war was lost. If he had not sustained a near-mortal wound, would he have been able to go through with his scheme to open his lines to a quick Allied thrust to Berlin before the Russians got there?

But the Japanese story is far more difficult to put together and assess, in some measure because of the reluctance of the Japanese themselves to confront the history, not always noble, of a losing war. Language, of course, is another problem, and it goes far to explain why the preponderance of works on the Pacific War have been told exclusively from the Allied side.

But over the years *MHQ* has been fortunate to publish articles that are, because of their emphasis on the Japanese experience, new and truly valuable contributions to military history. I would cite Theodore F. Cook Jr.'s account, unique when it appeared, of what happened in Tokyo when the government announced a declaration of war on the United States and Great Britain. (Pearl Harbor caught the average Japanese as much by surprise as it did Americans.) Joseph H. Alexander's "The Turning Points of Tarawa" views a struggle that was not initially hopeless for the island's defenders. Its outcome, Alexander points out, might easily have gone in their favor, had it not been for a single unlucky shellburst. And no document that has appeared in the magazine is more extraordinary than the memoirs of a former kamikaze pilot, Kanji Suzuki—a pilot who, through no fault or intention of his own, survived a suicide attack on an American ship.

Such firsthand accounts have always been a memorable feature of *MHQ*, and you will find them liberally scattered throughout this volume. Among my favorites are Alvin Kernan's description of how he stayed alive amid the fires and explosions of the sinking carrier *Hornet,* and David Balme's memoir of how, as a junior British naval officer, he discovered a naval Enigma code device on a captured German U-boat—a find that would go far to giving the Allies an advantage in the struggle for the North Atlantic. Then there are the twenty-six diary entries that a B-17 tail gunner named John Gabay made after each bombing mission over Europe. His matter-of-fact tone gives the terrifying sights that he records an unrelenting vividness.

Perhaps it is the subject matter they deal with, but military historians tend to be adept storytellers. You'll find some of the best here, people like Caleb Carr, Anthony Bailey, William Manchester, Antony Beevor, Carlo D'Este, Alistair Horne, Victor Davis Hanson, Stephen E. Ambrose, and John Keegan— to name just a few. *MHQ* has always been a writers' magazine. And what marvelous stories you'll find here, whether it is Manchester's description of the Battle of Britain, Thaddeus Holt's sad, brave tale of the real (but shunned) hero of Bataan, Edward P. King, Ambrose's minute-by-minute account of the taking of the Remagen Bridge, or George Feifer's resurrection of the crazy movie project that consumed the Nazi propaganda minister, Joseph Goebbels, as the Third Reich collapsed.

The last words on World War II will never be written. But in the meantime, here are some memorable ones.

I

THE GERMAN
BREAKOUT

1939–1941

POLAND 1939

CALEB CARR

Hitler's invasion of Poland on September 1, 1939, without a formal declaration of war, signaled the beginning of World War II in Europe. But his Polish campaign was, in a sense, a separate war, a dress rehearsal for the real one in 1940. It was the war Hitler won. Great Britain and France did come in two days later, but they could do little more than stand by while Hitler's armies—and then Stalin's—consumed Poland. That three-week war is chiefly remembered now (if it is remembered at all) as a laboratory for a new kind of mechanized warfare: blitzkrieg. The methods honed in Poland would be those used in France, Russia, and North Africa. But what goes largely unsaid—and it is a point that Caleb Carr emphasizes here—is how hard and well the Poles fought, with many fewer troops than the invaders, inferior equipment, and a strategic situation that was hopeless from day one, and that only became worse when the Soviet Union struck from the rear. As they learned to their sorrow, and it was a lesson repeated endlessly for both sides those next years: courage was not enough.

Caleb Carr is best known for his novels about crime in the New York City of the 1890s, *The Alienist*, *The Angel of Darkness,* and *Killing Time* (which appeared in *Time,* in Dickens-like installments). But as the readers of *MHQ: The Quarterly Journal of Military History* have long recognized, he is also a notable military historian.

IN THE LAST DAYS OF AUGUST 1939, THE GERMAN SEVENTH Armored Reconnaissance Regiment was moving east, along with the rest of the Wehrmacht. "Officially," recalled one officer in the Seventh A.R., "we were to take part in 'grand maneuvers under combat conditions.' Although live ammunition was being carried, we were issued only blanks. . . . Local people greeted us everywhere with flowers and drinks. 'Are you going to Poland?' we were asked. 'Of course not,' we replied. 'We're going on maneuvers.'"

On August 26, the Seventh A.R. reached the Polish border with Czechoslovakia, a nation recently occupied by German forces and now offering an excellent launching point for an attack into Poland. "Suddenly," the same officer went on, "the blank cartridges were exchanged for live ammunition. Now there was no longer any doubt: We were going to invade."

The attack was launched on September 1. The German navy shelled the contested port city of Danzig (Gdansk) in the north while the German army embarked on a huge pincer movement from north to south, aimed at the Polish capital, Warsaw. Although Polish resistance at the outset was disorganized—or nonexistent—the Germans soon found themselves fighting hard. Another German veteran wrote, "We admired our opponents for their national pride and commitment. They demanded our respect."

This is not the impression of the Polish campaign that has been generally fostered in the years since 1939. The German army's humiliation of France in 1940 and its early successes against the Soviet Union so stunned the world that the brief war the Wehrmacht waged against Poland is often seen as a mere dress rehearsal for those more momentous events. In hindsight, it seems impossible that little Poland, with its obsolete army and antiquated military tradition, could have stood even a remote chance against the world's most advanced military juggernaut. From this point of view, it is remarkable not that Germany defeated her eastern neighbor but that the campaign took as long as it did: seventeen days to decide the issue in the field, twenty-seven days to force the capitulation of Warsaw.

This assessment of the Polish campaign, while common, does little justice to either antagonist. In both the quality of their fighting and their occasional displays of tactical (if not strategic) ability, the Poles proved themselves a fighting force of far greater merit than, say, the French army that was sent reeling eight months later. And the German army in 1939 had not yet been transformed into the amazing war machine it would become in later years. That metamorphosis would actually begin during the heat of the Polish campaign, and constitutes a testament to the skill and innovative acumen of the German officer corps.

Perhaps the most erroneous impression created by many commentators (including Nazi propagandists during the war) concerning events in 1939 is that Germany's military leaders were eager to involve themselves in a war with Poland. To most German generals, such a conflict—Hitler's statements notwithstanding—meant war with Poland's allies: England and France. Vir-

tually no senior German officer faced that prospect with any certainty of ultimate success. The führer's ambitions were viewed with cultivated skepticism.

This attitude was not purely military in origin. During the previous year the
German army had seen its three top officers removed by Nazi intrigues. The
commander of the combined forces, General Werner von Blomberg, had been
replaced after his wife was falsely accused of once having been a prostitute. General Ludwig Beck, chief of the general staff, was removed after repeatedly voicing his belief that Hitler was taking Germany down a road toward world war
and ruin. Most ludicrous of all, the commander in chief of the army, Colonel
General Werner Freiherr von Fritsch, was falsely accused of homosexual activities by the SS. Tried and exonerated, Fritsch was nonetheless demoted. (He volunteered for hazardous duty in Poland soon afterward and was quickly killed.)

In the wake of this stunning attempt by Hitler to gain tighter control over
the regular army (always a hotbed of anti-Nazi sentiment), sixteen more German generals left the army and forty-four were given new assignments. In
nearly every case, these reassignments were made on the basis of political
sympathies. For example, General Beck's deputy chief of the general staff,
General Erich von Manstein—the German army's most gifted strategic planner but a man with little use for the Nazi party—was transferred to a divisional command.

Hitler apparently believed he could bring the army under his control
through such tactics, but he was soon proved wrong. For while the new commander in chief, General Walther von Brauchitsch, was slow to press his complaints against Nazi policies, he did eventually begin to press them; and the
new chief of the general staff, General Franz Halder, proved troublesome to
Hitler from the beginning. Halder's bristly hair and mustache, pince-nez, and
perpetual frown seemed to accentuate the contempt he felt for Germany's new
leaders—contempt that, by the end of the Second World War, would evolve
into open opposition and imprisonment at Dachau.

In this atmosphere of distance and disinterest at best, and distrust and hostility at worst, the German army received orders in the spring of 1939 to begin preparing operational plans for "Case White"—war with Poland. General
Halder assumed that to gain concessions from Poland, Hitler once again intended to use the army as an instrument of blackmail. This had been the
führer's tactic in dealing with the nations of Europe to date, and it had succeeded. Determined to undo the terms of the 1919 Treaty of Versailles, Hitler
had already reoccupied the Rhineland, achieved Anschluss with Austria,
taken the Sudetenland, and occupied the rest of Czechoslovakia—all without
firing a shot.

But Poland's attitude seemed to indicate a less propitious outcome to Hitler's latest round of brinkmanship. Following the First World War, Poland had been remade in a form that would have pleased her ancient warrior kings: Included within her borders were not only traditionally Polish territories but also healthy slices of German, Ukrainian, Russian, and Lithuanian lands. Hardest for the Germans to accept had been the creation of the "Polish Corridor," a wide swath of territory that ran north from Poland, severed East Prussia from the rest of Germany, and made an "international city" out of the port of Danzig. This region was largely inhabited by Germans, who after 1919 became Polish subjects. A good number of these people were military families, and more than a few German army leaders looked forward to the day when this humiliation would be reversed.

Nevertheless, nearly every senior German officer felt that if such reversal required war, Germany would have to wait to fight it. From its prescribed post-Versailles size of 100,000 men, the German army had recently expanded to well over a million, and would eventually grow to 4 million; but the expansion had come too fast, and the new soldiers lacked thorough training. The appearance of organized and armed SS military units—the force that would become the Waffen SS—was also of deep concern to Germany's regular army officers. How would these new soldiers, so thoroughly indoctrinated with Nazi dogma, so ferociously loyal to the party elite—and most important, so openly scornful of the regular army—behave in the field?

Even more crucial was the question of incorporating Germany's new military arms—the Luftwaffe and the panzer (armored) divisions—into the operations of the German army as a whole. In Germany as elsewhere, the debate over mobile armored warfare had raged ever since British tanks had made their presence felt in World War I. In England, Captain Basil Liddell Hart and Major J. F. C. Fuller had spent the decade of the twenties calling loudly but in vain for a new kind of army, in which masses of tanks would shatter linear fronts, race to the enemy's rear, and disrupt military and political control. It was warfare wholly unlike what had been the rule from 1914 to 1918. Fast and fluid, limiting destruction through mobility and seeking decision rather than devastation, mobile armored warfare represented a quantum leap in military thinking.

The idea was at variance with Britain's military tradition, as well as with that of the other victorious Allied powers, and was slow to take root. But in Germany it found fertile soil, for it must be remembered that the protracted attrition that was World War I was an anomaly in German (and especially Prussian) military history. Because of her geographic position—in a word, surrounded—Prussia's military goal since the days of Frederick the Great had consistently been quick, decisive campaigns that would allow her forces to turn speedily from one enemy to the next. Multiple-front wars were anathema to Prussian soldiers; protracted wars equally so.

The philosophy of mobility and quick decisions developed steadily in eighteenth- and nineteenth-century Prussia and was given its fullest embodiment by Helmuth von Moltke during his stunningly swift victories over Austria in 1866 and France in 1870–71. Thus the new armored tactics did not represent a departure from the German emphasis on quick decisions and mobility; on the contrary, they simply sped those processes up, to a point where—to older, more conservative minds—they were scarcely recognizable. But the link between blitzkrieg and Prussian campaigns of the past was real and evident, even if senior commanders could not see it.

Of course, the partisan attitude of many armored and air enthusiasts during the interwar years was not altogether helpful in easing the German army's old school into the new era of blitzkrieg. This was particularly true of the father of Germany's panzer tactics and divisions, General Heinz Guderian. Building on the theories of Fuller and Liddell Hart, Guderian envisaged a new style of warfare in which tanks were supported by motorized infantry, mobile artillery, and air power—an integrated force that could achieve decisive results at the *strategic* as well as the tactical level. Whole nations, he believed, could be brought to capitulation within a matter of days through the use of such a force.

Guderian was not a member of the Prussian military aristocracy. He was plainspoken to the point of bluntness—even, on occasion, rudeness—and his opinions of junior and senior officers alike were ill-shrouded. For example, General Beck, the much-admired chief of the general staff who had been dismissed by Hitler, had been to Guderian "a procrastinator," "a paralyzing element wherever he appeared," "a disciple of Moltke . . . [with] no understanding of modern technical matters." Recalled another armored commander, General Ritter von Thoma, following the Second World War, "It was commonly said in the German army that Guderian was always seeing red, and was too inclined to charge like a bull."

The fact that Adolf Hitler was one of Guderian's earliest converts to mobile-armored tactics did not help to win the panzer leaders' friends in the army high command. Attending one of Guderian's first panzer maneuvers, Hitler stated emphatically, "That's what I need. That's what I want to have." The issue was as yet a bit more complicated than that, and the development of first-class German tanks took much longer than Guderian would have liked. But the führer's support was both of immense value to the development of armor and an irritant to many of Guderian's superiors.

Such was the state of the senior German officer corps that was assigned, in April 1939, the task of preparing for the invasion of Poland: reluctant, politically disdainful (and because of that, distanced from the overwhelming majority of the German people), and finally divided on the future development of weapons and tactics. Fortunately for the Germans, the actual job of planning Case White fell to a small group of officers whose insight allowed them to make use of all the resources and talented men at their disposal—whether "old school" or new—in preparing a plan that was at once quintessentially Prussian and daringly advanced.

Overall responsibility for design and coordination of the attack was left, as was customary, to the commander in chief of the army, General Brauchitsch, and to the director of operations of the general staff, General Halder. Their design of the assault could well have come out of the pages of nineteenth-century Prussian history. Accepting the risks involved in stripping their western border of trained combat troops, Brauchitsch and Halder concentrated forty-two divisions into two army groups along the lengthy border around Poland and Slovakia to Pomerania. Army Group North was to cut the Polish Corridor and then advance southeast; Army Group South would engage the main Polish forces—hopefully before they could retreat behind the Vistula River—and then move to link up with Army Group North. This massive pincer thrust from north to south was centered on Warsaw. To achieve it, the Germans accepted the further risk of leaving their own center exposed to possible counterattack.

In the Moltke tradition, General Halder did not exclude field commanders and their staffs from contributing to Case White. Suggestions for the actual deployment and composition of armies were accepted (some willingly, others less so) from army group, army, and corps headquarters.

Command of Army Group South was given to General Gerd von Rundstedt, one of Germany's best-loved soldiers. Already in his mid-sixties, Rundstedt was a true aristocrat but even in appearance had a penchant for idiosyncrasy. In the words of his chief of operations, General Günther von Blumentritt, he "did not wear a general's or a field marshal's uniform, but preferred the simple jacket of the commander of an infantry regiment, with a marshal's shoulder badges and the regimental number 18. It often happened that young officers thus mistook him for a colonel and did not know that it was the field marshal who was standing before them, which Runstedt always accepted good-humoredly." Rundstedt was primarily interested in the movement of troops in actual battle. Peacetime staff planning and details held little fascination for him. Such an attitude placed immense responsibility on both his chief of staff and his chief of operations.

These posts had been secured by two of the most intellectually gifted officers in the Wehrmacht. Rundstedt's chief of staff was Erich von Manstein. The son of a Prussian artillery general, Manstein had been adopted in his infancy by his aunt and uncle—the latter a Prussian infantry general of noble lineage. Thus by blood and upbringing, Manstein was steeped in the Prussian military code. Behind his thin, penetrating eyes and beaklike nose worked a prodigious mind, one that would later spawn the remarkable German plan for the invasion of France and contribute significantly to Germany's early successes in Russia.

Manstein had many talents that made these successes possible, but one stood out above the rest: an unmatched capacity to fuse traditional Prussian strategy with the new armored tactics. He had broken step with many of his fellow military aristocrats by recognizing that General Guderian's new panzer divisions must not be slowed or hampered by the actions of infantry and artillery. (In fact, one of Manstein's most significant interwar achievements had been the development of mobile and self-propelled support artillery, which freed more tanks for the job of penetration and exploitation.) Faced with the task of planning the movements of Army Group South in the Polish campaign, Manstein quickly decided to concentrate most of the available armor in one of the group's three armies—the Tenth, under General Walther von Reichenau—in order to achieve a decisive breakthrough and the earliest possible encirclement of Polish forces west of the Vistula. The other two armies—the Fourteenth on the right flank, commanded by General Wilhelm List; and the Eighth, forming the group's left wing and commanded by General Johannes Blaskowitz—would play roles in this hoped-for envelopment, but the spearhead assignment went to Reichenau's panzers.

In this effort to blend the Prussian strategy of envelopment with modern armored tactics, Manstein was assisted by Army Group South's chief of operations, Colonel Günther von Blumentritt. The two men shared the same intellectual style, and during the months before the invasion they put in many extra hours attending to every detail of the operation. Manstein later recalled: "As often as not, the things that attract us to another person are quite trivial, and what always delighted me about Blumentritt was his fanatical attachment to the telephone. The speed at which he worked was in any case incredibly high, but whenever he had a receiver in his hand he could deal with whole avalanches of queries, always with the same imperturbable good humor."

Army Group North was given to General Fedor von Bock, a forceful and sometimes difficult commander, and comprised the Third and Fourth armies.

The Third Army troops were transported to their launching area in East Prussia by sea, under the guise of participating in a huge celebration of the German victory over the Russians at Tannenberg in August 1914. The Fourth Army, under General Günther von Kluge, was positioned in east Pomerania, opposite the Corridor.

General Guderian's Nineteenth Panzer Corps—the first unit that came close to embodying the panzer leader's ideas concerning armored operations—was placed under von Kluge. There was initially some resistance to the idea of including such a heavy armored force in the Fourth Army's operations, but Guderian's careful cultivation of Hitler soon had its desired effect, and the führer personally intervened to secure Guderian's role as the spearhead of the forces that would cut the Polish Corridor.

By August 20, the German army was ready. Yet despite the immense effort they had devoted to marshaling their forces, the German generals remained unenthusiastic. Throughout the summer, Chief of Staff Halder had secretly contacted the governments of both France and Great Britain, trying to relay the message that the army high command was powerless to stop Nazi designs because of Hitler's immense popularity with the German people. Only firm commitment on the part of the Western Allies, Halder said, could take the wind out of Hitler's sails. Halder's urgings fell on deaf ears.

On August 22, Hitler called his senior commanders to Obersalzberg for a "conference," which, as was often the case, degenerated into a long diatribe by the führer. The tone was set by Hermann Göring, who arrived wearing a comical jerkin, shorts, and long silk socks. "Up till now," Manstein later wrote, "I had assumed that we were here for a serious purpose, but Göring appeared to have taken it for a masked ball. . . . I could not resist whispering to my neighbor, General von Salmuth: 'I suppose the Fat Boy's here as a strong-arm man?'"

Informing the generals of secret negotiations with the Soviets that had produced a nonaggression pact (but not of the treaty's secret clause providing for the partition of Poland), Hitler spoke about his determination to redress by force the last remaining German grievance against the Versailles peace: the dismemberment of East Prussia and the subjugation of millions of Germans to Polish rule as well as, according to propaganda chief Joseph Goebbels, Polish abuse of them. Hitler claimed to have made proposals in good faith to the Polish government—all of them rejected. War with Poland was now a certainty. Hitler announced that he would probably order the attack for August 26:

> The destruction of Poland has priority. . . . I shall provide a propaganda reason for starting the war—never mind whether it is plausible or not. The victor

will not be asked afterward whether or not he told the truth. In starting and waging war it is not right that matters but victory. Close your hearts to pity! Act brutally!

The generals listened in depressed silence. One fell asleep.

✦

THE PREPARATIONS of the Polish army during this time of very real crisis revealed that while Polish commanders took the danger of invasion seriously, they lacked the skill and the character to meet the challenge. The Poles had a peacetime army of some twenty-three infantry divisions (which would grow to thirty on the eve of the invasion) and eleven cavalry brigades, plus two armored brigades; the latter were equipped with only small numbers of up-to-date tanks and many obsolete models. Still, the overall quality of this army was not to be dismissed: As Blumentritt wrote after the war, "The Polish officer corps was competent and courageous, and was highly regarded by the Wehrmacht."

But it was the cavalry that embodied the most outstanding features of Poland's military style, both good and bad. For hundreds of years, Polish horsemen had been among the world's finest, famous for their daring shock tactics and particularly for their terrifying night attacks. Napoleon had incorporated Polish lancers as an elite unit of his own Grande Armée. Yet pride in their success had made many of Poland's senior officers complacent. For example, the commander in chief of the Polish army, Marshal Edward Rydz-Smigly, had had his portrait painted against a background of charging Polish cavalry while his opposite numbers to the west were wrangling with the problems of mobile armored warfare.

Excessive pride also marred the Polish army's preparations for war with Germany. Geographically, Poland was in an almost hopeless situation. By seizing Czechoslovakia, Hitler had given his army three possible avenues of assault into Polish territory. The Poles' only real hope was to pull their defenses in from the very start—perhaps even as far back as the barrier of the Vistula—and fight a defensive war while waiting for France and England to force the Germans to disengage and attend to their western border.

From the start, however, such ideas were rejected by the Polish high command—in fact, they were rarely put forth for fear of the reception they would get. Some of Poland's most valuable industrial regions lay to the west of the Vistula, and the Corridor had become a symbol of the reborn and resurgent Poland. Few generals dared suggest that these regions be abandoned before even an attempt was made to defend them.

One who did have the courage to raise the issue was a General Kutzreba, director of the Polish Military Academy and commander of the Poznań army during the battle for Poland. While even Kutzreba's ideas were probably not radical enough to have prevented eventual disaster, his suggestion that the Polish army abandon not only the Corridor but the western section of the province of Poznań (bordering on Germany) might have given the Poles a better chance of concentrating their forces and successfully holding out until the pressure was relieved by their allies.

Instead, the Polish army spread its forces out along the entire border with Germany, from the Carpathian Mountains in the south, up past the Silesian border, on into the Corridor, and then east to the frontiers of East Prussia. Some seven frontline armies were formed out of the slender Polish resources in an attempt to hold the line everywhere. It was a prescription for disaster. Yet apparently not content with this gross error in judgment, the Polish high command next failed to pursue a rigorous program of fast mobilization, and spent their more imaginative moments planning for an eventual counterattack into Germany.

As he had said he would, Hitler ordered the German army to attack on August 26, and on the 25th German troops began to move toward the Polish frontier. But within hours an emergency message arrived at the headquarters of both army groups: The attack was canceled, and the troops were to be pulled back. Whether Hitler still had one or two eleventh-hour diplomatic tricks to try or simply balked when the moment of decision came is unclear— but despite the immensely difficult job of recalling five advancing armies, the German commanders were not displeased. As even Guderian said, "We did not go lightheartedly to war and there was not one general who would not have advocated peace." The mood at Army Group South headquarters was positively jubilant. Blumentritt recalled that "Rundstedt had some bottles of Tokay fetched from the town of Neisse to celebrate . . . this happy release."

The celebration was short-lived. On August 31, a terse new order was received by both army groups: "D = 1.9; H = 0445." And at 4:45 on the morning of September 1, 1939, the Wehrmacht swarmed over the borders of Poland.

✦

IN MOST AREAS, initial resistance was slight or nonexistent, owing to the slow Polish mobilization and to the fact that the Luftwaffe quickly destroyed Poland's air units. Whether the Polish planes were destroyed on the ground or managed at least to get into the air has been debated. The fact remains that within days the Germans had mastery of the skies. The German pilots, most

tasting combat for the first time, went on to smash bridges and rail lines leading to the fronts. General List's Fourteenth Army in the south met the stiffest
Polish resistance in the first days, but soon the Poles had collected their wits
and were fighting bravely everywhere.

While many historical accounts of the campaign portray the participation
of the Polish cavalry brigades as ludicrous, the German soldiers did not find it
so. Blumentritt recalled, "In the course of the campaign [the Polish cavalry]
gave several German divisions something serious to think about and distinguished itself by its great bravery." The horsemen "appeared like phantom
hosts to surprise us in the night."

The Germans were also plagued by the greenness of their own troops. Many
units were stunned or broken by the steadily stiffening Polish resistance and
were pulled together only by the determination and loyalty of their officers. As
a result of the bravery shown by all ranks of the officer corps, German casualties during the campaign were inordinately weighted toward that group.

Army Group North quickly discovered just how unprepared for war many
German soldiers were. Guderian remembered that when his panzers crossed
into the Corridor, the "Polish antitank gunners scored many direct hits."
Only by taking charge himself at the front was he able to restore order. His account of the first day's action went on revealingly:

> Shortly after midnight the 2nd (Motorized) Division informed me that they
> were being compelled to withdraw by Polish cavalry. I was speechless for a mo-
> ment; when I regained the use of my voice I asked the divisional commander if
> he had ever heard of Pomeranian grenadiers being broken by hostile cavalry. He
> replied that he had not and now assured me that he could hold his positions.

By the second day of the campaign, the Nineteenth Panzer Corps had
crossed its first obstacle, the Brahe River inside the Corridor, and its lead units
had reached the Vistula. Guderian's tireless peacetime promulgation of mobile armored warfare was beginning to bear fruit in the field.

Then, on September 3, occurred perhaps the most famous incident of the
entire Polish campaign. As Guderian's tanks—mostly fast training rigs armed
only with light artillery and machine guns, but including some heavier models—raced to close the Corridor, the renowned Polish Pomorska Cavalry
Brigade appeared west of the town of Graudenz. The Polish horsemen, Guderian recalled, "in ignorance of the nature of our tanks . . . charged them
with swords and lances." Polish losses were predictably heavy—"tremendous," in Guderian's estimation—yet the Germans did not sneer at the attack.

Rather, it was taken as further evidence of the enemy's immense courage and determination.

On September 4, the Polish Corridor was closed when Guderian's forward units made solid contact with the Third Army's Third Panzer Division, which was moving west out of East Prussia. Between two and three Polish infantry divisions and one cavalry brigade had been shattered in three days by the Nineteenth Panzer Corps, which had operated mostly on its own. Guderian's theories were triumphantly vindicated.

Hitler, in the meantime, had taken to rushing about the Polish front in the heavily armored train *Amerika,* seemingly oblivious to the dangers of battle. On the train the oppressive atmosphere that characterized all of the führer's headquarters dominated. "We have been living in the train for ten days now," wrote Hitler's secretary. "Its location is constantly being changed, but since we never get out the monotony is dreadful. The heat is unbearable . . . [and] to top it all, there is hardly anything worthwhile to do. . . . Obviously it gives the soldiers' morale a boost to see the führer in the thick of the danger with them, but I still think it's too risky."

On September 5, Hitler visited Guderian's corps and, impressed by the wreckage left in its wake—the smashed bridges and artillery—asked: "Our dive bombers did that?"

"No," Guderian answered, "our panzers!"

The former infantryman was, in Guderian's words, "plainly astonished." By September 6, the Nineteenth Panzer Corps was across the Vistula, moving faster than planned. While his superiors tried to decide what to do with an armored corps that had completed its primary assignment in just five days, Guderian spent the night contentedly in a castle chamber once used by Napoleon.

✦

AT ARMY GROUP SOUTH, meanwhile, armor was also providing the key to preventing the courageous but slow-moving Poles from organizing a coherent defense. As the Fourteenth Army began to smash its way through stubborn Polish resistance in the region of the Carpathians, the Poles in western Galicia made a surprisingly apt decision to fall back toward the Vistula before they were encircled. The main fear of both Rundstedt and Manstein was that such a move would lead to a generalized Polish retreat that would frustrate their aim of engaging the main Polish forces west of the Vistula.

This possibility was eliminated by the quick movements of the Twenty-second Panzer Corps under General Ewald von Kleist. Kleist—considered by Hitler to be one of the army's most "incorrigible" enemies of the Nazi party—

broke through the western Carpathians with the Second Panzer and Fourth Light divisions and raced toward the juncture of the Vistula and the San. Within days this speedy advance, along with Guderian's movements in the north, was to prove decisive in destroying any Polish hope of establishing a river defense.

Meanwhile, northwest of the Fourteenth Army, the Eighth and Tenth armies were advancing against heavy Polish troop concentrations in the Lódź-Radom region. The Tenth Army's job was to force an engagement with these troops as soon as possible; the Eighth was to cover the Tenth's left flank and prevent the Poles around Lódź and Radom from joining forces with the Poznań Army to the north.

Army Group South's ability to realize its goal of forcing the Poles to fight west of the Vistula was decided, according to Manstein, by "two factors which had appeared for the very first time in this campaign": the panzer divisions and the Luftwaffe. Reichenau's tanks tore open the Polish front line and, rather than assaulting the Poles from the front, were soon actually a good distance behind them. All attempts by the Poles to organize a systematic defense in the meantime were consistently prevented by the screaming Stuka dive bombers that continued to smash transport and communication lines without opposition.

During the first week of fighting, the Poles drew together in the vicinity of Radom. At this point, Rundstedt and Manstein decided to move quickly to encircle this pocket of enemy resistance instead of first gaining control of the Vistula and advancing on Warsaw, as originally planned. The accelerated pace offered by armored and motorized infantry movement meant that such an encirclement might be achieved without any significant alteration in the larger pincer concept of Case White. By September 9, the Radom pocket was closed, and though the Poles tried for three more days to break out, their fate was unavoidable. Seven divisions were lost, and the southern approach to Warsaw was suddenly wide open.

In the north, meanwhile, General Bock was giving thought to attaching Guderian's Nineteenth Panzer Corps to the Third Army, which was moving toward Warsaw. But Guderian protested that the Third Army was made up almost entirely of infantry—the usefulness of his panzers would be severely limited. The panzer leader formulated his own plan, which was to put the corps under direct army-group control and release it to the east, where, he claimed, it could quickly cross the Narev River and drive on to Brest Litovsk and the River Bug, the next significant barrier east of the Vistula. Such a move would invalidate the east bank of the Vistula as a Polish sanctuary; any

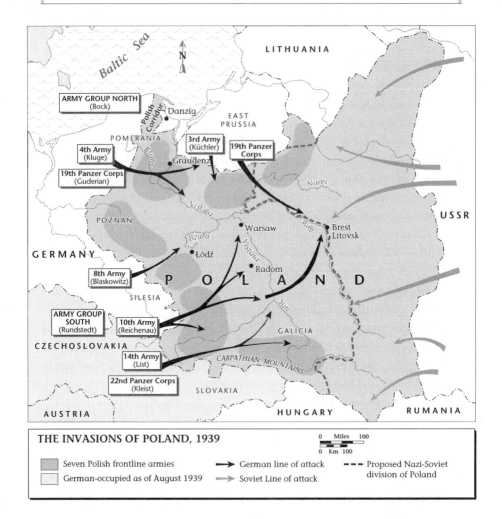

THE INVASIONS OF POLAND, 1939

	0 Miles 100
	0 Km 100

Seven Polish frontline armies   → German line of attack   - - - Proposed Nazi-Soviet
German-occupied as of August 1939   ⇢ Soviet Line of attack   division of Poland

*Germany poured five armies into Poland. The Poles were deployed too thinly and
tried to defend too much territory. Pincers isolated and then closed around their
seven border armies, as shown here. Panzers broke through to the rear, preventing
the Poles from establishing defense lines along the Vistula. On September 17, the
Soviets invaded, sealing Poland's fate: She was divided between the aggressors.*

Polish forces that were stationed there or managed to reach it would already
be encircled. The German plan for Case White had cast a wide net—and
Guderian's tactics offered them a chance to cast that net dramatically wider.

Von Bock approved the idea, and Guderian's Nineteenth Panzer Corps thus became, effectively, the world's first armored army: autonomous and freed from the constraints of coordinating its movements with the infantry. At the Narev, Guderian's troops encountered stubborn Polish resistance and once more displayed confusion, which their gregarious but tough commander again cleared up with numerous frontline appearances. Moving from unit to unit in a half-track rigged with a wireless radio, he organized a powerful assault, and by September 12 the Tenth Panzer Division had gotten across the Narev and was in a position to surround the Polish defenders. This freed the Third Panzer Division to race for the citadel of Brest Litovsk, and by the 13th the lead elements of the division had reached the city.

Still, there were surprises in store for the Germans—Army Group South had already learned this the hard way. Despite the fact that the first nine days of fighting had gone well, Manstein later recalled, he "still had a vague feeling that something was brewing on the northern flank of the army group." That "something" turned out to be the Polish Poznań Army. Though Manstein continually told the Eighth Army's chief of staff to be alert to the possibility of attack from the north, that army's attention remained focused on driving to the east. When the Poznań Army struck with surprising strength along the Bzura River on September 10, the Eighth Army was unprepared, and quickly called for reinforcements.

But Rundstedt and Manstein were, as Manstein later said, "by no means disposed to see the situation of Eighth Army restored by a reinforcement of its front." The Poles were displaying tactical daring and were enjoying some success—but they were only destroying their own strategic situation by attacking south rather than retreating toward their capital and the Vistula. Manstein went on to say: "Even if a local crisis—and possibly a serious one at that—were to arise here, it would have not the least bearing on the operations as a whole. On the contrary, it actually offered us the chance of winning a big victory."

Rundstedt and Manstein issued orders to the Tenth Army to move into position to cut the Poznań Army's lines of retreat eastward. They then flew to the headquarters of General Blaskowitz, the Eighth Army's commander, and directed the Battle of the Bzura from there. The Polish situation—again because of strategic ineptitude—was hopeless. The German Tenth and Eighth armies moved into position for another pocket encirclement, and the last nail was driven into the Poznań Army's coffin when Army Group North's Third Corps was detached to play a role in this encirclement.

One more shock, however, awaited the German army. On September 17, news that Soviet troops had entered Poland shot through the ranks of the Wehrmacht. Many a German soldier, junior and senior, wanted to know whom the Soviets had come to fight. But when word of the Russo-German agreement to partition Poland was received, as well as news that Russian troops were engaging Poles and quickly occupying Polish territory, the German soldiers returned to the task at hand. (One Polish officer fought the Germans in the morning and the Soviets in the afternoon, and escaped from both.) There was irony in the fact that many of these same German troops would have to fight in the not-too-distant future to conquer the areas of Poland taken by the Soviets; but such irony was unforeseeable.

At this point the situation for the Poles became hopeless. As the battle raged on the Bzura, Guderian's troops to the east prepared an assault on the citadel of Brest Litovsk. Kleist's panzers, meanwhile, had linked up with other advancing elements of Army Group North above the juncture of the Vistula and San Rivers. The Poles were faced with a double envelopment. On September 16, confident that the Twentieth Motorized and Tenth Panzer divisions could take Brest Litovsk, Guderian ordered his remaining forces to move farther south and link up with advancing elements of the Fourteenth Army.

On September 16, the Poznań Army capitulated, and the German Tenth Army reported the taking of 80,000 prisoners. The Eighth Army had taken 90,000. Although not as large as later German armored envelopments in France and Russia, the Battle of the Bzura set the pattern for those subsequent dramatic conquests. Of more immediate importance, it sounded the death knell for Polish resistance.

Already there had been ominous signs of what German occupation held in store for the Poles. Regular German army units were being followed into Poland by SS formations, whose job it was to root out members of the Polish nobility and government, as well as the intelligentsia and all Jews. As one Polish prisoner of war recalled, these Germans "began to select Jews 'by sight.' They avoided officers, but concentrated on privates and noncommissioned ranks, pulling out soldiers with 'Semitic' features and leading them away, to the accompaniment of shouts and face-slapping."

As to the British and the French, on whose efforts the fate of Poland ultimately rested, they had declared war on Germany soon after the invasion, as they were treaty bound to do. But neither ally had been able to offer anything more substantial by way of support. For if the German generals were somewhat startled by the speed with which they were able, through creative use of their panzer and air forces, to bring the Polish campaign to a climax, the British and French governments were even more so. There were no Allied provisions for launching a western relief attack within the two and a half weeks between the German invasion of Poland and the capitulation of the Poznań Army—thus the Poles were left to face their fate alone.

While the German troops east of the Vistula began to wrangle with the problem of pulling back to that river—everything east of it having been promised to Stalin by Hitler—the main body of Army Group South and the remainder of Army Group North prepared for the last task left to them: the taking of Warsaw. Under the civilian leadership of its determined mayor, Stefan Starzynski, the capital had been turned into a maze of barricaded streets. Such obstructions, however, would prove to be of as little value to the city as the influx of exhausted survivors of the Battle of the Bzura.

For the Germans had no intention of engaging in brutal street fighting. Assembling their artillery in a ring around the capital, they opened fire first on Warsaw's outer forts and defenses. Leaflets were dropped, calling for surrender and threatening the bombardment of the city proper. When no response came, the guns opened fire. By September 25, life in Warsaw had been brought to a standstill. As one German recalled:

> The mortars spoke incessantly, one battery after another, showering a hot rain of metal over Poland's capital, bursting in windows and tearing out window frames and doors. Watching by night we saw curves of colored fire flashing gracefully toward Warsaw. The earth quivered and our eardrums seemed about to split. . . . In all directions long smoky tongues of fire spurted up every second. In the heavens the clouds were as red as blood.

On September 27, the Poles offered to give in, and the shelling was immediately halted. On the following day the capitulation was signed, the Polish general in command of Warsaw telling the German conquerors, "A wheel always turns." Pockets of Polish resistance remained to be cleared up, and the job of conceding conquered territory in eastern Poland to Soviet troops proved complicated in spots. But by October 5, the German army had put Hitler in a position to parade victoriously through the streets of Warsaw. The Germans had taken hundreds of thousands of prisoners; Army Group South alone took more than half a million, at a cost of just over 6,500 officers and men killed.

The German synthesis of traditional Prussian strategy and advanced ar-

mored doctrines had brought about a stunning success. That synthesis was
best embodied in the person of Erich von Manstein, and it is therefore appropriate to record his final thoughts concerning the Polish campaign:

> In the German Wehrmacht it had been found possible [in Poland], with the
> help of the new means of warfare, to reacquire the true art of leadership in mo-
> bile operations. Individual leadership was fostered on a scale unrivaled in any
> other army, right down to the most junior NCO or infantryman, and in this lay
> the secret of our success. So far, the troops had had a purely military battle to
> fight, and for that reason it had still been possible to fight chivalrously.

That sense of chivalry soon became an irritant to Hitler and his Nazi
henchmen and caused the battle that the senior German officer corps was
forced to wage to become more than "purely military." Following the Polish
capitulation, General Blaskowitz, commander of the Eighth Army, became
military governor-general of the conquered territories. A soldier of the old
school, Blaskowitz had been appalled by the behavior of SS units in Poland.
As governor-general he set up military tribunals that sentenced SS soldiers—
including members of the Leibstandarte Adolf Hitler, the führer's pet unit—
to death for the crimes of murder, arson, and rape. This policy soon changed
when Austrian Nazi party officials arrived to take over the civilian administration of Poland.

But Blaskowitz had not been the only general to have run-ins with the SS
and other party organizations. Drawing on the experiences of his colleagues as
well as his own, Blaskowitz submitted a lengthy report to the commander of
the German army, General Brauchitsch, on Nazi behavior during the Polish
campaign. Hitler heard of the report but did not read it, choosing instead to
lecture Brauchitsch about the German officer corps's "outmoded conception of
chivalry."

Despite the inner tension between regular army officers and SS leaders, the
German Wehrmacht emerged from the Polish campaign transformed, battle-
tested, and ready. The crucial theories of air and armored power had been applied and vindicated; officers of all ranks had learned how to lead men under
fire; and an army whose quality had worried its own commanders (because of
the rapid expansion before the war) had proved itself a remarkable battlefield
force. The German officer corps had known that war with Poland meant war
with the world. Following the Polish campaign, some of those men might
still have been reluctant to face such an eventuality—but their reluctance was

now based not on doubts about the units under their command but on doubts about the sanity of their superiors. In France, Russia, and Africa, the methods honed in Poland would be expanded in scale and perfected in technique. And even during the closing months of the war, those methods would delay Allied victory to an extent deemed impossible by Allied commanders.

"ALMOST A MIRACLE"

ROBERT A. DOUGHTY

The collapse of France in the spring of 1940 came with an unexpected suddenness that almost defied explanation—though the explanations over the years have not been wanting. Was it the result of two decades of divisive politics and national dry rot that followed the debilitating victory in the Great War? Or were military miscalculations, abetted by incredible German good luck, a more immediate cause? In 1940, the French high command could not recover from its early mistakes, as it had a generation before; moreover, at this time, Germany was only fighting a one-front war and France had to take the brunt of the Nazi attack. In 1914, France could retreat to the outskirts of Paris, and time was on its side. That was no longer true. With the advent of mechanized warfare, France had only one battle to lose. The fatal confrontation came just three days after Germany invaded the West, on May 13, at a place that had already seen one of the worst defeats in French history: Sedan. Here, in 1870, the Prussians had surrounded and overwhelmed Emperor Napoleon III and his army. Now, just short of seventy years later, German Panzer columns erupted from the Ardennes Forest, spreading out over the old battlefield, and prepared to cross the Meuse River. The battle that resulted in a German breakout was decided by audacious leadership and the bravery of a few men. General Heinz Guderian's assessment of the Second Sedan—"almost a miracle"—was hardly an overstatement. But it was a miracle that could easily have gone the other way.

Robert A. Doughty is a colonel in the U.S. Army and head of the history department at the United States Military Academy at West Point. He is the author of two books on the French army and the fall of France, *The Seed of Disaster* and *The Breaking Point*. He is at present writing a book on the French army in World War I, tentatively titled *Pyrrhic Victory: French Strategy and Operation in the Great War.*

TWICE IN THE LAST TWO CENTURIES, THE DESTINY OF FRANCE has depended on the unfolding of events around the small city of Sedan, on the edge of the Ardennes near the Belgian border. In September 1870, the Prussians won a great victory at Sedan when they surrounded French forces and captured Emperor Napoleon III. In May 1940, the Germans won another great victory at Sedan when the Nineteenth Panzer Corps under General Heinz Guderian successfully crossed the Meuse River on both sides of the city and raced toward the English Channel.

It seems appropriate to take a closer look at this important crossing of the Meuse, for a great deal of fresh material about the campaign has recently become available. This includes personal accounts, daily logs, and after-action reports that provide a remarkable amount of information about the battle. Whereas a few years ago relatively little was available, we now have more information about this battle than about almost any other that has ever been fought.

Among the important insights provided by this new material is the recognition of how precarious the German victory at Sedan actually was. Although the Germans concentrated three of their best army divisions against one of France's weakest, only three of their six major crossings succeeded. Had the French managed to prevent even one of the three successful crossings—and they almost did—the scale and pace of the subsequent fighting would have been decidedly different. Guderian acknowledged in his memoirs how fortunate the Germans were by characterizing their success as "almost a miracle."

✦

GERMAN STRATEGY in May 1940 sought a swift, decisive victory by the launching of a massive attack through the Ardennes. Army Group A, commanded by General Gerd von Rundstedt, had responsibility for the main attack through the Ardennes and placed Panzer Group Kleist (containing the Nineteenth and Forty-first Panzer Corps and the Fourteenth Motorized Infantry Corps) and the Fifteenth Panzer Corps to its front. As commander of the Nineteenth Panzer Corps, Guderian was responsible for leading the main attack through the Ardennes and against the so-called hinge of the Allied rush into Belgium. This "hinge," the boundary between the French Ninth and Second armies, was just west of Sedan.

To accomplish its mission, Guderian's corps had to move more than eighty-five miles through the forests and rough terrain of Luxembourg and Belgium and then cross the Meuse near Sedan. The German offensive began at 4:35

A.M. on May 10, when the First Panzer Division crossed the bridge over the Sauer River at Wallendorf and entered Luxembourg.

While the leading German elements moved forward rapidly, massive columns to their rear moved ponderously through Luxembourg's narrow roads and thick forests. With more than 40,000 vehicles, General Ewald von Kleist's panzer group—as he later asserted—would have extended more than 625 miles if it had attempted to move along a single route. Despite intensive planning and numerous control measures, some German commanders in the long columns eagerly pushed forward and moved off their prescribed routes, thereby creating traffic delays for other units. The lack of discipline soon forced General von Kleist to threaten to execute those who violated road-march rules.

Fortunately for the Germans, the Allies did not identify the massive phalanx of forces moving through the Ardennes. Since the German columns were covered by a large number of antiaircraft weapons, very few Allied aircraft managed to penetrate deep enough to see the long lines of vehicles. Luck was also on the German side, for the few aircraft that did penetrate the air cover saw units on the periphery of the main thrust, not those in the center. Aerial reconnaissance thus provided only cursory information about a few widely separated enemy units in the Ardennes and reinforced the Allied perception that the main German attack was coming through central Belgium along the same route it had followed in 1914.

After moving across Luxembourg, the Nineteenth Panzer Corps encountered some spirited opposition along the Belgian border from a few companies of the Belgian Chasseurs Ardennais, a light-infantry force that used bicycles for transportation. The small group was able to delay the Germans for almost eight hours, but Guderian's forces soon were moving ahead. At Neufchâteau and Libramont, they easily pushed through French forces that were trying to cover the front of the Second and Ninth armies. The pell-mell withdrawal of the French under strong pressure enabled the Germans to seize crossing points over the Semois River, about six miles north of Sedan.

With hardly a pause, the Germans continued moving south, and at 10:10 A.M. on May 12, leading elements broke out of the woods about two and a half miles north of Sedan. Around 2 P.M., the first Germans reached the Meuse. It had taken them about fifty-seven hours to move across the Ardennes.

As the Nineteenth Panzer Corps approached Sedan, Guderian quarreled openly with his superior, Kleist. More important, the confident panzer leader ignored his boss's orders to cross the Meuse several miles west of Sedan, beyond the Ardennes Canal. Kleist wanted Guderian's corps to cross the river closer to the crossing site of the German Forty-first Corps at Monthermé, because the effect of two corps crossing close together would be greater than if they were separated.

Guderian, however, decided on his own to attack east of the canal instead. He considered the terrain near Sedan ideal for a relatively concentrated crossing, and he was concerned about French artillery fire from Charleville-Mézières if a crossing was made west of the canal. Although Kleist restated his order several times in the days prior to the crossing, Guderian never deviated from his intention to cross the Meuse closer to Sedan.

After the leading German elements reached the Meuse on May 12, Guderian became concerned about whether sufficient forces would be available for a crossing on the thirteenth. Many of his units were still moving forward through the rough terrain of Belgium. On the afternoon of the twelfth, he met with Kleist, who was angry about his orders being disobeyed. During this stormy meeting, Guderian insisted that the attack be delayed so his forces could be completely assembled. Kleist, however, insisted that the attack be launched the following day.

Much to Guderian's dismay, Kleist also informed him that aerial support would not be provided in the fashion already arranged by the Nineteenth Panzer Corps. Instead of the Luftwaffe delivering continuous and relatively low-level attacks, aerial support was going to consist of a short, concentrated bombing attack, which would be coordinated with German artillery preparation. Kleist believed this use of the Luftwaffe would cause the greatest damage to the French defenses.

Guderian had no choice but to abide by Kleist's order to attack the following day and to accept the modified method of aerial support. But after this meeting he became increasingly doubtful about the success of the river crossing. The daily log of the Nineteenth Panzer Corps includes a lengthy analysis of his concerns about the width, depth, and timing of the attack. The log notes, "The order of the Group [Kleist] . . . is completely different from the conception of the commanding general [of the Nineteenth Panzer Corps]. . . ." Almost as though readying a court case, Guderian prepared an argument for blaming Kleist if the crossing failed.

Nonetheless, after returning to his headquarters, he issued orders for the following day's crossing of the Meuse. The main attack was to be made by the First Panzer Division, which was reinforced by the Gross Deutschland Infantry Regiment. The division planned to make two major crossings about 500 yards apart just west of Sedan and a small third crossing in the "buckle" of the Meuse northwest of Sedan.

East of Sedan, the Tenth Panzer Division also planned two main crossings, one near Wadelincourt and the other southeast of Pont Maugis. West of Sedan and the buckle in the river, the Second Panzer Division prepared to cross on both sides of Donchery. Because the Second Division had experienced numerous delays in its move across the Ardennes, Guderian expected the Second Division to begin its attack after the assaults across the Meuse by the other two divisions.

If Guderian had known more about the condition of the French forces he faced, he might have been more confident of success. The units along the southern bank of the Meuse were part of the Second Army, commanded by General Charles Huntziger. With two army corps on line along the Meuse and Chiers rivers, the Second Army occupied defensive positions extending from a point west of Sedan to Longuyon, a distance of about forty-five miles, and had the mission of defending the zone across the southern edge of the Ardennes. Huntziger placed the Tenth Corps on the left and the Eighteenth Corps on the right.

As part of the Tenth Corps, the Fifty-fifth Infantry Division was responsible for defending along the Meuse at Sedan. The commander of the Fifty-fifth, General Lafontaine, placed his three regiments along the Meuse. However, after the Germans overran the French cavalry in Belgium, the French became concerned about the possibility of a German attack against the Sedan region. On the night of May 12–13, therefore, General Huntziger decided to increase the number of divisions along the Meuse and moved the Seventy-first Division into position where the Fifty-fifth's easternmost regiment had been. This relief-in-place permitted Lafontaine, on the thirteenth, to place two regiments along the river and elements of his third to their rear.

Of the three regiments in the 55th Division, the 147th Fortress Infantry Regiment occupied the key sector, extending from Bellevue to Pont Maugis. The regiment was a Series B unit, which meant it had only a small percentage of active-duty officers and soldiers and did not have a high priority for receiving modern equipment. When the Nineteenth Panzer Corps attacked across the Meuse on the afternoon of May 13, the First and Tenth Panzer divisions, as well as the Gross Deutschland Infantry Regiment, struck this single French regiment.

Despite the large forces that would be concentrated against the 147th, the terrain favored the defender. If the Germans emerged from the edge of the Ardennes to the north of Sedan, they would have to cross about two and a half miles of open terrain that sloped gently toward the Meuse and had several small villages spread across it. Although the Meuse was only about sixty feet wide, it could not be forded and thus served as a highly effective tank barrier. To the south there was a large flat area in the middle of a huge bend in the river. Several small hills dominated the southern edge of this flat area, but an even larger line of hills appeared to its rear, their tops about three miles from the Meuse. Farther east, just south of Wadelincourt, the line of hills was very close to the river and thus provided excellent positions for the French defenders. From here the French could direct heavy concentrations of artillery onto any exposed enemy forces in the huge open area to their front. (It is worth noting that on November 11, 1918, the American advance had reached these same heights overlooking Sedan.)

To defend his area, the commander of the 147th Regiment, Lieutenant Colonel François Pinaud, placed his three battalions on line. The 2/331st was on his left, the 2/147th in his center, and the 2/295th on his right. Each battalion commander further divided his area into three centers of resistance. Thus, if the infantry of the First Panzer Division managed to get across the Meuse, they would have to attack toward the high ground to their front and pass through three successive lines of resistance. And they undoubtedly would have to contend with heavy French artillery fire.

Along the banks of the river, which marked the principal line of resistance, the French had placed several blockhouses. Most of the forward defensive positions, however, consisted of small bunkers capable of providing only minimal protection against heavy enemy fire. The second line, along the small hills south of the Meuse, consisted of several large concrete blockhouses and essentially ran from Bellevue to Wadelincourt. Farther to its rear, the final line of defenses consisted of little more than shallow trenches and sparse fields of barbed wire. Despite months of preparation, several of the bunkers along the river and the second line were not completely finished; in addition, many lacked steel covers for their gunports, so that the enemy could fire directly into the bunkers.

Although the 147th Regiment had been in the Sedan sector since October, on May 10, only one company under Lieutenant Colonel Pinaud's command had been in its position for more than forty-five days. During the months of the Phony War, companies had been pulled from their positions and sent to the rear for training. When they returned to Sedan, they were assigned different positions. This unfortunate shuffling of companies disrupted efforts to improve defenses and prevented most of the defenders from being entirely familiar with their positions.

In addition, the cohesion of the battalions was weak. In the months before the German attack, commanders in the Second Army shuffled men from one battalion to another in an effort to add younger soldiers to battalions consisting primarily of older reservists. Before these personnel changes, the average age of a soldier in the 147th Regiment was thirty-one; a lieutenant, thirty-three; and a captain, forty-two. Shortly before the German attack, the battalions also received an infusion of replacements, which brought them close to their authorized strength. The commanding general of the Fifty-fifth Division later admitted that the cohesion of the division was "compromised" by personnel turbulence.

After the battle, General Grandsard, the commander of the Tenth Corps, complained that his forces did not have enough antitank weapons. He noted that the Fifty-fifth Division had only fifty-six modern antitank weapons along its approximately ten-mile front, or fewer than six weapons per mile. To make matters worse, these antitank weapons had been placed in blockhouses. After the initial assault of the German infantry pushed deep into the French position, many of the antitank weapons had to be left behind in the blockhouses and could not be used against the German tanks that crossed the Meuse the next day.

Other important weaknesses affected the performance of the Fifty-fifth Division. For example, the division had only 422 antitank mines. The 2/331st Infantry Battalion, which was in the area of Bellevue, put one minefield in its sector near Frenois, but it had only nineteen mines. Since most of the tanks of the First Panzer Division crossed through this area on May 14, even the smallest increase in numbers might have made a difference. Another critical weakness was in air defenses. When German aircraft struck the Sedan sector on May 13, the Fifty-fifth Division had only one antiaircraft battery in its immediate area, and it performed poorly.

Pinaud's regiment did have one noteworthy advantage—strong artillery support. The Fifty-fifth Division had eleven battalions plus two additional batteries of artillery in its sector. Three of these battalions provided direct support to the 147th Regiment. Three additional battalions arrived in the division's sector on May 12, raising the total number of artillery tubes to 174. If the Germans were to cross the Meuse successfully, this massive artillery support had to be neutralized.

Except for the French artillery, however, the initial odds favored the attacking Germans. The fortunes of war permitted them to concentrate a reinforced Panzer Corps against a French regiment with significant weaknesses. If the French artillery could be silenced or disrupted, the Germans had a reasonable chance of achieving success.

On the morning of May 13, Guderian waited anxiously for the launching

of the attack, scheduled to begin at 3 P.M. He still feared that Kleist's modi-
fied aerial-support plan placed the operation in jeopardy. But to his surprise,
German aircraft appeared over Sedan in the morning and began an extended
wave of attacks rather than a single concentrated barrage. Immensely pleased,
Guderian watched as the drawn-out aerial attacks disrupted the fire of the
French artillery.

Later that night he telephoned the German Luftwaffe commander respon-
sible for the flight and learned why a concentrated attack had not occurred.
Kleist's order had arrived too late to be implemented, and consequently the
Luftwaffe had abided by the previous plan. Luck had been with Guderian.

One can only speculate on how Kleist's plan, if implemented, might have
affected the German crossing of the Meuse; plainly, Guderian thought it im-
periled the whole enterprise. Even with the successful sustained bombing
Guderian had wanted, the German crossing would turn out to be an extremely difficult business whose overall success hung in the balance at more
than one critical juncture.

On the day of the crossing, Group Kleist was supported by almost 1,000
aircraft, most of them employed in the Sedan sector during the morning and
early afternoon. This huge number of aircraft delivered the largest aerial attack up to that date in military history. As hundreds of German aircraft circled Sedan and attacked French positions, the Fifty-fifth Division could put
up little defense.

The Luftwaffe attacks had an especially devastating effect on French ar-
tillerymen, many of whom manned easily identifiable artillery tubes. "Every
individual seen," one French battalion commander noted, "was followed and
machine-gunned by enemy fighters who defiantly confirmed their absolute
mastery of the air." The bombing also cut numerous telephone lines that the
French had not taken the precaution of burying; therefore, commanders at all
echelons soon lost contact with subordinate units.

As Guderian had hoped, the sustained bombing attacks slowly eroded the
Frenchmen's will to fight. Shortly after the attacks began, a few soldiers began
fleeing from the constant bombardment. Some were infantrymen who occupied positions near bunkers and were responsible for providing close-in security for them. By day's end, the trickle would become a torrent.

As German infantry and engineers assembled for the crossing of the Meuse,
French artillery fire became more sporadic and less effective. While it continued to inhibit movement along the northern bank, the lessening of its intensity enabled the Germans to complete their preparations. The aerial attack
had done its work.

Because of the late arrival of the attack order, some units in the First Panzer Division did not learn until around 1:30 A.M. that they were supposed to cross the Meuse on May 13. This left them very little time for last-minute planning and preparation, and some confusion continued to exist: The division was initially supposed to launch its attack at 9 A.M.; the attack time was changed to 2:15 and then to 3 P.M., but the division did not learn until 7 A.M. that the attack scheduled for 9:00 had been delayed.

As the infantry moved forward to their crossing sites, they trod the open fields in which much of the fighting between Prussian and French soldiers had occurred around Sedan in 1870. The French had been decisively defeated in that fighting, and it is noteworthy that the German soldiers moving across the same fields were about to participate in key actions that would soon lead to the same decisive results.

Engineer units were also moving forward, carrying rubber assault boats. French artillery fire forced the Germans to carry some of the boats forward on motorcycles with sidecars. Others were carried on trucks and arrived at the last possible moment.

Lieutenant Colonel Hermann Balck's First Infantry Regiment had the responsibility for making the main attack for the First Panzer Division. Shortly before the assault began, German tanks and 88mm guns fired at French bunkers near the regiment's crossing site at Gaulier, just west of Sedan. This silenced several of the bunkers. Almost precisely at 3 P.M., the Second and Third battalions of the First Infantry Regiment crossed the Meuse, the Second Battalion on the right (to the west) and the Third Battalion on the left (to the east). The First Battalion followed the two lead battalions.

Although several of the bunkers had been silenced, the engineers and infantrymen came under heavy machine-gun fire as they crossed. A few artillery rounds fell, but the enemy's guns were almost silent in comparison to the heavy fire before the sustained aerial attacks. The Seventh and Eighth companies led the Second Battalion across the river, losing several men in the crossing. When they reached the far side, the infantrymen initially hesitated under the heavy French fire. The battalion commander, however, had crossed the Meuse with the Seventh Company, and his presence and his demands for continued movement propelled the soldiers forward. During this momentary crisis and others to come, the courage and the presence of their leaders proved crucial to the eventual success of the Germans.

The daily log of the First Panzer Division described the forward movement of the First Infantry Regiment:

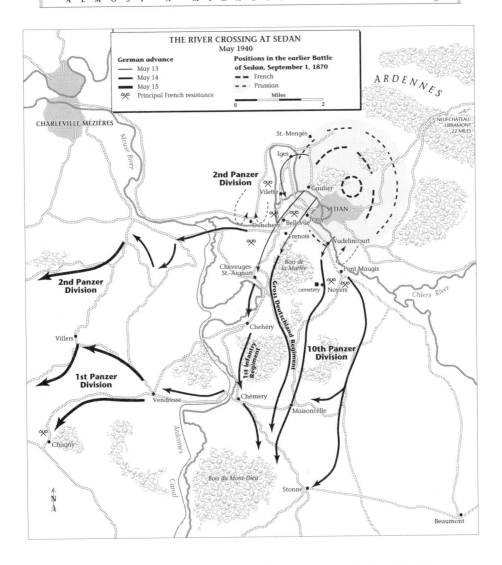

THE RIVER CROSSING AT SEDAN
May 1940

German advance
—— May 13
—— May 14
—— May 15
⚔ Principal French resistance

Positions in the earlier Battle
of Sedan, September 1, 1870
– – French
‑ ‑ Prussian

Miles
0   2

The German crossing of the Meuse in 1940 occurred near the site of the Pruss-
ian victory seventy years earlier. In the 1940 attack, three of the six main Ger-
man crossings were initially repulsed (broken arrows near Donchery and Pont
Maugis). Of the three successful crossings, the 10th Panzers' advance through
Wadelincourt met the stiffest resistance—some of it at the cemetery near Noyers.
The two remaining assault forces, the 1st Infantry Regiment and the Gross
Deutschland Regiment, were able to penetrate farther, to Cheveuges–St.-Aignan.
After the first hard day, the Germans regained momentum (larger arrows at far
left).

The first obstacles are overcome in a rapid advance, and the first bunkers rolled up. Despite this, French resistance comes back to life. Enemy artillery begins to shoot at the crossing points. The crews in the bunkers desperately defend against the advancing infantrymen. One bunker after the other, antitank guns, machine guns, and field fortifications are taken in individual combat and through the personal example of all the leaders who advance in front of their men. Antitank and antiaircraft [weapons] also play a tremendous role in the reduction of the enemy, and they destroy the French in relentless actions, sometimes at point-blank ranges.

The soldiers of the First Infantry Regiment continued moving forward and soon passed through the courtyard of the château of Bellevue, where Napoleon III's representative in September 1870 signed the surrender terms dictated by General Helmuth von Moltke. After capturing the two bunkers in this courtyard, the infantry continued to advance. Around 9 P.M. they reached the heights of La Boulette, from where the Prussian king William I had watched the decisive events of September 1870. Among the foreign observers with him had been General Philip H. Sheridan of the U.S. Army.

Around 10 P.M., elements from the First Infantry Regiment reached the small town of Cheveuges, about three and a half miles from where they had crossed the Meuse. There the soldiers halted and prepared to defend their narrow penetration.

The motorcycle battalion of the First Panzer Division also crossed the Meuse at 3 P.M. It crossed at the small island on the northeastern corner of the buckle, between St. Mengés and Iges. Around 6 P.M., the battalion reached a small canal at the base of the buckle, less than two miles from their crossing site. By the time the motorcyclists crossed the small canal, the First Infantry Regiment had cleaned out the opposition to its front, and the soldiers encountered no opposition. The motorcyclists quickly moved forward to join the leading German elements.

The Gross Deutschland Regiment tried to cross the Meuse at 3 P.M. but failed. This regiment was composed of soldiers from all parts of the German nation and was attached to the First Panzer Division for the Meuse crossing— about a half mile east of the First Infantry Regiment's crossing site. An elite unit that received special attention from Adolf Hitler, the regiment expected to do well; however, a hint of its future difficulties appeared when the boats for the crossing arrived at the last possible minute.

The men of the Gross Deutschland Regiment, however, were not as lucky as those of the First Infantry Regiment. The occupants of two French bunkers near the Gross Deutschland Regiment's crossing site courageously continued fighting and inflicted many casualties on the Germans. The regiment did not have tanks to assist it and tried to use its own self-propelled guns to silence the bunkers on the southern bank. When these guns proved ineffective, the regiment used the cover of the buildings on the northern bank of the river to move assault cannon forward, but these also failed. Finally, a heavy 88mm gun came forward and fired into the unprotected apertures of the French bunkers.

After several direct hits with the 88mm gun, the German engineers attempted to place assault boats in the river, but the determined French defenders halted them. A young German lieutenant and two engineers tried to cross the river despite the enemy machine guns and were killed. The 88mm gun opened fire again, and under its protection the Seventh Company of the Second Battalion finally succeeded in crossing the river. A platoon from the Sixth Company, with its platoon leader in front, moved across with the Seventh Company. Other elements of the Sixth followed.

As the two companies from the Second Battalion advanced under heavy fire, part of the Third Battalion also managed to cross the river. Although only half the battalion crossed, it quickly became embroiled in close-in, house-to-house fighting on the outskirts of Torcy, a small town on the southern bank of the Meuse, across from Sedan. The remainder of the regiment did not cross until later that night. Arduous as the regiment's task had been, it had still achieved one of the three successful initial crossings. Other German units had even less luck than the Gross Deutschland Regiment.

By 7 P.M., the First Panzer Division had crossed most elements of five infantry battalions and one motorcycle battalion—including elements from the Gross Deutschland Regiment. Even before elements from the First Infantry Regiment reached the French second line of resistance, German engineers began assembling two rafts for crossing the Meuse. To protect themselves, they worked behind the walls of a large factory that stood between them and the river.

By 7:20 P.M. the first raft was operating, and by 7:40, the second. To speed up the transport of men and equipment across the river, the engineers hooked the two rafts together and began ferrying units across. By 7:30, the engineers were working hard to construct a bridge just west of Gaulier. Shortly after 11 P.M., they completed the sixteen-ton pontoon bridge.

Before the bridge was completed, German engineers used the two rafts to transport reconnaissance vehicles, antiaircraft guns, and self-propelled guns across the river. Guderian refused to permit any tanks to be ferried across, however, even though they could have provided invaluable assistance to the infantry. The zealous armor commander preferred to keep the tanks together so they could be saved for the decisive thrust.

✦

EAST OF SEDAN, the Tenth Panzer Division planned on making two crossings, one near Wadelincourt, the other southeast of Pont Maugis. The main effort was the attack near Wadelincourt. Both the Second and Tenth Panzer divisions did not have their full artillery complement, for they had to send one of their three artillery battalions to the First Panzer Division, which was making the corps' main attack. Like the other divisions in the corps, the Tenth received its order late, but somehow managed to get its subordinate units moving forward on time.

The Tenth Division's two assaults across the Meuse encountered severe problems. French artillery fire destroyed most of the boats as the engineers rushed to unload them for crossing southeast of Pont Maugis. Heavy artillery fire also disrupted the other attack. It looked for a moment as if the attack by the Tenth Panzer Division was doomed to failure—and if that had happened at this third crossing point, the entire German operation might have been jeopardized.

However, in one of the most astonishing performances of the campaign, a few German soldiers opened a path for the division. An engineer staff sergeant by the name of Rubarth and his squad of assault engineers, together with a handful of infantrymen, successfully crossed the Meuse just north of Wadelincourt, and then destroyed seven bunkers, thus breaking through the main French defenses along the river. Sergeant Rubarth later gave a blow-by-blow account of their actions after crossing the river:

> [O]ur attack moves further forward toward the left in the direction of the railway line. From the railway embankment I and my men attack an enemy machine gun, whose position in open terrain has covered the fighting. The enemy next concentrates his artillery along the railway embankment, and we quickly attack the second bunker line with a few people. We must cross over about 165 yards of open terrain and a wire entanglement at the foot of the heights before us. The enemy's artillery follows each step. Then we stop before a bunker with two firing ports. We attack it from two sides. One Frenchman, who had left the bunker and aimed [his weapon] directly at me, was rendered harmless with a hand grenade. We press forward toward the bunker, moving through fieldworks, and do battle with the enemy. Lance Corporal Hose has meanwhile blasted open the entrance. The crew, which recognizes the uselessness of further resistance, surrenders. A [captured] French machine gun becomes a valuable weapon for us in another fight. We widen the breakthrough

point when we take out of the fight two bunkers to the left of us. The second, of which the crew had covered the firing ports, surrenders without resistance. The breakthrough of the second bunker line was thereby completely accomplished. One man who was injured is taken back by prisoners.

To the east of Sergeant Rubarth's crossing site, a squad of infantrymen led by Lieutenant Hanbauer also managed to cross the Meuse at Wadelincourt, destroy several bunkers, and open the way for the remainder of their battalion. Wrote one of the men accompanying Hanbauer:

At the railway embankment, they find an [enemy] field position which is firing. The lieutenant sneaks up to it, holding his pistol again. He charges it. The bolt goes forward. A click! The magazine is empty. Dammit! Those in the bunker have already heard the click. They turn around, are astonished, realize quickly what is happening, and start shooting. The lieutenant runs for cover. A hand grenade explodes just in front of the bunker. Another [German] soldier had recognized the situation immediately and wisely had thrown a grenade. Almost miraculously, our lieutenant was not hurt. He is lying three yards away and in the meantime has loaded his pistol. The rest of the uninjured Frenchmen surrender. There are three men, and they are taken to the entrance of Wadelincourt.

As Lieutenant Hanbauer and his men continued moving through Wadelincourt, they seized a machine-gun position and advanced toward the high ground to their front. The squad member's account continues:

It is now not much further to the top of the hill, which we absolutely must reach and clear of enemy. Everywhere small groups of French appear. They are disarmed and led back to the rear. Thus was trench after trench rolled up, machine-gun nest after machine-gun nest taken.

Just before the last few yards, a short rest is taken, and then we move forward with renewed energy and courage toward the top of the hill. Foxhole after foxhole appears before our eyes. Bewildered Frenchmen are crouched everywhere, pleased to be away from the terrible noise [of the fighting]. . . . More and more prisoners are taken. They are collected in a large bomb crater. . . .

Only seven of us find ourselves on the hill, all sides of which are now defended to ward off a French counterattack.

Thus, two small groups of soldiers managed to rescue the division from failure. By continuing to advance despite the heavy fire and overwhelming odds against them, they enabled two German infantry battalions to cross later on the thirteenth.

French soldiers remained in strong positions at Noyers and the World War I cemetery on the highest hills overlooking the crossing sites, and they continued to direct small-arms fire into the area around the sites. Throughout the night of May 13–14, the Tenth Division pushed small forces across the river and tried to expand its bridgehead, but the French could not be forced out of their positions. The German division was hampered by having sent its heavy-artillery battalion to support the First Panzer Division.

While continuing to push hard, the Tenth Panzer Division kept trying to construct a bridge at Wadelincourt. Despite losses from the French machine-gun and small-arms fire, the bridge was completed around 5:45 A.M. on the fourteenth, but traffic did not flow smoothly. After the French were finally forced off the high ground near Noyers, "technical difficulties" with the bridge forced the Germans to stop using it, and only one Panzer regiment eventually got across the Meuse on the fourteenth. The second Panzer regiment from the division did not cross until the early-morning hours of the fifteenth.

Of the three Panzer divisions in the Nineteenth Corps, the Second Division experienced the most difficulty crossing the river. The division did not reach the Meuse until late on the thirteenth after the other two divisions launched their assaults. Its initial attack was delayed by its late arrival and also by highly effective fire on its left flank from across the river. Until the bunkers between Vilette and Bellevue were captured, the division continued receiving heavy fire in its flank.

The Second Panzer Division tried to cross the Meuse on both sides of Donchery. After traversing a wide-open area, the men had to cross the river and then move up a steep hill on which numerous bunkers were located. In the initial attack, only a few men managed to cross safely—and the survivors soon had to swim back across. For the next several hours, the division's tanks fired at the French bunkers to its front on the southern bank, but the bunkers could not be silenced. Not until leading elements of the First Infantry Regiment from the First Panzer Division moved past Bellevue, turned right, and assaulted the bunkers from the rear could the Second Panzer Division get significant forces across the river. Elements from the 2/2nd Infantry finally managed to cross east of Donchery around 10 P.M.

At 9 A.M. on May 14, the division began constructing a bridge across the Meuse southeast of Donchery. French artillery fire from the west, however, prevented the Germans from finishing the bridge until 4 A.M. on May 15, approximately thirty hours after the division had moved forces across the river. On the fourteenth, tank battalions from the Second Division began using the bridge that the First Panzer Division had put up at Gaulier.

The three divisions of the Nineteenth Panzer Corps thus encountered varying degrees of resistance and achieved varying degrees of success. Of the six major crossings attempted (not counting the one by the motorcycle battalion), only three initially succeeded, two by the First Panzer Division (First Infantry Regiment and Gross Deutschland Regiment) and one by the Tenth Panzer Division. The Tenth Division succeeded only because of the remarkable achievements of two small groups of soldiers. The three failures—two by the Second Panzer and one by the Tenth Panzer Division—were repulsed relatively easily by French defenders, who suffered few casualties.

✦

THE KEY to the German success on the thirteenth was the First Infantry Regiment's successful crossing at Gaulier and rapid advance through Belle-vue and across La Boulette to Cheveuges. Under the strong leadership of Colonel Balck, the regiment opened a narrow and vulnerable hole in French defensive lines. The Gross Deutschland Regiment contributed significantly to the corps's success by expanding the narrow penetration made by the First Infantry Regiment. The chances of the Germans successfully breaking through all the French defenses, however, depended on their ability to expand the bridgehead before the French brought forward sufficient forces to halt their advance.

The day after the successful crossing of the Meuse, Guderian personally supervised the crossing of several hundred tanks at Gaulier, intervening on several occasions to give priority to specific units so they could cross more quickly. These tanks moved forward toward Chémery and Maisoncelle, arriving just in time to repulse the first French counterattack and then expand the extremely narrow and vulnerable bridgehead. That afternoon the First Panzer Division turned west from Chémery and moved toward Vendresse. While bitter fighting was going on at Vendresse, General Guderian met with the First Panzer Division's commanding general and operations officer and then decided to pivot the entire corps toward the west.

Of all the decisions made during the campaign, this one had the greatest effect on the fate of the French, who had expected the Germans to continue heading south. To make the pivot, the First Panzer Division continued pressing on Vendresse while the Second Panzer Division began moving west along the southern bank of the Meuse. Simultaneously, the

Gross Deutschland Infantry Regiment and the Tenth Panzer Division drove
south to occupy the heights of Mont-Dieu and defend the flank of the corps as
it turned west.

The extreme risk taken by Guderian can best be seen in the condition of
the increasingly exhausted soldiers of the First Panzer Division. Around
nightfall on the fourteenth, the following entry was made in the daily journal
of that division:

> The Armor Brigade reports heavy casualties and losses in personnel and
> matériel. Many officers have been killed or wounded. Only a quarter of the
> tanks can still be counted on to be combat ready. The lack of ammunition and
> fuel makes itself particularly noticeable.

Although the Germans continued pressing forward, the First Panzer Division's attack began losing momentum. On the fifteenth, a single French infantry company (reinforced by elements from the cavalry) at Chagny halted
most of the First and Second Panzer regiments. The panzers began advancing
again only after Colonel Balck's First Infantry Regiment managed to push
through the line of French defenses and open the way for them.

Farther north, tanks from the Sixth Panzer Division in the Forty-first
Panzer Corps finally broke through the French defenders at Monthermé early
on the fifteenth and rushed forward almost thirty miles before the end of the
day. During the same period, tanks from General Erwin Rommel's Seventh
Panzer Division advanced about fifteen miles west of Dinant. The combined
effect of these three breakthroughs shattered French forces along the Meuse on
the fifteenth.

On the morning of the sixteenth, French forces pulled back from the area
of the German penetrations and took up new positions along the Aisne River
to the south. By pulling back, they opened the way for the Germans, who
therefore had little or nothing in front of them as they raced toward the English Channel. Although the soldiers of the First Panzer Division were on the
verge of total exhaustion, an entry in its daily log concluded, "There is no
time for half stepping now."

Hitler and the German high command did not agree. As leaders in Berlin
became more and more concerned about the vulnerability of the left flank of
the German forces, Guderian received an order from Kleist to halt his advance
and await the arrival of follow-on forces. By moving into the open area on the
German left, these units could protect the flank against a French counterattack.

As usual, Guderian ignored the order. Recognizing the danger of giving the French time to recuperate, he prepared to continue advancing. When Kleist learned of this blatant disobedience, he met with Guderian at an airfield near Montcornet. During the sharp exchange between the two headstrong officers, Guderian offered to resign his command of the Nineteenth Panzer Corps, and Kleist quickly accepted the offer. The Twelfth Army commander, General Siegmund List, however, overruled Kleist: He refused to accept Guderian's resignation and permitted him to continue advancing west in a "reconnaissance in force." Thus was Germany prevented from losing a leader whose personal drive and brilliance was about to give her one of her greatest victories.

As the Nineteenth Panzer Corps began advancing to the west, there was little or nothing France could do to avoid defeat. What had seemed to Guderian to be "almost a miracle" soon took on all the characteristics of a French debacle.

"BLOODY MARVELOUS"

ANTHONY BAILEY

At the end of May 1990, fifty years after the "miracle" of Dunkirk, thousands of elderly British survivors thronged to the French Channel port for a week of reunions and commemorations. Some even made the trip in a flotilla of the "little ships" that had helped the Royal Navy in the rescue of badly beaten Allied troops. Dunkirk may have been a military humiliation, but almost 340,000 men did get away, including the professional core of the British army. (Even as waiting craft of all sizes and descriptions were carrying out the rescue, the new Churchill government debated whether to continue the war or to make indirect peace overtures to the Germans. Churchill and his hard-liners prevailed: The war would go on.) "Wars," Winston Churchill said soon after in the House of Commons, "are not won by evacuations." But this one may have been.

One notable observer at the Dunkirk anniversary celebration was the writer Anthony Bailey. Bailey watched thousands of veterans march creakily (or ride if wheelchair-bound) down streets once littered with rubble and corpses, and joined them in observances on the beaches where in endless patient lines they had inched toward safety in 1940. But mostly he listened to their stories: "I couldn't swim. I hung on to my haversack and kicked like hell"; "I was wearing my greatcoat, which was wet through and heavy, and they had a job hauling me into a small boat."

"Bloody Marvelous" was the headline in a London newspaper as the days of Dunkirk ended. It summed up the feelings of a nation—and of much of the world—at a time when Hitler's juggernaut seemed unstoppable.

Anthony Bailey was shipped from England to America as a small boy and spent much of the war's duration in Ohio, an experience he recounts

in his memoir, *America, Lost and Found*. He was for many years on the
staff of *The New Yorker*. He has written twenty-one books, including *In
the Village; Rembrandt's House; Major André; Standing in the Sun—a Life
of J. M. W. Turner*; and a forthcoming account of Vermeer's life and work,
A View of Delft. He lives in London.

IN THE LAST WEEK OF MAY 1990, THE WEATHER WAS FINE, AS
it was in 1940. The cool waters of the North Sea and the English Channel
were occasionally fretted by a brisk northeast breeze, but this caused no discomfort to the thousands of travelers on the big car ferries between Dover and
Calais. The voyage took just over an hour, enough time to listen to the safety
announcements (in English, French, and German), have a bite to eat, visit the
duty-free shop, and walk on deck to watch the White Cliffs fade and Cape
Gris-Nez grow distinct.

Eastward along the French coast toward Belgium, a pink-gray haze hung
over the oil refineries and steelworks of Dunkirk, thirty-nine sea miles from
Dover, where fifty years ago ascending clouds of black smoke formed for nine
days an unnerving landmark for the skippers of the motley craft (some without compasses) that were sailing to lift off the surrounded troops. Aboard the
ferry I crossed on this year, a good number of the passengers were elderly
men—many with wives or grown-up children—returning to the place where
they had evaded death or capture. Although a few make annual pilgrimages
to Dunkirk, many of those veterans of the British Expeditionary Force were
going back for the first time since 1940. This was to be the fiftieth anniversary of a military defeat that allowed nearly 340,000 vanquished soldiers to
get away.

While Hitler was hailing the end of "the greatest battle of world history"
and bells throughout the Third Reich tolled for three days in celebration,
Churchill growled at the House of Commons, "Wars are not won by evacuations." But probably this one was. After their stunning, swift punch through
the "impenetrable" Ardennes to the Channel coast, the Germans let many of
their quarry slip from their grasp. The professional core of the British army—
minus its tanks, vehicles, and heavy weapons—escaped. So did 110,000
French, though sadly many of them were summoned back to western France
and final surrender a few weeks later.

The urgently and brilliantly organized evacuation transformed the shambles of defeat into the groundwork for victory. "Bloody Marvellous" was a headline in the *Daily Mirror,* and the words were plucked from the lips of every man. The evacuation indeed involved the British public; its civilian representatives were there aboard yachts, barges, and paddle steamers. Fifty years later, the British have found it equally hard to escape being reminded by the press, radio, and television of the fall of France and the possibility—that 1940 summer—of German invasion. We have heard recordings of Churchill's speeches and seen film clips of Heinkels and Stukas dropping their bombs.

Much of Dunkirk was destroyed during those fateful days by bomb and shell, fire and explosion. The rebuilt city is like its former self, hardworking, friendly, unchic. The restored neo-Gothic town hall presides over postwar row houses and four-story apartment buildings put up in the devastated city center. A twenty-story, silo-shaped hotel and several huge dockyard cranes now dominate the skyline.

Dunkirk began in the early Middle Ages as a settlement of fishermen around a church, or kirk, on the dunes. Its harbor and canals sheltered some of the fleet that the duke of Parma mustered vainly in 1588 to help the Spanish Armada invade England. It was fortified by the great military engineer Vauban in the late seventeenth century while its corsairs, led by Jean Bart, wrecked the maritime trade of Louis XIV's enemies. The port is the third largest in France—with oil terminals and shipyards, locks that allow the passage of large ships into nontidal basins, and an intricate, accessible commercial waterfront in the heart of the town.

The tidal outer harbor is formed by two jetties, or moles. The mole on the east is the longest, with its base on the seawall that adjoins the beach running eastward. Along here is the "front" of Malo-les-Bains, a once-separate seaside community that is now one of Dunkirk's desirable suburbs. The beach stretches east to Zuydcoote, a village behind the dunes, and then Bray-Dunes, a tiny resort whose promenade and seafront buildings stand where the dunes used to be. A mile or so farther on is the Belgian border.

For Dunkirk's citizenry, the fiftieth anniversary of what they call *"la bataille"* is also the forty-fifth anniversary of V E Day. The last weekend in May was the centerpiece of eleven days of lectures, conferences, concerts, exhibitions, formal dinners, and fireworks. The French frigate *Jean Bart* was in the harbor, being visited by hundreds of Dunkerquois. Saturday, May 26, was specifically French Day, with a parade of *anciens combattants français.* Many of the older residents could not help remembering their days and nights in the cellars, under attack, fires raging, water cut off; the surrender that left them with a ruined town, docks full of sunken ships, streets and beaches littered

with the corpses of men and horses; and then the long despair and misery of
occupation, with German troops billeted in the houses of those who had survived, having to obey arbitrary German orders, and with only the occasional
sense of resistance to call back lost pride. As the town's mayor felt bound to
note while welcoming British visitors, the name Dunkerque for the French
symbolizes not just Nazi victory but French military defeat.

Even so, Anglo-French relations were remarkably cordial on this occasion.
British flags were to be seen all over town—the Union Jack flew alongside the
Tricolor, sometimes entangled with it, on the fifteenth-century bell tower in
the rue Clemenceau, which also houses the town's tourist office and war me-
morials. (In Malo-les-Bains, after the war, one street was renamed rue Winston Churchill.) *La Voix du Nord,* the leading regional daily paper, gave the
proceedings ample, evenhanded coverage. I had the impression that most of
the townspeople were by now unaware of the 1940 animosity between the Allies, which arose from the French feeling that the British had abandoned
them, the poor communications between the British and French staffs, the
British sense of French incompetence, and the French command's initial refusal to have anything to do with evacuation—and then its cry of despair:
"Why aren't you rescuing our men too!"

Most people seemed to be moved by the occasion—and those running ho-
tels, shops, and cafés clearly appreciated the boost in trade. At various ceremonies French speakers ended with *"Vive la France! Vive la Grande-Bretagne!"*
and the British replied with "Long live France! Long live the queen!" Now
and again one realized that Britain—never very far away—is closer than ever.
My hotel-room television lit up with a cricket match between England and
New Zealand.

British veterans and their wives were everywhere, in town-center bars, on
the front at Malo-les-Bains, and on the quayside of the Bassin du Commerce,
where many survivors of the fleet of Little Ships were rafted up. Some couples
had come not only to remember but for a holiday. The wife of one Welsh field-
ambulance man I met near the East Mole said, "We're staying for a week, but
we've had our money's worth already." Elderly Scotchmen filled the elevators
of one packed hotel—as did the fumes of scotch. One man had not only a flask
in his pocket but a creased army-issue map of this part of the coast. He pulled
it out to show me.

"I've never lost it. To tell you the truth, though, we were lost then. We
headed north over the fields—the clogged roads were murder. When we got
to the beach, we turned left."

Snatches of conversation could be heard: about the production cost of the

Sten gun ("nine shillings and six-pence"); about the sore crotch you got from marching in long johns; about the smell of dead horses; about gratitude for a deep Flanders ditch or for a hot cup of tea handed up to an exhausted soldier by a girl on a Kent railway station platform when his train from Folkestone paused.

Although I saw one man filling a small jar with beach sand as a souvenir, most of the veterans seemed to have their fill of memories. One or two still had bad dreams about the evacuation. Queued up in long lines zigzagging across the beach, waiting for the boats from the bizarre fleet to pick them up, the troops looked like ants, simple to crush. The dunes provided a bit of shelter from shellfire or the marauding Luftwaffe, with soft sand that was easy to dig into and that absorbed some of the impact of bombs. The beach, shelving gently out to sea, seems almost flat at low tide; it stretches out over half a mile, making embarkation difficult into craft of any size. Hence the need for shallow-draft boats; hence improvised piers formed by vehicles head to tail, on whose roofs and hoods the troops clambered out to deeper water. (The advantage of embarking from the beach was that it dispersed the troops and made them less of a target than they were on the East Mole.)

Many remember the coldness of those late-May nights—"You were glad of your greatcoat then"—but also their thankfulness for the dark, and for the fog and mist that grounded German planes for several days. Many recall the fearsome sound of a diving Stuka, with its banshee siren—the bright idea of the Luftwaffe's technical director, Ernst Udet. For some—the gunners especially—it was dreadful having to wreck cherished weaponry so it wouldn't fall to the Germans in working order. For many, of course, the hardest thing is still that their mates fell at their sides on the sand or, almost at the boats, sank beneath the surface. A lot couldn't swim. I met one man who said he'd received a letter from his girlfriend while waiting on the beach—the army postal service persisted! But when the field kitchens were abandoned, the troops were down to bully beef and so-called dog biscuits—"You had to suck those perishers for a long time before you could chew them up," one veteran told me.

The East Mole, soon severely damaged, was a combined breakwater and jetty, about three-quarters of a mile long. When the docks and inner basins became too difficult to use, it provided the best berthing for destroyers, minesweepers, and passenger steamers. Often bombed and shelled, with men lined up on it sometimes four abreast, its wooden deck had to be patched with gangplanks, hatch covers, and ward-room tables. Still, there were gaps. One BEF veteran told me he'd had to jump into the water while making his way out along the mole to a ship at the far end. "I couldn't swim. I hung on to my haversack and kicked like hell." I asked him—thinking of the weight of cans of bully beef—what was in his haversack. "I had my mouth organ, a gold watch for my wife, and a red velvet dress for my niece." I didn't ask how or where the last two items were obtained.

Some men brought away dogs, rescued from blitzed houses and abandoned farms; one brought along his new bride, a local girl. The piermaster in charge on the East Mole was a Canadian-born British naval officer, Commander John Clouston, who for over a week shouted at and generally encouraged the procession of battered men. Clouston supervised the embarkation of nearly 200,000 troops, but he himself was to be one of the 3,500 lost in the course of the evacuation. On June 2, returning to the mole from an overnight visit to Dover, he was drowned when a German plane sank the RAF launch he was on.

The mole now is solid concrete for the first half of its length from shore. This has a walkway on top and a locked gate where it joins the outer section— a breakwater formed of huge, jumbled-together blocks of concrete shaped like elongated Christmas puddings. (They would not be comfortable to berth against or board a ship from.) Along this outer half, tall navigation beacons are placed at intervals. The inner section is favored by Dunkirk anglers, who are also disposed at discreet distances with their rods, radios, and pouches of food and drink. A few strenuous walkers pace back and forth, stepping over the rods and taking deep gulps of the bracing North Sea air.

On the long beach, the activities of early summer were not interrupted by the anniversary. A few children played waist-deep in the chilly sea. A dozen Windsurfers, their bright sails like butterfly wings, planed back and forth. Families sat on the fine sand, sunning themselves. Yellow trucks trundled past, sweeping up litter. Along the promenades at Malo and Bray, people sheltered behind the café windbreaks, eating mussels and *frites* and drinking aperitifs. Children rode the carousels. In places old Christmas trees had been planted in the dunes to help hold them together, but at Bray, where the sand blew inland down the side streets, a high new apartment building was going up right on the dunes—not far from the spot where a giant concrete bunker, part of Hitler's anti-invasion wall, lay toppled, a lesson (one would think) about the perils of building on sand. At low tide at Bray, sand yachts raced over the flat surface of the beach. In a gully at the water's edge, I found the wooden ribs of a vessel, possibly the bones of a Thames barge, lost in the evacuation.

Behind the dunes, marshes long reclaimed from the sea stretch inland, now field and pasture, drained by ditches and canals. It is an almost Netherlandish countryside, not ideal for tanks, the narrow roads easily clogged by refugees and abandoned vehicles. It is where, in an increasingly tight perimeter, the rear guard (at first Anglo-French, then just French) held off the Germans long enough for all those troops to get away. This weekend, on rural roads and newer highways, the worries of some drivers were about the chances of being stopped by the gendarmerie and Breathalyzed, or of colliding with a British car whose driver had forgotten which side of the road he was supposed to be on.

Back in town, the Dunkerquois and visitors strolled around the quayside of the Bassin du Commerce. Here were displayed several aircraft engines that had been hauled from the sea by fishing boats—crumbling alloys and corroded steel like discolored coral. An excursion boat named *Elsa* was taking full loads of passengers on trips around the harbor. Most people had come to admire the Little Ships. Escorted by several Royal Navy vessels and a modern lifeboat, over 70 had made the crossing from England, representatives of the 700 or so that had helped the larger craft in the evacuation. Some 200 are still afloat, many just as houseboats, a few beyond hope. Most of those here were between-the-wars motor cruisers, with plumb-stem bows, upright wheelhouses, and little if any cockpits, clearly the objects of devotion expressed in paint, varnish, and elbow grease. They had romantic or homely names like *Wanda, L'Orage, Aureol,* and *Janthea.* Although none at this point is owned by anyone who made the 1940 passage, many had been to previous anniversary celebrations.

John Knight, the skipper of one, told me that in 1975 he was hailed from the quay by an Englishman clutching a large parcel in one hand; his other arm was missing. Would the skipper mind taking a package back to England for him? No, said Knight, if he didn't mind saying what was in it. Of course, said the veteran. He had just been walking on the outskirts of town, came to a familiar-looking cottage, and was peering over the hedge when an old lady asked, "Can I help you, monsieur?"

He said, "I was here in 1940."

"Ah," she said, "wait—don't go away." She went into a shed and came out with the mounting for a machine gun. "Here," she said, "you left this behind."

Knight's boat carried the mounting back, and he was invited to the ceremony at which it was officially returned to its regiment.

Sailing boats were in a minority in the Bassin, as they were in 1940, but several were the most conspicuous Little Ships. These were three big spritsail barges that had once carried such cargoes as grain, animal feed, and bricks around the south and east coasts of England. One, the *Ena,* had been abandoned by her crew on the beach here—they were taken off on a minesweeper as the Germans closed in. A late-arriving party of Royal Artillery gunners and

East Yorkshire infantrymen climbed aboard and sailed her home. Another, the *Pudge*, had reached Dunkirk under sail after the tug towing her hit a mine and sank. The *Pudge* now belongs to the Thames Barge Sailing Club. A sign in French in her rigging explained how she had rescued 200 French soldiers from the beaches. Underneath, on the deck, a steel bucket had been placed for donations toward her maintenance—pounds and francs equally accepted.

On Saturday evening I sat in a restaurant next to an elderly Englishman and his middle-aged son. The older man, Frederick Scott, spryly built, with a small, trim mustache, had been a staff sergeant in the Duke of Cornwall's Light Infantry, which had helped hold the perimeter until May 30. He said, "I got off the beach at Bray. I was wearing my greatcoat, which was wet through and very heavy, and they had a job hauling me into a small boat. From that, I was taken on board a minesweeper and, unscathed, straight back to Dover. Lucky!" Mr. Scott, who went on to fight in North Africa and Italy, seemed apprehensive about the speed at which his fellow veterans might be marching in the parade next morning. He said with a smile, "I hope they're all older than me."

On Sunday, *la journée Britannique,* I spotted Mr. Scott among the 4,000 veterans who paraded in the tree-lined Place Jean-Bart (where the large, sword-brandishing statue of the corsair had also survived 1940). There were speeches from Lord Kaberry, president of the Dunkirk Veterans Association, who said the dark cloud of fifty years ago had been blown away, and from Michel Delabarre, mayor of Dunkirk and French minister of transport, who reminded us of *"la prix de la liberté."*

A few veterans were wearing kilts, but most were in navy blazers or their best suits, many wearing berets, medals, and ribbons. Some had walking sticks or were in wheelchairs, pushed by friends or wives. Thousands of townspeople were on hand. A bugle played the "Last Post," a lady sold paper buttonhole poppies for British Legion funds, a British TV crew chased after Katie Adie, a star BBC news reporter, as she sought interviews and camera shots, and several wives sought Ms. Adie's autograph. The French sang "La Marseillaise" and the British, more loudly, "God Save the Queen." Interspersed with the bands of the Royal Green Jackets, the civilian but resplendently uniformed Lancastrian Brigade, and the South Wales Constabulary, the three battalions of veterans marched off toward the Town Hall, following their standards. They marched at a steady pace, not too fast, remarkably in step, swinging their arms. I caught Mr. Scott's eye, which twinkled. Once a soldier, always a soldier.

In the afternoon the ceremonies were on and off the beach at Malo-les-Bains. The Little Ships and their escorts came out of the harbor and formed a giant

circle, in the center of which a wreath was laid by an RAF air-sea rescue helicopter. The RAF's three-plane "historic flight"—a Hurricane, a Lancaster, and
a Spitfire—flew over at a slow rumble, followed by a dart past of RAF aerobatic-
team jets, streaming white smoke. Beside the 1940 battle memorial, not far
from the inshore end of the East Mole, prayers were said and hymns sung—
"Abide with Me"; "O God, Our Help in Ages Past"—though the wind made
the words indistinct.

Off the beach the Windsurfers continued to swoop back and forth, and
boys on skateboards rattled along the front. A man chased his dog; a mother
yelled at her small son; a passenger jet high overhead left behind a white trail
on its way east; and a French naval officer put out a hand to help a distinguished-
looking British veteran up the slope from the sand to the promenade. "Here
you are, sir," said the Frenchman. *"Merci,"* said the veteran. A second service
was held at the military cemetery. Later I heard that two veterans took sick
during the day and died.

I encountered few Germans in Dunkirk. It was not their occasion, now or
then. One pair I saw at a filling station made a point of speaking English to
the cashier. While most of the German army behaved as "correctly" as soldiers
can, several barbaric incidents not far from Dunkirk have not been forgotten.
On May 27, at the village of Le Paradis, ninety-seven men of the Royal Nor-
folks were taken prisoner and shot. On the twenty-eighth, sixty-six of the
Royal Warwicks surrendered and were massacred at Wormhout. Both these
atrocities were perpetrated by the same SS Leibstandarte Adolf Hitler regiment, commanded by Wilhelm Mohnke (who at this writing is still living,
near Hamburg, on a German army pension).

Yet no one I met at Dunkirk was conducting extensive postmortems. The
faults have been gone over time and again. It is the good fortune—Why We
Got Away—that still bemuses survivors. On one side, Hitler's crucial halt order, which delayed the German advance three days; Gerd von Rundstedt's
confirmation of Hitler's nervousness about the exposed flanks of the panzer-
led *Sichelschnitt* thrust; the vast surprise of such rapid success and the fact that
the German high command hadn't sufficiently considered what to do after the
breakthrough; and the gift of glory Göring demanded for his Luftwaffe, to
smash the Dunkirk pocket, which he failed to seize.

On the other side, a breathing space was afforded by the shock of General
Giffard le Q. Martel's British counterattack west of Arras (which added to
Hitler's nervousness), by the brave French defense at Lille, under General C.
S. Molinie, and by the unexpectedly long resistance of the forces at Calais and
the Dunkirk rear guard. The RAF and the Fleet Air Arm, often unseen by the

men on the mole and beaches, fought valiantly to keep the Stukas and E-boats at bay. Above all, there was Viscount Gort's perception in mid-May of looming defeat and his almost heroic single-minded grasp of the need for evacuation, and there was—back in Dover—Admiral Sir Bertram Ramsay's brilliant command of the evacuation, code-named Operation Dynamo. At that moment, British naval organization and energy matched that of the panzers.

General Heinz Guderian of the Nineteenth Panzer Corps later observed: "What the future course of the war would have been if we had succeeded at the time in taking the British Expeditionary Force prisoner at Dunkirk, it is now impossible to guess." As it was, one British gunner making his way to the beaches read an airdropped German leaflet that said, "The match is ended. Throw down your arms," and was able to reply truthfully, "Ended? We've only just kicked off."

AFTER DUNKIRK

BRUCE I. GUDMUNDSSON

The war in the West did not end with Dunkirk. Fighting in France continued for another three weeks, an interval that is rarely written about and one that was for the Germans much more than a mopping-up operation. France, outnumbered now, may have stood alone, but what remained of its army, some of its best and proudest units, did not give up easily. Germany suffered more than half its losses after the British left. As the military historian Bruce I. Gudmundsson points out, the Maginot Line actually did what it was supposed to do, and by the time of the final French surrender, the Germans had succeeded only in taking a few outlying bunkers, at considerable cost. Until the very end of "The Western Campaign" (as the Germans called it), Hitler prepared for a French counterstroke, a Marne-like miracle that never came. It was not the French army that collapsed but its generals. They ordered retreat at the very moment when their troops were doing the most damage to the invaders. No less a figure than Marshal Philippe Pétain, the octogenarian hero of Verdun and the new head of a government that had fled from Paris to Bordeaux, called for an armistice that was, like the 1918 version, actually an offer of surrender.

Bruce I. Gudmundsson is a former Marine who currently makes his living advising the Armed Forces on matters of tactics, policy, and structure. A frequent contributor to both the *Marine Corps Gazette* and *MHQ,* he is the author of several books, including *Storm Troop Tactics, On Artillery,* and *On Armor.* He is affiliated with the Center for War Studies at the University of Glasgow.

IN THE ENGLISH-SPEAKING WORLD, IT IS EASY TO BELIEVE THE last act of the great Blitzkrieg campaign of 1940 was the evacuation of the British Expeditionary Force from Dunkirk. It is with this heroic event (which ended in the early hours of June 4), and not the pathetic collapse of the Third Republic, that chapters in history books, episodes in television series, and lectures at staff colleges most often end. Because of this, it is easy to believe that whatever took place in the eighteen days that passed between the departure of the last boat from Dunkirk and the signing of the Franco-German armistice in the famous railroad car in the forest of Compiègne was but a footnote to an affair that had already been settled.

The Germans and the French see things differently. Well aware that over half of the German losses were taken out of play after Dunkirk, continental historians rarely make the mistake of dismissing the second half of what the Germans call "the Western campaign" as mere mopping up. They know that during the three weeks in which France stood alone against Germany, French tactical leadership was abler, French units more effective, and French resistance far stiffer than had been the case during the first half of the campaign. While no one imagines that the German thrust into the heart of France might have ended in a replay of the "Miracle of the Marne," those who look beyond Dunkirk know that it took the Germans a lot of hard fighting, as well as considerable operational skill, to deprive France of the remnants of her army.

The difficulties encountered in finishing off the French army came as no surprise to the Germans of 1940. Many, from Adolf Hitler himself down to the graying reservists who manned the Siegfried Line, had firsthand experience of the ferocity with which the French had defended their homeland during World War I. Those under forty had grown up with tales of the unyielding defenders of Verdun, the Chemin des Dames, and Hartmannsweilerkopf. So widespread was the German desire to avoid a direct confrontation with the French army that without exception, every one of the operational plans proposed to Hitler during the long winter of 1939–40 was aimed exclusively at the conquest of the geographical region known as the Low Countries. This covered all of Belgium, the Netherlands, and Luxembourg, as well as a long, thin strip of northern France. Such a conquest, Hitler hoped, would provide the bargaining chips needed to legitimize the Russo-German dismemberment of Poland, give Germany the air bases needed to threaten England, and provide a geographic buffer to protect German factories in the Ruhr Valley.

The plan that Hitler finally settled on was aptly called *Sichelschnitt,* "the cut of the scythe." Its definitive feature was the use of nearly all of the German armored and motorized divisions to drive across the northern edge of France, cutting off the Low Countries as effectively as a reaper's blade cuts a sheaf of wheat. Once isolated by this cut of the scythe, the Allied forces in the Low

Countries, including the armies of the hitherto neutral Belgium and the Netherlands, would be crushed between two powerful army groups. Though confident that neither the Belgians nor the Dutch could do much to prevent this maneuver, Hitler was deathly afraid of a French counterstroke, a massive attack that could leave his armored forces isolated on the Channel coast.

Hitler was particularly afraid of the French armored and motorized forces. As early as 1934, his protégé Heinz Guderian had noted that France had sufficient numbers of tanks, trucks, and half-track personnel carriers to assemble a mobile force that, to use the words of a Soviet general observing French maneuvers, "would make Genghis Khan green with envy." Lest these forces be used to break the German scythe before the harvest was over, Hitler decided to create a strong defensive line along the long chain of hills that marks the end of the Low Countries and the beginning of the great central plateau of France. This line would be established by muscle-powered infantry formations that Hitler ordered "laid like a string of pearls" behind the fast-moving armored and motorized troops.

✦

WHILE HITLER'S FEARS of a French counterstroke played havoc with his nerves, they turned out to be unfounded. Instead of interfering with the trap that the Germans were setting for the Belgians and the Dutch, the most up-to-date forces available to Hitler's enemies rushed into it. On May 10, 1940, the day the German offensive in the west began, four French armies, as well as the lion's share of the British Expeditionary Force, raced forward into the Low Countries. Twenty days later, this magnificent assemblage, which included more motorized divisions than the Germans had employed to conquer Poland, no longer existed. Some of the units that had escaped destruction in combat were awaiting evacuation at Dunkirk. The rest were back in the French heartland, licking their wounds and getting ready for the next round.

The French like to say that the "appetite grows with eating." This was certainly the case with Hitler. By the end of May, he had decided to undertake a second offensive in the west. While his generals believed that this second act of the great drama should aim at nothing less than the destruction of the French army, Hitler was somewhat more modest in his goals. Not yet convinced that the French of 1940 were any less dangerous than their fathers had been in the Great War of 1914–18, he set as the goal for the operation the seizure of the iron-rich province of Lorraine. Home to much of the French armaments industry, Lorraine was also the back door to the still formidable Maginot Line.

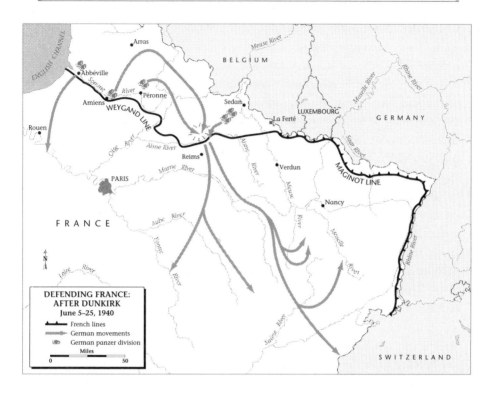

Except for a German advance along the coast, the Weygand Line (named for the French commander in chief) and the Maginot Line contained the invaders after Dunkirk. Meanwhile, panzer divisions converging on Reims encountered a huge traffic jam. Only after Weygand mistakenly ordered retreat on June 10 were the Germans able to break through and race for the interior.

Just how difficult the Maginot Line would be to pierce had been demonstrated to the Germans when, in the course of their initial attack, they ran into a small part of it. Thirty kilometers south of Sedan, the 71st Infantry Division, one of the first "pearls" to be laid in the wake of the "cut of the scythe," managed to take a small fort called La Ferté. For the Germans, the good news was they were able to capture the fort, the westernmost outpost of the Maginot Line, in less than two days. Whether the Germans could rely on their ability to repeat this coup was, however, another matter entirely, for the taking of La Ferté involved both Herculean efforts and considerable luck.

The bulk of the physical plant of La Ferté—a rabbit warren of barracks, kitchens, and magazines protected by concrete walls over eight feet thick—

was located so far underground as to be impervious to the heaviest bombardment. The only parts that showed above the surface were what the French nicknamed *cloches* ("bells"), the little steel cupolas that allowed French officers to observe the battle and French machine gunners to aim their weapons. These were likewise nearly impossible to destroy with artillery. For that reason, the heart of the German plan to take La Ferté consisted of getting small teams of combat engineers close enough to the bells to destroy them with explosive charges. This done, the defenders would still be hard to reach, but they would be blind and incapable of doing much damage.

To help the engineers cross the few hundred meters of ground dominated by the machine guns of La Ferté, the Germans assembled a grand battery of no fewer than 259 artillery pieces and put them under the command of the Austrian artillery virtuoso Colonel Robert Martinek. The nine heaviest pieces, 210mm siege mortars firing 250-pound shells, carved craters in the landscape. These would provide shelter for the engineers as they worked their way forward. The rest of the guns, which ranged from 88mm antiaircraft guns to 150mm field howitzers, were aimed at the bells. The physical effect on these thick steel cupolas was minimal. The few shells that actually made contact did nothing more than gouge the surface of the armor plate. The effect on the French machine gunners, who had to deal with the noise and vibration of as many as thirty near-misses every minute, was sufficient. For every time a French machine gunner turned his attention away from his field of fire, an opportunity was created for some German engineers to move a few meters forward.

On the first day of the attack, this technique allowed the Germans to knock out about half of the bells of La Ferté. Indeed, it worked so well that it took the French machine gunners and observers time to realize that they were under attack by something other than mere artillery fire. Whether the trick could be repeated on the second day, however, was never put to the test. Before the Germans could finish their assault, the hundred or so Frenchmen defending La Ferté were overcome by asphyxiation, as the air became poisoned by fumes from the electric generators and the smoke produced by the French machine guns.

Though the German propaganda machine tried to make the most of the capture of La Ferté, the disparity between the effort expended and the results obtained confirmed the German belief that the Maginot Line was more easily avoided than taken. Any penetrations necessary to the conquest of Lorraine should, as a result, be made along what would soon be called the Weygand Line. Named for General Maxime Weygand, Marshal Foch's former chief of staff who had recently been put in charge of all French forces fighting against Germany, this was a long series of defensive positions that, located mostly on the south bank of the rivers Somme and Aisne, stood opposite the German infantry divisions of Hitler's "string of pearls." They had come out of the hills to occupy the north banks of the rivers and canals that formed the great moat of the Weygand Line. Thus, the barrier that had been erected against a French counterthrust was to serve as the launchpad for Germany's second offensive in the west.

✦

GERMAN PLANS for this second offensive, with the code name of "Case Red," had started to take shape in the last week of May, when the German conquest of the Low Countries, though far from complete, was all but certain. The idea was to penetrate the Weygand Line in four places, at Abbéville on the Channel coast, at Amiens directly north of Paris, at Péronne just east of Amiens, and, closest to Lorraine, at Reims, some ninety miles east of Paris. Each of these penetrations was to be carried out by a strong armored corps, with two to four panzer divisions, reinforced with additional infantry, combat engineers, heavy artillery, and, in light of the fact that France could still put a thousand or more tanks in the field, units of antitank guns. Between these main attacks, the infantry would press forward, attacking across the rivers Somme and Aisne to keep the French from ganging up on the armored penetrations.

Deciding on a second offensive and carrying it out were two different things. The conquest of the Low Countries, and the defeat of the cream of the French and British armies, had taken nearly 65,000 men out of German operational units, had left over half of Germany's tanks in need of repair, and had worn the soles from untold thousands of jackboots. The infantry, which had led the way in every breakthrough, had been particularly hard hit and needed time to rest, refit, and integrate replacements. A logistics system, based on the heavily damaged Belgian rail network, had to be set up and, if the vast majority of German units were to move beyond their railheads, the 250,000 horses that had taken part in the "cut of the scythe" had to be given a few days of unhindered grazing.

Except for the fast-disappearing Dunkirk pocket, the Western Front was largely quiet. The week that connected May and June of 1940 was mainly used for consolidation of positions, reorganization of units, and the regrouping of formations. What little fighting there was involved bridgeheads, those places where the Germans had made a foothold on the south side of two narrow but militarily significant rivers, the Somme and the Aisne, that now

marked the northern boundary of French-held territory. The most hotly contested of these bridgeheads was at Abbéville, a town near the point where the
Somme flowed into the English Channel. Here, Charles de Gaulle's improvised armored division put to flight the better part of a German reserve division, including the List Regiment, in which a certain Lance Corporal Hitler
had served during the First World War. Here also the remnants of the British
Expeditionary Force, principally the Scots from the 51st (Highland) Division,
took part in a series of furious but ultimately futile attacks aimed at masking
the overall weakness of the French position.

This weakness was less a matter of numbers than of the peculiar interaction
of numbers and geography. To hold the 180 or so miles of the Weygand Line,
the French had to put nearly all of their sixty available divisions in line, with
nearly no reserves within or behind each division. The Germans, with ninety
or so divisions available for their attack, could match the French one for one
and still have thirty divisions left over. This numerical advantage translated
into the ability to make mistakes. If the Germans failed to break through in
one area, they could transfer their reserves to another. If, however, a single
French division was defeated, the entire line would be in jeopardy.

The French divisions varied greatly in quality. The best, with a high proportion of professional soldiers, a full set of weapons and equipment, and no
experience of the recent debacle in the Low Countries, were along the Aisne,
defending against the German penetration aimed at Reims. These divisions
also had the best terrain to defend, particularly the Argonne Forest, heavily
wooded uplands that had been successfully defended against German invaders
so many times before. Other divisions, particularly those hastily assembled from
the 130,000 men who had been evacuated from Dunkirk and returned to
France, were not so fortunate. These lacked the cohesion that only comes from
months of common service, had abandoned their heavy weapons along the road
to Dunkirk, and, most importantly, were convinced that nothing they could do
would prevent a repetition of the disaster they had just experienced. The majority of French divisions, however, were in a state that was neither excellent nor
deplorable. Adequately armed by the standards of the time, they were hampered
by the doctrine of a methodical *bataille de conduite* that left little scope for initiative. They were slow to react, usually more concerned with holding terrain or
maintaining liaison than with what the enemy was doing, and thus generally
unable to take advantage of German mistakes.

The initial German attack, launched on June 5, met some nasty surprises.
At Péronne, the Third and Fourth Panzer divisions ran into extensive minefields. Well covered by the fire of antitank guns and artillery, these minefields

deprived the divisions of 30 percent of their tanks and all of their forward momentum. At Amiens, the problem was the French "hedgehog" tactics, which allowed German tanks, but none of the other elements of the attacking armored divisions, to pass between a series of strongpoints.

✦

ALONG THE AISNE, the four armored divisions of Panzergruppe Guderian, the greatest concentration of German armor yet to be placed under a single commander, made a whole series of unpleasant discoveries. The first was the skill and high morale of the French divisions Guderian faced. In contrast to the irresolute defenders of Sedan, these divisions were full of infantrymen with a taste for close combat, gunners who realized that the bark (or, more precisely, the wail) of the Stuka was worse than its bite, and officers who knew when to throw out the book. As a result, when the German infantry made a penetration, they were met with immediate and violent counterattacks. When they assembled for an attack, their assembly areas were violently bombarded by French artillery. And, in at least one case, when the Germans massed their tanks for a breakthrough, they found that the obsolete field guns of the French divisional artillery, the 75mm field guns designed in the 1890s, made excellent antitank weapons.

At Amiens and Péronne, the result of these surprises was a modest degree of failure. The Germans still managed to move forward, but progress was slow. Along the eastern edge of the Aisne, in the dark forest of the Argonne, however, some German attacks met not merely with failure but with defeat. Near a village called Vandy, a German regiment that had penetrated four kilometers into the French position was hit with a series of fierce counterattacks by elements of the French 36th Infantry Division. By the time it had returned to its jumping-off position, this German regiment had lost nearly 971 officers and men, nearly a third of its effectives, to death, wounds, and, in nearly 400 cases, surrender. To the west of Vandy, the French 14th Infantry Division dealt with a similar attack, on a larger scale, in a similar way. In that case, more than 800 Germans, trapped between French strongpoints, chose surrender over continued resistance.

✦

ONLY AT ABBÉVILLE, at the western edge of the Weygand Line, did a German attack result in unqualified success. There, in what was to have been a subsidiary operation, the weakest of Germany's five armored corps (the XV Motorized Corps of General Hermann Hoth) punched through a French colonial division and, without the slightest pause, began its long ride down the Channel coast. The best-known member of this corps, Erwin Rommel, contributed to this victory in his usual manner, leading his armored division from the front and allowing nothing to stop the forward movement of his command. By June 9, the XV Motorized Corps had crossed the river Seine at a number of points, capturing the ancient city of Rouen and isolating the great port of Le Havre. Three days later, this latter city, defended by the same combination of French mechanized units and Scottish infantry that had proved so troublesome at Abbéville, surrendered.

The effect of this maneuver on the Allied leadership was considerable. The British, who were on the point of landing the 1st Canadian Division at Le Havre, decided instead to evacuate the few thousand British soldiers who remained on French soil. General Weygand became convinced that the line that bore his name had become untenable. Despite the fact that the Germans had been stopped on the Aisne and were paying dearly for every advance made in other sectors, he began preparations for a general withdrawal to the south. The French civil government agreed with General Weygand's assessment and ordered itself to abandon Paris.

While the breakthrough at Abbéville convinced both the French and the British commanders that they had lost, it failed to convince the Germans that they had won. Many, including both Hitler and his senior army officer, General von Brauchitsch, saw more danger than opportunity. To their minds, schooled in the German military tradition, such a penetration was cause not for panic or even retreat by the defenders, but for a riposte. They therefore imagined that at any minute the French strategic reserve, located somewhere north of Paris, would swoop down upon the vulnerable penetration, cutting off its lifeline and defeating its elements in detail. What they failed to realize was that the French had no strategic reserve. Having forgotten the teaching of Frederick the Great that "he who defends everywhere defends nowhere," the French had placed all their available forces either on, or just behind, the Weygand Line.

Hitler's eyes, moreover, were still on Lorraine, the prize that his acolyte Guderian had yet to win. Thus, instead of following the logic of the blitzkrieg and sending all available forces through the gap at Abbéville, Hitler sought to redeem Guderian's failure at the Aisne and the Argonne. He called off the attacks at Amiens and Péronne and sent the forces that had been fighting there, including two armored corps, to the Aisne. This brought to eight the number of German armored divisions trying to break down the back door into Lorraine and, as these eight divisions represented more than 80 percent of Germany's tanks, made it clear where Hitler's priorities lay. It also created a huge traffic jam that ensured that most of the tanks would not get to the front for three or four days.

Instead of the very real problems that the Germans were having on and behind the Aisne, General Weygand saw only dangers. The strange reluctance of the French air force, which enjoyed significant numerical superiority, to contest German control of the air meant that Weygand was unaware of the great traffic jam that had formed. The poor communications between forward French divisions and the various higher headquarters, as well as the practice of passing each message laboriously through the formal chain of command, ensured that General Weygand was also poorly informed about the degree to which the French troops on the Aisne had been able to resist and even repulse the German attackers. As a result, Weygand looked at the situation on the Aisne through the lens of earlier battles in the campaign and thus greatly underestimated the powers of resistance of his forces there. This led him to the fateful decision to order his most successful formations to retreat at the very moment that they were doing the most damage to the Germans.

On the evening of June 10, before the additional German tanks could go into action, the French forces on the Aisne received General Weygand's order to withdraw. Grudgingly, the hard-fighting French divisions complied, taking their equipment, their stockpiled supplies, and their prisoners with them. To keep the Germans from pursuing with too much vigor, they launched periodic counterattacks and, particularly in the heavily wooded Argonne, waged guerrilla warfare with snipers and small teams of Senegalese whose experience in jungle warfare had made them especially deadly in forests. In cases where Germans who had broken through in other sectors got in the way of this reluctant retreat, the erstwhile defenders of the Aisne attacked to the rear, convincing some Germans that the long-feared French counteroffensive was under way.

✦

THE FACT that this fighting retreat played on German nerves did not necessarily mean that it calmed French ones. The retirement of other French units from the Weygand Line had not gone nearly as well. Equipment and supplies were abandoned, bridges were blown up ahead of schedule, municipal officials sabotaged efforts at resistance, and drunkenness was rife. Even where discipline was maintained, the fact that no provisions had been made for such a retreat deprived otherwise formidable units of their capacity to fight. Such was the case of the crews of those Maginot Line forts located in the regions west of Metz and north of Strasbourg that Weygand had ordered evacuated on June

12. Without transport, food, or even rifles, and, having failed to acquire either the habits or the calluses so necessary to service as walking infantry, these once proud units were soon reduced to ragged bands of footsore refugees.

The evacuation of the Maginot Line forts was something that the French could not hide for long. Active German patrolling—which represented almost all of the activity of the German divisions opposite the Maginot Line—began to discover empty blockhouses within hours of the French departure. To Hitler, the message was clear. The capture of Lorraine was not only inevitable but could now be achieved with relatively modest forces. It was time, therefore, to look for other prizes. On June 13, the very same day that the commandant of Paris declared it an open city, Hitler reversed his previous directives. Instead of avoiding that great conurbation, with its historic ability to swallow whole armies, the advancing German forces should take possession of it. The next day, German infantry units, led by reconnaissance patrols on horseback and bicycles, entered the French capital.

While the fall of Paris overjoyed the Germans, it did little to change their overall approach to the campaign. Unaware of the chaos and despair that reigned in French units, in the French high command, and, particularly, in the French government, the Germans lived in fear of a swift reversal of fortune. Just as every step they had taken toward Paris had been haunted by fears of a second Miracle of the Marne, progress south and east of Paris evoked memories of the Franco-Prussian War, when, even after the French standing army had been defeated in the north, large-scale resistance erupted in the valley of the Loire. Spurred on by this specter, the Germans rushed to seize the places they considered necessary to such a revival. These included the harbors on the Atlantic coast, the great armaments center at Le Creusot, the frontier with Switzerland, and that part of the Maginot Line that dominated the valley of the Sarre, the only area north of Strasbourg where the French had not evacuated their forts. To get to these far-flung places, the Germans made full use of their armored and motorized formations, which they pushed to the mechanical and human limits of endurance.

The advantage was now entirely with the Germans. As had been demonstrated in both the campaign for the Low Countries and the breakthrough of the Weygand Line, the German fondness for dash and enterprise, initiative on the part of small-unit leaders, and decentralized, short-range firepower was certainly superior to the French love of highly schematic defenses, complex task organization, long-range engagement by fire, and written orders. As long as flanks were anchored and fronts were narrowed, the French units could make up for their deficiencies with an additional ration of courage, improvisation, or field craft. Once the slugging match turned into a pursuit, however, the French were completely outclassed. The German emphasis on thrusting boldly into the unknown, on leadership from the front, on the maintenance of tempo, and on the circumnavigation of centers of resistance paid huge dividends. The French emphasis on carefully synchronized movements hamstrung every attempt to offer resistance.

On the morning of June 14, while armored and motorized forces poured over the great central plateau of France, the Germans unleashed Enterprise Tiger, their long-awaited attack along the Sarre. Carried out by forces that had up to this point spent the campaign in comparative idleness, Tiger began with a hurricane bombardment in the style of 1918. Firing on the French forts were 259 batteries of artillery—more than 1,000 guns and howitzers. In a repetition of the tactics used at La Ferté, small teams of assault engineers crept forward, using the exploding shells as a screen as they cut paths in barbed-wire obstacles and laid their charges on observation turrets and firing positions. The forts responded with fire of their own—at long range against the German gun positions and assembly areas and, from scores of automatic rifles mounted in tiny steel turrets, at close range against the infiltrating pioneers.

As had been the case at La Ferté, the German shells, including those fired by the giant 420mm siege mortars, made little impact on the forts. In places, the bombardment did enable the attacking engineers to get within flame-thrower range of smaller outlying works, bunkers, and blockhouses held by one or two dozen men. For the most part, however, the first day of the German attack was a monumental failure. To capture a few platoons and to knock out a handful of machine-gun nests, more than 1,000 Germans had given their lives. The next day promised to be even worse, for the heavier German artillery pieces had run out of ammunition, and the Stukas, whose wail had always warmed the hearts of attacking German foot soldiers, were needed elsewhere.

During the long night that separated June 14 from June 15, the assault troops taking part in Tiger sat sullen in their bunkers, awaiting the canteens of ersatz coffee laced with schnapps that would signal the resumption of the attack, and unaware that, once again, German lives would be saved by a decision of the French high command. The forts that had held so well the previous day were to be evacuated; the big guns that had killed so many Germans, disabled; and the brave fortress troops sent into the interior of France, there to partake of the chaos.

Only Kafka could properly record the behavior of the school officials in Nancy who, with the Germans at the city's very gates, insisted on holding baccalaureate examinations in accordance with the peacetime schedule. Only Brueghel could capture the small-mindedness of the strawberry farmers who, with their town full of their tired, hungry, and often wounded countrymen, were chiefly concerned with getting their perishable crop to market. And it would take Goya to properly record the selfishness of the peasants who stood by the highways, selling water to refugees at five francs a glass, or the treachery of the mayor who arrested five French soldiers and turned them over to the Germans.

To many Frenchmen, including those who had made their reputations killing Germans, the confusion that reigned in the second and third weeks of June was far worse than the prospect of German occupation. The most august of those who held this opinion was Philippe Pétain, the hero of Verdun and, to the vast majority of Frenchmen, the first soldier of France. Just after midnight on the morning of June 17, Pétain, who had only been serving as interim head of the French government for a few hours, asked the Spanish ambassador to contact the Germans and ask for an armistice. At 12:30 P.M. that same day, Pétain made it clear in a short but powerful radio address that this armistice was, in all but name, an offer of surrender.

To those Frenchmen who had seen defeat with their own eyes, Pétain's broadcast made perfect sense. To those who were still undefeated, it was harder to fathom. At Clermont-Ferrand, in a region the Germans had yet to reach, General De Lattre de Tassigny, whose 14th Division had fought so well along the Aisne, asked permission to take the unit to a place where it could continue the fight: His was, perhaps, the only French formation that had actually increased its numbers, supplies, and stocks of weapons during the course of the campaign. This permission was denied. In London, Pétain's former protégé, Charles de Gaulle, recently promoted to brigadier general, saw no need to ask permission of anyone. His response to Pétain's broadcast was a broadcast of his own, inviting all Frenchmen on British soil to join him in repudiating the upcoming armistice.

The five days that passed between the French decision to sue for peace and the actual signing of the armistice were filled with little events but empty of great ones. For the Germans, concerned about the huge gaps that separated the walking infantry from the gasoline-powered formations, the chief activity seems to have been the forced march. Some French soldiers were likewise concerned about consolidating their positions. Believing that the upcoming armistice would, as armistices often do, grant each side the territory actually held, they continued to fight. Less enthusiastic French soldiers interpreted Pétain's broadcast as a grant of permission to lay down their arms.

What followed, in the week that passed between Pétain's radio address and the official ending of hostilities, was less end game than epilogue. Hitler, having achieved far more than he had hoped, set his mind to other things: plans for demobilization of the German army, schemes for winning the allegiance of French colonial troops in German prisoner-of-war camps, and, as might be expected, the continuing struggle with Great Britain. The German forces in the field, under Hitler's direct orders to avoid further losses, saw no particular advantage in taking yet another town or disarming yet another unit. In at least one case, the Germans went so far as to release French soldiers they had captured.

What fighting there was took place around those fortresses still in French hands. Along the largely mountainous border with Italy, the French fortress troops had no trouble stopping the offensive that had begun with the Italian declaration of war on June 10. Along the southern edge of the Maginot Line (which represented 40 percent of it), forts that had been left out of the evacuations of June 12 and 14 were somewhat harder pressed. All but one, however, held out until after the armistice had gone into effect. Even then, the garrisons refused to give up until ordered to do so by senior French officers who were brought in for that purpose. The surrender of the remnants of the Maginot Line was the last event of the Battle of France, the last occasion, in a campaign so full of similar occasions, where the French leadership, by grossly underestimating the power of resistance of its own forces, made things easier for the enemy. For the next four years, France would be ruled by many of these same leaders, men who continued to overestimate German capabilities. The view of German invincibility was not, however, universal. There were still those who believed that the Germans were not unbeatable and that, while the Battle of France was over, the battle for France had only begun.

"UNDAUNTED BY ODDS"

WILLIAM MANCHESTER

One hesitates to use that overworked word "decisive," but the Battle of Britain certainly qualifies. "Decisive" battles rarely decide, but this one did. It was not just history's first prolonged air engagement—if one counts the preliminary round for control of the English Channel, it lasted from July 10 to September 15 of 1940, more than two months—but it ended as Hitler's first major setback in the war. England would survive, and with a genuine leader: Winston Churchill. There would be no negotiated peace, the prospect that dangled as late as the weekend of Dunkirk. And the example of Britain's will to resist what had seemed until then an unstoppable Nazi juggernant would go far to inspire and energize the world's major noncombatant, the United States.

But as William Manchester makes clear, the outcome of the battle remained in the balance until the very end. It came as a result of an accident that can literally be blamed on the fog of war. What if a flight of German bombers had not become lost and by mistake dropped its bombs on London—which Hitler had declared off-limits? And what if Churchill had not retaliated by bombing Berlin? Few events in the history of war lend themselves so readily to counterfactual scenarios as the Battle of Britain. What if the Germans had taken British radar defenses more seriously? What if, in the beginning of September, they had finished off the destruction of the RAF airfields in the South of England instead of mounting an all-out assault on London? What if they had launched their invasion—Operation Sea Lion—when the British were on the ropes? And what if the commander of the Luftwaffe, Reichmarshall Hermann Göring, had not predicated his plans on bogus figures and his own propaganda?

William Manchester is the author of eighteen books, including *Death of a President* and *Good-bye Darkness*. This article is adapted from *The Last Lion: Defender of the Realm*, a work-in-progress that will complete his three-volume biography of Winston Churchill.

IN PREPARING ENGLAND FOR WHAT HE CALLED THE "BATTLE of Britain," Winston Churchill envisioned a mighty struggle on land between infantrymen, masterminded by generals and supported by mounted troops, armor, and sea power. Wars had always been waged that way. The world had never seen, or even imagined, a decisive conflict in the sky, fought in three dimensions by propeller-driven aircraft moving at 300 miles per hour while awed civilians, standing below, watched the white vapor trails of dogfights, the small dancing yellow flames of machine-gun bullets exploding against enemy fuselages, and, from time to time, the red flashes of exploding planes.

Scarcely anyone in responsible positions had even given serious thought to the challenges of aerial warfare. Professional airmen were an exception, of course, but all they knew for certain was that the aerial combat of 1914–18—the duels between individuals piloting wood-and-fabric biplanes while listening to the wind in the wires—had been rendered obsolete by advancing technology. Clearly, future combat would be far more complex. However, the most influential of the air-war prophets between the wars—Giulio Douhet in Rome, Lord Trenchard in London, Billy Mitchell in Washington, and Hermann Göring in Berlin—had made the wrong assumption. They believed that victory would belong to the air forces that launched the fastest, most powerful bombing offensives. Thus the Luftwaffe had leveled Spanish cities; the Italians, Ethiopian villages; the Japanese, Chinese cities; and the RAF, mutinous hamlets in Iraq. There was, air ministries told their governments, no defense against a knock-out bombardment from the sky.

Stanley Baldwin voiced that assumption in November 1932, when, endorsing unilateral disarmament, he told Parliament that there was no defense against "the terror of the air." In an uncharacteristically emotional speech he warned the House of Commons, and hence the country:

> I think it is well . . . for the man in the street to realize that there is no
> power on earth that can protect him from being bombed. Whatever people may
> tell him, the bomber will always get through. The only defense is offense,

which means that you have to kill more women and children more quickly than the enemy if you want to save yourselves.

That dogma still held after the fall of France. Even Churchill had come to believe that victory lay through offensive air power. On July 8, 1940, he told Lord Beaverbrook, the Canadian-born newspaper publisher and minister of aircraft production, that the "one sure path" to victory lay in bombing Germany into submission.

Air power had been crucial in the defeat of Poland, but little thought had been given to ways of countering it. During the phony war, RAF strategists, following the dogma Douhet had set forth in his futuristic novel, *The War of 19—*, had proposed sending fleets of bombers against industrial targets in the Ruhr. To their chagrin, His Majesty's Government vetoed unprovoked daylight raids. Dropping propaganda leaflets over the Reich addressed from *"Englische Arbeiter an Ihre Deutschen Brüder"* (English workers to their German brothers) was approved, but even this went badly; none of the raiders found their targets and, unescorted by fighters, suffered such heavy losses that the project was abandoned. Not until the night of May 16, with Guderian's panzers in Sedan, did the British send almost 100 bombers to pound industrial targets in the Ruhr. The RAF official history acknowledged that the bombardiers "achieved none of their objects." Most of the crews had jettisoned their bomb loads and returned to England. That should have given the air marshals pause. It didn't. In the words of the historian A. J. P. Taylor, they continued to believe that "bombing unsupported by land and sea forces could win a war."

Their faith in air offensives was not without dissenters. In 1937, a cabinet minister, Sir Thomas Inskip, facing the hard fact that Nazi Germany was winning the bomber race, argued that it really didn't matter. "The role of our air force," he said, "is not an early knockout blow but to prevent the Germans from knocking us out." The RAF, in other words, didn't have to win; it merely had to avoid defeat. The Air Ministry, appalled at this heresy, vehemently disagreed, but His Majesty's Government accepted Inskip's recommendation, and it was Britain's great good luck that the senior member of the Air Council agreed with it.

He was Air Chief Marshal Sir Hugh Dowding. In retrospect "Stuffy" Dowding is seen as the true hero of the Battle of Britain, though his colleagues and his countrymen were slow to recognize it. One reason lay in the nature of the man. He was difficult to like. Ever since Trafalgar, Britons had expected their military heroes to be men of action like Nelson, and Dowding was far from that. Tall, frail, and abstemious, he was a bird-watching widower whose career had suffered from tactlessness, unorthodox views, and a remarkable lack of social graces. In the mid-1930s his seniority entitled him to the RAF's highest post, chief of air staff, but his fellow marshals denied him it. Instead they sidelined him, or so they thought, as head of Fighter Command. If the war was going to be won by aerial bombardment, the only outcome they foresaw, there would be little glory for aircraft.

Ignoring them and their strategy, Dowding pursued his own goals with quiet tenacity. In his headquarters in Bentley Priory, an eighteenth-century mansion outside London, he organized Britain's antiaircraft defenses, presided over the RAF's change from biplane fighters to metal monoplanes powered by Rolls-Royce Merlin engines, pressed for all-weather runways at fighter fields, and took the first, historic steps toward military use of Radio Directional Finding (RDF), or radar, as the Americans later called it.

✦

RADAR WAS destined to be England's greatest shield in the critical months ahead. Dowding had championed it from the beginning. Before his promotion to Fighter Command, he had commanded RAF research and development, and while there had studied the RDF experiments of Robert Watson-Watt, a scientist at the National Physical Laboratories. Watson-Watt convinced Dowding and those around him that airplanes could reflect radio beams. The Nazis knew something about radar technology, but, seeing it as a reconnaissance device, they had entrusted it to their navy, and there it had languished.

In 1937, Dowding had ordered work begun along the country's eastern and southern coasts on a chain of twenty RDF stations, each with antennae that could detect the impulses of aircraft 150 miles away. At first the system relied entirely on 240-foot-tall towers. Two years later, technicians discovered that warplanes skimming the waves could slip under this net, so low-level beams were added. In addition, newly developed mobile radar stations blunted the risk from damage to fixed installations. By the spring of 1940, when the antennae had reached a height of 350 feet, Britain possessed a mesh of radio beams ranging from the tip of Scotland almost to Land's End; they comprised, as one Englishman later said, an "invisible bastion" against hostile aircraft.

This meant that two Battles of Britain would be fought, one by airmen in the sky and the other by radar crews on the ground. It was now possible to detect enemy aircraft while they were still as far as 150 miles away and flying at altitudes of up to 30,000 feet. Technicians studying monitoring screens would phone details on the range, direction, and size of advancing Nazi forces to the central operations room at Bentley Priory, where blue-shirted members of the Women's Auxiliary Air Force (WAAF), plotted their progress on a huge table map, using croupier rakes to move colored counters. Overhead, officers watching from a balcony radioed orders to the commanders of fighter squadrons, who then led their pilots aloft ("scrambling") and, when the Germans were sighted, peeled off for the attack against the enemy planes, or "bandits," as they were known in the RAF.

The commander of the Luftwaffe, Reichsmarschall Hermann Göring, issued his first operational directive for the battle on June 30. It would begin with a struggle for mastery of the sky over the Channel *(Kanalkampf)*. This was to be accomplished in July, setting the stage for the major assault on Britain, which would open with an intense, week-long *Adlerangriff* (Eagle Attack) and climax, in early September, with triumphant assaults on RAF fighter bases in southeast Britain.

Dowding believed that England's only hope of survival lay in radar and the RAF's single-engine fighters. He knew it was impossible for the RAF to destroy the great air fleets of the Luftwaffe, but that was never his objective. The Germans could not invade England as long as Fighter Command remained intact. Therefore, he would order his pilots to avoid direct combat with enemy fighters whenever possible, diverting them instead and then destroying enemy bombers stripped of their fighter escorts. The RAF would keep its Spitfires and Hurricanes in the sky until the autumn's worsening weather ruled out any possibility of a seaborne Nazi attack across the Channel.

The *Kanalkampf* opened on July 10, when some twenty Nazi bombers, escorted by some forty Me-109s, attacked a convoy off Dover and were challenged by two squadrons of Hurricanes and one of Spitfires. A single ship was sunk. Heavy fighting continued for a full month, most of it over the Channel and the southern coast of England. It was a testing time for both air forces. The RDF operators, still learning their skills, were finding that aircraft at tremendous altitudes disappeared from their scopes. RAF problems were compounded by the fact that a Luftwaffe squadron based on the French coast could cross the Channel in five minutes, while British fighters, rising to challenge them, needed fifteen minutes to reach their height.

After a fierce day of aerial combat, the Luftwaffe had lost seventy-five aircraft, the RAF fifty. That ratio, or something close to it, was to favor the British throughout the battle. A German victory would be impossible if the British could provide enough pilots. That, however, was by no means certain; in just three weeks of July, 220 RAF airmen had been lost.

The Royal Navy had no intention of withdrawing from the Strait of Dover without a fight. Heavily convoyed, all merchantmen flying the red ensign entered the Channel hugging the coast of Kent. Four Royal Navy destroyer flotillas—approximately thirty-six vessels—were stationed in the threatened area, with cruisers and battleships from the Home Fleet in the immediate vicinity. Nevertheless, by the end of the first week in August the bombers of Oberst Johannes Fink, the commander of the *Kanalkampf*, had sunk eight merchantmen and four Royal Navy destroyers. RAF coastal aircraft were vectoring the sky over the Channel. Dowding, less concerned about the loss of aircraft than pilot exhaustion—which led to pilot losses—took a hard line against daylight patrols. Grudgingly, the Admiralty barred the strait to destroyers in daylight. The merchantmen were given a choice: either they reached Dover at dusk, in which case they would be escorted at night, or they entered the Channel naked.

Twenty colliers took the risk. Because the Nazi navy was the one German arm with radar, one of their sets at Wissand, opposite Folkestone, identified the colliers off the Isle of Wight in the first moments of dawn on Thursday, August 8. A Luftwaffe strike followed. After the RDF station on the Isle of Wight picked up a strong blip, signaling the approach of a heavy raid, more than thirty Spitfires and Hurricanes formed an umbrella over the convoy. However, Fink, after luring the fighters away with decoys, sent in Stukas, which sank four ships and damaged seven others in less than ten minutes. The survivors scattered, tried to reassemble, and were attacked again, by a strong force of eighty-two Junker-87s escorted by Me-109s. Only four ships in the original convoy reached safety.

RAF pilots, learning on the job, discovered that they would have to flout some regulations if they wanted to live. First to go were the vee formations, impressive in prewar air shows but suicidal when enemy fighters, attacking out of the sun, maneuvered their machines behind British tails. For the same reason, the expensive sheepskin collars on the RAF's Irving flight jackets were cut off: if you wanted to survive, you had to be able to see over your shoulder. In addition, the best pilots scorned the regulation requiring their machine guns to be so adjusted that the bullets would converge 650 yards ahead of the aircraft. That was too far; pilots were spraying gunfire all over the sky. Veterans, knowing they had to get much closer, readjusted their Brownings.

During July, the RAF lost seventy aircraft and the Luftwaffe more than twice that—180, more than half of them bombers. On neither side was the damage significant, but British spirits were high. RAF pilots knew they were fighting for the very existence of their country. All Britain was aroused by the RAF's heroism. Thus the morale of flyers and civilians boosted one another.

✦

THE GERMAN raids grew heavier and more frequent. Afterward, those who fought in the sky were haunted less by memories of fear—their engagements lasted no more than ten or fifteen minutes—than by the relentless tension and fatigue. After a third or fourth sortie, men would fall asleep in their cockpits as soon as they had landed. Two or even three more sorties would lie ahead of them, and although they may have brushed death more than once, their weariness was so great that when dusk fell and darkness gathered, they had no immediate recollection of that day's fighting, not even of their kills. After the BBC's report of the latest score they would recover with the miraculous powers of youth and head for the village pub.

All England and all Germany—indeed, the entire world—anxiously awaited each day's scores, upon which the outcome of the battle—and the likelihood of invasion—seemed to hang. Number 10 Downing Street echoed with hurrahs after the Air Ministry reported, typically: "The final figures for today's fighting are 86 certain, 34 probable, 33 damaged. We lost 37 aircraft. 12 pilots being killed and 14 wounded." After dinner at Chequers on Saturday, July 13, John Colville, Churchill's private secretary, wrote in his diary: "Winston said the last four days have been the most glorious in the history of the R.A.F. Those days have been the test: the enemy has come and had lost five to one. We could now be confident of our superiority."

He believed it. He was citing the figures he had been given, and no one had deliberately deceived him. No one was deliberately misleading the führer either, but the numbers sent to his *Reichskanzlei* were very different. According to them, those days had been among the most glorious days in Luftwaffe history, and therefore clear evidence of German superiority.

In retrospect it is clear that the communiqués being issued by both sides were quite worthless. The trouble lay in pilots' reports. It was unrealistic to expect accuracy from excited twenty-three-year-olds struggling to prevail in a battle upon which so much hung. Their senses were distorted by multiple fears—fear of engine failure, fear of fire, fear of blind spots, and the overriding fear of being pounced upon at any moment by an unseen enemy. Few dogfights were simple. The skies were flecked with aircraft. Encounters frequently involved fighters and bombers, friendly and hostile, and sometimes it was impossible to tell which was which. Even when the air was free of the enemy, Dowding's pilots had too much on their minds: jammed guns, feeble oxygen supply, wavering compass deflection, and the endless stream of fresh information, much of it alarming, which was arriving through their earphones from the voice of their RAF sector controller below.

The RAF accepted its pilots' claims without question. However, British accounts of their own losses were always correct. That was not true of Luftwaffe reports. Announcing light casualties for the Luftwaffe and severe British losses was a mighty tonic for Reich morale, and Germans concluded that their airmen were winning the battle. After it was over, they assumed they had won it, just as, five years later, they assumed they were winning the war moments before they were warned that Allied troops were closing in on them.

One problem with deception is that the deceivers deceive themselves. That is what happened to the Luftwaffe's high command. "The Germans," as Churchill told Parliament, had "become victims of their own lies." The enemy had lost control of the battle's vital statistics, which, by the beginning of August, had become simply incredible. At one point, William L. Shirer, who was reporting from Berlin, observed dryly: "German figures of British losses have been rising all evening. First [they] announced 73 British planes shot down against 14 German; then 79 to 14; finally at midnight 89 to 17. Actually, when I counted up the German figures as given out from time to time during the afternoon and evening, they totaled 111 for British losses. The Luftwaffe is lying so fast it isn't consistent even by its own account."

At his Karinhall estate, Göring studied these bogus figures, counted the number of British ships sunk—and declared that the *Kanalkampf* had been a stunning German victory. After the French capitulation, he had been told that the Royal Air Force had been reduced to fewer than 2,000 front-line aircraft, of which between 500 and 600 were fighters. That was true—then. The reichsmarschall had written the sum on a pad of paper and pocketed it. In the fighting that followed he subtracted that day's losses, as reported to him, at the end of each day. In a Luftwaffe intelligence report dated August 16, he read that the British had lost 574 fighters since July, and that since their factories had provided them with no more than 300, they were left with about 430, of which perhaps 300 were serviceable.

As the remainder on Göring's pad approached zero, he was confident that the invasion could soon begin. But he would have despaired had he been shown the latest figures from ministry of aircraft production in London. In July alone British workers had produced 496 fighter planes—four times the monthly rate before Dunkirk. By the end of August, Beaverbrook would have 1,081 fighters available, with another 500 undergoing repair. Dowding, it seemed, would end the battle with more fighters than he had at the beginning.

✦

MOREOVER, THE WRECKS of aircraft downed over Britain could be recovered by Beaverbrook's Civilian Repair Organization (CRO). So efficient was "the Beaver's" CRO that by the end of summer, one third of Dowding's fighters had parts from crashed Hurricanes and Spitfires. Indeed, through CRO ingenuity, crashed German planes flew again as RAF aircraft. On August 10, Colville noted in his diary a comment by Churchhill that day: "Beaverbrook had genius, and, what was more, brutal ruthlessness." Never in his life, "at the Ministry of Munitions or anywhere else," had he seen "such startling results as Beaverbrook has produced." After studying the aircraft production charts, General Sir Henry Pownall, who was with them, "agreed that there had never been such an achievement." To be sure, it was a backbreaking job, and one from which the temperamental Canadian was forever resigning. Churchill wouldn't allow it. On September 2, at the end of one memorandum to the prime minister, Beaverbrook lamented, "Nobody knows the troubles I've seen." Beneath it Churchill minuted, "I do."

An elated Göring laid his statistics before Hitler, declaring that the RAF was helpless. The Reich, he said, had mastered the sky over the *Bach*—loosely, the brook, as he called the Channel. Now, he proposed preparations for the second phase of the battle: *der Adlerangriff,* the Eagle Attack—Germany's all-out air assault on England. Yet Dowding was noting in his journal that he still believed time was on England's side "if we can only hold on." In one day his pilots had claimed to have destroyed sixty German planes, and though he may have thought that figure suspect, he was impressed by the skill with which the young Englishwomen at his radar stations had interpreted the direction and ranges of the attackers. In the long run, if the RAF were to prevail, the performance of the WAAF would be crucial.

Britain had regretted the *Kanalkampf* sinkings but could spare the ships. At Chequers on August 9, a Friday evening, Churchill dined with some of his advisers. Even under the threat of invasion Winston cherished plans for British offensives: after the ladies had retired, he spoke at length about Charles de Gaulle's plan for an invasion of French North Africa, supported by the Royal Navy, at Dakar. His view of that day's losses in the Strait was philosophical: England, he said, would have to continue using her coastal vessels as bait, though he acknowledged that "the surviving bait are getting a bit fed up."

German tactics, when at their peak efficiency, were shocking. At Detling, near Maidstone, an RAF airfield was attacked just as the mess halls were filling. The operations tower was devastated, sixty-seven British airmen were killed, and twenty-two aircraft were destroyed on the ground. In another raid, near Oxford, two unescorted Ju-88 bombers arrived when the British fighters were on the ground refueling and rearming. The Germans destroyed forty-six aircraft, damaged seven others, and knocked out the maintenance sheds.

Luftwaffe airmen were as dangerous as ever. The blunders and mismanagement were committed by officers with higher ranks. Göring's intelligence was appalling. The Germans had only the vaguest understanding of the British defense system; indeed, at the outset they didn't know where key British airfields were. Operational maps did not distinguish between fields used by Fighter and Bomber Commands. The two factories where Rolls-Royce built the Merlin engines that powered Hurricanes and Spitfires were never bombed, though their location was no secret. Vital orders miscarried. Weather reports were unreliable. Staff work was slow and sloppy. When Göring summoned his generals he left orders that under no circumstances should they be disturbed; in at least one instance that led to conflicting orders. Worst of all, he adopted no coherent strategy, no priority of targets. After the war Adolf Galland, the ace who was one of his officers, wrote that "Constantly changing orders [that betrayed] lack of purpose and obvious misjudgment of the situation by the Command and unjustified accusations had a most demoralizing effect on us fighter pilots."

RAF radar baffled the enemy. Picking up its signals, German airmen reported British *"Funkstationen mit Sonderanlagen"*—radio stations with special installations. Nazi intelligence decided it was a communication system linking RAF pilots with ground controllers and concluded, on August 7, that, "As the British fighters are controlled from the ground by radio-telephone, their forces are tied to their respective ground stations and are therefore restricted in mobility"—which, had it been true, would have meant that resistance to mass German attacks would be limited to local fighters.

The commander of the Luftwaffe signals service, who was among the few Germans who understood the role of radar, urged that an attack on the RDF stations be given priority. A limited attempt on them, made on the day before the first major assault on the British mainland, was ineffective. At Dover the Germans rocked a radar pylon, but the 350-foot-tall lattice masts were almost impossible to hit; returning after an attempt to destroy four stations, the pilots reported total failure. Göring assumed that the British electronics gear and crews were deep underground and hence safe. (In fact they were in flimsy shacks beneath the towers.) He issued the order—"It is doubtful whether there is any point in continuing the attacks on radar sites, in view of the fact that not one of those attacked has so far been put out of action."

Nevertheless this was still the mighty Luftwaffe, its huge fleets *(Luftflotten)* of superb aircraft outnumbering the defenders by two to one. After the *Kanalkampf,* they completed plans for Eagle Day. The führer, unaware that Göring's figures were inflated, gave him the green light for *Adlerangriff.* Depending on the weather and other imponderables, the *Führerordnung* decreed, Eagle Day could begin as early as August 5. British intelligence officers in the code-breaking center at Bletchley Park relayed the decision to Churchill, and Dowding issued an order of the day to his men: "The Battle of Britain is about to begin. Members of the Royal Air Force, the fate of generations lies in your hands."

On August 6, the reichsmarschall set Eagle Day for August 10, a Saturday. The weather forced him to reschedule it for Tuesday, August 13, when heavy skies were expected to clear. They did: seventy-four Dornier bombers and fifty Me-110s took off, the clouds returned; Göring issued a recall order; they rolled away, and the offensive was officially on, targeting a 150-mile arc of southern England from the Thames estuary to Southampton. Commanding Eagle Day was Göring's ablest general, Field Marshal Albert Kesselring, who would send out 1,486 sorties against targets ranging from Scotland to Devon. By daybreak every radar tower was sending urgent warnings to the WAAF operations below.

Among those awaiting the onslaught were a dozen American war correspondents on the cliffs of Dover, including H. R. Knickerbocker, Edward R. Murrow, Helen Kirkpatrick, Quentin Reynolds, Whitelaw Reid, Virginia Cowles, and Vincent Sheehan. Their mood was fatalistic. Among them, Sheehan wrote, a "sense of inevitable tragedy had grown heavy." Some had been covering the spread of global conflict since the Japanese seizure of Manchuria in 1931. The Reich seemed invincible. They heard the familiar hum of the de-synchronized Messerschmitts, Heinkels, and Dorniers, which grew to a roar as the glittering wings of the great Nazi armada emerged from the dazzling sun-drenched mist over the Channel and approached a coast that had not seen an invader in nine centuries: Experience had taught them to expect another defeat for democracy.

✦

AND THEN, from RAF fields inland, they saw twenty-one squadrons of challenging Spitfires rising, Sheehan wrote, "like larks, glittering against the sun," maneuvering for position and attack. They heard the "zoom of one fighter diving over another . . . the rattle of machine-gun fire, the streak of smoke of a plane plummeting to earth, and the long seesaw descent of the wounded fighter falling from the clouds beneath his shining white parachute."

The scenes were repeated all that day and all week along the southern coast. Sheehan wrote: "In every such battle I saw, the English had the best of it, and in every such battle they were greatly outnumbered." Repeatedly "five or six fighters would engage twenty or thirty Germans . . . I saw it happen not once but many times." He remembered the Spaniards and the Czechs and wrote: "At Dover the first sharp thrust of hope penetrated our gloom. The battles over the cliffs proved that the British could and would fight for their own freedom, if for nothing else, and that they would do so against colossal odds. . . . The flash of the Spitfire's wing, then, through the mist glare of the summer sky, was the first flash of a sharpened sword; they would fight, they would hold out."

The battle reached a peak between August 24 and September 6, which became known to Fighter Command as the "critical period." In the first six weeks of fighting, Luftwaffe tactics had been tested by Dowding's strategy. He had ordered his pilots to avoid Messerschmitts—to flee from them if necessary—and go after the German bombers. Nazi fighters flying escort had been at a disadvantage; enemy bomber losses continued to be high; and, far more important, the RAF continued to be a force-in-being, warding off the threat of invasion.

In August this pattern changed. Kesselring massed a great concentration of Messerschmitts in the Pas de Calais. He meant to wipe out the sector airfields of Sir Keith Park's 11 Group—London's air defense—leaving the capital naked. During this time Churchill repeatedly visited RAF bases at Stanmar, Uxbridge, Dover, and Ramsgate. Colville noted that the prime minister was "full of admiration of the pilots" but thought it "terrible, terrible that the British Empire should have gambled on this."

On Thursday, August 15, the Germans had decided to test RAF Fighter Command's strength by attacking it from all sides simultaneously. For the first time Luftflotte 5, in Norway and Denmark, was assigned a major role. That was a mistake. Twelve RAF fighters, flying 3,000 feet above the raid, attacked out of the sun. The Germans lost sixteen Heinkels and six Ju-88s—a fifth of Luftflotte 5's bombers—and seven Me-110s. There were no British losses. Throughout the Luftwaffe that day became known as *der schwarze Donnerstag*: black Thursday.

In the south, however, that day's fighting was very different. Here the fields of 11 Group were the target. In Essex and Kent, fields at Martlesham, Eastchurch, and Hawkinge were hit; then the Germans attacked two aircraft factories near Rochester and fighter fields at Portland, Middle Wallop, West Malling, and Croydon. Before dusk the Germans had flown an unprecedented 1,786 sorties, and the total losses for both sides—109 aircraft—were the highest for any day of the battle. Each side suffered its highest losses for any single day. Churchill followed the fighting from the group headquarters, and he left, clearly affected. Climbing into his limousine with his closest military confidant, General Sir Hastings Ismay, he said, "Don't speak to me. I'm too moved." His lips were trembling—he was, in Colville's phrase, "fertilizing a phrase."

Five days later, when the most difficult and dangerous period in the battle was about to begin, he delivered his tribute to the RAF in the House of Commons:

The gratitude of every home in our island,
In our Empire, and indeed throughout the world,
Except in the abodes of the guilty,
Goes out to the British airmen who, undaunted by odds,
Unwearied in their constant challenge and mortal danger,
Are turning the tide of the World War
By their prowess and their devotion.
Never in the field of human conflict
Was so much owed by so many to so few.

On Friday, August 16, Kesselring continued to press the attack. Luftflotte 5 was grounded—grounded, indeed, for the remainder of the battle—but the Germans put up over 1,700 sorties, raiding fields almost at will. That Sunday the Germans lost seventy-one aircraft, nearly 10 percent of those committed. Nevertheless, after a day's lull they again arrived in force, undiscouraged by the costs of the offensive.

Göring summoned his *Luftflotten* commanders to Karinhall and ordered them to go after aircraft factories and rolling mills as "bottleneck" targets. Four days later he summoned them again to announce: "We have reached the decisive period of the air war against England." As in past conferences he was astonishingly ill-informed. He grossly underestimated the significance of Dowding's radar chain, thus assuring its continued immunity, and his summation of Luftwaffe accomplishments in the battle was wildly unrealistic.

Nevertheless Fighter Command's situation was critical. Unlike the enemy, Britain had no bottomless reserve of trained pilots. RAF bomber pilots were being retrained to fly Spitfires and Hurricanes. In a single week Dowding had lost 80 percent of his squadron commanders; one of their replacements had never even flown a Hurricane; after three landings and three takeoffs, he led his men into battle. Often pilots had logged no more than ten hours of flight before sighting an enemy fighter. In August, Fighter Command's "operations training period" was cut from six weeks to two. Some new pilots had never fired their guns. Some were boys in their teens.

Despite the Germans' losses, the ferocity of their attacks was unabated. On

August 15, Anthony Eden, Churchill's war minister, later recalled, he saw how "squadron after squadron of the Royal Air Force went up to engage the enemy and still the Luftwaffe kept coming. . . . As we listened and conjectured, things looked very stern, with the odds heavy against us."

But RAF gallantry was almost unbelievable. In peacetime exercises the RAF had established a hair-raising custom: they would attack enemy aircraft no matter how greatly they were outnumbered, defying five-to-one, even ten-to-one odds, and all England thrilled to this "Tally-ho!" tradition. Confronted by massive Luftwaffe fleets determined to force them to break formation, the seasoned Hurricane pilots of one squadron adopted a new, terrifying tactic. They simply pointed their propellers for France and flew straight through the enemy's bomber fleets—head-on, line abreast in a sawtooth line, deliberately adopting a collision course, challenging the enemy's courage by closing to fifty yards before sheering away.

The consequent closing speeds of well over 500 miles per hour left no time to aim. Accurate marksmanship was impossible anyway; the vision of each RAF pilot was obscured by streaks of tracer bullets, cordite clouds, onrushing contrails, and the fuselages of other crisscrossing aircraft. If he did register a kill at that range, his own plane would be scarred by the debris of an exploding German plane, smeared by its white coolant. But that was rare. More often the enemy pilots' nerves broke first. The spectacle of Hurricanes slashing diagonally across their noses, hurtling under their cockpits, or streaking past their wingtips was too much for all but the steadiest Luftwaffe airmen. They veered away and lurched out of formation, exposed to the machine-gun bursts of other British fighters.

The RAF pushed the limits of human endurance. Pilots slept in their cockpits between sorties, "undaunted by odds," in Churchill's words, "unwearied in their constant challenge and mortal danger." One Saturday, accompanied by his wife, Clemmie, his daughter-in-law Pamela, and Colville, he drove to Uxbridge, the frenzied headquarters of Dowding's No. 11 Group, controlling all the fighter squadrons in southeastern England. The rest of his party took a series of walks in the countryside, but he wanted to look into the faces of the airmen, talk to them, and hear their stories. That evening Colville wrote: "The P.M. was deeply moved by what he saw this afternoon at Uxbridge: he said what he saw brought the war home to him."

Mostly he had seen exhaustion. During the first three weeks of the battle one Uxbridge squadron had flown 504 sorties, spending more than 800 hours in the air. On a single day the squadron had scrambled seven times and flown fifty-three sorties. The enemy raids had been growing larger and more frequent, until by the weekend of Churchill's visit the pilots' time was almost completely occupied with flying, fighting, and sleeping. Awaking between 3:00 and 3:30 A.M. each July morning—it was about an hour later in August—they rolled out of bed unrefreshed, still tense, and were immediately put on twenty-minute standby. At the ring of the squadron bell or the bray of its klaxon they would pull on their flying boots and run to their aircraft in the gray, dank morning while struggling into their flight jackets.

The field would already be fully operational, with fire trucks, fuel wagons, ambulances, tents, a cookhouse, deckchairs for pilots waiting between sorties, and portable workshops for ground crews in position. On the landing strip each pilot began the final part of his hasty scramble ritual by slipping on his Mae West. His parachute came next, with ground crewmen kneeling to bring the straps together. Trotting heavily to the plane, the parachute slung beneath him like a cushion, he heaved himself up on the wing, swinging his legs with a loping effort to reach the cockpit and shoving the parachute beneath him on the bucket seat as he settled into a sitting position under the Perspex hood. On either side, ground crewmen were helping him with his safety harness. He wriggled his shoulders to loosen his shirt, already sticky with cold sweat. Whether he locked the cockpit open or shut was a matter of individual preference. Helmet on with built-in earphones in place, he checked his oxygen and radio leads, yanked on his flight gloves, and quickly scanned the bank of dials and gauges on the panel, making certain that the gunsight was on, the gun safety off, the oxygen available.

By now the cloud base would have risen to 5,000 feet and begun to fragment, promising a clear sky, a warm sun, and a slight breeze. In the control tower the base commander could see France; with binoculars he could even watch Luftwaffe aircraft circling on the far side of the Dover Strait. Here—and over there—the dry summer air reeked with the stench of high octane fuel. The pilot thrust his control lever forward to awaken the 1,175 horsepower in his Rolls-Royce Merlin engine. It was like flicking a baton to bring on the bass trombones; the tremendous surge of power shoved him in the back. (In emergencies override power was also available, a brutal abuse of the engine and a hammering racket, but worth another 20 miles per hour.) The needles on his panel began to jump and quiver, and the Merlin, beginning its idle, popped and belched. He slipped on his goggles, ready to go, though he didn't look up. There, he knew, over the thumb of Ramsgate, the sky would be huge and full of peril.

✦

SIR KEITH PARK couldn't move his airfields. If the Germans could knock them out by bombing and strafing, British fighters could neither take off nor land; the Nazis would command the air over southeast England, and Hitler's invasion could begin.

To protect his fields, he told his pilots to engage the enemy as far out as possible; the Germans responded by increasing the proportion of fighters to bombers. Spitfires and Hurricanes had to stay behind to provide air cover, and there weren't enough of them. The enemy onslaught was too great. Kesselring was putting up over a thousand sorties a day. Among the Luftwaffe aircraft was a new machine: the Messerschmitt-110. Though a disappointment in combat, the Me-110 possessed tremendous firepower; a flight of six 110s was armed with thirty machine guns firing armor-piercing and incendiary rounds, and twelve cannon armed with explosive shells.

Charging in from the sea each morning at an altitude too low for British antiaircraft guns, they would sweep the RAF fields in strafing attacks, wrecking repair shops, destroying hangars, ripping apart grounded planes, leveling operations buildings, and leaving airstrips unfit for landing.

RAF ground crews worked heroically, but before new craters could be filled in, a second flight of raiders would arrive. By dusk all British communications were paralyzed, and once the operations rooms were in ruins, the whole ground control system failed, leaving a shambles. One by one the advanced fighting fields were abandoned. And on the tenth day of the new Nazi offensive, September 4, a dozen Ju-88s slipped through Britain's fighter protection and hit the Vickers factory near Weybridge, destroying the works and inflicting 700 casualties. The output of Wellington bombers dropped from ninety a week to four, and normal production was not restored until the following year.

Duff Cooper reported to Churchill that British morale was "extremely high," but the public did not know what its leaders knew. Fighter Command was in crisis. Under Beaverbrook, British factories were producing 125 new fighters each week—twice as many as the Germans—but the Nazis were shooting down more than that. Dowding's aircraft reserve was shrinking. On the last two days of August the Nazi attacks reached a crescendo with 2,795 sorties. Their primary targets continued to be Eleven Group's vital sector stations at Biggin Hill and Kenley. By September 1, both were virtually useless. Hangars, aircraft repair shops, operations buildings, communications facilities—all were leveled. Of Eleven Group's seven major sector airfields, six had been demolished, and the five advanced airfields were hors de combat.

Meantime, Enigma decrypts admitted to only one interpretation: the

Nazis were ready to invade England. British intelligence had identified fifteen German supply dumps along the French coast between Dunkirk and the mouth of the Somme. Churchill told Parliament that the enemy could land almost anywhere: "Even the most likely sector of invasion, i.e., the sector in which fighter support is available for their bomber and dive bombers, extending from the Wash to the Isle of Wight, is nearly as long as the whole front in France from the Alps to the sea, and also upon the dangers of fog or artificial fog one must expect many lodgments or artificial lodgments to be made on our island simultaneously."

Incredibly, the German high command didn't grasp the implications of the Luftwaffe's successes. Even the demolishment of Britain's oil installations at Thameshaven provoked little comment. An exception was Generalfeld-marschall Feodor von Bock, one of the Wehrmacht's highest-ranking officers. Von Bock realized that the tide of battle had shifted; while preparing to move his army group headquarters from France to Poland, he tried to impress its importance upon his commander in chief, von Brauchitsch. Finding von Brauchitsch uncommunicative, Bock insisted that for the first time in the battle the Luftwaffe was making some real headway.

Every day now the Germans were coming in larger numbers, and they were threatening Britain's inner defenses. When, after a visit to Fighter Command headquarters at Stanmore, Churchill dined at Chequers with a group of military advisers, the enemy bombed Great Missenden, just four miles away.

By the first week in September the RAF was in desperate straits. Dowding's pilots were no longer permitted to pursue enemy aircraft out over the Channel. Because he lacked rested and refitted squadrons, he could no longer rotate them. In just two weeks he had lost 25 percent of his pilots, 60 percent of them experienced men. At that rate, Fighter Command would cease to be a disciplined fighting force in another week. The entire air-defense system of southeast England would have been destroyed.

Already the Luftwaffe could very nearly do what it pleased over the area Sea Lion had targeted for invasion. "If what Göring wanted was air superiority over southeast England for the invasion," Len Deighton writes, "then by 1 September it was almost his." Park wrote that "an almost complete disorganization made the control of our fighter squadrons completely difficult. . . . Had the enemy continued his heavy attacks [against fields and the control system] . . . the fighter defenses of London would have been in a perilous state." Group Captain Peter Townsend believed that "on sixth September victory was in the Luftwaffe's grasp." On September 7, he said, Wehrmacht divisions, panzers, and artillery "could have begun massive landings on British soil."

Describing the crisis to a secret session of the House of Commons, Churchill said that German "shipping available and now assembled is sufficient to carry in one voyage nearly half a million men." He told his listeners that:

> These next few weeks are grave and anxious. I just said in the Public Session that the deployment of the enemy's invasion preparations and the assembly of his ships and barges are steadily proceeding, and that any moment a major assault may be launched upon this island. I now say in secret that upwards of seventeen hundred self-propelled barges and more than two hundred seagoing ships, some very large ships, are already gathered at the many invasion ports in German occupation.

In a BBC broadcast he prepared the British people for the worst. If the invasion was coming, he told them, "it does not seem that it can be long delayed. The weather may break at any time."

> Therefore, we must regard the next week or so as a very important period in our history. It ranks with the days when the Spanish Armada was approaching the Channel, and Drake was finishing his game of bowls; or when Nelson stood between us and Napoleon's Grand Army at Boulogne. We have read all about this in the history books; but what is happening now is on a far greater scale and of far more consequence to the life and future of the world and its civilization than these brave old days of the past.

That first Saturday in September, the seventh, the Joint Intelligence Committee pored over a sheaf of reports: Enigma decrypts, aerial photographs, and accounts from agents on the Continent. Although they came from different sources, none known to the others, all agreed that the Nazi invasion could be expected to begin within twenty-four hours. Photographs revealed "a striking increase"—94 percent—in invasion barges. The Germans had ordered that all Wehrmacht leaves be canceled in twenty-four hours. Forty-eight hours after that, moon and tide conditions would be "particularly favorable" for enemy landings, the reports concluded. Warning of the "large-scale and disciplined" movement of troop transports toward forward bases on the Channel, the committee concluded that the last enemy preparations were complete.

In London the director of military intelligence told the chiefs of staff that the invasion was imminent. At Bletchley the Naval Intelligence Section concluded that the landings might begin the following day. The chiefs therefore ordered all defense forces in the United Kingdom to "stand by at immediate notice." The Air Ministry issued an "Invasion Alert No. 1" to all RAF commands, signaling the expectation that the Germans could be expected within the next twenty-four hours.

Yet to those who knew the führer and his Byzantine court, there was an air of uncertainty about the Reich's intentions. After listening to a recording of Hitler's most recent speech, Count Galeazzo Ciano, the Italian foreign minister, was baffled. Something about it was not quite right. He wrote in his diary that Hitler seemed unaccountably "nervous."

He was in fact furious. He was not accustomed to insubordination, but that is what it amounted to. The issue was Luftwaffe bombing. He had sent a directive to the Luftwaffe: "Attacks against the London area and terror attacks are reserved for the Führer's decision." He was still hoping to bring Churchill to the conference table, and he was also worried about reprisals against German cities. Confident that the Reich would never be subject to air raids, he had neglected the Fatherland's antiaircraft defenses.

Bombing cities was still an issue in 1940. Both the Hague and the Geneva Conventions—which the Reich was pledged to support—outlawed indiscriminate assaults on peaceful civilians. In May, when a flight of Heinkels had mistakenly killed nearly a hundred German women and children in the old university city of Freiburg im Breisgau, the Germans had blamed it on the RAF. A Nazi communiqué had reported it as an "enemy attack," Goebbels had condemned it as the *"Kindermord in Freiburg"* [massacre of the innocents], and the British traitor Lord Haw Haw had denounced it as a "perfectly substantiated atrocity."

Granting London immunity had never been popular in the Luftwaffe. As the autumn of 1940 approached with no victor in the skies over England, Göring repeatedly asked Hitler to reconsider. Discontent was particularly keen among German fighter pilots. In his postwar memoirs, Adolph Galland described London as a target "of exceptional military importance, as the brain and nerve center of the British High Command, as a port, and as a center for armament and distribution." He wrote: "We fighter pilots, discouraged by a task which was beyond our strength, were looking forward impatiently and excitedly to the start of the bomber attacks."

Although the Luftwaffe was approaching air superiority, time was on the RAF's side. September 15 had been fixed as the target date for Sea Lion, but already the weather was worsening; if England were to be invaded, the movement of barges and tugs could not be delayed.

The key event determining the outcome of the battle was a matter of chance. On the night of August 24, some 170 German Heinkels, ordered to bomb oil installations at Thameshaven and an aircraft factory at Rochester, had become lost. Before turning for home they jettisoned their bombs, and as it happened they were above London. Fleeing homeward, they left raging fires in several London boroughs, including Bethnal Green and East Ham.

Churchill saw his opportunity. He minuted the chiefs of Air Staff. "Now that they have begun to molest the capital, I want you to hit them hard, and Berlin is the place to hit them." That night—Sunday, August 25—eighty-one twin-engine Wellingtons and Hampdens carried the war to the heart of the Reich. The city was covered with dense cloud; only half the bombers found it. Damage was slight. Ten men were killed by a bomb that fell near the Goerlitzer railroad station, and the Siemens electrical works suffered a temporary loss of production.

However, no bomb had fallen on the capital of the Reich before. Shirer wrote in his diary: "The Berliners are stunned. They did not think it could ever happen. When the war began, Göring had assured them that it couldn't. . . . They believed him. Their disillusionment today is all the greater. You have to see their faces to believe it. . . . For the first time the war has been brought home to them."

Goebbels ordered German newspapers to carry the headline: *"Feiger Englischer Angriff* ("Cowardly British Attack"). The bombers came again on August 28 and again the following night, and after the third raid the headlines in the Nazi press read: *"Englische Luftpiraten Über Berlin!"* ("English Air Pirates Over Berlin!")

Hitler delivered a withering attack on the British leadership in Berlin's Sportpalast. Addressing an audience of social workers and nurses, he said, "The babbling of Mr. Churchill or Mr. Eden—reverence for old age forbids the mention of Mr. Chamberlain—doesn't mean a thing to the German people. At best, it makes them laugh." He then took up the bombings. "Mr. Churchill," he said, "is demonstrating his new brainchild, the night air raid." He had believed that such madness would be stopped, but "Herr Churchill took this for a sign of weakness." Now he would learn better: "We will raze their cities to the ground!" He shouted: "The hour will come when one of us will break, and it will not be National Socialist Germany!" The women leaped to their feet, joyfully shouting, "Never! Never!"

He knew, he said, that the British were wondering when his invasion would begin, and added:

> In England they're filled with curiosity and keep asking: "Why doesn't he come?" Be calm, he's coming! Be calm, he's coming!

Luftwaffe intelligence continued to be wildly inaccurate. Hitler was told that although "the prerequisites for *Seelöwe* [Sea Lion] have not been completely realized" in the past five weeks German airmen had shot down 1,800 British planes, which would have been double Dowding's total strength. However, the führer mused out loud at a working lunch, destruction of the RAF might be unnecessary; if their capital were subjected to terror bombing, the British might be seized by "mass hysteria," and the invasion could be canceled.

In lifting his ban and shifting the focus of the German air offensive, Hitler gave permission, wrote Alfred Jodl, the chief of the operations staff, "for the use of strong air forces in reprisal attacks against London." It meant monumental suffering for British civilians. It also meant defeat for Kesselring's strategy, for London's martyrdom would be England's salvation.

✦

ON THE CLEAR afternoon of Saturday, September 7, Göring, Kesselring, and their staffs stood on the cliffs of Cap Blanc Nez and watched their enormous formation of three Luftflotten—1,000 aircraft, a third of them bombers—cross the Channel and head for London, then the largest city in the world. It was an awesome spectacle. The enormous armada, covering 800 square miles and shutting out the sun, rose nearly two miles high.

The RAF had no warning that London was the target. At 4:00 P.M., Dowding was at his desk in Bentley Priory when British radar picked up the huge formation coming from Calais. In the past, Luftwaffe raids had split up upon reaching the coast, and British fighters were hovering at 20,000 feet, waiting for that moment to pounce. It never came. The armada, armed with huge new 6,500-pound bombs, crossed the east coast of Kent, near Deal, and headed straight for London, hitting Woolwich Arsenal first, then the Victoria and Albert Docks, the West India Dock, the Commercial Dock, and the Surrey Docks.

Behind them they left a flaming vision of apocalypse. Ships were sunk, catwalks mangled, cranes toppled, and great fires set that covered 250 acres and served as a beacon for a second heavy raid that night. More than 1,000 Londoners were killed. Because of a report that enemy parachutists were landing, the Home Guard issued the code word "Cromwell," signaling the beginning of an invasion, and church bells were rung all over England.

Luftwaffe raids on the capital continued on subsequent nights, but now the RAF was ready. The fighting in the air reached a climax on Sunday, September 15, which became known as Battle of Britain Day. Churchill witnessed it; because "the weather on this day seemed suitable to the enemy," he wrote, he and his wife drove to Park's headquarters at Uxbridge. They were taken to the bombproof operations room fifty feet belowground, which he compared to "a small theater," adding, "We took our seats in the dress circle."

There a gigantic map table and rows of light bulbs made the chaos in the sky overhead comprehensible. The defenders' commitment was total. When his visitor asked about reserves, Park looked grave and replied, "There are none." In Churchill's words, "The odds were great; our margins small; the stakes infinite." Like the battle of Waterloo, also fought on a Sunday, this was what Wellington had called "a close-run thing," but it ended in a great British triumph. At the end of the afternoon Churchill was told that 183 German planes had been shot down at a cost of twenty-six RAF aircraft, and though those figures were exaggerated, the significance of the day's fighting could not be. That evening, in a message to Dowding meant for enemy consumption, Churchill declared the British, "using only a small proportion of their total strength," had "cut to rags and tatters separate waves of murderous assault upon the civil population of their native land." Two days later he told Parliament, "Sunday's action was the most brilliant and fruitful of any fought up to that date by the fighters of the Royal Air Force."

The Germans had been badly stung, and they knew it. The high command of the Wehrmacht reported "large air battles and great losses for the German formations due to lack of fighter protection." The day's operations, involving over 300 bomber and 1,000 fighter sorties, were called "unusually disadvantageous," with the heaviest losses when the raiders were homeward bound. In addition, the invasion forces could not be kept at the ready because the RAF, hitting the Channel ports, was taking a mounting toll of German ships.

It was the death of Sea Lion. On September 17, Hitler postponed the invasion indefinitely on the ground that winter was approaching and the RAF was "by no means defeated." The German bombers would return to London for seventy-six consecutive nights, except November 2, but the führer had turned to maps of Russia. A German staff officer expressed relief at the prospect of "a real war."

HITLER'S D DAY

DAVID SHEARS

To the end of history, no doubt, arguments will continue about Hitler's plan to invade England in the summer of 1940—Operation Sea Lion. Was his threat genuine? Or was he merely trying to bluff Churchill's government into agreeing to a political settlement? The answer, according to David Shears, who interviewed many of the German participants after the war, is a little of both—and that may be why Sea Lion never happened. Hitler was serious enough to muster a huge invasion fleet at the just-conquered North Sea and Channel ports: So many barges were gathered there that the Rhine and the canals of Holland and Belgium were practically deserted through August and September, depriving German industry of needed war materials. Coastal batteries were built that were capable of shelling Dover, twenty-six miles across the Channel, and they did. But Hitler dawdled. The premature collapse of France had left him without a contingency plan for invasion. Strange as it may seem now, he initially feared that a successful invasion might cause the collapse of the British Empire—which, he felt, would benefit Japan and the United States more than Germany. So, in the weeks after Dunkirk, he pressed indirectly for a deal. It was only when he recognized that England was now prepared to fight to the end that he turned to the Sea Lion alternative.

Could an invasion have worked? In a brief accompanying article, Shears examines the two contradictory scenarios, the first by war gamers at Sandhurst and the other by a leading British military historian. (One is also tempted to mention Len Deighton's novel, *SS-GB,* which assumes that the Germans had not only brought off the invasion but that London had become a provincial capital of the Reich.) Perhaps the ultimate answer is that the two most crucial force multipliers, time and the führer's enthusiasm, were never on Sea Lion's side. In the event, Hitler's restless but obsessive mind was about to turn to Russia.

David Shears, a former British foreign correspondent, is now a free-lance writer and travel-book publisher. He divides his time between Washington, D.C., and the Outer Banks of North Carolina.

IT WAS A SUMMER TO REMEMBER. BASKING IN SUNSHINE, THE English countryside had never looked better. Cricket continued as usual at my 400-year-old school, and there was little to disturb a boy's preoccupation with bowling and batting. Although several of our younger masters had gone off to the war, classes went on with teachers taken out of retirement. To all appearances, the secluded little world of a Sussex boarding school remained wonderfully intact.

But even as teenagers we knew, as we heard the war communiqués, that our world hung by a thread. Hitler's panzer divisions smashed through the Low Countries and France. At Dunkirk, Britain's exhausted troops scrambled aboard every craft that floated, abandoning weapons and equipment on the beach. During those fateful days of May and June 1940, Britain felt suddenly naked, exposed to conquest by Germany's seemingly invincible might. Emotions were mixed; Britons felt exhilaration as well as fear. Paradoxically, the fall of France did not depress British spirits. Despite their peril, Britons were proud to stand alone as the "happy few." The new prime minister, Winston Churchill, like Shakespeare's Henry V before Agincourt, knew how to strike this chord in the national character. "There was a white glow, overpowering, sublime, which ran through our island from end to end," he wrote in his war memoirs.

Britons drew comfort from the fact that the Royal Navy was still vastly superior to the German fleet. But could its battleships protect the "sceptered isle" from invasion? Its admirals knew from recent experience off Norway how vulnerable surface ships were to air attack in coastal waters. How much air cover could the depleted Royal Air Force provide in the English Channel now that the Luftwaffe could move to forward bases in northern France? On June 4, the last day of the Dunkirk evacuation, the RAF had only 446 serviceable fighters, of which no more than 331 were Hurricanes and Spitfires.

As for the army, the Chiefs of Staff had just warned Churchill's war cabinet that if Germany succeeded in landing a mobile force firmly ashore, "the army in the United Kingdom, which is very short of equipment, has not got the offensive strength to drive it out." The British Expeditionary Force left 400 tanks, nearly 2,500 guns, and almost 64,000 vehicles in France. Two-thirds of the 963 tanks still in the United Kingdom were light vehicles of little combat value.

Neither side had foreseen or planned for a cross-Channel invasion. In the First World War, Britain had kept strong forces permanently stationed at home in case the Germans should cross the North Sea. But between the wars Britain let down her guard. When Germany rearmed in the 1930s, Britons were more alarmed by the new threat of bombing than by seaborne invasion. After war broke out in 1939, certain forces were placed within reach of the east coast, ready to deal with any possible landings. But that was all.

German military staffs were no better prepared. They were taken aback by the swift success of the blitzkrieg Hitler had launched on May 10. French resistance had crumbled with unexpected speed. Suddenly the Germans found their tank columns at the Channel and the Atlantic. It looked as if their newly revived 1914 sailors' ballad *"Wir fahren gegen Engelland"* ("We're Sailing against England") might finally come true. But a successful invasion of Britain depended on four main prerequisites: realistic plans, a large fleet of suitable landing craft, air supremacy, and Hitler's total commitment to the operation. At the time of Dunkirk, Germany had none of these. It was not until mid-July that the führer committed himself to an invasion plan, which came to be code-named *Seelöwe* (Sea Lion).

The German naval staff had produced a somber memorandum in November 1939, stressing the need to overcome British sea power and destroy the RAF before attempting to invade Britain. It suggested the east coast between the Tyne and the Thames rivers as the landing area—a distance of more than 250 miles—with the attackers crossing the North Sea from German ports. It ruled out Channel harbors for embarkation, since they would be too vulnerable to British attack. In any case, the German army at that time believed it would take at least six months of heavy fighting to reach Boulogne. Although the naval memo was referred to army and Luftwaffe staffs, it never went to the Oberkommando der Wehrmacht (OKW), the Armed Forces Supreme Command. Apparently Hitler did not hear of it until Grand Admiral Erich Raeder, commander in chief of the German navy, briefed him at a meeting on May 21, 1940, a day on which panzers were racing for the French coast. The führer, for various reasons, was full of hesitation.

Germany had practically no landing craft. Raeder was told on June 14 that no more than forty-five seaworthy barges could be mustered within a fortnight. To ferry its vaunted mechanized divisions to British beaches, the Wehrmacht would be forced to rely on strings of unwieldy barges, mostly towed by tugs at a likely speed of no more than two or three knots. It requisitioned nearly 2,000 such vessels from canals and rivers throughout northern Europe. These barges were designed for calm inland waterways and were quite unsuitable for the treacherous open seas of the Channel. Moreover, they would need to be converted into makeshift landing craft with the installation of bow ramps and reinforced decks.

Improvisation was the order of the day. Some farfetched ideas were canvassed: Professor Gottfried Feder of the Reich Economics Ministry came up with the notion of "war crocodiles" made of reinforced concrete. At least ninety feet long, these vehicles would cross the Channel under their own power and then crawl up the beaches on caterpillar tracks. Feder said that such floating fortresses could be built quickly, but naval architects doubted their seaworthiness, and his fantasy soon foundered.

More feasible were the ferries developed by Fritz Siebel, a German aircraft manufacturer. They used pontoons as catamaran floats, spanned by a sturdy deck. Powered by old aircraft engines driving air or water propellers, they were capable of carrying up to eighty tons of cargo or troops. Siebel actually built some 180 of these in 1940, along with 128 airscrew-driven barges. But the fact remained that most of the transport envisaged for Sea Lion comprised a motley fleet of barges that were unseaworthy and awkward to unload.

The German navy's scorn for these preparations was best expressed by Admiral Friedrich Ruge, then a commodore commanding a flotilla of minesweepers in the Channel. He told me in a postwar interview that one day in August 1940 he had been with army commanders watching a landing exercise. Both Field Marshal Walther von Brauchitsch, the army commander in chief, and General Franz Halder, the army chief of staff, were aboard one of his ships. According to Ruge, when the demonstration ended, Halder turned to him and asked what he thought of Sea Lion's prospects. Ruge did not mince his words. "Frankly, Herr General," he replied, "when I consider that you plan to cross the Channel at a somewhat slower speed than Caesar's legions 2,000 years ago, I don't think much of it." Ruge added that Halder was not amused.

Hitler, curiously enough, echoed the navy's doubts. He seemed even to welcome its misgivings. For they reinforced his own hesitations, which stemmed in part from his ambivalent view of Britain. Even in the heady days of June 1940, as he prepared to take the French surrender, Hitler nurtured no burning ambition to invade the British Isles. He believed London would soon come to its senses, realize the hopelessness of its position, and sue for peace. He would allow magnanimous terms, whereby Britain would return former German colonies and renounce British influence in Europe in exchange for an armistice sparing Britain and the rest of the British Empire. Although he had

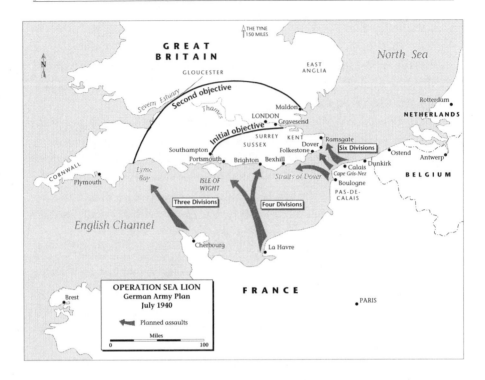

In November 1939, the German naval staff suggested a seaborne invasion from North Sea ports to a 250-mile stretch of Britain's east coast between the Thames and the Tyne rivers. In mid-July 1940, Adolf Hitler instead approved an elaborate army plan for a three-prong naval assault by six divisions landing between Ramsgate and Bexhill in the east, four divisions between Brighton and the Isle of Wight, and three divisions in Lyme Bay, toward Plymouth. In all, forty-one divisions would eventually seize the land from Gravesend to Southampton, then move as far as Maldon and the Severn Estuary. Cut off, London would fall, permitting an advance into Scotland. But by late August, Hitler had to bow to reality, limiting the assault to thirteen divisions landing on only eighty miles of coast between Folkestone and Brighton. Even this plan died, due to the Luftwaffe's failures and Hitler's preference for Soviet conquest.

few illusions that Churchill would accept such a settlement, he envisaged an alternative government led by David Lloyd George.

Lloyd George, who had led Britain to victory in 1918 and then campaigned on a "Hang the Kaiser" slogan, seemed an unlikely choice. But the former war leader had been fascinated by Hitler during a visit to Obersalzberg in 1936, when the Welshman was already in his seventies. Like some other

Britons in those days, Lloyd George then favored siding with Germany against Bolshevism. He called Hitler "a great man" and praised the Nazi leader's success in bringing down the unemployment rate. As late as October 1939, a month after the outbreak of war, Lloyd George was still urging Prime Minister Neville Chamberlain to heed peace proposals.

By then the disillusioned Chamberlain was no longer an appeaser. There remained some British politicians and intellectuals who felt bad about the Allied treatment of Germany after World War I. Some pacifists, notably on the Left and in the Church, still favored peace at almost any price. And there were those in all parties for whom Hitler, despite his duplicity and his pogroms, held a certain appeal. But their number and influence dwindled to a vanishing point after Dunkirk. Hitler's peace talk fell on deaf ears.

To the führer, Britain was a sideshow. He saw Sea Lion as a risky enterprise. He also had a well-known distaste for the sea—one German admiral remarked that Hitler felt seasick at the sight of a naval chart. Mastery of the Continent was his first objective. Once this had been achieved—from Poland to the Pyrenees—his thoughts turned eastward. His obsession then was to succeed where Napoleon had failed: to conquer Russia. But he had told his military chiefs in November 1939, "We can oppose Russia only when we are at peace in the West." As he had often stated in his book *Mein Kampf,* Germany must avoid a war on two fronts; to this end, Britain must be either invaded or brought to terms—preferably the latter. The "Aryan" British did not need to be humbled, like the despised Slavs; they just had to be kept out of the ring.

Precious weeks passed while Hitler stalled. If an invasion of Britain were to be mounted in 1940 with any prospect of success, it would need top priority, and a crash program to build seaworthy landing craft while the Luftwaffe gained mastery of the air. By late September, storms in the Channel would jeopardize amphibious operations.

Yet Hitler did not issue his Directive Number 16, ordering preparations for the invasion, until July 16, a month and a half after the end of the Dunkirk evacuation. Even then he sounded an uncertain trumpet.

"As England," he began, "in spite of the hopelessness of her military position, has so far shown herself unwilling to come to any compromise, I have decided to begin to prepare for, and if necessary to carry out, an invasion of England." The conditional words "if necessary" show that Hitler still hoped Britain would come to terms. Three days later he delivered to the Reichstag a ninety-five-minute speech that contained a vague "appeal to reason even in England." On an oddly plaintive note, he said it "almost causes me pain" to feel he had been fated to deal the final blow to the great British Empire, "an empire which it was never my intention to destroy or even to harm."

But to invasion-jittery Britons, these words dropped into a speech full of bombast and threats hardly sounded like a peace offer. On July 22, Lord Halifax, the British foreign secretary, dismissed the feeler by declaring that Britain would go on fighting "until freedom is secure." Evidently supposing that the British had missed the point, the Germans dropped leaflets containing a translation of Hitler's speech over Britain on the night of August 1–2. Headed "A Last Appeal to Reason," the leaflets were scorned by their finders. Derisive housewives raffled them to raise funds for the Red Cross.

The British, of course, had not been idle: Their aircraft factories were toiling around the clock, seven days a week, to turn out fighters. By early August, the number of Spitfires and Hurricanes had more than doubled. Britain's battered army, reduced to fifteen badly understrength divisions starved of tanks, guns, and transport, was getting reorganized and reequipped. A fledgling citizens' militia (Local Defence Volunteers, soon renamed the Home Guard) had been set up. To be sure, Britain's feverish preparations were often rudimentary. But every obstacle placed on an open field to block an enemy glider landing, every roll of barbed wire strung along a beach, made Britons feel a little more secure. They were so busy laying tank traps, building pillboxes, making Molotov cocktails, and removing signposts that they had little time to brood on their fears.

Some of the frenzy was fanned by alarmist intelligence. British decryptions of the Luftwaffe's Enigma-machine codes led London's Joint Intelligence Committee to warn that a full-scale invasion could come anytime after mid-July. Yet this scare was based only on the forward deployment of Luftwaffe squadrons to French bases. It lacked support from photoreconnaissance of Channel ports, which showed no concentration of invasion craft at that time. British Military Intelligence, not to be outdone, actually feared invasion might take the form of tanks ferried by motorboats. Naval Intelligence scoffed at this notion, but Admiral Sir Dudley Pound, the navy's first sea lord, argued that it should not be dismissed out of hand. He warned Churchill in a memorandum on July 10 that the Germans might be able to land 100,000 men, with England's east coast bearing the main weight of an invasion. The prime minister thought the figure pessimistic, but throughout July and August he kept Britain's main defensive strength in East Anglia, northeast of London. Only when the invasion fleet began its massive buildup in ports across the Channel early in September did Churchill shift his big battalions to the south.

Why did British intelligence forecast that the invasion would hit the east, not the south, coast of England? Two reasons are clear: First, the fact that no barges were then massing in Calais and Ostend suggested that no threat would come from that quarter; instead, Britons believed the Germans might sail out of Baltic ports, which were then beyond the range of British reconnaissance. Second, East Anglia, with its open beaches and flat hinterland, offered better tank territory than the shingled beaches of the south, which are mostly overlooked by cliffs or high downs.

German intelligence concerning Britain was amateurish, to say the least. The Germans overestimated British ground strength throughout July, August, and September by about eight divisions. They were ill-informed about the British order of battle and the locations of British units. Their only real success was in breaking Royal Navy ciphers, but this advantage ended in August when London became suspicious and changed the codes. Although the Germans dropped several agents into Britain, they were inexperienced men of few skills who conveyed little information before their capture. Tyler Kent, the cipher clerk at the American embassy who had betrayed Churchill-Roosevelt messages to the Axis powers, was arrested on May 18, long before Sea Lion was a serious undertaking.

If some of the British defensive expedients seem ridiculous, such as Home Guard volunteers training with pikes for lack of rifles, they were matched in absurdity by the Wehrmacht's barges and its plan to ship several thousand horses across the Channel to help unload artillery on the beaches. And Hitler's Directive Number 16—Sea Lion's original marching order—rates as one of the most unrealistic documents in modern military history. Its first fallacy was its proviso that the landing must come in the form of a surprise crossing. Given the slowness of the barges and the time they would need to form up, surprise was out of the question. Even if they could have made a speed of four knots in Channel waters—a generous assumption—those based at Ostend would have had to set out on the morning of the day before the invasion date; Dunkirk-based craft, with just a twenty-five-mile crossing, would have had to sail before sundown to make a dawn landing. With Channel currents running at up to four or five knots, the barges—towed in pairs—would have needed at least fifteen hours to make the journey. Ruge warned that the transport convoys would turn into a "pig pile" (*Sauhaufen*).

Second, the directive called for thirteen divisions to land on a broad front extending from Ramsgate in Kent to Lyme Bay in Dorset—a distance of 250 miles. The German navy insisted that there was no way it could protect such a wide zone. But the army was adamant. As late as August 6, Halder wrote in his diary that the navy's demand for a short front was "complete suicide" from the army's standpoint. Evidently expecting fierce resistance, he protested, "I might just as well put the troops that have landed straight through the sausage machine."

Third, Directive Number 16 was a soldier's, not a sailor's, document. It reads like an army river-crossing order, providing that "elements of the air force will do the work of the artillery and elements of the navy the work of the engineers." In other words, the Luftwaffe would soften up the defenses on the opposite shore, and the navy would provide the equivalent of pontoon bridges. Minefields would protect both flanks of the invasion area from the Royal Navy. Preliminary seizures of Cornwall or the Isle of Wight were to be examined (though such landings would hardly enhance the prospects of surprise). Finally, the directive decided on mid-August, just four weeks later, as the deadline for completing preparations for the whole operation. Considering the late start, this was utterly unrealistic.

Even the name, Sea Lion, was surely an error in judgment. Originally the invasion plan had been safely designated Lion (*Löwe*), but this was apparently changed by General Alfred Jodl, chief of operations at the OKW. According to one account, Jodl was noted for selecting code names far too suggestive of the actual operations, and Sea Lion was a clear example. Worse still, Reichsmarschall Hermann Göring sent the top-secret Directive Number 16 by radio to his Air Fleet commanders, trusting in his Enigma coding machines. It was promptly deciphered by the British code breakers, who thus gained a real coup—not only the code name Sea Lion but also Hitler's decision to set it in motion.

Admiral Raeder's reaction to Hitler's directive was predictable, and he lost no time in conveying it to the führer. The navy chief described the hazards presented by enemy mines, uncertain weather, lack of artillery support, and above all the British navy, which despite Luftwaffe attacks might be able to cut off the beachheads from reinforcement. Evidently the admiral's views again impressed Hitler, who acknowledged to his military chiefs on July 21 that invading Britain would not be a mere river crossing but a movement over sea-lanes commanded by the enemy—a truly English Channel.

Raeder pressed his objections at a crucial meeting with Hitler and the army chiefs on July 31 at the führer's Berghof mountain retreat. The doughty grand admiral began with an apparent show of support: He reported that the navy's preparations for Sea Lion were well under way. The necessary barges were being requisitioned and converted into makeshift landing craft. Along with tugs (many of which were merely trawlers), merchant ships, and other vessels, the invasion fleet should be ready and on station by mid-September. Minesweeping had already begun in the Channel, and given air cover and good weather, the task should take three weeks. Minelaying on the flanks of the invasion routes would start at the end of August. The navy would be able to execute Sea Lion on or after September 15.

But having said this, Raeder returned to the fray on the issue of a broad-front landing. He said the navy could not protect transports invading as far west as Lyme Bay from attack by British warships based at Portsmouth and Plymouth. He proposed instead that landings be confined to the Straits of Dover. He lectured the soldiers on the lore of the sea, telling them they must plan to storm the beaches when the tide was receding; otherwise the barges would keep floating off, and chaos would result. This requirement and two other tactical preconditions for a successful landing—the army's demand for a dawn touchdown and the need for enough moonlight to allow safe maneuvering—set close limits on timing. Raeder said there were only two periods when conditions would be right: between August 20 and 26, which was too soon, and between September 19 and 26, which was getting dangerously late in the year. All told, he concluded, it would be best to postpone Sea Lion until May or June 1941.

Hearing this plea for a six-month delay, Hitler might have thrown a tantrum. But the records of this key meeting show that he did not. And this in itself was further proof that the führer was less than wholehearted in his commitment to an invasion of Britain. In fact, Hitler had already secretly decided to attack the Soviet Union the following spring—at just about the time Raeder was now proposing to launch Sea Lion.

As the Berghof discussion proceeded, Hitler nonetheless clung to the hope of invading Britain by the autumn of 1940. He said all would depend on the air war, which could begin as soon as weather permitted. Redeployment of Luftwaffe squadrons to bases in northern France and the Low Countries had recently been completed. Halder's diary accordingly recorded this decision: "The air war will start now and will determine our ultimate relative strength. If the results of the air war are not satisfactory, invasion preparations will be stopped. But if we gain the impression that the English are being crushed and that the air war is . . . taking effect, then we shall attack."

Somewhat mollified, Raeder bundled his papers back into his briefcase and left the meeting. Sea Lion was still planned, but the navy's sober realism had been taken into account: Hitler had not yet accepted a six-month postponement, but the onus was on the Luftwaffe to fulfill the boasts of its vainglorious commander in chief, Göring. If it could not beat down the Royal Air Force, invasion would not be attempted.

But Raeder had been duped; he had not heard the full story. After the admiral had gone, Hitler confided his "smash Russia" obsession to his generals.

He thought that Britain was counting on the Soviet Union as a potential ally; with the smashing (*zerschlagen*) of Russia, London's last hope would be extinguished. Then Germany would be the master of Europe. Halder's diary records the führer's exultant command: "Decision: In the course of this drive of setting things right Russia must be eliminated. Spring '41." The die was cast for Operation Barbarossa. It was one of Hitler's momentous—and fatal—"unalterable decisions."

Does this mean that Sea Lion was just a bluff, that it was never a real threat to Britain? Field Marshal Gerd von Rundstedt, commander of the army group whose divisions were earmarked for Sea Lion, said in 1945, "I was always very skeptical about the whole affair. . . . I have a feeling that the führer never really wanted to invade Britain." His chief of operations, General Günther von Blumentritt, told B. H. Liddell Hart, the British military writer, "it was all regarded as a 'war game.' . . . Among ourselves we talked of it as bluff and looked forward to news that an understanding with Britain had been reached."

But these generals were talking after the war, as Monday-morning quarterbacks. I, too, talked with German officers at intervals during the postwar years, starting in 1946, and agree with William Shirer's observation that they had many axes to grind, notably "their principal theme, expounded at dreary length . . . that if they had been left to make the decisions Hitler would never have led the Third Reich to defeat."

If Sea Lion was mere bluff—which I do not for a moment believe—it was an expensive bluff. The fact is that for a two-month period, from mid-July to mid-September, Hitler was serious enough about Sea Lion to muster a huge invasion fleet at the Channel ports, at considerable cost to the German war economy: The arsenals of the Ruhr, like other industrial plants throughout the Reich, depended on barges for bulk transport. Halder admitted that the top priority accorded to Sea Lion was causing "economic derangement." And Raeder noted the severe impact of trawler requisitioning on German fisheries.

History records that all three German armed services became intensely preoccupied with Sea Lion in July, August, and September. The navy loyally played its part, despite its doubts. Just rounding up the barges, converting them, and providing them with crews was a Herculean task. Naval officers responsible had to improvise as they went along. Records vary according to dates and documents, but one official count showed that the navy requisitioned 1,910 barges, of which 1,490 clogged the Channel ports by September 19. Not only the Rhine but also Belgian and Dutch canals fell silent as the lumbering craft assembled along the coast from Rotterdam to Le Havre—and became sitting ducks for the RAF. In addition, by September 21 the navy found 166 steamers, just four short of the target figure. Tugs were at a premium, since three-quarters of the barges lacked their own power. By mid-September, more than 350 tugs and trawlers had arrived at the Channel harbors. In the naval bases of Kiel and Wilhelmshaven, only two tugs stayed behind. Only in one broad category of invasion craft—motorboats and fishing smacks—did the navy fall far short of its assigned goal: It could muster only about half the requisite 1,028 vessels of these types by September 19.

For those in the Low Countries and northern France, there was nothing phony about these intensive preparations. At Hitler's express order, the navy built heavy coastal batteries at the narrowest part of the Channel to cover the assault. The first battery, near Cape Gris-Nez, comprised four 38cm guns capable of bombarding Dover and was operational by August 1. Three more naval batteries with smaller guns followed within six weeks, and the army provided rail-mounted and other artillery. On August 22, the gunners opened up on a Channel convoy and claimed to have hit three out of thirteen ships, though none were sunk. They also fired twenty-four rounds on Dover, which responded with fire from a 14-inch gun mounted at Churchill's behest. More heavy guns were emplaced on the English side, and artillery duels ensued at intervals. The heaviest day, Churchill records, was September 9, when over 150 shells were fired.

After a slow start, the German army soon became wholly dedicated to Sea Lion. Depots, headquarters, and bases mushroomed in the countryside. Troops began intensive amphibious exercises on French beaches. The army's original plan, drawn up in July 1940, had been to ship six divisions from the Pas de Calais area, to land between Ramsgate and Bexhill; four divisions from the Le Havre area would attack between Brighton and the Isle of Wight: three others would sail from Cherbourg, in the Cotentin Peninsula, to open a third bridgehead farther west, in Lyme Bay; and two airborne divisions would spearhead the first-wave assault. All told, forty-one divisions were earmarked for the invasion in the July plan. The initial objective would be a line from Cravesend to Southampton including the North Downs of Kent and Surrey. The second goal would be a line from Maidon in Essex to the Severn Estuary at Gloucester, leaving London surrounded. Then London would be occupied and motorized divisions would strike northward, fanning out to Liverpool, Newcastle, and across the border to Glasgow and elsewhere in Scotland. Brauchitsch, the army commander in chief, reckoned the whole operation could be completed in a month.

When the navy said the army was being unrealistic, the generals accused

the admirals of prevarication. For a while Hitler sided with the army in fa-
voring a broad front, and it was not until the second half of August that the
führer ordered the army to bow to naval realities. Eventually the landing area
was narrowed to the eighty-mile stretch of coast between Folkestone and
Brighton, and the number of divisions was slashed by more than two thirds,
to thirteen.

But the army's eagerness persisted. Halder wrote in his diary on August 6
that "the only driving force in the whole situation comes from us." He evidently had more enthusiasm for Sea Lion than Rundstedt or Blumentritt, let
alone the navy. The army's exercises on the French beaches intensified; its engineers and tank crews devised ways of landing submersible tanks through
surf. But the generals' faith in flanking minefields to protect invasion craft
from attack was misplaced: British minesweepers would soon have cleared
channels to admit Royal Navy warships. Similarly, the army's reliance on
shore batteries to pulverize British defenses and keep the Royal Navy at bay
was optimistic, to say the least. The guns could cover most invasion craft only
part of the way. Only a few units—such as the Sixth Mountain Division,
which was to land near the White Cliffs of Dover—would remain within
range of the Cape Gris-Nez batteries.

So we come to the Luftwaffe, which by Directive Number 16 held the key
to Sea Lion. On July 21, Göring asked Hitler to permit "attacks on Britain's
fighter pilots, air force, aircraft industry, ports, industries, oil centers, and the
Channel area." Military staffs estimated that within a month these air assaults
would create the conditions for a landing. Göring even thought England
could be defeated by air power alone. He boasted that he could smash British
fighter defenses in southern England within four days and defeat the entire
RAF within two to four weeks. Even as late as September 5, when the Battle
of Britain had been raging for more than three weeks, a staff meeting was told
that "the *Reichsmarschall* is not interested in the preparations for Operation
Sea Lion since he does not believe the operation will ever take place." The
Luftwaffe had assigned half of its bomber force to supporting the landing
troops. But Göring was still confident that air power alone, without army intervention, would be sufficient.

His proud boasts were put to the test starting August 13, when the
weather permitted *Adlerangriff* (Eagle Attack) to begin. The epic tale of the
Battle of Britain does not need retelling. But we may recall that the Luftwaffe
shrewdly chose as its targets for that opening day the vital radar stations upon
which the RAF depended. Five were damaged, and one, on the Isle of Wight,

was knocked out for eleven days. Yet Göring was unaware of this success, and only three days later at Karinhall, his country estate, he told his top commanders that he doubted if it was worth continuing the attacks on radar sites. Accordingly, the Luftwaffe made only two more sorties directed at them—a serious blunder on Göring's part.

But his Luftwaffe staff soon caught on to another secret of the RAF's success—radar sector stations. Monitoring radio traffic between controllers at the stations and airborne pilots, the Luftwaffe realized the critical importance of these nerve centers in relaying radar and spotter intelligence to fighter squadrons. After suffering defeats in the air battles of August 15 and 17 (Germany lost 147 planes to Britain's 61), they switched tactics. Starting August 24, the stations were targeted for intense attack. Coming at a time when the RAF was already reeling from the weight of German numbers, this was a deadly threat. Although no sector station was totally incapacitated, two were badly damaged, and the strain was beginning to tell.

The ensuing fortnight was, for Britain, the worst period of the air struggle. During the two weeks ending September 6, 295 planes in RAF Fighter Command were totally destroyed and 171 seriously damaged. During the whole of August, 300 fighter pilots were lost, while the training schools graduated only 269. But then, in early September, came another providential German blunder. In retaliation for RAF bombing of Berlin, Hitler ordered the Luftwaffe to launch massive terror attacks on London. The capital blazed as German bombers stoked the fires—but the RAF sector stations were spared. Like the reprieve for the radar installations, this was a godsend. Battered Fighter Command bases in southern England could repair damage, replenish squadrons with new planes from the factories, and give pilots and ground crews a much-needed break.

Germany's Sea Lion planners recorded that Göring had not made good on his boasts. The German naval staff noted in its war diary on September 10 that "the indispensable precondition for the undertaking (Sea Lion) . . . has not been achieved, namely clear air command over the Channel." For Sea Lion to succeed, the Luftwaffe would have to switch its attacks from London to Portsmouth, Dover, and the British fleet. However, the navy did not want to suggest this to the führer, since, its staff noted, he shared Göring's view that the Blitz on London would be possibly decisive for the war, a strategy that might "make Sea Lion unnecessary."

Hitler and Göring were wrong; it would take more than bombing to break Britain's spirit. As firemen, air-raid wardens, and householders doggedly fought the flames, Britons did not quail; on the contrary, their sense of being hammered on the anvil hardened their resistance. Setting a "we can take it" example, Churchill's government and King George VI stayed put in London while bombs fell around them.

Throughout this tense period, Sea Lion remained very much alive. But while the RAF and British morale held out, Hitler could not set a D day (or S day, as the Germans called it) for invasion. The timetable was slipping, bringing Sea Lion in ever greater danger of foundering in the storms of autumn. Hitler had wanted *Adlerangriff* to start on August 5 and promised a definite decision a week or two later on whether to invade. But first the weather delayed large-scale air operations for ten days, and then the RAF proved harder to beat than Göring supposed. (The Luftwaffe's two-to-one defeat on September 15 was final proof, if any were needed, that "the few" had won the Battle of Britain.)

Indeed, the British were hitting back: not only by cheekily bombing Berlin but also with hit-and-run raids on the massed armada in the Sea Lion embarkation ports. During the night of September 14–15, the German naval staff noted, "the enemy continued their bombing attacks, directing their main effort on the coast between Boulogne and Antwerp. In Antwerp . . . considerable casualties are inflicted on transports—five transport steamers in part heavily damaged; one barge sunk, two cranes destroyed, an ammunition train blown up, several sheds burning." As these raids continued, the navy made an urgent appeal for stronger antiaircraft protection of the ports. For the RAF bombers, and the Royal Navy destroyers that joined in the bombardment, no more tempting targets could be found.

Such harassment was not making life easier for the German naval officers struggling to bring order to Sea Lion. But more threatening to the operation's prospects was the weather, which looked unpromising for the second half of September. The landing would need at least a week of calm seas; instead the forecast called for "a series of depressions in quick succession, with turbulent wind conditions."

Under the circumstances, Hitler had no alternative but to issue an order, on September 17, postponing Sea Lion "until further notice." It was yet another vague directive in that, ostensibly, it left the options open; the invasion fleet and all preparations were to be kept at the same state of readiness. The naval staff's war diary noted that "an order from the führer to carry out the operation is expected at any time and at short notice." Hitler still hoped that if he kept up the pressure—the invasion threat as well as the bombing of London—British morale would collapse.

Clues to Sea Lion's impending demise had begun to spread three weeks before Hitler's teletype went out from the OKW. A young German major in the First Panzer Division, based near Orléans in 1940, recalled long after the war that he was hauled out of a cinema as early as August 28 and told to report to his chief of staff.

"As I entered his office I was sure we were going to be told that Sea Lion had been given the green light," he told me in an interview. "So I asked the chief of staff, 'Are we on our way?' And he replied that I'd better sit down. Then he said: 'Yes, we're on our way, but not to England—to East Prussia.' So then we knew that Sea Lion was a dead duck."

The major was Johann Graf von Kielmannsegg, later a general who became a NATO commander. Since that episode occurred three weeks before Hitler issued his directive effectively killing Sea Lion, it shows that one panzer division, at any rate, knew which way the wind was blowing.

Hitler did not relax the navy's state of readiness until October 2, but his September edict instructed commanders to stop mustering barges at the ports and to start quietly dispersing larger concentrations of shipping. Some German destroyers and minelayers were moved away from Cherbourg to less-exposed bases such as Brest and Saint-Nazaire. On October 12, Hitler issued a further order shelving the invasion plan for 1940 but stating that Sea Lion might be revived the following spring or early summer.

By then, however, the führer was totally engrossed in Operation Barbarossa. Intoxicated by past military successes, imbued with dreams of Russian conquest, he had flouted his own maxim: no war on two fronts. If Hitler had delayed his Soviet adventure until Britain was neutralized, the history of World War II might have been very different. More German victories lay ahead, but Hitler's decision to sacrifice Sea Lion to Barbarossa put Germany on the road to disaster.

COULD SEA LION
HAVE WORKED?

DAVID SHEARS

Many have been tempted to speculate as to whether Hitler could have pulled off Operation Sea Lion if he had acted sooner. In the early 1970s, a group of senior British and German officers, including the Luftwaffe ace General Adolf Galland and the Battle of Britain pilot Air Chief Marshal Sir Christopher Foxley-Norris, met at Sandhurst to seek an answer. They umpired the first-ever war game on Sea Lion, organized by the *Daily Telegraph Magazine* and the Department of War Studies at the Royal Military Academy. Each side had a command room, and British and German officers played the respective wartime commanders. Hitler and Churchill were also represented. Decisions were passed to a main room, where they showed up as moves on a large landscape model of southeastern England and the English Channel.

Richard Cox, a former military correspondent of the *Daily Telegraph,* dramatized the results in his book *Operation Sea Lion.* His narrative account begins with an artillery spotter watching from Lympne Castle, a few miles southwest of Folkestone, as the first wave of German invaders moves ashore on September 22, 1940.

In Cox's scenario, based on the Sandhurst exercise, 8,000 Luftwaffe paratroopers and the first wave of seaborne forces succeed in establishing narrow beachheads in Kent and Sussex. The nine divisions in the initial German assault have little difficulty overcoming the skimpy beach defenses, and they capture both Newhaven, a few miles east of Brighton, and Folkestone. But they lack a functioning deepwater port at which steamers can unload heavy cargo. In the Channel, British motor torpedo boats and destroyers cause mayhem among the helpless barge trains. The Germans lose 449 barges and 28 steamers on S-Day—their term for D-Day—or roughly one-quarter of the whole Sea Lion fleet. The RAF loses 237 planes to the Luftwaffe's 333 downed aircraft.

On land, the German forces meet increasing resistance. The British recapture Newhaven. The invaders' seizure of Folkestone is of dubious value; its docks and cranes have been so effectively demolished by the retreating defenders that it can handle only two ships at a time. A few miles to the northeast, Dover is tenaciously defended. Although the German airborne troops are supplied by Junkers 52 transports landing at captured airfields, the army desperately needs to land its tanks and heavy artillery if it is to break out of the beachheads. Even with relatively calm seas, it is too rough to unload barges on the beaches without difficulty. Farther out to sea, the Royal Navy decides—after some initial losses—to keep its heavy ships out of the congested Channel waters, leaving the task of harassing the invasion fleet to fast-moving, smaller vessels. It can afford to do so, having started the action with fifty-seven destroyers to the Germans' ten. By the evening of September 23, the last three remaining German destroyers have been sunk. Admiral Raeder tells Hitler the navy cannot protect the convoy due to sail that night with the second echelon of 24,000 troops, 900 tanks, and vital stores. Hitler and the army commanders are furious, but the sailing is delayed. When the creeping barges are still ten miles off the British coast, two-thirds of them are wiped out by British destroyers' gunfire while air battles rage overhead.

By now the army realizes that the navy and the Luftwaffe have left their invading troops in the lurch. Ammunition is running out, and Hitler is finally persuaded to withdraw. Of the 90,000 men who had landed on S-Day, more than one-third have been killed or captured. Only about 15,000 manage to escape through Folkestone or aboard minesweepers from the beaches. More than 30,000 are taken prisoner by the British, and uncounted thousands more drown in the channel.

It is a plausible scenario.

Less plausible, in my view, is the grim alternative offered by Kenneth Macksey, a British former tank major who has written extensive military history and biography. In his 1981 book *Invasion: The German Invasion of England, July 1940,* he speculates that Hitler could have conquered Britain if Sea Lion had been launched in mid-July 1940.

Macksey begins by making the key assumption that Hitler, instead of hesitating, embraces Sea Lion with full fervor in late May rather than wait until July. Over Raeder's objections, Hitler decides to follow a strat-

egy of first beating down the RAF and the Royal Navy and then mounting a relatively small-scale invasion by sea and air.

After five days of hammering from the air, Britain is invaded. First to
land on the night of July 13–14 are Luftwaffe paratroops, dropping by
parachute and glider in the immediate vicinity of the planned bridgeheads. Then come the seaborne troops, landing on a twenty-five-mile
stretch of beaches west of Folkestone—between Hythe and Rye, just
across the East Sussex border—and scaling the heights between Dover
and Folkestone. Despite seasickness, these assault troops, brought over
in minesweepers and transferred to outboard-motored storm boats, are
largely successful. Some tanks are landed from barges as reinforcements
pour in. British resistance is weak. Defending troops have been partially
demoralized by cross-Channel bombardment. With their paratroops
knocking out some of the British shore guns, the invaders establish a
foothold up to 3,000 yards deep between Hythe and Dover.

Britain's counterattack is delayed while commanders try to size up
the situation. The Royal Navy, unable to obtain adequate air cover from
the hard-pressed RAF, comes under attack from dive-bombers and suf-
fers losses in newly laid minefields. Its forays into the Straits of Dover invasion lanes prove costly. Despite its superiority in numbers over the
German navy, the British fleet is unable to halt the enemy buildup on the
invasion front. As German troops fan out, refugees clog the roads.

On the afternoon of July 14, Luftwaffe officers manage to seize the
control building at the Hawkinge RAF station, just north of Folkestone.
There they find documents and maps, left intact by the fleeing controllers, that betray the command-and-control system of Fighter Command. General Albert Kesselring of the Luftwaffe orders massive
attacks on the sector stations the next day, with devastating effects on
RAF combat capacity. The first tank battles ebb and flow on July 15,
with heavy losses on both sides but an eventual victory for the invaders.
In the Channel, Churchill is desperate to halt the buildup. He throws
larger naval vessels into the fray, ordering cruisers as well as destroyers
to bombard the invasion ports. Battleships are summoned from Scotland
to take station off the east coast. The British meet resistance from German cruisers and win a naval victory. But the RAF's losses and the weakness of the British army are beginning to tell.

Churchill sends an agonized appeal to President Roosevelt. He has Roosevelt's sympathy, but the president cannot move faster than public opinion, and he is unwilling to intervene directly. With this last hope gone, Britain's doom is sealed. We do not need to follow each act in Macksey's unfolding tragedy: the German breakout, the decline of civilian morale, the belated and fruitless intervention of warships summoned home from Gibraltar, the continued destruction of remaining British tanks by German 88mm guns. Churchill accepts the inevitable, sends the royal family quietly out of London to await evacuation by warship from Liverpool, and tries to conserve what is left of the fleet to continue the fight overseas. Negotiations occur in Stockholm, an armistice is signed at the beginning of August, and Churchill and his cabinet follow their king into exile.

Macksey tells a gripping story, but I find it unconvincing. It goes without saying that Germany's chances of success were strongest in the post-Dunkirk weeks, when Britain was at her weakest. If the Wehrmacht had been able to put even a modest force ashore—and maintain it with supplies—it could have made short work of Britain's enfeebled army with its fifteen half-strength divisions denuded of armor and artillery. But this is an enormous if. First, we come back to that critical question of the invasion fleet. Macksey does not explain how, if Raeder was told on June 14 that no more than forty-five seagoing barges could be made available within two weeks, an adequate fleet of such vessels could have been mobilized by mid-July. Nor does he allow time for the conversion of requisitioned barges into makeshift landing craft. Even with a much-scaled-down invasion force, the task of commandeering, crewing, converting, and concentrating the necessary vessels at the Channel ports by such an early date would surely have overtaxed even German capacity.

Second, Macksey postulates the start of Luftwaffe nighttime air raids on Britain as early as June 5, with heavy daylight raids on Channel convoys beginning June 19 and the all-out Battle of Britain opening July 9. But he does not explain how the Luftwaffe could have managed to redeploy its fighters so rapidly to bases within range of Britain. In fact, the Luftwaffe was unable to exploit the newly captured airfields close to the Channel until late July. (Even then, bad weather delayed the start of Eagle Attack, its mass air assault, until August 13.) Without these forward bases, German bombers would have had to operate over Britain without fighter cover, making them easy prey for the RAF. Even with them, as General Galland has testified, it was difficult enough. His Messerschmitt 109 fighters operated from one of the air bases closest to Britain, but they were able to spend only twenty minutes in British skies before having to head home to refuel. "We felt we were on a leash," he told me in an interview. It is therefore hard to accept Macksey's suggestion that the Luftwaffe could have gained control of the skies over the Channel by the first week of July. Yet this is the key to his subsequent scenario.

Third, Macksey has German guns opening fire on Dover as early as June 29. But in the event, as we have seen, the 38cm coastal batteries capable of bombarding Dover, Hythe, and Folkestone were not emplaced until August.

Even if Hitler had been hell-bent on invading Britain soon after Dunkirk, he could not have made Macksey's mid-July deadline. It was just not feasible—and the longer he waited, the more impossible it became.

BARBAROSSA

WILLIAMSON MURRAY

In the first half of 1941, Hitler turned to the East, his intention all along, sending his armies first into the Balkans and Greece and then, on June 22, into the Soviet Union. Even though Great Britain remained unsubdued, it presented no immediate threat beyond annoyance: He was once again fighting what amounted to a one-front war, and his dream of establishing a German empire from the English Channel to the Urals seemed within reach. It would be a Europe free of the perceived contamination of the Jews and, as Williamson Murray writes, one "in which 'subhuman races' like the Slavs would live a life of Helot-like serfdom." On the plains of Russia, ideology would smash into ideology, revolution into revolution. Hitler could take care of England later.

So began one of history's great miscalculations. Hitler was perfectly aware of Napoleon's Russian calamity. He was determined to carry off his invasion in a different way—though ironically, the start of Barbarossa was only a day earlier than the anniversary of Napoleon's invasion. But instead of the Grande Armée's single march to Moscow, Hitler planned to attack in a lightning blow by over three million men along a two-thousand-mile front, overwhelming the armies of the Soviet dictator Stalin in a matter of weeks. It would not work out that way. As summer turned into fall, and the weather began to deteriorate, Moscow became as much an obsession for Hitler as it had been for Napoleon.

Conventional wisdom has it that the Russian winter doomed Hitler's invasion. But, Murray points out, decisions (or the lack of them) made long before the cold set in ensured the failure of Barbarossa. There was no way that it could have succeeded. But through an accumulation of blunders, Stalin almost turned the tide in Hitler's favor.

On December 5, just beyond the gates of Moscow, Soviet troops counterattacked, and the overstretched German divisions nearly gave way. Two days later, the Japanese bombed Pearl Harbor, and now the United

States was in the war. Hitler, who wanted Japan on his side and, more important, Japan's navy, declared war on the United States. But the events of early December would, as it proved, foreclose on his dream of empire.

Williamson Murray is a professor of history emeritus at Ohio State University, and, with Allen R. Millett, the author of the recently published *A War to Be Won: Fighting the Second World War.*

ON JUNE 22, 1941, THE WEHRMACHT INVADED THE SOVIET Union. Here was a moment, Adolf Hitler said, when "the world would hold its breath." He was right. The fate of Operation Barbarossa (the code name for the invasion) determined the course of World War II and the face of our world. The reasons for its failure have only recently become clear as historians have unraveled the monumental documentary evidence and cut their way through the legends and myths fixed in popular perceptions.

It is now beyond question that the German military deserves a full share of responsibility for its defeat: Its commanders endorsed Hitler's disastrous strategic and political approach in every respect. Moreover, their claims that they were largely ignorant of the "political" crimes of the SS have been revealed to be patently false; throughout the summer and fall of 1941, they actively and enthusiastically cooperated in the atrocities Nazi Germany visited on the Soviet peoples, particularly the Jews.

There are a number of explanations for the German failure that call for substantial rethinking. The foremost of these is that Hitler was almost entirely responsible for the defeat. That was, of course, the explanation the German generals offered after the war. There was some truth to their claims. Hitler was the driving force behind Nazi ideology—and the resulting atrocities—which did so much to alienate the Soviet population and to undermine whatever chance existed of weaning the Russians from Joseph Stalin's own murderous tyranny. Beyond that, Hitler failed to set clear goals for the invasion. He involved the Wehrmacht in a great spring campaign in the Balkans that seemingly delayed the start of Barbarossa by as much as five weeks. After the invasion of Russia began, he temporized for much of August as to what the next stage of the campaign should be. He overruled the army and diverted substantial forces from the central area of the invasion for a drive into the

Ukraine in September. And he ordered the resumption of the drive on
Moscow in late fall, just as the weather was about to turn against the Germans. But to lay all responsibility at Hitler's door is to misunderstand the nature of civil-military relations in the Third Reich. In effect, by 1941 the
leadership of the German army had completely sold out to Hitler and the
Nazi ideology. As a result, there is plenty of blame to go around.

One of the many truths that litter the landscape of history books is that
Mother Russia is so vast it is simply unconquerable. Did not the greatest military commander in history, Napoleon Bonaparte, fail? And, early in the eighteenth century, did not Charles XII of Sweden, no mean military commander
himself, meet the same fate?

But this explanation omits the German victory over Czarist Russia in
World War I. With the Treaty of Brest Litovsk in March 1918, and subsequent military advances, the German Empire won Finland, the Baltic States,
Poland, Byelorussia, the Ukraine, and the Crimea, and it left the rest of Russia in the throes of chaos. Perhaps we might not call this a conquest, but it
certainly represented a decisive military victory that would have permanently
altered the face of Europe, had not the megalomania of German military leadership resulted in total collapse on the Western Front later in the year. The
Germans succeeded by waging a limited but sustained campaign that placed
maximum strain on the Russian army, and a minimum one on the German logistic system. They also waged an exceedingly clever propaganda campaign
that exacerbated tensions and disharmonies within Czarist Russia. They finished off their efforts by shipping Lenin in a sealed train from Switzerland
back to Russia, as if he were a plague bacillus (which, in fact, he was).

The eastern campaign of 1914–17 stands in stark contrast to the German
campaign of 1941–45. In the former case, the Germans attempted to picture
themselves as liberators to many segments of Russian society, including the
Jewish ghettos of Eastern Europe. In World War II, racist Nazi ideology provided both the rationale and the driving force behind the invasion, as well as
the conduct of all military operations.

Hitler's ideological view of the world (and when we speak of Nazi ideology
we are speaking of Hitler's views) posited that race was the basic determinant
of human civilization. Virtually all human greatness derived from the Aryan
race; the German nation stood as the last bastion of that greatness. At the dark
end of the spectrum was the Jewish race, a parasitic and degenerative influence that threatened to destroy civilization. To reach their full potential, the
Aryan Germans had to widen the geographic bounds of the Reich far to the
east, gaining *Lebensraum* (living space) and expanding that close connection

with the soil on which all major civilizations depended. Hitler hoped eventually to create a German empire that would rule Europe from the Urals to Gibraltar, an empire free of Jews, in which "subhuman" races like the Slavs would live a life of Helot-like serfdom.

By 1941, a substantial portion of the German population—including most of the officer corps—fully subscribed to Hitler's conception of the world. From the first, the führer's planning for Barbarossa made no effort to hide the ideological nature of his crusade against the "Jewish-Bolshevik international conspiracy," centered in Moscow. From the infamous commissar order—that the army should shoot all commissars and other Communist officials when captured—to the murderous "special actions" against the Jews, Hitler made his intentions clear. And the senior army leadership not only acquiesced with their silence but in many cases cooperated wholeheartedly.

Even before Barbarossa was launched, the OKW (*Oberkommando der Wehrmacht*—armed forces high command) and the OKH (*Oberkommando des Heeres*—army high command) had issued decrees that dispensed with Germany's international and legal obligations. These were military decrees, not SS orders. Colonel General Erich Hoeppner, commander of Fourth Panzer Group and a participant three years later in the July 20 plot to assassinate Hitler, issued the following directive to his troops:

> The war against Russia is an important chapter in the German nation's struggle for existence. It is the old battle of the Germans against the Slav people, of the defense of European culture against Muscovite-Asiatic inundation, and the repulse of Jewish Bolshevism. The objective of this battle must be the demolition of present-day Russia and must therefore be conducted with unprecedented severity. Every military action must be guided in planning and execution by an iron resolution to exterminate the enemy remorselessly and totally. In particular, no adherents of the contemporary Russian Bolshevik system are to be spared.

A number of other senior generals, in particular Erich von Manstein and Walther von Reichenau, would issue even more bloodthirsty characterizations of the Eastern campaign as a racial crusade.

Such written approval translated into actual deeds. The SS Einsatzgruppen, detailed for the so-called special actions against Jews and Soviet citizens that turned out to be the first steps of the Final Solution, received extensive support, both direct and indirect, from the army. The Babi Yar massacre of over 33,000 Jews in September 1941, for example, received the complete cooperation of the army commandant of occupied Kiev. In turn, the commanders of the Einsatzgruppen wrote a series of notes of appreciation to senior army leaders expressing delight at the enthusiastic aid that army units rendered in the special actions.

The greatest indication of the army's acceptance of Hitler's ideological crusade lies in its brutal and callous treatment of its prisoners of war. Over the summer and fall of 1941, the army claimed to have captured 3.9 million Red Army soldiers. By February 1942, only 1.1 million remained alive, and of them only 400,000 were still capable of working as slave laborers. By the end of the war, barely 100,000 of these POWs had survived.

The German racial ideology, basic to the whole conception of Barbarossa, resulted in major miscalculations on the part of the Germans that made their victory impossible even before the invasion began. For one thing, senior Nazis from Hitler to the military leadership underestimated the capacity of the Soviet regime, its people, and its industries to put up a sustained and ferocious resistance. The Germans thought that all they had to do was, as Hitler put it, "kick in the door and the whole regime would collapse like a house of cards." This perception of the supposed subhuman qualities of the Slavic races contributed to faulty assumptions at the planning level that fatally undermined preparations for the invasion.

Even more disastrous for the Germans was the impact of this racial ideology on the Soviet people. If ever a regime were vulnerable to a political campaign aimed at undermining its popular support by causing internal dissension and revolt, it was Stalin's "workers' and peasants' paradise." By 1941, Stalin had killed millions of Soviet citizens; millions more remained in NKVD (secret police) slave-labor camps, where the inmates were starved and beaten to death at a rate only the Germans could match. Following Hitler's line, the German military assumed that Stalin's regime would crumble from internal dissension. In fact, the horror of Hitler's invasion policies, the callousness of German troops in their ideological crusade, and the extent of Nazi atrocities achieved the impossible: They drove the Soviet peoples back into the arms of their criminal leader.

Other factors in the German defeat sprang directly from the operational and logistic assumptions upon which the German military planned Barbarossa. The foremost of these was a belief that the Wehrmacht could catch the Red Army in the border areas and destroy it with a lightning blow. Thereafter, both OKH and OKW planners assumed, German troops would not face substantial, sustained resistance from the remnants of the regular army or called-up Soviet reserves. (This failure to properly gauge its enemy recalls the German army's intelligence blunders during the Battle of Britain.)

On the other hand, the force-to-space ratios of the funnel-shaped Russian theater were a factor that German planners were aware of from the beginning: The farther the German troops advanced, the fewer soldiers and weapons there would be for each kilometer of the widening front line. Any sustained Soviet resistance would cause increasing difficulties.

OKH planning originally targeted Moscow as the objective of the campaign, which Franz Halder, chief of the general staff, and most senior generals believed would guarantee the final breakdown of the Soviet regime. Hitler, however, argued in a series of conferences in December 1940 that, for economic and political reasons, the most important strategic targets were Leningrad and the Ukraine. From this point on, Halder, who had been burned a number of times in arguments with Hitler, left unstated what the strategic objectives of the campaign should be after the initial destruction of the Red Army in the border area. Instead, the OKH merely laid out the first stage of the advance, leaving the continuation of the campaign up in the air.

The largest gap in preparations for Barbarossa may have lain in logistics. Hitler, of course, gained widespread and justified notoriety for his penchant for moving his finger over maps as if enemy resistance, geography, and other such realities had no role. The logistic planning of the German military for Barbarossa fell entirely within Hitler's conceptions of the Jewish-Bolshevik regime's weaknesses and vulnerabilities; there appears to have been little connection between logistic and operational planning by German military planners. By November 1940, German logisticians had calculated that in the best case, they could supply German forces to a line approximately 600 kilometers to the east of the then-current Nazi-Soviet frontier. (As if to underscore the German military's lack of communication, Barbarossa's strategic planners envisioned a campaign of six to seventeen weeks, ending 1,750 kilometers from the starting point.) The fact that the Germans were able to push far beyond that 600-kilometer limit largely resulted not from Jewish-Bolshevik rot, as the Germans envisioned it, but, in the first months of the way, from gross incompetence on the part of the Soviet military leadership.

Ironically, the invasion itself might not have been possible without massive Soviet support of the German war economy in the year before June 22, 1941. The Soviets provided immense quantities of desperately needed grain, petroleum products, raw materials, and even rubber. Some historians have credited the Balkan campaign with having derailed Barbarossa by delaying the operation's original May jump-off date to June; however, the delay allowed the Soviets to provide more exports of fuel and other crucial materials—which in turn helped the Germans launch their invasion of the Soviet Union.

The logisticians calculated that after an advance of 600 kilometers (roughly to Smolensk), movement forward would have to halt for a considerable period of time to allow for resupply and the establishment of new forward supply dumps. Already the Germans had to make a number of overly optimistic assumptions. For example, they calculated that units engaged in fighting the Red Army would not expend more ammunition than had been fired in France. As a result, German troops crossed the frontier with only a basic load of ammunition. Given the rapid advance, and the low priority of logistic units, ammunition and fuel were in desperately short supply from Barbarossa's earliest days. German troops had to obtain food and fodder from the Russian and Ukrainian peasants, further damaging relations with the conquered population. Finally, the whole resupply effort depended on the repair of Soviet railroads, particularly the Smolensk-to-Brest Litovsk line. But since railroad tracks were generally secured well after the roads, repair work began only after considerable delays. And railroad-repair troops were given the lowest priority in the German army.

What the logisticians had to provide would have given any supply officer a nightmare. More than half the frontline divisions had shortages, or foreign equipment—everything from Czech tanks, French artillery, and Norwegian mountain guns to a hodgepodge of captured motor transport and civilian trucks seized from the newly occupied countries of western Europe. Moreover, Hitler had decreed the doubling of panzer and motorized infantry divisions; the army could do this only by scrounging equipment, especially supply vehicles, from every imaginable source. To get this force ready by June 22 required desperate efforts. Halder's entries in his diary suggest that providing the equipment for these new mobile formations would have forced a postponement of Barbarossa from the original May 15 date regardless of the campaign in the Balkans. All in all, the logistic system was supposed to transport huge amounts of fuel and supplies forward, all tailored for the vastly different weapons and vehicles with which the army was equipped.

✦

HOW, THEN, did the Germans get as far as they did? The true advantage that they enjoyed lay in the extraordinary quality of their officer corps and in the battle capabilities of their troops. This human edge rested on certain factors. German officers were selected by a demanding and thorough system, and the best were selected for, and schooled by, the general staff. The army prepared itself ruthlessly for combat and judged its performance by rigorous standards. The emphasis was almost entirely on operational and tactical (i.e., battlefield) performance. This narrow focus explains the German army's weaknesses in the political, strategic, and logistic areas. All of its battle skills had been honed by the run of success it had enjoyed from 1939 to 1941. In most respects, the Wehrmacht army of June 1941 was the finest fighting instrument the Western world has seen in the twentieth century.

The Germans were also helped by the Soviets' preparations (or lack thereof) to meet the invasion. Stalin started with the assumption that for political reasons his regime could not afford to lose territory. To do so might cause political consequences leading to the collapse of his regime. A series of war games in Moscow at the end of 1940 had suggested that there were considerable vulnerabilities in this area. Stalin's response was not to trade space for time, but instead to push more and more regular units of the Red Army up to the frontier to hold off any major German penetrations—exactly the place where they were most vulnerable. Yet Hitler had calculated incorrectly as well: The German panzers captured much of the Red Army that was mobilized by then, but the Soviet Union's capacity to mobilize more men proved stunning.

Stalin and his followers were so wrapped up in their own Marxist ideology that they missed the revolutionary nature of the Nazi regime, as ideological as theirs. As John Erickson has pointed out: "The failure to comprehend the essentials of German military doctrine in a tactical, operational sense . . . was the prime cause of disaster; the effect of this was and had to be devastating, for such a failure impeded and inhibited operational planning."

Exacerbating all the weaknesses involved in Soviet preparations were the devastating effects of Stalin's murderous purges of the Red Army's officer corps. The army leadership was in a state of abject terror. Not only had a substantial percentage of the best and brightest been liquidated, but the forward-thinking doctrine and tactical concepts developed by those "wreckers and traitors" were now deemed invalid.

Even so, the doctrine, training, and preparations of the Red Army were severely deficient compared with those of the German army. Despite its extraordinary level of toughness and willingness to sacrifice and suffer hardship, the Red Army was in no condition to stand and fight the Germans without relying on the spaces and distance behind it. Stalin had no understanding of the strategic and military realities that confronted his regime. He would learn—but at a catastrophic price.

The German hammer blow fell in the early hours of June 22. The last train carrying raw materials from the Soviet Union crossed into German territory barely two hours before the invasion began. Moscow did not send out the first alerts to the frontier districts until midnight on June 21–22. The warning never reached the frontline troops; across the length and breadth of the frontier, the German invasion caught the Soviets by surprise. The following exchange between a frontline unit and its headquarters captures the extent of that surprise:

Frontline unit: We are being fired upon. What shall we do?
Army headquarters: You must be insane—and why is your signal not in code?

Later that morning the German ambassador presented the declaration of war to an ashen-faced Vyacheslav Molotov, the Soviet commissar of foreign affairs. The confused and frightened Molotov plaintively commented, "Surely we have not deserved that"—as accurate a statement as he ever made, especially given the enormous economic aid that the Soviet Union had rendered to the Third Reich over the previous year.

The level of tactical surprise that the Wehrmacht achieved far surpassed German expectations. Luftwaffe bombers and fighters savaged the Soviet air force's frontline airfields, where aircraft were parked wingtip-to-wingtip. By noon of the first day, the ill-trained and ill-equipped Soviets had lost 800 aircraft on the ground and another 400 in the air.

The situation was no better for the Red Army. In Army Group North, General Manstein's LVI Panzer Corps broke entirely clear and within four days had rattled 200 miles forward to capture the Dvina crossings at Daugavpils. That was already more than half of the estimated maximum supply distance. Manstein proposed that Army Group North push its Second Panzer Corps up behind him and allow him to continue his rampage through the Baltic States. Both the panzer group commander and army group commander, however, opted for a more conservative broad-front advance, and some of the steam went out of the northern drive. Nevertheless, the speed of the German advance caused the Soviet position to fall apart in the Baltic and ended whatever possibility there might have been for a defense in depth in front of Leningrad.

If the situation was disastrous for the Soviets in the north, it was catastrophic in the center. Here two great panzer groups—the Third, under General Hermann Hoth, and the Second, under General Heinz Guderian—swung out from their jump-off positions in East Prussia and Poland to converge in a great encirclement behind Minsk. Meanwhile, the Soviet commander on the front, General D. G. Pavlov, proved completely incapable of handling the tasks confronting him.

Pavlov was one of the most slavish toads in the Red Army; returning from Spain, he had played a crucial role in persuading Stalin—on the basis of the supposed lessons of the Spanish Civil War—to disband the mechanized corps that one of the most prominent purge victims, Marshal Mikhail Tukhachevsky, and others had so laboriously built up in the 1930s. Now Pavlov passed on to his subordinate commanders the nonsensical orders issuing from Stavka (the Soviet high command) and Stalin in Moscow that the Soviet troops expel the German invader and execute offensive operations onto German territory—immediately. Not only did such orders have no relation to the calamity on the front, but they added to the chaos that was spreading throughout all levels of the Soviet command. Within weeks Stalin served up Pavlov as an example to the rest of the Red Army by having him shot. It was a thoroughly justifiable decision, but Pavlov's real crime had been the following of orders.

In late June, Guderian's and Hoth's surrounding of Minsk netted over 300,000 prisoners and vast amounts of booty. Still, there were disturbing signs in this first victory: Large numbers of Soviet troops managed to filter through the arms of the encirclement, while resistance proved unexpectedly tenacious. Guderian's panzers captured Smolensk on July 16, but Holt was not able to close off the encirclement until July 24, because Guderian's focus was on further advances. Another 300,000 Soviet prisoners of war, along with 3,205 destroyed or captured tanks and 3,000 guns, fell into German hands.

Only in the Ukraine did the Red Army put up a sustained, effective resistance. Nevertheless, by mid-July Army Group South was approaching Kiev. Across the board, the first four weeks of Barbarossa had brought the Germans enormous successes. Franz Halder trumpeted in his diary on July 3:

> On the whole, one can already say that the task of destroying the mass of the Russian army in front of the Dvina and Dnieper [Rivers] has been fulfilled. I believe the assertion of a captured Russian general to be correct that we can calculate on meeting east of the Dvina and Dnieper only disjointed forces, which alone do not possess the strength to hinder German operations substantially. It is, therefore, truly not claiming too much when I assert that the campaign against Russia has been won in fourteen days. Naturally it is not yet ended. The extent of the theater and the tenacity of resistance that will be conducted with every means will still claim many weeks.

But before the month was out, German operations inexorably ground to a halt. The lead elements, the panzer and motorized infantry divisions, were running out of fuel; they were also almost out of ammunition. Restrictions had to be put on the number of shells that artillery units could fire. On the primitive roads with their heat, dust, and deep glutinous mud when it rained, the German logistic system began to fall apart. By July 11—after just nineteen days—

25 percent of German supply vehicles had permanently broken down. The panzer divisions could not repair damaged tanks and other vehicles because parts were not getting through.

The panzer and motorized infantry divisions were now dangerously exposed; follow-on infantry formations were sometimes over a hundred miles behind the front line. Meanwhile, Soviet reserve forces were arriving in increasing numbers. Admittedly, the Stavka was largely wasting them in a series of furious but uncoordinated attacks on German spearhead units. But these counterattacks exacerbated the dangerous German shortage of ammunition. In turn, the need for ammunition placed a further strain on the diminishing number of supply vehicles, which drastically curtailed the Germans' ability to supply fuel to the front.

As late as the third week of August, Army Group Center was unable to build up fuel dumps for the renewal of the advance. Frontline units fired off ammunition as fast as it arrived, and the best units in the German army had to ward off ferocious Soviet counterattacks in a most precarious position and at heavy cost. By August 11, Halder was singing a very different tune in his diary:

> The whole situation shows more and more clearly that we have underestimated the colossus of Russia—a Russia that had consciously prepared for the coming conflict with the whole unrestrained power of which a totalitarian state is capable [something Halder knew about]. This conclusion is shown both on the organizational as well as the economic levels, in the transportation, and above all in the infantry divisions. We have already identified 360. These divisions are admittedly not armed and equipped in our sense, and tactically they are badly led. But there they are; and when we destroy a dozen the Russians simply establish another dozen.

The fighting around Elnya best underlines the extent of the German dilemma. In mid-July Guderian had seized this high ground as a jump-off point for an assault on Moscow. But as their doubts increased about whether Moscow would be the next objective, Guderian and his superiors began to advocate holding the salient for reasons of prestige. Soon massive artillery barrages, followed by wave after wave of Soviet attacks, broke on the German positions. The conditions under which the German infantry fought were nightmarish. Guderian noted that

> In most areas there was no depth to the line, such as in the area of the XX Army Corps's 78th Infantry Division, which was compelled to hold an 18-

kilometer front. No company or division had any reserves, and the enemy was able to creep within 25 meters of the German line. . . . The men in the dugouts had little contact with their commanders to the rear and to either side. . . . During four days' fighting up to August 26, the 78th Infantry Division had lost 400 men, and the overall casualty rate since the beginning of the war was 30 percent for the division. Most of the losses . . . were caused by 25 to 30 Russian guns that were firing an "unlimited" ammunition supply. A daily average of 2,000 shells fell on the 78th Infantry Division and on the night of 24–25 August 5,000 shells rained down.

Even with extensive reinforcements the German army was short 200,000 men in its combat formation on the Eastern Front. Twenty-one of the OKH's initial reserve of twenty-four divisions had already been detailed to combat; there were virtually no reserve divisions left. As alarming was the fact that only 47 percent of German tanks on the Eastern Front were still battle-ready; the rest were either disabled (30 percent) or out of commission and waiting for repair (23 percent). Not only had a large number of tanks already been lost, but almost all panzer divisions were well under strength too.

During August a lot of squabbling took place within the German high command, in particular between Hitler and the OKW on one hand and the OKH and the front commanders on the other. The former argued that the German army, rather than push eastward broadly, should focus its efforts on the Ukraine, to the south, and on Leningrad, to the north. Hitler emphasized his belief that Moscow held little significance either politically or economically. Moscow, he said, "is merely a geographical idea." But the OKH and the front commanders strongly advocated a resumption of the advance on Moscow. There were other serious quarrels within the senior leadership over tactical and operational issues, particularly over the number of Soviet troops escaping from the encirclements, but all of this squabbling seemed more a symptom of German troubles than a cause of them.

It is noteworthy that in all these August discussions, no one, from Hitler to the senior generals, was willing to examine the basic assumptions on which the Germans had launched their invasion. There were no discussions of the long-term implications of the campaign thus far, no apparent suggestion that the conquest of the Soviet Union might not be achieved in a year, no consideration of the need to prepare for a possible winter campaign, and no recommendation that the panzer and motorized infantry divisions be husbanded for refitting and reuse in 1942. Instead everyone simply agreed to push on into the depths of the Soviet Union regardless of the lateness of the season; the only disagreement was over which direction that advance should move.

By the end of August, the logistic situation at the front had greatly improved (in fact, tank strength was up to 75 percent), and Hitler had finally made up his mind: The next push would be toward Leningrad and deeper into the Ukraine; consequently, substantial forces would be drawn off from Army Group Center to support the advance of the army groups on either wing. By this time the advance, combined with tenacious Soviet resistance in front of Kiev and along the Dnieper, had created a gigantic Russian salient in the central Ukraine—one that was enormously vulnerable, to the north, from a thrust launched by Army Group Center and, to the south, from the advance of General Paul von Kleist's First Panzer Group down the Dnieper. In this dangerous situation, Stalin tied his commanders' hands by demanding that Soviet troops concentrate on defending Kiev rather than the dangerous flanks.

In early September the panzers began to roll forward, deep behind the forward edges of the salient. Stalin ordered his army commanders to stand and fight; on September 15, the German pincers closed behind Kiev, and the worst defeat of military history went into the books. The Germans claimed they captured over 665,000 soldiers (in addition to those killed); after the war the Soviets claimed that they had only 667,000 soldiers in the salient and that 155,000 escaped. No matter whose figures are correct, a disaster of immense proportions had occurred.

Meanwhile, Army Group North had closed on Leningrad and isolated Peter the Great's city, thus making possible the starvation of close to 1 million Soviet citizens over the upcoming winter. As if encirclement was not bad enough, Soviet authorities refused to allow evacuation of the Leningrad civilians or to stock food dumps for a possible siege. Moscow regarded both measures as an indication of defeatism on the part of those suggesting it, an offense punishable by death.

Now the period of relatively good weather was almost over, and winter was fast approaching. After the war, many German generals expressed surprise at the frigid conditions they had experienced in the Soviet Union—although several million German soldiers had fought on the Eastern Front in World War I, including a fair number of men who would go on to become high-ranking officers in World War II.

All of that seems to have played little role in the decision-making processes taking place. Hitler, the OKW, and the OKH staffs were all euphoric over the success of the Kiev operation. Army Group Center saw this as the opportunity to persuade Hitler to switch the emphasis back to the center for a swift advance on Moscow, to capture the Soviet capital before the onset of winter. With little discussion, the senior leadership now agreed: The forces diverted to the wings would return to Army Group Center, which would resume its advance on Moscow at the beginning of October.

No one questioned the logistic implications: The resumption of the advance, with its attendant massive military operations, would result in vast expenditures of fuel and ammunition. That, in turn, would prevent the buildup of supply dumps for the winter as well as take precedence over the shipment of much-needed winter clothing and winter lubricants. But in the aftermath of Kiev, there were few naysayers on the army staffs; after all, had not the OKH and Army Group Center been arguing throughout the year that the capture of Moscow would inevitably lead to the breakdown of Soviet resistance?

Hitler and the German high command agreed in mid-September to move directly to an offensive by Army Group Center against Moscow, code-named Typhoon. Yet the overall situation and state of the German army to the east should have called into question the wisdom of launching such an offensive. The supply situation was still precarious; the farther east the two armies advanced, the more difficult it would become to supply them in winter conditions. The commander of the Fourteenth Army reported on September 13 on the logistic situation in his area:

> At the moment [the supply situation meets] current consumption only. The transportation situation [does] not so far allow the establishment of depots sufficiently large to enable the troops to receive what they need in accordance with the tactical situation. The army lives from hand to mouth, especially as regards the fuel situation.

The condition of the panzer divisions underlines the state of units throughout the eastern theater after three and a half months of campaigning. More than half the panzer divisions committed to Operation Typhoon had less than 35 percent of their assigned fighting vehicles in operable condition.

Returning from the Ukraine, Guderian's Second Panzer Group launched the offensive on September 30. The other two panzer groups followed two days later. Given the lateness of the season, and the success that the Soviets had enjoyed in holding the Germans in the center, these blows caught the Red Army by surprise. On October 3, Orel fell to Guderian's 4th Panzer Division; the trams were still running as the German tanks rolled down its main thoroughfare.

The German advance came so swiftly and the Soviet collapse so suddenly that Moscow received its initial intimation of disaster through Hitler's speech in Berlin announcing the start of the "final decisive offensive." Stavka had no specific knowledge of what Hitler was talking about—except that communications no longer existed with Soviet armies facing Army Group Center. On October 5, Soviet reconnaissance pilots reported a German armored column twenty-five kilometers long advancing along the highway from Smolensk to Moscow—Napoleon's old route. Despite NKVD efforts to arrest the pilots as "panic mongers," their reports warned Moscow of the extent of the loss.

The Germans had ripped open the front line from Bryansk to Vyazma and encircled two enormous groupings of Soviet armies: in the north around Vyazma, the Nineteenth, Twentieth, Twenty-fourth, and Thirty-second armies; in the south, the Third, Thirteenth, and Fifteenth. The Germans claimed over 700,000 enemy captured in the two encirclements, not to mention the thousands who died in the so-called caldrons. The road to Moscow seemingly lay open.

The problem was that the weather closed in on the Germans almost immediately. The rains arrived as they always do at that time of year. In conditions of unimaginable misery, in a sea of mud, the German advance stopped. The Russians had their own problems: Stalin's rigid demands that every inch of territory be held, and the profligacy with which the Stavka had wasted their enormous armies, had brought the Soviets to the brink of defeat. But the month's reprieve gave the Red Army the time needed to concentrate its few reserves in front of Moscow.

The conduct of the capital's defense was turned over to General Georgy Zhukov, probably the best operational commander in World War II. Zhukov husbanded those reserves that arrived, funneling forward only sufficient forces to delay and keep back the Germans until winter took hold. His aim was to exhaust German forces so that he could deliver a telling counterblow when their offensive had, in every sense, run out of gas.

The Germans' persistence in spite of the season underlines the weaknesses of their military system. The exclusive concentration on operational concerns, on winning the next battle, to the exclusion of other vital ones—strategic, logistic, and even geographic—created the preconditions for the coming defeat. German intelligence made its usual contribution by estimating that, after the catastrophes of Bryansk and Vyazma, the Soviets were finally exhausted. The commander of Army Group Center, Field Marshal Fedor von Bock, concluded that the Wehrmacht "could now afford to take risks."

In a discussion with the chiefs of staff of Army Group Center, General

Halder hoped for six weeks without snow, to allow German troops to reach Vologda, Stalingrad, and Maikop. He suggested that while the observable situation appeared gloomy, "there was always the incalculable of luck in war." Moscow itself exercised a fascination on Halder and Bock, although the latter did not subscribe to the wide-ranging operations east of the capital that both the OKH and the OKW were planning.

In November the cold weather arrived. The fact that it froze up the glutinous mud returned some movement to the battlefield. But at the same time, the lack of winter-weight oils and winter clothing, and shortages in every other area, created a nightmare for German troops struggling forward. At times the cold was so intense that the troops had to start gasoline fires under their tanks to warm up the oil sufficiently so that the engines could turn over. (The Soviet units were better prepared with lightweight oil.) On the night of December 4, the temperature fell to 25 degrees below zero Fahrenheit; one regiment suffered 300 frostbite casualties. In these hopeless conditions, the advance halted at the gates of Moscow. The next day Zhukov shifted to a counteroffensive, and the entire German front threatened to fall apart.

✦

THE EXTENT of the German victories during the summer and fall of 1941 has obscured what little chance the Germans had for ultimate success in Operation Barbarossa. By their definition of the war as a *Vernichtungskrieg* (war of annihilation), to be waged with ruthless ideological vigor, Hitler and his military ensured that the Soviet people would have to rally around Stalin despite his tyranny. It was not that the Soviet Union was unconquerable. But the German campaign aimed not only at destroying the Jews but at enslaving the other Soviet peoples. On such an ideological approach rested the firm belief that the Wehrmacht could win the campaign in the space of four months. But the ideological preconditions, the commissar order, the extermination of the Jews, and the looting of the local population guaranteed that Soviet political cohesion would strengthen rather than break down.

The logistic and political weaknesses of Barbarossa were indeed extraordinary; as much as the battlefield expertise of the German troops, they delineated the "German way of war." Above all, what is surprising is that the German leadership seemed incapable of addressing alternative courses of action. Alternatives simply did not appear; the campaign was to be won by winter, so the senior German army leadership drove the exhausted, fought-out German troops onward to Moscow.

The question we should ask is not why the Germans failed to win, but rather why they got as far as they did.

II

THE GREAT
EAST ASIA WAR

THE
MIGHT-HAVE-BEENS
OF PEARL HARBOR

ELIOT A. COHEN

By the end of November 1941, the decision makers of Washington knew that war with Japan was coming, and probably in a matter of days. A message went out to Admiral Husband E. Kimmel, the naval commander at Pearl Harbor in the Hawaian Islands: "This is a war warning." His battleships were ready to steam into the Pacific for a confrontation with the Japanese navy, and an elaborate plan contemplated a clash somewhere between Midway and Wake Islands, perhaps as early as Christmas. Kimmel and his staff actually believed that war might break out on December 7, a Sunday—but on the other side of the Pacific. At the very moment when a six-carrier Japanese task force was bearing down on the islands, Kimmel was so consumed with his offensive scheme that he neglected taking any defensive measures. Surprise by the largest gathering of carriers up to that time was, as Eliot A. Cohen points out, "consistent with the Japanese style of operations." Surprise was something the United States should have been prepared for. It wasn't. The result on that Sunday morning was eighteen American warships sunk or damaged, including eight battleships, 2,400 dead, and almost 200 airplanes destroyed. The Japanese lost only twenty-nine planes.

In the intriguing essay that follows, Cohen points out that "Pearl Harbor could have been a draw, or even a marginal Japanese defeat. But it also might have been a considerably more dramatic Japanese victory." What is certain is that the disaster aroused and brought together an American public that had been divided about going to war. And, ironically, the loss of all those battleships forced the U.S. Navy to rely on the aircraft carrier—which it proceeded to turn into the dominant, and dominating, weapon of the Pacific war.

Eliot A. Cohen is a professor of strategic studies at the Paul H. Nitze School of Advanced International Studies at the Johns Hopkins University. He has written books and articles on a variety of military and national-security-related subjects. Cohen also directed the U.S. Air Force's official study of the Gulf War.

THE FAILURES OF COMMANDERS ON BOTH SIDES RAISED questions that, more then fifty years later, we are still trying to answer.

Could Pearl Harbor have gone differently? To ask this question is to ask three others as well: Could the attack have been avoided altogether? Could the United States have done better, exacting a heavier price from the Japanese attackers and suffering less damage? Could the Japanese have been even more successful than they were?

It is hard to imagine a peaceful outcome to the diplomatic conflict between Japan and the United States. Determined to counteract Japanese expansion in China and Southeast Asia, the Roosevelt administration had steadily increased economic pressure on Japan, first cutting off shipments of scrap steel in September 1940, and then, in July 1941, embargoing the export of gasoline suitable for aviation and freezing Japanese assets in the United States. For their part, the Japanese had decided to seize a vast area in Asia to guarantee themselves economic autarky, and they were determined to maintain their hegemony in China despite U.S. opposition. The fundamental incompatibility of American and Japanese objectives made the outbreak of war only a matter of time. This may not have been clear in mid-1941, but it was by autumn, at least to U.S. decision makers.

Still, was a surprise attack on the U.S. fleet stationed at Pearl Harbor inevitable? Although some senior naval officers in Japan disagreed with the strategy of Admiral Isoroku Yamamoto, commander in chief of the Combined Fleet of the Imperial Navy, it was consistent with the Japanese style of operations. And it made operational sense to disable the U.S. fleet so that it could not interfere with the contemplated six-month campaign to seize the Dutch East Indies, the Philippines, Malaya—the core of the new Japanese citadel.

Would the Japanese have called the attack off had they been discovered en route to Pearl Harbor? As early as January 1941, Yamamoto had declared that they might face the U.S. fleet sortieing to intercept his forces. And on November 17, he warned his officers, "You may have to fight your way into the target." The Japanese understood the long-term dangers posed by American power and were supremely confident in their own fighting ability. The attack was virtually inevitable.

✦

COULD THE UNITED STATES have anticipated that attack, and could Hawaii have been better defended? Much of the controversy surrounding the debacle at Pearl Harbor has focused on relations between Washington and Oahu, and on the processing of intelligence that might have warned of an attack. Some key information derived from code breaking was not passed from Washington to Pearl—for example, Japanese requests to their espionage operation in Hawaii for the location of U.S. warships and a last-minute warning that war was imminent. In the aftermath of the calamity, the local commanders and their defenders were understandably bitter about these lapses.

On the other hand, no information anywhere in the American intelligence system suggested an imminent attack specifically on Pearl Harbor, and even the requests about U.S. ships could be attributed just to Japanese attention to detail in gathering intelligence. And a lot of important information *was* passed to Pearl. For example, Admiral Husband E. Kimmel, commander of the Pacific Fleet, knew that Japanese diplomats were destroying their cipher machines on December 3. In fact, both he and the army commander on Oahu, Lieutenant General Walter C. Short, had been warned on November 27 about the prospects of war with Japan—the message to Kimmel began, "This is a war warning." Nor could any local commander claim it was inconceivable that Pearl Harbor would be attacked: The base had received generous allotments of men and matériel, and two studies by local airmen—one in March 1941, another in July—had indicated just how the Japanese might attack.

What *could* have been different was an immediate local warning, allowing the U.S. forces up to several hours' preparation for the fight. Rear Admiral Claude C. Bloch, the local base commander, had over seventy airplanes available on Hawaii (most, admittedly, were recent arrivals and still had maintenance problems); they could have patrolled the most dangerous avenues of approach to Oahu, which were generally known to be from the north and northwest, whence the Japanese attacked. Bloch made no such effort, later offering the specious defense that he could not have conducted reconnaissance in an entire circumference. Further, Hawaii had some of the army's first mobile radar stations. Early on December 7, about an hour before the first wave hit Pearl, operators actually detected the Japanese planes—which were mistaken for a flight of B-17s heading to Hawaii from the mainland. Errors in communication within Hawaii, and a poor alert system, prevented this vital information from triggering early air-raid warnings at the naval base.

Could defenses have been better? Here the answer is an unequivocal yes. In June 1941, Admirals Bloch and Kimmel had been warned that the Americans and British were able to launch air-dropped torpedoes that needed less than the previous minimum of seventy-five feet of water to level out. But Kimmel rejected the use of torpedo nets around the battleships, believing that the forty-foot-deep water at Pearl was too shallow for torpedoes and that the nets would prevent a quick sortie by the fleet. Torpedoes sank four battleships, including the *Arizona* and the *Oklahoma,* the only two permanently lost to the fleet.

As for air defense, the army's nearly 100 P-40s never had a chance to fight en masse over Oahu; the dozen or so marine Wildcats were also caught on the ground. Had the Japanese been forced to fight their way into the base, it is hardly likely they would have been able to launch their torpedoes, bomb, and strafe with anything like the accuracy they achieved. In fact, when their second wave of aircraft hit Pearl Harbor, it took twice as many losses as the first, even though the Americans were reeling from the initial attack.

Furthermore, had General Short not configured his forces primarily for an alert against sabotage, and had he taken the problem of air attack (rather than a purely naval invasion) more seriously, he might have deployed his antiaircraft batteries and kept his ammunition at hand, not locked away. Only four of the army's thirty-one batteries got into action at all, while navy batteries on the warships in harbor were firing within five minutes of the attack. Short's emphasis on the threat of sabotage also increased the damage, because planes were lined up wingtip to wingtip—and little provision (air-raid shelters, slit trenches, and the like) had been made for passive defense against air attack.

Had Short, Kimmel, and Bloch been more imaginative and flexible, or had Washington monitored their actions more closely, it is fairly easy to imagine a real battle taking place over Oahu. As it was, the Japanese lost twenty-nine aircraft, and another seventy-four planes were damaged—more than one-quarter of their force rendered hors de combat. A fierce defense might easily have doubled or trebled those losses.

More to the point, the American battleships (all eight of which were sunk or badly damaged) might have been largely saved, not only from torpedoes but from the high-level attacks (conducted at 10,000 feet) by Japanese bombers. Then the U.S. Navy might have attempted a more vigorous defense of Southeast Asia than it could under the circumstances. Rather than turning into a series of carrier engagements, the early battles of the war might have involved mixed forces tangling with each other.

Moreover, if Japanese self-confidence had been shaken by an abortive raid on Pearl Harbor, it is at least conceivable that the pace and audacity of their offensive in 1941–42 would have been curtailed. Ironically, this might have paved the way for bloody clashes at sea—leaving the United States *less* well off than it would be after the smashing victory of Midway in the summer of 1942.

✦

PEARL HARBOR could have been a draw, or even a marginal Japanese defeat. But it also might have been a considerably more dramatic Japanese victory. None of the American carriers in the Pacific—the *Lexington,* the *Enterprise,* and the *Saratoga*—were in harbor; the loss or crippling of even one would have altered U.S. strategy in the war. The *Lexington* played a crucial role in the Battle of the Coral Sea, in which she was lost but the Japanese carrier force was weakened in advance of Midway. The *Enterprise* was a key element of the U.S. carrier force at Midway. Had all three been badly damaged, it becomes hard to imagine the Solomon Islands campaign of 1942, which was necessary to protect the lines of communication to Australia and begin the process of grinding down Japanese air power.

The Japanese could not have determined whether the American carriers would be at Pearl Harbor; that was a matter of luck. But they could have thought through their strategy in the event of success; that was a matter of operational art, and here they failed. Had the Japanese wished, they could have stayed in the neighborhood of Hawaii for a couple of days, pummeling the submarine yard and setting ablaze the aboveground tank farm containing 4.5 million barrels of precious oil. Admiral Chester Nimitz, Kimmel's relief, would later argue that had the Japanese done so, the war might have gone on for another two years. But fearful of American carriers, not attuned to thinking about logistic targets (as opposed to the enemy's main force), and above all convinced that they had achieved their main goal, the Japanese steamed back west.

✦

IN THE WAKE OF Pearl Harbor, some writers have spun conspiracy theories to explain the surprise attack: The most durable—and least plausible—of these concerns President Roosevelt and his alleged desire to lure the Japanese into an attack on Oahu. Other people have suggested that Japanese success was inevitable—that there was no way of anticipating an attack on the morning of December 7, or even doing much to mitigate its effects. It's clear this isn't so. There was nothing inevitable about how Pearl Harbor turned out. The failures of the American commanders on the scene to provide for a plausible, if unlikely, blow resulted in the destruction that the United States suffered; the failures of Japanese planners and commanders to follow up their spectacular success allowed the United States, in a series of brilliant counterblows, to restore a balance in the Pacific within half a year of this debacle.

TOKYO, DECEMBER 8, 1941

THEODORE F. COOK JR.

Pearl Harbor caught the average Japanese as much by surprise as it did Americans. In Tokyo, on the other side of the international date line, it was a day later, already Monday, December 8, and all through that morning people gathered, full of unbelief, at any place where they could find a radio. After the great 1939 battles with the Soviets along the Manchurian border, a humiliation for Japan, most people expected an announcement of renewed fighting, especially at a time when Germany seemed to have Russia on the ropes at Moscow. But imperial aspirations had taken a new direction. Though the Japanese knew that relations with the world's foremost industrial power were deteriorating, few were prepared for war with the United States.

The events that day in the Japanese capital are virtually unknown in the West—as, indeed, is much of the Japanese experience in World War II. December 8, Theodore F. Cook Jr. notes, would be a day notable for public celebration and private doubts. After a radio announcer read the emperor's message declaring war on the United States and Great Britain—the actual "Voice of the Crane" was not for ordinary people to hear—crowds converged on the Imperial Palace and then stumbled home in the pitch-darkness of a first night of total blackout. For the Japanese, there was the sudden reassurance of righteousness. This was a racial war, but of a different sort from Hitler's. "We are the 'yellow race' our enemies talk about," a prominent editorial writer reminded them. "We are fighting to determine the superiority or inferiority of the discriminated-against peoples." In those first days and months, a tidal wave of victories swept over the Pacific and across Southeast Asia. "The Japanese," said one European commentator in Tokyo, "are panic-stricken by their own daring."

Theodore F. Cook Jr. is a professor of Japanese history at William Paterson University of New Jersey. He is co-author of *Japan at War: An Oral History*.

Remember December eighth!
On this day the history of the world was changed.
The Anglo-Saxon powers
On this day were repulsed on Asian land and sea.
It was their Japan *which repulsed them,*
A tiny country in the Eastern Sea,
Nippon, the Land of the Gods
Ruled over by a living god.

— KŌTARŌ TAKAMURA, POET

TOKYO WAS SILENT IN THE PREDAWN HOURS. A COLD, DENSE mist shrouded the city. It was December 8, 1941. Monday. A workday in the middle of the war. Fighting with China had dragged on since 1937. The country was tired. Over a million men of the Imperial Army, regulars and reservists, were deployed on the mainland of Asia. Actions were being fought with Chinese forces daily, while the frontier between the Soviet Union and Japanese-dominated Manchuria was bristling with troops.

The morning editions of the newspapers carried front-page stories about the frustrating deadlock in negotiations in Washington between the United States and Japan, reporting that the "German drive on Moscow continues." Those papers would remain unread by most of Tokyo, for they would soon be overtaken by events occurring halfway across the Pacific, on the island of Oahu—where, on the other side of the international date line, it was the morning of Sunday, December 7.

✦

AT 6 A.M. at the Imperial General Headquarters Army Information Bureau at Miyakezaka, sharp voices cried out, "Announcement!" Colonel Ohira, director of the Army Information Bureau, and Commander Tashiro, a Navy Information Bureau staff member, strode to a small platform in the briefing room as reporters scrambled to their places. Wearing a solemn expression,

Ohira read in a raspy voice: "From today at dawn, the Imperial Army and Navy are at war with the forces of the United States and Great Britain in the waters of the western Pacific." The brief statement was then repeated for the radio. The time in Hawaii was 11 A.M.; the attack on Pearl Harbor had ended one hour earlier.

"Special news! Special news! Imperial headquarters announcement!" The stillness was shattered as word went out by radio to all corners of the nation. At 6:20 A.M. the official announcement about the expanded war was followed by rousing strains of the "Battleship March" and other military songs. Not everyone had a radio, of course, but the music was soon blaring from shops and homes that did. Before long, streets echoed with vendors' bells signaling special editions from the newspapers.

A reporter from the *Asahi Shimbun* described the scene in Tokyo: "The tension of the Imperial City was perfectly matched to this historic morning. Those people who read the extra edition read it once, twice, and then three times. The Children of the Emperor stand unflinching, determined. People crowd in front of the radio shops. From those crowds, the ironlike spirit comes through."

War with the United States and Great Britain! But what did the announcement mean besides that? And if something had happened, where? Wasn't the "western Pacific" on Japan's side of the ocean? Studying the brief first announcement, people reflected on the dark clouds of crisis that had been gathering over Japan for many months. During almost all of 1941, Japanese relations with the United States and Britain had deteriorated and talk of war had gained strength as economic embargoes imposed by those Western nations and the Dutch East Indies took effect. Anxiety, foreboding, and a certain feeling of helplessness in the face of Western power loomed over Japan, adding to the frustration of the unending "China Incident"—as Japan preferred to call the fighting on the continent, rather than declare it a war and face further international sanctions.

But now Japan was at war with the Americans, British, and Dutch, as well as the Chinese. The country's enemies included the two strongest naval powers on earth—one of them the greatest industrial power ever. It was an electrifying thought, filled with great drama—and hidden terrors. Many Japanese had expected war, not with the United States, but with the Soviet Union, especially as the Germans neared Moscow. Indeed, at that very moment, army pilots in Manchuria were on three-minute alert, poised to attack the Soviet Union.

When dawn came on December 8, the mist soon burned away and the sky became unusually clear. "The sun rises brilliantly over the buildings," imperial adviser Koichi Kido, lord keeper of the privy seal, wrote in his diary. "To-day, I reflect that at last our nation is going to enter a great war with two great powers, America and England, as opponents. This dawn, air units of the navy have already raided Hawaii with their full force. I, who know this, have concerns whether it has been accomplished or not. Unconsciously, I pray to the sun; I close my eyes and pray." At 7:30 A.M. he learned from Prime Minister Hideki Tōjō himself about the great success of the "Hawaii surprise attack"; he entered in his diary, "Feelings of heartfelt gratitude for divine assistance." Most Japanese, however, would have to wait several hours to be told of the secret attack and its first results.

What was Emperor Hirohito doing this day? The emperor awoke at 2:40 A.M., "the silence of the frost-whitened Imperial Palace broken by Foreign Minister Shigenori Tōgō's dash to the palace," a news article would report. At 2:50 the head of the grand chamberlain's office came. "His Imperial Highness appeared in the crisp morning air and heard a report by Foreign Minister Tōgō for approximately one hour. The emperor had little time to sleep because he listened to reports from his subordinates on the situation in the western Pacific Ocean." At 7:22 A.M. the prime minister, "his face strained with tension, arrived with the other members of the Cabinet for a crucial meeting." Three hours later, the emperor attended the meeting of his Privy Council of senior advisers "and there directed the historic policy for the empire"—at least according to the news story. Despite the *Asahi Shimbun*'s concern that he may have lost sleep during the night, Hirohito "was truly self-composed, without the slightest indication of agitation," according to a grateful Kido, when the emperor met with his adviser between 11:40 and noon.

At noon, immediately following the tone at the hour, the national radio network broadcast an imperial rescript declaring war on the United States and Great Britain. This message, directly from the emperor to his people, was not delivered by him personally, since the "Voice of the Crane" was not for his people's ears to hear; it was read by Shigeru Nakamura, one of Japan's most renowned announcers. The effects were dramatic. One newspaper described a scene in Jimboch in the Kanda district: "People on hearing this abandoned their chopsticks, dropped their forks, removed their hats, took off their overcoats. No one ordered it, but all stood up somberly, bowed their heads, some sobbed in the extremity of their emotion. . . . Emotional scenes like this were observed all over the nation."

The declaration of war placed responsibility on the two Western nations for supporting and encouraging the Chinese, who had "disturbed the peace of East Asia." It accused the Western powers of pursuing "their inordinate ambition to dominate the Orient," not only by supporting the "regime which has survived in Chungking," but also by making "increased military preparations on all sides of Our Empire to challenge Us" and by striking at "Our peaceful commerce," severing economic relations.

"Patiently have We waited and long have We endured, in the hope that Our government might retrieve the situation in peace," declared the emperor's document. "But Our adversaries, showing not the least spirit of conciliation, have unduly delayed a settlement; and in the meantime they have intensified the economic and political pressure to compel thereby Our Empire to submission." This the empire could not allow.

"This trend of affairs would, if left unchecked, not only nullify Our Empire's efforts of many years for the sake of the stabilization of East Asia, but also endanger the very existence of Our nation," the emperor's message stated. "Our Empire, for its existence and self-defense, has no other recourse but to appeal to arms and to crush every obstacle in its path."

The rescript made no mention of the rules of international law, featured prominently in Japan's declarations of war against Russia in 1904 and Germany in 1914. Instead it clearly set a course toward redefining international order without any reference to rules made by the West.

The emperor did not deliver a historic speech in person, as President Franklin Roosevelt did before the U.S. Congress the next day. But an hour after the broadcast of the imperial rescript, Tōjō spoke from the rostrum of the Central Cooperative Conference; radio carried his address live to the nation. Like the rest of the crowd, Kōtarō Takamura, a noted poet and rightist intellectual, had assumed it would be a routine morale booster for the ongoing war with China. But government officials failed to show up on time; then word came that Tōjō was in an important conference at the Imperial Palace. The imperial rescript was read aloud at about half past eleven. Then they all received their scheduled box lunch. After lunch they heard the first results of the Pearl Harbor attack—still not announced to the general public. Takamura noted, "People applauded." At 1 P.M. precisely, the prime minister convened the meeting. The crowd bowed to the palace, and the imperial rescript was read again. Then Tōjō spoke:

"At this very moment our brave military and naval forces are defying death in the field of battle," he declared. "In spite of all that our empire has done, ardently desiring the preservation of the general peace of East Asia, our efforts have ended in a failure. . . .

"Our adversaries, boasting rich natural resources, aim at the domination of the world," Tōjō said. "In order to annihilate this enemy and to construct an unshakable new order of East Asia, we should anticipate a long war." But he called it "a heaven-sent opportunity" for the Japanese to prove they deserved to be hailed for building Greater East Asia. "The rise or fall of our empire and the prosperity or ruin of East Asia literally depend upon the outcome of this war. Truly it is time for the one hundred million of us Japanese to dedicate all we have and sacrifice everything for our country's cause. As long as there remains . . . this great spirit of loyalty and patriotism, we have nothing to fear in fighting America and Britain. Victory, I am convinced, is always with the illustrious virtues of our sovereign. In making known these humble views of mine, I join with all my countrymen in pledging myself to assist in the grand imperial enterprise."

Newspapers reported that many people wept as Tōjō spoke, and he was frequently interrupted by applause. The *Yomiuri Shimban* described banners that hung from the building declaring "Bury them! America and Britain Are Our Enemy" and "Advance! One Hundred Million Bullets of Fire!"

Following the speech, Takamura noted, "We passed a resolution and we then all went off to the palace, a line of some two thousand of us. Many groups were already there, and shouts of 'Banzai!' were delivered."

The evening editions of the newspapers all carried the imperial rescript and the prime minister's remarks in full. The *Asahi* and *Tōkyō Nichi Nichi Shimbun* headlines read, "Imperial Declaration of War against America and England." The *Yomiuri Shimbun* embellished, announcing, "Declaration of War Against Tyrannical America and England." The English-language *Japan Times & Advertiser* stated directly, "War Is On!" Articles reported landings in Malaya and advances in Thailand. The *Yomiuri* printed a map of the Pacific and a photograph showing mechanized vehicles moving down a road, with palm trees in the foreground, over the caption "In the Southern Area . . . our advance unit moves forward." Eight Japanese aircraft seem to have been added to the scene overhead.

American announcements from Hawaii were cited: "Japanese bombing caused great damage at the Pearl Harbor naval installation and Honolulu. Fires broke out at several places in Honolulu, but were immediately extinguished." NBC's broadcast was quoted: "Bombing by the Japanese Air Force is severe, but the U.S. Army and Navy still have control of the air and sea. The Japanese attack has been continuing for about three hours." The White House was said to have announced that "damage was extreme in the Oahu attack by Japanese forces."

All across the great capital, people moved toward the Imperial Palace. It was not instinct or mere curiosity that drove them; it was training—decades of preparation for such an event. Neighborhood leaders and others, wearing formal kimonos bearing their family crests, gathered at the gate where the emperor entered and left his palace, their hands spread wide as they knelt and bowed toward it. The newspapers recorded the activity in dramatic, present-tense style, the product of years of war reporting and experience with the officially preferred images and appropriate reactions for such occasions: "A Young woman bows low, her long black hair thrown forward over her face, tears of high emotion running down her cheeks, as the sun streams down. People grasp fistfuls of pebbles."

At the Meiji Shrine, a site of many imperial ceremonies in Tokyo, and at Yasukuni Shrine in honor of the war dead, similar scenes were recorded: "The reverent sound of steps on the white pebbles is heard. Elderly men bow down and beg as if speaking directly to their heroes' spirits." Bands struck up martial themes in squares and at military installations across the capital. Women from the Great Japan Patriotic Women's Association and members of the Reservist Association assembled and moved in local and district groups to predetermined destinations before the Imperial Palace and at the two shrines. A Noh performance with a patriotic theme was given at Meiji Shrine. Schoolchildren gathered and marched to honor the emperor at his palace. Donations began pouring in to organizations for the troops' welfare.

The next day's *Japan Times & Advertiser* gloated that at the American Embassy in Tokyo on December 8, "the Stars and Stripes was not streaming in the morning breeze." The report added that U.S. military attaché H. T. Cresswell and naval attaché Smith-Hutton were said to have refused comment, while the American ambassador, Joseph Clark Grew, canceled his game of golf with the minister from Denmark. At the British Embassy, opposite the Imperial Palace, "an irritated bulldog and a guard stood watch at the gate." The Americans and British would soon be repatriated.

The Italian and German ministers, on the other hand, expressed congratulations and confidence in Japan's ultimate victory. The newspapers made no mention of the Italian ambassador's mad rush to a Ginza tobacconist to buy out the last stock of English Dunhill pipes in Tokyo, only minutes before a limousine brought a leading Japanese industrialist and pipe aficionado bent on the same objective.

The stock market soared. The exchange leaders were stocks and commodities linked with the "Southern Area," such as natural rubber. Stock prices in shipping companies jumped sharply.

At 3 P.M. the radio broadcast nationwide a new song, prepared for the occasion by the Public Affairs Department of the Imperial Rule Assistance Association and entitled "Advance! One Hundred Million Bullets of Fire!" The broadcaster announced that the song would be played regularly and that the record would soon be available.

The city's lights, which had been increasingly subject to interruption from electricity shortages, were now under strict blackout regulations. Pursuant to an order announced earlier by the Tokyo Metropolitan Police at 5 P.M., all outside lights, including gate lamps, advertising, and decorations, were darkened. Night fell early in winter, and residents say the city seemed pitch-black from that moment on. As they stumbled home in the "too dark" evening, for many people it finally sank in that the moment for which they had drilled had arrived. The brilliant illumination of the Ginza, dimmed since the China war began, was now completely extinguished. It was likely to remain so until the end of the war.

✦

THERE WERE NO shouts of dissent, protests, or cries for peace—certainly not from the leftists, liberals, and others who had been largely driven from office or kept outside the circles of influence since well before December 1941. Even before war had broken out with China, right-wing terror, the threat of assassination, and active suppression by the "thought police" of the Home Ministry had stifled public expression of differing views. Prison and/or recantation was the fate of labor leaders, Communist party members, and the few resisters of military service. Political parties had been virtually merged into a cooperative coalition in support of the government.

Publishers of books, magazines, and newspapers had long been censored, and they exercised increasing skill at molding their pages to the views expressed by the authorities. Reporters had more than four years of experience in choosing the right ways to express patriotic emotion. In covering stories, they asked only the questions for which everyone knew the answers. Children volunteering to write to soldiers, parents offering up their sons, housewives pledging the family savings to the war-bond drives—all these received full coverage. For many, this was all the truth there needed to be. Indeed, on December 8, a coalition of newspapers declared plans for an "Assembly to Attack and Annihilate Britain and America" under their own sponsorship.

The newspapers, the articles and poems, and the official declarations of December 8, so full of determination and fervor, spoke of "the people's steel-hard nerves." Yet somehow there was a hollowness about them. Doubts among the people were as evident to some observers as the obviously political declarations of certain victory in a just cause. The Vichy journalist Robert Guillain, observing the people of Tokyo as they first learned of the opening of hostilities, detected their hidden emotion. He noted that "under their assumed impassivity they can barely control their stupefaction and consternation. They wanted this war and yet they did not want it. They talked about it all the time, out of bravado and in imitation of their leaders, but they never really believed in it. . . . Tokyo is afraid, the Japanese are panic-stricken by their own daring."

Novelist and critic Sei Itō had conflicting emotions, for personal reasons: Many of his friends and fellow writers had already been called up into the military, and he had made preparations against the day when he would be sent off to Manchuria. His diary entry for December 8, 1941, provides a remarkable barometer of his thoughts and emotional reactions.

Itō left home to post a letter a little after 1 P.M. on December 8; that's when he heard his neighbor's radio intoning the announcement of the "decisive air raid" on the military port at Hawaii and reports of the advances in Thailand. He was "taken by surprise," and rather than go back inside, he went off to see the town. As he went by bus and on foot through Shinjuku, Yotsuya, Hanzōmon, the Imperial Palace area, Hibiya, and the Ginza, before returning to his home at Nabeyayokochō, what struck him most was the lack of emotion. "Passengers on the bus are quiet. Not a one speaks of war." Near him was a youth who looked like an intellectual, with steel-framed glasses, wearing the uniform of an army sergeant. "As the bus throws us up against each other, I feel the urge to say, 'Finally it has begun, hasn't it?' but I keep silent, thinking I am the only one who seems to be feeling elated."

While the journalists might describe the Patriotic Women's Association, with their slogan-embellished sashes, engaged in their missions at the palace and the shrines, Itō noticed the women lined up at vegetable stands and sweet shops to get their allotments. He had learned only a week before that cakes, meat, miso, taro, and other food items would soon be placed on the ration-coupon list, joining such essentials as fish; he himself bought fried fish cakes.

At his house he prepared for the blackout and worked on his broken radio so he could listen to the evening broadcasts.

Shigeru [his eldest son, just in elementary school] is excited. . . . "Brave, aren't they!" he says. He cannot keep from talking. . . .

"Why does war happen?" Rei [his second son] asks in a carefree sort of way. Sadako [his wife] is talking to him.

I become happy, thinking they did a good job with the Hawaii air raid. Our side probably suffered great damage too. The paper said the Japanese air attack continued for three hours and suffered severe losses, but still sea and air control

of Hawaii was on our side. . . . Those who fall at Hawaii, I feel die for something!

Night comes. I am uneasy.

He was thinking about his own military call-up, now probably imminent.
Itō had expressed such concerns in his diary as early as December 1, when he
had wondered whether he would soon be "sleeping in hallways" like his fellow writers, called into military service with propaganda units and likely to
be sent abroad. He had evn gone out to purchase a good parka and a sheepskin
against the possibility.

As it became dark, Itō fell asleep, but his wife woke him at 9 P.M. and told
him the latest news:

> They inform us of the results of the air raid. Two battleships sunk, four se-
> verely damaged. Four large cruisers severely damaged. One aircraft carrier
> sunk. Brilliant! The Japanese way of doing it was excellent, as in the Japan-
> Russia War.

About ten that evening, a man came from the *Miyako Shimbun* and asked
Itō to make a few changes in his literary commentary that was scheduled to
run in the newspaper the next day. The following appeared in the paper on
December 9, 1941:

> This war is an absolute act. It is not merely an extension of politics or the re-
> verse side of politics. It is a struggle which the Yamato people had some day to
> fight in order to convince themselves from the bottom of their hearts that they
> are the most excellent people on the face of the globe. We are the "yellow race"
> our enemies talk about. We are fighting to determine the superiority or inferi-
> ority of the discriminated-against peoples. Our struggle is not the same as Ger-
> many's. . . .

But the author of these grand war aims was more concerned that evening
with the rumor his visitor had brought. "According to him," Itō wrote in his
diary, "there might be a call-up by the Navy. It might come for me. . . ." His
thoughts were with his family:

> Sadako falls asleep. I look at Rei and Shigeru. I am deeply moved when
> I look at them. They seem to be clinging to life. I want them to be able to sleep

through the night, every night, one by one. How long will I be able to watch them slumber with my own eyes like this? At 11:40 I go to sleep.

At the end of his entry for the day, Itō added:

IMPRESSION

Our fate is that we are not able to think of ourselves as a first-class people unless we fight the white first-class people of the world.

For the first time I come to realize with limitless loving tenderness the meaning of everything that is Japan and the Japanese.

There are many predictions about the outcome of this war, but I never even dreamed of attacking Hawaii. . . . Hawaii was unexpected, even for us. The Americans wouldn't have expected that either.

Many shared Itō's surprise and concern that day. Looking back nearly fifty years later, a former blacksmith who had become an auto repairman in the late 1930s remembered his feelings: "War with America? Why, I couldn't believe it. The only good cars I'd ever seen in Japan were Fords. Can't they understand that we can't beat America with the junk our auto companies are turning out? Those were my thoughts."

A transport sergeant, charged with keeping the army in China supplied, echoed those sentiments in his own recollections: "The only good trucks we had in the Japanese army in China were Chevrolets. We captured them at Shanghai and took them with us as we went along. Of course we had to manufacture all our spare parts in the field—out of tin sheets, scrap iron, and any metal we could lay our hands on—but they worked." Back in Japan when the war broke out, he couldn't imagine how they could have fought in China without them.

An officer in charge of an official diary at the Imperial General Headquarters recorded the following:

Having passed through the first day of the war, with the success of an ideal beginning of the war confirmed, including the strategy of sudden attack and the heightening of the nation's war spirit, as the war direction unit, our heightened emotion and gratitude are without limit. Yet, how to seek an end to this conflict is the most difficult part of this war. Gods and man unite and in that state of mind, for the first time, this will be achieved.

Air defense has been ordered for the entire imperial nation.

General Kazushige Ugaki, one of the architects of Japan's military politics in the decades before the war, also felt a warning appropriate. On December 8, 1941, he wrote in his diary:

> The beginning of this way is propitious. The curtain is drawn back. . . . Negligence is our most dangerous enemy. Win, and then make sure your helmet strings are tied tightly.

The war news that began pouring in dispelled most people's anxiety. The tantalizing early reports on December 8 were followed in only hours and days by bulletins of victories from across the Pacific: the American battle fleet sunk or disabled at Pearl Harbor; the pride of the British navy, the battleships *Prince of Wales* and *Repulse,* destroyed off Malaya by Japanese airplanes; landings at a dozen spots, with Japanese forces seemingly able to move anywhere at will. Within weeks the news was of Allied forces surrendering in the thousands; Hong Kong, Singapore, Rangoon, and Batavia in the Dutch East Indies falling into Japanese hands; Corregidor and Bataan undergoing siege; the Imperial Navy sweeping the Indian Ocean to attack Ceylon—all opposition apparently destroyed.

The spirits of the Japanese people were driven to a fever pitch of enthusiasm. Schoolchildren were especially joyful—after the conquest of Malaya and Singapore, they were showered with gifts of previously unobtainable natural rubber balls. But all Japanese were exuberant. Everything they saw in the first five months of the war seemed a confirmation of the decadence and inferiority of the West. Was it not clear that now, at long last, Japan would be able to establish its rightful place in East Asia?

Tokyo was transformed in the weeks that followed December 8. The Hibiya movie house, which in the fall had featured *Edison, The Man* with Spencer Tracy and *Mr. Smith Goes to Washington* with James Stewart, now was showing newsreels entitled *Naval Battle in Hawaii* and *The Landing on Borneo,* together with a movie about the romance between a Japanese man and Manchurian woman. In response to a professor's urgings, marchers clamored for the cleansing of the Ginza of all foreign words and phrases. In that spirit, the government officially abolished the term *Far East* as a notion from the "world of Anglo-Saxon order"; henceforth the goal would be to realize the ideals of the Greater East Asia War. The various patriotic women's associations all pledged themselves ready to fight "a hundred years' war" if necessary.

On New Year's Day 1942, the *Asahi Shimbun* used the whole front page for photographs of the air attack on Pearl Harbor; these first actual photographs of the raid to appear in a domestic paper had been held back as a New Year's present to the people of Japan. They showed the enemy fleet in Battleship Row, with the wakes of torpedoes, water columns rising from exploding bombs, and leaking fuel oil clearly visible, as well as Ford Island under attack in the heart of the harbor. The headline read: "Brilliant War History. The Annihilation of the American Pacific Fleet."

The newspaper announced that the eighth day of every month would be set aside in solemn dedication to the cause of the war, and the imperial rescript issued December 8, 1941, would be carried in each newspaper and read in ceremonies throughout the nation. The newspapers assured their readers that what they called the day that changed the world would be remembered forever.

✦

AND SO, BLINDED by the brilliance of the new jewels of their Empire of the Sun, many Japanese people set aside caution and concern and hurled themselves into the struggle. But in the end, the direct legacy of December 8, 1941, was a sweltering day in August 1945, when the emperor himself would finally speak on the radio, personally announcing his decision to end the war that had been declared so boldly that fateful morning.

THE OTHER PEARL HARBOR

D. CLAYTON JAMES

The Japanese conquest of the Philippines, once America's largest colonial possession, began with air raids on the archipelago's northern island of Luzon, on December 8, 1941—within hours of the sneak
attack on Pearl Harbor. Although General Douglas MacArthur's American and Filipino ground forces, as well as the small but grandiosely
named Far East Air Force, had been on full war alert since late November, they were caught completely off guard. Even after receiving confirmation of Pearl Harbor and of the bombing of towns in the northern
part of Luzon, the American high command in Manila inexplicably delayed response, time enough for Formosa-based Japanese bombers and
fighters specially equipped for long-distance flights to reach major airfields and quickly destroy 50 percent of U.S. combat airplanes on the
ground. The worst disaster occurred at the major American base, Clark
Field, where B-17 bombers had to be parked on the runway, without
camouflage, because of the softness of the surrounding soil. All were
destroyed, along with irreplaceable oil dumps. The Far East Air Force,
essential to the defense of the Philippines, was crippled on the first day
of the war.

Who was to blame? Was it the overconfident MacArthur, who did not
take reports of the havoc at Pearl Harbor seriously? Was it his too-
protective chief of staff, Richard K. Sutherland, who denied the air force
commander access to MacArthur that morning? To what extent was the
U.S. War Department responsible for the debacle? D. Clayton James,
MacArthur's biographer, reviews the circumstances and sequence of
events in the Philippines on December 8 hour by hour, and concludes
that explanations for Clark Field are multiple and, even now, inconclusive.

D. Clayton James is a professor emeritus in military history at the
Virginia Military Institute. He has written eight books, including a
three-volume biography of Douglas MacArthur.

THE RAID ON OAHU, DECEMBER 7, 1941, WAS WITHOUT QUES-
tion a surprise, but controversy still swirls over why "the other Pearl Harbor,"
the attack on Clark Field, Luzon, caught the defenders off guard later the
same day. With nine hours' advance notice of the Pearl Harbor assault, how
could the American command in the Philippines have lost most of its main-
line combat aircraft on the ground? Were American leaders in Washington or
in the Philippines more at fault? In the accounts of the Clark Field incident,
General Douglas MacArthur usually has been made the scapegoat. But were
there others who deserved blame? The story is a complicated one and made
more so by the scarcity of records. With such enormous attention focused on
Pearl Harbor, however, it seems fitting to reexamine the comparatively neglected and still-puzzling Clark tragedy.

On seven missions in November and December 1940, Japanese military
personnel flew commercial airplanes across Luzon, taking detailed aerial photographs of the installations where the bulk of American and Filipino armed
forces in the Philippine Islands were based. During the prior two decades,
Japanese immigration to the Philippines had increased markedly, and it is
now known that among the transient Japanese in the islands, particularly in
the Davao and Manila areas, there were numerous espionage agents. As on
Oahu, the Japanese had amazingly accurate intelligence data on the strength
and deployment of the Filipino-American ground, air, and sea units. Since the
Philippines offered little in strategic raw materials, the principal interest of
the Imperial General Headquarters in Tokyo was in the strategic location of
the archipelago in relation to a potential line of communications from the
East Indies, Malaya, and Singapore to the home islands of Japan.

In late July 1941, Lieutenant General MacArthur was appointed to head
the United States Army Forces in the Far East (USAFFE), with headquarters
in Manila. The Army Air Forces in the Philippines were reorganized in November as the Far East Air Force (FEAF), headed by newly arrived Major General Lewis H. Brereton. It was composed of the V Bomber Command under
Lieutenant Colonel Eugene L. Eubank, the V Interceptor Command under

Brigadier General Henry B. Clagett, and the Far East Air Service Command under Colonel Lawrence Churchill. By early December, many units were far from complete, with staffs and equipment still en route to the Philippines. Most of the air-defense equipment and crews had not yet arrived. Only two radar sets, one at Iba Field, a fighter base near the coast forty miles west of Clark Field, and the other on the edge of Manila, were in operation.

Brereton's command actually possessed more planes than did the Hawaiian department. Included were 35 Boeing B-17 bombers—the largest number assigned to any army air force—and 107 Curtiss P-40 fighters, as well as 135 older aircraft. Additional shipments of planes, crews, and equipment were scheduled for the islands, reflecting the concern of Washington officials over rising tensions in the Far East and the likelihood that the Philippines would be an early target of the Japanese. The threat was regarded as being so urgent that U.S. Army Air Forces leaders in Washington were considering the transfer of the remaining twelve B-17s in Hawaii to the Philippines. The Japanese, in turn, closely watched the rapid buildup of American air power in the Far East.

The major concentration of air resources was at Clark Field, the large air base northwest of Manila. Only Clark and the field under construction at Del Monte, on the southern island of Mindanao, could handle the heavy bombers. At Clark the bombers had to be parked on the field itself, without camouflage, because of the softness of the surrounding soil. In early December, the B-17s were divided between the two fields, with the next shipment of B-17s from Hawaii scheduled to be sent to Del Monte. Fighters were stationed at Clark and at several other fields around Manila and in central Luzon.

Under the most recent revision of the American Rainbow-Five war plan, formulated after the increase in air strength in the Philippines, the mission of the FEAF had been changed from purely defensive to offensive operations, "in the furtherance of the strategic defensive," including "air raids against Japanese forces and installations within tactical operating radius of available bases." The plan called for only limited offensive actions until a simultaneous conflict with Germany had ended in the latter nation's capitulation. Then the Pacific operations would be elevated to the strategic offensive level, including all-out tactical attacks and top logistical support to defeat Japan. Preliminary plans had been drawn up, however, for a B-17 attack on Formosa in the event of war with Japan. But the expectation was that Japanese forces would not attack until April 1942, allowing for further defensive preparations in the Philippines.

Meanwhile, on Formosa, Japanese forces gathered for an attack on the Philippines, to be carried out in coordination with the raid on Pearl Harbor.

The Imperial General Headquarters planned an intensive air assault on the airfields of Luzon, to occur several days prior to landings by ground troops. Its purpose was to protect the invading forces from the fast-growing FEAF. Operations in the vicinity of Clark Field and southward were assigned to the Japanese navy's Eleventh Air Fleet, a land-based unit on Formosa. The Fifth Air Group, under the Fourteenth Army, also located on Formosa, was to carry out attacks on targets in northern Luzon.

On the morning of December 8, 1941 (December 7, Oahu time), the planes of the Fifth Air Group took off from Formosa as scheduled and bombed Baguio, the Philippine summer capital, and other targets in northern Luzon at about 9:25 A.M. The report about this reached Brereton's headquarters at Nielson Field a few minutes later—about six hours after it had received reports of the Pearl Harbor attack. Radar reports of the approach of these Japanese planes toward Luzon prompted Eubank to send the B-17s at Clark Field aloft without bombs.

The planes of the Japanese Eleventh Air Fleet, which had been assigned the sites farther south on Luzon because of their longer range, were prevented by fog from leaving Formosa when planned. The land-based naval aircraft finally cleared their airfields at about 9:30 A.M.; the force consisted of 108 bombers and 84 Zeros. Their targets were Clark and Iba Fields. Because of the delay in launching the mission, the Japanese expected that the FEAF would have heard about the Pearl Harbor attack and would be prepared for them. Instead, due to an unfortunate sequence of events and bad luck, the FEAF planes were on the ground, virtually defenseless. The planes that had been ordered aloft earlier in the morning in response to reports of Japanese aircraft had landed to await further instructions and to refuel. Fighters from Del Carmen Field that had been ordered to cover Clark while its own fighters refueled could not take off because of a dust storm. Other fighters covering Clark earlier in the morning had already returned to Nichols Field and refueled in preparation for patrols over Bataan and the entrance to Manila Bay.

Before 11:30, FEAF headquarters at Nielson Field had begun receiving reports of approaching enemy planes, through radar contacts and observers who contacted the base. According to some accounts, this warning was relayed to Clark by teletype at 11:45; officers at Clark said they did not receive the message. The first report to get through to Clark arrived shortly after noon.

The first Japanese air action at Clark came at about 12:20 P.M. on December 8. By this time, headquarters had known about Pearl Harbor for nearly nine hours. But both heavy bombers and fighters were parked when a formation of twenty-seven Japanese bombers appeared overhead and the air-raid sirens went off. On the ground, B-17 pilot W. Dupont Strong heard "a low moaning sound" and then saw "a whole crowd of airplanes" approaching. He ran for cover: "By the time I hit the trench, the bombs had begun to hit the ground."

The initial assault was followed immediately by a second flight of bombers operating from 25,000 feet. They destroyed the communications center, damaged planes, and left other buildings on fire. As the personnel on the ground began to survey the damage, the attack most devastating to the parked aircraft started: Thirty-four Zero fighters strafed the field for over an hour. According to Eubank, "Most of the damage done to the aircraft was done by dive bombers and fighters." The antiaircraft weapons were old, few, and ineffective. With the communications system in ruins, Clark officials were unable to contact FEAF fighters patrolling over Bataan and Manila Bay, which could have challenged the Japanese. With the exception of 4 P-40s that were able to take off, the aircraft at Clark Field were destroyed on the ground, including the two squadrons comprising eighteen B-17 heavy bombers. "With complete disregard for their lives," Captain Allison Ind said later, the bomber crews "rushed out in a futile attempt to take the big machines off . . . One after another, these vitally needed, expensive, irreplaceable bombers collapsed in bullet-ridden heaps, or sagged to the ravenous flames that were consuming them." Hours later, First Lieutenant William (Ed) Dyess, a P-40 pilot from Nichols Field at Manila, flew over Clark and found that planes, oil dumps, and hangars were still "blazing fiercely. . . . It was a mess."

Meanwhile, a second Japanese force of fifty-four bombers and fifty Zeros assaulted small Iba Field. The attackers annihilated the radar installation and caught some of the planes of the Third Pursuit Squadron, which had been patrolling but had just returned to the base for refueling. The field was entirely destroyed, the result of an enormous commitment of bombs by the enemy. The Japanese would have been wiser to have deployed most of their large Iba attack force against other air bases, such as those at Manila—Nichols and Nielson fields.

By midafternoon of December 8, the strength in modern combat planes of MacArthur's air arm had been reduced by more than half. The seventeen B-17s that were on Mindanao when the Luzon raids occurred were all that remained of the original thirty-five heavy bombers, and at least fifty-five of the seventy-two P-40s on Luzon were lost. Another twenty-five to thirty-five older military aircraft of various types were destroyed. Only seven Japanese planes had been downed. Compared to personnel losses at Pearl Harbor, casualties had been moderate: about 80 killed and 150 wounded at Clark and Iba.

But the Far East Air Force, which MacArthur had counted on heavily in his plans for defense of the Philippines, had been eliminated as an effective combat force on the first day of the war.

✦

ALTHOUGH THE PEARL HARBOR attack was the subject of eight investigations and resulted in the removal of the top commanders in Hawaii, the Clark fiasco did not produce one official inquiry. It would not have been possible during the following months of combat in the doomed Philippines, but some officers assumed that a later inquiry would be conducted. However, the U.S. Senate's joint committee that in 1946 investigated the attack on Hawaii dismissed the Clark situation as being beyond its limited jurisdiction, and no other committee was set up to look into the matter.

The question of where to put the blame for the Clark Field disaster continues in a tangle of personalities and contradictory data. Major General Henry H. "Hap" Arnold, commanding general of the U.S. Army Air Forces, and his air staff in Washington must bear some of the blame because of the exaggerated importance they attached to the role that the B-17s could play in the defense of the Philippines. What possessed them to send their largest group of B-17s there without adequate radar protection is not known. MacArthur and Brereton, with only two radar sets in operation, had to depend on native North Luzon air watchers. Nor is it clear what role they envisaged the B-17s could perform if—as actually happened—the Japanese preceded their main landings with two weeks of devastating air assaults. The loss of the B-17s was regrettable, but their assignment to the Philippines without sufficient protection and without clearly formulated plans as to their proper employment was equally lamentable.

Recriminations among the Philippine high command were nonexistent in the aftermath of the Clark attack, perhaps because of the preoccupation with continuing enemy raids or a consensus that Washington's inadequate reinforcements to the islands was the underlying reason for the catastrophe. The only officer in the Philippines to be reprimanded by a Pentagon superior was Brereton, who received a blistering call on the afternoon of December 8 from Arnold: He demanded to know "how in the hell" such a veteran airman could have been caught by surprise after having nine hours' advance notice of the Pearl Harbor raid. General George C. Marshall, the army chief of staff, did not rebuke MacArthur, but he did remark to a reporter two weeks later, "I just don't know how MacArthur happened to let his planes get caught on the ground."

Arnold later stated that he was never satisfied with the explanations unofficially offered by all three principal figures in the affair—MacArthur, commander of American and Filipino ground and air forces in the Philippines; Brereton, the air chief; and Major General Richard K. Sutherland, MacArthur's chief of staff. In the following years, oral and written apologies by the key participants in the decision making at Manila were added to the few surviving official documents on the affair. But gaps and contradictions in the available evidence make it impossible to explain fully the reasons for the Clark tragedy or to determine definitively who was at fault.

The following is a brief reconstruction of the key developments on Luzon during the critical morning hours of December 8. At 2:00 A.M., a party at the Manila Hotel began to break up; it had been given in Brereton's honor and was a gala affair, considered by some veterans of Manila nightlife to be "the best entertainment this side of 'Minsky's.'" Forty minutes later, Asiatic Fleet headquarters in Manila received the news of Pearl Harbor, but, oddly, it did not inform MacArthur. At 3:40, Sutherland learned of the attack from a commercial-radio broadcast. He immediately notified MacArthur, who was in bed, and by 4:00 Brereton's headquarters at nearby Nielson Field had the news. The War Department's message officially confirming the existence of war with Japan was not received by MacArthur's headquarters until 5:30.

A half hour earlier, according to Brereton, he went to MacArthur's office, but Sutherland insisted that the general was busy and could not see him. Brereton then requested permission through Sutherland to launch a B-17 raid from Clark, shortly after daylight, against Japanese targets on Formosa. Sutherland responded that he could start preparations for the mission but that MacArthur would decide later when to begin offensive operations. According to Sutherland's account, he told Brereton—who agreed—that a photoreconnaissance mission should precede the raid because of the lack of data on possible Formosan objectives. At about 7:15, Brereton returned to USAFFE headquarters, where Sutherland again refused to allow him to speak with MacArthur. The air chief was simply told to stand by for orders.

About 9:30 A.M., reports of bombings of the Baguio and northeastern Cagayan areas reached FEAF headquarters at Nielson Field. Again Brereton called Sutherland to get permission to launch an offensive strike, but again he was refused. Ten minutes later, Sutherland telephoned Brereton and said that only the photoreconnaissance mission had been approved.

According to some accounts, MacArthur called Brereton at about 11:00 A.M. and said that the matter of offensive air action would now be left to his discretion as air commander; Brereton replied that he would shortly send three B-17s on a reconnaissance flight to Formosa, followed by a two-squadron B-17 raid after the photo mission's report was studied. On several occasions in later years, MacArthur emphatically denied that Brereton ever discussed a proposed Formosan raid with him.

The photo planes had been delayed in taking off for Formosa because additional cameras had to be flown up from Nichols Field at Manila; the plane carrying them arrived at Clark Field about ten minutes before the enemy bombers appeared overhead. The fog of war seemed to settle permanently over the Clark catastrophe, and even now the inadequate or contradictory evidence leaves moot many questions about the actual attacks as well as the prelude.

Brereton, MacArthur, and Sutherland each tended to stress different reasons for the disaster. Brereton argued that the deferment of the Formosan raid by Sutherland and MacArthur was the main reason the aircraft were caught on the ground, to which Sutherland responded that reconnaissance was necessary first and was delayed too long by FEAF headquarters.

MacArthur steadfastly denied knowledge of the proposed raid. In fact, he stated in 1954 that if he had known about the projected mission to Formosa, he would have rejected it:

> My orders were explicit not to initiate hostilities against the Japanese. The Philippines while a possession of the U.S. had, so far as war was concerned, a somewhat indeterminate international position in many minds, especially the Filipinos and their government. While I personally had not the slightest doubt we would be attacked, great local hope existed that this would not be the case. Instructions from Washington were very definite to wait until the Japanese made the first "overt" move. Even without such a directive, practical limitations made it unfeasible to take the offensive. The only possibility lay in striking from the air but the relative weakness of our air force precluded any chance of success for such an operation. . . . The enemy's air force based on excellent fields outnumbered ours many times. In addition, he had a mobile force on carriers, which we entirely lacked. Our basic mission directive had confined our operations to our own national waters so no outside reconnaissance had been possible. The exact location of enemy targets was therefore not known. Our air force was in process of integration, radar defenses not yet operative, and personnel raw and inexperienced. An attack under such conditions would have been doomed to total failure. . . .

MacArthur was undoubtedly correct in regarding such a mission as hopeless. Japanese records studied after the war showed that over 500 aircraft were stationed at twenty-five or more bases on Formosa at the time. Without long-range fighter escort, the two B-17 squadrons would have had little chance of success and certainly would have suffered such heavy losses as to preclude further raids.

In later statements, Sutherland chose to stress not the decisions of December 8 but rather an alleged disobedience of orders by Brereton before that day as the underlying reason for the Clark tragedy. Sutherland was a blunt-speaking, tough-minded professional who was given considerable leeway by MacArthur in speaking for the USAFFE commander. MacArthur viewed him as brilliant and able, if sometimes arrogant in dealing with others. Sutherland had a low opinion of Brereton but mistakenly assumed the air chief had finally sent all the Clark B-17s to the Del Monte base on Mindanao. On at least three occasions during the previous five days, MacArthur, through Sutherland, had ordered Brereton to transfer the B-17s to Del Monte. Only two of the four squadrons had been moved by December 8. Brereton's excuse was that he was shortly expecting another B-17 group to arrive at Del Monte and that the field there would have been too crowded to handle the remaining Clark B-17s.

In addition to emphasizing, like Sutherland, the tardiness in moving the heavy bombers to the south, MacArthur also stressed the responsibility of the War Department in the disaster through its failure to provide adequate reinforcements for the Philippine defenses. It was true that the United States had never provided the personnel or matériel adequate for a successful defense of the Philippines, despite Washington's acceptance of War Plan Orange since the early 1920s. This plan went through many revisions, thereby losing any sense of emergency, but consistently called for a defense of four to six months by the Philippines garrison in case of a Japanese attack, at the end of which the Pacific Fleet was expected to achieve a breakthrough to the islands with reinforcements. Whereas Washington officials and MacArthur were slow to grasp the urgency of reinforcing the Philippines, the enemy was quick to pounce before the American buildup progressed further. "Our intelligence estimates had calculated that the Japanese aircraft did not have sufficient range to bomb Manila from Formosa," stated Washington's last message before the war, warning MacArthur only against sabotage, not attack. A B-17 navigator at Clark Field was still convinced years later that "our generals and leaders committed one of the greatest errors possible to military men—that of letting themselves be taken by surprise. That error can be exceeded only by treason."

Nevertheless, when all the evidence is sifted, however contradictory and incomplete it may be, MacArthur still emerges as the officer who was in overall command in the Philippines that fateful day, and he must therefore bear a considerable measure of the blame. His self-confidence and optimism tended to lull others into an unjustified feeling of security. What happened on November 27, 1941, on each side was revealing: That day, Japanese officers on a warship off Formosa were making final plans to invade the Philippines as soon as weather permitted, and a large Japanese task force was secretly departing from the Kurile Islands, heading eastward; its carrier planes would make the attack on Pearl Harbor. Meanwhile, MacArthur was assuring Admiral Thomas C. Hart, commander of the Asiatic Fleet, and Francis B. Sayre, high commissioner of the Philippines, that there would be no attack until spring. Unfortunately, the War Department became mesmerized by MacArthur's unrealistic reports about the combat readiness of the Philippine defense forces. On November 28, Marshall sent MacArthur an exuberant reply to such a message: "The Secretary of War and I were highly pleased to receive your report that your command is ready for any eventuality."

MacArthur failed to permit his air commander, Brereton, free access to him. It was MacArthur who allowed Sutherland too much authority, and the chief of staff would three times deny Brereton's plea for guidance on the morning of December 8. MacArthur and Brereton still could have decided how to disperse the B-17s remaining at Clark Field.

Even as MacArthur met in Manila with Admiral Hart and Vice Admiral Thomas Phillips, the British naval commander at Singapore, on December 5 and 6, the USAFFE commander expected the Japanese attack would not come until after January 1. Phillips died when Japanese bombs sank his flagship four days later.

Had MacArthur been on better terms with Hart (the former thought the latter was interfering with his air force in the matter of offshore air patrols), he might have learned of the Oahu air raids an hour earlier from Asiatic Fleet headquarters, the first to receive the radio message. As it was, MacArthur underestimated the Japanese attack on Pearl Harbor, thinking the enemy must have suffered a serious setback afterward.

Neither was MacArthur's chief of staff guiltless. Sutherland protected his boss so completely from every distracting interruption that he made air, naval, and ground commanders furious by denying or delaying their access to MacArthur, until the chief of staff deemed it necessary. Sutherland also considered himself somewhat of an authority on air matters, having had some limited flying experience. General George C. Kenney, MacArthur's air commander from 1942–45, would clash with Sutherland on more than one occasion; he later said he could understand how the arrogant chief of staff cowed and thwarted Brereton, who was never able to sit down and talk it out with MacArthur on the fateful December 8. Brereton felt the need for quick action and could have transmitted this to MacArthur. The planes need not have been caught on the ground. They could have been sent to Java or Australia to be used against long-range strategic targets.

If, as some accounts indicate, MacArthur did telephone Brereton at about 11:00 A.M. and tell him that the execution of offensive air action would be left to his discretion, the nagging question that remains is why MacArthur hesitated about seven hours in reaching that decision. Brereton was never blamed for the Clark disaster by MacArthur, who felt that nothing could have saved the day for the FEAF. (Ironically, Brereton's last major part in the war would be in Europe as commander of the ill-fated First Allied Airborne Army, which was involved in Operation Market-Garden in September 1944.)

In retrospect, if Sutherland had not blocked Brereton from seeing MacArthur, a conference of the two commanders, in view of MacArthur's opposition to a raid on Formosa, would probably have concluded with the decision to send the heavy bombers at Clark down to Mindanao that morning. As attested to by Captain Chihaya Takahashi of the Japanese Eleventh Air Fleet, "The Japanese feared mostly that, at the time of the first attack, the American planes would take refuge in the southern areas, therefore making the campaign very difficult." The helpless position of the American heavy bombers on the ground was therefore an exhilarating sight to the attackers, and it resulted in the one fact about which no researchers disagree: the destruction on the first day of war of one of the most formidable obstacles to the Japanese conquest of the Philippines.

KING OF BATAAN

THADDEUS HOLT

Two days after the Clark Field raid, the Japanese came ashore in northern Luzon, and then in other parts of the main island of the Philippines. There was no longer an air force to stop them, and they were virtually unopposed. By early January 1942, they had seized most of the island, including the capital, Manila; "Filamerican" troops withdrew to the peninsula called Bataan, a place that would shortly become part of the American mythology of nobility in defeat. Their aim was to hold out there and on Corregidor Island at the entrance to Manila Bay as long as possible—presumably until aid came. But MacArthur—who did not enjoy his finest hour in the Philippines—had left behind enormous stocks of food that he should have moved into Bataan long before the final retreat. The defenders fought on for three months. The "Battling Bastards," they called themselves: "No mama, no papa, no Uncle Sam / And nobody gives a damn."

Meanwhile, under orders from Washington, MacArthur escaped to Australia, in order to command all Allied forces in the South Pacific. Desperate efforts to get supply ships past the Japanese blockade failed. Finally, on April 9, 1942, disobeying MacArthur's orders to hold out, Major General Edward P. King Jr. surrendered the starving and disease-ridden remnants of the Bataan defenders. The enemy was breaking through everywhere and King knew that any further resistance would mean wholesale slaughter. So, though he knew he was destroying his career, he tried to save his men. King could not have known how brutally their Japanese captors would treat them. The defeat in the Philippines may have been the low point of World War II for the United States, but "Back to Bataan" became a rallying cry.

Thaddeus Holt is a former deputy undersecretary of the army, a lawyer, and a writer on military subjects.

BATAAN. THE VERY WORD IS HOLLOW, SORROWFUL, DISTANT, LIKE a dim echo of Roland's horn that the king heard afar, and, hearing it, knew his paladins were slain. It was a modern Roncesvalles or Thermopylae, where brave men held back the hosts of darkness till they were overcome at last. But at Bataan there was no pointless slaughter at the end. When their commander was satisfied that nothing more his men could do would make any difference, he did not ask them to go on and be butchered. On the seventy-seventh anniversary of Appomattox, defying orders and expecting to be court-martialed for what he did, he surrendered more men than have ever been yielded up by any other American general. No soldier in our history has shown more moral courage, yet he is all but unknown.

✦

BORN IN ATLANTA in 1884, Edward Postell King Jr. grew up wanting to be a soldier. Any boy in that time and place was reared on tales of the Lost Cause—of ragged and starving men fighting to the bitter end, giving up only when they could go no farther, overcome but unvanquished—and Ned was grandson and nephew of Confederate officers. However, the family wanted him to be a lawyer, so he took his law degree at the University of Georgia and went to work for his uncle, the founder of the great Atlanta firm of King & Spalding. But Ned King was no more meant to spend his life hunched over deed books than had been another law clerk turned artilleryman, Winfield Scott, a century earlier; after a few unsatisfactory years at the bar, in 1908 he secured a commission in the regular army.

He had a brilliant career. In the Great War, he earned a precocious Distinguished Service Medal (DSM) as principal assistant to the chief of field artillery. In the slow interwar days, he had the usual assignments of a recognized comer: Leavenworth as student and as instructor, both the army and the naval war colleges, the War Department, all interspersed with troop duty. In the late 1930s, as a colonel, he was director of the War Plans Section of the Army War College; and in 1940 he became a brigadier general.

King was short and stout, with a full head of reddish-brown hair and a generous mustache. He was a well-read man; a graceful writer; a religious man who took his Christianity seriously; a man of scrupulous courtesy toward fellow officers and enlisted men alike; an officer whose men were ever in his mind; but withal a robust fellow with a quick hearty laugh, a sly sense of humor, and a merry twinkle in his gray eyes. Men respected him and liked to work for and with him. "A brave and gallant soldier and a perfect gentleman," said his friend and boss, General Jonathan M. Wainwright.

As one of the army's top planners, a master of artillery, and an officer with experience at the highest level in the raising of the great citizen army of 1918, Ned King might well have been one of the major figures of World War II. But fate did not turn that way. Perhaps in recognition of King's 1917–18 training experience, his first assignment as a general officer was to the Philippines, where General Douglas A. MacArthur was organizing the new Philippine Army. When war broke out in December 1941, King was MacArthur's second-ranking ground officer, after Major General "Skinny" Wainwright.

American strategists had always known that the Philippines could not be effectively defended, and for decades the plan in case of attack had been to withdraw to Bataan, a peninsula on the west side of Manila Bay, and to hold out there and on Corregidor and the other fortified islands at the entrance to the bay, denying the Japanese fleet the use of Manila for as long as possible. MacArthur persuaded Washington to scrap those years of planning and authorize him to try to defeat the Japanese on the landing beaches with his half-trained forces. Predictably, many of his raw Filipino troops fled before General Masaharu Homma's ruthless veterans of the war in China; moreover, despite ample warning, his air force had been destroyed on the ground at the outset. Reverting hastily to the traditional plan, MacArthur managed to withdraw his force (accompanied by unexpected thousands of civilian refugees) safely into Bataan in early January 1942.

Bataan is a rounded peninsula twelve to fourteen miles wide at the main defensive line (called the Orion-Bagac line), and from that line to the end of the peninsula is about the same distance: a roughly circular area of some 200 square miles, or somewhat larger than Brooklyn and Queens together. It is mountainous, with peaks that rise more than 4,000 feet around the crater of a huge ancient volcano at the center. Except for a strip of open sugarcane fields along the east coast, in 1942 it was covered with a dense hardwood jungle notable for its many enormous thorns. Apart from a network of trails that the engineers had cut through the jungle, its only highway was the East Road, running down the east coast to the village of Cabcaben on the southeastern corner of the peninsula. From Cabcaben the road continued across a wooded shoulder of the mountains and back down to the little port of Mariveles at the south end, opposite Corregidor. There it became the West Road, running through jungle and mountains up the western side of the peninsula to the west end of the Orion-Bagac line. The nerve center of the defense was in the area called Little Baguio, where the East Road crested the high ground between Cabcaben and Mariveles. Here were the flimsy headquarters buildings, the main ordnance and engineer depots, and a cluster of open-air structures where the sick and wounded were treated, known collectively as General Hospital no. 1. (There was also a no. 2, on the East Road close to Cabcaben.)

The army was "Filamerican": some 66,000 Filipinos and 12,000 Americans, as of the onset of the last battle. Most of the rank and file were Filipinos: seven small divisions of the new Philippine Army, with American and a few Filipino senior officers, Filipino junior officers, and American advisers; the Philippine Scouts, crack professional regiments with American officers and Filipino enlisted men; the Philippine Constabulary, likewise American-officered but a gendarmerie rather than a military force. The only wholly American outfits were the 31st Infantry Regiment; the grounded airmen, now recycled as infantry; and various specialized units, such as a small tank force and two antiaircraft battalions of the New Mexico National Guard. The army was organized into two small corps: I Corps on the left, under Wainwright, and II Corps on the right, under Major General George M. Parker. Skinny Wainwright was an old-time cavalryman who went where the action was. Parker, in poor health, was less energetic and seldom visited the front.

Initially the army occupied the Abucay-Mauban line, an advanced position some eight to ten miles forward of the Orion-Bagac line. Here the Philippine Army troops began to fight well, showing that the disastrous performance of many units at the start of the war had simply reflected lack of training at all levels. (As King always emphasized in his orientation lecture to newly arrived officers—and as was abundantly proved by the brilliant performance of the Philippine Scouts throughout the campaign—the Filipinos were brave and hardy fighters, superb soldiers when properly trained and led.) Between January 7 and January 26, 1942, the Japanese pushed the defenders back to the Orion-Bagac line. Some Filipino units still crumbled under pressure, but their performance was sharply better, and the attackers took severe losses. After that, Homma received a succession of unpleasant surprises as the skill and confidence of the Philippine Army increased. When he tried to emulate a successful tactic of his colleague Tomoyuki Yamashita in Malaya, by landing forces on the coast far behind I Corps's front, the defenders wiped them out in what was called the Battle of the Points. When he tried to break through on the II Corps front, the defenders threw him back in the Battle of Trail 2. He attacked on Wainwright's front, and some of his forces broke through; but they were quickly surrounded and methodically liquidated in the Pocket Fights. By mid-February, the Philippine Army had become, in one American officer's words, "battle-hardened, vicious, disease-ridden, jungle-fighting experts."

Homma's army was now in bad shape. A counterattack could have retaken Manila from him, he said later. Nowhere else had the tide of Japanese conquest met this kind of resistance, and he was behind schedule and getting pointed questions from Tokyo. Humiliated, he retired to lick his wounds, call on imperial headquarters for reinforcements, and plan another offensive while starvation and disease did their work among the defenders.

Starvation and disease were his key weapons. For in reality, Bataan was not a campaign but a siege. The defenders were on half rations from the beginning, because MacArthur had left behind enormous stocks of food that he should have moved into Bataan long before the retreat. Soon the ration was less than half. They ate the cavalry horses. They ate carabao and mule. They ate monkey. They ate dog, iguana, and snake. As February and March wore on, the men grew thinner, weaker, sicker. They knew that the final Japanese onslaught was just a matter of time. They realized MacArthur's assurances that help was on the way were lies. When they heard a Roosevelt "fireside chat" on the radio in February—he talked about Europe and barely mentioned them—they knew they had been written off. The "Battling Bastards," they called themselves: "No mama, no papa, no Uncle Sam / And nobody gives a damn." But they held on.

Major General King—he got his second star soon after the war began—was MacArthur's chief of artillery. In any combined-arms ground unit of division size or greater, the chief of artillery is the most important officer after the commander, and on Bataan that was assuredly true of King. Before the war he had ensured that his officers were familiar with the terrain. He supervised emplacement and fire patterns, juggled the ammunition supply, reorganized units. He devised schemes to make the Japanese believe the defenders had more guns than they did—including an old Filipino ruse, firing black-powder charges from bamboo tubes. The artillery was crucial in slowing down the enemy at the Abucay-Mauban line, and it received a letter of commendation from MacArthur for that work. In the Battle of the Points, King ingeniously used the terrifying power of the huge Corregidor harbor-defense mortars in an infantry-support role. The Japanese recognized King's artillery as their most formidable opponent. In a 1943 interview Homma told the Tokyo newspaper *Mainichi*, "By far the greatest number of our wounded were hit by shrapnel, testifying to the fierceness of the enemy bombardment." Another Japanese general said the defenders' artillery "was so accurate and powerful that the Japanese Army feared this most."

In his tunnel headquarters deep inside "the Rock," as Corregidor was called, MacArthur seems to have gone into a blue funk after his initial failures. Incredibly, only once did he visit Bataan. His friend President Manuel Quezon of the Philippines proposed that the islands be neutralized, with both American and Japanese forces to withdraw, and MacArthur passed this idea on to Washington with apparent approval. On February 9, a shocked Roosevelt issued a direct order to MacArthur: The Americans in the Philippines must fight to the end.

In early March, at Roosevelt's direction, MacArthur escaped to Australia. He reorganized the forces in the Philippines into four separate units, each reporting directly to him in Australia through a chief of staff left on Corregidor. The troops on Bataan became "Luzon Force." Wainwright was moved up to command it, with King as his artillery officer. At I Corps, Wainwright's place was taken by tough, hard-swearing Major General Albert Jones, an old friend of King's. (In line with some long-forgotten joke, King always called him "Hones," pronounced "Ho-ness," supposedly a Spanish pronunciation of Jones.) Before leaving, MacArthur awarded King his second DSM for his brilliant performance, and his parting advice to Wainwright was that the artillery was "the best arm you have."

Washington changed MacArthur's command structure and put Wainwright in command of all forces in the islands, giving him a third star. From Australia, MacArthur radioed Roosevelt's no-surrender order to Wainwright, with the injunction that "the foregoing instructions from the President remain unchanged." On March 21, Wainwright moved to MacArthur's old headquarters on Corregidor and gave King, as next senior general, command of Luzon Force.

By then the men on Bataan were walking skeletons. Beriberi and scurvy had set in. Dysentery and hookworm were rampant. About 75 to 80 percent of the frontline soldiers had malaria—1,000 men a day were entering the two overcrowded field hospitals—and the quinine supply was running out. One-fourth of the men were barefoot, and at least 90 percent of their clothing was unserviceable by normal standards.

Thirteen days after King took over, on Good Friday, April 3, Homma's final offensive opened with a fierce onslaught on the left of Parker's II Corps. Dazed by an overwhelming artillery and air bombardment, the sick, hungry men broke and the front gave way. King sent in reserve units, but the next day Parker's line broke again. King committed more reserves, but on April 5, Easter Sunday, the Japanese overran the key position of Mount Samat, overlooking the lines of both I and II Corps. Wainwright came over from Cor-

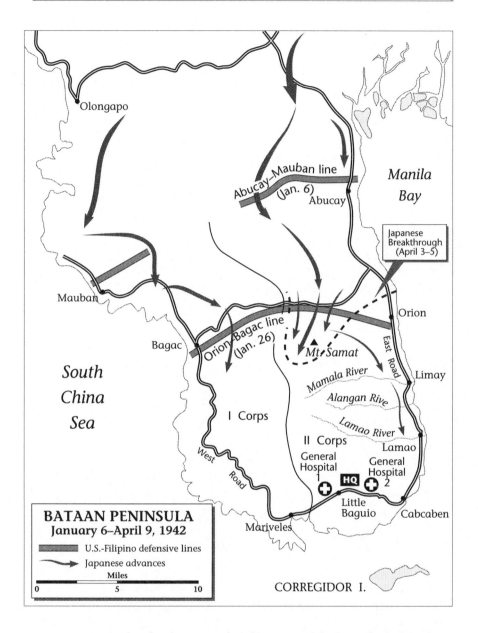

BATAAN PENINSULA
January 6–April 9, 1942

Olongapo

Abucay-Mauban line (Jan. 6)
Abucay

Manila Bay

Japanese Breakthrough (April 3–5)

Mauban

Orion-Bagac line (Jan. 26)

Bagac

Orion

East Road

Mt. Samat

Limay

South China Sea

Mamala River

Alangan River

Lamao River

I Corps

II Corps

Lamao

General Hospital 1

General Hospital 2

West Road

HQ

Little Baguio

Cabcaben

Mariveles

▬▬ U.S.-Filipino defensive lines
→ Japanese advances
Miles
0   5   10

CORREGIDOR I.

In January 1942, the Japanese pushed the Bataan defenders eight to ten miles back from their initial position, the Abucay-Mauban line, to the Orion-Bagac line. I Corps, in the western part of the peninsula, and II Corps, on the eastern side, held out until the final enemy offensive, on April 3–9. King's surrender took place near Lamao.

regidor for the day while a counterattack was organized for the next morning. On April 6, as the counterattack was being launched, King asked his staff what percentage of the army was effective—which he defined as anyone who could carry his weapon for 100 yards without resting and still shoot. On that definition, said the staff, it's about 15 percent—in the units that are still cohesive, that is. When the counterattack ran headfirst into the attacking Japanese, it broke like a wave against the shore. The Japanese pushed on, and by nightfall on April 6 they had irrevocably split II Corps off from I Corps and were positioned to roll the former up into Manila Bay.

April 7 opened with another fierce bombardment, and II Corps began to disintegrate. Parker stayed far behind the front and played little further role, and Brigadier General Clifford Bluemel—in some people's view, "the meanest man in the United States Army" and a natural leader of the sort that believes his men should be more afraid of him than of the enemy—took charge of the II Corps front by default. Rifle in hand, he rounded up stragglers and formed a line along the Mamala River, some four miles south of the original line. But by nightfall even he had to conclude that his weary men, many of whom had not eaten for two days, could not hold there. He ordered an overnight withdrawal to the Alangan River, two and a half miles farther south.

That afternoon of April 7, King sent his chief of staff, Brigadier General Arnold Funk, across to the Rock to brief Wainwright. He told Funk not to mention the word "surrender." Funk got back at about 4:00 P.M. He had told Wainwright "that the II Corps had disintegrated, that there was nothing but confusion at the front lines, and due to the physical condition of the I Corps, the fall of Bataan was imminent." Wainwright, bound by his own orders, had ordered King through Funk to fight to the end. He also directed that Jones attack eastward to relieve II Corps. Impossible, said Jones, when King passed this order on. The men are too weak, and it would take eighteen hours to reposition them in any case. King, Wainwright, and Jones conferred by telephone, and finally Wainwright left it to King's judgment. That ended that. King told Jones to start a phased pullback to avoid being outflanked on the east.

Dawn of April 8 found a handful of confused and bone-tired men defending Bluemel's line at the Alangan. By late afternoon Bluemel had to order another fallback two miles to the next river, the Lamao. II Corps by now had utterly collapsed. The roads and trails were clogged with dazed, bewildered men, savaged by Japanese planes, thinking only of escape. Communications were breaking down, but such fragmentary information as King received pointed only one way. He called Corregidor: If you want any troops sent over to the Rock, get them tonight or it will be too late. Corregidor wanted the 45th Infantry, a veteran Philippine Scouts outfit from Jones's front. The mass rape at Nanking in 1937 was fresh in mind, and King wanted to send the hospital nurses over too. Initially at least, Corregidor said no. King determined to send them anyway.

In this or a later conversation, King told Lieutenant Colonel Jesse Traywick, Wainwright's assistant operations officer, that the situation looked hopeless. Traywick relayed this to Wainwright, then told King, as he later recalled, that Wainwright replied: "Tell them not to surrender. We can't surrender. We've got orders from the president of the United States."

"I'll do my best to carry out my orders," replied King, his voice sounding "very upset" to Traywick. "But the break is so great that it looks hopeless. I'll keep in touch with you."

Obviously Wainwright was unwilling to take the responsibility of disobeying MacArthur and the president, even though he plainly knew as well as King did that only surrender could prevent a massacre of Luzon Force. So King shouldered the responsibility alone. For the rest of that terrible day and night, King and Wainwright played out a charade: Wainwright pretended not to know what King was doing, and King avoided putting him in the position of knowing until it was a fait accompli. It was as if both Nelson and his admiral were regarding each other with telescopes to their respective blind eyes.

King's problem now was to hold the Japanese far enough back that they would not be firing into the hospitals, and long enough to get the nurses out and destroy the public property. (Under the laws of war, you can destroy your weapons, equipment, and other public property to keep them from falling into the enemy's hands right up to the moment of surrender, but not thereafter.) In midafternoon he called his senior commanders together and told them to prepare to destroy all their weapons and equipment, except motor transport and gasoline, when he gave the word.

At about 6:00 P.M., King learned of Bluemel's situation on the Alangan. (By then Bluemel was falling back to the Lamao, which in turn he would soon conclude he could not hold.) King was now at the absolute bottom of his manpower barrel. The only combatants not yet thrown in were the antiaircraft gunners of the New Mexico National Guard who defended Little Baguio against Japanese planes. They were tough, brave men, many of them Navajos, Apaches, and other tribesmen, but they had no infantry training, were sick and hungry like everyone else, and had been at their guns for forty-eight hours already; some batteries had fought off as many as twenty dive-bomber attacks. No matter; there was nobody else. At 7:00 P.M., King told their commander, six-foot-six Colonel Charles G. Sage, who a short while before had been a newspaperman in Deming, New Mexico, to destroy their antiaircraft weapons, pick up rifles and bayonets, and go form a line at Cabcaben.

Later that night, there was an incident that approached black comedy. It had begun earlier in the week when MacArthur, from his comfortable office in Australia, radioed orders to Wainwright that would bear comparison with the zaniest emanations from the Berlin bunker three years later. They involved a complicated two-pronged attack by both corps to wrest Olongapo on the west coast from the Japanese, there either seizing supplies that would "rectify the situation" or breaking up into guerrilla units. ("The ones who planned this action and the person who issued this order must have been totally ignorant of the situation and the condition of the troops on Bataan," snorted Bluemel after the war. "It sounds like an order issued in a map problem, being solved in a comfortable room where food and cigarettes are plentiful.") MacArthur had told Wainwright to order this operation when food ran out on Bataan. That night, on all Bataan, there was enough food left for one last half-ration issue to the troops. At about 10:30 P.M., Wainwright dutifully passed this order to King.

No doubt cursing inwardly, King called Jones. Hones, he asked, knowing full well the answer, "have you got any troops that are capable of launching a counterattack?" Of course Jones said no. So King took the responsibility of withholding the order.

At about 11:00 P.M., King sat down with Funk and Colonel James V. Collier, his assistant operations officer, for their final conference. Outside, in Collier's words, "The road, the one road around Bataan, was jammed with Philippine Army troops, arms thrown away. They were like a mass of sheep. . . . Thousands poured out of the jungle like small spring freshets pouring into creeks, which in turn poured into a river."

King, Funk, and Collier went over the situation in exhaustive detail, turned it all over, thrashed it all out. They kept getting back to the same bottom line: Nothing that could be done would prevent the Japanese from being in Mariveles by nightfall on April 9. And that would be the end of Bataan and the death of the army.

That being the case, from now on those sick, half-naked, desperately hungry men would be dying for no purpose.

King's orders were unambiguous. He was to keep fighting. (The 75th Article of War: "Any officer . . . who, before the enemy, . . . shamefully abandons or delivers up . . . any . . . command which it is his duty to defend . . . shall suffer death or such other punishment as a court-martial may direct.")

Court-martial or no, Ned King was not going to let his men die without purpose. We will open negotiations with the Japanese, he told Funk and Collier.

King called in the two other general officers who were at Little Baguio—Parker of II Corps and Brigadier General James Weaver, commander of his small force of tanks—and told them that he was sending a flag across the lines at daylight. He would take this action on his own responsibility. He spoke of the potential massacre of the thousands of sick and wounded in the hospital; of the tens of thousands of civilian refugees, mostly women and children; of the fact that he was out of touch with the front; of the fact that "only 25 percent of our men are on their feet," and that at most he could not hold longer than one more day. As Weaver recalled it, King said further: "Corregidor has sent over a list of stuff they want us to send out. I want to send the nurses and they've refused that. I shall send them anyway. Is there anything else any of you can think of? My career is over."

"I never pitied a man so much," recalled Weaver. "I admire Ned King—a fine soldier—very studious. He looked at each of us." Is there any possibility of any help? Weaver asked. None whatsoever, said King; the Air Corps promised to send a strike from Mindanao, but it never arrived.

King called Jones to tell him of the decision, while Parker called Bluemel. Jones had been trying unsuccessfully to move out the troops Corregidor wanted.

"I hate to tell you this, Hones," said King, "but I'm surrendering at 6:00 A.M. They're shelling the hospital. Parker's gone. There's nothing else I can do. Put white flags all along your line. You'll have to destroy your artillery and machine guns and stand by for further orders."

"I don't see what else you can do," said Jones. "I'll spike the artillery, all right. But I'm going to hang on to my machine guns in case of sudden attack, just in case the Japs don't recognize the surrender."

"I'm giving you orders to destroy them," said King. "I don't give a damn what you do, these are your orders."

"Don't worry about me," said Jones. "I'll take care of it. At the last minute we can throw the bolts into the jungle."

"Use your judgment, Hones," said King. His voice was "hopeless—quavering," Jones recalled.

At that moment—it was 11:40 P.M.—an earthquake smote Bataan, shaking the mountains and trees to their roots, as if God himself were setting his

seal on the death warrant of the army. ("Even the earth is shaken by our decision," said one of King's party.)

At midnight King's staff gathered around him. "Quietly, calmly, but
tersely," as Collier recalled it, he said:

> I did not ask you here to get your opinion or your advice. I do not want any
> of you saddled with any part of the responsibility for the ignominious decision
> I feel forced to make. I have not communicated with General Wainwright be-
> cause I do not want him to be compelled to assume any part of the responsibil-
> ity. I am sending forward a flag of truce at daybreak to ask for terms of
> surrender. I feel that further resistance could only uselessly waste human life.
> Already our hospital, which is filled to capacity and directly in the line of hos-
> tile approach, is within range of enemy light artillery. We have no means of or-
> ganized resistance.

He did not have a white horse and a saber and someone to ride up and down
the lines to rally the troops, he said wryly. There was just no way to continue
the fight. "There was not a dry eye present," recorded Collier.

✦

COLONEL EVERETT WILLIAMS, King's chief of artillery, and Major Marshall Hurt of the operations staff volunteered (both were bachelors) for the ul-
tradangerous job of trying to pass through the lines and make contact with
the Japanese. King gave Williams a typed page of orders: Find the Japanese
commander, present my compliments, ask for a time and place where he and
I can meet. If he won't receive me, ask his terms for surrender. Ask for particular consideration of the large number of sick and wounded in the hospitals;
of the fact that our force is disorganized and my staff and I can best pull it together for further movement to prison camp; of the fact that these sick, hungry men cannot move on foot and I have saved transportation for them; and of
the vast number of civilian refugees who are unconnected with our forces.
Leave at whatever time you think will get you to the front lines at daylight.

At 1:30 A.M. the order went out to begin destroying property. Now began
a Götterdämmerung. The navy had already started the destruction: Soon its
installations at Mariveles were lighting the sky with their Games, shore facilities were being blown up, ships being scuttled. Some ordnance officers had
jumped the gun and started blowing up ammunition even as King, Funk, and
Collier were conferring; now they began to set off all the ammunition. Tanks
were wrecked, fieldpieces were ripped apart, some cannon were blown to bits
by firing them double-loaded. It was "like the end of the world, fantastic, re-

verberating, reminded me of *Fantasia,* the Night on Bald Mountain, a night of Hell," recalled one of Sage's New Mexicans. The supreme moment was at 2:10 A.M., when the TNT warehouse and main ammunition dump at Little Baguio detonated with a string of stupendous blasts. The earth heaved, trees rocked in the ground, the sky was filled with multicolored pyrotechnics, masses of hot metal fragments rained down, one of the flimsy headquarters buildings was wholly blown away. One officer said to his foxhole mate that the explosions reminded him of something Sibelius might have composed.

With the big dump blown, it was safe to move about. Williams and Hurt set off in a reconnaissance car with a motorcycle escort, up the East Road against the current of the human flood.

At about 2:45 A.M., MacArthur's absurd Olongapo project raised its head again. Jones phoned to report that Brigadier General Lewis Beebe, Wainwright's chief of staff, had just called him to ask about it. When Jones had said he had received no orders, Beebe had told him he probably soon would.

That was disturbing. Did Wainwright mean to take direct command of I Corps with the surrender already under way? King called Wainwright. The connection was bad. Wainwright, hard of hearing, gave Beebe the phone. "I want a definite answer as to whether or not General Jones will be left in my command regardless of what action I may take," said King. After two or three minutes, the officers with King heard him say "You bet, Skinny; thank you very much," and he hung up. Corregidor could not agree to a surrender because of MacArthur's orders, he told them (and of course he had not asked for that), but there would be no interference with any element of his command. King went on to say, as one witness recalled, "that if he survived to return home he fully expected to be court-martialed, and he was certain that history would not deal kindly with the commander who would be remembered for having surrendered the largest force the United States had ever lost."

✦

ON THROUGH THE NIGHT continued the orgy of destruction. The bus carrying the nurses from General Hospital No. 1 took hours to push its way to Mariveles through the human swarm jamming the road, and one nurse later recalled that the sky was alight the whole time. (The nurses made it safely to Corregidor.) Finally, at about 6:00 A.M.—when, according to plan, Williams and Hurt would have crossed the line, white flags would be appearing, the die would be irrevocably cast, and Wainwright could truthfully tell MacArthur that he could do nothing to stop it—King put in a call to Wainwright. For some reason, Wainwright was not available.

"All right," said King, probably speaking to Beebe,

I'll talk to you. Tell General Wainwright for me that I have decided to surrender Bataan. The Japanese attack has broken the center of the line, they are pouring on all trails toward both the east and the west coasts and I have nothing to stop them. This decision is solely my own, no member of my staff nor of my command has helped me to arrive at this decision. In my opinion, if I do not surrender to the Japanese, Bataan will be known as the greatest slaughter in history.

Beebe reminded him of the order for the Olongapo attack.

"With what?" retorted King.

At the same time, Funk was giving the news to Lieutenant Colonel Traywick, who was the night duty officer. It was Traywick who actually broke the news to Wainwright. Traywick quickly called back to say that Wainwright said not to do it. It's too late, said Funk. There was no more communication between King and Corregidor.

Toward 9:00 A.M., Hurt reappeared at headquarters. After a hair-raising adventure, he and Williams had reached the commander of the Japanese force attacking down the East Road. The commander was to meet King near the village of Lamao. Williams had been kept behind as a token of good faith.

King said a prayer, and was ready to go. Hurt led the way with Collier in a jeep, followed by King and two aides in a second jeep. They flew white flags made from a bedsheet. King had put on his last clean uniform—like another general, seventy-seven years before.

When he was a nineteen-year-old amateur cannoneer dreaming of being a soldier, Ned King had been one of the crew that fired the minute guns for the state funeral of John B. Gordon, Georgia's grand old man, Lee's last corps commander, "the Hero of Appomattox." As a youth he surely had heard at least once Gordon's oft-delivered, stirring lecture on "The Last Days of the Confederacy." Through King's mind now passed Lee's words on that other April 9, when Gordon had told him that he had "fought my corps to a frazzle": *Then there is nothing left to do but to go and see General Grant, and I would rather die a thousand deaths.*

Arrogant and truculent, the Japanese would not discuss terms. Homma would not even see King; he sent a staff colonel. Over and over King emphasized the needs of the men, their desperate condition, how numerous they were, how he had ordered his transportation saved and would undertake to carry them to any designated place. The Japanese would not even talk about it.

Will you not just assure me that my men will be well treated, King asked.

The Japanese colonel drew himself up and said loftily, "The Imperial Japanese Army are not barbarians."

It was the best King could do. He handed over his pistol.

By a supreme irony, Roosevelt rescinded his no-surrender order that very morning.

✦

THE IMPERIAL Japanese Army are not barbarians.

Do not try to tell that to the survivors of Bataan.

King could not have known, of course, that the Japanese not only would refuse to let many of his men ride to prison in the vehicles he had so carefully ordered saved, but would harry them up the East Road, sick, skeletally thin, desperately hungry, gasping for water in the blazing Philippine sun, stumbling from beriberi, their ragged garments drenched in their own diarrhea—Japanese clubbing them, bayoneting them, beheading them—in a march of death that would kill some 650 Americans and 5,000 to 10,000 Filipinos. He could not have expected their first destination, Camp O'Donnell, with its loathsome open latrine trenches and one water spigot for thousands of men, where in a few weeks another 1,600 Americans and at least 15,000 Filipinos would die. He could not have expected the next three years, the freight cars and hell ships in which men suffocated, the coal mines where they slaved, the gratuitous beatings by sadistic guards. He could not have expected the deliberate starvation, sometimes only a spoonful of rice a day. He could not have known that barely a third of the Americans he surrendered on April 9, 1942, would ever see home again.

For some weeks, in the first dumbfounding shock of this barbarity, he wondered whether he had done the right thing. When Jones joined him after hiking part of the death march, he thought King had "no spirit—mentally sick." King soon recovered, and he and Jones did manage to ameliorate to some small extent the horror of Camp O'Donnell before they and other senior officers were sent to a separate camp. But throughout the first years of imprisonment, King had recurrent seizures of black depression.

After the war, King repeatedly apologized for not suffering in the same prison camps as his men—as if that had been within his control. He and his fellow senior officers certainly suffered. Wainwright soon joined him in prison, having yielded Corregidor and the rest of the forces in the Philippines less than a month after King's surrender. Eventually, generals and some colonels were moved to Formosa, later to Manchuria. They were systematically starved, harassed in innumerable ways both gross and petty, forced to labor in the fields, allowed negligible communication with the outside world. Both Wainwright and Jones were beaten. King never was, but he injured his hip in Manchuria, and for lack of proper medical attention it never healed properly.

Both King and Wainwright spent the war thinking they were despised back home. Moreover, King expected to be court-martialed for disobeying orders. Everybody else, officers and men, knew that what King had done was not only right but an act of supreme courage. "He was faced with a terrible situation and he made a brave and determined decision," said Wainwright after the war. "To my mind [King was] the hero of the show," said General Weaver. One of King's regimental officers wrote, "It is my honest opinion that there was no greater hero on Bataan than he." After they got home, Jones wrote to King: "The American people will probably never realize the service you performed at the surrender. It took a great man to steer a true course through the troubled sea of heroics and traditional emotions. Thousands of Bataan heroes owe their lives to you. The future attitude of the Filipinos to our Government largely will be based upon your humane and excellent estimate of that situation and your brave decision."

King's and Wainwright's worries, of course, proved unfounded. Atlanta gave her native son a hero's welcome after the Japanese surrender. But for the rest of the country, Wainwright alone was the symbol of the gallant defense of the Philippines. He stood behind MacArthur on the *Missouri*. He got the Medal of Honor, four stars, and an army command to go with it, a ticker-tape parade up Broadway, receptions by the Senate and the House, and a book contract complete with ghostwriter. Almost nobody heard of King.

"My career is over," Weaver remembered King saying at that last meeting, and so it proved to be. King had taken care that no one else was tainted with his decision, and he did all he could to ensure that his people, from privates to Jones and Bluemel, got the medals and other recognition they deserved. But there was no recognition for King himself, the man who had fought skillfully to the end and then saved thousands of lives. Bataan and Corregidor joined the Alamo and Fort Sumter and the Little Big Horn in American legend, but somehow the adulation showered—and justly so—on Wainwright was allowed to substitute for recognition of them all. After a few wrap-up paperwork assignments, King retired in late 1946.

The blame for this shabby treatment—about which King never complained—lies squarely on Douglas MacArthur's shoulders. Jealous and ungenerous, for the rest of his days MacArthur sought to divert attention from his own performance in the Philippines by denigrating the men he had left behind. Right up through the publication of his memoirs on the eve of his death in 1964, he was still carping about the failure to carry out his crackpot Olongapo scheme. He barely mentioned King in his memoirs and praised him not at all. Wainwright's honors were contrary to MacArthur's wishes. George C. Marshall, army chief of staff, and Secretary of War Henry L. Stimson wanted Wainwright to have the Medal of Honor after the fall of Corregidor in 1942, but MacArthur snidely refused to recommend it. Even Wainwright's invitation to the ceremony on the *Missouri* was pressed on MacArthur by Washington.

When MacArthur came home in 1951 after Truman fired him, the War Department thoughtfully brought King to Washington and gave him a ringside seat for MacArthur's address to Congress. King—who had sharply defended his old boss—went up to speak to MacArthur, but the latter affected not to know him. "There was no recognition in his eye," as King put it, and he had to introduce himself. "I believe he does not like to be reminded of Bataan," wrote King to Bluemel.

✦

IN RETIREMENT KING lived in a small cottage on the Georgia coast, with summers in the North Carolina mountains. He devoted himself to innumerable volunteer causes, especially the Red Cross. (A friend told him once that people were imposing on him, getting him to do all this pro bono work. I'm living on a pension that they are paying for, King responded; I owe them something in return.) In some local demand as a speaker, he repeatedly sounded a few simple themes: Never again let the country fall into the unpreparedness that made Bataan possible. Do not forget the men who suffered for you. Do not forget the loyalty of the Filipinos. And do not trust the Japanese, and never believe their promises; in forty years they will be as great a threat as ever.

He died in 1958 and was buried in one of the loveliest spots in America, the shady, moss-grown churchyard of St. John's-in-the-Wilderness, in Flat Rock, North Carolina, near Carl Sandburg's home. On his stone are seven fitting words from St. Luke: *He that humbleth himself shall be exalted.*

III

WORLD
AT WAR
1942–1943

THE CHANNEL DASH

MICHAEL H. COLES

If only the victors write history, it is also true that the victors seem to have the only heroes. Nothing could be further from the truth, of course. Think of the Japanese Zero pilots who endured long flights over water in impossibly constricted cockpits to attack Clark Field in the Philippines. Or to cite a later episode in this section, the valiant doomed defenders of Tarawa, who came so close to denying the United States an essential island stepping-stone. Can there be a better case in point than the tale of the daring escape in February 1942 by the Nazi battle cruisers *Scharnhorst* and *Gneisenau* and the heavy cruiser *Prinz Eugen*?

The three ships had been trapped for almost a year in the French port of Brest, where they were under constant attack by RAF bombers. They were not only vulnerable but idle; Hitler felt that they would be of more use defending Norway or threatening the convoys that supplied the Soviets. But what was the best escape route? The Germans chose the shortest—but also the most risky: a dash through the Straits of Dover. Hitler reasoned that he not only had the advantage of surprise—always a bane for the Allies—but that the British were incapable of making and executing quick decisions. This was one time, as it proved, when he was not wrong. The breakout of the three ships would be aided by a tragicomedy of errors on the other side. For the British public, the Nazi ships' escape, much of it in broad daylight, was almost as mortifying as the fall of Singapore two days later.

Michael H. Coles, a former British naval pilot, is a visiting fellow at International Security Studies at Yale and a writer of military history.

BRITISH NAVAL PLANNING FOR WAR AGAINST GERMANY traditionally relied heavily on the Royal Navy's demonstrated ability to control
its enemy's only exits from the North Sea: the English Channel and the narrow passage between Scapa Flow and Norway. For a few fleeting hours during
the winter of 1942, however, Great Britain lost command of the Channel. In
a daring maneuver, the German battle cruisers *Scharnhorst* and *Gneisenau* and
heavy cruiser *Prinz Eugen* steamed in broad daylight through the waters the
British had always deemed their own.

In London shortly after the incident, a *Times* editorial thundered:

> Vice Admiral Ciliax has succeeded where the Duke of Medina Sidonia failed:
> with trifling losses he has sailed a hostile fleet from an Atlantic harbour up the
> English Channel and through the Strait of Dover to safe anchorage in a North
> Sea port. Nothing more mortifying to the pride of sea power has happened in
> home waters since the seventeenth century.

Naval air power was also affected. After the potential of naval aircraft was
first demonstrated in World War I, there was considerable dispute during the
interwar years regarding proper control over the new weapon. Advocates of an
independent air force argued that the air was indivisible, while navies insisted
that they retain command of all maritime activities. In the United States and
Japan, the admirals were successful in preserving their air arms; in Britain,
the Royal Navy lost control of all aviation to the new Royal Air Force, and it
was not until 1937 that it regained only the shipborne portion. However, it
took the German navy's 1942 "Channel Dash" to demonstrate convincingly
the folly of dividing command of maritime aviation.

✦

GERMANY'S 1940 OCCUPATION of Norway and defeat of France greatly reduced Britain's natural geographic advantages, since the choke points that for
so long had frustrated Germany's ability to wage war in the world's oceans
were suddenly unblocked. Brest and Saint-Nazaire provided access to the Atlantic, while the fjords of Norway furnished surface-vessel and submarine
bases well outside the North Sea. A major German victory on land had inflicted a significant setback on Britain's position at sea.

Nevertheless, it was not until the beginning of 1941 that the *Scharnhorst*
and *Gneisenau*—fast, modern, 32,000-ton battle cruisers carrying nine eleven-
inch guns and numerous smaller weapons each—were able to evade the Royal

Navy's arctic patrols. For two months they menaced British shipping in the North and South Atlantic. Then, in late March, their initial mission completed, the two ships entered Brest.

Significant as access to a French Atlantic port may have appeared to German naval planners, the ability of the RAF to subject it to constant air attack greatly reduced the effectiveness of the Brest-based squadron. In addition, destruction of most of Germany's Atlantic supply vessels significantly restricted the big ships' range. These factors, together with maintenance problems, would keep the *Scharnhorst* and *Gneisenau* close to Brest for the rest of 1941. Even so, the two battle cruisers, joined in June by the Bismarck's consort *Prinz Eugen,* remained a constant threat to Britain; never sure when they might sortie into the Atlantic again, it had to maintain significant naval strength at Gibraltar and Scapa Flow in readiness.

During the second half of 1941, the disposition of the large surface ships became a frequent topic of discussion between Adolf Hitler and his naval commander, Grand Admiral Erich Raeder. The führer, concerned about the battle cruisers' vulnerability in Brest, felt they would be of more use in Norway, where they could deter a feared British attack against that country while threatening Allied convoys supplying the Soviets via Murmansk. Raeder, on the other hand, argued that by remaining in Brest the squadron represented a continuing menace to vital British routes to the south.

In Hitler's opinion, however, the squadron was like a cancer patient whose life can be preserved only by major surgery, however risky. It was his threat to order the idle ships decommissioned and their guns and crews used in defense of Norway that finally persuaded the admirals to chance the surgery; by the end of the year, discussion was focusing on the route to be taken.

Raeder recommended a breakout to the north around Scotland, telling Hitler that the shorter Channel route was too risky. Raeder's pessimism was not shared by his operational commanders, including Vice Admiral Otto Ciliax, who would command the squadron during the passage. The Channel route was preferable, they persuaded Hitler, pointing out that it was shorter and that escort by small vessels would be possible, air cover available, harbors of refuge nearby, and the enemy battle fleet far away.

On January 12, 1942, the German navy presented Hitler with its plan for the big ships' passage through the Channel, which depended on three principal elements: careful clearing of British minefields, high-density air cover, and surprise. Mines had always ranked high on the list of reasons that heavy naval units could not force their way through the Channel. Still, Commodore Friedrich Ruge, the minesweeper commander, was unexpectedly optimistic.

Absolute safety could not be guaranteed, but he felt that a deepwater passage could be cleared without attracting too much attention.

Readily understanding the need for effective air cover, Hitler directed the Luftwaffe to do everything it could to ensure the safety of the ships. Despite pressing demands on its strength from other theaters, the Luftwaffe proved surprisingly cooperative, possibly recognizing that removal of the battle squadron from Brest would reduce the intensity of RAF attacks on the Atlantic ports and therefore the associated air-defense requirements.

Hitler also seized on Ciliax's idea of a nighttime departure, essential if surprise was to be maintained as long as possible. He countered the arguments of his advisers, who feared annihilating daytime air attacks in the Strait of Dover, by saying that past experience indicated the British were incapable of making and executing lightning decisions. In this case at least, the führer knew his enemy better than many of his admirals did.

Information from U-boats in the North Atlantic indicated that good weather conditions would be likely in mid-February: little moonlight and low clouds, resulting in poor visibility. Tides and currents also would be favorable then. The ships would leave Brest on the evening of February 11, pass Dover at noon the following day, and arrive in Germany's North Sea ports twenty-four hours after departure. As the *Times* would later comment, "The German plan combined audacity in action with accurate and patient organization in advance."

Surprise was, in the final event, tactical rather than strategic. As early as April 1941, an RAF analysis of possible enemy naval movements had predicted an attempt by the *Scharnhorst* and *Gneisenau* to reach Germany via the Channel, and a plan for opposing action by bombers, torpedo bombers, and light surface craft had been prepared and circulated. Crucially, the plan, code-named Fuller, assumed a night passage through the Channel's narrow waters. Regular photoreconnaissance of Brest began, and several submarines were stationed off the harbor to report any movements. Unfortunately, requirements in other theaters caused these to be reduced to one by year's end.

All intelligence available by late January pointed toward the likelihood of a breakout in the near future. A British Admiralty "appreciation" on February 2 stated in part, "We might well . . . find the 2 battle cruisers and the 8-inch cruiser with 5 large and 5 small destroyers, also, say 20 fighters constantly overhead . . . proceeding up Channel." It added, "Our bombers have shown that we cannot place much reliance on them to damage the enemy, whilst our Coastal Command T/B [torpedo/bomber] aircraft will not muster more than 9." The following day, the Admiralty warned its various opera-

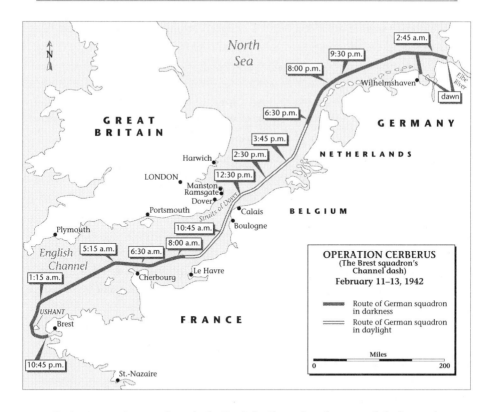

*Beginning its journey through the English Channel under cover of darkness, the
German squadron cleared the breakwater at Brest at 10:45 P.M. on February 11.
The line shows its route—the darkest portion indicating its travel during the night.
As the white portion shows, the ships daringly passed through the Straits of Dover
(where they were first fired on) in broad daylight. After uncoordinated, ineffectual
attacks by the British navy and Royal Air Force, the German ships reached their
home ports at dawn on February 13, their pace slowed only by three mines.*

tional commanders and the RAF's Bomber, Fighter, and Coastal commands
that a breakout was likely and requested all commands to bring the Fuller
arrangements into force.

By February 7, six destroyers, ten torpedo boats, over thirty minesweepers,
and numerous smaller vessels had reinforced German naval forces already in
the Channel. The next day, the RAF's Coastal Command determined that
weather and tidal conditions favored a movement anytime after February 10,
with the Channel the likely route. At this time, therefore, the British could
assume with some confidence that the German fleet would soon break out,

and that it would move through the Channel; the only uncertain element was the precise time of departure. Nevertheless, both the Royal Navy and the RAF had become convinced that the ships would try to pass through the Strait of Dover at night, which argued for a daytime departure from Brest. Reports from an agent in that port, warning urgently that the likeliest time of departure would be around 11:00 P.M. during a new-moon period, either were never seen by the Admiralty or were disregarded.

Coastal Command, whose torpedo bombers probably represented the greatest threat to the German fleet, did very little other than institute night patrols by radar-equipped aircraft over the western approaches to the Channel. A squadron of Beaufort torpedo bombers was ordered to move south from Scotland, but it was unable to do so because of bad weather. None of the other antishipping squadrons were moved nearer to Dover, and, in view of the high level of secrecy surrounding Fuller, none of the pilots concerned were told about the possibility of a breakout or the ships they might encounter.

Bomber Command, normally unwilling to divert resources from its strategic offensive against Germany, reluctantly designated a strike force to prepare for action against the battle cruisers; but on February 10, without telling anyone, it ordered half of the strike force to stand down and extended the remainder's notice from two hours' standby to four. Significantly, however, it did arrange to lay ninety-eight magnetic mines off the Dutch coast, in what Enigma decryptions and captured enemy charts indicated were the paths just swept by Ruge's coastal forces.

The Admiralty, its capabilities stretched to the limit, took what minor defensive measures lay within its means. Vice Admiral Sir Bertram Ramsay, commander in chief at Dover, was placed in tactical command of a skimpy fleet consisting of two fast minelayers at Plymouth and Portsmouth, eight motor torpedo boats (MTBS) at Dover and nearby Ramsgate, and half a dozen elderly destroyers based at Harwich. At Ramsay's request, these surface forces were augmented by six naval Swordfish torpedo planes. These obsolescent biplanes were moved to an RAF fighter field at Manston, near Dover, and placed under joint RAF-navy command. The minelayers sowed new fields off the French coast, but Ruge's forces discovered and swept them just before the heavy ships passed through. Because of the continuing threat represented by the German battleship *Tirpitz*—which had been moved north to Trondheim in mid-January and was thus ideally situated to attack Soviet-bound convoys—and the Admiralty's quite logical unwillingness to subject an already badly stretched fleet to the risk of German air attack, the British did not shift any major units based at Scapa Flow. Such concern would have been heightened by the recent destruction of the capital ships *Repulse* and *Prince of Wales*. Fast, modern naval aircraft, manned by well-trained Imperial Japanese Navy crews, had taken less than two hours to sink two of the Royal Navy's most powerful ships.

In essence, therefore, it was the RAF, strongly resenting any diversion of resources from its strategic-bombing mission, that had the primary obligation to detect any movement of the German squadron, and that would play the most important role in stopping it if it did move. The Royal Navy's role was effectively to act as the goalkeeper: to provide what force it could to prevent the enemy ships from passing through the narrow portion of the Channel, by which time any breakout would be more than half completed. No one person was in charge of British defenses; indeed, it would have been hard to divide responsibility better if that had been the intention.

The breakout, which the Germans code-named Operation Cerberus, began on the evening of February 11. Just as the ships were about to put to sea, a major RAF bombing raid began. The Germans were extraordinarily lucky: Not only did the bombs cause no damage to the ships, but, more important, the returning bomber crews confirmed that they were still in harbor, presumably for the night. At 10:45 P.M., the three heavy ships and six escorting destroyers cleared the Brest breakwater and headed into the Atlantic, before entering the English Channel.

Already off Cherbourg by 6:30 A.M., still in the dark, the squadron was joined by an additional escort of E-boats, which would be relieved at intervals throughout the day. About an hour later, the first of the escorting fighter aircraft, Messerschmitt Bf 109s and 110s and Focke-Wulf 190s, arrived.

General Adolf Galland, Germany's veteran fighter leader, had meticulously prepared air cover for the operation. More than 250 day and night fighters, controlled by flexible, on-the-spot command arrangements and supported by sophisticated communications, were dedicated to the naval squadron's safety. Some sixteen fighters would be over the warships at any one time, keeping as low as possible to avoid detection by British radar. Other aircraft were kept on immediate alert at various bases along the French coast. Crucial to the whole plan were Luftwaffe pilots and communications specialists aboard the ships, in constant contact with Galland's command post ashore, to give local direction to the fighter effort.

The German air-defense plan also involved secret and relatively untried electronic countermeasures designed to jam British radar. Beginning several weeks before the breakout, in order to reduce suspicion, the interference gradually increased so that by early February it had become a daily phenomenon, which the RAF assumed was a result of atmospheric disturbances. These countermeasures greatly reduced British ability to detect the ships as they entered the narrow portion of the Channel.

As dawn broke over the German capital ships, at 8:20 A.M., Admiral Ciliax could not believe that he had gotten this far undetected. A number of factors had combined to frustrate early discovery, evidence either of German good fortune or poor British planning. First, with the assumption that no movement was likely that night, HMS *Sealion*—the lone submarine covering the entrance to Brest—had withdrawn to recharge her batteries. If the British air raid had not delayed the squadron's departure, the *Sealion* might well have reported its movement.

Enigma, normally such a reliable source of information on the movement of German surface vessels, also failed to provide timely intelligence. Traffic decrypted through February 10, while indicating that departure was probable, had given no precise indication of timing. Unexpected decoding delays then caused a backup so that signals received February 10 through 12 were not available for three crucial days, by which time the German ships were safe in their home ports. As noted earlier, vital human intelligence also never reached its proper destination or was disregarded.

Coastal Command's plan to detect any movement of the German fleet called for nightlong patrols along three lines: Brest to Ushant, that island to Le Havre, and Le Havre to Boulogne. On the night of February 11, the air-to-surface vessel (ASV) radar of two of the night patrols, never very reliable at the best of times, failed just at the moment the German squadron was passing the respective patrol lines. The third patrol was recalled due to weather conditions. By the time the various commands became aware that coverage of the western Channel had been seriously compromised, it was too late. Adding to British misfortunes, photoreconnaissance of Brest at dawn on February 12 was hampered by low clouds and thus unable to discover that the ships had departed.

Responsibility for air coverage of the Channel now shifted to Fighter Command's morning Spitfire patrols. The pilot of the first of these sorties caught sight of a number of small craft leaving Boulogne, but lowering clouds made visibility so bad that he returned home, assuming the ships he had faintly seen were a routine coastal convoy. The German squadron moved on, unseen, just below him. After this first patrol came two more pairs of Spitfires, one on routine reconnaissance and the other investigating extensive enemy fighter activity over the Channel. Both sorties spotted the enemy squadron, but neither fully understood its significance. Slavish adherence to radio silence meant that not until the planes landed, soon after 11:00 A.M., did Fighter Command realize that the German capital ships were not only at sea but already fast approaching the Strait of Dover.

About twenty minutes elapsed before the Spitfire reports had traveled up the chain of command to Fighter Command headquarters, thence to the Admiralty, and finally to Ramsay's command at Dover. The Fuller plans—calling for coordinated attacks by aircraft, surface vessels, and shore batteries, all well supported by the RAF's 550 available fighters—were then finally set in motion.

Meanwhile, in spite of effective enemy jamming, as early as 9:30 A.M. British coastal radar had picked up plots of circling aircraft near the French coast and moving slowly eastward. Amazingly, in view of the known possibility of a breakout, no alarm was sounded. It was not until after 10:00 A.M. that fast-moving, large radar echoes, surrounded by smaller, faster blips, provided unmistakable evidence that major surface vessels with substantial fighter escorts were moving up the Channel. Then difficulties finding a secure telephone delayed getting this information to Ramsay's Dover command for another forty minutes. Even so, despite the lack of any official confirmation, Ramsay alerted his scanty surface forces and the six Swordfish at Manston, informed the army-manned shore batteries at Dover, and—without authority to give orders to the RAF—suggested that Coastal Command bring its own torpedo bombers to readiness.

Even so, it was past noon on February 12 before Admiral Ciliax first heard the sound of British gunfire as shore batteries engaged his ships in the narrowest part of the Channel, between Dover and Calais. The firing was uneven, impeded by reduced visibility and German evasive action. Thirty-three rounds were fired, but there were no hits.

Surface forces most immediately available to Ramsay were the five motor torpedo boats based at Dover, commanded by Lieutenant Commander E. N. Pumphrey. He left harbor just before noon. With the uncooperative Germans appearing from nowhere in broad daylight, Pumphrey hastily abandoned complex plans for a coordinated night attack by his MTBs and the Manston Swordfish. Once clear of the narrow waters, Ciliax had increased speed to close to thirty knots, so that Pumphrey had to coax the maximum performance from his little fleet. The first enemy sighting was the E-boat escort and then, as the German smoke screen momentarily cleared, the massive gray shapes of the three heavy ships.

With one of his boats already out of action from engine failure due to the high-speed chase, Pumphrey determined he would be unable to pass ahead of the enemy and must attack through the E-boat screen. Torpedoes were fired at a range of between 4,000 and 5,000 yards, but because of weapon malfunctions and Ciliax's evasive maneuvers, none found their mark. Then, assisted by two accompanying motor gunboats that laid a protective smoke screen of their own, all the MTBs withdrew to Dover, suffering superficial damage and no casualties. Meanwhile, the three MTBs from Ramsgate had also put to sea, but they never caught up with the Germans.

At the Manston RAF base, Lieutenant Commander Eugene Esmonde, commanding the six Swordfish torpedo bombers of the Royal Navy's 825 Squadron, had previously been told to prepare his planes for a night strike as the German ships passed by Dover. Such an attack, though dangerous, was within the elderly biplanes' capabilities. Indeed, British naval aviators were given extensive training in night torpedo attacks, despite their difficulty, because of the operational limitations of their aircraft. On the other hand, a daylight attack against heavily armed battle cruisers with substantial fighter cover would be extraordinarily risky. Esmonde, however, was a particularly experienced pilot. It was he who had led the final and successful air attack on the *Bismarck,* an operation for which he had recently been decorated.

Just before noon, a message from Ramsay at Dover informed Esmonde that the *Scharnhorst* and *Gneisenau* were approaching the straits. At the same time, the alert reached the five RAF fighter squadrons designated to escort the Swordfish, but this was amid great confusion because the officer with the Fuller plans had locked them in his safe and gone on leave. Adding to the chaos was incorrect information that the German ships were traveling at only twenty-one knots.

Even so, it would take the Swordfish, flying at ninety knots, their maximum speed when armed with a torpedo and carrying a crew of three, a dangerously long time to catch the enemy as he headed eastward. Told that some of the fighter escort might be late, Esmonde decided to take off at 12:20 P.M. and circle over the coast for a few minutes while awaiting them. Just as he was about to start his engine, he was told that the enemy's speed was now estimated to be twenty-seven knots. Haste was therefore essential. Over the coast five minutes later, with still no sign of his escort, Esmonde was becoming desperate when at last ten Spitfires appeared.

The fighters, from the RAF's 72 Squadron, were the only ones to rendezvous with Esmonde that day. The pilots, told only to escort some Swordfish, knew nothing of this engagement going on below in the Channel. Esmonde circled for a few more minutes; then, realizing there would be no more escorts, he dropped down to fifty feet to cover the twenty-three miles separating his planes from the enemy ships. The weather was closing in, and a lowering cloud base and poor visibility hampered coordination between the Swordfish and their escorting Spitfires, already complicated by the big difference in the speeds of the two aircraft. Moreover, the lack of radar in any of his planes meant that Esmonde could not use the clouds as cover (as he had during his 1941 attack on the *Bismarck*) without running an unacceptable risk of losing his targets.

The planes soon came into contact with the Luftwaffe screen. Outnumbered and, in the case of the Fw 190s, outclassed, the Spitfires fought valiantly but could not prevent the German fighters from attacking the Swordfish. Esmonde's planes, now committed to their torpedo runs, made easy targets as they flew straight and level just above the waves.

Soon they were over the E-boat and destroyer screen and had to face intense fire from the entire German fleet. The battle cruisers' eleven-inch guns aimed their heavy projectiles into the sea ahead of the Swordfish, creating lethal walls of water through which the badly damaged craft had to fly. The tail of Esmonde's aircraft was on fire and half his lower wing shot away. Finally a German fighter blew away his top wing, and his plane, out of control, crashed into the sea—though not before he dropped a torpedo aimed at the *Scharnhorst*. However, it did not strike its target.

So died Eugene Esmonde, who had flown against the Germans in France and Norway, had led the first torpedo attack on the *Bismarck,* and had survived the sinking of the *Ark Royal.* A citizen of the Irish Republic, he had owed no allegiance to Britain or to its king. His mother received his posthumous Victoria Cross at a Buckingham Palace investiture on St. Patrick's Day.

As the second plane passed over the destroyer screen, its gunner was killed by an enemy fighter. Sublieutenant Edgar Lee, the observer, tried to take over the gun but was unable to move the gunner's body. His pilot, Sublieutenant Brian Rose, managed to drop his torpedo about 1,200 yards from the *Prinz Eugen,* despite severe wounds from shell splinters. His engine failing and his main tank losing fuel rapidly as a result of cannonfire, he turned away astern of the enemy ships before crashing into the sea some 500 yards beyond the screen. Lee managed to get Rose out of the plane and into a life raft, from which they were later rescued.

The third Swordfish—its three crew members all wounded, its engine missing two cylinders, and its top wing on fire—astonishingly attempted two attacks. Although injuries caused the pilot, Sublieutenant C. M. Kingsmill, to abandon his first run on the *Scharnhorst,* he recovered and was able to alter course and aim his torpedo at the *Prinz Eugen* before crashing into the sea.

British MTBs rescued all three crewmen. The remaining three Swordfish were last seen attacking against continuous heavy ship and air defense. Nothing more is known of them; none of the nine crewmen survived.

The attack was over at 12:45 P.M., twenty minutes after Esmonde's planes took off. None of the torpedoes had found their targets. Only five of the eighteen men who set out survived, three of them badly wounded. Fifteen minutes later, two more Spitfire squadrons arrived over the scene, having taken off too late or lost their way. By then, that phase of the battle was over.

More than an hour and a half after the abortive Swordfish attack, Ciliax received his first setback. At 2:30 P.M., a heavy shock from an underwater explosion rattled the *Scharnhorst.* Her lights fading slowly, the ship gradually came to a standstill as the *Gneisenau* and *Prinz Eugen* roared past. The *Scharnhorst* had hit a mine laid by Bomber Command. In such an event, the breakout plan called for Ciliax to transfer his flag, together with his Luftwaffe liaison team, to an attendant destroyer. Jumping onto the heaving deck of the escort vessel, the admiral and his staff raced off in pursuit of the rest of his squadron. The crew of the *Scharnhorst* rapidly repaired the damage, and the ship was soon able to resume full speed. She overtook the other ships before long, though Ciliax would not return to the *Scharnhorst*'s deck until dawn on February 13.

Six destroyers commanded by Captain C. T. M. Pizey now represented the Royal Navy's last hope of intercepting the Germans. In the words of a survivor, they were "ancient destroyers, really only junk for the scrapyard, on their way to meet the most powerful and modern naval squadron of all." Already at sea in exercises off Harwich, Pizey's squadron set course at noon, believing there was ample time to intercept the Germans, whose speed was assumed to be only twenty knots. Learning at 1:00 P.M. that the enemy was actually making twenty-eight knots now, Pizey realized that he would be unable to catch the ships unless he moved at full speed along the most direct route—which lay right through a known minefield. Shortly after the course alteration, one of the destroyers had to return to Harwich with engine trouble. From 1:30 P.M. on, the little fleet was shadowed by a German reconnaissance plane and subjected to several bombing attacks. RAF fighters detailed to escort Pizey's force failed to find it.

At about 3:15, when Pizey's destroyers were twenty-two miles west of the Hook of Holland, his radar picked up three large echoes some ten miles to the southeast. Deteriorating weather and particularly low visibility helped cover his approach as he turned on a course to intercept. Large numbers of aircraft from both sides were now appearing in and out of the clouds in the vicinity of the German squadron. Several German aircraft assumed Pizey's ships were friendly and fired their recognition signals, while some of the British planes mistook them for the Germans and attacked them.

Sighting the enemy at 3:42 P.M., Pizey immediately turned to attack. The three destroyers of the first division—the *Campbell, Vivacious,* and *Worcester*—approached to within just over a mile and a half, under a hail of fire from the German battle cruisers and destroyers, before the *Campbell* and *Vivacious* turned to launch their torpedoes at the *Gneisenau.* The *Worcester,* failing to see the *Campbell*'s turn, came in even closer, under heavier and more concentrated fire, before launching torpedoes at the same target. By this time the battle cruiser was turning away, and all three sets of torpedoes missed. Hit in both boiler rooms, the *Worcester* came to a standstill right under the muzzles of the enemy guns.

The second division—the destroyers *Mackay* and *Whitshed*—attacked the *Prinz Eugen,* which in turn was taking radical evasive action to avoid bombing attacks. Neither ship's torpedoes found their target, and the two vessels then returned safely to Harwich.

A further decrease in visibility helped shield the *Campbell* and *Vivacious* as they disengaged from the enemy, exchanging gunfire with some of the escorting destroyers. As they withdrew, they came upon the *Worcester* drifting in the water, badly flooded and on fire. The *Campbell* stopped to pick up survivors and tried to take the damaged ship in tow, while hampered by attacks from friendly as well as hostile aircraft. By this time, however, the *Worcester* had managed to raise steam in one boiler. Pizey took his two undamaged ships back to Harwich to replenish their ammunition. The *Worcester* limped home, arriving in port at dawn the following day.

While Pizey's destroyers were making their gallant but abortive torpedo attacks, the RAF was also throwing most of its available strength into attempts to halt Ciliax. His chief of staff, Captain H. J. Reinecke, later recalled that the British seemed to be using anything with a propeller that could carry bombs. These air attacks lasted from about 2:45 to 6:15 P.M. Although 242 Bomber Command aircraft and 28 torpedo bombers of Coastal Command took part, escorted by 398 fighters, only 39 bombers and 16 torpedo bombers were able to locate the enemy. By early afternoon, pilots were reporting ceilings of 1,000 feet or less and visibility of under 1,000 yards, conditions that contributed greatly to the difficulty of finding and attacking the German squadron. As visibility worsened, aircraft that were able to spot the enemy tried to gain enough height to make effective attacks, only to find themselves in the clouds, unable to see their targets. Armor-piercing bombs designed to be dropped from a high altitude had little effect on the heavily armored war-ships when released below the cloud base.

Several factors other than weather also accounted for the RAF's failure to mount an effective attack: lack of training in antishipping work, delays in getting the bomber force airborne, and communications errors. In addition, many of the bomber crews had not been told the importance of the targets they were going after—indeed, what the targets actually were. Those who did find the enemy attacked "incessantly and with tenacity," according to General Galland. However, only two of the smaller German escort vessels suffered any damage. The torpedo bombers fared no better: Thirteen torpedoes were dropped but no hits resulted. Summarizing the air attacks after the event, Galland noted that the RAF had been sent into action without sufficient plan-ning, a clear concept of the attack, or systematic tactics. The obsessive secrecy that surrounded the Fuller plans certainly had a price.

As dusk fell and the air attacks gradually petered out, Ciliax and his staff began to relax for the first time since they had left Brest. The peaceful inter-lude was brief. At about 8:00 P.M., while just north of Vlieland, the *Gneisenau* hit a mine. Damage was only slight, however, and she was able to continue in the company of the *Prinz Eugen,* with only a slight reduction in speed.

Worse damage occurred an hour and a half later, when a massive underwa-ter shock indicated that the *Scharnhorst* had struck a second mine, which in-flicted more serious damage than did the first. With her engines stopped, the huge vessel drifted in the dark waters off the Dutch coast. It took nearly an hour for her crew to get two of her three engines working, and then she was able to limp along at only twelve knots, with her fire-control apparatus and important navigational equipment out of order and over 1,000 tons of water in her bilges. Unfortunately for the British, they had lost contact with the en-emy squadron and, in any event, had exhausted their available resources. As dawn broke and the German coast came in sight, Ciliax and his staff rejoined the *Scharnhorst* as she came slowly into Wilhelmshaven; at about the same time, the *Gneisenau* and *Prinz Eugen* entered the mouth of the Elbe.

In the eyes of the admiral and his subordinates, the operation appeared a complete success. German casualties were minor, while it was estimated that the British had suffered a badly damaged destroyer (the *Worcester*) and lost over sixty aircraft. Captain Reinecke recalled, "We knew we had twisted the lion's tail, and that the British didn't like it."

Indeed, the British did not like it. The writer Harold Nicolson, a member of Parliament, recorded in his diary that people were more distressed about the Germans' exploit than they were about the loss of Singapore two days later. Responding to criticism in the House of Commons, Prime Minister Winston Churchill took the position that although the breakout was a tactical success for the enemy, the abandonment of Brest by the German capital ships represented a strategic gain for the British. Subsequent events largely confirmed this analysis, but the *Times* refused to accept it, instead questioning whether a chance had been missed to send something like a quarter of the German navy to the bottom of the Channel, "where its effectiveness in the battle of the Atlantic would need no dialectical estimation."

As frequently happens when a British government has to explain an embarrassing event, an eminent jurist was asked to convene a Board of Enquiry. The resulting report by a High Court judge, A. T. Bucknill, implied that the main blame for the fiasco lay with the Germans, for choosing to make the passage by daylight when they were expected at night. The report also concluded that the forces available to the British were, even with adequate warning, insufficient to cripple the German squadron. In fact, any rational analysis would have determined that the chances of sinking the three ships in the Channel were remote. The sustained firepower of two British battleships and two cruisers with eight-inch guns had earlier proved insufficient to sink the *Bismarck,* which was finally scuttled. The *Scharnhorst* and *Gneisenau* were horses from the same design and construction stable. As for British bombers, their crews were trained to bomb cities at night from high altitude, not fast-moving ships at sea—unlike the specially trained Japanese crews who had made the lethal attack on the *Repulse* and *Prince of Wales* off Malaya.

Nowhere did the report seriously question the divided-command arrangements, under which the navy could only suggest to the air force that it bring its planes into readiness. But as Stephen Roskill pointed out after the war in his official history, "the organization for the control of all the various sea and land forces involved did not prove adequate to the occasion. . . . A specially created command was essential to the efficient and flexible control of all our forces."

Although the Bucknill Report covered the immediate and obvious reasons for the debacle of February 12, 1942, it failed to deal with more fundamental historical causes. It wasn't long before the outspoken admiral of the fleet, Sir Roger Keyes, drew attention to the more basic structural flaws that had permitted the German success. The event, he said, was a cruel humiliation that emphasized the folly of those who twenty-four years earlier had deprived the navy of its large and highly efficient air service and who still tolerated dual control of naval air power. "Aviation," said Keyes, "is of vital importance to the Navy. . . . There should be no dual responsibilities. . . . The Navy must be left free to develop, train, and control the naval air service it needs." The

Channel dash did indeed have at least one positive impact: From 1942 onward, the Fleet Air Arm was largely reequipped, mostly with American-made aircraft.

As it turned out, Churchill's assessment was probably right: The passage of the enemy battle squadron, though a tactical success, resulted in a strategic gain for the British. Back in their home waters, where the Royal Navy had always preferred to contain a German fleet, the three ships proved to be much less of a threat than they had been on the French Atlantic coast.

As early as the night of February 26–27, an RAF bomber raid inflicted heavy damage on the *Gneisenau,* which was subsequently withdrawn from service. Scuttled at the end of the war to block the approaches to the harbor at Kiel, she was later used as scrap steel by the Soviets.

The *Scharnhorst* eventually reached Norway, where she joined the battleship *Tirpitz* and remained a threat to convoys to the Soviet Union. On December 26, 1943, she was sunk by the Royal Navy's battleship *Duke of York* during the Battle of the North Cape, the last pure gunnery duel between battleships. It took the *Duke of York* and her consorts more than two hours to sink the German vessel, during which time she survived direct hits from over a dozen fourteen-inch shells, many eight-inch and six-inch salvoes, and some eleven torpedoes. Only 36 of her crew of nearly 2,000 were saved.

On her way to Trondheim, the *Prinz Eugen* was torpedoed by a British submarine. She managed to return to Kiel and, following repairs, spent the rest of the war in German waters, lending gunnery support to the German army against the Soviets in 1945. Ceded to the U.S. Navy at the end of the war, the *Prinz Eugen* went to San Diego; on board was the same Captain Reinecke who had helped Admiral Ciliax manage the breakout four years earlier. She was subsequently used as a target during atomic-bomb tests at Bikini Atoll.

What happened on February 12, 1942, can be summarized as follows: For thirty years, the admirals respectively responsible for British and German naval strategy had assumed it would be impossible for a German battle fleet to pass through the English Channel. It took an Adolf Hitler, essentially a land person, to challenge that assumption, while an accumulation of British political and strategic errors created the circumstances that permitted the challenge to succeed. The Royal Air Force had some of the tools but few of the skills needed to stop the German breakout. The Royal Navy had most of the skills but few of the tools; more important, it lacked the command authority to conduct a unified defense of Britain's vital maritime approaches.

PATROLLING GUADALCANAL

WILLIAM H. WHYTE

At the beginning of June 1942, with the American carrier victory at Midway, the balance in the Pacific war shifted (though not as abruptly perhaps as some historians would have it). The Japanese bite-and-hold strategy, which would end with the invasion of the Hawaian Islands and the isolation of Australia, had been checked but not yet fatally so. Their advance had depended on a methodical island-hopping timetable but now it was the turn of the Americans to counter with an island-hopping strategy of their own.

It began, somewhat uncertainly, with the August 7 landing by U.S. Marines on Guadalcanal, an island in the Solomons that controlled the sea lines of communication between the United States and Australia. The six-months' struggle may have been small by the standards of the war on the Russian front, but it had, as has been so often (and rightly) pointed out, an epic quality—a struggle, charged with racial hatred, not only between determined equals but against the jungle. In the end it was the Americans who came off with the advantage, but barely. Hunger, disease, and a debilitating sense of isolation would do in the Japanese as surely as they had the American defenders in the Bataan jungle.

One of the marines who fought through the entire campaign was a 1939 Princeton graduate named William H. Whyte (who would be known in the future for his keen observations of American social mores). He acted as the intelligence officer for Lieutenant Colonel William N. McKelvy, a hard-drinking old-line professional marine who commanded the Third Battalion, First Marine Division. Whyte here describes some of the everyday engagements that characterized the Guadalcanal fighting as much as the bigger battles, and gives a memorable picture of a tough enemy whose morale showed signs of cracking. It was October, a time when the campaign was still far from decided, though beginning to tilt in favor of the Americans.

William H. Whyte left Guadalcanal at the end of the campaign with a serious case of malaria that lingered for years. He spent the rest of the war lecturing and writing at the United States Marine Corps Staff and Command School at Quantico, Virginia, on the fighting qualities of the Japanese soldier. On the basis of the stories he had written in the *Marine Corps Gazette,* he was hired by *Fortune* magazine after the war ended. Whyte, who died in 1998, was the author of the classic study of corporate conformity, *The Organization Man.* This account of his Guadalcanal experiences is taken from his final book, *A Time of War.*

WE WERE WELL INTO THE GUADALCANAL CAMPAIGN AND STILL we had no decent maps. This didn't deeply concern McKelvy because he couldn't read maps anyway. But he did love a touch of showmanship, and when he discovered that one of our men, Corporal Wike, was a pretty fair draftsman, he decided to have some fun.

I instructed Wike to draw up a battalion map using all his skills at lettering. It was a handsome affair, completed in a tent at night by the light of an acetylene lamp, full of redundant details. The lettering was especially impressive. "North Coast of Guadalcanal-Lunga Area," it said. "Third Battalion, First Marines, Lt. Col. William N. McKelvy commanding."

McKelvy loved it and he would drag me along with him on visits to other units, ostensibly to inspect their maps. Our visit to his best pal, Colonel Lenard Cresswell, commanding the First Battalion, was a case in point.

"Where are your battalion maps, Charlie?" McKelvy asked.

"Battalion maps?"

"Charlie, you should have a battalion map like this," at which point he signaled me, the straight man in this performance, to reach into the aluminum container I happened to be carrying and unroll Corporal Wike's work of art. Cresswell and all the others would be suitably impressed. McKelvy, of course, would then stride away, shaking his head in feigned disbelief at the map-making ignorance of his fellow battalion commanders.

McKelvy spent hours looking at the maps we collected as the campaign wore on, though most of them were fairly useless. He would brood over possibilities these maps seemed to suggest to him. It was another rare performance—the great American strategist making his plans; a foeman worthy of the steel of those Japanese strategists across the river, who were no doubt studying their own maps.

During the lull following the September 12 Battle of Edson's Ridge, we began serious efforts to improve our knowledge of Japanese positions and Japanese morale through sophisticated patrolling beyond our perimeter. Patrolling heretofore had not been one of our strengths. A few days after we landed, a captured Japanese sailor told us the whereabouts of a number of Japanese soldiers and sailors and said they might be ready to surrender. Our division intelligence officer, Lieutenant Colonel Frank Goettge, decided he would lead a twenty-five-man patrol to locate this unhappy pocket of Japanese fighting men. He and his party, which included the surrendered sailor, left by boat the night of August 12. The minute they stepped ashore, Goettge was killed by enemy fire—as was the Japanese sailor. Except for two or three survivors, the rest of the patrol was wiped out as well.

The Japanese sailor probably told us the truth, as far as he knew it. The fact is, Japanese prisoners—they were enlisted men, never officers—were usually in a state of shock, trembling and sometimes making hand gestures, pleading to be killed. One of my jobs was to take the captured soldiers up to division headquarters, where they would be interviewed by Major Edmund J. Buckley, a former missionary fluent in Japanese and a true expert. "The war is over for you," he would say. "The lieutenant here tells me you have fought well." That was always well-received and had an enormous effect on the prisoner. Buckley would continue with soothing words, and soon the prisoner would begin telling us what he knew.

The prisoners were confined to an enclosure near the field hospital. The sign said Camp Tojo, or something very much like it. The sergeant in charge was a jolly fellow, and he became quite friendly with his guests. He gave his prisoners considerable freedom. One morning, I was awakened by a touch on the shoulder and found a Japanese soldier staring at me. "My God," I thought to myself, "they've broken through." But, of course, they had not; the Japanese was a prisoner, and he simply wanted to collect my laundry to be cleaned at the Tojo Laundry.

Generally, we treated the prisoners with kindness. Occasionally, though, they were shot, much to the chagrin of those who had hoped to interview them. Invariably, these killings were committed by rear-echelon troops seeking to demonstrate misplaced valor.

Division commander Major General Alexander A. Vandegrift became so

impatient with what he perceived to be our lack of patrolling skills that he assigned Lieutenant Colonel William J. Whaling, executive officer of the Fifth
Marines, to form a special unit of men for scouting and sniping. Most of his
men had been hunters in civilian life, and many of them became serious characters in the great Marine Corps tradition.

I don't recall Whaling's operation having much effect on us. We went
ahead with patrolling, learning our lessons along the way. Jungle patrols were
damn hard work. I described this situation in a letter to Dad [William Whyte
Sr.] and Margaret [Whyte's stepmother]:

> When the battle dies down there is ceaseless patrol activity in the jungle—
> a sort of no-man's land. The terrain is fascinating—steep grass-covered coral
> ridges, deep ravines you have to climb down hanging onto vines like a monkey
> to keep from falling. The trees are tremendous—giant dilo trees as high as 180
> feet and banyan and eucalyptus trees almost as large.
>
> You have no idea of how tiring a patrol is. The heat is terrific and because of
> security measures you're loaded down with ammunition, grenades, emergency
> rations, machetes, etc. We usually carry two weapons, one of them a Thompson
> or Reising submachine gun.
>
> Trying to get up the slippery banks of the many mountain-fed streams (tor-
> rents after a rain and it always rains in the mountains) is the worst part as you
> have to keep your weapons out of the mud.
>
> Last but not least are our jungle friends—the Nips. You have to watch every
> clump of bushes for snipers and machine guns. You also have to listen to the birds
> and distinguish between the real McCoy and the phony bird calls the Japs use.
>
> We ran into a bunch of Japs some time ago. I had a patrol of six and myself.
> Our mission was to locate the Jap positions as our offensive began at dawn the
> next day. We spotted one area in front of a 75mm gun a friend of mine had
> taken the breechblock out of earlier (while the Japs slept). His patrol was
> pumping tommy guns at them, so we swung north and went through the jun-
> gle up the beach and went along the ridges to the north, finding two Jap 37mm
> guns emplaced and camouflaged at a bend in the road. As the gun crew was
> obligingly sleeping or eating somewhere we tinkered with the guns with the
> aid of a screwdriver until it would take a mechanical genius to put them back
> together again (still have a breechblock as a souvenir).
>
> We then skirted the coral formations (caves, etc.) along the shore until I
> spotted what appeared to be a Marine standing up behind a sort of coral "igloo"
> with a gun port in it about 20 yards away. Then I heard the Jap birdcall signal
> (one long note, one short) and the Marine turned around and saw me. For a Ma-

rine he looked very, very Japanese. I shot at him with my .45, missing him quite completely. I ducked for cover (as my Nipponese was likewise doing) and the rest of the patrol flopped down into firing positions behind logs, trees, etc.

We had evidently surprised the gun crews of the 37mm, for they started rushing around for cover by the little coral "igloos." Fortunately all three men on our left had Thompsons and three Japs who tore across for cover were literally torn to shreds. The rest of the Japs started shooting (at what I don't know as their shots came nowhere near us) and jabbering quite excitedly. A couple stuck their heads up to see what was going on. The man on my right got one and I got the other.

Finally all shooting stopped but a machine gun to our left opened up. As we were about ¾ of a mile away, we knew that an exit would not be injudicious. We threw our grenades and then withdrew one by one, the remaining men increasing their fire to make it sound like we were being reinforced.

The Japs on our left must have thought we were a small army, as they never bothered us. We must have sounded like one! Six men, three Thompson submachine guns, three Reising submachine guns, five rifles, three .45 caliber pistols plus a weird assortment of grenades, knives, and wire to fix up booby traps. The men were all ready to go and get the Jap headquarters and were grinning broadly as they pulled out their knives and looked at me as if to ask could they rush in. As later events proved, the place was honeycombed with machine-gun positions so I still believe discretion is the better part of valor!

I didn't mention in my letter home that we did lose one of our men, Pfc Dix, to enemy fire during our withdrawal.

We had two patrols that day. The second was led by my old friend from officers candidate school, Harold "Ramrod" Taylor. He commanded our battalion's mortar platoon, and for days he and the men in their observation post had been looking in vain for some Japanese 37s that were hurling shells at our position. But all they could see were the white cockatoos endlessly fluttering above the foliage that screened us from the enemy positions.

Taylor marched into McKelvy's tent and asked permission to take a patrol out there and destroy the guns. It seemed preposterous—the enemy was solidly entrenched on the steep ridges. There was undoubtedly a heavy screen of forward observers and snipers, not to mention close infantry support of the gun positions. However, McKelvy, like everyone else, was sick of the shelling, so at last he gave in to Taylor's request.

Ramrod asked but one thing—twenty-four hours to lay his plans. He was a perfectionist, and he wanted to make this patrol as perfect as he could. He spent the rest of the day with me, the intelligence officer, minutely examining a recent aerial strip of the territory across the Matanikau River. Yet even with the use of stereo glasses there was no clue to any enemy activity. Shell holes, native tracks, Melanesian huts, yes—but no telltale blast-flattened grass or fresh trails. Witn no indications to go on, the two of us could only examine the enemy capabilities, and by making a study of the terrain, list them in order of probability. We even made a mud castle showing what we knew of the Japanese positions on the other side of the river.

Since the shells were high-velocity 37s, all deeply defiladed (deeply sloped) places could be eliminated. What we were looking for were spots with moderate defilade and covered ravines leading to them for supply routes. We finally picked five locations that seemed to fulfill our requirements and numbered them on the photos. It was now midafternoon, time for the Japanese gunners to begin throwing their usual four o'clock salvos at the ridges. By listening carefully to this gunfire, we were able to eliminate two of our locations as being too far south.

So now we had three possible locations. We then determined a route that would allow Taylor to pierce the enemy screen of observers and snipers, bypass strongpoints, and reach our target locations under cover. We also figured out a primary and alternate route to get the hell out of there if things went wrong.

We set out at the same time (I described the results for my patrol in my letter home). Taylor and his little group of volunteers—everybody wanted to go with Taylor—cautiously paddled across the river in a rubber boat at dawn, silently alighted on the west bank, and crept slowly through the dense canebrake. Wordlessly, the men followed in file behind Taylor as he skirted along the wooden slopes of a ravine that he knew would lead him near Location No. 1. At length he reached it, took out his aerial photograph, checked it to make sure of just where he was, and then sent his first scout forward to reconnoiter the spot.

The scout crawled slowly up the little gully until he had come almost to the top, but looking around he saw no gun—only a pile of dried grass. It was then that a small breeze stirred and he caught the sickly muskish odor of sweat and Japanese perfume. Crawling up the grass pile, he brushed some grass away—and stared straight into the muzzle of a Japanese 37.

He summoned the rest of the patrol, and they came forward immediately. It was at that crucial moment they heard the sharp barking of a dog. To their horror Taylor and his men peered down into a ravine and saw that the barking was coming from a mean-looking cur who was frantically trying to awaken his Japanese masters who were peacefully sleeping in their bivouac at the bottom of the ravine.

Determined to profit from this display of typical Japanese overconfidence, Taylor told his men to sit tight at Location No. 1 while he lone-wolfed it to Location No. 2. Arriving there he was greeted with the sight of another 37, visible at close range through its camouflage. As he approached the gun, Ramrod looked down into the ravine at a group of native huts and saw four Japanese soldiers watching his every move. Taylor hesitated for a moment and then waved at them cordially. Just as cordially, the Japanese waved back. As they lazily watched him, Taylor calmly removed the vital parts of the gun's breechblock, stemming his instinctive desire to shoot and run. The gun dismantled, he waved again to his new friends and walked back slowly along the ridge, hunching over to make himself as diminutive as possible.

Reunited with his men, he tarried only long enough to leave a calling card—a message of greeting—in the gun barrel. He and his men followed the main withdrawal route and re-entered our lines, mission accomplished.

Two days later, McKelvy asked that we repeat our patrols, with Taylor following the same route. This was an incredibly stupid mistake.

We pushed off before dawn, again by rubber boat. Ramrod's group turned left and began climbing the steep ridge. I turned right with my patrol, heading on a different route for Point Cruz. Ramrod and I had agreed there was a strong chance that there were some high-ranking Japanese officers there. Capturing them would be a great coup.

Eventually, we came upon a sudden opening in the thicket, and there, just in front of us, stood a dozen Japanese soldiers. They had been cooking something over a fire, and they were as surprised to see us as we were surprised to see them. We had the drop on them and opened up with everything we had. Both sides fired; both sides missed.

My men were not all for rushing forward to capture or kill these soldiers. Instead, we opted for discretion, moving across the sandbar to the safety of our own positions. I was taken to see "Red Mike" Edson, a colonel commanding the Fifth Marines, who was readying his men for an attack. I told him what I had seen and emphasized the dangers of his Point Cruz position.

"Thank you," Edson said. "You've had a hard day, lieutenant, so why not relax a little and let me carry on and run the regiment." It was about then that I shuddered. You never can help shuddering, just a little, when you've done something like this. I had volunteered, and I was lucky.

Not so Ramrod. When we were fighting our way out of Point Cruz, we thought we heard some whistling noises, maybe signals from Taylor. They were shots, and some of them must have killed my friend.

We learned later that the Japanese had been waiting for Taylor's patrol at

Location No. 1. When they attacked, Taylor turned to his men and told them to run for the river while he held off the Japanese. They refused. He ordered them to leave. Reluctantly they left him and headed for home. From the sound of the heavy firing it was obvious that Taylor was preventing the Japanese from making any kind of pursuit. About the time his men reached our lines, the firing stopped. It meant one thing—Taylor was dead.

We mourned his loss. We berated our complicity in going along with McKelvy's insistence of retracing the route of Taylor's first patrol. In the end, we insisted McKelvy put Ramrod in for a Navy Cross. He didn't want to—he never sought recognition for any of his men—but this time we refused to back down. Ramrod Taylor received a Navy Cross (and when the battle was over and we were headed home, so did Bill McKelvy).

Through these combat patrols (and the interviews with prisoners captured during them) we compiled some helpful information about our enemy. Colonel Clifton B. Cates, our regimental commander, put a lot of it together in an intelligence report dated September 6, 1942.

[Japanese officers] all carried sabers and automatic pistols of various makes, ranging in caliber from .25 to .38. The Nambu automatic pistol (model 1925), cal. 7mm, was found on several officers. The 8mm cal. of the same make was carried by many of the noncommissioned officers.

The individual soldier carried two types of rifle—one . . . the model 1905 and the other, the model 1919 of the same make. [The standard Japanese rifles of WWII were the Ariska Model 38 (1905) 6.5mm and Model 99 (1939) 7.7mm.] Bayonets are carried by every soldier and are very sharp, and with a hooked ring to catch opponent's blade. In hand-to-hand fighting, it was noted they held their bayonets in their hands and used them as swords. They all carried hand grenades and used them frequently, but they had a very small bursting radius.

The Nambu light machine gun (cal. 7.7mm) was an effective weapon, and they used light and portable grenade throwers (model 1899) to considerable advantage.

In general, Cates said, the Japanese equipment is far inferior to ours in every respect. With the exception of their 7.7mm machine gun—the Nambu—their weapons look like our 1898 vintage. Cates might have added that the Marines who landed on Guadalcanal were still carrying the old bolt-action 1903 Springfield rifle, itself a pretty good carryback to 1898 vintage. When the Army troops relieved us, they carried the new semiautomatic M-1s, giving them, on paper at least, a lot more firepower. Our Reising submachine gun was a loser too. It was a flimsy weapon, constantly jamming and breaking down. Those of us who carried it popularly called it the "Rusting gun." We gave up on it early on, and thereafter trusted the old Thompson submachine gun to balance things out.

The pack carried by individual Japanese soldiers was always scrupulously clean. We found it contained camouflage nets for helmets and shoulders with twigs and grass woven into them; a three-piece set of cooking utensils; two or three cans of food, sweet cakes, bread, and rice; an extra pair of shoes, either sneakers or hobnailed; underclothes, socks, and toilet articles.

Almost every soldier carried a diary, something we did not allow on our side. Sometimes, we found, they carried opium. In some of the packs were small Japanese flags with writing scrawled on them. Each soldier carried a first-aid kit containing two sterile triangular bandages and two picric acid gauzes for burns. Officers and noncommissioned officers carried heavy leather dispatch cases, with notebooks and crude maps.

Their tactics, Cates reported, were puzzling. In the first fight, the Battle of the Tenaru, the Japanese relied on the surprise of a quick assault in large numbers and supporting fire from heavy and light machine guns and portable grenade throwers. Rather than keeping low to the sandpit, which closes the mouth of the Tenaru River, they charged standing straight up with small intervals between them. On receiving our fire, they continued to expose themselves with utter disregard for life. Those who were able to reach this side of the river were in great confusion and for the most part leaderless. The officers who led the advance across the sandbar were the first to be shot.

They showed a tendency to bunch up, so that sometimes three or four machine guns were placed so close together they were within bursting range of one of our heavy mortar shells. Five men were seen taking cover around the same tree. They were experts at camouflage, but their marksmanship was poor.

Reduced to desperate conditions, many Japanese lay among their own casualties, played dead, and when marines drew near rose up to throw hand grenades at them. Suicides were numerous when capture became evident. During hand-to-hand combat, the Japanese emitted wild yells and brandished their weapons fiercely.

✦

CATES NOTED SOMETHING we had found again and again—Japanese, close up, had what we found to be a distinctive odor. "You can actually smell a Jap at a good distance," is the way Cates put it (it is possible, I suppose, that they could smell us too). "They use some kind of powder which permeates the atmosphere and our men on the front lines can sometimes tell when they are near. The odor is a sweet sickening one, but it is perfume compared to a dead Jap [after] a few hours exposure to the hot sun." The smell, two days after the battle of the Tenaru, made a lot of us lose our lunches.

I took a stab at examining Japanese fighting skills, with some criticism of our own performance, after one of my patrols, and I put it down in writing (a copy of which is reproduced in Cates's unpublished manuscript).

General Estimate:

1. Most noticeable fact was—amazing lack of precautions taken for security. Patrols got within 15–20 yards of enemy groups and opened fire first. Enemy propensity for leaving guns unattended inexplicable. Either morale at such a state they don't give a damn, or else on basis of previous experience in Java and Malaya totally unprepared for enemy patrol activity. Evidently expected us to remain behind our barbed wire defenses, as had previous opponents.

Terrain ideal for use of large vine-covered trees as CPS [command posts]. High ground to south of beach as plenty of high knolls and ridges commanding all approaches to bivouac areas and gun positions. (Enemy does use birdcall warning system—one long, one short—enemy approaching but does not exploit it fully.)

2. Enemy tactics: Terrain superb for long range sniping. High ground descending steeply to river in vicinity of bend offers covered positions with FULL VIEW OF OUR LINES AND ACTIVITY BEHIND OUR LINES. Sniping could be done at range of 150–1,000 yards with an abundance of lucrative Marine targets always in sight. Yet, despite the fact the enemy was bivouacked in this area, there is no evidence of any sniping. Rather they evidently kept close to the caves they had constructed in the sides of the ravines.

NOTE: Observing from enemy territory, our camouflage and camouflage discipline is almost nonexistent. Enough activity and noise could be observed of our lines and of the ridges behind to keep a dozen enemy CPs snowed under sending dope in. If bush hides our bivouac areas, enough yelling and shouting is furnished to give away the position. Sandbag emplacements were very easy to spot and a continual flow of traffic over the ridges was always in evidence. Jeep drivers' racing of motors accurately designated the course of our roads. On the other hand, all enemy positions . . . were skillfully camouflaged with leaves and branches. However, the enemy nullifies the camouflage effect to a great extent by engaging in loud and excited jabbering back and forth when under fire.

3. Enemy morale: Low. Members of outposts probably physically weak and

suffering from hunger, and probably very unhappy about the whole thing. They made no effort to retrieve their dead comrades lying within 200 yards of them, nor did they take advantage of their excellent observation at the mouth of the Matanikau River to harass us with sniping.

We all believed we were beginning to win this crucial battle, but we still had a long way to go.

✦

McKELVY'S THIRD BATTALION fought in several important engagements during the campaign. Early in November, General Vandergrift commended McKelvy and the Third Battalion for "noteworthy performance of duty during the period October 9, 1942 to November 1, 1942."

THE DAY
THE *HORNET* SANK

ALVIN KERNAN

An equally intense naval struggle took place in the waters around Guadalcanal. Among the actions, as desperate as they were costly to both sides, was the Battle of Santa Cruz, on October 26, 1942. This time it was the Japanese who won on points, as it were. They sank one carrier that day, the *Hornet,* and damaged another, the *Enterprise*. But they lost a hundred planes, and with them, an elite group of naval aviators. The Americans could replace the ships, planes, and pilots; the Japanese, increasingly, could not, and it would prove the difference in the naval war.

Alvin Kernan was a nineteen-year-old petty officer on the *Hornet,* already a veteran of Midway, an "Airedale" whose job was to prepare carrier aircraft for strikes. He was in the ordnance shack, just below the flight deck where he could see nothing, when the first bomb struck, and a plane crashed suicidally into the ship: "A bright red flame came like an express train down the passageway, knocking everything and everybody flat." After several torpedo hits the great ship went dead in the water. Somehow Kernan managed to survive the next six hours and be rescued. After spending the rest of the war on various carriers, he went on to become director of humanities at Yale and dean of the Graduate School at Princeton. His harrowing account of the day the *Hornet* sank is one of the notable memoirs *MHQ* published in its continuing series, *Experience of War*. It is excerpted from Kernan's *Crossing the Line: A Bluejacket's World War II Odyssey*.

A LITTLE AFTER 0900, THE PUBLIC ADDRESS SYSTEM BROKE the quiet of the ship with an announcement from the bridge. "Enemy aircraft at fifty miles and closing." An unbelievably short time later we heard, "Stand by to repel attack by enemy aircraft," and almost instantly the five-inch guns located at the corners of the flight deck began firing—*bang-bang-bang*—in their heavy slow rhythm, not nearly fast enough it seemed to us. These battles developed speedily, and with the 5-inchers still firing, the old Oerlikon one-point-ones began going off with their much faster but still deliberate rhythm.

In the ordnance shack, just below the flight deck, we could see nothing, only listen, feel the vibrating steel deck, and slide back and forth with the steep turns of the ship that came in quick succession. When the new 20-millimeter guns spaced along the catwalks began their continuous rapid firing, we knew the attack had commenced and that the dive-bombers were coming down and the torpedo planes—for the Japanese still used them to deliver the big blows with deadly accuracy—were making their runs at water level. Someone had mounted a .30-caliber machine gun in a railing support just to starboard of the island, and when I heard it clattering away, I knew they must be close. A bomb went off with a great flat bang that shook the ship deep in her bowels where it had penetrated before the delay fuses—contact forward, inertia aft—fired. Then another, and the elevators jumped up in the air and came down, locked, with great bangs.

Then, just up the passageway, past the dive-bomber ready rooms, near the admiral's quarters, there was a huge explosion. A bright red flame came like an express train down the passageway, knocking everything and everybody flat. A Japanese plane, hit, had suicidally crashed the signal bridge and then ricocheted into and through the flight deck just forward of the area where we were sitting. Its bombs rolled around and did not go off, but its gas tanks had exploded. We got up and ran to the other, after, end of the passageway and by a ladder there up onto the flight deck at the after end of the island. There the one-point-one gun crews were down in a bloody mess. Their magazines had been stacked in a circle behind them, and bullets from a strafing plane had caused them to fire at knee level into the gun tubs.

We rushed back down the ladder and stood there hesitating whether to go back up on the flight deck or take our chance below. Two great heavy thuds raised and then dropped the entire ship, torpedoes going home one after another on the starboard side, below the waterline—the death wounds of the ship, though we didn't know it at the time. The *Hornet,* turning at a sharp angle, shook like a dog shaking off water and began to lose speed instantly and list to starboard, which was terrifying, for you were still alive only so long as the speed was up and the ship was answering. You sense it in the soles of your feet, and it began to feel noticeably different at once, sluggish and dull, the rhythm off, and then another delay-fused bomb went through the flight deck just aft, through the hangar deck, to explode with a sharp sound somewhere deep below, followed by an acrid smell and smoke curling up out of a surprisingly small hole. The rudder was now jammed, and as the ship began to turn in circles, all power was lost. The fire hoses stopped putting water on the fires that now were everywhere.

Fire was behind us, and the flight deck was too exposed, so we went down on the hangar deck, already listing sharply to starboard, with the edge of the deck in the seawater that was running into the midships elevator pit. I ran down a long ladder and skidded into the bulkhead, for the steel deck was covered with oil. The forward bulkhead of the hangar deck exploded and the motor and cockpit of a burning Japanese torpedo plane crashed through and fell into the forward elevator pit. Its bomb failed to explode, but its gasoline now caught fire and the deck around the wreck began to glow red.

It had already done tremendous damage when it crashed into the gun sponsons on the bow of the ship, probably after the pilot was killed while making his run on the port bow, or perhaps he was an early kamikaze, carried away with the sight of the enemy ship so close and filled with battle will to obliterate it. One of the compartments he hit on his way through the ship was a blanket storage, and his plane had set the blankets afire and scattered them burning and smoldering the length of the hangar deck. The navy had fine white blankets with blue bands—these were officers' blankets—and the smell of burning wool mixed with fuel oil remains my dominant sensory impression of the day.

The guns stopped firing. The first strike was over, but by now the ship was dead in the water, and you had to be careful, so steep was the angle of the hangar deck, not to slide on the oily surface out one of the openings and into the water on the starboard side where the torpedoes had hit below the waterline, flooding the compartments below. The island and bridge hung menacingly out on the starboard side, seeming about to topple over and take the ship with them. There was fire forward where the plane had crashed through, the deck was red with heat, and several bomb holes in the deck were pouring out smoke. Among the burning and smoldering blankets dotted about the deck were bodies, some terribly burned, others dismembered, some appearing unharmed. The burns were the worst to see, huge blisters oozing fluid, the tight charred smelly flesh, the member sometimes projecting as if straining for some final grotesque sexual act. A place not to linger, but there was now all-hands work to be done here.

Damage control managed to correct the list somewhat, but power and electricity were still gone, and firefighting had to go on by hand with buckets and a fire-retardant powder. The cruiser *Northampton* came up to tow the *Hornet,* sending over her steel towing cable to be attached to the anchor chain after the anchor was unshackled. The huge, water-filled ship actually began to move, until the cable broke on the *Northampton* end and dropped in the water. There was no power on the *Hornet* capstan to haul it in, so it was dropped.

A second attempt was made using a two-inch steel cable that was stowed in the well of the midships elevator pit of the *Hornet,* an ominously dark and slippery place by now, partly under water. This cable, hundreds of feet long and tremendously heavy, had to be uncoiled and passed, like some huge stiff greasy snake, by hand to the bow of the ship, where it was secured before being sent over to the *Northampton.* Everyone in the area was rounded up for this job, and we formed a solid line up the hangar deck, slipping and sliding, heaving in rhythm, trying to move the dead weight of this steel boa constrictor. From time to time the guns would go off again and everyone dropped the cable and took cover. But after a while we did manage to get the cable forward, and a boat from the cruiser picked up the end to begin towing preparations again.

No planes would ever land or take off from the *Hornet* again, and the air divisions, my own squadron included, provided free hands for the grim task of gathering the dead and wounded. I worked for a time on the flight deck helping to carry the injured crewmen from the gun mounts and the bridge to a corner on the high port side forward where the doctors had set up a hospital and rigged some awnings to protect the wounded from the brilliant sun that never stopped shining all day.

As I started back across the flight deck, the guns began firing again as a single dive-bomber made a run on us. I lay flat on the deck, covering as much of my body as possible with my tin hat, trying to work my way into it, and thinking for the first time that I was likely to die, and resenting it, feeling that at nineteen I really hadn't had a chance to do most of the things people do, and vowing to do them if I survived. From that moment to this, life has continued to seem a gift—overtime in a way—and all the more enjoyable for it.

The bomb missed, and I ran to shelter in a compartment in the island where hundreds of other sweating frightened men were huddled behind thin steel bulkheads. By now the ship felt terribly heavy. Power had not come back on and nothing worked any longer.

All this time the *Enterprise* had remained visible in the distance while hiding under a squall from the Japanese planes, but around noon she too came under attack. The antiaircraft shells made the sky black and the ship twisted and turned. In the end she caught three bombs, but no torpedoes, and continued to operate her flight deck. Our strike groups, having heavily damaged one of the Japanese carriers, *Shokaku,* but not sunk her, were returning. The *Enterprise* would take her own planes aboard and as many of the *Hornet's* as possible, but the others would have to land in the water, their crews picked up by the destroyers serving as plane guards. So now the *Enterprise* picked up speed and moved away to the north, preparing to land planes. On her deck the pilots taking off were shown a famous message chalked on a board: "Proceed without *Hornet."*

As she became smaller and then went hull down on the horizon, the war moved away from us, and with an awful feeling of loneliness we turned to the business of survival. Three destroyers moved in alongside us on the high port side, only a few yards away, with their masts and yards swaying wildly back and forth as they tried to maintain station in the swell while passing hoses over to fight the fires aboard the carrier. The *Hornet* did not move at all, but the lighter destroyers, pitching and rolling, from time to time would crash against us with a terrible clang. The rigging would catch in the catwalk above and tear away when they rolled back, and their radar and fire control were being battered and broken in the process.

Lines were passed across, and when possible we began to pull the wounded over to the destroyer, some in wire stretchers, others sitting in a boatswain's chair. Speed was crucial, since we expected to be attacked again, and the destroyer had to cut loose if that happened. Men stood by the connecting lines with axes. Those of us on the lines pulling the chairs and stretchers over to the destroyer ran down the hangar deck with the line, and then ran up again, hoping to God that we wouldn't slip and go crashing into some piece of unyielding iron or go skidding out into the water coming in on the starboard side. Fires still burned forward, bodies lay around the deck, no time or need to move them. Below, the work went on to try to restore some power, but the Japanese torpedoes were real killers, in contrast to our own inept weapons, and there were no flickering lights, which would have indicated that the dynamos were starting up again.

The ship was now the business of her crew, particularly the engineers and the damage control groups, and the airedales had nothing to do. We were assembled again on that ghoulish hangar deck, where I asked an officer if the smoking lamp was fit. Under stress, he was annoyed by the question, and there was a danger of fire, so he snarled that surely a sailor could go one day in his life without smoking. I muttered something about "What if it's the last day?" and got away with it in the confusion of the moment.

I decided that things did not look good, and that we were probably going to abandon ship, so it was time to prepare. I could not bear to leave all the bright new guns that I had polished so nicely that morning, so I made my way up to the ordnance shack, picked one out, and put it in a sack, just in case. Encouraged by my own bravado, I then did something extremely foolish and dangerous. I made my way down through several hatches and dark decks to my locker. The water sloshed ominously on the low sides of the compartments, but my locker was on the high, dry side of the ship. I had no trouble and stupidly felt no fear of the ship rolling over and sinking. A pillowcase held my basic gear, including a suit of whites in case we went some place where there was liberty, but a diary I had been keeping for some time—contrary to regulations—was reluctantly left behind. In a moment I was back again on the hangar deck, the envy of all my friends for having salvaged some clothes, answering muster. The airedales were to be taken off since they served no useful purpose on the ship any longer.

About 1500 the destroyer *USS Russell,* one of the firefighting destroyers alongside, stretched cargo nets between the two decks. The *Hornet* sat heavy and still, filled with the seawater that would take her down, but the *Russell* rolled and pitched. When she came into the *Hornet* she crushed the net and anything in it between the sides of the two ships. Trial and error, after a few people got caught, taught the right way to do it. The trick was to jump just as the *Russell* began to roll out, being careful that your foot landed on one of the tightening ropes, and not on the holes between, for there wasn't time to recover and make your way slowly up a loosening net. If you did it right you landed on the rope and its stretch would pop you like a trampoline onto the deck of the *Russell* and into the arms of several of her crew. Carrying my pillowcase filled with my contraband pistol and my liberty whites, I leaped for my life and made it with a great bound of exhilaration. Tricky, but better than going into the oily water where anything could happen.

At the best of times in war a destroyer is a small and crowded ship, and as about four hundred additional men squeezed aboard, every space above and below deck was filled to the point where it literally was difficult to move. Just as I got aboard, another Japanese strike, launched from their surviving carriers, roared in. The *Russell* cut her lines, pulled away at high speed, and started firing her antiaircraft guns. Looking for a place with some protection, I crawled under the mount of the after 5-inch gun, which swung around above me, the bolts holding the gun to the swiveling mount missing me by what seemed no more than a quarter of an inch. The firing directly above and the clang of the hot shell as it came out of the breech was too much for me, and I crawled out thinking what a real mess it was going to be if a plane came in strafing, with the deck absolutely filled with people who couldn't move without going over the side.

In a moment one did, just as I forced my way into an after deckhouse already crammed with sailors trying to cover up their heads. The enormous power the ship was turning up gave a speed of about forty knots and forced the stern deep in the water, forming a huge stern wave that made it impossible to see anything aft except the wall of water. The destroyer was not hit, but it seemed as if we were all going to go down because the incoming Japanese torpedo planes made their run on the *Hornet* from behind the *Russell,* zooming along on the wave tops and then juking up and down at the last moment. The carrier took more bombs and one additional torpedo, making her death certain. In the same attack, the *Northampton,* trying to avoid a spread of torpedoes aimed at her, dropped the last towing cable, ending that slim hope of saving the *Hornet.*

Fortunately, no plane came near us, and the destroyer's officers began sorting us out, making sure that each bunk was filled in six-hour shifts, putting the injured below deck near the sick bay, arranging for each group to appoint one man to come to the galley to draw food twice a day. The Torpedo Six ordnance gang, about seven or eight of us by now, found ourselves aft on the starboard side, sitting on a narrow deck with our backs to the after deckhouse bulkhead and our feet outboard to the rail resting in the scupper. It was an uncomfortably wet place at high speed, but there was, just above our heads, a rail welded to the bulkhead to which it was possible to tie yourself, even when hanging onto a full pillowcase, which I began to curse but refused to give up.

The very long day of October 26, which I always celebrate privately, was drawing toward sunset. We were still circling the *Hornet,* but as it became clear that no power could be raised and that the effort to tow was finished, the command was given to abandon ship, and the crew began to go over the side on ropes and to jump into the water. There was no room for any more survivors on the *Russell,* so as the other ships moved in to pick up the rest of the crew, the *Russell* turned south and began withdrawing. The Battle of Santa Cruz was over, and sitting on the deck, cold and exhausted, looking back at a tropical sunset with the smoking carrier sitting there at an odd, lumpy angle, I for the first time considered the possibility that we might lose the war. The *Hornet* had been such a big and powerful ship, and yet only a few hits in a brief space of time had been enough to finish her. Then too it was already apparent, as it would be crystal clear after we knew all that went on that day, that the U.S. Navy had fought ineffectively.

But the navy would be back, and even in going down the *Hornet* was tougher than we thought. Still later that evening our own destroyers went back to finish her off with torpedoes, but once again the American torpedoes failed. Some missed, some failed to explode, and those that hit did not sink her. The destroyers then turned their five-inch guns on her, starting more fires, but still, after several hundred rounds, they failed to put her down. By then the Japanese surface fleet was getting close—they were still trying to force a surface battle—and the American destroyers withdrew, leaving the scene of the battle and the hulk of the *Hornet* to the victors in the battle. She was too far gone to be salvaged, though, and a few of the superb Japanese long-lance torpedoes at last blew the bottom out of her, and she went down in more than three miles of water to where she must still be sitting, as beautiful and proud as ever.

THE BATTLE THAT NEVER HAPPENED

DAVID M. GLANTZ

By the late autumn of 1942, the Berlin-Tokyo axis seemed to be reeling on all fronts. The Japanese were giving way on Guadalcanal and Australian and American troops were pushing over passes of the Owen Stanley Range in New Guinea. In Egypt, the British had broken through at El Alamein, and the Allies had landed in French North Africa. And at Stalingrad the Russians had launched a vast counteroffensive, Operation Uranus, that aimed to trap an entire German army in the ruins of the city. Stalin was by now vigorously pressing the Western Allies to re-establish themselves on the European continent in 1943—what became known as the Second Front.

On the Eastern Front (which was of course the First), it has for long been believed that, beginning with Stalingrad, the Germans suffered an unbroken series of defeats leading to the fall of Berlin, and with it, that of Hitler and his Thousand-Year Reich. Only now, with the opening, however erratic, of the Soviet archives, are we beginning to form a different picture of what actually did happen on the Eastern Front. The German retreat, though it eventually ended in defeat, was masterful (and is still being studied in detail by the American army). The Soviets also experienced major reverses. But they were covered up, and forgotten. For the Soviet government, history was important only as propaganda.

The worst of those setbacks was the operation called Mars, the twin of Uranus, that was the centerpiece of Marshal Georgy Zhukov's Soviet strategic designs that fall. Zhukov's aim was to pinch off the Rzhev salient, a dagger still pointed at Moscow a year after the failure of Barbarossa. Operation Mars would last three weeks, from November 25 until December 15, 1942, would leave the salient practically undented, and would cost Stalin's most illustrious general some 500,000 casualties. The defeat and others like it, David M. Glantz writes, "would be cloaked in obscurity and silence" for more than fifty years. It was, in fact, Glantz who discovered the existence of Mars while doing research in the Soviet military archives.

Colonel David M. Glantz, U.S. Army (ret.), is editor of the *Journal of Slavic Military Studies* and one of the world's foremost authorities on the Eastern Front in World War II.

HISTORY STATES THAT THE TITANIC BATTLE OF STALINGRAD ALtered the course of war on the German Eastern Front and set the Wehrmacht and German Reich on their path toward utter and humiliating defeat. History has accorded enduring fame to the victors of Stalingrad, and after its winter campaign of 1942–43, the Red Army seemingly never again suffered strategic or significant operational defeat. The architects of the Stalingrad victory entered the annals of military history as unvanquished heroes who led the subsequent Soviet march to victory. Foremost among them was Marshal of the Soviet Union Georgy Konstantinovich Zhukov, the hero of Moscow, Stalingrad, Kursk, and Berlin.

History, however, has misinformed us. The muses of history are fickle. They record only what was reported and ignore what was not. From the fall of 1942 on, the Soviet combat record resembles a seamless, unblemished march to inevitable victory. In fact, numerous Soviet failures and defeats punctuated the Red Army's victorious march. The flawed historical mosaic elevated the reputations of victorious Soviet commanders such as Zhukov and I. S. Konev to almost superhuman proportions, covering up the fact that, after all, they too lost battles, and sometimes big ones.

Operation Mars, originally planned by the Soviets for late October 1942, but postponed until November 25, remains the most glaring instance in which the historiography of the German-Soviet War has failed us. Operation Mars was to be a companion piece to Operation Uranus, the code name for the Soviets' Stalingrad strategic counteroffensive. By conducting operations Mars and Uranus, the Soviet Stavka (Headquarters of the High Command) sought to regain the strategic initiative. Planned and conducted by Marshal Zhukov and a host of other famous Soviet generals—and appropriately named for the Roman god of war—Operation Mars formed the centerpiece of Soviet strategic designs in fall 1942. Its immense scale and ambitious strategic intent made it at least as important as Operation Uranus and perhaps more so. But Mars might as well have been a battle that never happened.

Today, using German and Soviet archival materials, we can correct this historical oversight and properly commemorate the sacrifices of the half million Red Army soldiers and the many Germans who became casualties during the operation, a figure that exceeds the military death toll of the United States' armed forces throughout the entire war.

In late September 1942, key Stavka political and military leaders formulated a strategy to reverse the fortunes of a war that had been largely running in Germany's favor. Their plans reflected the bitter experiences of the prior eighteen months and the military realities they faced. During 1941, the Germans had advanced to the very gates of Moscow before Soviet counteroffensives saved the Russian capital. Despite subsequent Soviet successes in winter, German forces remained menacingly close to the city. Undeterred by its setback at Moscow, the following summer the German army once again attacked, this time across southern Russia to the banks of the Volga River at Stalingrad, threatening not only the city but the oil-rich Caucasus region. After spectacular gains, by October 1942 the German offensive bogged down in the ruins of Stalingrad and on the northern slopes of the Caucasus Mountains. Having once more underestimated the resilience of the Red Army and the imposing geographical challenges of the immense theater of war, the Wehrmacht again faced the wrath of a Soviet winter counteroffensive. The only question was: Where?

Marshal Zhukov played a significant role in planning Operation Mars; he had earned Stalin's trust through his tenacity and many victories. A former cavalry officer, Zhukov had gained much of his reputation as a fighter in action against the Japanese in August and September 1939. Forces under his command had utterly routed Japanese forces at the Khalkhin River in eastern Mongolia, a defeat that later contributed to the critical Japanese decision to remain aloof from the German-Soviet War. Few now recall, however, the ruthlessness of Zhukov's assaults along the Khalkhin River, which cost him about 40 percent of his attacking force and had prompted sharp criticism from the Red Army general staff.

After beginning the war as chief of the Red Army general staff, Zhukov received field command and was instrumental in bloodying the Germans' nose in the terrible battles around Smolensk in July and August 1941. In September, Stalin relieved Zhukov of his command along the Western axis and dispatched him to Leningrad, ostensibly because Zhukov disagreed with Stalin's disastrous decision to defend Kiev. After Zhukov had stabilized Soviet defenses around Leningrad, in October Stalin summoned him to Moscow; he needed a fighter to halt the German juggernaut. Zhukov responded by planning and leading the victorious Soviet Moscow counteroffensives in winter 1942.

In spring and summer 1942, he commanded Soviet forces along the Moscow axis. While the Germans were advancing on Stalingrad, Zhukov orchestrated several offensives against German forces in the central sector of the front, including a major attack on the Rzhev salient in August, which was a virtual rehearsal for Operation Mars.

Zhukov's combat experiences at Smolensk and Moscow in 1941 and 1942, and west of Moscow in summer 1942, compounded by frustration over his inability to achieve total victory in those operations, prompted him to insist that the war would be won or lost along the Moscow axis. In short, Zhukov thought that German Army Group Center, whose forces were lodged in the Rzhev salient menacingly close to Moscow (about 100 miles away), posed the greatest threat to Moscow and the Soviet war effort. In his view, the Rzhev salient, about ninety miles square and a legacy of the chaotic fighting of winter 1941–42, represented a dagger aimed at Moscow—because it contained Army Group Center's powerful German Ninth Army. Therefore, argued Zhukov, the Soviet Union could best achieve strategic victory in 1942 by smashing the German Ninth Army in the salient and, thereafter, all of German Army Group Center.

Zhukov knew that this would be no easy task. General Walter Model's German Ninth Army had erected strong defenses around the salient and had fortified all cities and towns along its periphery, including the key cities of Rzhev, Belyi, and Sychevka. The Germans had also fortified the rivers flanking the salient and had cleared timber from the main north-south and east-west roads and rail lines. Zhukov and Model both understood that whoever controlled the roads would control the salient. Although heavy forests and swamps dominated the salient's western and central regions, the Germans had cleared enough terrain to permit both firm defense and the maneuver of mobile tactical and operational reserves within it. In addition, by late October, the dirt roads and many rivers crisscrossing the salient should be frozen or close to frozen.

Zhukov also realized that General Model would be a formidable opponent, for he too was a fighter. Model had delivered a stinging rebuff to Soviet forces in the region in winter 1941, and combat in 1942 provided Model's forces with a keen appreciation of every inch of terrain in the region. Nevertheless,

Zhukov was convinced that his forces, together with the massive strategic reserves the Stavka had assembled at near-frenzied pace in summer 1942, were strong enough to permit the Red Army to deliver two major, mutually supporting strategic counteroffensives—one, which he advocated, against German Army Group Center and the other, which others supported, against overextended German Army Group South at Stalingrad.

During the Stavka's strategic deliberations, Zhukov emphasized Soviet force superiority in the decisive central sector of the front. Here the Soviet Kalinin and Western Fronts, supported by the Moscow Defense Zone, fielded almost 1.9 million men, more than 24,000 guns and mortars, 3,300 tanks, and 1,100 aircraft, in every category more forces than were deployed in the Stalingrad region. (Of this number, Zhukov employed around 720,000 men and 3,375 tanks and self-propelled guns in Mars.) Zhukov argued that eradication of the threat to Moscow would inevitably contribute to success in the south as well. Should either Soviet offensive falter, Stavka reserves could develop and exploit the other offensive.

Stalin accepted Zhukov's recommendations, and on September 26, 1942, the generalissimo ordered that major strategic counteroffensives be conducted at both Rzhev and Stalingrad. Appropriately, Zhukov would command the former, and his contemporary, General A. M. Vasilevsky, would command the latter. Vasilevsky, then chief of the general staff and deputy minister of defense, was a consummate staff officer and a protégé of a former chief of the general staff, Marshal B. M. Shaposhnikov. At the outbreak of war, Vasilevsky had been chief of the general staffs Operations Directorate, and, because of his obvious talents, he rose from colonel to colonel general in only four years. His wartime accomplishments as key general staff planner and "fireman" in vital operational sectors had won Stalin's confidence—and an appointment for him, in July 1942, as chief of the general staff. Vasilevsky's calm demeanor and keen intelligence tended to moderate both Stalin's and Zhukov's excesses.

With Stalin's formal approval, the general staff, Zhukov, and Vasilevsky planned twin two-phased strategic offensives and assigned each of the four operations the code name of a planet. In Operation Mars, planned to commence in late October, forces of the Kalinin and Western Fronts would encircle and destroy the German Ninth Army in the Rzhev salient. Two to three weeks later, in Operation Jupiter, the remainder of the Soviet Western Front would join the offensive and help destroy all German forces east of Smolensk. Vasilevsky's initial operation, code-named Uranus and tentatively timed for mid-November, was to envelop German forces in the Stalingrad region. In Operation Saturn, set to begin in early December, Vasilevsky's forces would seize Rostov, destroy remaining German forces in the great bend of the Don River, and cut off German forces withdrawing from the Caucasus.

Although Operation Mars was slated to begin on October 28, rainy weather delayed the usual October freeze and forced postponement of the operation until late November. The subsequent Stavka directive to Red Army generals I. S. Konev and M. A. Purkaev—both under Zhukov's command—ordered their Western and Kalinin Fronts "to encircle the enemy Rzhev Grouping, capture Rzhev, and free the railroad line from Moscow to Velikie-Luki." To do so, three of Konev's armies (a Soviet army consisted of eight to twelve divisions or brigades and was somewhat larger than a German corps) were to attack the Rzhev salient from the east, and three of Purkaev's armies were to attack from the west and north. The 6th Tank and 2d Guards Cavalry Corps (a Soviet corps was roughly the size of a German panzer division) would spearhead Konev's advance, and the 1st and 3d Mechanized Corps would exploit Purkaev's attack. Each of the tank corps numbered more than 200 tanks. To ensure success, the Stavka provided extraordinary additional armor, artillery, and engineer support for Zhukov's two attacking fronts. In fact, Zhukov's more than 3,300 tanks and 10,000 guns and mortars exceeded the firepower the Stavka allocated to Vasilevsky to carry out Operation Uranus.

The plan for Operation Mars bore all the characteristics of a Zhukov-style offensive operation. To maximize pressure on the Germans, his forces would attack simultaneously in all sectors. By launching his main attacks against the base of the Rzhev salient from both east and west, Zhukov sought to envelop German forces in the salient with frontal assaults, without having to conduct complex maneuvers with his mobile forces across the difficult terrain and in the harsh weather conditions. To achieve quick success in his attack sectors, Zhukov ordered his front commanders to mass their forces and commit all of their armor early in the battle. By late November, the long-awaited cold weather finally arrived, and rivers, streams, and swamps froze, permitting operations to commence. However, the ensuing constant snowy weather hampered mobile operations, hindered artillery observation, and grounded supporting aircraft on both sides.

Soviet forces struck early on November 25, simultaneously in all offensive sectors. Preceded by a vicious artillery preparation, infantry and supporting tanks of the Western Front's 20th and 31st Armies struck hard at German XXXIX Panzer Corps units dug in along and north of the Vazuza and Osuga Rivers northeast of the vital German railhead of Sychevka. Numbering well over 200,000 men and 500 tanks, the two Soviet armies faced about 40,000 German defenders. Despite this numerical superiority, the violent Soviet attack achieved only mixed results, since German forces occupied strong defenses, and Soviet forces had to assault across generally open and rolling terrain at a time when incessant fog and driving snow showers reduced the effectiveness of the Soviet artillery preparation.

North of the Osuga River, three Soviet 31st Army rifle divisions numbering almost 20,000 men and supported by more than 100 tanks attacked the strong defensive positions of the German 102d Infantry Division. Soviet infantry clad in winter white advanced in echelon, their ranks interspersed with supporting tanks. German artillery, machine-gun, and small-arms fire tore into the advancing troops as antitank weapons picked off the accompanying armor. For three days, and at a cost of more than half their riflemen and most of their tanks, the Soviets hurled themselves in vain at the 102d Division's prepared defenses. Faced with this determined resistance, the 31st Army's assault collapsed, and, despite Zhukov's and Konev's exhortations, it could not be revived. Three of the 20th Army's rifle divisions attacking between the Vazuza and Osuga Rivers met the same grisly fate. Despite strong armored support, their attacks stalled after suffering frightful losses. Undeterred by the initial failures, Zhukov and Konev insisted the attacks continue to support operations farther south—and the carnage increased.

To the south, along the banks of the Vazuza, a single rifle division of the 20th Army achieved signal, if limited, success. The division, supported by a brigade of around fifty tanks, crossed the frozen river, tore through forward German positions, and seized two German-fortified villages on the river's west bank. Exploiting the opportunity, the army commander quickly moved another division across the river and into the breach. Fierce fighting raged all day in the rolling open country west of the river as Soviet infantry struggled to overcome pesky German village strongpoints and expand the bridgehead. It was critical that they do so, for the Soviets planned to commit an additional rifle corps and two mobile corps into the breach to exploit the operation westward. All day, exhorting, cursing, and cajoling, Soviet commanders urged their men on. By day's end, although the bridgehead was still too small, Konev ordered the 20th Army's second echelon and mobile force to advance the next morning.

This decision, however, turned out to be premature and ill-advised. Defending German forces from the Fifth Panzer and Seventy-eighth Infantry Divisions fought with grim abandon. Small German combat groups of infantry, tanks, and artillery in company and battalion strength fiercely defended the numerous log and stone villages that dotted the generally open, rolling, and snow-covered fields west of the Vazuza River. Attacking Soviet forces lapped around these strongpoints, overcame some, but left many as deadly obstacles strewn throughout their rear. The Germans reinforced their sagging defenses by ordering the 9th Panzer Division, then camped west of Sychevka, to march to the sounds of the guns and plug the developing breaches.

On the night of November 25–26, while Soviet riflemen strained to expand their tenuous bridgehead, Soviet second echelon and exploitation forces struggled forward. Under constant German artillery fire, more than 200 tanks, 30,000 infantry, and 10,000 cavalrymen, with their accompanying logistical trains, moved forward in darkness, along two frozen dirt roads, through light forests to the east bank of the river. Since both roads had been chopped up by artillery fire, and too many forces were using them at the same time, chaos ruled supreme. The reinforcing infantry and tanks clogged the Vazuza crossing sites as harried officers tried in vain to clear the way for the advancing armor and cavalry. Although the rifle corps crossed the river, the tank and cavalry corps could not. It was midday on November 26 before the 6th Tank Corps's armor could go into action, and the mounted troopers of the 2d Guards Cavalry Corps remained east of the river until November 27. To Zhukov's and Konev's utter frustration, offensive momentum was already flagging. Furthermore, their reinforcements had already suffered light casualties and were disorganized after the chaotic night march.

The Germans experienced the full wrath of the Soviet assault on November 27. While German reserves maneuvered into blocking positions along the open terrain on either side of the critical Rzhev-Sychevka road, German frontline forces desperately but skillfully defended their fortified village strongpoints, severely disrupting the attempted Soviet armored and cavalry exploitation. After noon, the Soviet 6th Tank Corps, attacking in brigade columns of about fifty tanks each, with infantry riding on the tanks, lunged between and, in some cases, over the German strongpoint defenses, followed on horseback by the troopers of the 2d Guards Cavalry Corps. The German village defenses smashed the Soviet attack into fragments. Nevertheless, three Soviet tank brigades ran the gauntlet and crossed the vital Rzhev-Sychevka road into the forests beyond; a fourth did not make it. The more vulnerable Soviet cavalry suffered frightening losses as they galloped through the snow and withering German fire across the road into the German rear. The Germans responded by counterattacking from north and south, along the Rzhev-Sychevka road and against the exposed flanks of the exploiting Soviet forces.

In two days of fighting, the 5th Panzer Division had suffered more than 500 casualties, and the 78th Infantry Division reported, "All units severely weakened and great losses in equipment and weapons." The cost to the Russians was obviously higher, for the Germans counted at least fifty destroyed Russian tanks, and the fields in front of their positions were littered with Russian dead.

By nightfall on November 28, it was clear to all that the Soviet attack had faltered. Although the bulk of the 20th Army's armor and cavalry had reached the forests across the Rzhev-Sychevka road, the attrition had been staggering, and German counterattacks along the road had slammed the door on their withdrawal. Worse still, the exploiting tankers and cavalrymen were no longer within the range of supporting artillery, since there was no room for it in the bridgehead. Zhukov and Konev, however, were undeterred. They ordered their beleaguered tankers to organize a breakout to the west during the night of November 28–29, while exhorting their forces in the bridgehead both to support the breakout and to widen the gap in German lines. Zhukov's continued grim optimism was conditioned, in part, by his stubborn refusal to admit defeat and by the striking success Soviet forces seemed to be achieving elsewhere.

Along the western flank of the Rzhev salient, the Soviet 41st and 22d Armies had made striking progress in the first three days of battle and appeared close to reaching deep into the defending Germans' rear area. Once they had done so, Zhukov believed, the temporary difficulties along the Vazuza would become irrelevant.

The 90,000 men and more than 300 tanks of the Soviet 41st Army struck early on November 25, after an artillery preparation had smashed the defenses south of the fortified town of Belyi. Advancing across the frozen, forested swamps into more open terrain along the main dirt road that traversed the western flank of the salient, the Soviet riflemen and tanks easily overcame forward German defenses, then lunged through the villages along the road and into the light forests in the German rear. At dawn the next day, the Forty-first Army commander ordered his 15,200-man and 224-tank-strong 1st Mechanized Corps into action. Commanded by the experienced General M. D. Solomatin, it made spectacular initial progress. Moving slowly through the heavy and virtually roadless forests, the tank force had torn a hole twenty kilometers wide and nearly thirty kilometers deep in the German defenses by nightfall.

Despite the difficulty encountered in keeping some sort of order during the advance through the forest depths, General Solomatin's tank brigades succeeded in reaching the key communications road linking Belyi with the German rear area.

Despite this seemingly dramatic success, the 41st Army's attack plans almost immediately went awry. Although ordered to avoid a prolonged struggle for the city of Belyi, army forces were irresistibly drawn to the enticing target. Thinking that Belyi was ripe for the taking, the army commander launched attack after frontal attack on the town. Furthermore, when the attacks failed, the army commander diverted precious forces to Belyi from his exploiting mechanized corps. Despite his exertions, however, Belyi could not be taken.

Meanwhile, the exploiting Soviet armor attempted to sever the crucial road running northwest into Belyi, which was the only German resupply route into the city. Now opposed by company and battalion groups from the 1st Panzer Division, the Soviet mechanized corps commander urgently requested reinforcements for his flagging attack. His superiors, however, denied the request and committed his reinforcements to the battle for Belyi. All the while, the army's overextended mechanized force fought a bitter, daylong struggle along a thirty-kilometer sector of the key Belyi road. The following day, Soviet hopes for exploitation were dashed when fresh German armored reserves reached the battlefield. The fortunes of battle were clearly turning, and initial Soviet success had been squandered in the futile battle for Belyi. Soviet forces in the German rear went over to the defense and awaited the inevitable German counterblow.

Meanwhile, General Harpe was frantically assembling reserves to contain and, ultimately, defeat the Soviet offensive. Relying on the 1st Panzer Division to hold the Belyi strongpoint and the thin defenses along the Belyi road, Harpe requested and received three panzer divisions from higher headquarters. To reach the battlefield, however, these divisions had to march long distances over difficult routes in the harshest of winter conditions. Until they arrived, German fortunes in the Belyi region remained in the balance.

While battle raged around and south of Belyi, German forces to the north were also under heavy attack. On November 25, the Soviet 22d Army, with more than 50,000 men and 270 tanks of Major General M. E. Katukov's 3d Mechanized Corps, assaulted up the Luchesa River valley. Attacking along a narrow corridor flanked by forests and frozen swamps, Soviet forces tore a gaping hole through German defenses and drove German forces eastward up the valley. The Germans committed elements of the Grossdeutschland Division into the fray to slow the Soviet advance. Heavy fighting raged as Soviet forces drove toward the road running north from Belyi. Although the Germans were unable to close the yawning gap created by the 22d Army's attack, the often impenetrable terrain, deteriorating weather, and skillful German defense took a heavy toll on the advancing Soviets and halted them short of their goal. By November 30, the Soviets occupied a salient eight kilometers wide and almost fifteen kilometers deep in the German defenses. But, try as they did, the 22d Army's forces could not overcome ferocious German resistance and reach the critical Belyi road.

The tense situation along the Luchesa River was only exacerbated by Soviet pressure against the northern extremity of the Rzhev salient. There, on a broad front along the northern extremity of the Rzhev salient, on November 25 the 80,000 men and more than 200 tanks of the Soviet 39th Army launched Zhukov's secondary attack. Although Soviet forces achieved some initial success in the partially wooded countryside, they were unable to exploit it because of skillful action by German tactical reserves. By November 30, this struggle, too, had degenerated into a series of grinding Soviet attacks that achieved only limited gains.

Zhukov, Konev, and Purkaev alternated between elation and frustration over the results of the first five days of operations. The Western Front's main attack in the east had clearly faltered. Although the 20th Army's mobile forces occupied precarious positions astride the critical Rzhev-Sychevka road, the 31st Army's attack had utterly failed, and the 29th Army had not yet joined the assault. Nevertheless, both the 41st and 22d Armies had made real gains, and Konev still had significant reserves, including an additional tank corps of almost 200 tanks, which he could commit in the 20th Army's sector. Consequently, Zhukov instructed Konev to reinforce the 20th Army with 31st Army divisions and to withdraw his exploiting armor and cavalry from their exposed position west of the Rzhev-Sychevka road. After regrouping, he was to continue his assault. Meanwhile, the two Soviet armies west of the Rzhev salient would develop their attacks in support of the 20th Army. What Zhukov did not know was that the German command was preparing to strike back in the sector where Zhukov's forces had achieved their greatest success.

West of the Rzhev-Sychevka road, Konev's mobile forces, now isolated and starved of ammunition and logistical support, attempted to break out to the east on the night of November 29–30. The desperate night attack cost the tank corps nearly all of its remaining 100 tanks, and the more fragile cavalry were mercilessly slaughtered by heavy German fire.

Zhukov was bitterly disappointed. His 20th Army had lost more than 30,000 men and 200 tanks in five days of vicious combat. Losses in the 31st Army were just as severe, and little had been gained by the effort. Even more disconcerting, on the west side of the salient, the 41st Army's seemingly certain victory also soon degenerated into catastrophic rout, and the 22d Army soon faced frustrating stalemate.

South of Belyi, the Soviet 41st Army's worst fears materialized. Not only were the Germans able to hold on to Belyi, but they orchestrated an effective counterstroke. The situation began deteriorating after December 1—after Soviet forces had gone on the defense. First, the German 1st Panzer Division and the newly arrived 12th Panzer Division regained firm control of the Belyi road and began applying unremitting pressure to Soviet defense lines southeast of the city. Even more devastating for the Soviets, the German 19th and 20th Panzer Divisions began concentrating south of the Soviet Belyi salient. It was no mean task, since every German movement was contested by the terrible weather conditions, the abysmal roads, and intense resistance by Soviet partisans. Despite the difficulties, on the morning of December 7, the two German divisions struck the 41st Army's southern flank, while the 1st Panzer Division and Grossdeutschland Division attacked southward from Belyi.

In three days of intense fighting, the combined German force slashed through the 41st Army's rear and encircled the bulk of the army southeast of Belyi. The glorious Soviet thrust had degenerated into an inglorious trap. Soviet commanders did what they could to organize a breakout, but all initial attempts to escape failed. The encircled Soviet forces then dug in and waited anxiously for news of success in other offensive sectors.

Soviet progress farther north in the Luchesa valley promised no relief. Despite strenuous efforts, Soviet forces in that sector could achieve little more. Having lost about half of its initial manpower and even more of its tanks, the Soviet 22d Army lacked the strength to expand its penetration. Nor could the Germans eliminate it. Although intense fighting ebbed and flowed for days, the stalemate endured. Farther north, the Soviet 39th Army continued its slow progress at the northern apex of the Rzhev salient against stout German resistance, with little prospect for victory.

Zhukov responded to the depressing news from the Belyi sector with characteristic resolution. Unwilling to admit defeat, he orchestrated a massive buildup of forces in the 20th Army's sector. Between December 2 and 10, he reinforced the army with a fresh tank corps and several divisions from the 31st Army, hastily reconstituted the 6th Tank Corps with tanks received from the Stavka reserve, and reinforced the adjacent 29th Army to twice its original strength. While the fighting raged on at Belyi, he ordered the 20th and 29th Armies to resume their assaults on December 11, in concert with a fresh drive in the north by the 39th Army, which he reinforced with a stream of divisions from the 30th Army in the Rzhev sector.

On the morning of December 11, massed Soviet infantry from the 20th and 29th Armies, backed by remaining infantry support tanks, resumed their

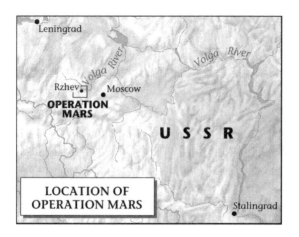

attacks from and south of the Vazuza River bridgehead. Despite withering German fire, Konev committed the almost 350 tanks and 20,000 men of his new 5th and refurbished 6th Tank Corps into combat. So hastily organized was the attack that many of the new tanks had not received their coat of white camouflage paint. Attacking desperately across a four-kilometer sector into the teeth of reinforced German antitank defenses, the Soviet 20th Army lost about 300 tanks in two days of incessant and deadly combat.

Although the carnage was frightful in the attack sectors of both the 20th and 29th Armies, Zhukov and Konev urged their forces on. The assaults continued for three days before collapsing in utter exhaustion on December 15. By that time, all from the lowliest private to Zhukov himself realized that defeat was at hand. If the carnage along the Vazuza did not confirm that reality, the fate of the 41st Army at Belyi would.

The 41st Army's encircled force of about 40,000 men, now led by General Solomatin of the 1st Mechanized Corps, held out southeast of Belyi for as long as humanly possible. Finally, dwindling logistical stocks demanded action. On the night of December 15–16, Solomatin destroyed his remaining armor and heavy weapons and thrust westward with his remaining infantry. Running the fiery gauntlet, Solomatin saved what he could of his corps and its accompanying infantry forces. The cost, however, was devastating. The German 1st Panzer Division alone counted 102 Soviet armored vehicles destroyed, and Solomatin reported more than 8,000 of his 12,000 troopers killed and wounded and most of the corps' 200-plus tanks destroyed or abandoned. The toll in the remainder of the 41st Army was equally grim, totaling more than 200 tanks and tens of thousands of riflemen.

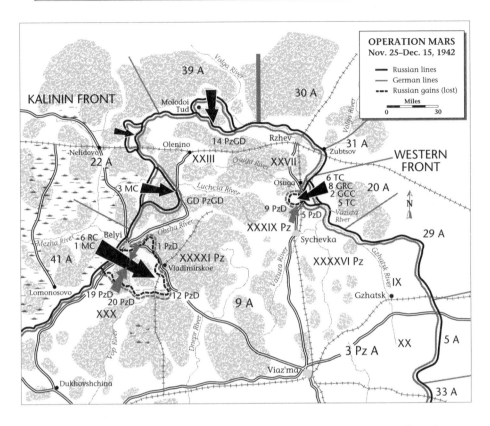

To the Soviets, the German-held Rzhev salient was like a dagger pointed at the Soviet capital (see location map at left). Hitler agreed and ordered his forces to hold the salient at all costs. To do so, the German 9th Army needed to defend critical communications routes along the salient's flanks that connected it to its parent Army Group Center. Zhukov threw his armor-heavy 41st, 22nd, and 20th Armies against the salient's eastern and western base to smash German defenses, sever communications, and envelop the bulk of the German 9th Army (above). With characteristic stubbornness, and at tremendous human cost, Zhukov had his forces pummel German defenses in an operation that he hoped would ultimately destroy all of German Army Group Center and become a turning point in the war. By tenacious and skillful counterattacks, the Germans thwarted the Soviet offensive and dealt Zhukov the most disastrous defeat of his illustrious career.

Even the twin catastrophic Soviet defeats along the Vazuza River and at Belyi did not completely destroy Zhukov's resolve, for he continued to attack with his 39th Army in the north until mid-December. Despite Zhukov's stubborn defiance of reality, by December 15, Operation Mars was a shambles. Stalin, the Stavka, and perhaps even Zhukov himself knew well that Mars was at an end. Furthermore, long before, Stalin had abandoned any hopes of launching Jupiter. By early December, the bulk of Stavka reserves were already en route to reinforce Vasilevsky's successful Operation Uranus at Stalingrad.

Zhukov had conducted Operation Mars in characteristic fashion. The Soviet assaults were massive and unsparing in manpower and matériel. Discounting the harsh terrain and weather conditions, he relied on pressure across the entire front and simple maneuver by his powerful mechanized corps and tank corps to achieve victory. Zhukov's methods, however, failed. Skillful German tactical defense by small but tenacious combat groups, which exploited terrain and man-made obstacles to a maximum, bottled up attacking Soviet mobile forces before they reached key objectives in the German rear area. In the process, the Germans inflicted maximum casualties on the Soviets by separating attacking Soviet infantry from their supporting mobile forces. Avoiding panic and holding only where necessary, the German command slowly assembled the reserves necessary to counterattack and achieve victory. Nevertheless, German victory was a "close thing." While causing catastrophic Soviet casualties, the German divisions themselves were fought to a frazzle. It was no coincidence that several months later, Model asked for and received permission to abandon the Rzhev salient. He and his army could ill afford another such victory.

Operation Mars cost the Red Army nearly half a million men killed, wounded, or captured. Individual Soviet combat units were decimated in the operation. The Soviet 20th Army lost 58,524 men out of its original strength of more than 114,000 men. Solomatin's 1st Mechanized Corps lost 8,100 of its 12,000 men and all of its 220 tanks, and the accompanying 6th Stalin Rifle Corps lost more than 20,000 of its 30,000 men. Soviet tank losses, correctly estimated by the Germans at around 1,700, exceeded the total number of tanks the Soviets initially committed in Operation Uranus at Stalingrad. In Western armies, losses such as these would have prompted the removal of senior commanders, if not worse. In the Red Army they did not, for when all was said and done, Zhukov fought, and the Red Army needed fighters.

Although far less severe than those of the Soviets, German losses in the operation were grievous, too—losses they could ill afford given their smaller manpower pool and the catastrophe befalling them at Stalingrad. For example, the 1st Panzer Division suffered 1,793 casualties, and the 5th Panzer 1,640, while losses in the infantry divisions along the Soviet main attack axes were even greater. The overall Soviet casualty toll, however, was at least tenfold greater than the total German loss of around 40,000 men.

✦

THE MANNER in which Operation Mars was fought and the carnage the operation produced has few parallels in the later war years. For grisly results, its closest peer was the famous Soviet frontal assault on the Seelow Heights during the April 1945 Berlin operation. Not coincidentally, it too was orchestrated by Zhukov. Unlike the case of Mars, however, the victorious conclusion of the Berlin operation required no alteration of the historical record to preserve Soviet pride or commanders' reputations.

The legacy of Operation Mars was silence. Stalin and Soviet history saw to it that Vasilevsky's feat at Stalingrad remained unblemished by the Rzhev failure. Zhukov's reputation remained intact. Stalin and Soviet history mandated that he share credit with Vasilevsky for the Stalingrad victory. Zhukov gained a measure of revenge over German Army Group Center at Kursk in the summer of 1943 and in Byelorussia in the summer of 1944. Ironically, however, it would be Vasilevsky who, as key Stavka planner, would play an instrumental role in finally crushing that German army group in East Prussia in January 1945. Such is the fickleness of history.

Soviet military history ignored other notable Soviet defeats during the later war years. Among those operations, which, like Mars, would be cloaked in obscurity and silence, were the failed Soviet Central Front offensive of February–March 1943 in the region west of Kursk, the abortive Soviet Byelorussian offensive of fall 1943, and futile Soviet attempts to invade Romania in May 1944 and East Prussia in the fall of 1944. This silence was possible because each of these Red Army defeats occurred at the end of a major Soviet strategic advance, when the overall Soviet victory masked the local failure to vanquished Germans and history alike and shrouded the events in a veil of anonymity that has endured for more than fifty years. That cloak is finally being lifted.

EIGHTH ARMY EYEWITNESS TO EL ALAMEIN

GEORGE GREENFIELD

The third of the great Axis setbacks of 1942 (four, if you count Guadal-canal, which the Marines had almost cleared by the end of the year) was El Alamein. If this struggle in the western desert of Egypt did not in-volve the numbers of Stalingrad or the majestic ships of Midway, it was, in terms of generalship, a masterpiece of timing by the British Bernard Law Montgomery. Luck aided him. His famously resourceful opponent, Field Marshal Erwin Rommel, was on sick leave in Germany; even as he was rushing back, his temporary replacement would die of a heart at-tack. At midnight on October 23, by the light of a full moon, Mont-gomery unleashed a mass artillery bombardment, followed by infantry probes. Except for the hundreds of aircraft, the battle at this stage had all the marks of a World War I setpiece attack. Montgomery, as John Kee-gan has written, "rightly judged that the British armored divisions lacked the flair to out-German the Germans." Only when his troops had made substantial dents in the Axis line did he send his armor through. Hitler radioed Rommel his predictable not-a-step-is-to-be-yielded com-mand; Rommel disobeyed. The 2,000-mile retreat of his Afrika Korps across Libya to Tunisia began.

One British soldier at El Alamein was an intelligence officer named George Greenfield; in a period of days he was twice blown up by land mines and nearly killed by a shell splinter, but came through unscathed. The following piece memorably evokes the small incidents from which a big battle is compounded.

George Greenfield was a London-based writer, the author of numerous books. This account of his part at El Alamein is excerpted from his memoir, *Chasing the Beast*. Greenfield died last year.

THE BUFFS WAS THE THIRD-OLDEST INFANTRY REGIMENT IN the British army, dating back to the trained bands raised by Queen Elizabeth in the sixteenth century. It celebrated its battle honors on April 23, which happened to be Elizabethan poet William Shakespeare's birthday as well. Each year on that date, the surviving officers hold a reunion lunch at the Duke of York's Barracks in London.

Some years ago at the lunch, someone suggested I write a book to explain what it was like to be plucked from the academic world and thrust into the reality of war. I leaped at the idea. Luckily, Charles Daniels, my orderly fifty-odd years before, was still a friend. He had kept a diary—strictly against my orders—that he still had and thus was able to check my flagging memory of battles long ago.

The Battle of El Alamein against the *Afrika Korps* in late 1942 was a turning point in World War II—in Winston Churchill's words, "the end of the beginning." I was fortunate—in another phrase of Churchill's—"to march with the Eight Army" and to survive.

✦

MY MAIN JOB as battalion intelligence officer was twofold: to gather and to distribute as much information as my section and I could discover. Large-scale maps of our desert locale, pinned to map boards and covered in acetate, had to be marked up in red grease pencil for the enemy and blue for our own side. Thirteenth Corps issued maps of the entire corps area, which reached us via divisional and brigade headquarters. Each in turn added to or altered the markings so that when the maps finally reached us at the sharp end, they looked like the meanderings of a drunken spider, which had dipped alternate feet in red and blue. The information we gained through our own observation and patrols went back in turn via brigade and division to corps headquarters.

Things were beginning to stir. Lieutenant General Bernard Law Montgomery had arrived to take command of the Eighth Army. To show his broad-mindedness, he took to wearing an Australian slouch hat with the left brim pinned upward until a message arrived from the Ninth Australian Division headquarters saying they were rather particular about who was entitled to wear their special headgear. Obediently, for once, the vain little man substituted a Royal Tank Regiment beret, which he retained until the end of the desert campaign and beyond.

Brand-new Sherman and Churchill tanks were unloading at Port Tewfik and Port Said to replace the aging and worn-out Valentines. There were also brand-new heavy guns for the Royal Artillery. The Highland Division arrived, or "Highway Decorators" as they quickly became known from their habit of painting old petrol cans with the initials "HD" and using them as route markers. The rest of us claimed, quite inaccurately, that we knew our way around the desert without the need of reminders. Night patrolling intensified, and "line-straightening" operations took a greater toll in killed and wounded. Deception plans were rife: Dummy tanks began to appear in squadrons close behind our divisional headquarters, and the recorded sounds of tanks grinding along and changing gear were amplified—to be heard by and to confuse the enemy.

At last it was the night of October 23, 1942, the evening of the full moon. On our immediate front a Royal Sussex battalion would launch the assault, leaving the start line and moving through gaps that had been cut in the broad minefield at night by the sappers and then concealed. The Second Buffs would follow up and take over the attack after the first wave stopped. We were to press on for several hundred yards, if we could, and establish a bridgehead so that the next day the Seventh Armored Division's tanks could burst into the open spaces beyond.

At nine o'clock, the battalion began to stir. A message arrived for the colonel saying that the Bren carriers and Scorpions, converted tanks with a device attached to the front for exploding mines, were in position a thousand yards back and would be coming forward to clear avenues in the minefield once the bridgehead was established. For some minutes men played quietly with their weapons, slowly opening and closing the bolts of their rifles, adjusting their bayonet frogs, and feeling their ammunition pouches to make sure that their rounds were still there. Everyone seemed to be keyed up, waiting.

Behind us the guns along the thirty miles of front were silently pointing upward. The signal—a quick jerk by each number one gunner—came and the night stillness was smashed by the concerted roar of the guns. Shells whistled over the heads of the infantrymen, whirring like wild geese in flight, and all along the enemy positions the flashes of their bursts flickered on the skyline. The volume of fire increased until all sounds mingled so that from one point of view could be heard the explosion of one salvo, the airborne rush of another, and the firing of a third. The giant drum notes of noise beat a continual tattoo along the enemy line, where we knew men winced and crouched as the shells fell among them with a vicious shriek. And now gunners sweated in the moonlight as they fed the guns, and gun barrels grew hot, and the air smelled bitter with the fumes of the exploded charges. Still they went on firing as battery relieved battery and troop relieved troop all down the British line.

With so many guns and so many men and so many shells spread along a wide front, there is always a risk of error, just as linking up several orchestras, out of sight of one another, can lead to a cascade of false notes. So it was in our immediate front. The plan was for a creeping barrage that would come down about two hundred yards ahead of the Royal Sussex regiment's start line and move forward like a protective curtain as the men on the ground moved forward. According to the plan, as our leading troops reached the enemy's defensive positions, they would still be crouching and shaken under the impact of the barrage. Alas, human error played its part. The opening salvos from the gunners well behind us landed right on the start line. Many in the battalion were killed or wounded by friendly fire before they had time to fire a shot in anger at the foe.

Naturally, there was wild confusion and, worse, a brief delay. Some platoons had lost their officers, others had been decimated. By the time they had formed up again, the tanks had plowed ahead. Not for the first time, the infantry was going into battle largely unsupported.

Monty had arranged for a printed sheet to be handed out to the assaulting troops. In his schoolboy clichés, he spoke of "hitting the enemy for six out of Africa" and wished us Godspeed in our efforts. We read it by the bright light of the full moon, crumpled it up, and threw it aside in disgust. It might be an interesting game to a general sitting safely in his trailer well behind the lines, but it was somewhat more serious to those at the sharp end. Besides, seeing the casualties from the Royal Sussex and our own D Company being rushed back to the nearest field-dressing station—continuing Monty's own metaphor—this was not a game of cricket.

✦

FROM THEN ON, the first night of the Battle of El Alamein was a blurred kaleidoscope. The barrage at last lifted and, as we trudged forward through the gaps in the minefield, our deafened ears gradually functioned again, and we could pick up the high-pitched rattle of German machine guns and the lower, slower sound of our Bren guns and medium machine guns. One moment, I was charging toward an Italian *sangar*, the built-up, usually circular defense posts that the Italians preferred to trenches. I was waving a Beretta pistol that, a week or two earlier, I had sliced from the belt of a dead officer. A dark shadow ahead fired a burst that whipped wildly overhead. I fired a couple of rounds back. The dark shadow disappeared. Whether I had hit, or even killed him, I shall never know.

The next moment, it seemed, I was with our medical officer, Captain Isaac Shragovitch. A short, stocky man of great strength, he was a Canadian and had come to Britain with their forces in 1941. He wanted to get frontline experience and, after months of inactivity, transferred to the Second Buffs as medical officer when the battalion was mobilizing for the desert. He was squatting alongside one of our corporals, who was lying on his back.

"Hey there, George," he said to me.

"What's up, Shrag?" I replied.

"This poor guy. Just given a shot of morphine. The stretcher-bearer got a tourniquet on him. See all that blood?" He indicated an area of black saturated sand with his flashlight. "The leg's virtually off. Shell splinter or something. It's only hanging on by this shred of flesh. Here, George do something useful. Sit down and cradle the lower part with your knees. I'm going to cut it clear and then we can get him back to the FDS [field dressing station]. Risk of gangrene if we hang around."

So I squatted down and grabbed the leg. The thighbone had been sliced clean through by the shell splinter, and the doc only had to make one swift cut to free the upper stump. Then they bundled the now unconscious corporal onto a stretcher and began to move away.

I was left cradling the unattached leg in my hands. "What do I do with this, Shrag?" I asked weakly.

"Keep it as a memento," he said.

I had never realized how heavy a leg is, especially when it is wearing an ammunition boot. Thirty or more pounds in weight, concentrated bone, muscle, and flesh packed into a narrow cylinder. With effort, I shifted the leg onto the sand, as reverently as I could, and went my way.

Colonel J. P. Williams was buzzing around like a blue-arsed fly, sometimes getting ahead of his own men in his brave impatience. I knew he was naturally courageous, but he was also desperate to win a medal. He had been in the desert for more than two years and had nothing to show for it. Williams was regular army, the war would not last forever, and rapid promotion in peacetime tended to follow the man with the decorations. It was a dangerous combination.

The night continued and gradually the forward tempo decreased. The tanks of the Seventh Armored Division had ground to a halt, our leading infantry companies had reached a massive minefield, and it would be daylight in another two hours. My orderly, Charles Daniels, ever cheerful, had been darting about like a sparrow at a feeding table, and he was now helping to convert a captured *sangar* into a night stop for the intelligence section. The moon had gone down, and the sky was at its darkest. I arranged the sentry list in case of a surprise return attack, which was most unlikely, pulled my great-coat collar up, and lay back, my head comfortably lodged on what I took to be an old bedroll.

I fell almost at once into a deep, untroubled sleep. Two hours later, waking in a gray dawn in time for stand to, I discovered my head had been resting on the chest of a dead Italian, lying on his back, legs outstretched. I noticed without really registering the fact that the corpse was wearing thick, white woolen socks. Some days later, as I had been wearing the same pair of khaki socks for more than a week without once removing them, Daniels suggested I needed a change, and he produced a pair of white socks. Gratefully, I un-wound my short puttees, unlaced and removed my boots, peeled off the dirty socks, and pulled on the white ones. They fitted snugly. After a while the penny dropped, and I asked Daniels where he had found them. After a little evasion, he confessed to stripping the dead Italian of his boots and socks. Nei-ther fit Daniels, so I benefited. The socks were a useful addition to my meager wardrobe.

That dawn, the tanks turned round and began to rumble back toward and beyond the original start line. We did not then know it, but Monty, sensing a stalemate in the south of the Alamein line where we were had decided to group all his armor in the north for a knockout punch once the infantry had cleared the way. We watched them go, their radio masts whipping in the gray air, as the massive vehicles lurched to and fro on the twisting path through the minefields. The gaps were never cut in a straight line but in zigzags of varying length, so that, once the stanchions and the guiding wires were removed, the enemy could not just hit on the right bearing and then drive straight through. Now we felt isolated, alone.

A day or so later, the colonel was getting bored with all the inactivity. Al-ready, he had viewed the battle scene by walking into no-man's-land in sunny daylight, with me keeping a safe distance behind. He called me forward and told me to hand over my map board so that he could study the terrain then oc-cupied by the Italian *Folgore* Division, one of Benito Mussolini's crack air-borne units. He was waving the board around, its acetate cover reflecting the sun's rays in all directions, while I cringed behind him. The obvious hap-pened. There was a burst of machine-gun fire from in front. I flung myself down and groveled in the shallowest of sandy depressions. I looked up to see the colonel staring at me with contempt. Still standing erect, he turned round and walked slowly back to our lines. I followed him, almost crouching on all fours, expecting at any minute the fatal burst that would tear my back apart.

The next morning, when I reported to battalion headquarters, Colonel Williams said briskly: "Right, Greenfield. A spot of reconnaissance, I think." He pointed a forefinger at the map. "See this narrow wadi, here. Turns out into open ground—there and there. But it's a blind spot. Half the *Afrika Korps* could be lurking there and we wouldn't have a clue. So you and I'll take a Bren carrier and have a 'shufti,' what?"

The man is an idiot, I thought. If a reconnaissance had to be made, and I believed that the idea was due more to his inner urge to be up and doing than to military need, it should be carried out by the battalion intelligence officer, not the officer commanding the whole unit. Besides, I had studied the map carefully that morning and recalled a symbol in red (the enemy color) denoting an 88mm gun dug in opposite the exit to the wadi. I certainly was not looking for a medal for gallantry, posthumously awarded. So, reluctantly, I climbed into the front of the Bren carrier, alongside the driver, while the colonel occupied the space behind him.

We reached the wadi and began threading a path toward the area where it opened out. Fifty yards short, I muttered to the driver under the crunching noise of the tracks, "Take it easy, slow down." Our progress dwindled to a crawl.

"Come on," Colonel Williams shouted, impatiently. "We'll be all day."

The pace quickened slightly, but when we were about twenty yards from the opening, I kept muttering to the driver, "Slower, slower."

The colonel could take it no longer. "Halt!" he shouted. "For God's sake, Greenfield! You keep farting around like this, it'll be dark before we finish. Here, you take my place. I'll do the navigating."

We changed places and set off again at a brisk pace. We had hardly traveled ten yards when there was a rending, earsplitting crash. The left side of the carrier dropped and a pillar of smoke and sand dust rose on that side. I vaulted over the other side and lay flat in the sand. The *Afrika Korps* always set one or more machine guns beside an eighty-eight, so that troops bailing out of a wounded vehicle could be shot down as they ran. But nothing happened for a few moments, and I cautiously stood up, crouching.

Peering around, I saw the left front of the carrier had slipped into a sizable hole. The blast had flung a section of the heavy track, more than six feet in length, several yards away. Christ, I thought, we ran over a Teller mine, the deadliest kind of mine in the desert war. The colonel was huddled on the floor of the front compartment, moaning softly. There was a green sheen on his face. (We learned later that one leg had been broken a dozen times between ankle and thigh and had to be amputated.) The driver was shaken, and the stout gear lever had wrapped itself around his ankle so that he could not move. The ankle was later found to be broken, but he was a stolid countryman and in good spirits.

I had to do something about the colonel. He was obviously suffering great pain and he might have serious internal injuries. Looking to my left, I saw a partially concealed tank about one hundred yards away. Its side was painted with the Kent Yeomanry insignia. Tanks, I knew, always carried morphine vials. Besides, with its powerful transmitter, the tank could radio a message back for medical help. The only snag, as I discovered while I trotted toward the tank, was having to cross a minefield to reach it.

In theory, the weight of a man was insufficient to set off an antitank mine. On the two other occasions I had to cross an uncharted minefield, the theory proved itself, as fortunately it did this time. Panting, I leaned against the tank, which was sheltered behind a small bump in the desert. The turret opened and a young officer with long, fair hair popped his head out. He had seen us go up on the minefield and had tried to wave us away, but the colonel was too intent on a bunkered forward progress, and his back blocked my forward vision. Yes, they had morphine to spare, he said. Give the wounded man this much, and try to get him to keep it under his tongue as it dissolves. And, yes, they would radio back at once to their headquarters, which would pass the message by radio to ours.

Back at the smashed carrier, I managed to get the colonel, half conscious from the shock, to take the drug. He was still huddled in the bottom of the vehicle with his knees drawn up under his chin. His left leg looked like jelly, as if only the ankle puttees and the long stocking were holding it in place. I did not risk moving him, with the chance of aggravating his injuries and causing him more pain. The driver was sitting there stoically. His broken ankle was clearly hurting him, but he smoked a cigarette and made a joke or two as we waited for help to arrive.

Half an hour later, it came, in the shape of Captain Shragovitch, driving his jeep, accompanied by a fifteen-hundred-pound medical truck. Shrag had a stretcher assembled, and the medical orderlies expertly lifted the colonel out of the broken carrier and into the truck. The two orderlies and the immensely strong Shrag managed to tug the twisted gear lever clear of the driver's ankle and release him from his seat. He hopped into the back of the truck, which was ready to drive away.

As Captain Shragovitch was organizing the removal of the wounded, I noticed that the backs of his chunky calves were almost brushing a black, thread-like wire running parallel to and about six inches above the ground. I went rigid. It was part of an antipersonnel mine. If the wire were pushed forward or backward, it would tug against the safety catch on top of the covered mine. Once released, the percussion cap would spring the mine about a foot upward, then it would burst, scattering a curtain of flying steel splinters. Half a step back from Shrag and we would both lose feet, legs, hands, and arms—if we were lucky. More likely, we would both be killed and the occupants of the truck severely wounded.

I took a pace nearer him and, as casually as I could, said, "Shrag, for Chrissake don't move backward. Take half a pace forward, in fact."

He began, "What the hell . . ."

But I interrupted: "You're almost standing on an AP [antipersonnel] mine, you clown."

The good doctor leaped ahead like a startled hare. When he turned around, I explained the significance of the thin, black wire. By now the truck was ready to move off, we waved it away, and Shrag carefully placed one foot after the other over the wire and returned to the safety of the track. He proposed, and I seconded with alacrity, that, for medicinal purposes of course, we should each have a snort from the brandy he always carried in his jeep for emergencies. We were both, no doubt, suffering from recent shocks to our respective constitutions. We each downed a large tot, and then it occurred to Shrag that I might have undergone two shocks, one with the colonel and now with the mine. I accepted without too much demur but pointed out that my father had told me the perils of drinking alone. So I insisted that he join me, which he did.

Then he decided we ought to get back to battalion headquarters. He soon had the jeep careening along the narrow, zigzag path through the minefield. Two hundred yards from home, he swung a little wide on one bend, there was an enormous thump and crash, and the front wheel next to where I was sitting shot straight up into the air about eight feet. We had gone over another mine. Luckily, we always followed regulations by covering the floors of jeeps with heavy sandbags. Doc and I both felt the shock, but the sandbags absorbed most of it. The fact that the part of the vehicle to run over the mine was an extension to the main body was also fortunate. By then a sobered-up couple, we trudged the last part of the journey on foot.

Perhaps a couple of days after I had almost been blown up twice, the battalion had moved and the intelligence section was completing its new office, which consisted of a pit alongside the 1,500-pound truck. Daniels was helping to pull the truck's canvas cover—tilt, as we called it—over the hole to provide shade. I was squatting on the step of the truck, studying the map on its board, and Sergeant Mike Henderson was standing up, peering over my shoulder. There was a sudden scream and an immediate earsplitting crash. A jagged hole appeared in the map board; the sergeant jerked like a hooked fish. He clapped his hand to his thigh, and blood welled through his fingers. An enemy shell had landed out of the blue. Its blast knocked Daniels back into the pit he had dug. We patched Henderson up with his field dressing, and he was quickly evacuated to the nearest advance dressing station.

When the hubbub died down, I felt a slight itching on my left elbow. There was a two-inch rip in the roll-up of my shirtsleeve that, as I pulled the sleeve down, was repeated every few inches. The shell splinter had sliced through the map board and through the bulk of my rolled-up sleeve to strike the sergeant's thigh. If I had been squatting five or six inches to my left, it would have struck me in the heart.

Most men in action secretly think they are invulnerable. Otherwise, the strain of battle would be unbearable. Indeed, experienced observers know that the first look that crosses a man's face when he is wounded is one of surprise that he, of all people, should stop a bullet or shell splinter. But, having survived unscathed two mine explosions and one freak shell burst, I was beginning to suffer the dangerous delusion that God was not only an Englishman but that the initials G. G. did not merely stand for "Good God" but for "George Greenfield" as well.

Lieutenant Colonel Williams was soon replaced by Lieutenant Colonel Hubert Percival, seconded from the Highland Light Infantry. Sandy-haired, with an almost ginger mustache, he was a man at ease with himself, dry, laconic, and not liable to flap like his predecessor. He had received the Distinguished Service Order for a previous action and so had nothing to prove. He quickly won the confidence of his officers and men. For the first time since leaving England, our leader was a real man.

The measure of the man was evident early on. The battle in the south of the Alamein line, after being static for its first nine days, was beginning to move forward. The main forces in the north were pounding their way through *Afrika Korps* defenses and minefields, while our diversionary attacks were keeping one panzer division away from the major action. On this occasion, two or three days after Percival's arrival, I had been on the go for more than twenty-four hours, moving around no-man's-land, mainly on foot, to check enemy sites and pick up information from returning night patrols. I was so tired on return to headquarters that I unrolled my sleeping bag, climbed in without even taking off my boots, and fell asleep at once. I must not have moved during the night for, when I rolled out of the blankets and stood up, a big, black scorpion came prancing out behind me, tail cocked, pincers aggressively thrust out. Just then, Percival emerged from his trench.

"Sir, sir," I shrilled, "there's been a scorpion in my bedroll all night!"

"Well, if it's female," he said, "you'd better marry it."

Whenever he and I went on a reconnaissance together, he would give me general directions in a casual voice and then let me get on with it, a refreshing change from his predecessor. Our only problem was that he disliked smoking, and I was hooked on the weed. On one occasion, when we were away from battalion headquarters for most of the day, picking our way between soft sand patches in a jeep, I found that the pack of cigarettes that I could have sworn was on a shelf in the back of the jeep was not there. We drove cautiously along and stopped to use binoculars. I was gasping for a cigarette and told Percival. I should have been suspicious when he nonchalantly produced a pack of cigarettes and offered to sell me one for a shilling. I jumped at the offer. At the next halt, the price had doubled, and each time it doubled again. By the time we got back to headquarters, I owed the colonel twelve pounds, sixteen shillings—more than two weeks' pay for a lieutenant. Being the man he was, the colonel handed me back the half-empty pack of cigarettes, which he had indeed swiped from the jeep, and let me off the debt. I should have forsworn smoking at that moment, but, alas for these leathery lungs, the filthy habit was to persist for the next fifty years.

Many of us who had grown up with General Montgomery, first in the Twelfth Corps and then South-Eastern Command, thought he was out of his depth against a battle-hardened opponent with panache like Erwin Rommel. As the stalemate persisted into the eighth and ninth day, our private doubts grew. But then luck, or force of arms, or military skills, or a combination of them began to prevail. The little man, of whom Churchill was later to say, "Unbeatable in battle and unbearable in victory," was on his way. Under cover of darkness, Rommel began to withdraw his troops in an orderly fashion from the north end of the battle line. In the south, where the Forty-fourth Division remained, the enemy opposite us, mainly the Italian *Ariete* Division with a few units from the tougher *Folgore* Division, fled in disorder. Operation Supercharge, the westward advance to drive the German and Italian forces out of North Africa, had begun.

It was a hectic period; unconnected episodes as bright as lanterns remain in the memory. A squadron of the Free French Brigade was lined up in its Bren carriers at the near edge of a broad minefield. They were too impatient to move in a single file along the path cut through the minefield. So, with the trumpet blast of "La Marseillaise," they drove straight forward in a line. The explosions were like the bass notes of a giant organ. Some of the carriers drove only five yards into the minefield before blowing up; some managed ten, a few fifteen yards. It was a combination of idiocy and bravery to match the charge of the Six Hundred, but, as the French general dryly remarked then, "It is magnificent, but it is not war." In less than a minute the carriers, intended to be a mobile screen for our soft-skinned vehicles, were left lurching and smoking in ruins dotting the minefield. The unnecessary casualties had to be evacuated at risk to the medical staff's lives.

We reached a kind of crossroads where a north-south track bisected one running east-west. Alongside it was a dump of brown, cardboard boxes. The boxes were crammed with contraceptives, each in its little brown paper packet. What on earth were they doing there? In my own experience and from observation, men in action tens of miles from civilization, where the nearest female would be a dead she-camel caught in a minefield, find that the urge to survive subsumes the sexual drive. As battalion intelligence officer, I had a duty to keep in close touch with all the companies, but I never came across or even heard a vague rumor of any homosexual relationships developing. When the troops saw the heaped-up boxes, they laughed, muttered something about "half his luck," and promptly rolled the condoms over the muzzles of their rifles to keep out the sand.

Later the same day, we suddenly came to understand the purpose of all those contraceptives. Making a sweep northward, I spotted a crashed aircraft in a dip not far from the track. I told my driver to approach it in the jeep—but cautiously. It might be a decoy, with a desperate squad from the *Folgore* Parachute Division dug in close by, prepared to fight it out on a last-man, last-round basis. But as we approached, it was evident that there was no one outside the aircraft. We could see it had been shot down by the Royal Air Force from the row of bullet holes across the front screen and the strips of waxed cloth hanging off the wings. They were marked with the sign of the Red Cross, as was the fuselage on both sides.

"Bit saucy, that blue job pilot," the driver remarked.

"Take a look inside," I said.

The stench of death engulfed the plane. It must have been there for three or four days, and the hot sun beating down on two dozen dead bodies still sitting in their seats, slowly going black in the face as putrefaction set in, had accelerated the process. Apart from the pilot and co-pilot, there were only women on board, young women, several of them with long blond hair. I saw some strange sights in my six years of military service, but this was the most macabre of them all.

It confirmed rumors that had circulated round the Eighth Army for many weeks. This was—or had been—a brothel plane. Under the guise of a Red Cross hospital aircraft, its task was to take prostitutes from Europe, some of them no doubt from the fatherland itself, to an administrative area behind the front line. A row of tents would be set up, and men from the *Afrika Korps'* fighting units would be brought back for a few moments of satisfied desire. And, to guard against venereal diseases, the boxes of contraceptives would be required.

✦

BY NOW, PRISONERS were becoming a problem. In the north, Rommel withdrew his mainly German troops in good order, always keeping slightly ahead of our pursuing armor. But in the south the retreat was a shambles. As far as we could see, the Italian officers had abandoned their men. Hungry, thirsty, many of them barefoot, they lined the tracks, pleading with us to take them prisoner and set them up in a nice camp with regular meals and plenty of water. But our orders were to keep pressing northwestward, gradually moving toward the coastal road. We could not even commandeer their rifles and other weapons, as the jeep and the 1,500-pound truck would bog down under the great weight. All we could do was detach one capable private soldier to lead them back toward divisional rear echelon. One wag lined them up like a drill sergeant, made them march in step, and taught them the words and melody of a popular jingoistic song, "There'll Always Be an England." The splendid Italian baritones, few of whom knew even a smattering of English, lustily sang, each man, no doubt, hoping to create a good impression with his captors.

On the whole, our men behaved well toward them, but there were exceptions. Once, I had halted the column and was busy trying to work out bearings on prominent features to discover our exact position on the map. Attempting to do too many things at once, I did not concentrate properly on a couple of questions asked by a member of the intelligence section.

"Do you know the Italian for water, sir?" he asked.

"*Aqua,* I think."

"And for watch?"

"God knows. The French for 'clock' is *horloge.* Try *orlogio.*"

I went on with my map calculations, and then the penny dropped. I jumped out of the jeep and walked some way down the track. There was my man standing by the trackside as the prisoners shambled by, holding up a *chagul* in one hand. A *chagul* was a bag shaped like a hot water bottle but made of thick calico or webbing. It was filled with water, now more plentiful after the breakout, and hung on the outside of trucks and jeeps. The water very slowly seeped through to the outside and the desert breeze kept the contents cool. He was shouting *"Aqua?"* and then, pointing to his wrist with the other hand, *"Orlogio."* He was already doing well from the bartering. Four or five handsome wristwatches were strapped above his left wrist. A watch for a mouthful of cold water—it must have seemed a worthwhile exchange to the thirsty prisoners.

I ordered him to hand them back to their owners, an impossible task, but at least he would not score from the deal. And then I told our new intelligence sergeant to put him on extra duties for the next week. For years afterward in peacetime, I would look closely at the pictures of property dealers and black marketeers in the newspapers to see if the market enterprise shown by a Buff on that occasion had reaped its due reward.

✦

OUR BIGGEST PROBLEM was with senior Italian officers and in particular their generals. We overran one headquarters to find silk-lined tents and the staff, from the commander on down, dressed in their best silk uniforms, ablaze with medals, each with a leather suitcase packed, awaiting capture. One tall, imposing general refused to surrender to me, a mere lieutenant. He would only hand himself over to an officer of equivalent rank. As he spoke fairly fluent English, I explained that our generals were rather too busy fighting a war to attend to the niceties of military etiquette, so he could either surrender to me and get transport back to civilization or stay on indefinitely in the desert, without food and water. He said he would report me to the Geneva Convention, but I did not stay awake at night worrying. Indeed, while I had originally been thinking of sending him back in a comparatively comfortable spare jeep, I now arranged for the tailgate of a bumpy truck to be lowered and for the bemedalled captive to be shoved without ceremony up into the vehicle, where he had to stand, swaying precariously as it lurched along the ruts of the road.

And so it went on until the colonel, who had attended early morning orders at brigade headquarters, returned and took me to one side. He quickly explained that the coastal road, which we were due to reach later that day, was already clogged with too many tanks and trucks. If units bunched up too much on the one narrow road, it could make a field day for the *Luftwaffe* and its dive-bombing Stukas. So the orders were that the brigade, which had suffered severe casualties on the opening night of the battle, would be withheld.

It would withdraw into reserve outside Alexandria and eventually be broken up. Whatever position we had reached at twelve noon that day would be our farthest move westward. The battalion would then halt, regroup, and withdraw to safety. But I was not to pass the information on to anyone at all. The enemy sent over reconnaissance aircraft every day, and we had to give the impression of a normal advance.

I was more frightened in the next three hours than I had been throughout the war up till then and, looking back, than I was to be ever again. To have come so far without a scratch . . . to have had several near-misses, it would be just my luck, I felt, if a "stay behind" desperate group of the enemy were to come bursting out of cover and gun down my jeep. It was, after all, the lead vehicle of the whole battalion. Or maybe they would be crafty and let me through unharmed before tackling the trucks of the main body, knowing they could always pick me off afterward at their leisure. It would have been more comforting to confide in Daniels or one of the other members of the intelligence section, but I had to maintain secrecy.

The minute hand of my watch crept round the circle. Ironically, the expanse of soft sand that had held up our progress on previous days had given way to a flat, hard area, and the jeep could bowl along at twenty miles an hour or more, pressing farther on its journey into fear. The last quarter-hour was almost unbearable. We had seen nothing untoward all morning, no crashed aircraft or burned-out tanks. And that made the arid landscape all the more sinister. Five minutes to the hour, then two minutes to the hour, and at last both hands on my watch stood vertically to attention. I told the driver to halt and turn the jeep round. Surprised, he did so. I stood up and, waving both arms, gave the signal to about-turn.

For us, the battle was over.

STALINGRAD

ANTONY BEEVOR

Stalingrad was not only the first major Soviet victory in an Eastern Front war already a year and a half old but a psychological turning point. Antony Beevor calls it "the most pitiless, and perhaps the most significant battle in modern history," a conclusion hard to argue with. The battle may have been unavoidable. Hitler wanted to protect the flank of his drive southward to the Caucasus Mountains and the oil fields of the Caspian Sea, and he saw Stalingrad merely as one of the anchors for that flank. (Climbers actually planted the Nazi flag on Mount Elbrus, the highest peak in Europe, and patrols reached the Caspian.) But the battle might never have taken the obsessive form it did had Stalingrad's name been different.

Beevor, one of our best younger military historians, describes Stalingrad's special terrors. In September, when fighting began, General Friedrich Paulus, commander of the German Sixth Army, told Hitler that he would need ten days to reduce the city on the Volga, an estimate that, in the next five months, was soon forgotten. By the time fall arrived, it had turned into the longest close-quarters struggle in history. "Rattenkrieg"—rats' war—German soldiers called it. "One speaks about death," one man wrote home, "as one does about breakfast." A building might be a sandwich of Germans on the top floor, Russians in-between, and more Germans on the ground floor. Underneath the corpse-packed rubble Soviet assault squads equipped with explosive charges roamed the sewers. The hand grenade became king, and the flamethrower its court chamberlain. Here was trench warfare gone vertical, but with concentrations unheard of even in World War I. On a front five kilometers wide, five infantry divisions might attack, plus tanks and planes. It was as if Hitler, who increasingly took charge of the battle, had reverted to the ethos of the old Western Front, where he had served as a corporal. Zhukov let him do so, while with deceptive care he and the Soviet chief of staff, Alexander Vasilievksy, prepared the two-pronged assault, Uranus, that would trap and swallow the Sixth Army. Hitler refused to believe that the Soviets had the reserve armies left to mount an operation like Uranus—but then he also forbade mention of winter. As it turned out, Zhukov would launch both Uranus and Mars in the snow. The success of one would allow the failure of the other to be forgotten.

Antony Beevor is the author of *Stalingrad* and such books as *Crete: The Battle and the Resistance* and (with Artemis Cooper) *Paris after the Liberation*. He is writing an account of the 1945 siege of Berlin. Beevor lives in London.

JUST BEFORE DAWN ON THE MORNING OF AUGUST 23, 1942, THE Sixteenth Panzer Division moved out of its bridgehead on the right bank of the River Don. Lieutenant Colonel Count Hyazinth von Strachwitz's battalion of the Second Panzer Regiment was the point unit. The regiment descended from the oldest cavalry unit of the Prussian army, the Great Elector's Life Guard Cuirassiers. Strachwitz, who enjoyed the good looks of a matinee idol, had a reputation to maintain. In the rapid advance to the Marne of 1914, his light cavalry detachment had pushed so far to the front that the men could make out the towers of Notre Dame. This time he wanted not just to reach the Volga, but to seize a crossing point as well before the Soviets recovered from their surprise.

The rock-hard steppe may have offered fast going, but tank commanders standing erect in their turrets, wearing goggles against the dust, had to keep an eye out ahead for hidden gullies invisible to the driver. For the first twenty kilometers, the panzer crews sighted few enemy soldiers. The slightly rolling terrain of dry, rough grass seemed eerily empty.

Around midday, after a flurry of radio transmissions, the divisional commander, General Hans Hube, suddenly halted his headquarters. Engines were switched off to conserve fuel. Soon the insect-droning of a small airplane could be heard. A Fieseler Storch appeared. It circled, then came in to land alongside the command half-tracks. The pilot climbed out and strode over. It was General Wolfram von Richthofen, the commander in chief of the Fourth Air Fleet.

Richthofen, in shirtsleeves and with his uniform cap pushed back, exposing part of his shaved head, greeted Hube curtly. He told him that on orders from the führer's headquarters, all of Fourth Air Fleet's resources were to be diverted to the Stalingrad front. "Make use of the day!" he added. Two hours later, the panzer crews looked up to see waves of Junkers 88 and Heinkel III bombers, as well as squadrons of Junkers 87 Stukas, flying toward Stalingrad. A mass of aircraft-shaped shadows passed across the steppe.

On their return, the Stuka pilots sounded their sirens to greet the advancing troops. The panzer crews waved back exultantly. In the distance, they could already see the columns of smoke rising over the city.

That same evening, Strachwitz's armored vehicles halted on the high bank above the Volga, almost a mile across and "as calm as a great lake." The tank crews gazed through their binoculars toward Asia. They had reached the designated boundary of the Third Reich's eastern territories. Messerschmitt fighters performed victory rolls above their heads. Many soldiers thought the war was won. To their right, the city of Stalingrad blazed from the first of Richthofen's air raids, which killed 40,00 civilians. The only resistance the panzer crews faced came from antiaircraft batteries manned by female gun crews barely out of high school. "We had to fight shot for shot," the division reported, "against 37 flak positions manned by tenacious fighting women until they were all destroyed." Thus began the most pitiless, and perhaps the most significant, battle in modern history.

The feverish moods of optimism and doubt just before the Battle of Stalingrad were similar to those of the previous summer, during the first weeks of Operation Barbarossa. "The vastness of Russia devours us," Field Marshal Gerd von Rundstedt had written to his wife just after his armies had successfully completed the Uman encirclement. With an advance of more than 700 kilometers, the Wehrmacht had conquered huge territories, yet the horizon seemed just as limitless. The Red Army had lost more than two million men, yet still more Soviet armies appeared. "At the outset of the war," General Franz Halder wrote in his diary on August 11, 1941, "we reckoned on about 200 enemy divisions. Now we have already counted 360." Hitler was angered to find that although the door to the Soviet Union had been kicked in, the structure was failing to collapse as he had predicted. Russian soldiers were not like the French in 1940. All too many of them refused to acknowledge defeat.

Bad communications also took their toll. The railway tracks, which were a slightly broader gauge than found in Germany, had to be relaid, and instead of the highways marked on their maps, the armies had found dirt roads, whose choking dust could turn to glutinous mud in a brief summer downpour. Whole columns were brought to a halt until the ground dried. In many marshy places German troops had to build their own corduroy roads of birch trunks laid side to side. The farther they advanced into Russia, the harder it was to bring supplies forward. Panzer columns racing ahead would sometimes have to stop because of lack of fuel, and even when the mechanized artillery managed to keep up, the resupply of shells could never be guaranteed.

Adolf Hitler changed his mind about the main axis of advance again early in September. He at last agreed to an attack toward Moscow, yet the forces for Operation Typhoon were not ready until the very end of the month. There was little time left to achieve a decisive outcome before the Russian winter started in earnest. When General Friedrich Paulus, Halder's chief planner for Barbarossa, had raised the question of winter warfare earlier, Hitler had forbidden any mention of the subject.

The balance of power—geopolitical, industrial, economic, and demographic—swung decisively against the Axis in December 1941, with the failure to capture Moscow and the American entry into the war, yet this was not clear at the time. One should not forget the Allies' despair in the summer of 1942. The Japanese had inflicted humiliating defeats in the Far East, the Red Army appeared to be at the point of collapse, and Field Marshal Erwin Rommel was advancing toward Alexandria. The psychological turning point of the war would come only in the following winter with the battle for Stalingrad, which, partly because of its name, obsessed both Hitler and Stalin. The battle would become a personal duel.

When on the morning of June 1, 1942, the plan for the invasion of the Caucasus was presented at the führer's headquarters in the Ukraine, Hitler hardly mentioned Stalingrad. As far as his generals were concerned, the city was little more than a name on the map. The first phase of Operation Blue, the code name given to the next phase of the German advance, was to capture Voronezh to secure the left flank. The second was to catch the bulk of the Soviet forces in a great pincer movement west of the Don and destroy them. The Sixth Army would then move toward Stalingrad, but not occupy it, to secure the northeast flank, while General Ewald von Kleist's First Panzer Army and the Seventeenth Army advanced into the Caucasus. After Field Marshal Fedor von Bock had finished his outline, Hitler spoke. He made it all sound so simple. The Red Army was finished after the winter fighting, and the recent fighting around Kharkov had again confirmed German supremacy.

On June 28, the Second Army and the Fourth Panzer Army, which were deployed around Kursk, attacked due east toward Voronezh. More by happenstance than strategy, the desperate resistance of the Red Army at Voronezh started a phase of concentrating defenses on cities, rather than arbitrary lines on the map. Stalin at last allowed Marshal Semyon Timoshenko's armies to pull back to avoid encirclement, but they had been so badly mauled that on July 12 a new army group command—the Stalingrad Front—was established by Stavka (general headquarters) directive. Although nobody dared write or voice the defeatist suggestion that the Red Army might be forced back as far as the Volga, a suspicion began to grow on the Soviet side that this was where the main battle would have to be fought. The most significant evidence was the prompt dispatch from Saratov to Stalingrad of the Tenth NKVD (People's Commissariat for Internal Affairs) Rifle Division.

Those summer days seemed glorious for German front-line regiments unaware of the significance of Voronezh. "As far as the eye can see," a war correspondent wrote in his diary, "armored vehicles and half-tracks are rolling forward over the steppe. Pennants float in the shimmering afternoon air." Commanders stood fearlessly erect in their tank turrets, one arm raised high, waving their companies forward. These times were especially intoxicating for young officers in panzer divisions, racing over the steppe to take Rostov-on-the-Don. The recovery of their morale with the spring weather, the new equipment, and the great success at Kharkov in May had ended unpleasant thoughts of the Russian winter.

Hitler, however, could not restrain his impatience. He had not counted on being delayed at Voronezh, and although panzer divisions streaked ahead in sudden breakthroughs, they were also brought to a halt at crucial moments due to a lack of fuel. This represented a doubly goading delay for the führer, with his eyes constantly straying across the map to the oil fields of the Caucasus.

His feverish mood pushed him into the most disastrous change of plan. The central stage of Operation Blue had originally been a rapid advance by the Sixth Army and Fourth Panzer Army toward Stalingrad to cut off Timoshenko's retreating troops, before the attack was launched against Rostov and across the lower Don into the Caucasus. Hitler was so desperate to speed the attack into the Caucasus that he decided to run the two stages concurrently, which greatly reduced the concentration of force.

Rejecting Halder's advice, he diverted General Herman Hoth's Fourth Panzer Army southward and also deprived the Sixth Army of the XL Panzer Corps, thus slowing its advance dramatically—many have argued fatally—into a slow, frontal assault on Stalingrad. Consequently, Paulus's advance guard did not reach the edge of the city until the end of August, and his divisions were not ready to launch a full assault until the second week of September. At a conference at Hitler's *Werwolf* headquarters at Vinnitsa on September 8, Paulus estimated that the capture of the city would take about ten days and that he would then need "fourteen days of regrouping." What he had completely failed to appreciate was that Richthofen's destruction of the city from the air had turned it into a jumble of rubble, ideally suited to a desperate defender.

While Paulus was at Vinnitsa, General Vasily Chuikov was summoned by Commissar General Nikita Khrushchev and General Yeremenko to be appointed commander of the Sixty-second Army, defending the city. Comrade Chuikov, said Khrushchev, looked at him and said that he had understood correctly.

They all knew that to hold on they had only one resource greater than the Germans', and that was human life. "Time is blood," as Chuikov put it later, with brutal simplicity. Discipline was to be merciless. Senior officers had started to slip back over the river, abandoning their men, many of whom, as Chuikov realized, also wanted "to get across the Volga as quickly as possible, away from this hell." He made sure that NKVD troops controlled every landing stage and jetty. Deserters, whatever their rank, faced summary justice. Chuikov also recognized that the Soviet defenders had to fight in the closest possible quarters to reduce the German advantage of tank and air superiority. They must also exploit the German reluctance to fight at night, for the same reasons, but also to wear the enemy down through physical exhaustion and stress.

Paulus launched a series of set-piece offensives that managed to seize great chunks of the city. The first, on September 13, took the southern part; the next, starting on September 27, seized the northern salient right up to the factory district of Stalingrad along the Volga bank. During that month alone, the Sixth Army expended 25 million rounds of small arms ammunition. But all the time Paulus's troops suffered constant casualties during what they described as the *"Rattenkrieg,"* or rat's war.

Fighting in Stalingrad itself could not have been more different from frontline existence out on the steppe. It represented a new form of warfare concentrated in the ruins of civilian life. The detritus of war—burned-out tanks, shell cases, signal wire, and grenade boxes—was mixed with the wreckage of family homes—iron bedsteads, lamps, and household utensils. Vasily Grossman wrote of the

> fighting in the brick-strewn, half-demolished rooms and corridors of apartment blocks, where there might still be a vase of withered flowers on a table, or a boy's homework open on the desk. In an observation post, high in a ruined

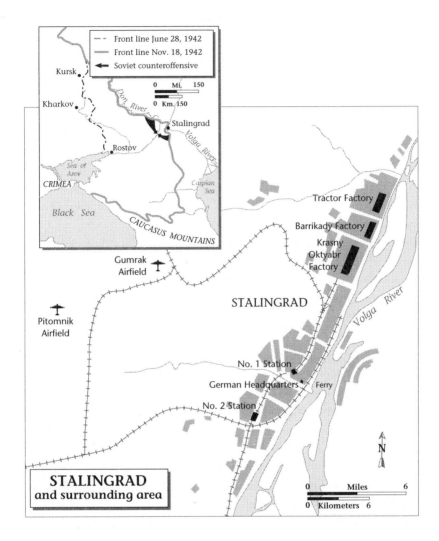

Front line June 28, 1942
Front line Nov. 18, 1942
Soviet counteroffensive

Kursk

Kharkov

Don River

Stalingrad

Rostov

Volga River

Sea of Azov

CRIMEA

Caspian Sea

Black Sea

CAUCASUS MOUNTAINS

Tractor Factory

Barrikady Factory

Krasny Oktyabr Factory

Gumrak Airfield

STALINGRAD

Volga River

Pitomnik Airfield

No. 1 Station

German Headquarters

Ferry

No. 2 Station

N

STALINGRAD
and surrounding area

Miles

Kilometers

From the end of June 1942 until the middle of November 1942, German armies gobbled up vast portions of the steppe of Southern Russia (inset). The map of Stalingrad and the area surrounding the city on the Volga shows some of the principal landmarks around which fighting ebbed and flowed for five months.

building, an artillery spotter with a periscope might watch for targets through a convenient shell-hole in the wall, sitting on a kitchen chair.

German infantrymen loathed house and street fighting, and they did not adapt nearly as well as their Soviet opponents. On the whole, the German infantryman seems to have found such close quarters combat, which broke all conventional military boundaries and dimensions, psychologically disorienting. During the last phase of the September battles, a large brick warehouse on the Volga bank near the mouth of the Tsaritsa was "like a layered cake" with Germans on the top floor, Russians below them, and more Germans underneath them. The enemy was often unrecognizable. Every uniform was impregnated by the same dun-colored dust.

German generals had not envisaged what awaited their divisions in the ruined city. The decision to assault Stalingrad had deprived them of their great blitzkrieg advantages of armored mobility. It also reduced them to the techniques of the First World War, even though their military theorists had argued that trench warfare had been "an aberration in the art of war." The Sixth Army, for example, found itself having to respond to Soviet tactics by reinventing the "stormwedges" introduced in January 1918: assault groups of ten men armed with a machine gun, light mortar, and several flamethrowers for clearing bunkers and cellars.

Chuikov's plan was to funnel and fragment German mass assaults with "breakwaters." Strengthened buildings, manned by infantry with antitank rifles and machine guns, would deflect the attackers into channels, with camouflaged T-34 tanks and antitank guns waiting half-buried in the rubble behind. Most of the fighting, however, consisted of lethal little conflicts. One of Chuikov's officers wrote that the battle was fought by assault squads, generally six or eight strong, from "the Stalingrad Academy of Street Fighting." They armed themselves with knives and sharpened spades for silent killing, as well as submachine guns and grenades. (Spades were in such short supply that men carved their names in the handle and slept with their head on the blade to make sure that nobody stole it.) The Stalingrad sewer system no longer worked, so Chuikov promised: "We shall strike at him from under ground." The assault squads sent into the sewers were strengthened with flamethrowers and sappers brought in explosive charges.

The Germans were more frightened during the hours of darkness, and stress accelerated their exhaustion. The German foot soldier, the *Landser*, had a special fear of the Siberians from Colonel Nikolay Batyuk's 284th Rifle Division, who were considered to be natural hunters. "If only you could understand what terror is," a German soldier wrote in a letter captured by the Russians. "At the slightest rustle, I pull the trigger and fire off tracer bullets in bursts from the machine gun." The Russians also kept up the tension by firing flares into the night sky from time to time to give the impression of an imminent attack.

The Soviets used both their two-engine night bombers, which attracted the fire of every German flak battery on the front, and large numbers of maneuverable little U-2 biplanes, which were used to drop small bombs during night raids. The worst part was the eerie change in sound. In the distance, the U-2 sounded like one of its many nicknames, the "sewing machine." Then, as the pilot approached his target, he would switch off the engine to glide in like a bird of prey. The only sound then would be the swishing of air through its struts, until the bomb fell. The aircraft's psychological effect was considerable. It attracted more nicknames than any other machine or weapon used at Stalingrad. Other names included "the duty NCO," because of the way it crept up unannounced, the "midnight bomber," the "coffee-mill," and the "railway-crow."

"One house taken by the Russians, one taken by the Germans," scribbled Vasily Grossman in his notebook just after his arrival. "How can heavy artillery be used in such a battle?" He soon discovered the answer. Soviet artillery massed on the far side of the Volga did not attempt to shell German frontline positions. Their purpose was to hammer enemy lines of communications and, above all, smash battalions forming up for attack. Fire was directed by Soviet artillery observation officers who were concealed like snipers at the top of ruined buildings. The Germans, well aware of the danger they represented, treated them as a high-priority target for their own snipers or antitank guns.

During house- and bunker-clearing, no weapon was more necessary than hand grenades. Red Army soldiers called them "pocket artillery." They were also effective in defense. On Chuikov's orders, grenades were stocked ready to hand in recesses dug into the side of every trench. Another useful weapon, often as dangerous to the user as to its intended victims, was the flamethrower, based on a crudely fashioned carbine stock with a barrel and nozzle.

Red Army soldiers also proved enthusiastic improvisers, inventing gadgets to kill Germans. New booby traps were dreamed up, each more ingenious and unpredictable in its results than the last. Angered at their inability to fight back against the Stuka attacks, Captain Ilgachkin, a battalion commander, decided with one of his soldiers, Private Repa, to construct their own form of antiaircraft gun. They fastened an antitank rifle to the spokes of a cart wheel, which in turn was mounted on a tall stake driven into the ground.

Another device was dreamed up by Vassili Ivanovich Zaitsev, who soon became the most famous Russian sniper in Stalingrad. Zaitsev's idea was to attach the telescopic sight from his sniper's rifle to an antitank gun and then take on machine-gun nests, shooting a shell right through their loophole. But he soon found that however exact his gun-laying, the charges in the mass-produced antitank shells were not consistent enough for precision shooting.

The garrisons holding the fortified buildings so central to Chuikov's strategy suffered great privations when cut off for days at a time. Some of them included young women medical orderlies or signalers. These garrison soldiers were less likely to be soaked to the skin or suffer from trench foot, unlike their counterparts out in the steppe. Instead they had to endure dust, smoke, an overwhelming cacophony of noise, hunger and, worst of all, thirst. The city had been without fresh water since the pumping station was destroyed by the Luftwaffe in the August raids. Knowing the consequences of drinking polluted water, desperate soldiers shot at drainpipes in the hopes of extracting a few drops.

Supplying forward positions with food was a constant problem. One antitank detachment had a Kazan Tartar cook who filled a large army thermos with tea or soup, fastened it to his back, and crawled up to the frontline positions under fire. If the thermos was hit by shrapnel or bullets, the hapless cook was soaked in tea and soup. Later, when the frost became really hard the soup or tea froze and he was "covered in icicles by the time he got back."

Women medical orderlies, most of them students, were among the bravest people on the ruined battlefield. Their sacrifices were often wasted through the subsequent treatment of their charges. The casualties they carried or dragged over the rubble and down to the edge of the Volga had to wait until long after nightfall. They were then loaded like sacks of potatoes onto the supply boats, empty for the return crossing. When the wounded were off-loaded on the east bank, they were frequently abandoned for hours without water, food, or care. Survival was far from guaranteed even after reaching one of the score of field hospitals on the east bank of the Volga. Conditions in Red Army hospitals, despite the presence of some of the finest Russian doctors, resembled those of a meat-processing factory.

In the great battle of attrition, the shipments of wounded to the east bank had to be matched by fresh "meat for the cannon" taken across the Volga into the city. The Stavka drip-fed the Sixty-second Army with reinforcement divisions as their predecessors were shot to pieces. The new battalions were marched forward at nightfall for embarkation under the eyes of the NKVD troops. They could only stare across in silence at the city on the skyline opposite lit by fires, and try to ignore the smell of burning and of corpses decomposing under the rubble. Patches of the river were still aflame with oil. There were also NKVD detachments on many of the ships, ready to shoot anyone who dived overboard in a final desperate attempt to avoid his fate on the west bank.

The Soviet authorities were quite ruthless in their discipline and summary justice, none more than Chuikov. "In the blazing city," he wrote, "we did not suffer cowards, we had no room for them." The first six weeks of the battle were the hardest in establishing a ferocious discipline. The political department of the Stalingrad Front only felt able on October 8 to report to Aleksandr Shcherbakov in Moscow that "the defeatist mood is almost eliminated, and the number of treasonous incidents is getting lower."

That the Soviet regime was almost as unforgiving toward its own soldiers as toward the enemy is demonstrated by the total figure of 13,500 executions, both summary and judicial, during the Battle of Stalingrad. This included all crimes classed by the commissars as "extraordinary events," from retreating without orders to self-inflicted wounds, desertion, crossing over to the enemy, corruption, and anti-Soviet activities. Red Army soldiers were also deemed guilty if they failed to shoot immediately at any comrades seen trying to desert or to surrender to the enemy.

The most significant number of desertions occurred from batches of civilian reinforcements drafted in from districts close to the front. For example, a large proportion of the ninety-three deserters from the 15th Guards Rifle Division had been citizens of Stalingrad evacuated to Kranoarmeisk. "These men were completely untrained and some of them had no uniforms. In the haste of mobilization, their passports were not taken from many of them." This, the report to Moscow acknowledged, was a serious mistake. "Clad in civilian clothes and having passports, they easily managed to get back over the Volga. It is necessary and urgent to take passports from all soldiers."

Even day-to-day administrative policy confirmed the impression of soldiers as discardable items. New boots, uniforms, and equipment were reserved entirely for new armies being formed in the rear. For frontline soldiers at Stalingrad, replacement items did not come from the quartermaster's store, they came off the bodies of dead comrades. Nothing was wasted. Men sentenced to death had to strip before they were shot on the lip of a shellhole. Soldiers were even sent forward at night into no-man's-land to strip corpses to their underclothes.

On Monday, October 14, 1942, Paulus launched the heaviest attack yet on the factory district of northern Stalingrad. The offensive began on a narrow front, using every available Stuka in General Richthofen's Fourth Air Fleet. Concentrated German artillery and mortar fire smashed into dugouts, and phosphorus shells set on fire any remaining combustible material. "The fighting assumed monstrous proportions beyond all possibility of measurement," wrote one of Chuikov's officers. "The men in the communication trenches stumbled and fell as if on a ship's deck during a storm." Commissars seem to have felt an urge to become poetic in what they saw as the terrible majesty of mass death and destruction. "Those of us who have seen the dark blue sky of Stalingrad in these days," Dobronin wrote to Shcherbakov in Moscow, "will never forget it. It is threatening and severe, with purple flames licking the sky."

Shells striking solid iron installations in the factory workshops produced showers of sparks visible through the dust and smoke. General Viktor Zholudev was buried alive in his bunker by an explosion, a common fate during that terrible day. Soldiers dug him out and carried him back to army headquarters. Others seized the weapons of the dead and fought on.

The dust-covered German panzers smashed right into the huge sheds of the tractor plant like prehistoric monsters, spraying machine-gun fire all around and crunching the shards of glass from the shattered skylights under their tracks. During the close-quarters fighting that followed, there were no clear front lines. Bypassed groups of Zholudev's guardsmen would suddenly attack as if from nowhere. In such conditions, a wise German medical officer sited his dressing station inside the armored safety of an extinct smelting furnace.

During October, while Paulus's weakened divisions reduced the Soviet bridgehead on the Volga bank, Chuikov suddenly realized that his army had become the bait in an enormous Soviet trap.

The original idea for Operation Uranus, the great counterstroke at Stalingrad, dated back to Saturday, September 12, the day that Paulus met Hitler at Vinnitsa. Marshal Georgy Zhukov had been summoned to the Kremlin at the moment of crisis. There, in Stalin's office, overlooked by recently installed portraits of Aleksandr Suvorov, the scourge of the Turks in the eighteenth century, and of Mikhail Kutuzov, Napoleon's dogged adversary, Zhukov had to explain why all their attempts to counterattack on the northern flank above Stalingrad to help Chuikov's army had failed. Stalin told Zhukov and Aleksandr Vasilievsky, the chief of staff, to examine every option.

The city of Stalingrad, Zhukov argued when they came back the next day, should be held in a battle of attrition, with just enough troops to keep the defense alive. Then while the Germans focused entirely on capturing the city, the Stavka would secretly assemble fresh armies behind the lines for a major encirclement, using deep thrusts far behind the point of the apex formed by Paulus's advance. The flanks to the rear on both sides were held by weak Romanian divisions.

The gigantic preparations were carried out in great secrecy. On October 17, Don Front headquarters gave the order that all civilians "within 25 kilometers of the front line" must be evacuated by October 29. Civilians were drafted into a construction corps more than 100,000 strong, repairing roads and bridges along the Saratov-Kamushin-Stalingrad route and all others leading to the front.

The main assault, nearly two hundred kilometers west of Stalingrad, would be launched southeastward from the Serafimovich bridgehead, a seventy-kilometer stretch south of the Don, which the Romanian Third Army had not had the strength to occupy. This point of attack was so far to the rear that the bulk of German panzer forces in and around Stalingrad would not be able to get back in time to make a difference. Meanwhile, an inner strike would cut down from another bridgehead south of the Don at Kletskaya. South of Stalingrad, another armored thrust would attack northwestward to meet up with the main assault around Kalach. This would mark the encirclement of Paulus' Sixth Army and part of Hoth's Fourth Panzer Army. Altogether some sixty percent of the entire armored strength of the Red Army was allocated to the operation.

The Red Army was unable to conceal preparations for such a huge offensive from Richthofen's air reconnaissance squadrons, but it managed to mask the scale. This, combined with the previous incompetent counterattacks of Soviet tank brigades, convinced the German general staff that nothing more was planned than an attempt to threaten their lines of communication.

Uranus was launched on November 19 in freezing fog. Once the Fifth Tank Army had broken through the Romanians its two tank corps raced southeastward. On November 20, two mechanized corps broke through south of Stalingrad. Paulus's armored divisions were unable to disengage rapidly from the fighting in the city and were then sent due westward, back across the Don.

Only on November 21 did the Germans comprehend that the Soviet objective was one of total encirclement from the south. By then it was too late. The following day, the whole of the German Sixth Army and a major part of the Fourth Panzer Army, altogether nearly three hundred thousand men, were trapped in a skull-shaped *Kessel,* or cauldron, extending from Stalingrad out into the open steppe. Hitler refused any idea of withdrawal from the Volga as soon as *Reichsmarschall* Hermann Göring, with breathtaking irresponsibility, asserted that the Luftwaffe could resupply "Fortress Stalingrad" by air.

Paulus's twenty-two divisions were doomed. They did not have the fuel nor the physical strength to break out and fight their way across an increasing width of snow-covered steppe. Field Marshal Erich von Manstein organized a rescue attempt early in December, although without great hope of success. Four days later, Zhukov and Vasilievsky countered with another offensive, Operation Little Saturn, smashing through the Italian Eighth Army high on the Don flank. This threatened Manstein's whole position in southern Russia. A start to the evacuation of the Caucasus coincided with the end of all attempts to rescue Paulus's starving and frozen men.

✦

THE SIXTH ARMY celebrated Christmas "in German fashion although in far-off Russia," convinced that Hitler could never abandon them. They had no idea how far Manstein's forces had been forced to retreat. Their "historical function," in Hitler's words, was to hold on by the Volga until the tide of war changed. But they did not know that even Manstein now needed to exploit their forced sacrifice, evacuating the Caucasus, while they tied down seven Russian armies.

The Junkers 52 transports, frozen on the ground and shot at in the air as they crossed the increasing stretch of Soviet territory to reach the *Kessel,* provided only a small fraction of the Sixth Army's needs. The cold became terrible, with temperatures often down to between minus twenty and minus thirty degrees centigrade. When bandages around frostbitten hands and feet were unwrapped, toes and fingers sticking to the material simply came away. One soldier wrote home to say that while he was asleep, mice had managed to gnaw two toes from his senseless foot.

The remaining draught animals were slaughtered to provide a few hunks of tough meat in *"Wassersuppe,"* water soup. The combination of hunger, stress and extreme cold upset the metabolism of the soldiers. As a result, their bodies could absorb only a fraction of the pitiful nourishment they received. This accelerated starvation dramatically reduced their already lowered resistance to disease, of which the biggest threat was typhus, transmitted by lice. "Lice are like the Russians," an infested panzer-grenadier lieutenant wrote home. "You kill one, ten new ones appear in its place."

On January 10, 1943, the German Sixth Army awaited the Soviet *coup de grace* from seven Soviet armies with mixed emotions. "One speaks about death as one does about breakfast," one man wrote home. "Ordinary soldiers continued to trust the word of Hitler," said the officer who took over the command of Strachwitz's tank battalion. They still believed the stories of the SS Panzer Corps' coming to their rescue and of air-landed reinforcements.

The future was bleakest for the Soviet citizens serving in German uniform in the Sixth Army. The NKVD at Don Front headquarters was shaken to obtain from prisoner interrogations an idea of the scale of the "treason." German accounts certainly seem to indicate that a considerable proportion of those attached to Sixth Army divisions—fifty thousand before the encirclement—were now fighting in the front line. Many officers testified to their skill and loyalty. "The Tartars were especially brave," reported an officer in the factory district of Stalingrad. "As antitank gunners using captured Soviet weapons, these Russians were proud of every Soviet tank they destroyed. They were fantastic guys." The battle group commanded by Lieutenant Colonel Mäder, based on two grenadier regiments from the 297th Infantry Division at the southernmost point of the *Kessel*, contained no less than 780 "Russian combat volunteers," nearly half his force.

The opening bombardment on January 10 was so intense that Colonel Ignatov, an artillery commander, was prompted to remark with grim satisfaction, "There are only two ways to escape from an onslaught of this character—either death or insanity." The *Landser*, their fingers so swollen from frostbite that they could hardly fit inside the trigger guard, fired from shallow foxholes at the waves of riflemen advancing with long spike bayonets fixed. Russian T-34s, carrying infantry like monkeys on the backs of elephants, lurched across the steppe. The high winds that cut through any clothing had blasted the recent snow off whole areas, exposing the top of the almost colorless grass. Mortar shells rebounded off the frozen earth and exploded as airbursts, causing far more casualties. The German Communist Erich Weinert wrote, "The dead are lying, grotesquely twisted, their bowels hurled out, most of them with bandages on their hands and feet, still soaked with yellow anti-frostbite ointment." The Sixth Army's resistance, when one considers its physical and material weakness, was astonishing. The most telling measure lies in the Soviet casualties suffered during the first three days of fighting. The Don Front lost 26,000 men and more than half its tank force.

The Sixth Army could not possibly resist the pressure. A lack of fuel during the retreat made the evacuation of the wounded more difficult than ever. Incapacitated soldiers piled in trucks that had ground to a halt just froze to death in the open. Even those who reached Pitomnik, west of the city, were far from certain of being saved. "The airfield," noted a young officer, "was chaotic: mounds of corpses, which had been dragged from the hospital tents and bunkers; Russian artillery bombardment; air strikes and landing Junkers transports." Lightly wounded soldiers and deserters, appearing like a horde of beggars in rags, rushed the aircraft as they landed in an attempt to board. The weakest were trampled underfoot; the cargo being unloaded was thrown aside or ransacked. The *Feldgendarmerie* (military police), rapidly losing control of the situation, opened fire on numerous occasions.

In the chaos at Pitomnik, a chance coincidence might save a wounded man's life, picking him out when hundreds were left to die in the snow. Alois Dorner, a gunner with the Austrian Forty-fourth Infantry Division, wounded by shell splinters, was appalled by the scenes. "Here was the greatest misery I have ever witnessed in my life. An endless crying of wounded and dying . . . of whom the majority had not had anything to eat for days." Dorner, who had not eaten since January 9, was also expecting to die when on the night of January 13, the Austrian pilot of a Heinkel 111 passed by and happened to ask where he came from. "I'm from round Amstetten!" he replied. The airman called over a member of his crew, and together they carried Dorner to the plane.

Casualty clearing stations at this time were so overcrowded that patients shared beds. Often when a severely wounded man was carried in by comrades, a doctor would wave them away because he already had too many hopeless cases. The shortage of plaster of Paris meant that doctors had to bind shattered limbs with paper. "The casualty rate from wound shock rose higher and higher," recorded one surgeon. Diphtheria cases also increased greatly. The worst part was the accumulation of lice on the wounded. "With spatulas we had to scrape the lice off bodies on the operation table and fling them in a fire. On eyebrows and beards they were clustered like grapes."

The retreat accelerated. News of Soviet tank attacks now caused "panzer panic" in German ranks. There were hardly any more antitank guns left with ammunition to resist them.

At times, the sky cleared completely, and the sun on the snow was blinding. As evening fell, the shadows became steel blue, yet the sun on the horizon was a tomato red. The condition of almost all soldiers, not just the wounded, was terrible. They limped on frostbitten feet, their lips were cracked right open from frost, their faces had a waxen quality, as if they were already dead. Many did die. Exhausted men slumped to the snow and never rose again. Those in need of more clothes stripped corpses of clothing as soon as they could after the moment of death. Once a body froze, it became impossible to undress.

On the sectors that had not yet been broken through, starving men were too exhausted to go outside the bunker to hide their tears from their comrades. "I am thinking about you and our little son," wrote an unknown German soldier in a letter that never reached his wife. "The only thing I have left is to think of you. I am indifferent to everything else. Thinking about you breaks my heart." Out in the fire trenches, men were so cold and weak that their slow, uncoordinated movements made them appear as if they were drugged.

Because of the lack of fuel, it was impossible to save more than a part of the hundreds of wounded left in the field hospital at Gumrak. As dawn broke on the morning of January 22, Russian infantry could be seen in the distance, advancing in extended line "as if on a hare shoot." As the enemy approached to within rifle range, officers from Ninth Flak Division who had been responsible for the airfield packed into the last vehicle, a staff car. A hundred meters down the road they found a soldier from the field hospital who had had both legs amputated trying to propel himself along on a sled. The Luftwaffe officers stopped and tied his sled to their back bumper as he requested, but it overturned almost as soon as they started again. One lieutenant suggested that he cling onto the hood, since there was no room left inside. The wounded man refused to hold them up any longer. They were by then within range of the Russian infantry. "Leave me!" he shouted. "I haven't got a chance anyway." The Luftwaffe officers knew that he spoke the truth. Anybody who could not walk at this point was already as good as dead. They drove on and the crippled soldier slumped in the snow by the side of the icy track, waiting for the Russians to arrive and finish him off.

The loss of Gumrak airfield effectively meant that the air bridge had collapsed. Whenever Luftwaffe planes flew over, men looked up longingly and continued to gaze at the sky well after the tiny dot had disappeared. The remnants of the Sixth Army pulled back into the city.

The conditions in Stalingrad in the makeshift hospitals were even more appalling than at Gumrak, with around 20,000 wounded packed into cellars under the ruins of the city, to say nothing of the sick, who may well have brought the total to 40,000. Some 600 badly wounded men were packed into the cellars of the Stalingrad theater, with no light and no sanitation. "Moans, calls for help, and prayers," wrote a doctor from the Sixtieth Motorized Infantry Division, "were mixed with the thunder of the bombardment. A paralyzing smell, smoke, blood, and stench of wounds filled the room." There were no more bandages, no medicine, and no clean water. "It is impossible to describe the human misery, the filth and the hopelessness that I saw," wrote an officer from the 297th Infantry Division, "and nobody could do anything to help these pitiful men."

Of the 91,000 men still left alive at the time of Paulus's surrender at the end of January 1943, nearly half died of disease and starvation by that spring.

By the time the last Stalingrad prisoners of war were returned to West Germany in 1955, no more than 5,000 had survived the Stalinist camp system run by the NKVD.

The German losses were gruesome. So were Romanian losses. But more than half of the one million people who lost their lives in the Stalingrad campaign were Soviet citizens. Forty thousand civilians died in the city itself. Another 60,000 died as slave laborers in Germany. Yet 10,000 civilians, including 1,000 children, managed, unfed, to survive in holes and sewers through five months of battle. This is still the hardest aspect of the battle to comprehend.

The Red Army suffered the worst slaughter. Chuikov, believing in his dictum that time was blood, had never shrunk from spending human reserves to that end. The Germans had never been able to comprehend this reckless prodigality with life. Nor could they fathom the Russian refusal to give up. "Father," a German corporal had written home at the height of the battle in the city, "it's impossible to describe what is happening here. Everyone in Stalingrad who still possesses a head and hands, women as well as men, carries on fighting."

DIARY OF
A TAIL GUNNER

JOHN GABAY

"The barracks are kind of empty tonight. The kid that sleeps next to me won't be back . . . Today was a sad one. Our radioman, Charley Gunn, went on his first raid with another crew and all hands failed to return. There was a cable waiting for him—his wife gave birth to a baby boy. He'll never know."

This was the daily experience of a twenty-three-year-old staff sergeant from Brooklyn named John Gabay. A tail gunner on a B-17, he saw worse in the air: bunkmates bailing out in a ball of fire, planes carrying friends going down in a fatal spiral. Gabay belonged to the 94th Bomb Group, 331st Bombardment Squadron, of the Eighth Air Force. He was stationed at the Rougham base, just outside the English town of Bury Saint Edmunds in East Anglia. In the fall and winter of 1943–44, Gabay, a former high-school swimming champion, kept what he called his "little black book." After each mission over German-occupied Europe—he figured that they averaged eight hours and forty minutes—he would return to his barracks and, sitting on his bunk, write down entries while the harrowing events of his day were still fresh.

Some years ago, Gabay's son, Thomas, showed up at the *MHQ* offices with a large loose-leaf notebook crammed with memorabilia, records of the 94th Bomb Group, and, most important, the typescript of John Gabay's diary. What follows is a mission-by-mission account, twenty-six in all, of a period in the air war against Germany when results did not yet balance against the terrible costs.

John Gabay returned home a hero, with a Distinguished Flying Cross and three Oak-Leaf Clusters. In April 1945, he learned that his twenty-one-year-old brother, Eugene, also a tail gunner in the Eighth Air Force, had died over Germany: In the last month of the war, on his twenty-seventh and last mission, flak killed him. Gabay worked twenty years for the New York City Sanitation Department. He married and had twelve children. He died on June 8, 1986, just short of his sixty-fifth birthday.

1. GELSENKIRCHEN, GERMANY

November 5, 1943 (B-17 382—"Horrible Hanks") TARGET: *Synthetic-oil refineries in Ruhr Valley* TEMPERATURE: *—43° F.T. (FLIGHT TIME): 5:15 E.T. (TIME OVER ENEMY TERRITORY): 1:35 ALTITUDE: 28,000 feet* BOMB LOAD: *10 500-lb. HE (HIGH-EXPLOSIVE BOMBS).*

Today was my first mission. Our group (the 94th Bomb Group, with twenty-four planes) made the run on the target first. We went over Holland and immediately saw three Me-109s. Later on we saw ten FW-190s, two Ju-88s, one Me-110, and several more 109s. I fired at a 109 coming in at 6 o'clock. I must have come close as he peeled off and dove away quickly. Flak was very intense and pretty accurate (fourteen solid minutes). Our ship was hit several times (two holes in left wing flaps, several in fuselage, severed oil line in number three engine and bent the prop). Oil covered ball turret and wheels. I could hear the pieces of flak hit—concussion driving the ship several feet upward. We were very lucky to get out of the Ruhr Valley. One of the waist gunners got the bends. He screamed a lot with the pain. Now the 109s moved in for another battle. My guns worked perfectly. I was holding them off pretty good. As we crossed over Belgium, our P-47s met us and scattered all the enemy fighters. We lost one bomber in that last fight. Bombs went through the wing of another ship but they made it back OK.

This was my first raid and it was with an old crew. They had twenty-four missions and were uneasy to have a rookie flying tail gun. But when we landed, they all came back and shook hands with me and said I did OK.

2. MÜNSTER, GERMANY

November 11, 1943 (B-17 846—unofficially called by the ground crew "Lucky 13") TARGET: *Marshaling yards in heart of city* TEMP.: *—28° F.T.: 6:00 E.T.: 1:55 ALT.: 24,000* BOMB LD.: *2 tons incendiaries*

It seemed at first to be a pretty easy mission. As we entered the Dutch coast we were met with light flak. Then our P-47s showed up and we had no trouble at all till we reached the target. Flak wasn't too heavy, but our bomb-bay doors wouldn't open. We finally got them open and got rid of the bombs in Germany. Our escorts stayed with us as long as they could—engaging in several dogfights. They had to leave us over Holland and then the fun began. About 50 FW-190s and Me-109s attacked us from every direction. We couldn't close our bomb-bay doors so they picked on us thinking we were crippled. One FW dove straight down from 1 o'clock high and let go with his cannons. He put a hole in our left wing big enough to crawl through. He also blew off a piece of the vertical stabilizer over my head. The Fort [Flying Fortress] on our wing burst into flames and only five got out—one chute was on fire. They were from our barracks. A 109 came directly at me and I know I hit him as he rolled over in a dive and disappeared. Another one came in low at 8 o'clock and Chauncey [the nickname of Ben Carriere], our ball gunner, hit him and he burst into flames and went down. Several FW-190s kept coming in at the tail and I hit one; he rolled over and I lost him. The Fort on our other wing burst into flames and went into a spin. Didn't see any chutes. Flak burst under our ship and concussion knocked us up about fifty feet. As we reached the Channel an FW-190 followed up low at 5 o'clock and Chauncey knocked him into the water. We made it back OK—but our new ship was a wreck.

This was our crew's first raid together. Got back OK.

3. RJUKAN, NORWAY
November 16, 1943 (B-17 012—no name) TARGET: *Power station (world's largest heavy-water plant)* TEMP.: *–45° F.T.: 10:05 ALT.: 12,000 BOMB LD.: 5 1,000-lb. HE*

A very long dull uninteresting mission over the North Sea. It was intensely cold. My heated gloves and boots went out shortly after takeoff and I had to keep banging my hands and feet for about nine hours to keep from getting frostbite. As it was, the tips of the fingers on my right hand were frostbitten. Saw some fishing boats as we approached the Norwegian coast. A very picturesque scene. Then we flew over the icy mountaintops—up through the fjords—very pretty. We had to make two runs on the target as we got there a little early. After we dropped the load, we turned right and passed along a valley. On the top of the mountain I saw several men shooting at us with rifles and machine guns. As we left the coast we were met with light inaccurate flak. One FW-190 made a feeble pass at us, then called it a day. We made it back OK— not much gas left.

4. PARIS, FRANCE
*November 26, 1943 (B-17 798) TARGET: Ball-bearing factory on the
Seine River TEMP.: −36° F.T.: 6:30 E.T.: 1:35 ALT.: 24,000 BOMB LD.:
3 tons demolition bombs*

Five minutes after crossing the Channel, we saw our escort—eight P-47s and
eight Spits [Spitfires]. Number four engine was going bad and had to be
feathered but we continued on anyway. We were twenty minutes from our target when we ran into heavy cloud formations, which meant we couldn't see
our target. As we got closer to Paris, the flak batteries sent up very heavy flak.
They couldn't see us but they had our altitude right on the nose. We made a
run on the target but couldn't see it due to the heavy cloud cover. That meant
we couldn't drop our bombs on Allied territory unless we could see and pin-
point the target, and the target must be military. We got a big flak hole in the
tail coming out of the target area. One ship cut through our formation and almost hit us. I called the pilot and he dropped our ship and then pulled up
quickly. It was quite a jolt—our radioman almost went through the top
hatch. The waist gunner floated through the air and both landed on the ball
turret, disconnecting their oxygen hoses. The ammunition in all the gun positions was upset; mine came out of the boxes and hit me in the head. I had
about 100 rounds in each gun that were usable.

We could no longer keep up with the formation so we had to leave and go
down. Our low group got hit hard by several FW-190s and Me-109s. Our escort was too high to see it. It was the British Spits. There were several dogfights later on—one B-17 got hit and was burning badly. He left the
formation, then blew up—bombs and all. The crew were good friends of
mine. By this time we were all alone over enemy territory, and our number
one engine started to go bad. We were struggling to reach the Channel with
the probability of ditching as close to the English coast as possible. Meanwhile seven FW-190s came out of nowhere and began to stalk us. They stayed
just out of range, then broke off as we reached the Channel. They must have
been out of ammunition. We dropped our bombs in the Channel. A little later
we saw the White Cliffs of Dover, then our number one engine died. But we
made it on two engines. My face and chin were frostbitten. We got back OK.

5. BREMEN, GERMANY
*November 29, 1943 (B-17 846—"Lucky 13") TARGET: Heart of city—
docks TEMP.: −64° F.T.: 7:45 E.T.: 2:20 ALT.: 28,500 BOMB LD.: 2.5
tons mixed*

After [I finished] cleaning and checking guns someone stole the bolt from one of my guns and I had to get a new one at the last minute. Hard to believe.

When our formation was completed, we went up through the North Sea, then came down right over Bremen. Flak was very heavy. Ship on our left had its wing blown off. Didn't have time to see if anyone got out as fighters hit us hard. Our P-47 escort jumped on them and the battle began. I called out an Me-210 at 5 o'clock low to Chauncey and he almost got him. I fired at an FW-190 and saw him blow up just as a P-47 pulled over the tail. I figured he might have got him first. There were dogfights all over the sky. Vapor trails were heavy and broke up our formation. We ended up in two different groups, which weakened our firepower. Our escort of P-38s and Spits never showed up—again. Our Cq [communication] equipment and radio compass were shot out. I never saw so many different types of enemy fighters trying to get our group. There were Me-410s, 210s, 110s, 109s, FW-190s, Ju-88s and 87s. About 150 in all, and all of them trying to outdo each other. It must have been an Iron Cross day. Ju-87s tried dropping parachute bombs. All our guns were going at the same time. It felt like the ship would come apart. I fired at anything within range. I know I hit a few as I saw several break off and dive. We made it back OK, but I had frostbite on my face, chin, and knees. They wanted to put me in the hospital but I went into a fit and got off with only one day grounding. Went to confession before takeoff. It made the raid easy.

6. BORDEAUX, FRANCE

December 5, 1943 (B-17 846—"Lucky 13") TARGET: Focke-Wulf Airdrome and Repair Plant TEMP.: −27° F.T.: 9:45 E.T.: 4.30 ALT.: 21,000 BOMB LD.: 2.5 tons HE

For a change I was pretty warm on this mission. I always wanted to see the south of France but the cloud cover was so great that I couldn't see much—in fact, it was so bad we couldn't drop our bombs. We had P-47 and P-38 escort cover over the Brest peninsula. We circled our target outside of Bordeaux and a bunch of 190s came at us through the clouds. They hit the last Fort in our group. It caught on fire, pulled out of formation, rolled over on its back, went into a dive, and exploded. Nobody got out. We had several attacks at our tail. I was beginning to think the Jerries knew me. We used plenty of evasive action and it worked pretty good. One Focke-Wulf came in so close, I could see his face. I poured it to him and he rolled over burning, ending up outside of Bill's window. He poured it to him and when he started to slip lower, Chauncey in the ball blasted him, and as he went down everybody was hitting him till he blew up. He must have misjudged his attack and found himself too close and panicked. Our two groups were too close and fighters flew in between them, which made it difficult to fire at them. We had a small fire in the bomb bay but Bill put it out in a hurry. We were within seventy-five miles of Spain and over seven hours on oxygen. Got back OK.

7. KIEL, GERMANY
December 13, 1943 (B-17 846—"Lucky 13") TARGET: Heart of city TEMP.: −28° F.T.: 8:10 E.T.: 0:56 ALT.: 24,200 BOMB LD.: 2.5 tons HE

We flew up through the North Sea and just as we entered the enemy coast, about forty Ju-88s appeared out of nowhere. They flew alongside our formation on both sides, but just out of range. After several minutes of this, they began to peel off and four of them attacked our ship from the tail. They came in close, one at a time. The flame from the cannons, tracers from their machine guns, and rockets from under their wings made the situation a bit hairy. All I could do, besides being scared, was to spray each one as they came in and call for evasive action. I hit the second one and he rolled over and burned. I saw my tracers slam into the cockpit of the third. I may have hit the pilot, as the ship started to go out of control. I poured more into it, knocking off the canopy under the nose. It looked like a leg hung out of the ship for an instant, then fell out. Then the ship went into a spin. More Ju-88s flew alongside of us, out of range. Some of them waved to us. It was shaky waiting for them to attack. Then they came at us. Our pilot used plenty of evasive action and all guns were firing. The ball turret in the ship next to us was blown out. Several ships were hit hard. We had several flak holes, machine-gun holes, and a couple of 20mm-cannon holes in the right wing. A squadron of P-38s showed up for a change and the bandits scattered. One bomb got hung up in the bomb bay but C. L. [Claude Chambers, the bombardier] managed to dump it after a few minutes. Leo was annoyed that I didn't put in any claims. I don't like the hassle.

Today—December *13th;* Our Crew—*#13;* Bombs Away at *1300*—Another Lucky Day

8. BREMEN, GERMANY
December 16, 1943 (B-17 037) TARGET: Docks—heart of city TEMP.: −38° F.T.: 8.30 E.T.: 1:30 ALT.: 24,000 BOMB LD.: 3 tons mixed

We were supposed to have plenty of escort—P-38s, P-51s, and P-47s—but we were late and missed them. When we saw the P-38s they were passing us on their way home—not a nice feeling. Flak over the target was extra heavy. The sky was black with flak-burst smoke and I could smell it through my oxygen mask. The noise was cruel and the concussions were murderous. Every ship in the group must have had flak holes—we had plenty. When we came out of the target area, the fighters were waiting for us. I never saw so many. They were hiding over the stale flak smoke. Our crew led the Eighth Air Force on this raid. We had two direct attacks at the tail but they didn't press them. The low group in our wing got hit very hard. One of the Forts blew up. The Jerry that got him gave some exhibition of flying. He was something special. We had a British radar officer on board. His job was to confuse the German radar [by throwing bundles of aluminum foil out the waist-gun windows]. It didn't work. The weather over the Channel was bad and especially over our field. We made the landing on the first try but nearly collided with another Fort. There were two crack-ups later on. Our ship was a mess—full of holes. I thought the crew chief was going to cry. We were told at interrogation that Bremen put up more flak today than any city up to now. Big Deal! Got back OK!

9. BREMEN, GERMANY
December 20, 1943 (B-17 212) TARGET: Heart of city—docks TEMP.: −42° F.T.: 6:30 E.T.: 1:55 ALT.: 24,000 BOMB LD.: 3 tons HE

It's Flak City again! Today we took a cameraman with us. He got some good shots—he also got frostbite. P-47s escorted us for a while, then we picked up P-51s. Saw several dogfights around us. Our escort did a good job. Saw them knock down a few Focke-Wulfs. Flak over target was extra heavy, as usual. It knocked out our number one engine so we had to leave formation and hit the deck and try to make it back alone. We had a few attacks, but two P-51s saw us all alone fighting off two FW-190s and down they came and scattered the bandits. By this time we were passing over Wilhelmshaven and heading out over the North Sea, but not before running into some very accurate flak. We made it back OK. Had several holes in fuselage, nose Plexiglas, vertical stabilizer; number three engine quit just as we touched down.

10. SAINT-OMER, FRANCE
December 24, 1943 (B-17 846—"Lucky 13") TARGET: Rocket-gun sites and factories TEMP.: −28° F.T.: 5:45 E.T.: 0:23 ALT.: 18,800 BOMB LD.: 2.5 tons HE

This was a most secret briefing. We were told it was a most important raid. Everything that could fly was in the air. We were to try and hit scattered rocket installations, which meant we had to do individual squadron bombing. Flak was light and there were no fighters. This was hard to believe. As we had our bomb run, flak started to get a little heavy but not too accurate. Still no fighters! This was truly a milk run.

✦

Saint-Omer is just south of the Belgian border, close to the English Channel. The installations, which looked like ski jumps, were for the not-yet-operational V-1 "buzz bombs."

11. Ludwigshafen, Germany
December 30, 1943 (B-17 846—"Lucky 13") Target: Nazis' largest chemical works F.T.: 9:00 E.T.: 4:00 Alt.: 24,000 Bomb Ld.: 2 tons incendiaries

This raid was deep into Germany. Our escort was pretty good—P-47s, P-51s, and Spits. Flak was very heavy over the target. Just as we crossed the French coast, about fifteen Me-109s hit us. They only made one pass, then attacked a B-24 group below us. They shot them up pretty bad—a few of them went down. Our ball-turret gunner passed out for a few minutes. We thought we lost him. But he came to and let us know he was OK. I think the stiff was sleeping. During the raid, we ran into six different heavy flak areas. A gunner in the next barracks, his twenty-fourth mission, got hit in the neck with a piece of flak and was killed instantly. We had scattered fighter attacks in and out. Not too heavy but constant. When our escort was around they chased them. Got back OK!

12. Bordeaux, France
January 5, 1944 (B-17 846—"Lucky 13") Target: Airdrome and repair plant Temp.: –35° F.T.: 7:45 E.T.: 4:30 Alt.: 20,300 Bomb Ld.: 3 tons HE

We crossed the Channel to France, then headed south along the French coast to our target. It was a clear day and we could see the ground, which didn't happen often. We flew over the city of La Rochelle and ran into moderate but inaccurate flak. I could see the flashes from their gun batteries. They also tried to cover the town with smoke pots, thinking we were going to bomb it. We met a few P-47s but they left us in a few minutes. A lone 109 attacked a Fort lagging behind. They had their own private war till we started the bomb run. Then the flak came, heavy and accurate. I could hear the bursts and hear the chunks of steel ripping into the ship—a sickening sound. Fighters came through their own flak and attacked us. We were flying Purple Heart Corner again and the FW-190s attacked our ship in threes and fours. [Purple Heart Corner was the low outside position on the formation, and one that enemy fighters found easy to isolate.] I know I damaged some. It was a running fight for almost an hour. We lost an engine and couldn't keep up with the group. About the same time another Fort lost an engine and we both hung together till we reached the Brest peninsula, then he couldn't stay with us and lagged back. When he was about 800 yards back, two black-and-silver FW-190s attacked him and blew him in half. I didn't have time to look for the chutes as both fighters came at us at 6 o'clock level. I poured it to them—a wing came off one and the other burst into flames. The pilot insisted I claim them. We got a few light flak bursts before we left Brest. We were all alone—then I saw a Fort below us ditch. We got back OK. Ship had several flak and machine-gun holes. Had three big holes in the tail and broken side window.

✦

THIS WAS THE *mission for which Gabay was awarded the Distinguished Flying Cross.*

13. FRANKFURT, GERMANY
January 29, 1944 (B-17 846—"Lucky 13") TARGET: Industrial center TEMP.: –45° F.T.: 7:50 E.T.: 2:45 ALT.: 24,000 BOMB LD.: 2.5 tons HE

According to briefing, today's raid was supposed to be the heaviest of the war. We crossed the Channel and over the enemy coast at Belgium. Flew over Brussels, then cloud cover became 10/10 [no visibility whatsoever]. On this raid we were to have Spits first, then P-47s, P-38s, and P-51s. As usual, the Spits didn't show. The rest of the escort was fairly good—P-47s the best, as always. They also always seem to be the most aggressive. About twelve 109s tried to hit us but the P-47s broke it up. When they had to leave, the group in back of us got hit by a massive attack of about sixty 109s. Nine Forts went down together. Frankfurt was supposed to be heavily defended by flak batteries. We brought along bundles of metallic paper and threw it out during the bomb run. It must have worked as the flak was heavy but very low. We had little trouble getting home. A few feeble attacks. Number *13* is over. Got back OK.

14. Brunswick, Germany

January 30, 1944 (B-17 498—"Passionate Witch II") Target: Me-110 factory Temp.: –26° F.T.: 7:30 E.T.: 3:45 Alt.: 21,000 Bomb Ld.: 2.5 tons HE

The last time the Eighth Air Force went to Brunswick they lost sixty Forts. Today, only twenty. We were fairly close to Berlin. Had to skirt several flak areas but ran into three heavy ones, plus the flak over the target. Escort was fairly good—P-47s always there, but again the Spits didn't show. We had heavy contrails at this altitude and a lot of haze, which made it hard to see enemy fighters. Had several near accidents—weather was brutal. We threw out metallic paper on bomb run but this time it didn't work. Flak was pretty accurate. Several dogfights erupted—nice to see but a little hairy at times watching to see if the enemy could break through and get at us. They did a few times but it wasn't bad. Got back OK.

15. Wilhelmshaven, Germany

February 3, 1944 (B-17 846—"Lucky 13") Target: Sub pens Temp.: –47° F.T.: 7:00 E.T.: 1:30 Alt.: 24,500 Bomb Ld.: 2 tons incendiaries

It seems we made this raid the hard way, under very bad weather conditions. We had complete 10/10 cloud cover up to 20,000 feet. We had fairly good escort for a while. We ran into heavy but not so accurate flak as we crossed the enemy coast. On the bomb run the bomb-bay doors stuck so Mike [Jankowski, the engineer and top-turret gunner] had to crank them down—in time to drop on target. Flak was heavy, but over on our left. We were to come out by way of the North Sea. A sleet storm reached our altitude and we couldn't see to stay in formation so we got orders that everyone was on his own. Ice was forming on our wings as we let down through the storm. The last thing I saw before the weather enveloped us was a Fort running into the tail of another and chewing it up so bad the gunner fell out over the North Sea. I couldn't see anything else as the weather closed in around us. We dove at great speed trying to get to warmer air. The ice soon broke away from the wings and we didn't hit anything—so far so good! We broke out through the clouds about 200 feet over the North Sea along the Frisian Islands. Now plenty of 20mm was bursting around the tail and left waist—couldn't see where it was coming from. Then weather opened up and saw soldiers running for their gun positions. We opened up on them—saw about twenty go down like rag dolls—got out of there fast. Was a bumpy ride home. Found myself in midair several times.

16. FRANKFURT, GERMANY

February 8, 1944 (B-17 498—"Passionate Witch II") TARGET: Heart of city TEMP.: –47° F.T.: 8:40 E.T.: 4:00 ALT.: 27,500 BOMB LD.: 2.5 tons HE

We were leading the low squadron of a new group deep into enemy territory. Twenty minutes after we crossed the enemy coast, we ran into some very accurate flak. Saw some fighters but P-47s kept them busy. Flew at pretty high attitude. As soon as we started our bomb run I saw a group of Me-109s at six o'clock low and leaned up to keep an eye on them and in so doing, pulled out my oxygen hose without knowing it. I passed out and hit my head on the armor plate. But before I passed out, I vaguely remember trying to plug the end of the hose back where it belonged, but I just couldn't reach it. I thought it was hanging out the rear of the ship for several miles and I kept trying to pull it back in. The flight surgeon said a man could only live for about ten minutes without oxygen at this altitude, but according to the crew, they were trying to contact me for over twenty minutes. Bill Geier [the waist gunner] crawled back to the tail and found me slumped over, no oxygen and my face purple. He immediately gave me emergency oxygen and artificial respiration as best he could. I started breathing again. When I came to, I tried to fight with him but I had no strength. I straightened out in a few minutes but was groggy all the way home. I'm sure it was a miracle that I made it. Crew said I was shooting at fighters but I don't remember any of it.

17. BRUNSWICK, GERMANY

February 10, 1944 (B-17 498—"Passionate Witch II") TARGET: Heart of city TEMP.: –48° F.T.: 8:50 E.T.: 3:50 ALT.: 23,700 BOMB LD.: 3 tons

I don't know how to start this one. I'm very tired. They told us at briefing the plan was to send 200 Forts deep into Germany as a decoy to lure up enemy fighters so our escort could try to knock out the Luftwaffe. It didn't turn out that way. As soon as we crossed the enemy coast, we ran into swarms of enemy fighters. (At interrogation everyone agreed over 300 fighters at one time pounded our group.) I knew we were really in trouble when about 150 of our escort showed up and immediately dropped their belly tanks so they could mix it with the enemy. That meant they couldn't stay with us very long—and the raid was just beginning. The Luftwaffe must have put up every fighter they had. . . . Fighters hit us from every angle. I saw Forts and fighters blowing up, Forts and fighters going down smoking and burning, wings coming off, tails coming off, the sky full of parachutes. . . . One guy floated into a low Fort—he was churned up by the propellers and took the Fort with him. It just rolled over into a dive. The sky was so full of tracers, 20mm cannon shells exploding, and even rockets. Steel was ripping into our ship with sickening sounds. There were times when I was afraid to shoot for fear of hitting one of our own planes or some poor guy in a parachute.

We were leading the high squadron of nine planes—only two of us got back. They attacked the tail four abreast and four deep—sixteen at a time. Their wing guns lit up like Luna Park [in Coney Island]. These guys were not fooling. There were countless dogfights. The P-47s at times were badly outnumbered but they did a great job and stayed with us until the very last minute. A couple of them asked for a heading home and said they were sorry they had to leave, but they were very low on fuel. When they left, the fighters became even more aggressive—if that was possible. All guns were firing at the same time. The whole ship was vibrating. I was shooting at everything that came in range. I think I hit a few but was too busy to see what happened as another attack was already starting, then another, etc. I know Chauncey got an FW-190. Ju-88s flew over us dropping aerial bombs, but it wasn't effective. At one time there must have been 200 fighters above us in dogfights. I saw 2 P-47s go down but I saw the 47s shoot down several Jerries.

The battle let up for about five minutes and about that time Chambers, our bombardier, called out large formations of fighters at twelve o'clock high. We all thought they were our escort coming in force from England to help. But it turned out to be FW-190s and Me-109s—about 150 of them. Now the fun really began. We had no more escort. Forts and fighters were going down all around us. Our ship got slammed with 20mm cannon and machine-gun slugs—a miracle none of us were hit. At the end of the battle, 20 P-47s showed up and put up a magnificent battle. Flak over the target was heavy, but not bad on the way home. We made it back OK. But there are a lot of empty beds tonight. This old Fort really took a beating—I don't know how it stayed in the air. The damage—half the nose blown out; six feet of the vertical stabilizer blown off; tail cables severed; all my windows blown out; one 20mm went through left side of tail above my hands and blew up just outside my window. All in all, ground crew counted 136 holes. But we made it back OK.

18. PAS DE CALAIS, FRANCE

February 13, 1944 (B-17 498—"Passionate Witch II") TARGET: Rocket sites TEMP.: −15° F.T.: 4:00 E.T.: 0:35 ALT.: 12,500 BOMB LD.: 3 tons HE

We did squadron bombing today. Our crew led the low squadron. Each squadron had different targets. We flew over six or seven flak areas. Flak wasn't heavy but what they threw was right in there—medium to light but very accurate. It killed a navigator in our squadron. I didn't see any fighters— friendly or otherwise—on the way in, but I could hear every burst of flak. Maybe I'm thinking too much about flak. At least with fighters you can fight back. France looked so peaceful and quiet until "Bombs away." Forts were coming and going, dropping bombs on their own individual targets. I wondered what the heck was so important down there. The ground was covered with bomb bursts and once in a while big explosions—a hit, I guess! One B-24 got hit bad by flak and flew in our formation all the way home. Coming back saw some fighters near the Channel, but they ignored us. Thanks a lot.

19. ROSTOCK, GERMANY

February 24, 1944 (B-17 498—"Passionate Witch II") TARGET: Heart of city TEMP.: −8° F.T.: 10:25 E.T.: 3:30 ALT.: 12,000 BOMB LD.: 2.5 tons HE

Today I put in my longest combat mission—in time. It wasn't too bad. I guess after Brunswick, nothing is too bad, or maybe I'm flak happy and beginning to enjoy this sport. I hope not. We had to hit our secondary target because of heavy cloud cover. The Luftwaffe sent up several different types of fighters—Me-109s, 110s, 210s, Ju-88s, and FW-190s. There weren't too many of them. We had several attacks but the fighters left us and attacked other groups. I hope it was because we were pretty good. Some of the other groups got hit bad. A lot went down. Later on, one Fort in our group went down—saw only three chutes. But the fighters kept after it till it blew in half. Ju-88s were shooting rockets at a high group. They would stay out of range and then their wings would light up with a large orange flame and out came two rockets like a large ball of flame. Then the Forts would turn left or right to evade them. Saw several German patrol boats along the Danish coast. I think we were flying too low again.

20. REGENSBURG, GERMANY

February 25, 1944 (B-17 704) TARGET: Aircraft assembly plant and ball-bearing factory TEMP.: −26° F.T.: 10:30 E.T.: 5:45 ALT.: 14,000–17,000 BOMB LD.: 2.5 tons HE

Another long haul into the fatherland. As we crossed the French coast, the radioman got a report that the Fifteenth Air Force came up from Italy and just hit the same target we were going after. We went in anyway. We ran into several flak areas in France. I was flying with a different crew and felt uneasy all the way. As soon as our escort left us, the wing in the back of us got hit hard by 109s and 190s. Two Forts went down—nine chutes came out of one and three from the other. The second Fort went out of control and the fighters wouldn't give the crew a chance to bail out. It caught fire and went into a steep dive. Wings and tail fell off and I saw the fuselage hit the ground. These raids lately are too low—the flak gets more and more accurate. We flew over Luxembourg and then into Germany. The Reich was covered with snow, a pretty sight—peaceful and quiet looking. I could see the Alps on our right and in the distance we could see the target still burning from the earlier raid by the Fifteenth.

As soon as we started our bomb run, the flak really came up. Our bomb-bay doors wouldn't open so the engineer came out of his top turret to hand-crank the doors open. As he did, flak ripped off the dome of his turret. The flak bursts were very loud and pieces of steel were ripping into our ship. I just happened to look up and saw an eager 109 come at us through the flak. I poured a long burst at him and saw him smoke and roll over in a dive. I may have got him. One Fort was blown up by flak over the target—no one got out. We started our long haul back—no escort all the way; could see Frankfurt and Stuttgart still burning from previous raid. Saw a lot of smoking Forts trying to make it home. Over France, we were hit hard by two different flak areas. Flak ripped through our nose, wing, windshield, and tail—getting a wee bit nervous. We had sporadic fighter attacks all the way home, but they didn't press too hard. I guess they were getting tired and frustrated. As we neared the Channel one odd-looking Fort tried to turn back and the CO [commanding officer] called some Spits that had just happened to be flying nearby to pick him up and bring him back to England. He had to be a Jerry. [It was probably a B-17 captured intact by the Germans, but there is no indication that the Spitfires forced it down.] I didn't care too much for the crew I was with today. They got too darned excited under fire and I can't stand that—had to keep telling them to simmer down. But we made it OK.

21. BERLIN, GERMANY

March 6, 1944 (B-17 252—"Sweaty Betty") TARGET: Heart of city TEMP.: −26° F.T.: 8:40 E.T.: 4:35 ALT.: 21,000 BOMB LD.: 2.5 tons HE

I've finally got my wish—a raid on Big B. Somehow I'm not as anxious, but I'd like to get it under my belt. Our crew led the 94th, then just as we crossed into Germany, we had to lead the 3rd Division over the target. It was just like any other rough raid over the Reich, except we got a double Scotch at interrogation and had our pictures taken when we landed. Our command pilot [who sat in the copilot's seat] was Colonel Thorup [one of the air base commanders].

We crossed the Channel and entered Holland and ran into light but very, very accurate flak and met our escort, P-47s at this point. When we left we had some eager attacks by about thirty 109s and 190s. We managed to keep them honest till our escort of P-51s showed up. Then the dogfights began. The sky above us was full of vapor trails in one massive dogfight. Several fighters were knocked down—mostly Jerries. Meanwhile, the group just in back of us lost eight Forts in one pass by about sixty 109s and FW 190s. Several parachutes filled the sky—couldn't keep track as fighters came at us. Then the 51s came and everybody was shooting at somebody. What a mess! As we started our bomb run, very heavy flak filled the sky. I could hear every burst around us, and the steel hitting our ship and the ship jolting up and down and sideways with the concussions. I saw the city—big and beautiful and then it was burning. What a shame! We dropped our bombs and got the heck away as soon as we could, as the flak was murder. Our left wing was hit bad. Saw several (about five) Forts go down over the target. I think the flak is beginning to get on my nerves. When we left the flak area, we were met by another escort—P-51s. Very comforting. As we left Germany into Holland, we again ran into light flak, but extremely accurate. A few more fighter attacks, a few more dogfights, then the Channel and sighs of relief—we made it OK. Tonight BBC said the Eighth lost sixty-eight bombers. Oh yes, I flew right waist gunner today. Protocol called for an officer in the tail on lead ships. The crew was leery about this and so was I, but he did OK—whoever he was.

22. BRUNSWICK, GERMANY

March 15, 1944 (B-17 704) TARGET: Heart of city TEMP.: −28° F.T.: 7:45 E.T.: 2:50 ALT.: 21,000 BOMB LD.: 2 tons mixed

I flew with [Lieutenant] Senior today. As usual, they put him in Purple Heart Corner again. None of the brass like him but he was an excellent pilot and the crew loved him—that's good enough for me. It was his last mission—it was also Stan Kyowski's last. He's the waist gunner. I thought it would be another rough one but this time Brunswick wasn't too bad. I know now why the crew loved the pilot. When the group ran into flak he would pull away from the formation till it was past the flak area. He would only do this when there were no fighters around and he was flying low and outside. This broke all the rules—but he didn't care. We crossed the Dutch coast and some light but accurate flak came up. Our escort, a large group of P-38s, was all around us. At one time, about fifty fighters tried to break through but the 38s were all over them so they couldn't concentrate too much on us, although they managed to get in a few whacks. The Fort in front of us got it and went into a spin—only one chute came out. Saw a couple of hundred fighters mixing it above us. Jerries and P-38s were going down. Then a group of P-47s go into it and really broke it open. I still think they're the best. I know they must have the most courage. Coming back was uneventful—pockets of light flak way off and a few feeble fighter attacks. Our escort made this one pretty easy. Got back OK.

23. MUNICH, GERMANY
March 18, 1944 (B-17 252—"Sweaty Betty") TARGET: Railroad marshaling yard TEMP.: −32° F.T.: 10:05 E.T.: 5:45 ALT.: 20,000 BOMB LD.: 2 tons incendiaries

Another long haul but the escort was pretty good—P-47s, 51s, and 38s. Over France ran into several light and inaccurate flak pockets. As we entered Germany, I could see the Alps in the distance. Der Fatherland was covered with snow—lovely sight. Just as I was beginning to appreciate the scenery, some heavy flak woke me up to reality. We ran the gauntlet of flak and fighters from Augsburg to Munich. Flew the waist again today. Too dull—not like the tail. Got a few shots in, nothing much. Over the target, starting with the bomb run, the flak got very, very accurate and heavy. Pieces of steel ricocheting inside the ship, the loud noise of the flak bursts, the jostling of the plane, the wishing I was somewhere else. A few seconds after the bombs dropped, a burst of flak exploded outside my gun position, knocking me flat on my back, cutting the gun barrel in half, and destroying the armor plate. No one was hit—I don't know why! A foot higher and I would have lost my head. By the way—could see the bombs hit the railroad yard—Locomotives and freight cars were coming up in the air, end over end. Got back OK.

✦

ON MAY 24, 1944, *the "Sweaty Betty" was hit by flak and badly damaged over Berlin. The pilot nursed the plane back to the English Channel, where he ditched it. All the crewmen were picked up.*

24. BRUNSWICK, GERMANY

March 23, 1944 (B-17 925) TARGET: Heart of city TEMP.: −38° {F.T. omitted} E.T.: 3:05 ALT.: 21,000 BOMB LD.: 2 tons incendiaries

My pilot finished up on the last raid, so today I flew with a new pilot, Lieutenant Butler, a West Point man and a real stiff. We started over Holland and missed our escort—we were too early. Ran into a few light but accurate flak areas. The crew were new and inexperienced and they really showed it. They kept tying up the intercom with a lot of nonsense till I lost patience and told them to stay off the wire unless they had something important to say. It worked for a while. We were deep in Germany and ahead of schedule and no escort in sight. Just as we started our bomb run, contrails appeared overhead—about fifty of them. They flew in fours, just like our escort. I tried to convince the crew that those fighters were FW-190s but they insisted they were P-47s. This was hard for me to take. Just then a bunch of fighters, Me-109s, came up from below and attacked the group in back of us. I saw three Forts go down burning on the first pass. Then the fighters from above dove on us and the fun began. I warned the crew they were enemy fighters but I was the only one shooting. They hit us hard and two Forts went down quickly and several others were hit, including ours. It was a rude awakening to the crew. All the time the dumb pilot was VHF [very high frequency] instead of intercom and couldn't hear the attacks called out. The Fort on our right wing was hit and burst into flames. It rolled over and almost collided with us. It blew up a few seconds later. No one got out. I didn't get in any good shots as most attacks were either head-on or from above. Flak was heavy over the target, but not accurate. We hit a flak area a short while later that was very accurate. Our escort came just as the Jerries hit us again. One Fort in our group was blown in half.

We passed through a strip of the Ruhr Valley and the flak was murderous. We took several hits. A ship on our left started to burn badly after taking a solid flak hit. I saw six get out. Then the flaming ship went out of control. It slid right through the group. All of the Forts pulled up but ours as the dopey pilot was still on VHF, and couldn't hear me call. The burning ship just missed the tail by about three feet. I could hear the roar of his engines. It leveled off—four more got out, then it rolled over and broke up. We made it back OK. No thanks to the pilot, and I sure told him so.

25. CHERBOURG, FRANCE

March 26, 1944 (B-17 498—"Passionate Witch II") TARGET: Rocket sites TEMP.: −26°; F.T.: 5:00 E.T.: 0:20 ALT.: 20,500 BOMB LD.: 2.5 tons HE

Almost crashed on takeoff. Getting close to the end now and things are getting a little hairy. Briefing was for Leipzig but somehow it was scrubbed—thank God! We crossed the French coast and made a right turn. Flak very heavy, but off to our left. French must be sending it up. Started our bomb run as soon as bombardier spotted target. All bombs weren't dropped on time. Saw them hit ground and miss target. A few fighter attacks didn't amount to much. The Channel always looks good coming home—so do those White Cliffs of Dover. This was supposed to be my last mission but have to make one more as they raised them to thirty. Since I had twenty-three when they upped them, I only have one more to go. Made this one back OK.

✦

ON APRIL 29, 1944, "Passionate Witch II" went down over Berlin, hit by flak. There were no survivors.

26. CAZAUX, FRANCE

March 27, 1944 (B-17 540—"Miss Donna Mae II") TARGET: Airdrome TEMP.: −5° F.T.: 9:15 E.T.: 4:50 ALT.: 12,000 BOMB LD.: 2.5 tons HE

I flew with Gavit today. He's a good pilot. It looked as though the mission would be scrubbed as a heavy fog rolled in. Takeoff was delayed two hours. What a way to sweat out my last raid. We finally took off and could barely see the wingtips, the fog was so thick. We climbed through the fog for half an hour, along with hundreds of other ships. We were all sweating. Finally broke through at 10,000 feet. We formed up and crossed the Channel; France was as clear as a bell. I saw fires and smoke on the ground where other bombers hit. But we had another two and a half hours to target. Crossed Brest and flew over the Bay of Biscay. German warships threw some flak up—very inaccurate. There were scattered dogfights all the way down—P-38s, P-51s, P-47s against Ju-88s, FW-190s, Me-109s, and 110s. We had a few attacks but they weren't pressed. By the way, our target is near the Spanish border. We dropped our bombs right on target this time. At this low altitude we shouldn't miss.

Hangars went up and so did the oil dump. Plenty of heavy smoke. Not much flak. We crossed Brest and some 109s dove out of the sun and hit us hard. Saw one Fort go down. Got in some shooting—not very good. P-47s arrived and scattered the Jerries. Can't believe this is the last mission. Made it back OK. Had a celebration in the barracks. I was the first to finish from the barracks— fifty-two didn't make it.

CHURCHILL
AND HIS GENERALS

ELIOT A. COHEN

Like Hitler, Winston Churchill had an abrasive relationship with the military men around him. They quarreled with him, they sulked, they resisted what they perceived as his attempts to micromanage. But unlike their counterparts in the German general staff, they did not live in fear of their leader. (Churchill also did not compromise them, as Hitler did, with huge bribes.) Alan Brooke, the chief of the Imperial General Staff, could note angrily in his diary that "without him England was lost for a certainty, with him England has been on the verge of disaster time and again . . ." On the verge, perhaps, but Churchill never took his country across the line of calamitous no return. Churchill, for his part, could remark, on watching his chiefs of staff file out of a meeting, "I have to wage modern war with ancient weapons." As Professor Cohen writes here, "Churchill's uneasy relationship with his generals stemmed, in large part, from his willingness to pick commanders who disagreed with him—and did so violently." He may have made their lives miserable, yet he was not, like Hitler, determined to crush their independence. Could they have won the war without him?

At a time when Churchill's war leadership is increasingly coming under attack, Cohen sees a need to confront the revisionists. Did Churchill have a coherent strategy? Was he, in fact, powerless to alter the great decisions of history? And, ultimately, what is strategy, what role should it play in war-making, and who should direct it? (Churchill had no qualms about the matter of direction: "At the summit," he wrote, "true strategy and politics are one.") In the process, Cohen reflects on what went wrong with our Vietnam strategy—and why, though Desert Storm was an operational masterpiece, it was far from being a strategic one. History does matter, and perhaps some of our recent presidents should have paid

attention to the Churchillian example. As Cohen concludes, "It is difficult to quarrel with the results."

Eliot A. Cohen is professor of strategic studies at the Paul H. Nitze
School of Advanced International Studies at the John Hopkins University. He has written books and articles on a variety of military and
national-security-related subjects. Cohen directed the U.S. Air Force's
official study of the Gulf War.

FEW HISTORICAL FIGURES ESCAPE REVISIONS OF THEIR
worth as statesmen. This is particularly true of wartime leaders, and especially true of Winston Churchill. Although some presidents and prime ministers have had their reputations go up (James Madison, for example) or
remain the same (Lincoln comes to mind), such reexamination usually chips
away at the historical statuary rather than polishes it. In the case of Churchill,
the critique is particularly interesting, because it goes not only to the question of the character and personality of the British leader, but to the essence of
the activity in which he engaged: the creation of strategy.

"There are times," wrote G. R. Elton, "when I incline to judge all historians
by their opinion of Winston Churchill—whether they can see that no matter
how much better the details, often damaging, of man and career become
known, he still remains, quite simply, a great man." Judged by Elton's standards, many contemporary historians fail. For the past several decades,
Churchill's war leadership has come under increasingly severe attack. Actually,
the current spate of criticism represents merely one of several waves of postwar
attacks on Churchill as warlord. The first disparaging assessments came primarily from military authors, and in particular Churchill's own head of the
British army, Chief of the Imperial General Staff Alan Brooke, who also chaired
the Chiefs of Staff Committee, which consisted of the uniformed chiefs of all
three services. The publication of his diaries in the late 1950s shocked readers,
who discovered in entries Brooke himself retrospectively described as "liverish"
that all had not gone smoothly between Churchill and his generals.

In fact, Brooke had withheld some of the more pointed criticisms of the
prime minister, which he often wrote after late-night arguments with
Churchill. If anything, his anger at the prime minister grew as the war went

on. On September 10, 1944, he wrote in his diary (in an entry not included in the published version):

> [Churchill] has only got half the picture in his mind, talks absurdities and makes my blood boil to listen to his nonsense. I find it hard to remain civil. And the wonderful thing is that 3/4 of the population of this world imagine that Winston Churchill is one of the Strategists of History, a second Marlborough, and the other 1/4 have no conception what a public menace he is and has been throughout the war! It is far better that the world should never know and never suspect the feet of clay on that otherwise superhuman being. Without him England was lost for a certainty, with him England has been on the verge of disaster time again. . . . Never have I admired and despised a man simultaneously to the same extent.

Others expressed themselves in language more temperate but had, one suspects, opinions no less severe.

Many of the field marshals and admirals of World War II came away nursing the bruises that inevitably resulted from dealing with Churchill. They deplored his excessive interest in what struck them as detail that was properly military, and hence not his business; they feared his imagination and its restless probing for new courses of action. But perhaps they resented most of all his certainty of their fallibility. Norman Brook, secretary of the cabinet under Churchill, wrote to General Sir Hastings Ismay, the former secretary to the Chiefs of Staff, a revealing Churchillian observation: "Churchill has said to me, in private in conversation, that this [improvement in civil-military relations in this war over the last] was partly due to the extent to which the generals had been discredited in the First War—which meant that, in the Second War, their successors could not pretend to be professionally infallible." Or as Churchill himself wrote when deprecating the American proposal for appointing a single supreme commander for the war in northwest Europe:

> This all looks very simple . . . and appeals to the American sense of logic. However, in practice it is . . . not sufficient for a Government to give a General a directive to beat the enemy and wait to see what happens. . . . The General may well be below the level of his task, and has often been found so.

One broad criticism of Churchill as warlord has it that he meddled, incurably and unforgivably, in the professional affairs of his military advisers. A second wave of criticism comes from those who have pored over the documents at some distance from the actual events. Thus, the historian David Reynolds describes Britain's decision to fight on in 1940 as "right policy, wrong reasons." He deplores with mock pathos the fate of "young whipper-snappers who have the temerity to read the documents and then ask awkward questions!" Other historians have had less resort to humor. Martin Kitchen writes that Churchill was "seldom consistent and was easily carried away." Small wonder, then, in the words of Sheila Lawlor, that "the conduct of war emerged, not from any one 'grand plan' or strategy, but out of a series of conflicting and changing views, misunderstandings, personal interests, and confusions." In the end, Kitchen says, Churchill, "like all men, however great, was powerless to alter the great decisions of history."

For the new historians, Churchill's sins have to do less with bullying and meddling—few late-twentieth-century scholars are inclined to carry a brief for generals—than with lack of foresight or inability to stick to a plan. When Churchill was right, it was for the wrong reasons; if he changed his mind, and he did so frequently, it was a sign of febrile instability; if he described the strategic position of the Allies in compelling prose, it was a sham that covered up chaotic forces that he had neither the wisdom nor the fixity of purpose to master. Thus we have two indictments no less severe than those of the generals: Churchill failed as strategist because he did not devise a coherent strategy for the war. (Perhaps no one can, some of these historians might argue.) In that case, Churchill deserves removal from his pedestal because he misled his contemporaries and at least one succeeding generation into believing otherwise.

One may sympathize with both sets of critics. The generals, after all, suffered the indignities of working with a man who kept them up late day after day, while hounding them with questions of detail. Even less forgivable were such barbs as his remark about confronting, in the person of his chief of the Imperial General Staff, "the dead hand of inanition," or his observation, on watching the Chiefs of Staff file out of a meeting, "I have to wage modern war with ancient weapons." Bearing the responsibilities they shouldered, knowing better than anyone else the strains suffered by a force all too often fighting at a disadvantage, they seethed with discontent, and small wonder. The historians have some excuse as well for their impatience. The stifling weight of pro-Churchill orthodoxy that dominated not only historiography but public opinion for decades after the Second World War provoked a natural reaction from a later generation naturally skeptical of politicians. All the more irritating to many professional historians have been the contemporary political leaders who have declared their reverence for Churchill. Surely, some

denizens of faculty clubs and senior common rooms must think, anyone ac-
claimed as a hero by Dan Quayle, Caspar Weinberger, or Margaret Thatcher
cannot deserve the uniquely glorious reputation of Winston Churchill.

✦

THE GENERALS may have suffered from their excessive closeness to a man
who made excruciating demands upon their energies, time, and patience. The
dons may have let the temptations of donnish life, which rewards swipes at
historical orthodoxy and deprecates the Great Man theory of history, get the
better of them. But a deeper explanation for the antipathy of these two groups
to Churchill lies, I suspect, in their picture of what it is to make strategy. The
generals have in mind a concept of civil-military relations to which we still,
amazingly, pay lip service: a world in which civilians provide resources, set
goals, and step out of the way to let professionals do their professional work.
In such a view, a politician has no more business getting involved in strategy
than a dental patient has in mixing the amalgam that goes into a cavity.
Brooke's exasperation speaks for more than one military leader:

> After listening to the arguments put forward during the last two days I feel
> more like entering a lunatic asylum or nursing home than continuing with my
> present job. I am absolutely disgusted with politicians [sic] methods of waging
> a war!! Why will they imagine they are experts at a job they know nothing
> about! It is lamentable to listen to them!

The anti-Churchill historians, on the other hand, either think that strategy
cannot exist or that, when done properly, it consists of pristine and unchange-
able blueprints. Most of them see so much muddle and inconsistency that
they find the idea of any fixed policy laughable; others scorn statesmen for failing to reduce the problems they confront to the neatness of a graduate term
paper.

Five years after the Gulf War, in which politicians (seemingly) left military
matters in the hands of generals and won a stunning victory thereby, such
views may seem more attractive than they might have in the early 1940s. In
fact, both groups misgauge the real problem of formulating strategy, which
Churchill himself described more aptly than anyone. It has become the fashion to scorn Churchill's memoirs of the First and Second World Wars for not
being true accounts of his activities and their consequences. Such caution is
well taken, but Churchill's writings in these volumes, and in his biography of
Marlborough, have a second and more lasting merit as reflections on the nature of war statesmanship. In Churchill's view, war statesmanship focused at

the apex of government an array of considerations and calculations that even those one rung down could not fully fathom—a view shared, interestingly enough, by free France's irascible leader, General Charles de Gaulle. War, Churchill wrote in *The World Crisis,* "knows no rigid divisions between . . . Allies, between Land, Sea, and Air, between gaining victories and alliances, between supplies and fighting men, between propaganda and machinery, which is, in fact, simply the sum of all forces and pressures operative at a given period. . . ."

Churchill's profound sense of the uncertainties inherent in war suggests he would have found the notion of a blueprint for victory at any time before, say, 1943 an absurdity, bred of unfamiliarity with war itself. Moreover, Churchill believed that the formulation of strategy in war did not consist merely in the drawing of state documents sketching out a comprehensive view of how the war would be won, but in a host of detailed activities that together amounted to a comprehensive picture. In other words, Churchill struck a middle position between those who would deny the possibility of strategy at all (as opposed to mere military opportunism) and those who would reduce it to a blueprint. In the latter category fell the American military leadership, which bitterly resisted any attempt to deviate from the basic strategy of an invasion of northwest Europe in 1943. Churchill successfully opposed them, persuading President Roosevelt to adopt first the invasion of North Africa in 1942, and then the follow-on campaigns in Sicily and Italy in 1943.

What were the practical consequences of the Churchillian approach to strategy? What exactly is it to make strategy in wartime? One set of activities, of course, has to do with the broad decisions of war: in the case of World War II, when to launch the invasion of France, what weight to place on strategic bombing as a means of defeating Germany, or how much emphasis to put on aid to the Soviet Union. But undergirding these high-level strategic decisions, on which historians traditionally lavish a great deal of attention, are other, less visible but no less important activities. They involve decision-making about matters of detail—important detail, but detail nonetheless. They may be illustrated by episodes from the war.

Perhaps the most important of these activities was a continuous audit of the military's judgment. Churchill, as his generals often complained, kept a close eye on many matters of military detail. On March 30, 1941, for example, he sent General Ismay a note regarding an exercise called VICTOR, which had occurred from January 22 to 25 of that year, under the auspices of the then commander of Home Forces, General Alan Brooke. Churchill's query went as follows:

1. In the invasion exercise VICTOR, two Armoured, one Motorised, and two Infantry Divisions were assumed to be landed by the enemy on the Norfolk coast in the teeth of heavy opposition. They fought their way ashore and were all assumed to be in action at the end of 48 hours.

2. I presume the details of this remarkable feat have been worked out by the Staff concerned. Let me see them. For instance, how many ships and transports carried these five Divisions? How many Armoured vehicles did they comprise? How many motor lorries, how many guns, how much ammunition, how many men, how many tons of stores, how far did they advance in the first 48 hours, how many men and vehicles were assumed to have landed in the first 12 hours, what percentage of loss were they debited with? What happened to the transports and store-ships while the first 48 hours of fighting was going on? Had they completed emptying their cargoes, or were they still lying in shore off the beaches? What naval escort did they have? Was the landing at this point protected by superior enemy daylight Fighter formations? How many Fighter airplanes did the enemy have to employ, if so, to cover the landing places?

The purpose of Churchill's query became clear in the third paragraph:

3. All this data would be most valuable for our future offensive operations. I should be very glad if the same officers would work out a scheme for our landing an exactly similar force on the French coast at the same extreme range of our Fighter protection and assuming that the Germans have naval superiority in the Channel.

Clearly, Churchill feared that such exercises fed an altogether excessive assessment of enemy capabilities, and one that, if taken seriously, could paralyze the British high command from acting in any way save defensively.

Brooke replied on April 7, giving the figures noted by Churchill, including estimates of enemy loss rates (10 percent in crossing, 5 to 10 percent on landing), plus the assumption that the Germans would consume fuel and food found on British soil. Churchill responded a few weeks later, noting how much more difficult than this British landings in Greece had proven, and continuing to press his inquiries. British forces had trickled ashore in Greece that same March (under the watchful eye, it must be noted, of the German military attaché, whose country was still at peace with Greece). It took a full month for the British to transport 31,000 lightly equipped soldiers, a force perhaps half the size of the notional German invaders of VICTOR. The British landed without opposition, yet found themselves logistically taxed by

the difficulty of simply setting up a base in a foreign country. With this contemporary experience (admittedly in far rougher terrain and in an undeveloped country) in mind, Churchill found the notion of the Germans flinging
ashore a far larger force in the teeth of opposition in two days to be questionable, at the very least. He noted, for example, that on the last two days of the
exercise the British were credited with 432 fighter sorties, and the Germans
with 1,500—although the Germans had farther to fly. He inquired about the
amount of warning of an invasion that was assumed and asked (without receiving an answer) why the Germans should have been assumed to capture
large quantities of fuel on landing in Britain. Gamely enough, Brooke continued to reply, until the exchange petered out in mid-May.

What is the significance of this episode? It is noteworthy, first, that the
commander in charge of the exercise, Brooke, stood up to Churchill and not
only did not suffer by it but ultimately gained promotion to the post of chief
of the Imperial General Staff and chairman of the Chiefs of Staff Committee.
But more important is Churchill's observation that "it is of course quite reasonable for assumptions of this character to be made as a foundation for a military exercise. It would be indeed a darkening counsel to make them the
foundation of serious military thought." At this very time, in April of 1941,
the chiefs of staff were debating the dispatch of armored vehicles to North
Africa. Churchill was arguing—against the position of several of his military
advisers (including the chief of the Imperial General Staff, or CIGS, Sir John
Dill)—that the risks of invasion were sufficiently low to make the TIGER
convoy to the Middle East worth the attempt. TIGER went through, losing
only one ship to a mine, and delivered some 250 tanks to hard-pressed British
forces.

By no means did Churchill always have it right. Early in the war, for example, he persistently exaggerated the damage done to German U-boats by
the Royal Navy, although he did so in part as a way of keeping up British
morale. But initially he did support offensive tactics against German submarines—such as the organization of hunter-killer groups—rather than the
sounder course of escorting convoys and picking off the U-boats as they attacked their prey. His persistent attempts to bring Turkey into the war—a
policy that absorbed a great deal of diplomatic effort, as well as substantial
sums of cash and amounts of military matériel—came to naught. Many of his
schemes, and in particular his persistent clamor for operations against northern Norway, could not meet the test of military practicability.

But it is no less true that Churchill often caught his military staff when
they had it wrong. More than once, the military judgment of First Sea Lord

Sir Alan Cunningham proved no less defective than that of his political superior. In the spring of 1944, for example, Churchill beat back a Royal Navy plan for a postwar force founded on the premise (in the words of the naval staff's paper, "The Empire's Postwar Fleet") that "the basis of the strength of the Fleet is the battleship. . . . This war has proved the necessity of battleships, and no scientific development is in sight which might render them obsolete." Throughout the war Churchill deplored the navy's obsession with the battleship, even after the destruction of most of the heaviest German ships and the entrance into the war of the powerful U.S. Navy.

In a similar vein, Churchill regarded the products of the superb British intelligence system with a combination of interest and skepticism rare in political leaders. When the Joint Intelligence Committee (JIC) suggested in September 1944 that Germany would collapse by December, Churchill disagreed vigorously and, as it transpired, correctly. The intelligence professionals of the JIC had by this point access to outstanding information, and the experience of five years of war in which to sharpen their judgment. After noting that the Germans had suffered approximately a million casualties in the first half of 1944 alone, and pointing to reverses around the circumference of the German position in central Europe, they argued that Germany would probably not be able to sustain the war to the end of the year.

They were proven wrong. Churchill's acidic reply to the JIC on September 8 is a masterpiece of critical analysis of an intelligence estimate by a policy maker, beginning with the opening line, "I have now read the Report and have not noticed any fact in it of which I was not already aware," and concluding with the correct prediction: "It is at least as likely that Hitler will be fighting on the 1st January as that he will collapse before then." But Churchill also went out of his way to defend intelligence operatives. On at least one occasion he personally intervened to make sure that the cryptanalysts of Bletchley Park—"the geese who laid the golden eggs but never cackled"—had all the administrative support that they required.

Churchill exercised one of his most important functions as war leader by holding the calculations and assertions of his subordinates up to the standards of a massive common sense, informed by wide reading and experience at war. When his military advisers could not come up with plausible answers to these harassing and inconvenient questions, they usually revised their views; when they could, Churchill revised his. In both cases, British strategy benefited.

✦

OF ALL THE responsibilities that come the way of statesmen at war, the most important may be the selection of those who direct the armies and fleets. Few cares rest heavier on the war statesman, and few present greater difficulties. In the case of deciding on a major operation, a war statesman can consult his own right reason and reams of planning and intelligence material; he has the benefit of advice prepared by large staffs, and he can turn to a variety of experts for their views. The task of picking generals is far more difficult. The commander who excelled at one level of war leadership may prove incompetent at another, and rarely can a statesman discover the abilities and weaknesses of his military subordinates except by trying them in new tasks. A prime minister (or, for that matter, a president) may find his ability to seek counsel limited by the cliques in which generals often gather, and by their tendency to shelter one another from the wrath of disappointed superiors. Moreover, in wartime the cost of firing a general is high, for they become popular figures upon whom public hopes and fears are built.

Churchill's uneasy relationship with his generals stemmed, in large part, from his willingness to pick commanders who disagreed with him—and did so violently. The two most forceful members of the Chiefs of Staff, Brooke and the first sea lord, Sir Alan Cunningham, were evidence of that. If he dispensed with Dill, he did so with the silent approval of key officers, who shared his judgment that the CIGS did not have the spirit to fight the war through to victory. As Ismay and others privately admitted, however, Dill was a spent man by 1941, and hardly up to the demanding chore of coping with Churchill. As Ismay later recalled, "The one thing that was necessary, and indeed that Winston preferred, was someone to stand up to him, instead of which Jack Dill merely looked, and was, bitterly hurt." If Churchill were to make a rude remark about the courage of the British army, Ismay later recalled, the wise course was to laugh it off or to refer Churchill to his own writings. "Dill, on the other hand, was cut to the quick that anyone should insult his beloved Army and vowed he would never serve with him again, which of course was silly." Dill was fired in November 1941, and left office on Christmas Day of that year.

Churchill's relationship with Brooke was the most explosive of all his dealings with his military subordinates, but he and Cunningham, who replaced the ailing Sir Dudley Pound as first sea lord in 1942, had one almost as tense. Some of Churchill's field commanders suffered particularly from his impatience, above all Archibald Wavell and Claude Auchinleck, the hapless commanders in the Middle East in 1939–41 and 1941–42 respectively. Although Wavell orchestrated a brilliant campaign against the Italians in 1941, his silence in the face of Churchill's barrage of memoranda urging action, and the failures in Greece and Libya, doomed him. Like his predecessor, Auchinleck found himself axed by Churchill, and in large part for the same reason: an apparent reluctance to engage the enemy.

The tension between Churchill and his Middle East commanders stemmed in part from differing perspectives. The prime minister was preoccupied with the sacrifices made to sustain the armed forces in the Middle East, including the sending of convoys at great risk through the Mediterranean. Having, moreover, a larger sense of the imperatives of coalition warfare—keeping both Russians and Americans convinced that Britain could and would bear its share in defeating the Axis—he needed success in the desert. Furthermore, because Churchill was an avid consumer of intelligence, particularly decrypts of Rommel's communications, he knew just how badly off the Afrika Korps was (or claimed to be), and this made his irritation at the failure of his commanders to crush the Germans all the more intense.

It was not enough, of course, to pick good commanders. As a war leader Churchill found himself compelled to prod them as well—an activity that occasioned more than a little resentment on their part. Indeed, in a private letter to General Claude Auchinleck shortly before he assumed command in the Middle East in June 1941, Dill warned of this, saying that "the commander will always be subject to great and often undue pressure from his government." Clearly, Churchill felt one of his most important responsibilities was the goading of his commanders into action; and if Alan Brooke resented this pressure, he at least responded to it better than did Dill.

More important yet was the role played by Hastings Ismay, who served as the secretary to the chiefs of staff and the indispensable link between the irascible prime minister and his harried chieftains. As Ismay later described his role: "I felt that my job was to interpret, repeat to interpret, the prime minister to the Chiefs of Staff, and the Chiefs of Staff to the prime minister." This task Ismay performed superbly. One suspects that in his absence the rancor between Churchill and the Chiefs of Staff might have exploded disastrously. Indeed, Ismay recalled in 1964 that in advance of the Quebec summit of 1943 the Chiefs of Staff were on the verge of a collective resignation. Ismay "stepped into the breach" and formally resigned, only to have the resignation ripped up and relations at least temporarily restored.

The permeation of all war, even total war, by political concerns should come as no surprise to the contemporary student of military history, who has usually been fed on a diet of Clausewitz and his disciples. But it is sometimes forgotten just how deep and pervasive political considerations in war are. Take, for example, the question of the employment of air power in advance of the Normandy invasion. As is well known, operational experts and commanders split over its most effective use. Some favored the employment of tactical air power to sever the rail and road lines leading to the area of the proposed beachhead, while others proposed a systematic attack on the French rail network, leading to its ultimate collapse. This seemingly technical military issue had, however, political ramifications, because any attack (but particularly one targeted against French marshaling yards) promised to yield French civilian casualties. Churchill therefore intervened in the bombing debate to secure a promise that French civilian casualties would be held to a bare minimum. "You are piling up an awful load of hatred," Churchill wrote to Air Chief Marshal Tedder. He insisted that French civilian casualties be kept to a maximum of 10,000 killed (versus initial projections of as many as 160,000). Reports were submitted throughout May that listed the number of French civilians killed and (callously enough) "Credit Balance Remaining." By the end of May, German reporting indicated that some 6,000 Frenchmen had perished in the bombing—considerably fewer than Churchill had feared.

One way in which the permeation of even apparently minor tactical decisions by political concerns occurred under Churchill was through the balancing of risks. Thus, Churchill presided over discussions in the summer of 1943 over whether or not to use strips of metal chaff (code-named WINDOW) to confuse German radar. The trade-offs were exquisitely painful: On the one hand the head of the Royal Air Force believed that bomber crew casualties would go down by a third if the British used chaff; on the other hand, those responsible for Britain's fighter defenses argued that should the Germans use the same device, night fighter defense would become ineffective for as long as half a year. Although the calculation hinged on technical judgments, it came down, in the end, to an assessment of how much risk the British would run to save their own men's lives and inflict greater damage on the enemy. Such a calculation was, perforce, political and was made by political authority.

✦

"AT THE SUMMIT, true strategy and politics are one," Churchill wrote in his multi-volume account of World War I, *The World Crisis*. The civil-military relationship and the formulation of strategy are inextricably intertwined. A study of Churchill's tenure in the high command of Great Britain during the Second World War suggests that the formulation of strategy is a matter more complex than the laying out of blueprints. As any observer of government or business knows, conception or vision makes up at best a small percentage of what a leader does: It is the implementation of that vision that requires unremitting attention and effort. The debate about the wisdom of some of Churchill's judgments (for example, his desire to see large amphibious operations in the East Indies) is largely beside the point. His activity as a strategist emerges in the totality of his efforts to shape Britain's war policies and to mold the peace that would follow the war.

The Churchillian model of civil-military relations is one of what might be called an uneven dialogue—an unsparing (if often affectionate) interaction with military subordinates about their activities. It flies in the face of the contemporary conventional wisdom, particularly in the United States, about how politicians should deal with their military advisers. In that view—seemingly ratified by the way in which the United States conducted the Gulf War— civilian leaders set objectives, provide resources, and get out of the way, leaving the generals to their business. Not really an accurate depiction of how even that one-sided war was waged, this model of civil-military relations does not work in serious, sustained conflicts.

Churchill's pattern of relationships with his generals resembles that of other great democratic war statesmen, including Lincoln, Clemenceau, and Ben-Gurion, each of whom drove their commanders to distraction by their supposed meddling in military matters. These men varied greatly in their previous military education, ranging from Churchill—who had not only a formal training but vast experience in government before, during, and after the First World War—to Lincoln, whose main military experience was a month's militia duty in the Black Hawk War. But all four intuitively understood the preeminence of politics in the conduct of war. Clausewitzians by instinct if not by education, these men recognized the indissolubility of political and military affairs, and refused to recognize any bounds to their authority in military activities. In the end, all four provided exceptional leadership in war not because their judgment was always superior to that of their military subordinates, but because they wove the many threads of operations and politics into a whole. And none of these leaders regarded any sphere of military policy as beyond the scope of his legitimate inspection.

The penalties for a failure to understand strategy as an all-encompassing task in war can be severe. The wretched history of the Vietnam War, a conflict in which civilian leaders never came to grips with the core of their strategic dilemma—the conduct of a war that was both conventional and revolutionary in its nature—illustrates as much. President Johnson, in particular, left strategy for the South Vietnamese part of the war in the hands of General William Westmoreland, an upright and limited commander utterly unsuited for the kind of conflict in which he found himself. Westmoreland was not called to account for his operational choices, nor did his strategy of attrition receive any serious review for almost three years of bloody fighting. At the same time, the president and his civilian advisers ran an air war in isolation from their military advisers, on the basis of a weekly luncheon meeting from which—until halfway through the war—men in uniform were excluded.

A Churchillian leader fighting a Vietnam War would have had little patience, one suspects, with the smooth but ineffectual chairman of the Joint Chiefs of Staff, General Earle Wheeler. He would, no doubt, have convened all of his military advisers (and not just one), and would have badgered them constantly about the progress of the war, and about the acuity with which the theater commander was pursuing it. The arguments might have been unpleasant, but at least they would have taken place. Perhaps no strategy would have made the war a winnable one, but surely some strategic judgment would have been better than none.

Nor can strategy simply be left to the generals, as they so often wish. Here, perhaps, contemporary observers of foreign policy and civil-military relations have indeed forgotten the lessons of the First World War, that generals can get it wrong. In America's most recent and successful war, in the Persian Gulf, politicians abdicated their responsibility to shape a war's conclusion, leaving matters in the hands of a volatile theater commander and a politically adept but reflexively cautious chairman of the Joint Chiefs of Staff. As a result, the war ended with virtually no thought for what a postwar Iraq would look like, and before the destruction of those elements of the Iraqi army most essential to the maintenance of Saddam Hussein's regime. The Gulf War offers evidence as well of the frequent diversity of military views—for example, the split before the war between army and air force generals over the efficacy of a strategy heavily reliant on air attack. If politicians hear only authoritative strategic estimates, the chances are that other views have been suppressed, not that they do not exist.

The Churchillian way of high command rests on an uneven dialogue between civilian leaders and military chiefs (not a single generalissimo). It is not comfortable for the latter, who suffer the torments of perpetual interrogation, nor easy for the former, who must absorb vast quantities of technical, tactical, and operational information and make sense of it. But in the end, it is difficult to quarrel with the results.

THE TURNING POINTS
OF TARAWA

JOSEPH H. ALEXANDER

Important as Guadalcanal may have been in countering the Japanese thrust into the South and Central Pacific, its capture hardly put the Allies on an express track to Tokyo. By midsummer 1943, they had advanced barely 200 miles in the Solomons and on New Guinea; strategy floundered. At that rate, someone observed, we would not reach Japan until 1960. That torpid pace clearly called for a change, and it came at the Quebec Conference in August, when one of the U.S. Navy's chief planners, Rear Admiral Charles M. Cook Jr., universally known as "Savvy," made a radical proposal. Instead of advancing island by costly island, he suggested, why not surge ahead in thousand-mile leaps that would bypass many of the strongest Japanese citadels? The original timetable envisioned the surrender of Japan in 1947 or 1948; Cook's plan, which was enthusiastically adopted, would accomplish that twenty-seven to forty months ahead of schedule (with a little help from a pair of atomic bombs).

The test of the new timetable came at Tarawa Atoll in the Gilbert Islands on November 20, 1943. The Gilberts, in the Central Pacific, were the farthest outposts of the Japanese empire, and the centrally located Tarawa Atoll was the key to their possession. The main island of that atoll, Betio, also had a landing strip that could accommodate bombers—in effect, a stationary aircraft carrier. But Betio, less than three miles long, was jammed with pillboxes, gun emplacements, camouflaged foxholes, and a garrison pledged to fight to the death. It did. Of the 4,600 men stationed there, 99.7 percent would die. But those heroic defenders would take more than a thousand equally heroic marine attackers with them. The story of the Battle of Tarawa has been told often—from the American side. But Joseph H. Alexander makes the unfamiliar familiar: The result was even closer than most people imagine. By piecing together accounts by the few survivors, translations of war diaries and unit histories, captured documents, and ULTRA radio intercepts, he describes the struggle as the Japanese experienced it. Think of the World War I Western Front without a no-man's-land. Tarawa's outcome might easily have gone in their favor, had it not been for a single unlucky shell burst.

Joseph H. Alexander served for twenty-eight years in the Marine Corps, including two combat tours in Vietnam, and retired as a colonel. He is the author of *Utmost Savagery: The Three Days of Tarawa.*

THE FIRST OF FOUR TURNING POINTS IN THE BATTLE OF Tarawa occurred at 8:55 A.M. on D day, November 20, 1943, when the ragged lines of eighty-seven American assault amphibian vehicles (officially "landing vehicle tracked," or LVTs) approached Betio Island's fringing coral reef. Both sides watched intently. Could these strange "little boats on wheels," as a Japanese survivor of the battle would describe them, negotiate the coral wall at low tide? In a series of nearly ninety violent collisions, the LVTs hit the reef, slowed, then crawled over the barrier to rumble the remaining quarter-mile ashore with their landing force of 1,500 Marine Corps riflemen and combat engineers. At this improbable sight, one Japanese *rikusentai* (naval infantryman) exclaimed, "The god of death has come!"

Yet the Japanese had surprises of their own to spring. The Americans were astounded to find that the Imperial Navy defenders had survived the greatest bombardment of the war to that point with most of their major weapons and all of their fighting spirit intact.

Both sides had much at stake. For the United States, defeat at Tarawa could derail the newly conceived Central Pacific campaign and fatally undercut national confidence in the largely untested doctrine of amphibious assaults against heavily defended beachheads. Tarawa for the Japanese was a proving ground as to whether their isolated garrisons could keep American invaders at arm's length until the Combined Fleet could sortie from Truk and force the long-sought "Decisive Battle."

The American side of this landmark battle has been told often. Here for the first time is the Japanese perspective, pieced together from the few survivors' accounts, translations of Japanese war diaries and unit histories, captured documents, and ULTRA radio intercepts.

Compared to the more notorious Japanese bastions of Truk and Rabaul, little-known Tarawa seemed an unlikely site for the first large-scale, opposed amphibious assault of the war. The British Crown Colony of the Gilbert Islands, of which Tarawa was a part, had been an easy conquest for Japanese naval forces in the second week of December 1941. Small teams of *rikusentai* seized Makin and Tarawa without opposition, then departed, leaving only observation units and light security forces. But the Gilberts ceased being a backwater in August 1942, when the Americans executed a submarine-launched raid on Makin in order to relieve Japanese pressure on the Guadalcanal beachhead. While tactically inconclusive, this two-day raid galvanized Imperial General Headquarters (IGHQ) into building up forces in that distant quarter. Within a week, the Yokosuka 6th Special Naval Landing Force, 1,500 strong, sailed for Tarawa. In six weeks construction troops had a bomber strip under way on Betio, the key island of Tarawa Atoll.

There remained much to do in preparation for an American invasion. During autumn 1942, Army Chief of Fortifications Lieutenant General Tokusaburo Akiyama toured Japanese island outposts from the Lesser Sundas in eastern Indonesia to the Gilberts and found disturbing levels of unpreparedness. Sobered by the American invasion of Guadalcanal, Akiyama found the Gilberts, truly the farthest outposts of the empire, to be equally vulnerable to an unexpected offensive. He also stated the obvious: Tarawa, with its central location, bomber strip, and natural defense features, was the key to the Gilberts.

To the extent possible, IGHQ accorded Tarawa's defensive preparations top priority and supplied generous amounts of naval troops, weapons, fortification materials, and labor. Betio became a formidable citadel, and the garrison's operational mission evolved to simply resisting an American landing for a minimum of three days, until the Combined Fleet could arrive.

Admiral Mineichi Koga flew his flag as commander of the Combined Fleet on board the superbattleship *Musashi* in Truk harbor at this time. In August 1943, Koga issued his Third Stage Operational Policy, which included *Hei* Plan #3, counterattack guidelines should the Americans invade the Gilberts. In that event Koga hoped to take advantage of his geographic position to assemble submarines, surface forces, air units, and a counterlanding force from throughout the Pacific.

Koga's *Hei* plan had flaws. The Combined Fleet was already critically low on fuel. Further, the Imperial Navy suffered from a lack of strategic intelligence. An American offensive was in the wind—but where? Twice Koga sortied his fleet into the Central Pacific in response to false alarms, consuming precious fuel to no avail. When Admiral William F. Halsey landed the 3d Marine Division on Bougainville on November 1, 1943, Koga decided to reinforce Rabaul with his heavy cruisers and—most critically—the last 173 qualified naval aviators in his command. Halsey's daring carrier-based air raids on Rabaul in early November damaged eight Japanese cruisers and killed about 150 pilots. This emasculated the Combined Fleet for the winter. Koga still had the fleet carrier *Zuikaku* with him at Truk, but without its air group he would not risk his superbattleships. The Tarawa garrison likely never knew it, but from this point they were truly on their own.

The Americans would face an all-navy force in the Gilberts. In February 1943, IGHQ had redesignated Tarawa's original *rikusentai,* the Yokosuka 6th, as the 3rd Special Base Defense Force, with responsibility for manning the bigger guns and most of the fourteen tanks. Then came the 111th Construction Battalion, commanded by Lieutenant Isao Murakami. With Betio's bomber strip already well under way, Murakami's large, talented force—similar in organization and can-do spirit to the American naval "Seabee" battalions—began building gun emplacements, magazines, and command posts. Murakami's force had stopped in Kwajalein en route to take on board the first two (of four) 8-inch guns. Antiaircraft systems went up first; then the big coastal defense emplacements, followed by hunkers and pillboxes. Then it was time for more fighting men.

On March 17, 1943, Commander Takeo Sugai arrived on Betio Island with his newly formed Sasebo 7th Special Naval Landing Force. Tarawa would be the first and last fight for the Sasebo 7th. Formed in Japan, on Kyushu, only six weeks earlier, the unit contained a mix of combat veterans, new volunteers, and old hands recalled to service. Those men whose reports of Tarawa have survived reflect this variety of combat experience. Commander Sugai, a Naval Academy graduate who would prove to be a resolute combat fighter, was off the active rolls as recently as 1940, serving as a professor in a Kobe merchant marine school. Warrant Officer Kiyoshi Ota served in the landing force that seized Hainan Island in 1940. Petty Officer Chuma, a trained antiaircraft gunner, served previously in Batavia, Saigon, Makasssar, and the Celebes. Petty Officer First Class Tadao Onuki, a tank commander at Tarawa, was a truck driver in the expedition by the Japanese Fourth Fleet that seized Rabaul from the Australians in 1942. All hands—veterans and rookies alike—benefited from intensive weapons training at the Tateyama Naval Gunnery School near Yokosuka before embarkation.

Freshly promoted Rear Admiral Keiji Shibasaki took command of these

disparate elements at Tarawa on July 20, 1943. Shibasaki hit the ground running. Troops trained all day, then helped build fortifications and obstacles half
the night. Training invariably involved live firing exercises. To ensure fire discipline among his many machine gunners along the shoreline, Shibasaki ordered the fronts of the pillbox embrasures sealed shut to force the crews to
concentrate only on their assigned field of fire, typically enfilade fire along the
seaward sides of barbed wire entanglements or other obstacles.

Shibasaki is often remembered for his boast to the native Gilbertese that "a
million Americans cannot take Tarawa in a hundred years." He may well have
said that, but his purpose surely would have been to boost the morale of his
own garrison—several thousand young Japanese sailors on a crowded equato-
rial island at the very farthest reaches of the empire, waiting for the inevitable
American invasion. Already sickness had taken a toll. Shortly before the battle Shibasaki had to send Lieutenant Murakarni back to Japan with several
hundred acutely ill troops.

Shibasaki faced other problems trying to integrate the defense of Betio. His
career experiences would hardly have made him (or any flag officer) an expert
in the complex details of fire control, heavy ordnance, mine warfare, tactical
communications, air operations, or fortifications engineering. Sensing this,
the navy division of IGHQ dispatched in August 1943 a "defense combat
team" of experts under the distinguished Namizo Sato, dean of the Naval
Mine School. Sato would have served Shibasaki better had he stayed more
than just a few days at Tarawa, but he had little incentive to linger: The place
was hot, unhealthy, and subject to bombardment. While the garrison dutifully planted antiboat mines along the obvious landing points on Betio—the
southern, western, and eastern beaches—they left the northern shore for last
and never mined the lagoon entrance in the belief their coastal defense guns
would command that narrow passage. But Shibasaki ran out of time. The invasion occurred while he still had more than 3,000 mines waiting to be sown.

Shibasaki's hopes of further enhancing Betio's defenses were frustrated
when U.S. submarines increasingly began to interdict Japanese cargo ships
along the extended route from the home islands to the Gilberts. From August
to November, Shibasaki looked in vain for a special delivery of 25mm dual-
purpose (antiair and antiboat) machine cannons and—especially—*cement*.
Warrant Officer Ota admitted during his initial POW interrogation that "the
weak point in the defensive installations was that all the pillboxes were not as
yet converted [from logs] to concrete."

U.S. Navy ULTRA intercepts reveal that Shibasaki expected the cargo ship
Mikage Maru on November 20. His concern for the safe arrival of this ship

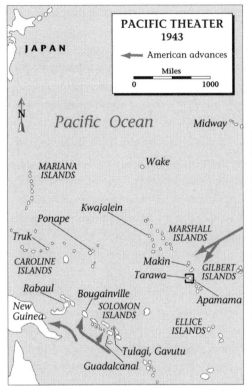

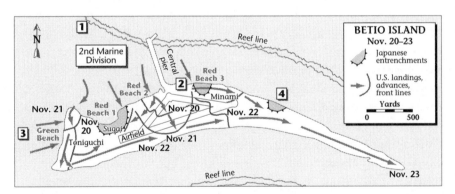

The map of the Pacific Theater in 1943 shows the two-pronged American advance, island-hopping toward Japan. Tarawa Atoll, in the Gilberts, was protected by submerged reefs. The four turning points (numbered) of the three-day battle for the main island, Betio, were: 1. American LVT passage over the reefs ringing Betio; 2. Rear Admiral Shibasaki's death; 3. the American taking of the west coast, covered by naval gunfire; 4. failure of the Japanese attack on the third night.

(with its presumed cargo of weapons and cement) amid the gathering storm of preliminary bombardments may account for the strange sight that greeted the vanguard of the U.S. Southern Attack Force as it cautiously approached Tarawa from the west the night of November 19. Betio was suddenly pinpointed by a series of flashing signals in a strange code from the equivalent of masthead lights. The garrison evidently thought their ship was at hand. Instead it was the enormous American task force, steaming dead toward the island.

Despite this unpleasant shock, the Japanese opened the battle before dawn on the twentieth. There were 4,601 of them on Betio: 2,571 *rikusentai,* 30 mechanics in the 755th Air Group detachment (abandoned in haste the previous day by their pilots), and 2,000 civilians in the 111th Construction Battalion. The landing force component of the U.S. Southern Attack Force consisted of the 2nd Marine Division, which numbered around 19,000 men. Of these, 5,000 would execute the amphibious assault on D day, and a total of 7,000 more would hit the beach—or try to—before D-plus-3.

Sentries on Betio lit the darkness with a red warning flare. At 5:07 A.M., the big eight-inch guns opened up on the American ships, including the vulnerable transports, still full of troops and unwittingly anchored well within range (due to strong currents and inaccurate navigational charts). But the Japanese crews couldn't capitalize on their advantage. In the only really effective gunnery sequence of a long, frustrating morning, U.S. battleships opened a devastating counterbattery fire that blew up a magazine, destroyed three of the guns, and damaged a fourth. In a matter of minutes, all four of Shibasaki's prized eight-inch batteries had been taken off the board. The lagoon entrance was suddenly accessible to the enemy.

Shibasaki notified his superior commanders at 5:59 A.M. that an American task force was bombarding the island and launching landing craft. Thirty minutes later Admiral Koga activated *Hei* Plan #3 to counterattack the Gilberts. Nine long-range submarines were already under way from the Carolines to the Gilberts, alerted by preliminary sightings of the converging American task forces. In the Carolines, Colonel Manjiro Yamanaka, commanding a 1,500-man army regiment known to Japanese strategic planners as the Ko Detachment, received urgent orders to prepare for embarkation on board two destroyers for a counterlanding operation in the Gilberts.

When early dawn revealed the southern horizon covered with fifty American warships, including three battleships (plus five escort carriers out of sight over the horizon), Commander Sugai assembled his subordinates and conducted a ceremonial burning of the Sasebo 7th's colors. There would be no retreat, no surrender, for the *rikusentai.*

Stung by the abrupt loss of his main batteries, Shibasaki ordered his secondary coastal defense guns—four 140mm shielded mounts, and a half dozen pedestal-mounted 80mm deck guns—to open up on the enemy fleet. Yet Shibasaki was poorly served by his coast-defense gunners. Against dozens of U.S. ships clearly within range, arrayed broadside, and barely making steerageway as they bombarded the island, the Japanese gunners could record only a long series of near-misses.

Ordnance failures further frustrated the Japanese. As American landing craft approached the island, the Japanese fired shells with airburst fuses calculated to inflict maximum damage on troops—but the shells had been overloaded with explosives, which vaporized the shrapnel, simply "dousing [the invading Marines] with hot sand." One of the 140mm batteries nailed the USS *Ringgold* (DD 500) dead center with two rounds—but both shells proved to be duds. Given this reprieve, *Ringgold* would contribute materially to the second turning point of the battle several hours later.

Shibasaki's relief from these setbacks came from a strange quarter. American inexperience in coordinating carrier air strikes and naval gunfire led to two deadly lapses wherein all firing ceased for roughly thirty minutes at a time. The lapses gave the Japanese defenders ample time to shake off the effects of the pounding and move forces and ammunition from the south shore to the threatened north shore—negating some of the tactical surprise the Americans had earned by attacking through the lagoon to approach Betio from the north.

During the second pause—from 8:55 A.M. to 9:25 A.M.—*Ringgold* and her sister ship, the USS *Dashiel* (DD 659), in Fire Support Section Four honored the cease-fire order angrily. As the only gunships in the lagoon, they could see that the Marine assault waves were still twenty-five minutes from touchdown on the beach. Shibasaki grasped the opportunity to rush more troops from the south shore to the endangered northern coast. Petty Officer Onuki used the lull to maneuver his Type 95 light tank out of deep cover and into a good firing position overlooking the north shore.

At 9:35 A.M., the communications ship *Katori Maru* in Kwajalein recorded this urgent message from Shibasaki:

> Enemy is approaching all over the shore north of the pier, inside atoll, with more than 100 amphibious tanks within visible sight. Later, 200 or more landing craft observed. Inside the atoll . . . four or more destroyers and minesweepers have entered and are making bombardment to cover the landing force. Other parts of the fleet are outside the atoll. . . . Several tens of carrier planes

and float planes are used by enemy for air superiority. All of our forces are in high morale, having decided to fight until death.

"We could see the American landing craft coming toward us like dozens of spiders scattering over the surface of the water," said Warrant Officer Ota. But Shibasaki and Sugai berated their troops out of their shock. Now the Americans were fully within range of every weapon on the island. The guns of the *rikusentai* would not disappoint their commanders. Fire lashed out at the Americans from a hundred narrow embrasures and ports. Onuki commenced firing the 37mm gun from his tank turret. "There we broke our silence," he said. "Under roaring fires, enemy craft wrecked, American soldiers went down one after the other, went falling into the sea."

Petty Officer Chuma's Type 88 dual-purpose 75mm gun had proven ineffective against the enemy's fast-flying aircraft, but now, firing horizontally, fifteen rounds per minute, the crew had a field day against the slower LVTs and landing boats. Chuma's pedestal-mounted gun was one of four on the island's northwest shore that would eventually be overrun by infantry. But for a glorious hour that morning, these gunners accounted for most of the destroyed American landing craft. The U.S. Marines lost only eight LVTs in the initial shocking assault, but at least half of these blew up, with great slaughter, from direct hits by Chuma's coolly firing battery.

On the northeastern shore that morning, a 127mm dual-purpose gun crew displayed equal virtuosity, sinking consecutively four landing craft as they approached the reef laden with light tanks. While cheered by this success, Shibasaki could only curse his fate that the same gun had been out of action an hour earlier when other enemy landing craft delivered fourteen Sherman medium tanks to the reef, where they rumbled over the coral and advanced through the shallow water beyond. One Sherman foundered in a submerged bomb crater, but the others made it ashore unmolested by anything greater than small-arms fire.

Once ashore, however, the Shermans encountered the *rikusentai*'s well-served field guns and light tanks. A single 75mm mountain gun knocked out three Shermans as they rumbled inland, unescorted by riflemen. One plucky Japanese light tank, engaged in a losing duel with a Sherman near the western shore, launched a dying, final 37mm round, a phenomenal shot, right down the barrel of the opposing tank. The Sherman survived, minus its main gun, and served in the reduced capacity of an armored machine gun. The Japanese had never seen tanks this large, but their spirited defense whittled away at the Shermans until only two were left operational by dusk on D day.

Throughout the fire of all these field guns, and fully integrated with the vicious cross-stitching of the Japanese machine guns, fell hundreds of rounds of well-aimed indirect fire. American survivors would curse the effectiveness of Japanese mortar fire on D day. In fact, the Japanese had no mortars on Betio, just the squat but deadly Type 92 70mm howitzers and the ubiquitous 50mm grenade-throwers. (The Americans erroneously—and dangerously—called the latter "knee mortars." In fact, if fired from the knee, their recoil would break a man's leg, as some U.S. troops with captured weapons found out the hard way.)

The American gamble of converting lightly armored, mechanically frail logistic vehicles into assault craft worked to the extent that 1,500 Marines forced a shallow series of toeholds along the north shore—identified by the landing force as Red Beaches One, Two, and Three, from west to east. But with their LVTs increasingly knocked out of action by point-blank fire and their reserve troops piled up along the reef in deeper-draft boats, the Americans realized the battle would now be won or lost by their ability to get sufficient forces ashore via the 500-yard wade from the reef to avoid being overwhelmed by local counterattacks. Over the next twenty-four hours, three separate battalion landing teams tried to reinforce the beaches on both sides of the pier by such desperate wading. Japanese machine gunners, maintaining their disciplined fire sectors, had a tabletop shooting gallery against the Americans struggling through the shallows. Hundreds of Marines fell to this unremitting fire; those who made it ashore often arrived weaponless and in tactical disarray.

As D day sped toward its early tropical sunset, the U.S. commanders knew they were in great danger. Fifteen hundred of the 5,000 Marines who had crossed the reef that day lay dead or badly wounded. The survivors clung to scattered pockets, out of communication with one another, and grimly aware they faced an equal number of Japanese whose forte was night fighting.

At this critical point, in the late afternoon of D day, occurred the second turning point of the battle of Tarawa. Western military historians have surmised for the past half century that Admiral Shibasaki died on the third day of the battle and that the expected Japanese counterattack did not materialize the first night because the heavy bombardment shredded Japanese wire communications. Translation of detailed Japanese accounts, however, reveals the surprising fact that Shibasaki died the first afternoon, along with his entire staff. This loss clearly affected the ability of the Japanese to orchestrate a counterattack the night of D day.

The coup de grace came from the fortunate USS *Ringgold* and her sister destroyer. Both ships steamed dangerously close to the north shore, enjoyed uncommonly good communications with the Marines on the eastern flank, and delivered well-directed fire on a day otherwise marked by inexact naval gunfire support. From his improvised defensive position, Warrant Officer Ota estimated the ships to be only a thousand yards offshore, marveling that "with the naked eye we could clearly see the American sailors on the destroyers' decks."

According to Japanese accounts, Admiral Shibasaki realized by mid-afternoon on D day that his concrete command post was the only safe refuge for his hundreds of wounded men. In a humane but fateful decision, he ordered his entire staff to evacuate the shelter and follow him across the island to an alternate site. The two destroyers, firing for some time at Japanese gun positions within the same target area, received sudden reports from their shore fire-control party of enemy troops in the open. The ships switched to multiple salvos of airburst-fused shells, any one of which could have made quick work of exposed troops. Japanese accounts indicate a "large-caliber shell" caught Shibasaki in the open, killing him instantly.

The garrison's communicators studiously avoided reporting Shibasaki's death. At 4:30 that afternoon, the *Katori Maru* received its last message from the garrison, which simply reported: "Enemy under support of fleet and aerial bombing have entered . . . the harbor and are continuously landing men and matériels. We are fighting them near the north-south line leading to the pier."

The early death of Shibasaki and his staff left Commander Sugai in command of the Betio defenses, but Sugai was bottled up in his deadly "pocket" in the northwest. Lieutenant (jg) Tamikichi Taniguchi, commanding the Second Company of the Sasebo 7th, was likewise in dangerously close contact with the assortment of Marines on the western beach.

Only Lieutenant (jg) Goichi Minami, commanding the Third Company on the east, had it in his power to win or lose the battle the first night. The U.S. Marines were particularly vulnerable on that flank—barely 600 troops scattered along a shallow enclave running west from the Burns-Philp Wharf at the eastern edge of Red Beach Three past the base of the main pier to the precarious position, at the edge of Red Beach Two, of Colonel David M. Shoup, commanding the assault forces ashore. Lieutenant Minami easily had three times that number, counting both *rikusentai* and armed construction workers, and he had only to penetrate 400 yards along the beach to cut off the lifeline of the pier and overrun Shoup. No major American force in the Pacific War was ever as vulnerable as the exhausted elements of the Second Marine Division that first night at Tarawa. But young Minami, in his initial exposure to combat, was no substitute for the fiery Shibasaki. Japanese forces remained essentially immobilized at the moment of their greatest opportunity.

The third turning point of the battle occurred shortly before noon on the second day along the western end of the island, designated by the Americans as Green Beach. This phase of the battle took place between two company commanders, Lieutenant (jg) Taniguchi of the Sasebo 7th, and Major Michael P. Ryan, commanding an unlikely assortment of survivors ("Ryan's Orphans") from four different landing teams. Taniguchi's men still occupied a daunting series of pillboxes, gun emplacements, and camouflaged foxholes, but their fields of fire were oriented westward. Ryan attacked north to south from his initial toehold on the western edge of Red Beach One. More significantly, Ryan, in the expediency of close combat, had discovered the deadly combination of fire and maneuver that would spell the doom of Japanese garrisons in the Central and Western Pacific for the remaining two years of the war: Sherman tanks covered by infantry, improvised assault squads of flamethrowers and demolition experts, and a shore fire-control party with a working radio. Responsive naval gunfire spelled the critical difference. Ryan's team called in major-caliber naval fire within fifty yards of the Marines. In less than an hour the Americans had swept the entire west coast. The Second Marine Division finally had a covered beach over which to land reinforcements fully intact.

Ryan's achievement became a critical turning point in the battle, because the Japanese could not recover from the annihilation of Taniguchi's company and the subsequent loss of Betio's broad western shoreline. Its loss meant the Japanese would henceforth be blind to American reinforcements approaching Betio from the west. The Americans' constant aerial strafing, naval bombardment, and increasingly effective shelling from the artillery of the landing force prevented Sugai and Minami from executing any deployments to reinforce the west during daylight. This must have been keenly galling to Commander Sugai. The Marines presented absolutely perfect targets—paddling ashore for over an hour in eighty-four rubber boats from the western reef, backlit throughout by the setting sun—yet no Japanese were in a position to fire an aimed shot with any weapon, not even a rifle.

The final turning point in this bloody contest occurred the third night, when Commander Sugai and Lieutenant (jg) Minami finally mustered forces on the eastern flank to counterattack the same 1st Battalion, 6th Marines who had landed with such impunity the previous evening.

This was a sensibly planned, well-orchestrated series of night attacks—not at all the sake-soaked *"Banzai!"* charges typically characterized by Western historians. Initial probes found the seams between American units and the location of their automatic weapons. This accomplished, a force of some 500 to 700 *rikusentai* then struck those sectors of the Marine lines at 4:00 A.M. Such a concentrated attack delivered along the north shore the first night could have devastated the American landing force. By the third night, however, the Marines had tipped the balance in their favor.

Prearranged naval gunfire and artillery concentrations blanketed the eastern approaches; star shells kept the battlefield in constant illumination. More than half these Marines had fought the Japanese in the Solomons; their lines bent but did not break. Individual troops proved their mettle in primeval hand-to-hand fighting with knives and bayonets. The attack failed at great loss to the Japanese. Warrant Officer Ota's account is instructive:

> Each man was so loaded down with hand grenades we could hardly walk. . . . 'READY!' We disabled the safeties on our hand grenades. 'ATTACK!' We rushed all together here and there. I completely forgot my wounded knee. The dark night was lighted as bright as day. There were heavy sounds of grenade explosions, the disordered fire of rifles, the shrieks, yells, and roars. It was just like Hell. The night battle was over in half an hour. Altogether, about 750 of us had entered the night attack. Almost all were killed, but I was somehow still alive.

The failure of their counterattack broke the back of the Betio defenders. A few hours of residual fighting on the fourth morning cleaned out the last pockets of resistance. Many of the surviving *rikusentai* chose to die at their own hands. Warrant Officer Ota and Petty Officer Onuki somehow survived having their respective bunkers scorched with flamethrowers and flattened by charges of TNT and were captured.

Elsewhere in the Gilberts, the U.S. Army's 27th Division overran Butaritari Island in Makin Atoll; a Marine reconnaissance unit landed by rubber boats from a transport submarine to wrest Apamama Atoll from its small Japanese garrison; a fresh Marine landing team ran a force of 175 *rikusentai* to ground on Buariki Island, Tarawa Atoll, and, in savage jungle fighting reminiscent of Guadalcanal, killed them all on November 27. The U.S Central Pacific Force had recaptured the entire Gilbert Islands in exactly two weeks.

Admiral Koga's *Hei* Plan #3 had failed. Only his fleet submarines achieved any degree of success, notably the sinking of the escort carrier USS *Liscome Bay* (CVE 56) off Makin by *I-175*. But the Southern Attack Force sank *I-35* off Tarawa on the fourth day of the battle, and other U.S forces sank *I-40* in the northern Gilberts two days later.

Koga, shaken to his roots by the devastation wreaked earlier on his carrier pilots and heavy cruisers at Rabaul, never stirred from Truk. His decision to ignore the threat to the Central Pacific and reinforce the northern Solomons in effect not only cost him his chance for the "Decisive Battle" in the Gilberts but led as well to his being outflanked and forced to vacate Truk by the subsequent (and nearly immediate) U.S. invasion of the Marshalls. IGHQ would retain Koga in command of the Combined Fleet, however, until his death in a plane crash shortly after the Marshalls campaign. The Fourth Fleet's emaciated force of destroyers and light cruisers never left the Marshalls. Colonel Yamanaka's Ko Detachment deployed from Ponape to Kwajalein, but waited there in vain for final orders to execute their counterlanding in the Gilberts. Admiral Koga canceled *Hei* Plan #3 on December 4.

Admiral Shibasaki and his men fulfilled their side of the plan in spades, holding the American landing force at bay for the requisite three days. The last *rikusentai* very likely died with eyes searching the western horizon in vain for the sight of the expected Japanese battleships. Shibasaki received a posthumous promotion to vice admiral; the emperor commended the doomed garrison. They had paid a fearsome price: 4,455 died. The bulk of the 146 prisoners captured by the Marines on Betio were Korean laborers; only nineteen were Japanese. Two were survivors of the sunken submarine *I-35;* several others were civilian members of the 111th Construction Battalion—carpenters, masons, a barber, some "pick and shovel men." Only 8 were *rikusentai* from either the Sasebo 7th Special Naval Landing Force or the 3d Special Base Defense Force. The 2,571 *rikusentai* at Tarawa thus suffered a fatality rate of 99.7 percent.

The *rikusentai* nevertheless sold their lives dearly. The American landing force sustained 3,400 casualties (including 1,115 killed) in three days, roughly 30 percent of the assault elements of the 2nd Marine Division who were able to land while the battle still raged. This savage fighting in such a compressed time and space—more than 5,500 Japanese and Americans killed in seventy-six hours within a space smaller than that occupied by the Pentagon building and its parking lots—would remain the haunting hallmark of the battle.

Tarawa became a pivotal milepost in the Pacific War. The Americans learned from their many mistakes, validated their previously unproven amphibious doctrine, and rolled "on to westward," an increasingly invincible juggernaut. The Japanese tried desperately to devise countermeasures, including the increasing use of special suicide attack units, but never again would they hold an American landing force in such dire jeopardy as they did the first night at Tarawa.

THE KWAI
THAT NEVER WAS

STANLEY WEINTRAUB

If there was a genuine disaster that Churchill presided over, it had to be the capitulation of Singapore to the Japanese in February 1942. More than 100,000 Empire troops went into captivity, many of whom would soon end up working on the so-called "Death Railway." The Japanese had pushed on through Siam (today's Thailand) and Burma, right up to the borders of India, which they intended to bring into their sphere. But a major logistical problem now facing them was how to get men and supplies to Rangoon. An ocean voyage around the Malay Peninsula was not only long but faced the danger of attacks by Allied planes and submarines. The answer was to build a connecting rail line through the malarial swamps and jungle uplands of Burma, and POWs and civilian conscripts offered a ready-made free labor pool. Men starved, succumbed to disease, and died by the thousands, their remains consigned to funeral pyres. Those who attempted to escape and were recaptured, were forced to dig their own graves before they were shot. And all the while, as Stanley Weintraub writes, "flocks of expectant vultures watched from the tops of tall teak trees."

The "Death Railway" was completed by the summer of 1944, but because of Allied air raids, it carried little traffic. After the war, two Thai Rivers, Kwae Yai and Kwae Noi, became collectively immortalized as a novel and movie called *The Bridge on the River Kwai*. In 1958, the movie garnered seven Academy Awards. But, as Weintraub notes, Hollywood's version of how the infamous bridge on the "Death Railway" was built, and then destroyed, was more romantic than the actual story. The grisly conditions of the Japanese prison camps in Southeast Asia never even made it to the cutting room floor. They were simply too unpleasant to be seen. The noted photographer John Sargeant, who spent four harrowing years in the camps, accompanied the director of *The Bridge on the River*

Kwai, David Lean, as an adviser to the movie. "He never once listened to me," Sargeant said.

That all goes to prove that history may make movies; movies may make history; but movies are *not* history.

Stanley Weintraub is the author of *Long Day's Journey into War: December 7, 1941, The Last Great Victory: The End of World War II,* and, most recently, *MacArthur's War: Korea and the Undoing of an American Hero.*

FLOWING FROM LOWER BURMA, THE THAI RIVERS MAE KHLANG (Kwae Yai, or Little Kwai) and Kwae Noi intersect near Khanchanaburi, west of Bangkok. Since a best-selling novel of the mid-1950s and an unforgettable film made from it, they have been imagined collectively as the River Kwai. In his account of bridge-building on the Kwai ordered by the Japanese in World War II, the French novelist Pierre Boulle experienced none of the horrors he fictionalized, nor did Xan Fielding, his translator, or the two screenwriters who removed the narrative even further from reality. Yet the fictive events, conflating novel and cinema, have become "history."

The River Kwai bridge that has erroneously become identified as the "Bridge on the River Kwai" is an eleven-span steel-and-concrete structure at Tamarkan, near Khanchanaburi. (In fact, the true bridge on the Kwai, now gone, did stand at this site.) The large existing bridge had been cannibalized from Java by the Japanese in 1942. Dismantled into eleven spans, each twenty-five feet long, the bridge was shipped in sections to Bangkok, then floated upriver on the Kwae Yai and hauled to the site by elephants—and by prisoners of war. Japanese railway arithmetic held that eighty POWs, whatever their physical condition, equaled one elephant.

There were six steel bridges on the Kwai in addition to that one. There were also more than 680 wooden crossings, most of them tremblingly rickety and carrying no rails, but some higher and longer than the one that became known as the "Bridge on the River Kwai." Of the nearly 700 bridges stretched over 265 miles of malarial swamps and mountainous jungle, in the popular conception the one at Tamarkan seems legitimized as "the bridge" by its size and by the huge cemetery nearby, where thousands of prisoners of war who perished building the Burma "death railway" are buried. Local entrepreneurs have only fueled the myth: for tourists there are now River Kwai train rides, boat excursions, bus tours, sound-and-light shows, T-shirts, souvenir railway spikes, and a museum.

A wood-fired Japanese pony engine and a diesel truck with flanged wheels for rail-riding stand as monuments on a length of track near the bridge site. A bronze plaque informs that the railway, nearly 300 miles long, was built between October 1942 and October 1943. Trains from Bangkok make a special stop at it. A travel poster boasts, "Tourists will definitely have the joy of their life cruising along the real River Kwai on their way to pay a visit to the Chungkai War Memorial Cemetery."

Even the cemetery misleads. From mid-1942 into October 1943, when the railway and its bridges were constructed, an estimated 12,568 (of some 61,000) POWs died in the effort, and at least seven times that many civilian laborers, mostly Tamils from Malaya. To take the film or the novel as a representation of reality is to ignore the huge civilian labor force drafted by the Japanese with false promises of good wages and working conditions. There were 220 mass graves for civilian draft laborers along the Khlang and the Kwae, and thousands of individual burial sites quickly swallowed up by the humid tropical jungle, which could rot an elephant's carcass down to tusks and bones in two weeks.

POW labor was available because in February 1942, the British had surrendered Singapore to a numerically inferior force that had outguessed and outmaneuvered the combined British and Commonwealth colonial garrison. To the contingent of POWs were added survivors from such sunken warships as the Australian *Perth* and the American *Houston,* and Dutch and other defenders of the sprawling Netherlands Indies. To carry on a campaign intended to seize Burma and then India, the Japanese had to send troops and matériel into Rangoon in southeastern Burma, a long voyage around the Malay Peninsula subject to air and submarine attack. A rail line connecting existing trackage around Bangkok and around Rangoon would speed the buildup while safeguarding men and matériel. But it would have to go along jungle rivers and tropical highlands.

However costly in manpower that might have seemed, it was a price easy to pay. A surplus of POWs existed, all expendable in the furtherance of the Greater East Asia Co-Prosperity Sphere. A Japanese who committed the ultimate shame of surrender was rejected at home. The deaths of such prisoners altered only their fleshly status, for they were, to the Japanese, already spiritually dead.

Even if building materials were in place and equipment and tools were available, the directive from Tokyo to construct a railway and its bridges would have been audacious. The Japanese had neither bulldozers nor steamrollers, nor cranes nor jackhammers, often not even wheelbarrows. Prisoners broke up earth for mounding the railway bed, or for bases for bridges, with pickaxes, shovels, and hoes, sometimes moving soil and rock in buckets or in burlap stretched on poles. Crushing stone—in tropical heat that weighed on the body like an affliction—was often attempted with a sledgehammer by men who, starved into skeletons, weighed hardly more than the hammer. To break up boulders, POWs used hand drills and inserted dynamite sticks, then ran for cover.

Most prisoners had developed malaria; many suffered dysentery, beriberi, pellagra, dengue fever, scrub typhus, and—worst of all—tropical ulcers from insect bites or injuries, which after festering in the rank filth could lead to gangrene and the crude amputation of a limb. Quickly rotted or shredded, clothes hardly existed. Fortunate prisoners had shoes. Most worked in crude loincloths. Flocks of expectant vultures watched from the tops of tall teak trees.

Conditions even as described by Boulle were inappropriate for a bigbudget feature film, but Carl Foreman devised a script from the novel, working on it in England, where he lived in self-exile. Blacklisted in the United States, he had become unemployable after the McCarthyite hearings on the "Hollywood Ten" and alleged Communist infiltration of the American film industry. Another blacklisted writer who had retreated to England, Michael Wilson, rewrote the screenplay for Sam Spiegel, the producer, and David Lean, his director, but after its translation to celluloid the credits listed neither Foreman nor Wilson. Instead, the name of Boulle, the novelist, appeared, although he could neither read nor write English, for the film could not be distributed nor shown with the names of the banned. As a result an Academy Award for best screenplay in 1957 honored the wrong person, and only in 1985 were the true writers, denied onscreen credit a generation earlier, finally acknowledged—posthumously—and their families awarded their Oscars.

The Bridge on the River Kwai collected seven Academy Awards, one of the highest totals ever, for Best Picture, Best Director, Best Screenplay, Best Actor (Alec Guinness), Cinematography (Jack Hildyard), Film Editing (Peter Taylor), and Best Musical Score (Malcolm Arnold, whose "Colonel Bogey March" theme remains unforgettable).

Also unforgettable, even to those who know the film only by reputation, is Pierre Boulle's fictional colonel. His sterling qualities as a leader of men derive from British snobbery and his sense of the virtues of discipline, so long as the discipline emanates from his side rather than that of the enemy. Boulle's

Colonel Nicholson had impeded the escape of his men from Singapore to the Dutch East Indies because his commanding general had signed a surrender. To fight on would have violated orders from above. Nicholson had ignored the first Japanese attempting to take his surrender because they were only privates and "could not speak a word of any civilized language." With rare personal courage, Nicholson endures savage abuse to establish to his captors that under the *Manual of Military Law* he retains the authority to issue orders to his men—and when he establishes that, he issues his own version of each enemy order, invariably harsher than what the Japanese intended. "The main thing," he explains to Clipton, the medical officer, "is to make the lads feel they're still being commanded by us and not by these baboons. As long as they cling to this idea, they'll be soldiers, not slaves."

The forbidding march through the jungle to which the British POWs are subjected leads to a site along the river where they are ordered to build a railway bridge. Since such a span has no purpose without rail trackage to and from it, the implication is that other work parties of POWs exist, but the narrative largely isolates Nicholson's men in order to focus upon them. He has two other surviving officers. Major Hughes had been a mining company official in Malaya, and Captain Reeves a public works engineer in India. It is crucial, Nicholson tells them, that the construction be done well. Colonel Saito and his marginally civilized Japanese might be used to "shoddy, amateur work" but the British represented the continuity of Western technology.

All of Nicholson's efforts are directed at efficient operation under the most primitive conditions. His exasperation is even worse than that of enemy overseers when his men are deliberately slack or incompetent "under an ostentatious show of willingness." Nicholson is beaten and tortured when he forbids officers to do manual work, but when he is not on the scene his men's effectiveness declines, and the Japanese engineer in charge reduces individual quotas for filling the railway embankment by 33 percent. Even curses and blows fail to accelerate the work, and, anxious about an anticipated high-level inspection, Saito is forced into a concession. He announces that since December 7, 1942, will mark the first anniversary of Japan's entry into the war, he will grant a general amnesty. Henceforth officers "would devote themselves to supervising their men's activity so as to ensure the maximum efficiency."

While the work on the bridge and approaches proceeds, far to the west in Calcutta the commander of Force 316 (patterned on the real-life Force 136, a British special forces unit based in India) plans to slip agents into the area to see that the rail link to Burma never becomes viable. At the River Kwai site, however, Captain Reeves, loyally following Nicholson's lead, investigates the proposed location of the bridge and finds it "utter folly," as he puts it, to build on the quagmire there. The pilings "would just go on sinking." Further, the "hopeless" Japanese engineer seems to Reeves unconcerned about the quality of lumber used, "hard or soft, rigid or flexible, or whether it will stand up to any stress laid on it. It's an absolute disgrace, sir." Moreover, the Japanese incompetent has no working plans except to lay "a plank across a ditch" a hundred feet above the water. "It'll never stand up, sir. I'm absolutely ashamed to be taking part in such sabotage."

Force 316 would have been pleased with the enemy's ideas for the bridge, but not the proud Brit POWs, who appeal to the Japanese ("these apes") for more efficient reorganization of working squads. "It's an absolutely rotten show," Reeves agrees, caught up in the spirit of the challenge. "In India, where the climate's just as bad as this, and the ground's much harder, the coolies get through one and a half cubic yards quite easily."

Nicholson arranges to "have a word with Saito," which results in the latter's "shameless loss of face"—a humiliation so complete that beads of sweat break out over Saito's contorted brow. Japanese soldiers, he finally declares, would have built the bridge faster and better.

Nicholson tactfully agrees, pointing out that the Japanese were used to having their own officers commanding them. "But I hope to show you the true worth of the British soldier quite soon, Colonel Saito. Incidentally, I ought to tell you that I've altered our men's quota."

As Saito charges him with insubordination, Nicholson interrupts calmly: "I've increased it from one cubic yard to one and a half. It's in the general interest, and I felt this step would meet with your approval."

Dumbfounded, Saito begins to yield when Nicholson suggests, his tone unchanged, "We've still got to fix the quota for your men working on the line. At first I thought of putting it at one cubic yard so as not to overtire them, but don't you think it would be best if we made it the same as the British soldiers? That will create a healthy competitive spirit. . . ."

"The Japanese soldiers' quota," Saito screams, "will be two cubic yards!"

With satisfaction, Nicholson salutes and withdraws. (In fact, few Japanese soldiers did manual work on the railway, for a quarter of a million civilian laborers had been drafted to supplement POWs.)

"What fools they are, sir!" observes the medical officer ("a strange glint in his eye as he spoke") with irony lost on the colonel. "To think that, without us, they would have built their bridge in a swamp and it would have capsized under the weight of their trains loaded with troops and supplies!" The colonel's face remains "inscrutable."

Thanks to Nicholson, Hughes, and Reeves, "the methods of Western civilization" continue to triumph over the "primitive empiricism" of their captors. Performing the actual labor, the men in the ranks suffer injury, brutality, sickness, even death, but the survivors go on, their "punishing tasks" accomplished "with zeal and cheerfulness" although "more or less naked" and resembling "a slave gang." "With a satisfied eye," Nicholson watches the bridge take form, and Saito cannot altogether conceal his astonishment and admiration. The impressive span appears likely to be finished ahead of deadline.

Having surveyed the area with the help of Thai partisans, Force 316 has other ideas. Reporting back, commandos advise against employing the RAF because at most, aerial bombs might damage only a few arches of a wooden bridge. Explosives laid at the site, however, could "blow the thing sky-high and shatter the piles at water-level, and [one could] also time the explosion for when a train is actually crossing the bridge. . . . Here they'll have to detour in the line and build the bridge all over again—not to mention the loss of a train and its load of war material. What a show! I can just see it. . . ." Another in the mission exclaims, "I only hope the Air Force chaps won't have a go at it, sir, before we do." As for the POWs, "The natives had quite a lot to say. . . . They had seen them working almost naked in the scorching sun, working without break and under strict surveillance. . . ."

"If only they knew we were in the offing, sir," one sapper observes to Colonel Green, the fictional Force 316 commander, with complete misunderstanding. "If only they knew this bridge of theirs was never going to be used, it might raise their morale." But the POWs cannot be told. "They'd start trying to help us and might give the whole show away by having a go at the bridge themselves . . . the only result would be terrible reprisals."

More and more men working on the bridge and approaches suffer from jungle scourges. Obsessed about completing the bridge before the deadline, Nicholson, however, prowls Clipton's hospital enclosure drafting laborers who might be abusing sick privileges—men with malaria and temperatures of only 104, and with jungle sores not requiring amputation. Even if a man is "not at the top of his form," says Nicholson, he can make himself useful for the "finishing touches."

Sarcastically, Clipton ventures, "I suppose you're going to have the thing painted, sir?"

"Don't even think such a thing, Clipton," says the colonel testily. "The most we could do would be to give it a coating of lime—and a fine target that would make for the planes, wouldn't it! You seem to forget there's a war on!"

"You're quite right, sir. There's a war on."

Lying, Nicholson pulls the careworn medical officer aside to warn that Saito might empty the hospital entirely, and Clipton yields by discharging a quarter of his patients. Uncomplaining, they straggle back to complete the last yards of the bridge and the finishing details essential to Anglo-Saxon craftsmanship.

For Force 316 the destruction of the bridge is simply a textbook operation. A team of two could lay a plastic charge in half an hour while making the detonator invisible. But Nicholson, prowling the site, chances upon the commandos. In vain they explain who they are, and their orders; Nicholson angrily launches himself at them before they can plant their device properly. When the charge explodes, a little damage is done, and the engine and two coaches of an approaching train slip the rails and plunge into the river, but the bridge remains intact. The third man in the force, at a distance with Thai irregulars, and with a powerful mortar, prevents his companions, wounded by Japanese fire, from being captured alive. As their bodies, and Nicholson's, were being carried away by Japanese soldiers, he reports on return to headquarters, he had planted a shell right among the group. "A stroke of luck! Both our chaps were blown to pieces. . . . Believe me, sir . . . I didn't want to leave the job half done, either. All three of them, I should have said. The colonel as well. There was nothing left of him. . . . After that, sir, I fired all the shells I had. . . . We sprayed the ground pretty thoroughly. . . . The stuff was falling a bit indiscriminately, on the rest of the company rushing out of the camp, on the derailed train, in which everyone was shrieking, and also on the bridge. . . . There was no more ammo, nothing else to fire. So we retired. . . . I took the only line of conduct possible. It was really the only proper action I could have taken."

"The only proper action," his colonel concedes.

That was the novelist's rendering. The screenplay required a more upbeat ending. Irony is wasted on most moviegoers. "Two men lost. Some damage done but bridge intact thanks to British colonel's heroism," Force 316's report had conceded understatedly in the novel. In the film, Nicholson is killed by a commando mortar shell, but he falls very conveniently onto the detonator's plunger and blows up the bridge in a shattering climax, while Clipton, the medical officer, cries, "Madness! Madness!" The waste of war is emphasized by having one of the dead Force 316 men be an American whose war ideals are only "to go home." For box-office reasons the Thai partisans include several sexy young women, one of whom begins a chaste romance with the doomed American. And, necessarily, the actors appear too well fed.

The film script suggested a theme reflective of "Hollywood Ten" sensitivities—collaboration. When Nicholson commits his men not only to building the bridge but to doing it in the most professional—rather than in the most subversive—manner possible, he is guilty of the sin of collaboration with the enemy. If war is madness, deliberate, voluntary collaboration is utter insanity. In the film Nicholson explains that POWs legally cannot refuse to work. But to the colonel the work for the Japanese becomes a monomaniacal enterprise, even a technological monument to distant England. He compares the bridge and its components to the first London Bridge and the great elms felled to build it. He even has a commemorative plaque affixed to mark the achievement as that of British soldiers.

In the screenplay the commando whom the colonel recognizes at the end (and to whom he shouts a shocked "You!") is an American escapee from the camp, a violator of the code. The commando recognizes the lone figure proudly surveying his achievement as the collaborator responsible for such stylish assistance to the enemy. The denouement appears morally appropriate, the creator unintentionally destroying his own creation while struggling to save it from the commando saboteurs.

In fact, the bridge—or bridges—across the Khlang and the Kwai were never destroyed beyond repair by Force 316 or the RAF. The Japanese engineer described as incompetent by Pierre Boulle in the novel was in reality Hiroshi Abe, a lieutenant who before the war was supervising the laying of track for the first of what are now the famous high-speed "bullet trains." The big bridge that Abe took, in recollection, to be the basis for the fictional one was a wooden span 100 yards long over a gorge more than thirty yards deep. "Without the elephants we couldn't have done it," he recalled. In neither film nor novel are there any elephants, and they were rare in the building of the actual bridge as well. Abe's bridge was near the Thai border with Burma, far from Bangkok, and used Burmese civilians and Japanese soldiers, as well as British prisoners. POWs, he claimed, were "physically weak . . . and only given the job of turning the pieces [of large boulders] into rocks of just the right size or [of] digging up soil. . . . That movie . . . is complete fiction and idealizes the behavior of British prisoners. . . . In the movie, the Japanese rail unit was in charge of managing captives. That wasn't the way it was. Our unit specialized in building bridges and only borrowed prisoner labor."

His deputies, Abe claimed, would go to a prison camp along the river and ask, "Can we have three hundred workers today?" A guard unit would escort the POWs to assigned tasks—some for digging, some for cutting wood. "In the movie the British volunteer to build the bridge for us. They say, 'The Jap Army's way of doing things is all wrong. Let us do it!' Nothing like that happened and they never built us a great bridge. William Holden and his [commando] team were supposed to have sneaked behind the lines and blown the bridge up. That didn't happen either."

In a fashion, Abe was honest. His underlings did most of the dirty work. As John Stewart—a slight, bespectacled British noncom—recalled, if the required prison labor failed to materialize, a squad of army engineers led by a corporal entered the POW huts to drag out additional prisoners, whatever their condition. *"Jodan desuka?"* the Japanese soldier would shout. "Is this a joke? I need three hundred, not two hundred." More bodies for the daily funeral pyres would result, and hardened to the sight, Stewart remembered a memorable day at the bridge when a Japanese colonel, pleased with the progress, offered him a precious cigarette. Neither had the means to light it, but behind a nearby hill smoke was rising.

"A score of bodies were burning. Flesh bubbled, and limbs writhed. I bent down, with one hand protecting my face from the heat, and with the other picking out a burning twig." The colonel backed away in horror. After Stewart lit his cigarette, his unlikely companion asked how such a thing could be done "from the fire that's consuming your friends."

It was, Stewart replied, a nothing-to-be-done thing: *"Shigata ga nai koto."* The colonel lit his own cigarette from Stewart's.

Later a cameraman and technical adviser on David Lean's film crew, Stewart knew that since most of his advice was ignored in view of box-office necessities, that memory could be kept to himself.

On one personal inspection of the hospital huts, Abe eliminated from forced labor the swollen beriberi cases, the diphtheria victims, those with maggoty and putrid flesh, and the entire "jungle ward," where cases of smallpox, meningitis, and typhus were isolated. But he ordered out all the feverish malaria patients who were not actually delirious. "In war orders must be given until final victory," he explained to a British officer whom Stewart accompanied. "Sometimes these orders are very hard, very painful. You must remember that the Emperor himself wants this railway to be built. As far as you are concerned, *shigata ga nai.* . . . Tomorrow you will find fifty more men."

Stewart would write that Abe was hanged for war crimes, but he only got the verdict right. The sentence was commuted, and Abe survived his imprisonment. Long after his release from death row in Changi Prison in Singapore, where thousands of British POWs had been herded in February 1942, he admitted, "For us Japanese, becoming a prisoner was itself the greatest shame imaginable. It was the same as death. . . . I had to build that bridge. I felt genuinely sorry for the captives, but I was in no position to actively improve their conditions. We had to have human labor because we didn't have machines. . . . The prisoners didn't exactly work. They resisted in silence. Officially they worked three hours in the morning, had an hour of rest, then worked four hours in the afternoon, but they were just skin and bones. They couldn't labor any more than that."

The worst period was the "Speedo" summer and early autumn of 1943, when the railway was pushed to completion and guards used their only word of English—Speedo—to hurry up the work. Neither illness nor injury moved the Japanese to pity. To them, illness was also shameful. As a POW doctor on the railway, Constantine Petrovsky remembered the enemy philosophy was "if you're sick you're finished." The Japanese would permit hospital time only when something was visible, like a maggoty, gangrenous infection or a broken limb. After all, a lieutenant told his group, "You prisoners. You finished. Your people don't want you. You die."

Much of the "Speedo" period was also the monsoon season, which lasted for six months, beginning in late May. During the worst of it, no work could be done; thus the monsoon spared the very lives it made miserable. Stewart remembered the monsoon's "operatic extravagance" at times when nothing not rooted to the ground seemed in danger:

> Bolts of lightning illuminated the jungle like magnesium flares. As the thunder exploded, the air itself felt shattered into its different elements, ionised and unstable. The metallic reek of ozone obliterated all the jungle odours. The wind howled in the jungle canopy. . . . Shafts of rain lashed our fragile shelter. . . . With every short respite, fat clouds of steam wreathed the undergrowth and crept up to the canopy. The air itself became aqueous, and in the vaporous silence we slowly came back to life.

Neither film nor novel makes much of the monsoons and the soggy respites they purchased from the railway. In fiction, the season vanished.

Although Boulle's bridge is mythical, there was a Chungkai (or Songkrai) Camp for POWs just south of the Kwae at Khanburi, now Khanchanaburi, and a bridge was built there. Boulle did his homework. Allied prisoners suffered far more than either novel or film could capture, and they were forced to dig, break up, and carry one-and-a-half cubic meters of soil and rock daily, with guards using meter sticks to measure completion of quotas. There were memorable British officers dedicated to the well-being of their men in captivity in Burma, two of the most notable being the Australian combat surgeon Lieutenant Colonel Edward ("Weary") Dunlop, a figure of awesome dedica-

After the British surrendered Singapore in February 1942, the Japanese planned a campaign to bring Burma and India into their sphere. A major logistical problem facing them was the need to send men and matériel to Burma. If they were sent by ship—the long way, around the Malaya Peninsula—Allied subs and planes could attack the convoys. A rail route extending the existing line into Burma, built by POWs and civilian conscripts, seemed the obvious answer.

tion and courage at the Hakhan Nayak prison camp, and Lieutenant Colonel Philip Toosey, at the Nahon Nayak Camp near Bangkok, who assumed charge of POWs in Thailand at the Japanese surrender. Perhaps the officer closest to those in the ranks doing forced labor on the railway was Lieutenant Colonel Harold H. Lilly of the 5th Battalion, Sherwood Foresters (Nottinghamshire and Derbyshire Regiment). "Everybody knew his name," C. R. Eber of the

Singapore Volunteers, a Eurasian private among the POWs, recalled, "Even the Japanese respected him."

Eber, in an oral history interview done in the early 1980s, recalled being marched the last eighty-five miles to Khanburi in broiling sun and oppressive heat. Many prisoners collapsed; he fell and expected to be abandoned but was given aid by a British medic and recovered. "Packed like sardines in a field—no shelter at all," Eber recalled, they were promised by Lilly, who addressed them, "I'll see if I can get you a rest tomorrow."

The next morning the Japanese commander ordered them off toward a labor collection point for the railway. As medical corpsman Anthony Daniels recalled, the officer declared in his limited English, "You must help Nippon!" Colonel Lilly insisted, "My men are not in fit condition to march. They are all exhausted and have blisters on their feet. They must have some rest."

"Do you know I can have you shot for refusing to march?"

"You had better shoot me now because my men are not going to march."

"Weary" Dunlop recalled a similar confrontation after he ordered his men to rest and insisted that they could not work. When a pistol pressed to his ribs failed to change Dunlop's mind, the gun-wielding Japanese officer conceded, "You are a very foolish man. I could have killed you. But you are a brave man too." Although he was a surgeon rather than a fighting officer, his authority over his men was afterward unchallenged by the Japanese.

In Lilly's case, his men did not march that day, but they had little choice after that if they wanted their teacup-sized rice ration. Yet Lilly was no Nicholson, intent upon asserting the superiority of Western civilization as he saw it. He was trying to protect lives, even at the cost of his own.

The next day, dawn to dusk, Lilly's men were marched for fifty miles through virgin jungle, bitten by mosquitoes, leeches, and whatever else crawled or flew. "We wrapped our legs in large leaves," Eber recalled, "to protect them." Muddy pools were their only water, and their food was rice, cooked along the way, and tea. After two more days they were encamped at a site near the river, where they built bamboo enclosures, each one to shelter, shoulder to shoulder, 200 men. It would be their "standard of accommodation" for a year. They were fifty miles south of Moulmein in Burma, possibly the site of Lieutenant Abe's bridge. There were Gordon Highlanders, a Cambridge regiment, Royal Fusiliers, and Singapore Volunteers. Lilly was their only officer; below him in rank were sergeant majors. (Most officers remained in Changi Prison.) At nearby camps were Tamil Indian laborers from Malaya. Some guards were Korean; others were members of the rebel Indian National Army recruited from former POWs. All wore Japanese uniforms.

With the railways and its bridges slated for completion by October 1943, in time for a new offensive in Burma, any prisoner reasonably sound was compelled to work. Some were carried to the site in stretchers. (Magnanimously, they were given two days off at Christmas 1942.) In February 1943, additional British officers were sent to lead working parties. Men fell out at dawn each morning with their hand tools, to march to a work site. Dressed in G-strings or loincloths, each carried a tool and a gunnysack with rice and scrounged edibles, from wild chilies to boilable insects. Now and then they hid a few dynamite sticks to throw into the river and explode fish onto the bank. Rations would be reduced even from their starvation minimums, and men sought out, to grill on camp or jungle fires, such delicacies as snakes, monkeys, iguanas, cats, and dogs. Carl de Souza recalled his work unit "stripping the jungle clean" for things to mix into the rice porridge or stew they prepared three times daily—leaves of plants such as wild spinach or passion fruit were prized to extend the daily "ten spoonsful" of rice.

The railway embankments followed the course of the Kwai, their crowns topped with excavated and broken rock. When guards looked away, POWs laid rails on "sleepers," or ties, of dangerously soft wood, hoping for rapid deterioration in the muggy climate. Low, often flooded, areas required rock columns to level the trackage to embankment height; where the columns broke above water level, the prisoners fitted into them upright long logs to support the bed of the bridge. Neither novel nor film observes that a flat-bottomed rail weighed about seventy pounds per yard and came in twenty-four-foot lengths. A rail was a massive weight for emaciated men to wrestle into position for spiking onto the wooden sleepers. The work was brutal.

Despite Abe's assertions of professionalism, he did not have much engineering expertise under his command to spread along the length of the railway. Some gradients were too steep for underpowered locomotives to pull overloaded carriages, and some curves were too sharp and could—and did—pitch trains into ravines. No real-life Reeves or Nicholson had work crews improve the line.

The last bleak meal of the prisoners' day (always rice) was cooked in near-darkness after they returned to camp, usually singing en route to keep spirits up. Morale boosters were needed all the more when planes overflew them as they worked and they could see the circular red insignia identifying the enemy. More than anything else, the planes suggested that the bad times had not turned around, a perception reinforced into 1943 by the news gleaned from improvised radios (whose discovery could mean death for owners and listeners). The British and ANZACs, both well represented along the Kwai, had retreated deep into Egypt; the Russians had fallen back as far as Stalingrad; the Japanese were swarming into New Guinea and the Solomons. And in Burma, the British had been pushed westward nearly to the Indian border.

Removed from hiding places, the radios were played long after dark, usually in the stinking latrines from which guards kept their distance. Each evening, as work details approached their camps, their rising voices became recognizable to the sick and dying in the hospital enclosures, chorusing "There Will Always Be an England," "Pack Up Your Troubles," and other familiar songs that suggested home, even to men who had never seen England.

A quartermaster sergeant might shout as they marched, many painfully barefoot with jungle sores, something like, "Today is my doctor's wedding day." (The men cheered.) "I think I will give him three thousand pounds as a gift." (More cheers.) "On second thought, I think it's best to put the money back in the old hope chest." And, Eber remembered, their troubles temporarily forgotten as they jeered the pretended miserliness, "We booed." The efforts by all to keep morale up in appalling conditions may have reinforced their will to live. Other than the overwork, brutality, and disease that, Eber estimated, cost five lives a day at his base camp until the railway was completed, the problem was "waking up after dreaming of home to find I was still a prisoner. . . . We knew there was no escape." Rather, there was the "bamboo fence"—which meant no fence, only the forbidding jungle. Australian POWs recalled the escape of several mates who were captured three days later, forced to dig their own graves, then publicly executed. But for them and actor William Holden, the dark, dense, nearly impenetrable jungle was daunting enough. Former British POW Eric Wilcox recalled in his 1995 memoir *The Railway Man* that some escapees, sick, starving, and spent, gave themselves up knowing full well that they would be shot.

In July 1944, with the line and its bridges completed but little traffic moving in daylight because of Allied air raids—the Japanese by then had few aircraft to spare for local defense—the fittest survivors were sent to transit camps to be readied for shipment to Japan for work in the coal and copper mines. It was unsafe to be too healthy. Some of those en route to Japan drowned when their troop ships—"cesspools," recalled Petrovsky—were sunk by American submarines. Some who survived the mines in southern Kyushu were unfortunately aboveground when atomic bombs blasted Hiroshima, near Petrovsky's camp, and camps near Nagasaki. Perhaps the luckier ones, too weak for the long ocean journey, remained along the Kwae and the Khlang to maintain the railway and bridges until the Japanese surrender—which came, fortunately, as the Japanese in Thailand were receiving instructions to kill all remaining prisoners before the end of August 1945.

Reclaimed by jungle borers and tropical rot, most of the bridges the prisoners built have not survived as well as the novel and the film made from it. However much both romanticize the realities, they contribute something that the facts alone might not. They illumine the conflict of contrasting racial—or racist?—pride that was so prominent a feature of the war, the mutual misunderstandings of disparate cultures; the dehumanizing impact of war, whatever one's side or its perceived rightness; and the indomitability of the human spirit. Best-sellerdom and box-office film receipts do not diminish the saga—even the tragedy—of the Kwai.

ORDE WINGATE: REBELLIOUS MISFIT

CHARLES BERGES

"He was a very difficult man," Charles Berges begins his article about Orde Wingate, the British general who organized and led the fabled "Chindits" in the backcountry of Burma. That assessment may even be a bit of an understatement. Wingate was one of those notable British military eccentrics—"Chinese" Gordon of Khartoum fame comes to mind—whom only a colonial army could produce, and his exploits ranged from Palestine to Ethiopia to Burma. Personally fearless, he mixed savage discipline with inspiration: If his men revered him, his fellow officers resented (loathed might be a better word) his unorthodox ways as well as his knack for winning over people in high places. Winston Churchill was one of them, and it was the prime minister who brought Wingate to Quebec in the summer of 1943 to air his plan for neutralizing the Japanese threat. (This was the same conference where "Savvy" Cook hatched his Great Leaps Forward scheme.)

There were three main stops in this difficult man's career, and at each he left achievement behind him. In Palestine during the late 1930s, Wingate, an ardent Zionist, taught Jewish settlers how to fight back against Arab raiders—and got himself, for neither the first nor the last time, in hot water. ("My favorite madman," the Jewish leader Chaim Weizmann called him.) In Ethiopia in 1940, Wingate's irregulars swept through the country forcing garrison after garrison of Italians to surrender; Wingate would lead the deposed Ethiopian emperor, Haile Selassie, back into his capital, Addis Ababa. But it was in Burma in 1943 and the first months of 1944 (he died in an airplane crash) where Wingate made his lasting reputation. When he arrived in Delhi in April 1942, the Japanese were surging through Burma toward India. They could be stopped, Wingate maintained, by putting a force behind the lines to disrupt their communications and invasion plans. Wingate's "Chindits"—

named after the mythical winged lions whose likenesses adorned Burmese temples—would give Great Britain its first success, and a much-needed one, in Southeast Asia.

Charles Berges is a physiotherapist in Brooklyn Heights, New York, and frequent contributor to *MHQ*. He served in the Korean War and, with medical groups, treated wounded guerrillas on the Afghan border.

HE WAS A VERY DIFFICULT MAN. HE GAVE THE IMPRESSION OF one who sets out deliberately to make enemies, a practice at which he had amazing success. Insolent to superiors, sneering and contemptuous of peers, often harsh in his dealings with subordinates, he made only the most grudging concessions to the social imperatives of a rigid military caste. Slovenly in the extreme, with appalling views on personal hygiene, he was a living affront to an army in which appearance and decorum weighed heavily. Ordinary minds hated him with an enduring passion; larger ones ignored the rudeness and listened to the genius behind the gibes, for he was a mesmerizing speaker—gifted with clarity of mind and precision in expressing thought, able to hold the attention of the best minds and most influential people of his time. His intolerance of the views of others and his certainty of the rightness of his own stemmed from his belief that he was the chosen instrument of divine will. Fearless in action, he led from the front, and his courage and messianic zeal inspired all who followed. Whatever the role—tactician, organizer, or trainer—he performed brilliantly. He was Orde Wingate, one of the most colorful Allied commanders of World War II.

Born in India in 1903, the son of an army colonel, Wingate was raised in England after his father's retirement. Both of his parents were deeply religious and members of the puritanical Plymouth Brethren, a Christian sect that adhered more strongly to the punishments of the Old Testament than the forgiveness found in the New. The young Orde and his five siblings were raised in a Spartan environment of study and prayer. Friendships outside the family were discouraged, and tutors visited the home to expand on the elementary education provided by Wingate's mother. The children received an excellent but insular education. The Old Testament was a living presence in their home and had a tremendous impact on young Wingate, who would remain devout all his life.

In time, Wingate became a student at the great British public school Charterhouse. His family permitted no socializing, and he could make no friends. Wingate was barely remembered as an undersized, unkempt, unhappy boy with a ferocious glare. His father's influence secured him an appointment to the Royal Military Academy at Woolwich, the artillerist's equivalent of Sandhurst, where his slovenliness, poor scholarship, and scornful demeanor nearly got him expelled. A severe dressing-down by the school commandant brought Wingate to his senses, and he applied himself and graduated in 1923, the sixth generation of his family to serve the Crown.

In 1927, having demonstrated proficiency in Arabic, which he acquired during a year of intensive study, Wingate was posted to the Sudan Defense Force. This assignment came about through the intercession of a famous cousin, Sir Reginald Wingate, former governor-general of the Sudan. Wingate was to spend six years with the Sudan Defense Force, training his command, patrolling, and trapping ivory poachers and slave traders. Wingate got on well with the Sudanese and the Ethiopians just over the border. While in the Sudan he began to develop the qualities that later became his hallmarks: a phenomenal eye for terrain, mastery of the art of ambush, and the ability to inspire troops.

In 1936, Wingate, then a captain, was posted to Palestine as an intelligence officer, part of the reinforcement of a garrison that was beginning to feel besieged. Great Britain had governed Palestine since 1919 under the mandate of the League of Nations. Britain's championing of a Jewish homeland, as expressed in the Balfour Declaration of 1917, had stunned and angered the largely Muslim population of Palestine. There were periodic outbreaks of violence against Jewish settlers, but adroit handling by the British kept the problem manageable.

This relative calm ended in 1933 with the rise of National Socialism and the expulsion of Jews from public life in Germany. By 1936 the movement of Jews to the Holy Land had increased from a few hundred a year to tens of thousands. Palestinian Arabs were alarmed and outraged by the number of arriving Jews, and there were similar reactions in Lebanon, Syria, and Transjordan. Well-armed and well-led Arab bands began cross-border raids on Jewish settlements (kibbutzim), British police posts, and army convoys. Assassinations of settlers and moderate Arabs became commonplace. Counterguerrilla activity was rarely effective. By official order, the police could only leave their barracks and troop convoys could only travel on the roads in daylight. The night belonged to the Arabs.

In Palestine, Wingate was surrounded by sites and terrain familiar to him from his boyhood study of the Bible. A short walk, a glance in any direction, brought him to an Old Testament locale. He was entranced with the land and the people, finding the Jews far more intelligent and stimulating than his brother officers (he rarely missed an opportunity to tell them so). He was in instant sympathy with the Jews and their Zionist cause. The British army and police at that time were generally pro-Arab. There was probably justice enough in both camps, but for a man of Wingate's confrontationalist nature, the choice was easy—he was a Zionist zealot within a month of his arrival.

Wingate never had trouble meeting influential people, and he easily moved into the circles of the Zionist elite. At parties in Haifa, his first post, he would approach a member of a group and, without preamble, speak at great length on the future of Zionism and his own role in that future. His hosts, who knew he was an intelligence officer, were suspicious but also intrigued by his passionate views. He was soon on warm terms with the Zionist leadership, men such as David Ben-Gurion and Chaim Weizmann (who called Wingate "my favorite madman"). Eventually, the Jews embraced him and endured his constant criticism of their political passivism and lack of fighting spirit. To *Hagana,* the Jewish underground army, he became *Hayedid* ("The Friend"), someone to be cherished and forgiven for his excesses. They were far more tolerant than Wingate's fellow officers, who reacted with rage to his Zionist advocacy and taunts about the army's inability to deal with Arab raiders.

By 1937, the Arabs were regularly sabotaging Britain's Iraq-to-Palestine oil pipeline. Wingate arranged a meeting with the commanding general, Archibald Wavell (later field marshal, viceroy of India, and a staunch Wingate supporter), to discuss the problem. Wingate suggested a roving commission for himself to gather information on Arab strength, staging areas, and infiltration points.

Gaining approval, Wingate set off on an inspection tour of probable border crossings and the nearby kibbutzim that were bearing the brunt of Arab attacks. He was as impressed with the determination and discipline of the settlers as he was appalled by their defensive posture. He preached a policy of bringing the fight to the enemy. Following a severe Arab attack, *Hagana* agreed, with great misgiving, to an armed probe of Arab territory.

Wingate led a party thirty miles into Arab-controlled territory, to a village known as a raider stronghold. Positioning his men for an ambush and instructing that there was to be no firing until all of the enemy was in the bag, Wingate proceeded to the village outskirts and began shooting. His fire was answered by a fusillade as armed Arabs ran straight into the trap set for them. Five were killed and the rest captured. Questioned in fluent Arabic by this terrifying officer, the survivors disclosed the location of their arms cache. Wingate then led his force back to their settlement, Hanita. A future Israeli war hero and defense minister, the then teenage Moshe Dayan described the settlers' elation at their successful first fight. Amid the excited talk and jubilation, Wingate sat quietly in a corner, stark naked, munching onions, combing his body hair with a toothbrush, and writing a report.

With Wavell's backing, Wingate weathered the official furor over this incident and was permitted to return to northern Palestine for further intelligence-gathering missions, which to him meant armed forays into Arab territory. At his request, *Hagana* sent him their best and brightest, who, along with British volunteers, were formed into twenty-man squads, half British, half Jewish. These units were dubbed Special Night Squads (SNS) by Wingate and were very successful at ambushing Arab columns.

Combining accurate intelligence on the movement of infiltrators with Wingate's cunning in divining enemy intentions, the SNS conducted ambushes on raider columns and surprise attacks on their strongholds. These actions were usually well-planned, brief, and very costly to the Arabs. When the British police expressed skepticism over the high enemy body counts, Wingate began laying out the corpses in front of the nearest police station, with a request for identification. The Arabs acknowledged his ruthless efficiency by putting a one-thousand-pound price on his head, but Wingate proved elusive. He survived a bomb attack that destroyed his car, and during a particularly savage action he was wounded by friendly fire but refused evacuation until the fight was won. Wingate earned his first Distinguished Service Order for this engagement.

To further improve the efficiency of his SNS units, Wingate was allowed to set up a training school at Ein Harod. The course was brief and to the point: lectures by Wingate, drill and arms training, then active patrolling with experienced squad members. Wingate is remembered by the SNS members with whom he served as an arresting figure, unshaven and unwashed, dressed in a soiled uniform and his trademark sun helmet, usually with a Bible under his arm. The air of command was unmistakable. He was on easy terms with the British officers and men and warmer ones with the Jews, who were permitted to call him Orde when he was off duty. But on operations that he personally led, Wingate was a savage disciplinarian, quick to strike a man for lack of stealth or poor shooting. He imbued the settlers with a confidence in their martial skills, and with Wingate they never lost an engagement. They saw themselves as the cadre of a future Jewish army; he saw himself as its commander.

In late 1938, Wingate, at the request of Chaim Weizmann, went on leave to Britain to plead the Zionist cause. While he met many influential people, the only real result of the trip was to put his career in jeopardy. The British were supporting an essentially pro-Arab policy in Palestine; because of the empire's enormous Muslim population, Zionism was not a cause they could appear to be abetting. Events then moved rapidly. In mid-1939 Wavell was transferred and his successor, hearing of Wingate's political maneuvering in London, assigned him to a desk job in Jerusalem. The SNS was turned over to another officer and quickly disbanded, and the Ein Harod school was closed. Wingate was then posted to an antiaircraft brigade in England. Deemed a security risk, he was forbidden from returning to Palestine. To Wingate, no punishment could have been more severe. His Zionist friends had to argue him out of resigning his commission and returning to Palestine as an illegal immigrant.

Still in the army, Wingate was saved from military limbo by his old mentor, Archibald Wavell, who was then serving as British commander in chief of the Middle East. Wavell had Wingate transferred to Cairo, where he was needed to wage a guerrilla war in Ethiopia.

In 1935, Italy had launched a massive attack on Ethiopia from their colonies of Eritrea and Somaliland. The population was subjected to heavy aerial bombardment and the liberal use of mustard gas, to which Ethiopian levies, armed with old rifles or spears, were unable to respond. Still, they managed to hold out for seven months before their country was overrun and their emperor, Haile Selassie, was forced to flee. He then made a famous and quite futile speech to the League of Nations, begging them to honor their pledges of protection to small countries.

The Italians found Ethiopia to be an uncomfortable possession. Huge sums of money invested in fortifications, roads, bridges, and public works brought trifling returns. There was no oil and few minerals. Foreign investors were not interested in Italy's new possession. Above all, the populace had never been pacified. A brutal reign of terror instituted by Italian General Rodolfo Graziano was followed by the far more humane administration of the Duke of Aosta, but the damage had been done. The people seethed with hatred, and the Italians found themselves in control of little more than their bases and forts.

✦

AFTER FRANCE'S surrender and the Battle of Britain in the summer of 1940, the focus of World War II shifted to the Middle East. Italy had entered the war in May, and with the French in Syria and North Africa neutralized, the large Italian army facing France was free to pursue other objectives.

Britain feared an advance on the Sudan and then Egypt. Many officials in the Sudan believed Italian occupation to be inevitable, and they were comforted that control would be exercised by the gentlemanly Duke of Aosta, whom some knew personally. In October, Orde Wingate, now a major and no gentleman at all, arrived in the Sudanese capital of Khartoum.

Following discussions in Cairo in August 1940 with Wavell and Anthony Eden, Prime Minister Winston Churchill's war minister, Wingate was ordered to establish liaison with Haile Selassie, then in Khartoum; build a force to invade Ethiopia; and raise the indigenous tribes against the Italians. They all understood that to be successful, this force would have to operate under the banner and person of Haile Selassie. In order to conduct his mission, Wingate was given a million pounds' credit and a Godspeed.

In Khartoum, Wingate immediately established a rapport with the emperor, who had been languishing resignedly in the Sudanese capital for months. He recognized a different sort of British officer in Wingate, who in turn saw in Haile Selassie a man and a cause that he could gladly serve and champion.

Wingate's energy produced extraordinary results in the torpid atmosphere of Khartoum. The Frontier Battalion was formed for Wingate's use by detaching one company from each battalion of the Sudan Defense Force. He also had thousands of Ethiopian refugees transferred to Sudan from Kenya and formed into Patriot battalions, then arranged for British officers and noncommissioned officers to train them. Jewish doctors were brought in from Palestine to bolster the meager medical staff. Thousands of camels were purchased for the transport of arms, ammunition, and explosives.

Wingate then recruited a staff of volunteer British officers, whom he interviewed while lying naked in bed, combing his body hair. Although disturbing and offensive, he got the revolt moving. One of Wingate's officers was Wilfred Thesiger, destined for fame as an explorer. He cataloged Wingate's rudeness, ruthlessness, and savage temper, then summed up his leadership as "completely inspiring."

Months earlier, a tiny British group, Mission 101, had penetrated deep into Ethiopia to test the waters of rebellion and to determine if the tribes could put aside their mutual hostilities for the common good. To evaluate the possibilities, Wingate flew into Ethiopia and landed at an airstrip that had been cleared on a tabletop mountain. He barely made it. After talking with some of 101's men, two attempted takeoffs failed; Wingate's plane was not able to reach flying speed, and the pilot was braking within feet of the mountain's edge. He suggested Wingate get out, as a crash was very likely. Wingate replied: "Spare me this nonsense. You understand aerodynamics. I understand the Will of God. Take off." The plane cleared the edge of the cliff with inches to spare.

Gideon Force, as Wingate named his command, entered Ethiopia in January 1941. The Sudanese Frontier Battalion, hastily trained Ethiopian patriots, British mortar and Bren gun sections, and a propaganda unit equipped with loudspeakers comprised the force. A base was set up at the foot of the Gojjam Escarpment, where the emperor, complete with retinue and bodyguard, would wait while Wingate moved forward. Haile Selassie was the fire under the Ethiopian revolt, and no chances could be taken with his safety. After spotting Wingate's column, which included a lengthy camel caravan, Italian aviators reported the advance of a very large force. Far to the east, British and Indian troops were attacking Eritrea from the north and Ethiopia from the south.

Gideon Force's advance was essentially an exercise in maneuver, improvisation, and bluff. With only a few hundred soldiers, Wingate had to operate against well-garrisoned, fortified towns commanding the roads from the Sudanese border through the capital at Addis Ababa and beyond. Mutually supportive satellite forts ringed the towns. The besieged always heavily outnumbered their attackers. Still, Wingate was lucky—Ethiopian spies and captured Italian mail reported low enemy morale. He planned to harass the lines of communication, pen the Italians in their forts, and prevent them from sending reinforcements to their units fighting in the east. But his enemy displayed a strong tendency to evacuate, and Gideon Force was too small to hold them. Wingate consequently adjusted his tactics and would cut up the columns of frightened Italian soldiers as they tried to retreat through open country.

In his first combat action in Ethiopia, at the town of Burye, Wingate committed his entire force in a daylight attack, which convinced the Italians that a great host was surrounding them. Gideon Force kept up a steady fire that night and the next with mortars and machine guns. Loudspeakers harangued the Italians' native levies, demanding they desert or face the wrath of the emperor. The Royal Air Force bombed the town, the only time Wingate received air support during the campaign. It was enough. On the third morning, the garrison, 5,000 strong, evacuated eastward in trucks, armored cars, and on foot, constantly harassed and frequently ambushed.

Debra Markos, the capital of Gojjam Province and Wingate's next target, held 11,000 troops led by a more aggressive commander, who ordered counterattacks to restore his position. But a steady stream of deserters provided

Wingate with precise intelligence, and these Italian sallies found only empty ground.

Constant night actions around Debra Markos, many led personally by Wingate, were launched to keep up the pressure. Fifty-man groups would creep up to the Italian picket lines, unleash a shower of grenades, charge in with fixed bayonets, then melt away. Enemy reaction was met with fire from constantly shifting positions, with Wingate often serving a mortar himself. He made the night a hell for the enemy.

After three weeks of punishment and further discouraged by news of British successes in Eritrea and eastern Ethiopia, the Italian garrison evacuated the town, leaving their supplies intact. Wingate took the surrender from an Italian army doctor. What followed was pure *opéra bouffe*. In Wingate's entourage was a reporter from the *Christian Science Monitor* who was fluent in Italian. As the party toured the fort, a telephone rang, and Wingate immediately told the reporter to impersonate the doctor and report the presence of a full British division. The result was the abrupt abandonment of two Italian positions guarding a crossing of the Blue Nile.

On April 6, Haile Selassie arrived in Debra Markos and, with Wingate at his side, raised the Ethiopian flag. On the same day, British forces commanded by Lieutenant General Alan Cunningham entered Addis Ababa and sent word that the emperor would not be immediately welcome in his own capital. This unfortunate circumstance arose from Cunningham's fears for the safety of the huge number of stranded Italian women and children in the city. Italian soldiers left armed to keep order had twice fired into crowds of Ethiopians, and Cunningham feared a massacre if the emperor returned before order was restored.

Haile Selassie, however, recognized the political consequences if he was denied access to his capital. Wingate, who had received a direct order from General Cunningham to prevent a return by all means short of force, immediately suspected a plot to turn Ethiopia into a British protectorate. He knew the right course of action. He was the emperor's man; the emperor must be restored in his capital. Wingate recalled as much of Gideon Force as could be spared to guard the roads and provide an escort. On May 5, five years to the day after the Italian takeover, the emperor returned as undisputed ruler of Ethiopia. He was led into the city by a Patriot battalion, at whose head, riding a gray horse, was Orde Wingate. Presented with a *fait accompli,* General Cunningham made a graceful speech of welcome, to which the emperor graciously responded. The populace was ecstatic, and there was no violence.

The campaign was not quite over. North of Addis Ababa, a large Italian force had been brought to bay in the fortress of Agibar by a few platoons of Gideon Force and local Ethiopian patriots. On his arrival, Wingate sent a runner to the Italian commander, informing him that the Duke of Aosta had surrendered, and it would be entirely honorable for him to do the same. However, if he chose to hold out, the British would leave, and the beleaguered defenders would eventually have to surrender to the Ethiopians. Realizing what was implied, the commander agreed, asking only for proper military honors. Fourteen thousand troops, led by their officers, marched past an honor guard of a dozen ragged Patriots and laid down their arms at collection points guarded by Bren gunners. Wingate addressed his small Ethiopian force, reminding them sternly that, as Christians and soldiers of the emperor, no harm should come to their former tormentors on the long march to Addis Ababa—and none did.

During the five-month campaign Wingate had performed magnificently. He had planned and raised a scratch force, inspired them with his magnetic leadership, and carried them to the liberation of their country and the restoration of their hereditary ruler. He had also stepped on every available toe. His superiors admired his military skills—and urgently wished him elsewhere. Gideon Force was disbanded. Wingate, then without a command, left Addis Ababa for Cairo, never to return.

If Wingate hoped for official recognition from Middle East Command headquarters for his exploits, he was to be bitterly disappointed. Ethiopia had been a sideshow within the larger sideshow of the East African campaign; few staff officers were familiar with it. Britain's attention was on the disastrous evacuations from Greece and Crete and Lieutenant General Erwin Rommel's activities in the Western desert. Wingate was disliked and generally ignored, left to plod from office to office, proposing guerrilla operations in Libya and the Balkans that aroused little interest. Reduced from colonel to his substantive rank of major, exhausted, ill with malaria, lonely, and depressed, Wingate tried to take his own life by cutting his throat. An officer in the next hotel room heard the thud of his body hitting the floor and broke down the door in time to save his life. When well enough to travel, Wingate was shipped back to England, broken in spirit. His military career seemed almost certainly to have reached its end.

Wingate had few friends, but they were devoted, and none more so than his physician, Benjamin Kounine. It was Kounine who nursed Wingate back from a hysterical wreck to the hard, confident soldier he was. He also introduced Wingate to the outstanding clinician of the time, Lord Horder, who was King George VI's personal physician and had immense influence in medical circles.

When Wingate completed Kounine's course of treatment, he was examined by Horder, who pronounced him sane, responsible, and fit for duty. The recommendation of the king's physician carried the day with a medical review board, and Wingate, chafing for suitable service, was returned to the active list. Yet who would have him? Wingate had as many enemies at the War Office as elsewhere. No one requested his services. The problem seemed unresolvable.

Of course, it was Wavell who once again provided the solution. Wingate's former Middle East commander was now the British commander in chief in India and was desperately seeking a way to stop the Japanese, who, having taken Malaya and Singapore, were advancing rapidly through Burma to the Indian border. With things in his command looking increasingly grim, Wavell sent for Wingate. Arriving in Delhi in April 1942, Wingate found, as had Wavell, a command wallowing in despair and hopelessness. Routed time and again by the Japanese, Allied forces had lost their confidence and had become convinced that they could not compete in the jungle with their ferocious opponents.

But Wingate was at his best in apparently hopeless situations. Promoted to brigadier general and asked to devise his own mission, Wingate studied everything he could find on Japanese culture and tactics. He recognized the Japanese as an experienced, dedicated foe who must be met in brutal jungle and mountain terrain, where the goodwill of the population could not be taken for granted.

Several weeks of study, travel, and observation resulted in the "Memo on Long Range Penetration and the Re-Conquest of Burma." In it, Wingate posited that, since the Japanese controlled nearly all of Burma, they would naturally begin preparations for the invasion of India. The best way to frustrate their plans was to insert a force far behind their lines. Such a force, supplied by air and in radio contact with its headquarters, would lay waste to enemy communications and destroy small garrisons and supply depots. Large enough to pack a punch, yet small enough to disperse and melt into the jungle if attacked, the force could completely disrupt Japanese invasion plans. Over the vehement objections of his staff, who not only disliked Wingate but also believed that the operation had no value, Wavell approved the plan and ordered Wingate to organize and lead such a mission.

In the months that followed, India Command witnessed a "Wingate whirlwind," as the new brigadier raged through various headquarters with demands for men and matériel. The bureaucracy tried to obstruct his plans, but eventually Wingate got his men and supplies. Code-named 77 Indian

Brigade, Wingate's force consisted of three battalions—one British, one Ghurka, and one Burmese—with only the last having substantive experience in the jungle. The unit's training in central India was merciless. Everyone was taught to do everyone else's job; everything and everyone moved at the double. There were no amenities or days off, and eventually there was no sick call. Many, particularly in the rather overage British battalion, failed and were dropped from the force. The remainder became hardened troops and developed a strong esprit de corps. So great was the influence of Wingate's personality on his men that they could accept his warning that sick and wounded would be left to the mercies of the jungle and the Japanese. When not supervising the training of his troops, lecturing them personally, or fighting with staff officers, Wingate had himself flown in a bomber over the route he proposed to take. Finally, he styled his men "Chindits," a corruption of the Burmese word for a mythical winged lion whose likeness adorned Burma's temples.

In February 1943, the Chindits, totaling 3,000 men, 1,000 mules, along with some bullocks and elephants, entered Burma from Assam and proceeded eastward to the Chindwin River, the outer border of Japanese-held territory. Wingate sent a small unit across the river with little attempt at concealment. A larger group of 1,000 men with mules crossed noisily sixty miles downstream and received an airdrop of supplies in broad daylight. Twenty-four hours later, Wingate led the main force across at night at the first point. His stratagem worked; the Japanese assumed the initial passage was a feint and directed their attention downstream.

For the next three months, Chindit columns, linked to each other and their aerial supplies by radio, ranged through the Burmese jungle. On roughly parallel tracks, the columns were fingers that could be formed into a fist. They attacked enemy garrisons, blew up bridges and railways, destroyed enemy stores, laid mines, ambushed Japanese positions, and moved constantly. Wingate was everywhere, demanding better discipline, longer marches, less rest—and, above all, tighter security and unceasing vigilance. A column sweating through thick jungle would suddenly come on their commander squatting under a tree, balefully eyeing each man as he passed. The irreverent nicknamed him "Bela Lugosi," but the point was made; they were always under Wingate's gaze.

The expedition moved ever deeper into enemy territory. In March, the Chindits crossed the Irrawaddy River, greatly increasing the danger to themselves. Initially, Japanese reaction had been slow and confused, compounded by the multiple columns and Wingate's tactic of having dummy supply drops considerable distances from his command. But now the majority of two of the five Japanese divisions in Burma were committed to the hunt. Inevitably, the noose grew tighter, while the Chindits became weaker from wounds, fever, hunger, and exhaustion. Realizing that his force was in danger of annihilation, Wingate broke the Chindits into prearranged dispersal groups. Pack animals were slaughtered, and all bulky weapons and supplies destroyed.

Abandoning their casualties was particularly ghastly to all. Whenever possible, they had been left in or near Burmese villages with money in their pockets, sometimes with notes to the Japanese local commanders appealing to their chivalry in the treatment of gallant foes. Usually, conditions demanded that their comrades, with the worst possible conscience, simply leave them propped against a tree. The Chindits scattered and made their bids for safety, some still in cohesive fighting units. One column marched straight north into China, where they were royally entertained and eventually flown back to India. Some fought their way out of Burma. Wingate himself led his own party, the Japanese close behind, in a swim across the Chindwin into the welcoming arms of a Ghurka patrol.

Chindit losses were appalling. Fully one-third of the force succumbed to wounds, disease, the jungle, or Japanese prison camps. Enemy losses were not high, and the matériel that was damaged was soon replaced or repaired. Yet the gains were quite real; Wingate had maintained a large force deep in enemy territory for months, supplied entirely by air. Much had been learned about Japanese tactics and the techniques of aerial resupply. Perhaps most important, the Chindits had disproved the conventional wisdom that the British could not compete in the jungle with the Japanese. The enemy had been met there and kept off balance, bewildered, and frequently outfought. Wingate had held the initiative. The result was a terrific boost in morale for all Allied forces in Southeast Asia.

The press also took notice of this first British success in the East. It was made to order—a daring operation deep behind enemy lines, led by a charismatic officer with the face and attributes of an Old Testament prophet. To his credit, Wingate never played to the press, yet tales of the Chindits and their commander made front pages on newspapers throughout the Allied world. The "Clive of Burma" had captured the public imagination, nowhere more so than at No. 10 Downing Street. Winston Churchill, fed to the teeth with the timidity and procrastination of the Indian command, reacted with enthusiasm to the Chindit expedition and ordered Wingate home for consultation.

What followed was one of the many episodes in Wingate's life that almost seem to have been scripted in Hollywood. Still dressed in tropical uniform, he arrived at the prime minister's residence on the eve of Churchill's departure for the Quadrant Conference in Quebec. Over dinner, the two discussed the Far Eastern situation. Churchill was so struck by Wingate's grasp of problems and his bold plans for their resolution that he decided on the spot to bring him to Quebec to meet President Franklin Roosevelt and the American and British chiefs of staff. In a *coup de théâtre* he clearly relished, Churchill arranged to have Wingate's wife escorted to Edinburgh for a surprise reunion with her husband, then to the Clyde docks, where their ship waited. As Churchill later wrote, "The *Queen Mary* drove on through the waves, and we lived in the utmost comfort in her, with a diet of prewar times."

Wingate conducted himself very well at the August 1943, Quebec conference, particularly with the American chiefs of staff, who were anxious to heat up the Burmese war in order to relieve pressure on Lieutenant General Joseph Stilwell and his Chinese forces in northern Burma. Wingate's proposal to operate several brigades simultaneously in long-range penetration operations met with their approval. Wingate wanted a large fleet of transport aircraft for delivering supplies and light aircraft for ferrying out wounded. The chief of the United States Army Air Forces, Lieutenant General Henry "Hap" Arnold, met Wingate's demand and added a fighter and bomber component for close support. He also sent his personal representative, Colonel Philip Cochrane, a first-class fighter pilot and the real-life model for Flip Corkin of the *Terry and the Pirates* comic strip.

Breezy, informal, with a trademark "fifty-mission" cap perched on the back of his head, Cochrane was as flamboyant as Wingate. They detested each other on sight. With time, however, mutual disdain developed into mutual regard, and they worked very well together. It was Cochrane who suggested the use of troop-carrying gliders to land Chindits where desired. The First U.S. Air Commando was born, some eleven squadrons, later characterized by Southeast Asia commander Lord Louis Mountbatten as the finest example of inter-Allied cooperation of the war. While the Commando remained under American control, it was designed to work exclusively with the Chindits—in effect, it was a private air force complementing Wingate's private army. Wingate's cup was nearly full; he was to command six brigades, and he was now a major general with a triple Distinguished Service Order (the second for Ethiopia). Churchill added a final present before the return to India—the right of direct access to the prime minister at any time.

With the great freedom of movement provided by Cochrane's planes now available to him, Wingate developed the stronghold concept, a fortress situated in very difficult country close to the enemy's line of communication. Not approachable by road or river, it was first positioned and then supplied entirely by air. It required its own water supply and enough flat land nearby for an airstrip. Chindit columns would issue forth from the stronghold, lay waste to enemy installations, disrupt road and river traffic, ambush Japanese units, then retreat to their well-entrenched fortress if attacked by superior forces. There would always be a powerful garrison in the stronghold, and a floater battalion around its periphery, to give early warning and to attack an enemy thrust from the rear. Aerial reconnaissance had identified several locations that met the necessary requirements.

✦

NEEDLESS TO SAY, Wingate and his plans met with hostility from many British officers. Aside from the customary animosity that his approach always engendered, many senior officers believed that long-range penetration on Wingate's proposed scale was a blunder, that "Chinditry" was a mere adjunct to regular operations. The Burma front had the lowest equipment priority of all Allied theaters, and the officers feared Wingate's lavishness would denude and cripple regular operations. The staff strove mightily to hold back the requested men and machines, but with Mountbatten's firm support, Wingate received six brigades for his second expedition. He was very sparing in his use of the Churchill card, but his enemies knew he could play it, and they all feared the "old man" in London.

Wingate's ferocious training methods were again successful in molding soldiers into Chindits. He was feared more than loved and trusted more than either. Officers who earned his regard could expect rapid promotion; Michael Calvert, who had brilliantly led a column in the first expedition, was a brigadier at barely thirty. Junior officers who incurred Wingate's displeasure could be, and occasionally were, broken to the ranks.

Operation Thursday, as this new expedition was named, began in February 1944, with the dispatch of one brigade on foot from Assam through the jungle toward Indaw, an enemy railhead and airfield near the Irrawaddy River. Japanese trains from Indaw carried most of the matériel being transported from Mandalay to Myitkyina, the objective of Stilwell's Chinese forces. Two brigades were to be flown in by glider to "Broadway" and "Piccadilly," locations near Indaw that were considered suitable for strongholds. The mission of Thursday was to cut all road, rail, and river traffic to the Japanese facing Stilwell, attack them from the rear, and create the maximum confusion on the north Burma front. Three additional brigades were held in readiness as reinforcements or to exploit future opportunities.

The airlift was set for March 5. Troops, mules, and weapons were assembled at an Indian airfield and loaded into gliders. As tow planes revved their engines for an early evening flight, a fresh aerial photograph of Piccadilly was shown to Wingate and a gathering of high-ranking officers. It revealed a geometric pattern of teak logs completely covering the proposed landing zone. It was later learned that the wood had been laid out to dry by Burmese loggers, but at the time it was assumed to be a Japanese antiairborne defense. Wingate conferred with his principal field officer, Michael Calvert, who opted for taking both brigades into Broadway at once. Seventy CG-4 Waco gliders, packed with men, weapons, and earth-moving equipment, took off in brilliant moonlight.

The overloaded Wacos, towed in pairs by each transport, were difficult to control, and several broke their towropes and crashed in the jungle. The first to land at Broadway was Calvert and his crew, who dashed about madly setting flares to establish an approach path. Gliders were coming in from several directions, sometimes colliding or landing on top of each other. Many skidded into the trees. The luckiest landing of the night was a bulldozer-laden Waco that had its wings torn off by trees. As it stopped, the top-hinged forward compartment swung its occupants up as the bulldozer was catapulted beneath them. An imperturbable American engineer officer started the machine and immediately began clearing wrecked gliders and smoothing the landing zone.

For Wingate, many hours of sitting by a silent radio taught him the horror of high command. After ordering the operation, he was powerless to alter the chain of events that followed. The first radio signal, "Soya Link," was the code for serious trouble, and the very worst was assumed. Wingate was nearly at the breaking point when, at daybreak, a second message, "Pork Sausage," announced success. The Japanese had not been waiting, Calvert had established a defensive perimeter, the main force was safe, and the airstrip was ready to receive cargo planes. Dozens of C-47 Dakotas arrived at Broadway that day with men, mules, artillery, and ammunition and took out the injured on their return flights. When Wingate flew in for an inspection, he had reason to be pleased. Within the allotted thirty-six hours, Broadway contained a garrison of 11,000 men; was well-protected by bunkers, wire, and artillery; and had strong air support close at hand—all 200 miles behind enemy lines. It was a tremendous achievement.

During the next two months, Chindit columns operating from Broadway and two additional strongholds—"White City" and "Aberdeen"—ravaged the Japanese rear areas, ambushing convoys, destroying supplies, and completely stopping the flow of reinforcements and matériel to the Japanese in northern Burma. The fighting was savage, usually hand to hand, with frequent simultaneous bayonet charges. Aerial attacks on Broadway were met with heavy antiaircraft fire and fighter support. Land thrusts on the strongholds met heavily entrenched and wired positions well-defended by artillery, mortars, and flamethrowers.

Attacks on these positions were always repulsed and the attacking units usually destroyed. The Japanese were operating under two great disadvantages: They had no real idea of the size and strength of the Chindits, and they had developed a fatal overconfidence born of their nearly effortless conquest of Malaya and Burma in 1942, which caused them to attack with insufficient strength. At the point of launching a great offensive into Assam (which resulted in their double disasters at Imphal and Kohima), they felt no need to reinforce their line-of-communication troops to deal with the threat to the Year.

The Chindits had accomplished their several missions quickly and with relatively small loss to themselves. Their success had proven the merit of Wingate's vision of long-range penetration and the effort he had expended in developing it. Tragically, he did not live to see his theories vindicated. Since the start of Operation Thursday, he was almost constantly airborne, flying from conference to conference. On March 24, the B-25 Mitchell bomber in which he was flying crashed, and all on board were killed. After an arduous journey, a search party found the wreckage. Everything had been smashed and burned beyond recognition . . . except a huge sun helmet.

So stunning was the loss of Wingate to the Allied cause that the authorities briefly considered suppressing the news. Some staff officers shared the jubilation of the Japanese. To Chindit officers who had worked closely with Wingate as well as soldiers who knew him only from parades, the sense of personal bereavement was profound.

Chindit columns continued to fight, chiefly on Stilwell's front. Their commanders were brave and competent but lacked Wingate's vision, charisma, and easy access to the highest levels. In August, Lord Mountbatten reluctantly acquiesced to the desires of the high command. Noting that the entire army was now "Chindit-minded," he signed the order for the force's dissolution. The strongholds were abandoned, the units returned to regular infantry duties. What happened in Burma had happened before in Palestine and Ethiopia; without the direct, personal intervention of their creator, the creation was soon dissolved.

In death, Wingate's good name and reputation were savaged in the British official war history. His exploits and character were denigrated in lengthy and condescending passages that were repeated for no other figure. Officialdom would have its revenge. Officers who had been bested in confrontations with Wingate wrote the history of the Burmese war, and their hatred extended beyond the grave. A distinguished veteran of both Chindit expeditions, Sir Robert Thompson, summed up the disparagement as "a hatchet job by little men who could not have competed with Wingate either in military argument or in battle."

The Japanese held quite a different view of Chindit operations, as interviews with high-ranking commanders immediately after the war revealed. Japan had no plans for the invasion of India; Burma was the last in a series of concentric defense rings emanating from Japan. The Japanese offensive was planned to become defensive from 1942 on, and they believed that their Chindwin River defense line was quite adequate. Wingate's first expedition and penetration was a rude shock. The Japanese commander, General Renya Mutaguchi, realized that the Chindwin line was untenable and, in order to forestall any British offensive, he would have to attack over the river into Assam. Of course, Wingate could not possibly have intended this effect, yet it was, nevertheless, profound. Mutaguchi had never imagined a counteroffensive through his lines on the Chindwin, and he did not have the reserves on hand to deal with it nor, due to Wingate's success with false trails, did he know where to find his foe.

Likewise, the second expedition was a complete surprise to the Japanese. The Chindits were in position several days before their location was known. The Japanese chief of staff for their southern army, General Numata, admitted that the Chindits devastated the lines of communications to both Stilwell's front and the Assam offensive and contributed materially to the Japanese failures.

In summing up the qualities of a remarkable soldier, one can do no better than quote the appreciation of Chindit column commander Bernard Fergusson:

> He seemed almost to rejoice in making enemies, but he was a military genius of a grandeur and stature seen no more than once or twice a century. Secondly, no other officer I have heard of, could have dreamed the dream, planned the plan, obtained, trained, inspired and led the force. There are men who shine at planning, or at training, or at leading; here was a man who excelled at all three, and whose vision at the council table matched his genius in the field.

IV

THE
SECRET WAR

GOTT MIT WHOM?

DAVID BALME, AS TOLD TO
JOHN MCCORMICK

"Gott Mit Uns" ("God is with us") was long a German military slogan, but on May 9, 1941, *He* was definitely on the other side. That was the day when a group of British convoy escort vessels depth-bombed the Nazi submarine U-110 to the rough surface of the North Atlantic and took its crew prisoner. Few ordinary individuals have an opportunity to influence great events, but a young Royal Navy sublieutenant named David Balme belongs to that select number. What he found as leader of a boarding party would alter the course of the naval war, though it was a secret he could not reveal for years. Recently, in England, John Mc-Cormick, an American neighbor of Balme, talked to him about his exploit. Though Balme was in his mid-seventies, he had never before told his own story.

David Balme, after retiring from the Royal Navy not long after World War II, had a career in finance. John McCormick was for many years a professor of comparative literature and writing in a number of American universities.

THE ANNALS OF WAR AT SEA OFFER FEW EVENTS TO COM-pare with a single episode that unfolded in the mid-Atlantic on May 9, 1941. For its complexity, the secrecy it demanded, and its strategic value, that episode only now is taking its proper place in the history of the Second World War. Allied shipping losses to German U-boats by May 1941 had become cat-astrophic; disaster loomed for Britain and the entire Allied effort. When the British destroyer *Bulldog* recovered intact the German naval decoding ma-chine "Enigma" from the surfaced submarine U-110, however, the outlook for Allied merchant shipping underwent a true sea change in every respect. The episode of the Enigma machine proved to be a defining moment in a long war, one without which triumph must have been significantly and perhaps fatally protracted.

Bulldog was the senior ship of the 3rd Escort Group, which included the destroyers *Amazon* and *Broadway,* and an armed merchant cruiser, *Rampura,* commanded by Commodore Joe Baker-Cresswell and based in Iceland. On May 7, 1941, Baker-Cresswell was ordered to relieve the preliminary escort group of Convoy 318, bound from Liverpool for Halifax. The convoy had been under U-boat surveillance virtually from its point of departure, and on May 8, a twenty-year-old Royal Navy sub-lieutenant, David Balme, in *Bulldog,* saw *Ixion* torpedoed by *U-94* (which had survived fifty-five depth charges). Here, based on a series of interviews, is his account of the action.

✦

"WE WERE SAD about losing *Ixion,* but even sadder because she was loaded with Scotch whiskey. We had a busy night, now that we knew we were being tracked by a wolf pack. The next morning, May 9, we lost two more ships at almost the same time. *Bulldog* headed for the position from which the torpedoes must have been fired, as did *Broadway. Auberetia,* a corvette that had joined us, made an Asdic [sonar] contact and dropped a pattern of depth charges. Smith, commanding, thought he had missed, and dropped another pattern. It did not miss.

"I learned later that Smith's patterns had broken vital gauges in *U-110,* ruptured fuel tanks, damaged the electrical system, and ripped out the stop cock of the buoyancy tanks. Out of control, she shot to the surface, broaching not far off our starboard bow. We opened fire and turned to ram, as did *Broadway.* From intuition, and from inspiration based in experience, Captain Baker-Cresswell abruptly swerved and ordered *Broadway* also off her collision course. Why not board her and, if possible, take her in tow back to base?

"Under our fire, the *U-110* crewmen could not man their deck-gun; pouring out of the hatch, they leapt or fell, wounded or dead, into the sea, Lemp, her notorious captain, among them. Captain Baker-Cresswell ordered, 'Cease-fire and away the boarding party.'

"That meant me. One of my duties was to command that party, although we had never had time to drill. *Bulldog* lay to, about one hundred yards to windward of *U-110.* The sea was calm, for the Atlantic, only the usual long swells. The first lieutenant ordered 'Lower away' and then 'Slip,' and our five-oared whaler, clinker-built, was under way. Under way for what? I wondered. My orders were to recover all code books and papers I could find.

"At the tiller, my thought of scuttling charges the Germans must have set before we could even get to our prize would not go away: therefore I steered for the windward side of the boat, as faster than to the more seamanlike lee-ward. That meant we had an unpleasant time of it, working ourselves up the slippery side of the boat and finally securing the whaler.

"All that was busy preliminaries, but now I had starkly to face the fact that, alone as never before in life, I, David Balme, was duty-bound to climb that conning tower and descend into what? Remains of the German crew to greet me? Or scuttling charges rigged to explode as I opened the hatch? My previous seven years of training could not dull the vividness of such mental images. 'Stop thinking. Do it,' I told myself. I climbed the conning tower, and at the top I took my Webley revolver out of its holster. I had never fired it in my life.

"I am still haunted by my climb down that last vertical ladder, fifteen feet into the bowels of *U-110*, now with the revolver holstered. I felt there must be someone below trying to open the sea-cocks, or setting the detonating charges. But no one was there. There must have been complete panic in *U-110*, and she was left to us as the greatest prize of the war. But I still wake up at night fifty-six years later to find myself going down that ladder.

"I made a preliminary reconnoiter in the blue emergency lighting. Not a German to be seen, but I could hear an ominous interior hissing between the rumble of depth charges not far off. Depth charges could detonate any scut-tling charges. I called my men down, to learn that the whaler had been dashed to driftwood against the hull of the U-boat.

"I signaled to *Bulldog* that the U-boat looked seaworthy and could be towed. Baker-Cresswell sent the motorboat to remove any booty, and booty there was. Everything was lying about just as if one had arrived at someone's house after breakfast, before they had time to make up the beds. Books and gear were strewn about. My men formed a chain to pass up all books and charts except leisure reading.

"Meanwhile the telegraphist found the W/T office [radio compartment] in perfect condition: no one had so much as tried to destroy books or apparatus. Code books, signal logs, paybooks, and general correspondence were all in-tact. A coding machine, too, was plugged in as though it had been in use when abandoned. It resembled a typewriter, hence the telegraphist pressed the keys and reported to me that the results were peculiar. The machine was secured by four ordinary screws, soon unscrewed and sent up the hatch to the motorboat alongside.

"At about 1430, when we had been aboard for two hours, I was sitting at the captain's desk eating a sandwich sent over from *Bulldog* and going through all the papers when I came on a sealed envelope. It turned out to be the June settings of the coding machine, the Enigma. The May settings probably were in Lemp's pocket when he perished. Later, the July settings were captured from the German trawler *Lauenberg.*

"Now *Bulldog* closed *U-110* and we tried to secure a towing wire. It parted just as *Bulldog* steamed off to investigate a reported U-boat contact. This was a desolate and forlorn moment. There I was, with my boarding party, aboard *U-110* in the middle of the Atlantic, alone with no ship in sight, and with wind and sea gradually rising. With no more movable gear to collect, I battened down the hatches, and we waited.

"Happily, *Bulldog* returned in an hour, and we set about securing another tow, with the great help of the chief bosun's mate, who arrived by motorboat. The two held, and at about eighteen thirty we returned to *Bulldog,* having spent some six hours in *U-110.* Now *Bulldog* set course for Iceland with our unique prize, but our hopes turned black when *U-110,* laboring in a heavy sea, sank at about eleven hundred the next day.

"We could not have known then that the loss of *U-110* was the best possible outcome to the entire episode. Assuming that *U-110* had been destroyed, the Germans not only failed to realize that *U-110* had been captured; they also failed to realize that their precious Enigma machine with its codes had fallen into the hands of British Intelligence. And because the survivors of *U-110* had been rushed belowdecks of ships in the area, as late as 1981 Admiral Dönitz refused to believe that Enigma had been fatally compromised. It is also worth noting that some 400 men in the convoy and escorts knew of the U-boat's capture, [but] not one revealed that fact until the end of the war."

✦

THE FULL SIGNIFICANCE of *Bulldog*'s coup was not lost on Bletchley Park, British code-breaking headquarters. Complacent about the security of Enigma, the Germans under Dönitz had directed all U-boat activity by radio signal, organizing their *Graue Wölfe* (wolf packs) or directing individual U-boats with extraordinary efficiency. But when the Allies possessed the necessary rotor codes, Allied shipping losses dropped hearteningly, and in the months when they did not, losses rose. In the summing up, however, one British analyst could say that the Germans had "radioed themselves to death": while Jürgen Rohwer, a leading German naval historian, has written, "There were many factors which influenced the outcome of the decisive Battle of the Atlantic, but I would put the Enigma at the top of the list. . . ." That German slogan from earlier wars, *"Gott mit Uns"* ("God is with us") was put in question by the apparent coincidences of May 9, 1941. If Gott was with anyone that day, He was with the British.

For "courage and initiative," Baker-Cresswell was awarded the DSO [Dis-

tinguished Service Order], Balme the DSC [Distinguished Service Cross].
King George VI assured David Balme after the ceremony in 1941 that were it
not for the risk of tipping off the enemy, the two officers would have received
honors more appropriate to their deed, but that this would be put right after
the war. No such outcome could occur, however, owing to the continuing security required during the next forty-five years of the Cold War. It is only today that the whole story can be told. Now, in their age, both men may rest
content in the knowledge that their actions of May 1941 shortened a war, an
achievement given to few men, ever.

DECIMA MAS

PAUL KEMP

For Italy, the Second World War was an unrelieved disaster. Its dictator, Benito Mussolini, had exalted colonial aspirations but his revived Roman Empire was all decline and fall. He attacked France in June 1940; the French, though reeling from Hitler's assault, threw his army back over the Alps. That same year the British restored Haile Selassie to his throne in Ethiopia and sank three battleships at the Italian naval base in Taranto—a carrier operation that may have been the original inspiration for Japan's Pearl Harbor raid. The following year the Nazis had to bail Italy out, first in Libya and then in Greece. (In return, Italy sent two reluctant armies' worth of men to the Eastern Front, where they were predictably chewed up, mostly in the battles around Stalingrad.) The Italian people never showed enthusiasm for Mussolini's imperial designs, and by the summer of 1943, Italy had resigned from the war, only to be ravaged by two invading occupiers, the Germans and the Allies.

Bright moments were few, but if you were to look for exploits worthy of a war adventure movie, a *Guns of Navarrone* in reverse, those of the Decima MAS—the 10th Light Flotilla—approached the stuff of legend. A unit that specialized in naval sabotage, the Decima MAS relied on human-guided torpedoes, speedboats that exploded on contact, and frogmen who attached warheads to ship hulls. Its water-borne commandos put two British battleships out of action—something the Italian navy never accomplished—and sank or badly damaged almost thirty ships. Posing as salvage men, Italian operatives raised a scuttled tanker in a Spanish harbor close to Gibraltar and fitted the ship with an underwater door, through which they launched their human torpedoes. And when Italy left the war, the leaders of the Decima MAS were preparing for a raid on New York harbor. It was to have taken place on Christmas Eve 1943. Think of the movie that could have been made from *that* exploit.

Paul Kemp is a British naval historian.

EVERYTHING MUST HAVE SEEMED PERFECTLY NORMAL TO Admiral Sir Andrew Cunningham on the morning of December 19, 1941, as he stepped out onto the quarterdeck of his flagship, HMS *Queen Elizabeth,* for colors. The signalman and his assistant were standing by the ensign staff ready to hoist the ensign, the Royal Marine band and guard were fallen in, and the ship's officers and other ratings of the duty watch were in their positions. Ahead, a bustle on the quarterdeck of HMS *Valiant* indicated that similar ceremonies were under way. It looked like the beginning of an ordinary day for the two battleships of the British Mediterranean Fleet, harbored at Alexandria.

Yet Cunningham and every other man aboard those battleships knew that the ceremony was a farce, intended to deceive the prying eyes of Axis agents ashore and Italian air reconnaissance. The truth was that overnight the balance of naval power in the Mediterranean had shifted. At 10:15 P.M. on December 18, Italian "human torpedoes" had penetrated the defenses of the harbor and laid explosive charges beneath the two battleships and a tanker, which was anchored alongside a destroyer. The subsequent explosions had caused considerable damage, rendering the four ships unfit for further operational service without substantial repair. (How well the ingenious deception worked is debatable, but the Italians could not confirm how successful the attack was until the men who were captured while carrying it out were released following the armistice of 1943.)

The Italians responsible for this audacious attack came from the 10th Light Flotilla—the Decima MAS (10th Motoscafo Armato Silurante, or "torpedo-armed motorboats")—a unit that specialized in naval sabotage using explosive speedboats, human-guided torpedoes with detachable warheads, and assault frogmen. Armchair historians commonly deride the Italian navy's operations during World War II, ignoring its successes with minelaying, anti-submarine work, and convoy escort duty. In such areas, the Italians were highly efficient and well regarded by their opponents, but the exploits of the Decima MAS in particular were unequaled examples of heroism and cold-blooded determination. The unit's operations ranged the length and breadth of the Mediterranean, and by the end of the Italian government's participation in the war, it had plans to attack Allied bases even as far away as New York and Freetown, Sierra Leone.

✦

NAVAL-SABOTAGE WEAPONRY originated in World War I. It was developed primarily by the Italians, whose navy sought ways to attack the Austrian battle fleet, lying in safety behind the nets and minefields protecting its main base at Pola (now Pula) in the northern Adriatic. To penetrate the defenses at Pola, two young naval officers in Venice devised a weapon known as the *mignatta,* or "leech." This was basically an old torpedo fitted with a 385-pound warhead. Two operators would swim alongside and, by means of handholds, guide the torpedo to the target ship, where they would detach the warhead and secure it to the hull using magnetic clamps. The operators would then swim away with the *mignatta.* The weapon was first used on the night of October 31, 1918, to sink the Austrian dreadnought *Viribus Unitis.*

Development of such weapons did not stop during the interwar years. Research concentrated on improving the *mignatta,* which eventually reemerged with the name *siluro a lenta corso, or* "slow-running torpedo." The SLC was about twenty-two feet long and carried a 660-pound detachable warhead. It was carried in pressure-tight containers welded to the deck of a parent submarine and was released near a harbor entrance. The operators sat astride the SLC and rode it to the target. Then, instead of attaching the warhead magnetically, they suspended it from cables secured to the bilge keels.

SLC was the formal name of the weapon, but to its operators it was the *maiale,* or "pig." This unflattering nickname was coined by one of the early operators, Major of Naval Engineers Teseo Tesei, who had once been forced to abandon an SLC that plunged out of control. His first words on reaching the surface were "That swine got away again!" The name stuck.

There was also development of high-speed, explosive motorboats, based on the rapid torpedo boats the Italians had used to great effect in World War I, sinking two Austrian battleships. One such craft was the MTM *(motoscafo turismo modificato o migliorato,* or, "modified tourist motorboat"), a roughly eighteen-foot-long speedboat packed with 660 pounds of explosive. The operator would aim the MTM at the target ship, run it in at high speed (up to thirty-three knots), and bail out when he was sure that the craft would strike home. He would then paddle away on a small raft. There were a number of derivatives of the MTM, but all had the same principle: a large explosive charge, high speed, and means for the operator to abandon the craft before the explosion.

The Decima MAS also trained assault frogmen to exit from submarines in order to mine ships in harbor. Two devices were favored: a 4.4-pound magnetic limpet mine and a larger, 44-pound device with a small propeller that would detonate the charge only when the target ship had attained a speed of five knots. This was to confuse the enemy about how the explosion had happened.

The Italians had originally formed the Decima MAS in the mid-1930s, during the Abyssinian crisis. The Italians feared that the stronger British Mediterranean Fleet would prevent them from reinforcing their armies in East Africa. This prompted the need to develop a secret weapon that could be rapidly deployed to carry destruction into the enemy's camp and thus reduce the British advantage. In fact, the British stood by during the Italian conquest of Ethiopia, and the naval-sabotage unit was disbanded. In July 1939, however, it was hurriedly re-formed, this time under the name of the 1st Light Flotilla, as war with Britain and France loomed ever closer. Only in March 1941 was the name Decima MAS revived; the flotilla was then split in two, one half dealing with underwater operations and the other with surface warfare.

The earliest Decima MAS operations were distinctly unsuccessful. Two SLC launches against Alexandria in August and September 1940 did not take place because the SLC's "parent" submarines were sunk by British aircraft. The first SLC launch against Gibraltar, also in September 1940, was abandoned when Italian air reconnaissance found the harbor to be empty. In another operation against Gibraltar, on October 30, two of the three SLCs broke down. Their crews were able to swim ashore; as arranged, they were met by Italian agents and returned to Italy. The third craft, operated by Lieutenant Gino Birindelli and Warrant Officer Damos Paccagnini, managed to get within seventy yards of the battleship HMS *Barham* before grounding on the bottom. With their air supply nearly exhausted, the two men had no choice but to abandon the SLC and swim for safety. Both were eventually picked up by the British. Whatever stories they may have told their interrogators were swiftly dispelled later in the morning when the warhead of their SLC detonated, leaving the British in no doubt regarding what had happened.

Experience is a great teacher, and the Italian planners were learning fast. Lieutenant Commander Junio Valerio Borghese, commander of the assault submarine *Scirè,* felt that an advance base was required near Gibraltar, where the SLC crews could rest and observe the target area until just before an operation. The Italian tanker *Fulgor,* which had been interned at Cádiz since 1940, was the perfect sort of base, and personnel were soon sent, incognito, overland with stores and supplies to equip the tanker for her new role. But the *Fulgor* was moored in Spanish waters, so her military use by the Italians was an infringement of Spanish neutrality.

While the underwater arm of the Decima MAS had been attempting to strike at both ends of the Mediterranean, the surface arm had not been idle.

Air reconnaissance revealed that the Royal Navy was using Suda Bay in Crete as an anchorage. This seemed a perfect opportunity to use the MT attack boat, a smaller version of the MTM but equally effective. On the night of March 25, 1941, the destroyers *Crispi* and *Sella* sailed from the Aegean island of Stampalia with MT boats slung in their davits. Six miles off the northeast side of the entrance to Suda Bay, the destroyers hove to and lowered six boats into the water. The mission was now under the command of Lieutenant Luigi Faggioni in the leading MT boat. Unbelievably, Faggioni was able to lead the six craft slowly, with throttled-down engines, through the boom defense at the entrance to the bay without being spotted. Then he went forward alone to reconnoiter the harbor. To his satisfaction, he picked out the silhouettes of the cruisers *York* and *Carlisle,* the tanker *Pericles,* and a number of other ships. He then returned to his men and assigned targets.

Shortly after 6:00 A.M., the peace of Suda Bay was shattered by the roar of engines as the MT boats went on the attack. HMS *York* was struck by two boats, piloted by Lieutenant Angelo Cabrini and Mechanic 3rd Class Tuilio Tedeschi. The explosions blew open the port side of the ship around the machinery spaces. To prevent her sinking, she was hurriedly towed into shallow water by HMS *Hasty* and beached. The *Pericles* was the next ship to be hit. When Mechanic 2nd Class Lino Beccati's MT boat crashed into her side, her cargo spilled out into the bay and caught fire.

The remaining three MT boats did not do so well. Two broke down. Faggioni launched his own boat at the *Carlisle,* just getting under way, but he misjudged the increasing speed of the cruiser, and his boat missed her stern by a matter of a few feet. All six operators who successfully abandoned their craft in time were subsequently taken prisoner by the British.

Overall, however, the operation against Suda Bay boosted the Italians' confidence. Plans were immediately stepped up for an attack on the port of Valletta at Malta, the British naval base in the center of the Mediterranean and a major threat to the Axis powers. This operation was complicated. The attack force—commanded by Commander Vittorio Moccagatta, the new overall commander of the Decima MAS—initially comprised nine MT-type explosive motorboats, carried on the escort vessel *Diana.* The *Diana* would drop the MT boats about twenty miles outside the entrance to Valletta's Grand Harbor; then a motor torpedo boat under the command of Lieutenant Commander Giorgio Giobbe, the Decima MAS's attack-boat expert, would guide them in.

It was not clear how the attack boats could breach the net defenses barring the entrance to the harbor, until reconnaissance revealed that the weak point lay under St. Elmo's Bridge at the western side. Here there was no proper boom, only nets suspended from the bridge. Another boat with two SLCs aboard was therefore added to the force. One SLC, under the command of Major of Naval Engineers Tesei (the man who had nicknamed the SLC), was to blow away the nets. That explosion would be the signal for the MT boats to attack. Meanwhile, the other SLC was to turn into Marsamxett Harbor at nearby Manoel Island and go for the British submarine base there. Two standard motor torpedo boats were included for recovering the MT operators after they had abandoned their boats.

It was a daring plan and showed the offensive spirit of the Decima MAS. But the Italians did not know that the Malta defenses were equipped with radar, which would rob them of their greatest asset—the protection of darkness. Sure enough, on the morning of July 27, 1941, when the *Diana* hove to twenty miles from the Great Harbor, Malta radar picked her up. There were other problems as well. Tesei was not able to destroy the nets. Then, when one of the MT boats making the attack run crashed into the St. Elmo Bridge and exploded, the left-hand span fell into the water and blocked the harbor entrance. By that time, the British defense system was fully alert. Hurricane fighters were in the air, destroying several boats, with heavy casualties.

Malta was a disaster of huge proportions: One torpedo boat had been sunk and another captured. All nine MT boats had been sunk along with the torpedo boat carrying the SLC, both of which had been lost. Fifteen men had been killed and eighteen taken prisoner. But it was more than just the number of men who had been lost. They included the commander of the Decima MAS, Moccagatta; its explosive-motorboat expert, Giobbe; and one of its most experienced SLC operators, Tesei. Such men were hard to replace.

Command of the Decima MAS was assumed by Borghese, who had been captain of the submarine *Scirè*. He realized that radar had changed everything. The explosive-speedboat tactics so successful at Suda Bay were now merely suicidal. So he concentrated on further development of SLC operations and on the assault frogmen, also known as "Gamma men."

Meanwhile, in the western Mediterranean, the men of the Decima MAS had made their first use of the *Fulgor*, moored at Cádiz, as a base against Gibraltar. The SLC crews were sent overland from Italy to Cádiz, where the *Scirè* joined them on May 24, 1941. She remained overnight in the harbor at Cádiz before leaving early the next morning. Unfortunately, this operation was to prove no more successful than its predecessors. The *Scirè* launched the SLCs at Gibraltar on May 26 from the same position as before. This time, since air reconnaissance had found the naval harbor empty, the SLCs were directed against merchant ships lying in the roadstead. One of the SLCs broke down, and the crews of the other two found it impossible to handle the heavy charges, so they abandoned them. The men swam ashore and were quickly sent back to Italy. Nevertheless, Borghese refused to consider the attack a failure. His men had proven the value of the *Fulgor* as an advance base and had also perfected the evacuation routes from Spain. Moreover, the fact that no alarm had been given meant that another attack could be mounted quite quickly.

An operation on September 20 finally brought success at Gibraltar. The *Scirè* collected six SLC operators from the *Fulgor* and launched them at 1:00 A.M. Two of the two-man teams found it impossible to penetrate the defenses of the naval harbor and found targets instead in the commercial anchorage. Lieutenant Amadeo Vesco attached his team's warhead to the 2,198-ton tanker *Fiona Shell,* and Lieutenant Decio Catalano attached his team's to the 10,893-ton dry-cargo vessel *Durham.* The third team, led by Lieutenant Licio Visintini, succeeded in entering the harbor through the north entrance. Visintini intended to head for a cruiser moored at the south end of the harbor but found the patrols too vigilant. Instead he selected the 8,145-ton tanker *Denbydale,* lying alongside the harbor's detached mole.

All three crews successfully ditched their SLCs and returned to Spain, where their contact, who was nominally a consular official in Barcelona, waited to greet them—and to deflect any unwanted attention from the Spanish authorities. At 9:00 A.M., the Italians had the satisfaction of hearing their warheads explode: The *Fiona Shell* was sunk, the *Denbydale* damaged beyond repair, and the *Durham* driven ashore.

Although this last submarine-based attack had been a success, it was the only one of four to have ended conclusively. Borghese and the other planners realized that using a submarine to launch the SLCs limited the number of operations and the number of operators, since the submarine could carry only three SLCs. It seemed to make sense to launch future operations from the Spanish mainland, not just to manage the evacuations from there. So they acquired a safe house in La Línea, Spain, to use as a base for teams of assault frogmen, who would swim from the beach into the commercial anchorage and plant their limpet mines on one of the increasing number of merchant ships in the area. The Gamma men would then return to Spain and await their next mission.

✦

IN THE MEANTIME, Borghese had turned his eyes eastward, in particular to the port of Alexandria, where, behind minefields and net defenses, lay Admiral Cunningham's flagship, HMS *Queen Elizabeth,* and the rest of the British

Mediterranean Fleet. This operation would follow the same plan as earlier, unsuccessful attacks on Alexandria.

On December 3, the *Scirè* had sailed from La Spezia, on the northwestern Italian coast; on December 9, she had collected the three SLC crews at Leros, in the Aegean. At 8:47 P.M. on December 18, Borghese had brought the sub to the surface within a mile of the heavily patrolled entrance to the harbor. By a stroke of luck, some British destroyers were entering the harbor, so the three SLCs simply had followed them through the harbor entrance without hindrance. At 10:15 P.M., the three SLCs had come together on the surface, well inside the harbor, and immediately commenced their attack runs.

The SLC manned by Lieutenant Luigi de la Penne and Chief Petty Officer Diver 1st Class Emilio Bianchi had taken HMS *Valiant* as their target. During the run in, Bianchi, who was having problems with his breathing apparatus, had been swept off the SLC and had swum to a buoy. De la Penne had carried on alone but had been unable to attach the 660-pound charge to the *Valiant*'s hull without help, so he had dropped the warhead on the sea bed a few feet below her hull. He then had sunk the SLC and, unwilling to leave Bianchi, joined him on the buoy, from which they were taken prisoner by a very surprised British patrol. The other two SLC crews—Captain of Naval Engineers Antonio Marceglia with Leading Seaman Diver Spartaco Schergat, and Captain Vincenzo Martellotta with Leading Seaman Diver Marion Marino—had successfully laid their charges under the *Queen Elizabeth* and the tanker *Sagona* (which, as an added bonus, had the destroyer HMS *Jervis* alongside), respectively.

Meanwhile, de la Penne and Bianchi, after a brief interrogation aboard the *Valiant,* had been sent ashore in the custody of the civil police. When Admiral Cunningham had heard of their capture, he had ordered that they be returned to the *Valiant.* At the same time he had ordered that drag chains be hauled along the ships' hulls to dislodge any explosive charges. But at about 6:00 A.M. on December 19, the charge under the *Sagona* had gone off. De la Penne and Bianchi, who had become somewhat restive in captivity, had sent a message to the *Valiant*'s commanding officer, Captain Charles Morgan, to the effect that his ship would blow up in five minutes. The explosion had been as punctual as it was devastating. Four minutes later, the warhead under the *Queen Elizabeth* had exploded as well.

Six brave men had put two battleships, one destroyer, and a tanker out of action. None of the SLC men were killed; all became prisoners of war. It was the success of this attack that caused Winston Churchill to demand that the Royal Navy adopt similar measures, to attack the German battleship *Tirpitz*.

The British developed the Chariot, based on the SLC, as well as a two-man midget submarine; they operated successfully for the rest of the war.

As for the Italians, Borghese was immensely heartened by the attack. In May 1942, after new crews were trained, he sent the submarine *Ambra* with three SLCs to repeat the operation. However, finding that the defenses at Alexandria had been considerably strengthened, they abandoned the mission.

In August 1942, he attempted one more operation in the eastern Mediterranean. The *Scirè,* carrying a party of Gamma swimmers, was sent to attack Haifa, a port in Palestine that had suddenly become important to the British, who were at the time falling back before the seemingly inexorable Axis advance in Egypt's Western Desert. The *Scirè* signaled on August 9 that she was off Haifa and that the harbor was packed with transports, submarines, tankers, and destroyers. But she was not heard from again. Not until after the Italian armistice was it pieced together that the sub had been sunk by the British trawler *Islay,* with the loss of all her crew and the Gamma men.

The Haifa failure effectively marked the end of the Decima MAS's involvement in the eastern Mediterranean. With the collapse of the Axis forces in the Western Desert following the Battle of El Alamein, attention shifted back to the western Mediterranean, to Gibraltar and the North African port of Algiers, where an Anglo-American army was pouring ashore. However, the Decima MAS did not quit the eastern Mediterranean without one more blow against the British. Throughout August and September 1942, torpedo-boat patrols were made off the North African coast to disrupt Allied shipping movements. These patrols proved largely fruitless, but on August 29 they torpedoed the destroyer HMS *Eridge,* inflicting irreparable damage.

✦

MEANWHILE, IN GIBRALTAR, using the name of Conchita Ramognino, the wife of one of its officers, operatives for the Decima MAS had bought the needed safe house. Known as the Villa Carmela, it was the perfect sort of place. The house overlooked the commercial anchorage, and the garden sloped down to the beach only 500 yards away from where the nearest Allied merchant ships were anchored. Frogmen were smuggled into Spain by various means, and by July 1942 a twelve-man team had assembled. On the night of July 13, the men, each carrying three 4.4-pound mines and wearing a camouflaged diving suit, descended to the beach and swam toward the crowded anchorage. The current was strong, and a number of the divers lost their mines; nevertheless, they managed to damage four merchant ships totaling 9,546 tons—the *Meta,* the *Shuna,* the *Empire Snipe,* and the *Baron Douglas.* But the Spanish authorities proved unusually vigilant in this instance, and as seven of the divers were staggering up the beach at La Línea on their return, they encountered a patrol of the Civil Guard. Their presence was clearly an infringement of Spanish neutrality that could not be overlooked, and they were immediately arrested. However, their detention was brief, and all twelve were eventually smuggled out of Spain.

The Decima MAS leadership then decided that what was needed was a ship that the Gamma and SLC men could leave and reenter at will without arousing the suspicions of the Spanish authorities. Lieutenant Licio Visintini found the ideal solution: the 4,995-ton, Italian-registered tanker *Olterra,* lying scuttled and interned at Algeciras, six miles from Gibraltar. Under cover of a salvage operation to raise the ship for sale to a Spanish buyer, the Italians brought the *Olterra* up and moored her at the end of a breakwater extending northward out of the harbor at Algeciras.

Visintini's plan was to set up a fully equipped workshop in the *Olterra's* hold, where SLCs would be assembled and tested. Using the salvage operations as a cover, Italian workmen cut an opening into a small compartment in the bow, allowing access to the sea. When the ship was restored to her normal trim, the opening was below the waterline, and the bow compartment was flooded. But the main hold remained dry. Thus the *Olterra* had a perfect exit-and-reentry compartment. SLCs could be slung on pulleys in the bow compartment. When it was time to launch an attack, they could be lowered into the water to pass out of the ship through the opening in the bow. They could do their job, then return to the *Olterra* the same way.

While conversion work on the *Olterra* was proceeding, the Italians were moving SLCs, spare parts, and other supplies into Spain. The question of how much the Spanish authorities knew of what was going on is hard to answer. Certainly they were aware that the Italians were using Spanish territory as a base from which attacks could be launched on Gibraltar, but it is doubtful whether they were aware of the extent of the operation. Their attitude seems to have been one of outward ignorance so long as they were not provoked or had their neutrality visibly flouted.

The British had not been idle in upgrading the Gibraltar defenses. Patrols had been stepped up and the number of searchlights increased. Around the gates to the harbor proper, the net defenses had been toughened, and small explosive charges, sufficiently powerful to kill any person within range, were dropped into the water at regular intervals. The Gibraltar Naval Diving Party had been set up, and its members were kept busy checking the bottoms of ships arriving from Spanish ports as well as making frequent bottom searches of ships anchored in the bay. Thanks to this increased vigilance, only one

British ship, the *Ravenspoint,* was sunk during a raid on the night of September 14, 1942, by three Gamma men from the safe house.

The night of December 5 was selected for the first *Olterra* operation. Visintini was to lead the attack, and he could hardly believe his luck when the battleships *Nelson* and *Rodney,* accompanied by the aircraft carriers *Furious* and *Formidable* and a host of cruisers and destroyers, entered the harbor that evening. Faced with such a cornucopia of targets, he postponed the attack in order to go over the SLCs once again and make sure that everything was in perfect order. Visintini planned to attack the battleship HMS *Nelson* himself. Ensign Girolamo Manisco would attack the *Formidable,* while Lieutenant Vittorio Celia would attack HMS *Furious.*

On the night of December 7, as the SLCs nosed out of the *Olterra* and made their way across the bay, the crews noted that the British defenses were more than usually alert. Nonetheless, when Visintini saw the bulk of the *Nelson* ahead, he went straight for her. He and his crewman, Petty Officer Giovanni Magro, were spotted by a patrol boat, which dropped explosive charges. Both men were caught in the explosion and killed outright. Next, Manisco's SLC was picked up by a searchlight as he approached the detached mole and attracted a hail of gunfire. Manisco and his crewman, Leading Seaman Dino Varini, abandoned their craft and swam to an American merchant steamer nearby, where they were taken prisoner. With the defenses now thoroughly on the alert, Celia and his crewman, Petty Officer Salvatore Leone, stood no chance of carrying on with their mission. Celia turned about and, after being pursued by numerous motor launches, finally reached the safety of the *Olterra,* only to realize that Leone was missing, having fallen off the SLC during the return dash across the bay.

The failure of the attack in no way reflected on the bravery of the operators. The next day, the bodies of Visintini and Magro were recovered from the harbor. The Royal Navy buried them at sea with full naval honors, apparently none the wiser as to where they had come from. Manisco and Varini gave no clue, telling their captors that they had been brought from Italy by the submarine *Ambra.* This tale was close to the truth. The *Ambra* had, in fact, taken three SLCs and a party of ten Gamma swimmers to Algiers on December 10 to attack the mass of Allied shipping in the port. That operation had been extremely successful, sinking one merchant ship, the *Ocean Vanquisher,* and damaging three others (although the sixteen Italians had been captured). However, the Allies learned quickly, and the Italians had to abandon a similar operation against Bône in April 1943 because that Algerian harbor's defenses had been strengthened.

Gibraltar now became the focus of Decima MAS operations. More SLCs were covertly sent to the *Olterra,* along with new crewmen and a new commanding officer, Lieutenant Commander Ernesto Notari. On May 8, 1943, three SLCs, each carrying a double warhead, slid out of the *Olterra* and made their way across the bay. Notari rode the first; Cella, the second; and Lieutenant of Naval Engineers Camillo Tadini, the third. This attack was a complete success. They sank the *Camerato* and damaged the *Pat Harrison* and *Mahsud.* The three crews returned safely to the *Olterra,* while other Italians left frogmen's equipment strewn about the shore at La Línea to deceive both the British and the Spanish about where the attack had come from.

Notari did not rest. He wanted to smuggle an SLC into the harbor at Gibraltar by attaching it to the hull of a ship entering the port. The water carrier *Blossom,* which made a daily trip from Gibraltar to Algeciras, seemed suitable. The SLC could be attached while the *Blossom* was bunkering at Algeciras, and then it would simply hang on for the return voyage. The wash of the ship normally would make it nearly impossible for the crew to remain astride the SLC during the passage, so Notari's men devised special shields to protect them.

But before this audacious plan could be put into effect, Notari launched another SLC raid, using the same three crews, on the night of August 3, 1943. This time, the SLC men encountered a new menace—barbed-wire netting hanging down below the ships' sides, invisible in the darkness. Nevertheless, the three teams succeeded in attaching their warheads to the American liberty ship *Harrison Gray Otis,* the Norwegian tanker *Thorshovdi,* and the British merchantman *Stanridge.* All three ships were damaged. The three SLCs returned safely to the *Olterra,* but once there Notari realized that his crewman, Leading Seaman Diver Andrea Gianoli, was not aboard. It turned out Gianoli had fallen off the SLC during the attack and been picked up and taken aboard the *Harrison Gray Otis.* He had just been transferred to the custody of a naval motor launch when he had the satisfaction of hearing his charge go off.

This was to be the last operation carried out against the British by the Decima MAS. Notari and the other SLC men returned to Italy, leaving the Olterra in the hands of her "proper" mercantile crew. Mussolini had been overthrown on July 25, 1943, and since then the government of Marshal Pietro Badoglio had been negotiating surrender terms with the Allies. On September 3, an armistice was signed, and Italy was officially out of the war.

There were other developments. The British had been observing the *Olterra* from their vantage points atop the Rock of Gibraltar and were sure that the tanker was the source of the attacks, but they could not prove anything. They applied diplomatic pressure to the Madrid government, and after the departure of the SLC crews, Spanish officials had boarded the *Olterra*. They had secured the ship, forbidding any of the crew to leave.

On September 22, a Spanish naval officer stationed at Algeciras boarded the *Olterra* and, claiming to be acting on orders from the Spanish government and the Italian embassy in Madrid, ordered the destruction of all compromising material. Italian consular officials tried in vain to shove the three remaining SLCs out the door of the secret compartment. Then they managed to destroy two of them with scuttling charges. But the third was found intact by the British when they assumed control on October 10. By then, the *Olterra*'s engineer officer, Paolo Denegri, deciding to throw in his lot with the British, had told security officers at Gibraltar all he knew of the tanker's activities.

While attention was on Gibraltar in the western Mediterranean, a lone Gamma swimmer had been achieving considerable success in the east. Decima MAS planners had identified shipments of chromium, a vital war commodity exported from Mersina (now Mersin), Turkey, as an objective for their operations. In June 1943, Lieutenant Luigi Ferraro was sent to Mersina under diplomatic cover. Based at nearby Alessandretta (now Iskenderon), he would select a likely target, swim out from the beach to plant his mines, and then return. In this bold-faced but simple manner and with a total disregard for the neutrality of Turkish soil, Ferraro sank three ships totaling 15,900 tons and damaged a fourth by early August, when he stopped.

When hostilities between the Italians and the Allies ended, one of the most daring operations ever conceived by the Decima MAS had to be abandoned. Borghese had been working for months on plans to attack shipping in New York. To do this he had the large oceangoing submarine *Leonardo da Vinci* modified to carry a CA-type (two-man) midget submarine in a well on her forward casing. The midget submarine, the *CA.2,* carried a crew of three and was armed with eight 220-pound charges slung outside the hull. Along with the *CA.2,* the *Leonardo da Vinci* would carry a group of Gamma assault frogmen. The operation called for the big sub to release the midget and the Gamma group outside New York Harbor. The Gamma men would help the CA.2 through the nets and into the Hudson River, where they would be free to attack any targets of opportunity. For greater psychological impact, the attack was scheduled for Christmas Eve 1943. If it had been successful, similar operations would have been launched against Freetown in Sierra Leone and ports in South America. But these operations were not to be.

The armistice brought a cruel dilemma for the officers and men of the Decima MAS: whether to obey the orders of the legitimate Italian government and become part of the cobelligerent Italian forces fighting with the Allies, or to join the forces of the Italian Social Republic, the rump Fascist state set up by Mussolini in northern Italy. The force was effectively split into two.

The majority chose to obey the orders of the legitimate government and ended up participating in a number of operations alongside their old adversary, the Royal Navy. In June 1944, a mixed force of Gamma swimmers and British Charioteers (operating the British equivalent of the SLC) raided La Spezia and sank the hulks of the cruisers *Bolzano* and *Gorizia* to prevent their use as blockships by the retreating Germans. In April 1945, an all-Italian force, but using British Chariots instead of the SLCs, attacked Genoa and immobilized the incomplete aircraft carrier *Aquila,* again preventing her use as a blockship. In contrast, those who chose to stay with the Fascist regime found their efforts continually frustrated by lack of material resources—in their flight north they had to abandon most of their stores—and by the superiority of the Allied forces ranged against them.

The exploits of the Decima MAS are an example of what courage and bravery can achieve in the face of seemingly overwhelming odds. In a war in which technology occupied a position of growing importance, their exploits were a remainder of an age when character and bravery counted for everything. After Visintini was killed at Gibraltar, his diary was found aboard the *Olterra.* The last entry read:

> I believe that I have done everything possible. My soul is at peace and I dedicate myself entirely to this operation. Before I depart I offer a prayer to God that our operation may bring victory and peace to Italy and to my family. Viva l'Italia!

SABOTAGING
HITLER'S BOMB

DAN KURZMAN

In the race for the Bomb, nobody on the Allied side could be sure whether Germany was ahead or behind. Those in charge of the American Manhattan Project to build an atomic weapon eyed with suspicion a heavy-water plant at Vemork in Norway—heavy water being necessary to create a chain reaction in an atomic reactor. Since the Nazis had swept through Norway in the spring of 1940, the small and precious supply of heavy water that the Vemork plant produced had been going to Germany, a sure tip-off that its physicists were up to something. Whatever it was, their task would not be made easier if they were deprived of heavy water. Knowing where that plant was located was one thing; getting there and destroying the heavy-water-filled concentration cells in the electrolysis building were quite another. A first attempt to reach Vemork in November 1942 failed. Later, in February 1943, a team of six saboteurs, all Norwegians, parachuted into a nearby wilderness area; they were to join a group already in place and attempt the seemingly impossible. (Stalingrad had just fallen and the U.S. army in North Africa had recovered from the Kasserine Pass setback; success at Vemork could only add to the Nazi reverses of that month.) The saga of the Norwegian demolitions experts began with the crossing of a frozen mountain wasteland and the scaling, in the dark, of a sheer cliff. In case they were captured at the top, each carried a cyanide pill.

Dan Kurzman is the author of *Blood and Water: Sabotaging Hitler's Bomb,* from which this article was adapted. His most recent book is a biography of the prime minister of Israel, the late Yitzhak Rabin.

LIKE A FAIRY-TALE CASTLE FORTRESS, THE NORSK HYDRO heavy-water plant in the village of Vemork in southern Norway stood defiantly at the edge of a sheer precipice. It overlooked the valley town of Rjukan, which lay darkly nestled amid snow-splashed mountains about seventy-five miles west of the capital, Oslo. The plant seemed impregnable, but by the summer of 1942, Allied leaders decided that it had to be destroyed.

The Germans, who had invaded Norway in April 1940, were attempting, it seemed, to build an atomic reactor, which could trigger a bomb, using heavy water made at Norsk Hydro as a principal ingredient. No Allied military objective had greater priority than the destruction of this plant.

How close was Germany to producing a bomb? Allied nuclear scientists didn't know. But they did know that many German scientists, especially the physicist Werner Heisenberg, were their professional equals and might well be running ahead in the nuclear race. And particularly alarming were British and Norwegian intelligence reports that more and more canisters of heavy water were being exported from the Norsk Hydro plant to Germany—the first concrete evidence its scientists might be working on a bomb.

Heavy water, or deuterium oxide, was vital to a bomb. The compound of oxygen and the heavy isotope of hydrogen, it has twice the mass of ordinary oxygen and hydrogen and works as a slow-motion mechanism. It thus moderates the speed of the neutrons set free in an atomic reactor and permits these elementary atomic particles to achieve a chain reaction that could split the nuclei of a fissionable element and cause an explosive release of atomic power. (The Germans didn't know then that the more accessible graphite would also moderate the speed.) Shortly after the American scientist Harold Urey discovered heavy water in 1932, the Norsk Hydro electrolysis plant began churning out the substance as a by-product of fertilizer and selling it to laboratories around the world.

It was no wonder that soon after Brigadier General Leslie R. Groves was appointed in September 1942 to head the Allied effort to build an atomic bomb, known as the Manhattan Project, he began to urge his superiors to order an air attack on Norsk Hydro. But Norwegian Resistance leaders in London pressured the British to oppose such a raid, which, they argued, could result in heavy civilian casualties. Meanwhile, President Franklin D. Roosevelt, prodded by Groves and some of the general's scientists, who feared data leaks by London, decided to withhold nuclear information from the British (a policy later rescinded). Now, feeling no obligation to consult with the United

States, Prime Minister Winston Churchill went ahead on his own and ordered British forces to launch Operation Freshman, an assault by glider-borne commandos on the Norsk Hydro plant. The details would be kept secret even from the "ungrateful" United States.

To pave the way for this raid, four British-trained Norwegian commandos flew to Norway on October 18, 1942, in what was called Operation Grouse. They parachuted into the glittering white wilderness of the Hardanger Plateau, a craggy, windswept fairyland of waterfalls, frozen lakes, and rivers—the most intimidating mountain area in northern Europe. For fifteen days, the men struggled on skis through raging blizzards, lost, half-starved, dragging behind them a load of supplies on a sled they luckily found (one of them, a native of the area, recognized it as his long-lost childhood sled). Finally, they reached the spot where the Freshman gliders were to land. They broke into a log cabin and began their wait.

On November 19, two Halifaxes revved up at an air base in Scotland, each connected to a Horsa glider that would carry seventeen men, including one officer, and took off into the dreary skies toward southern Norway. Only one Halifax would return. It lost its glider—which crashed into a mountain near Stavanger on the southwest coast of Norway, nowhere near the rendezvous with Grouse—when the rope pulling it snapped. The second Halifax and its glider crashed into a mountain farther south. All seven members of the Halifax crew were killed, but miraculously, twenty-three of the men in the two gliders survived, most with severe injuries. Several from each managed to seek help from local farmers, who persuaded them to give themselves up, arguing that language barriers and constant Nazi patrolling precluded escape.

What happened to those survivors would only come out in war crimes trials held after the war, trials that resulted in the hanging of those who played a direct role in their murders. Ordered by Hitler to kill captured commandos and saboteurs, even men in uniform, Gestapo agents poisoned or strangled three of the British, stamping the Adam's apple of one of them. Another victim was shot in the back, and fourteen more were led one by one to an execution site at the bottom of a hill, where they were shot. According to a German witness, the sergeant in charge of the firing squad motioned to the first prisoner to remove his army jacket. The squad would feel better if they were shooting a "saboteur" rather than a uniformed soldier. Almost mechanically, the man obeyed, taking off his jacket slowly, sleeve by sleeve, as if struggling for every moment of life still left to him.

After he was shot, another prisoner met the same fate even as he waved a photo of his wife and children, pleading with the squad for mercy. The last man executed, the most seriously wounded, was shot after being carried on a stretcher to the blood-soaked killing site and placed sitting against the rocky surface of the hill. The bodies were then thrown into a nearby pit.

The last five prisoners had reason for hope, since their German interrogator treated them with kindness and promised that they would live out the war in a prisoner-of-war camp. The interrogation went on for weeks. They apparently confirmed that their objective had been Rjukan when the interrogator indicated that the Germans already knew, having found a map at one of the crash sites with the name of the town encircled.

The men were blindfolded and told they were to speak with officials from Berlin before being sent to a POW camp. These officials, it seemed, did not want to be identified. *"Achtung!"* the squad commander cried, and the prisoners stood at attention in respect for the distinguished visitors. The crack of gunfire split the air, and there were more bodies to be hurled into a pit.

All the survivors of Operation Freshman were now dead.

✦

DESPERATION SWEPT through the halls of British intelligence when search planes returned to base on the afternoon of November 20 without having spotted the missing Halifax and the two gliders. Operation Freshman, intelligence officials agreed, had clearly ended in disaster. A new mission had to be launched without delay, whatever the cost. For every drop of heavy water trickling out of Norsk Hydro could mean that Hitler was that much closer to victory in the war. And the desperation grew when the Germans issued a communiqué the following day: The Britons had been captured and "wiped out to the last man."

British intelligence leaders, supported by their Norwegian counterparts, decided that a group of British-trained saboteurs must now try to blow up the heavy-water plant. When one agent of the U.S. Office of Strategic Services in London found out about it, he scoffed, according to another agent, that "this was some devious British scheme . . . to cover an ulterior objective." But the skeptics did not know Lieutenant Joachim Ronneberg, a Norwegian saboteur working for the Special Operations Executive (SOE) in London, who would lead the next commando raid.

A handsome, charismatic figure, Ronneberg, twenty-three, had worked for his father's shipping firm before the war. He joined the Resistance when the Germans overran Norway and proved himself a courageous and imaginative commander. He fled to Britain in order to join the SOE, vowing to return to Norway with arms to fight the Nazis. Now he reveled in the opportunity—even if he was being asked to lead men on a possible suicide mission.

His superior, Colonel Leif Tronstad, a Norwegian scientist who headed SOE's Norwegian section, said that the mission could help determine the outcome of World War II, since heavy water would permit the Germans to build a bomb powerful enough to "destroy half of London." The commando team wouldn't have much time for planning, Tronstad said, but fortunately four of their friends were already in Norway waiting for them, having originally been sent as a "reception committee" for the Freshman group.

Ronneberg immediately selected the five men who would share with him the passion—and danger—of the mission, which was code-named Gunnerside. He chose as his second-in-command Lieutenant Knut Haukelid, a muscular, highly intelligent man from a prominent Norwegian family whose twin sister was a well-known actress, Sigrid Gurie. The other four choices were Lieutenant Kasper Idland and Sergeants Fredrik Kayser, Hans Storhaug, and Birger Stromsheim. All had fled Norway via Sweden or nearby islands; from there, Royal Air Force planes flew them to Britain.

Within a few days, the six commandos were training at a secret camp, Number 17, near London, where a wooden model of the Norsk Hydro plant had been erected in a small building, complete with the eighteen high-concentration cells that turned out the fluid. Over and over, the men practiced handling explosives, laying charges, fashioning detonators, timing themselves down to the last split second. They studied aerial photographs and diagrams of every building, of every German military station in the area, of almost every square yard of terrain. Underlining the price of failure, the men were issued a cyanide pill enclosed in a rubber capsule, which they were to stick to the roof of their mouth if they were about to be captured. When bitten, it would bring death within three seconds.

Finally, on February 16, 1943, they climbed into a plane, flew to Norway, and parachuted to earth, hoping to meet the four Grouse commandos who had long been waiting for the British, and now the Norwegians, to join them in an attack on the heavy-water plant. But as they disentangled themselves from their parachutes, Ronneberg and his men realized that they had landed far from where the advance party was supposed to greet them. All anyone knew was that they were on the Hardanger Plateau, perhaps twenty miles from the Grouse camp.

The commandos now set out to find Grouse, but soon a storm howled through the mountains, and the men, blinded by the blizzard, could no longer find their way. They holed up in an abandoned hut for three days, then put on their skis, which had been dropped with them, and dragged themselves along hour after hour, day after day.

Adding to their trials was an encounter with a poacher who was hunting for reindeer, whose meat he would sell on the black market. Should they shoot him to prevent his reporting their whereabouts to the Germans? Ronneberg decided to let him go—and even supplied him with money and a few bars of chocolate. But he threatened to report the man's illegal activities to the Germans if he betrayed the group. (Eventually, the Germans in the man's home village learned that he was passing chocolate around to children and guessed he must have obtained it from the British, since none was available in wartime Norway. The black marketeer was thus forced to betray the commandos, though only after their mission had ended.)

When the storm finally lifted, the commandos put on their skis and set out to search for their Grouse comrades. As they were about to traverse a steep slope, one man suddenly sighted two dots, which soon turned into human figures on skis, edging down the great white valley below and then climbing toward them. Were they Germans . . . or perhaps Grouse men? The two strangers were so heavily clothed and bearded that they were unrecognizable. Concealed behind boulders, the commandos watched as the men skied up a lower slope and took turns scanning the area through binoculars.

Ronneberg ordered Haukelid to find out who they were; he had trained with the Grouse men in Britain. If they turned out to be strangers, he should say that he was hunting reindeer. Haukelid removed his rucksack, put a pistol in his belt under his camouflage suit, and started toward the hillock where the two men were standing. Ten minutes later, after climbing the slope from their rear, he found himself about fifteen yards behind them. He leaned on his ski poles, breathing in the clear air and marveling for a moment at the great panorama of white emptiness.

With one hand gripping his pistol under his camouflage suit, Haukelid coughed loudly and the strangers wheeled around, also with pistols in their hands. Haukelid exchanged stares for a moment with two hollow-eyed, yellow-complexioned men with unkempt beards. Suddenly cries of joy echoed through the valley as the two Grouse commandos, Lieutenant Claus Helberg and Sergeant Arne Kjelstrup, wildly embraced Haukelid.

✦

THAT NIGHT, February 23, 1943, no one starved in the cabin where the Grouse men had been hiding. For months they had survived on scraps of food they found in abandoned huts, and on reindeer they occasionally killed and devoured in their entirety. Now the Gunnerside guests had brought with them raisins, chocolate, and other delicacies that their hosts had tasted only in their dreams. It was a feast to savor, complete with spirited talk about old friends and colleagues in England, about recent miseries and joys and hopes for the future—though all realized there might not be one.

The next morning, the men perused the wrinkled maps and diagrams that Ronneberg spread before them. Nine of the men would attack the heavy-water plant, their leader announced. Only the Grouse radio operator, Lieutenant Knut Haugland, would stay behind so he could keep British intelligence informed. Ronneberg would lead a four-man demolition team including Kayser, Idland, and Stromsheim, while Haukelid would head a five-man covering party, with Storhaug and three Grouse commandos—Helberg, Kjelstrup, and the Grouse leader, Lieutenant Jens Anton Poulsson.

The "castle" these men would attack was perched on a massive shelf of rock carved out of the nearly vertical side of a 3,000-foot mountain. About 450 feet below, in a deep gorge, flowed the Maana River, which served as a kind of protective moat, while over 1,000 feet above, water from dams and lakes surged through penstocks into the turbines of the company power plant. This plant stood just behind the electrolysis building, where water dripped through a gradual, mazelike concentration process that started on the fifth floor and trickled from one metal, sausage-shaped cell to another, floor to floor, to a room in a corner of the basement. Here the fully concentrated heavy water drained into the cells that the commandos hoped to destroy.

The question was, how would the men get to the "castle," get in, and get away? One option: climb down the north side of the Maana River gorge, cross the ice-encrusted river, climb up the almost vertical south face to the single-track railway that was used to ship machinery from Rjukan, and follow it around a ledge to the electrolysis building.

The alternatives were no more promising. They could try to cross a narrow suspension bridge that spanned the ravine and led almost directly to the building. But since sentries guarded the bridge, the attackers would have to shoot them, and within seconds every German in the vicinity would rush to the scene. Moreover, Ronneberg stressed, the Nazis based in Rjukan would grab civilian hostages and shoot them in the morning.

A third alternative was to sweep down an icy flight of stairs that began at the mountain summit and descended along the penstocks feeding the power plant. But this whole area overlooking the shelf complex was heavily mined and studded with machine guns, booby traps, and antiaircraft guns.

On February 26, after moving his men to a cabin closer to the plant, Ronneberg made a startling discovery. In one photo of the almost vertical cliff, he noted that in places small trees and shrubbery sprouted from it. He passed the photo around. Where trees grow, he said, a man can climb.

At nine o'clock on the following morning, February 27, with the weather fortunately "mild and clear," Claus Helberg slipped on his skis and set off on an exploratory mission. As he skied along the road to Rjukan, he suddenly spotted a possible route that twisted down through the juniper bushes to the river. The commandos could climb down from here, cross the river, and then, with luck, scale the opposite cliff to the railroad ledge.

Helberg made his way down toward the river, and in the gorge, day seemed to turn into night. Except for a strip of morning sky, light had been blocked out by the walls of stone that enclosed this desolate, eerily silent corridor. On the other side of the river, Helberg found what he dared not believe he would find— a "somewhat passable way up the factory side." As Ronneberg's photograph had shown, small trees and bushes poked out of ancient cracks in the wall.

The Gunnerside men were elated when Helberg returned that evening with the news. Yes, they could make it to the railroad track. They would leave the cabin at 8:00 P.M. the following night and try to reach the heavy-water plant about 12:30 A.M. Before departing, they put on British army uniforms under their white camouflage suits, in the hope of preventing reprisals against local civilians. They wanted the Germans to believe that British soldiers, not Norwegians, were the saboteurs.

✦

AS THE NINE commandos slid down the steep mountainside after leaving their cabin, their skis almost invisible under the soft snow, they suddenly glimpsed the "castle" glowing faintly in the moonlight filtering through a slightly overcast sky. Their objective was no longer a photo or an "X" target on the map, but a seemingly unassailable concrete fortress. The wind blew in relatively warm gusts, turning the snow and ice into slush. Would the river ice still form a solid bridge across the gorge?

The commandos skied cautiously along the slick Rjukan road, then, following Helberg, climbed to a parallel secondary road. Here, along the roadside, they dug a shallow snow depot, where they hid their skis and poles, excess equipment, and camouflage suits, which they would retrieve after the operation—if they managed to get away.

Weighted down with pistols, tommy guns, grenades, knives, ammunition, and explosive charges, the saboteurs, with Helberg in the lead, returned to the main road and climbed down toward the river at about 10:00 P.M. When Helberg reached the bottom of the gorge, the sound of splashing water reinforced fears that the warm air had melted the river ice, which, in fact, was breaking up. Helberg led the others along the narrow riverbank, searching for an ice bridge. He finally found one, but about three inches of water already flowed over it.

While his comrades watched tensely, he dipped one foot into the water until it reached the ice, then gradually pressed down with both feet. He gingerly treaded across the bridge, barely able to balance himself on the slippery surface, and finally reached the opposite bank. Since the ice had held, he motioned to the others to follow.

Now the commandos were faced with the greatest obstacle of all. Stretching almost straight into the sky was the wall of rock. They could not even see the railroad ledge that rimmed it about 150 yards above the river. They found footholds in the bare rock along the barely visible path that Helberg had earlier discovered, and they edged up the cliff face, their fingers poking into cracks or holding on to narrow ledges. About a third of the way up, Kasper Idland dangled from a ledge by the fingers of one hand as he drew the other hand along the rock face, feeling for a handhold. He spotted one, just as his strength was about to give out. He had to swing like a monkey toward some shrubbery a short distance away, releasing his hold with one hand just as he grabbed the branches with the other. Just then, a gust of wind swept by, a moment too late to claim the first casualty of Gunnerside.

Inch by agonizing inch, the saboteurs rose toward the railway ledge, and finally near-paralyzed fingers locked onto its outer edge. One by one, the men crawled to horizontal ground, then helped drag those behind across the threshold. Exhausted, they collapsed beside the track for several minutes, gasping for breath, mesmerized, it seemed, by the sound of the plant turbines whining over the intermittent roar of the westerly wind. All nine had made it.

Ronneberg glanced at his watch. It was a few minutes after eleven. He ordered his men to start moving in a single file along the track toward the plant, which was about half a mile away. They halted at a transformer shed about 500 yards from the gate leading to the plant. Now they could see the suspension bridge and watch the guard change. At midnight two guards marched from their barracks nearby the bridge and relieved those on duty there. A half-hour later, the commandos would attack.

At exactly 12:30 A.M. the men re-formed, with Knut Haukelid's covering group in front, followed by Ronneberg and the demolition party. The column halted about 100 yards from the gate, and Ronneberg ordered Haukelid and Kjelstrup to advance alone and break the lock, while the others covered them. Those behind held their breath as the two advance men edged their way along the track. When they reached the gate, Kjelstrup took a pair of shears from his pocket and cut through a link in the padlocked iron chain.

All five members of the covering group now rushed through the gate into the yard and lay prone in preassigned positions. Helberg covered the gate; Kjelstrup, the penstocks; Storhaug, the suspension bridge. Haukelid and Poulsson crouched behind two storage tanks about twenty yards from the guard barracks.

Meanwhile, the demolition team of Ronneberg, Kayser, Stromsheim, and Idland stealthily moved along just inside the fence and cut the chain on a second gate that would serve as an alternative escape route. They then headed for a steel door of the electrolysis building leading to the basement, where the highly concentrated heavy water filled metal cells. Ronneberg tried the door handle. It was locked.

Explosives could blow the door open but would alert the Germans, who, amazingly, were not guarding or patrolling this area. Ronneberg ordered Stromsheim and Idland to rush up a nearby stairway to the first floor. Maybe they could open the door there and get to the basement. Ronneberg and Kayser then dashed around the building in a frantic search for a cable tunnel they had been told about in training.

Suddenly, they came to a window, blacked out except for pinpoints of light escaping through it in thin beams. Ronneberg peered through one of them and his heart raced. There, several feet below the window, he saw two rows of cells standing upright like tin soldiers, and an elderly civilian sitting at a desk behind them. They had to be the heavy-water cells! Ronneberg thought of breaking through the window but feared the Germans would hear the noise and investigate.

The two commandos ran along the wall until they saw a ladder that led to a narrow opening just below the first floor. Removing a flashlight from his pocket, Ronneberg leaped up the ladder and slid into the opening headfirst, followed by Kayser. It was the cable duct. The two men inched forward through the tunnel, which was so narrow they couldn't turn their heads around. The journey over a tangle of rusty pipes and snakelike cables seemed endless. What if they ran into an obstacle they couldn't get past? How would they crawl back when they could barely move forward? This duct might be their coffin.

Suddenly, when the pair had crept through almost the full thirty yards of tunnel, Ronneberg heard a loud clang just behind him. Kayser's pistol had slipped out of his holster and landed on a pipe. Both men froze until the echo faded.

Kayser retrieved the pistol and the two men continued their snail-like advance. Finally, the beam of Ronneberg's flashlight blended with a dull glow at the end of the tunnel. Soon they reached a ladder inside a basement room adjoining the heavy-water chamber. They climbed down and, with pistols drawn, approached a set of double doors that led to the chamber.

Ignoring a sign on one of the doors warning, in German and Norwegian, "No Admittance Except on Business," Ronneberg cautiously turned the doorknob and, to his surprise, found the door unlocked. He opened it just enough to peek inside at the watchman, who was still seated at a desk, his back to the door.

Kayser burst in first, waving his pistol, and cried in Norwegian: "Put your hands up! If you resist, I'll shoot you!"

The guard turned around in his chair, then stood up, trembling, with hands raised. He gaped in shock at the intruders, as if at an apparition. While Ronneberg locked the double doors from the inside, Kayser aimed his pistol at the man's head and pointed to the British army insignia on his sleeve.

"We're British soldiers," he announced again in Norwegian.

Meanwhile, Ronneberg put on rubber gloves to protect himself against an electric shock and went to work placing the charges on the eighteen heavy-water cells. As he moved from cell to cell, wrapping a twelve-inch charge around each one, the guard, who was apparently an Allied sympathizer, Gustav Johansen, observed him admiringly. At one point, he warned Ronneberg about the dangers of the electrolysis process. He should be careful, Johansen said, because lye might leak through his gloves.

When Ronneberg had placed charges on about half the cells, a sudden crash of glass broke the tense silence. Kayser aimed his pistol at the window, which now framed a partially shattered pane, fearing the worst. But he saw a familiar face suddenly pop into view, somewhat obscured by jagged triangles of glass—Birger Stromsheim. Stromsheim was equally surprised to see his comrades inside.

Ronneberg ran to the window to help Stromsheim climb through it and cut his hand on the glass. He had been through so much without suffering a scratch. And now, at this crucial moment, he had to worry about stopping the blood, which soaked his glove and would make it difficult to place the charges. Fortunately, Stromsheim was also trained to do the work.

They should take care not to short-circuit, Johansen said, or there might be an explosion.

That was just what there was going to be, Kayser exclaimed.

When all the charges were in place, Stromsheim checked them over twice while Ronneberg, wiping away the blood from his cut every few seconds, coupled the eighteen fuses so he would have to ignite only nine of them. He

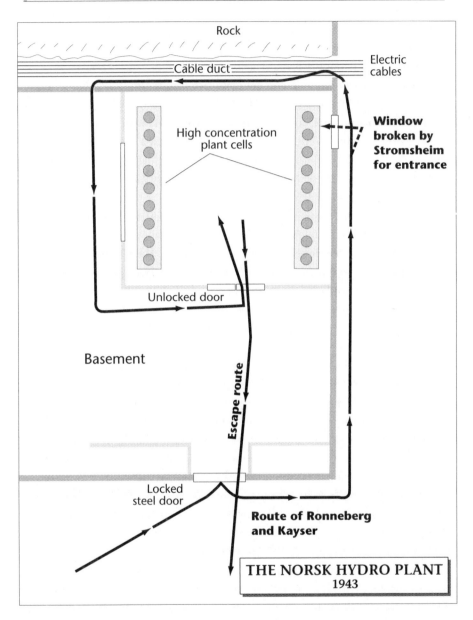

Rock

Electric
cables

Cable duct

Window
broken by
Stromsheim
for entrance

High concentration
plant cells

Unlocked door

Basement

Escape route

Locked
steel door

Route of Ronneberg
and Kayser

THE NORSK HYDRO PLANT
1943

*Arrows trace the route to the heavy-water cells that Ronneberg and Kayser fol-
lowed. After crawling through a cable duct to the basement, they surprised the
lone guard, a Norwegian who did not resist—and in fact offered friendly advice. Joined by Stromsheim, they laid their charges, lit their fuses, and ran for
their lives.*

would ignite two-minute as well as half-minute fuses, just in case the shorter ones did not work. Nothing could be left to chance.

As Ronneberg was finishing his work, Johansen, who had been ordered to rush to the second floor as soon as the fuses were lit, suddenly cried out that he couldn't find his glasses. Would Ronneberg please help him find them? He could hardly see without them. Ronneberg stared at the man incredulously. This was a life-and-death moment, not only for his team but perhaps for the Allies. A German guard could appear at any second and sound the alarm. Yet, with Stromsheim busy with the explosive charges and Kayser in the next room opening the steel door to the yard with a key he had taken from Johansen, the watchman expected Ronneberg to drop the fuses and look for his glasses!

But the saboteur saw before him an elderly gentleman, no doubt a good Norwegian, who was probably working there to keep his family from starving. And how could he work without his glasses, which were virtually irreplaceable in the austerity of Nazi-occupied Norway? The man could have been his father.

"Where the hell did you put them?" Ronneberg asked.

And he dropped his fuses and went to search for the man's glasses. After scanning the room, he found a glass case in a corner. Picking it up, he handed it to Johansen, who thanked him profusely. But hardly had Ronneberg returned to his work when the watchman called to him again.

His glasses were not in the case, he said in a broken voice.

Ronneberg paused for a moment. And again he quickly glanced in every corner, then thumbed through reams of paper piled on the man's desk. Finally, he found the glasses—hidden between the pages of a book.

Again Johansen expressed his deep gratitude. But Ronneberg had no time for amenities. He was about to light a match to ignite the longer fuses when Stromsheim, who was working near a staircase, rushed to Ronneberg and whispered that someone was coming down the stairs.

Ronneberg froze. It was probably a German guard. His good deed could end in catastrophe. He and Stromsheim drew their pistols, and Kayser covered Johansen with his gun to make sure he would not betray them. The footsteps grew louder. A shadow finally appeared against the staircase wall. Guns were aimed. And then the shadow suddenly became a man—the Norwegian night foreman, Gunnar Engebretsen. He gazed at the three trespassers in shock. While Stromsheim and Kayser covered the two civilians, Ronneberg lit a match and ignited the two-minute fuses. Then, as he lit the thirty-second ones, he cried:

"Let's go!"

Kayser shouted to the two workers, who were standing by the stairway: "Run to the second floor as fast as you can or you'll be blown to bits!"

Ronneberg added: "And keep your mouth open or your eardrums will burst."

Then Ronneberg, Kayser, and Stromsheim dashed through the steel door and into the yard, where they met Idland, who had been standing guard. Hardly twenty yards from the building, they heard an explosion, muffled by the competing sounds of machinery rhythmically grinding away in the yard. Half a ton of heavy water had suddenly "evaporated."

"At last there was an explosion," Haukelid would report in his memoirs, "but an astonishingly small, insignificant one. Was this what we had come over a thousand miles to do?"

Poulsson would agree in his own memoirs: "There was a bang. A distant, faint blast. We looked at each other. This couldn't possibly be the real thing."

But then they concluded that perhaps it was. For the heavy-water apparatus was, after all, situated in the insulated basement of the electrolysis plant.

✦

THE GERMANS apparently didn't think the "faint blast" was the real thing, either, for according to Haukelid, none reacted for several minutes. But then, from behind the two storage tanks where he and Poulsson were hiding, they saw the door of the guardhouse open. An unarmed German stepped out with flashlight in hand, sauntered to the electrolysis building about fifty yards away, and tried the steel door. It was locked. He then strolled back to the guardhouse, and the two commandos groaned in relief.

But in a moment the German reappeared, and this time he moved toward the two storage drums that hid the two commandos from view. Haukelid grabbed a hand grenade and held it ready to be thrown, with his left middle finger in the safety-pin ring. And Poulsson aimed his tommy gun at the approaching soldier.

As he gradually advanced, the German swung his flashlight from side to side along the ground. Poulsson had a strong urge to shoot; but Haukelid whispered to wait.

Poulsson lowered his weapon, but raised it again when the man directed his beam on the ground just behind them. If the beam explored the foreground, it would surely reveal the two commandos. But at that moment, the German swung the flashlight around and returned to the guardhouse, closing the door behind him. All kinds of noises were always spewing out from the electrolysis building and the power plant behind it. Nothing special on this night, he apparently felt. Perhaps the snow had exploded a land mine.

Haukelid and Poulsson waited a few minutes to give Ronneberg's party time to escape from the electrolysis building, if they hadn't already left it, then ran to the yard gate. About 300 yards outside the gate, they found the others waiting for them. The nine men, all in perfect shape except for Ronneberg's cut hand, embraced and joked. Now they had only to retreat the way they came.

As the men made their descent, which they found far easier than the climb, they worried that the Germans would turn on their powerful illumination system and trap them in the gorge. What they didn't know was that the guards, though realizing what had happened a short time after the explosion, couldn't find the switch until it was too late. But when flashlight beams began dancing in the night, the saboteurs, who reached the river after about half an hour, were sure the Germans had discovered their line of retreat. They merely had to follow the trail of blood that dripped from Ronneberg's injured hand.

Staggering to the main road, the men hid behind brush along the roadside as cars packed with German officers and Norwegian plant executives from Rjukan zipped past. They finally reached the spot where they had hidden their skis, coveralls, and excess equipment and began the long trek to safety. Five of them would ski across 400 miles of mountainous, German-controlled territory to neutral Sweden, while two would make their way to Oslo, where they would work in the underground before skiing to Sweden, which welcomed refugees from Norway. All these men would ultimately fly to Britain in RAF planes. Another pair would remain in the Norwegian mountains to organize Resistance groups.

Though every member of Gunnerside survived, Claus Helberg came closest to disaster. After reaching Oslo, he returned to the Hardanger Plateau area to recover weapons the commandos had stored in various places and was sighted by a group of German soldiers. For hours they chased him on skis until only one pursuer remained. Finally, Helberg halted, and the two men faced each other like ancient gladiators who knew that one of them must die. They both fired simultaneously—and missed. But while the German ran out of bullets, Helberg still had four. The hare began chasing the hound, and the latter, apparently hit, collapsed in the snow.

Helberg then skied away, but in the dark plunged over a cliff and broke his arm. He managed to reach a village and move in with a friend, only to learn that German soldiers were occupying the next room. In the morning, he went to a German field hospital and talked the unsuspecting doctor into treating his arm, then moved into a hotel—where two of the most powerful Nazis in Norway were staying. Helberg and other Norwegians were arrested for "vacationing" instead of working for the Third Reich. The Nazis never suspected he was one of the wanted saboteurs—even after the pistol he was hiding dropped to the ground between the legs of one of the guards. Helberg explained meekly that it wasn't loaded. The guards confiscated the weapon but didn't bother to report him. On the way to a prison camp, Helberg leaped from the bus, dodging a flurry of bullets, and took refuge in a mental asylum, where, not surprisingly after his hairbreadth escapes, he felt at home. He finally skied to Sweden and then flew on to Britain.

Despite the destruction caused at Norsk Hydro by the explosion, the Germans rebuilt the heavy-water plant in several months. But the delay in production was enough to disrupt Germany's nuclear program and perhaps seal its fate. General Groves, however, having little faith in British-directed sabotage raids, again urged that American planes bomb the plant, and the United States now pressured Britain to agree despite the opposition of the exiled Norwegian government, which still feared civilian casualties.

On November 16, 1943, the American raid took place; 388 bombers, B-17s and B-24s of the Eighth Air Force, based in England, headed for Norway. Orders called for the force to drop its bombs between 11:30 and 11:45 A.M., when the workers would be at lunch in their well-protected basements. But twenty-two Norwegians, mainly women and children, died, many when a makeshift bomb shelter in Vemork sustained a direct hit. Even though 828 bombs were dropped, only two apparently hit the electrolysis plant. The heavy-water cells were untouched.

Nonetheless, the raid was a strategic success, since it finally convinced the Germans that they should transfer the heavy water and equipment to Germany. Learning of the move, several Norwegian saboteurs, including Knut Haukelid, reluctantly agreed to blow up a ferry carrying the shipment across a lake located a few miles from Rjukan. The shipment was to be sent from the opposite shore by train to a port, where it would be placed aboard a vessel bound for Germany. When so much was at stake, the saboteurs could not refuse British pleas to undertake this operation.

But they did much soul-searching as they contemplated the certain death of passengers who would be aboard the ferry—children, friends, even relatives. One saboteur was only able to stop his mother from boarding the vessel by saturating her food with a laxative. Those plant engineers involved in the plot also faced great danger, and one of them would only avoid arrest by having his perfectly normal appendix removed on the day of the scheduled explosion so he wouldn't be suspected of complicity.

Haukelid and two other saboteurs sneaked aboard the ferry the night before it was to sail and set the charges in the hold. They scrambled to safety just before the train carrying the heavy water arrived at the lake. Hours later, on the morning of February 20, 1944, as the ferry, carrying more than fifty unsuspecting passengers, chugged toward a distant shore, the bomb exploded, sending the craft to the bottom of the lake within minutes. Twenty-seven people were picked up by lifeboats or craft sent from shore, but twenty-six went down with the ferry, together with the shipment from Norsk Hydro.

✦

THERE WERE OTHER factors impeding the development of a Nazi atomic bomb, but the heavy-water sabotage was the coup de grace that ended Germany's nuclear dream. Hitler was misled by his scientists into believing that a bomb-building project was impractical and that nuclear energy would be useful mainly to power submarines. They feared, as the German nuclear scientist Carl von Weizsäker explained to me, that the führer would "have their heads" if he thought a bomb could be built and they then failed to produce one in six months.

However, if the German scientists had achieved a chain reaction with Norwegian heavy water, indicating that an atomic bomb could indeed be built, they might have summoned the courage to ask for a massive nuclear project. The problem was that the Allied attacks on Norsk Hydro blocked the effort. As Kurt Diebner, a German atomic scientist, would lament after his country's surrender, "It was the elimination of German heavy-water production in Norway that was the main factor in our failure to achieve a self-sustaining atomic reactor before the war ended."

BEACHHEAD LABRADOR

W. A. B. DOUGLAS

In the war with Germany, weather forecasting gave the Allies an edge that is often overlooked. The weather patterns that developed in the Arctic and over the North Atlantic would sweep across Europe in a matter of days, and their influence on events was hardly marginal. To be denied this information was to be blinded. Both sides set up weather stations on the east coast of Greenland and on the island of Spitsbergen. The opposing weathermen fought skirmishes and took casualties— though at times, when winter storms became notably severe, they also assisted one another. (Those were, as John Keegan has pointed out, the northernmost military incidents that have ever taken place.) By 1943, as the Battle of the North Atlantic swung against them, the Germans increasingly found themselves at a disadvantage in the weather war. The Allies sank their weather reconnaissance ships and shot down information-gathering planes (whose range was limited in the first place.) Submarines also sent in weather reports through Enigma code machines. But not knowing that the Allies had captured both machines and their code books, the U-boats gave away their positions and were often sunk.

As it became apparent that an Allied invasion of the European continent was only a matter of time, the Germans were forced to take increasingly big risks to gather weather information from the other side of the Atlantic. One of the most daring is the subject of the article that follows. It is also an account of the single armed German landing on North American soil, by the crew of the *U-537*. In October 1943, they would spend twenty-eight hours on an unpopulated stretch of Labrador shore, an occurrence that only came to light early in the 1980s, as well as the reason for their landing. On an informed hunch, W. A. B. Douglas, formerly the official historian of the Canadian armed forces, journeyed to that remote bay, and he describes here the remarkable discovery he made.

The payoff of the weather war came a little more than seven months after the *U-537*'s nervous hours in Labrador. The original Normandy landings had been scheduled for June 5, 1944, but when a huge storm blew in from the Atlantic, they had to be postponed for at least a day and perhaps longer. For all the Germans knew, the wretched weather could go on for days, and they concluded that there was no prospect of an invasion until the middle of the month or early in July. They relaxed their vigilance. But Allied control of the North Atlantic allowed them to detect a slight break in the weather that the Germans could not have known about. D day could go forward on the morning of June 6. The ability of the supreme commander of the operation, Dwight D. Eisenhower, to exploit that famous break in the storm gave the Allies the advantage they most needed (and one they might not have enjoyed under fairer skies): surprise.

W. A. B. Douglas was the official historian of the Canadian armed forces from 1973 to 1994. He is the co-author (with Roger Sarty) of the forthcoming official history of the Royal Canadian Navy in World War II.

ON SEPTEMBER 18, 1943, THE SUBMARINE *U-537* SLIPPED OUT of Kiel, Germany, and headed for the western North Atlantic on her first operational patrol. On board as supercargo was a scientist, Dr. Kurt Sommermeyer. Accompanying him, crammed into the U-boat's hull, were ten large canisters filled with nickel-cadmium and dry-cell high-voltage batteries, designed to withstand the cold, as well as the necessary equipment to record, encode, and broadcast weather information. The captain of the *U-537* was Lieutenant Commander Peter Schrewe, whose unique and dangerous task was to set up an automatic weather station on the coast of Labrador. It would be the only such equipment the Germans ever placed on North American soil.

With the inevitable Allied invasion of western Europe looming, the Germans continually sought the data they needed from the Atlantic Ocean to predict the weather over continental Europe, and the Allies continually tried to stop them. Manned weather stations—for example, in Spitsbergen, Norway, and Greenland—were vulnerable to detection and attack. Weather flights by aircraft were limited by the range of the planes and by the weather itself. Submarines detailed as weather-reporting ships were often sunk—unknown to the Germans, they gave away their positions when they sent in their reports using the Enigma code, which the Allies were able to read. Alternatives had to be found.

Both sea- and land-based automatic weather stations had been developed early in the war, by Ernst Plötze, a professor at the University of Freiburg, and Edwin Stöbe, an engineer from Travemünde, near Lübeck. Such stations could be placed in areas where manned equipment was difficult or impossible to establish and maintain. They did not expose any personnel to the danger of attack and were difficult for an enemy to locate.

The equipment carried by the *U-537* was designated *WFL-Wetter-Funkgerät (land)*, or weather-reporting station, land-based type-number 26, the sixth in a series of twenty-one such stations manufactured by the Siemens company in cooperation with the German navy and the Ministry of Transport's Office of Meteorology. (Other stations were put into operation in or below the eastern Arctic, north of Norway.)

WFL 26 was capable of measuring, with reasonable precision, atmospheric pressure from 950 to 1,050 millibars and temperature from twenty degrees below zero to thirty degrees Celsius (four below to eighty-six degrees Fahrenheit). Wind direction and speed were determined by indicators inside a specially designed instrument, which had an elastic coupling to avoid transmitting vibrations to the system. A cylinder with alternating insulated and metal strips, representing alphabetical and numerical signs in Morse code, relayed instrument readings when it rotated, through lightweight contact needles that set off two letters for each character of measurement. This had to occur ten times over a period of 80 to 120 seconds, to make sure the readings were received successfully. A Lorenz LO 150 FK-type transmitter, with a peak output of only 150 watts, used a frequency of 3,940 kilohertz to broadcast the report to receiving stations in northern Europe every three hours from about 4:30 A.M. to 10:30 P.M. Greenwich Mean Time. A mechanism switched the transmitter on for about three minutes at a time: one minute for warming up and two for transmitting. This was a very advanced concept for its time, and postwar comments in a U.S. Navy technical report about captured German equipment suggest it had not been matched by meteorological scientists in the Allied countries.

Schrewe recorded in his war diary that he intended to go as far north as possible along the Labrador coast to avoid being spotted by Eskimos. After a stormy transatlantic passage, in which he lost his antiaircraft-gun mounting over the side in heavy seas south of Greenland, the U-boat commander took

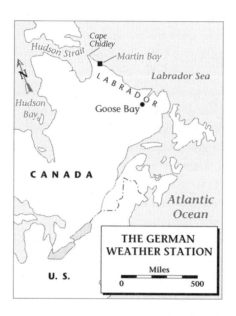

*The Germans placed the weather station at Martin Bay near the northern tip of
Labrador to minimize the chance of detection.*

his bearings at Cape Chidley, located at the northern tip of Labrador and the
entrance to the Hudson Strait, and then went south about fifteen nautical
miles. On October 22, Schrewe navigated safely through the treacherous and
only partly sounded channels leading between Home Island and the Avayalik
Islands and then just south into Martin Bay.

He evidently did not know that in late October the annual migration of
harp seals attracted every hunter within reach to that region; however, luck
was with him. Not only did no hunter report seeing the boat, but he also
missed, by exactly one week, a rare coastal sweep from Goose Bay by a PBY
Canso amphibious plane of the Royal Canadian Air Force's 162 Squadron.

For the next twenty-eight hours, the *U-537* lay at anchor, all hatches
open—a sitting duck if there had been an attack—while the crew manhandled the 220-pound canisters, along with a tripod and mast, into rubber boats
and then onshore over a small gravel beach. Luck still held for Schrewe: He
apparently escaped detection by a vessel—most likely a local fishing boat—
that one of his patrols spotted sailing past the bay. Without any other interruption, the men toiled to erect the weather station 400 yards or so inland

from the beach, on a hill about 170 feet high. At 5:40 P.M. on October 23, having ensured that the station was functioning properly, Schrewe weighed anchor and set off in the *U-537* for a tedious and sometimes terrifying anti-shipping patrol in his assigned area, off Newfoundland. On December 8, the U-boat finally returned to base at Lorient, in northwestern France, without having had any success against Allied shipping. (The *U-537* was later transferred to the Pacific to attack Allied shipping there, and she was sunk with all hands in the Pacific on November 9, 1944; of those on board during the trip to Labrador, only Dr. Sommermeyer and one other person are known to have survived the war.)

Subsequent reports indicate that the weather station sent out normal transmissions for a few days, but then there was apparent jamming on that frequency (about which nothing more is known; no evidence has yet turned up that the Allies learned about the equipment). In July 1944, another U-boat, the *U-867,* reportedly set out from Norway to erect a second weather station in Labrador but was sunk en route by Royal Air Force planes.

The *U-537*'s special mission was a well-kept secret. For more than thirty-five years, only a handful of German seamen and scientists knew about it. Persistent research in the late 1970s rescued the episode from oblivion, but it was not until 1981 that various pieces of the puzzle fell into place. Since then, people reading initial accounts of the weather station have provided further details, leading to additional speculation.

How did the story come to light? After retiring from the Siemens Corporation in the late 1970s, an engineer named Franz Selinger decided to write a history of the German weather service. Among the late Dr. Sommermeyer's papers, he found photographs of one weather station and a U-boat that did not fit in with the eastern Arctic installations he had previously been able to identify. Selinger relentlessly followed up on two clues in the photographs: the U-boat was missing the usual antiaircraft-gun mounting, and the landforms did not seem right for the eastern Arctic. Deducing by their appearance that they must be on the Labrador coast, he contacted the Directorate of History at Canadian National Defence Headquarters to see if there had been a German weather station there, but neither Canadian nor U.S. archives could produce evidence of one. He also turned to the German naval historian Jürgen Rohwer, whose knowledge of U-boat data is encyclopedic, and through him was able to obtain information from the son of Dr. Sommermeyer. Finally, having identified the *U-537,* he located the U-boat's logbook at the German military archives in Freiburg, which brought to light specific details of the cruise.

Later, he learned more from Werner Bendler, who claimed to be the only surviving crew member from the 1943 expedition (having left the crew before the U-boat was sunk).

Selinger wrote to me in 1980 to see if there was any information in the Canadian military archives about the weather station. Nothing could be found. Now the Canadian Coast Guard took an interest in the matter. Captain J. Y. Clarke, then director of fleet systems and an old shipmate of mine, offered passage to Selinger and me in the icebreaker *Louis S. St. Laurent,* on her annual Arctic cruise in the summer of 1981. This generous assistance enabled us to visit Martin Bay by helicopter from the icebreaker on July 21. After one heart-stopping circuit when nothing could be seen on the ground, we found the remains of the weather station.

We were not, however, the first to come across it. Others had been there and removed most of the attractive material—the radio transmitter and copper wire, for instance. Nevertheless, the canisters, tripod, and mast, and some dry-cell and nickel-cadmium batteries, preserved through all weather conditions for thirty-eight years, remained there for us to identify—though some of the contents had been knocked over, strewn about, and in some cases destroyed.

The Germans had shrewdly painted the words "Canadian Weather Service" on the canisters, so looters had evidently been deceived into thinking this was Canadian government property (and thus, obviously, fair game). After reading about the weather station, a geomorphologist from Carleton University in Ottawa sheepishly admitted that he had come upon the site in 1977 while making a geological survey of the Tomgat Mountains, had assumed it was related to postwar defense, and had been meaning to ask the Department of National Defence about it. None of this detracted from our satisfaction in discovering the site.

The first automatic weather station ever erected in North America, it offers incontrovertible evidence of the only landing by German armed forces on North American soil during World War II. The remaining pieces of this weather station are now in the possession of the Canadian War Museum in Ottawa, still awaiting a suitable occasion for display as an unusual footnote to the history of the war.

THE DECEIVERS

THADDEUS HOLT

Normandy caught the Germans by surprise, and the reason wasn't just the weather.

As the Allies prepared to take the war to Berlin and Tokyo, an unlikely assortment of intellectuals, some of them in a decidedly unheroic middle age, fashioned a worldwide network—net might be more to the point—of deception. Their object was to plant information largely true but false in crucial particulars, information that would convince the enemy to deploy troops to meet a bogus threat, away from the main point of attack. Deception, at which the Allies became masters, could be both tactical and strategic. On a tactical level, specialists could create fake airplanes, tanks, landing craft, supply dumps, or army camps. "They could," writes Thaddeus Holt, "produce the sounds, and even the smells, of an armored unit starting up. They could replicate radio traffic." At El Alamein, the deceivers fooled Field Marshall Erwin Rommel "into believing that the main weight of General Bernard Montgomery's armored striking power was on his left rather than on his right, where he delivered his knockout punch."

Strategic deception was the tactical version writ large. In the months leading up to D day, the Allies created notional—fake—divisions, corps, armies, and even an army group. (Some were real, to be "reassigned" from phantom D days to the real ones, as was the leader of the notional army group, George S. Patton.) In the early months of 1944, the Germans, thanks to deception efforts, estimated that there were fourteen Allied divisions in Egypt and Libya (there were actually three), training to invade the Balkans—thus tying up twenty-two of their divisions in Greece and Yugoslavia, divisions that would have been better used in France or Russia.

In the North Pacific, notional American landing forces in Alaska and the Aleutians kept 80,000 Japanese troops pinned down in the Kurile Islands. But the greatest success of the deceivers was in persuading the Germans that the Normandy landings would not be made in Normandy—and no one was more taken in by the strategic hoaxes than Hitler. The führer came to believe that the main Allied landings would come at the narrowest point of the English Channel. Convinced that Normandy was only a feint, he kept an entire army in the Pas de Calais all through June and July. By the time he realized that he had been duped, it was too late.

There is a quality that few accounts of World War II seem to grasp, and one that goes beyond the apparent domination of weaponry. That is human intelligence, and the way it can affect outcomes. It's sometimes a relief to think that people do not change; only technology does.

Thaddeus Holt is a lawyer and former Deputy Undersecretary of the Army. A frequent contributor to *MHQ,* he is the author of a major study of deception in World War II, the forthcoming *By Guile and By Valor.*

LONDON, July 27, 1944—At first light this morning, the 59th ("Rattlesnake") and 17th divisions—the cutting edge of Lieutenant General John P. Lucas's U.S. Fourteenth Army—together with the 55th Division of Lieutenant General W. D. Morgan's British Fourth Army, swarmed across the Strait of Dover and smashed into France to link up with a surprise predawn parachute and glider assault by the U.S. 9th ("Thunderstorm") and 21st ("Hurricane") and British 2nd airborne divisions. In view of the weakening of German forces in the Pas-de-Calais district so as to contain the Allied bridgehead in Normandy, military analysts anticipated a quick seizure of Antwerp and Brussels, followed by an all-out drive on the Ruhr.

Lieutenant General Lesley J. McNair, commander of the First U.S. Army Group and chief, under Supreme Commander Dwight D. Eisenhower, of this, the decisive Allied assault on Hitler's Festung Europa, expressed satisfaction over the opening phase of the attack. So did his old friend Lieutenant General George S. Patton Jr., recently announced as commander of the U.S. Third Army, part of Lieutenant General Omar N. Bradley's Twelfth U.S. Army Group in Normandy. "My motto is hold 'em by the nose and kick 'em in the pants," said Patton. "While we hold that bastard Rommel's nose in Normandy, Whitey McNair is going to kick his tail all the way to Warsaw."

Don't remember any such news story? Well, how about this:

SÈTE, France, June 20, 1944—Troops of the 6th Airborne Division of Lieutenant General Alexander ("Sandy") Patch's U.S. Seventh Army this morning completed consolidation of the beachhead opened by yesterday's landing in southern France. German news broadcasts speculated that the next objective would be Toulouse and a linkup with Major General Lloyd R. Fredendall's task force, which hit the beaches near Bordeaux three days ago.

Don't recognize that either? Try one more:

ADAK, Alaska, June 16, 1944—Bursting out of the North Pacific fog, Yanks and Canadians yesterday kicked in Tojo's back door, invading the northern outposts of the Japanese homeland itself.

Under overall command of Lieutenant General Simon B. Buckner Jr., units of the U.S. 108th ("Skullbusters"), 130th, and 141st divisions stormed ashore at Paramushiro, while the U.S. 119th ("Wildfire") Division and a Canadian brigade struck the adjacent island of Shumushu. Paramushiro and Shumushu are the northernmost islands of the Kuriles chain.

First reports suggested that resistance was light. "We know they are there in strength, though," said one colonel, who declined to be identified. "Digging them out won't be easy."

Likewise unfamiliar? Well, no wonder. These were phantom D days, D days that never were—except in the minds of Allied strategic-deception operators and their victims, the Axis intelligence services. The D day threatened in the Pas de Calais was Operation Fortitude South II. Building on a superbly successful earlier deception, Fortitude South, it helped keep much of the German Fifteenth Army away from the Normandy bridgehead. The threatened June 1944 D day in the south of France was Operation Vendetta, and that in the Bordeaux region was Operation Ironside. Their purpose was to help ensure that German forces in those regions were held there and not sent to reinforce the defenders of Normandy. All were part of a comprehensive plan called Bodyguard. Meanwhile, on the other side of the world, Operation Wedlock, the threatened D day in the Kuriles, was designed to distract Japanese attention, and divert Japanese resources, from Admiral Chester W. Nimitz's assault on the Marianas.

That summer of 1944, when the tide of victory had turned and the Allies launched the offensives that would carry them to Berlin and Tokyo, was the finest hour of the assortment of colorful characters that developed and supervised Allied strategic deception. Bodyguard and its components culminated the work of Brigadier Dudley Clarke of the British army, whose "A" Force perfected the techniques of deception, and of Colonel John Bevan, whose London Controlling Section orchestrated British deception worldwide. And Wedlock marked the serious entry on the scene of the Special Section of Joint Security Control, under Bevan's American opposite number, Colonel Newman Smith, which was to orchestrate deception worldwide for the United States.

✦

GENERAL (LATER FIELD MARSHAL) Sir Archibald Wavell, in the early part of the war the British commander in chief in the Middle East, had served under General Sir Edmund Allenby in 1917–18, and had learned from that legendary figure the value of deception and surprise. Late in 1940, Wavell decided to systematize deception by appointing an officer to take charge of it for his whole theater, responsible only to Wavell himself. For this purpose, he recruited to his headquarters in Cairo an officer already noted for imagination and resourcefulness, Lieutenant Colonel (eventually Brigadier) Dudley Clarke. This turned out to be one of Wavell's greatest contributions to the Allied cause.

Clarke was a regular soldier, merry-eyed, humorous, a talented raconteur, with a spooky knack of suddenly appearing in a room without anyone having noticed him come in. He had a passion for secrecy, and the very existence of his unit—deliberately given the nondescript name "A" Force—was known to almost no one. He set up shop originally in a converted bathroom in Wavell's headquarters building in Cairo, and subsequently in a building at 6 Kasr-el-Nil that had housed one of the Egyptian capital's more fashionable bordellos. (According to one of his officers in later years, "Before the full expansion of 'A' Force took place, Clarke courteously permitted the ladies to remain in business on an upper floor.") Over the next several years, he worked out the theory and practice of deception—especially strategic deception—in a comprehensive and systematic way. More than that: Most of the other major practitioners of the art of deception on the Allied side learned their trade with "A" Force or followed Clarke's principles, even though he himself remained throughout the war in the Mediterranean and the Middle East. (When Wavell was transferred to India in 1941, he recognized that Clarke was irreplaceable and bequeathed him to his successors, appointing as deception officer in India Lieutenant Colonel—later Colonel—Peter Fleming, who in civilian life was an explorer, best-selling author, and all-round adventurer, and may have been in some respects an inspiration for his brother Ian's fictional character James Bond.)

"A" Force conducted both tactical and strategic deception. At the tactical level, Clarke's specialists had at their disposal an extraordinary array of contraptions to fool Axis reconnaissance. They could mimic airplanes, landing craft, guns, and vehicles of all kinds. They could make a tank look like a truck, or vice versa. They could imitate airfields, supply dumps, motor pools, encampments. They could produce the sounds, and even the smells, of an armored unit starting up. They could replicate any desired type of radio traffic. They had dummy paratroopers who could be dropped in great numbers to simulate an airborne assault, complete with the sound of small-arms fire and the flashing of Very lights apparently fired by officers to signal to their men. "A" Force played a great part in the victory at El Alamein, fooling the Germans into believing that the main weight of General Bernard Montgomery's armored striking power was on his left rather than on his right, where he delivered his knockout punch.

But it was in stategic deception that Clarke's genius truly flowered. As fully developed by 1944, his system worked in simplified form as follows: Beginning with the object of the deception—what it was intended to make the enemy do (not *think, do;* that was one of Clarke's cardinal principles)—Clarke would devise a "story" to be implanted in the enemy's mind. Working from a meticulously detailed scenario and timetable constructed from this "story," he would allow the enemy to learn, one at a time, bits and pieces of information—largely true, but false in crucial particulars—calculated to lead him little by little to the desired conclusion, and thence to the desired action. Information—"food-stuff," in the lingo of the business—was fed to the enemy by every imaginable channel. Dummy tanks, airplanes, and landing craft would be set out for the benefit of his air and ground reconnaissance. Phony radio traffic, meticulously designed to duplicate the characteristics of real traffic, would simulate units talking to one another, engaged in training exercises, changing locations. Leaves would be canceled and borders would be closed at times consistent with the launching of an imaginary operation. Fake maps and other documents would be left where the enemy would find them. Rumors would be planted in the bazaars of the Middle East, among resistance forces in Axis-occupied territory, and in the cocktail-party chatter of the diplomatic corps in neutral capitals; sometimes, indeed, actual requests or demands would be made to neutral governments in support of purely bogus activities. Anything that could occur to the exuberant ingenuity of the deceivers was fair game, with two firm exceptions: As a matter of the highest policy, they would never give false information to the Allied press, and—a rule of Wavell's—nothing must be done that would interfere with the soldiers' mail from home.

The most colorful, if not always the most important, of channels to Axis intelligence was called "special means." This referred to controlled leakage of information; most romantically, it was a cover term for what are commonly called double agents—people whom the enemy believed to be their own spies but whose messages actually emanated from the Allies. Some of these were actual agents who had "turned" either voluntarily or to escape hanging; many were purely fictitious characters supposedly recruited by the original agents. By means of seemingly clandestine wireless sets, or by messages in invisible ink sent to cover addresses in neutral countries, they would provide their Axis case officers with such information as their Allied handlers wanted passed. But special means also included calculated indiscretions, planted rumors, and all other forms of controlled leakage (though these later came to be distinguished as "related means").

Central to Clarke's methods on the strategic level was the "notional order of battle." (*Notional,* a word much in vogue with British academic philosophers of a couple of generations ago, is a favorite term in the deception business and was probably introduced either by Clarke or by Wavell himself.) This was an imaginary list and disposition of Allied forces in the relevant theater—usually far more numerous than the true forces, and differently disposed. Hopefully, if the Axis command believed that this was the real Allied order of battle, and that the Allies intended to use these forces in a wholly different way from their actual plans, they would make faulty dispositions that would inure to the Allies' benefit—such as deploying, in order to meet the bogus threat, forces that might otherwise have been used to counter the true Allied operations.

Such an order of battle obviously had to be inflated with nonexistent units. The first of these, suitably enough, was "A" Force itself, which began life as a notional brigade of a notional force called the Special Air Service—forerunner of the real SAS, paradigm of the Green Berets and other special forces the world over. Over time, Clarke added such bogus British formations in the Middle East as the Ninth Army (which in fact was merely a few administrative units), Twelfth Army (totally notional), 20th Armoured Division (in reality an armored brigade and a large number of dummy tanks), and so on, joined after the United States entered the war by such imaginary American units as the 16th and 22nd divisions. The Germans duly entered all these into their rosters, and by the late spring of 1944 they estimated that there were some fourteen Allied divisions in Libya and Egypt alone, when the true number was three. What with this threat, together with the activity of Yugoslav guerrillas and the distant but growing threat of the advancing Soviets, the Germans at that vital time had some twenty-two divisions tied up in the Balkans that could have been put to far more productive use in France, Italy, and Byelorussia.

✦

UNDER CLARKE'S and Wavell's inspiration, the former's methods were eventually extended to the top level of the British command, and thence to the American high command as well. In October 1941, Clarke visited London and gave an account of his activities to the British Chiefs of Staff. Impressed by his accomplishments, they decreed the appointment of an officer, to be called the controlling officer, who would report to them and be responsible for preparing and executing cover plans at the London level. The first controlling officer did not get the bureaucratic support he needed, and he asked to be relieved in May 1942. His replacement was Lieutenant Colonel (later Colonel) John H. Bevan, in civilian life an investment banker in the City of London, who had had intelligence experience in the 1914–18 war and had been involved in tactical deception in the Norwegian campaign.

Johnny Bevan proved to be the ideal choice for controlling officer. Courtly, gracious, modest, widely respected, multitalented, essentially unmilitary, and quintessentially Establishment (Eton and Christ Church; he and Field Marshal Harold Alexander were married to sisters, daughters of an earl), he had come favorably to Churchill's notice as a young officer back in 1918, and was a great friend both of Churchill's chief of staff, General Hastings ("Pug") Ismay, and of his fellow bird-watcher, Field Marshal Sir Alan Brooke, chief of the Imperial General Staff. By a happy chance (if chance it was), his appointment coincided with a personal message from Wavell, now commander in chief in India, to Churchill urging the prime minister's "personal consideration" of a "policy of bold imaginative deception worked between London, Washington, and commanders in the field by only officers with special qualifications." This was just the kind of thing to appeal to Churchill's buccaneering side. He circulated Wavell's message to the Defence Committee of the Cabinet. In response, the Chiefs of Staff renamed Bevan's office the London Controlling Section (usually referred to as the LCS), and gave him worldwide responsibility for developing overall deception policy, for approving and coordinating theater deception plans and their execution, and in general for carrying out "any matter calculated to mystify or mislead the enemy wherever military advantage may be so gained." And they invited "the Americans to set up a parallel organization in Washington, which should maintain close liaison with their colleagues in London."

In late August 1942, the American Joint Chiefs of Staff set up an entity called Joint Security Control (known usually as JSC). Partly, no doubt, this was in response to the British invitation. Partly it reflected dismay over security leaks in connection with Operation Torch, the forthcoming invasion of North Africa. And to a now indeterminate degree it reflected the initiative of Lieutenant Colonel (later Colonel) William Baumer, a young officer on the army General Staff. Baumer was a man of parts, with several published books and a master's degree from Columbia to his credit, who early perceived the value of deception and for the next two years tirelessly agitated for it in the face of his seniors' skepticism. Headed by the chiefs of military and naval intelligence, JSC was responsible for protecting the security of information as well as for implementing and coordinating—not planning—deception operations. It did not get planning authority till late 1944, and it never got the sweeping authority enjoyed by the LCS.

In October 1942, the first top-level inter-Allied deception conference took place in London. As well as completing cover and deception plans for Torch, the meeting worked out inter-Allied arrangements for future deceptions. In December and January, Bevan visited Washington, and the final division of authority was agreed on. The British LCS would handle Europe, the Mediterranean, the Middle East, and India-Burma. The American JSC would handle the Western Hemisphere, the Pacific, and China.

On the tactical level, military deception was an old American tradition, going back at least to 1779, when George Rogers Clark approached Vincennes carrying far more flags than the size of his force would warrant, so as to multiply his manpower in British eyes. In the Civil War one thinks of the wooden "Quaker guns" and scarecrow sentinels at Manassas Junction and Harrison's landing in 1862, of "Prince John" Magruder's theatrics at Yorktown and Gaines' Mill, of the empty trains bearing "reinforcements" that covered P. G. T. Beauregard's retreat from Corinth, of Nathan Bedford Forrest in 1863 marching the same two guns round and round till his opponent thought himself hopelessly outnumbered, of Stonewall Jackson's "Mystify, mislead, and surprise" (a favorite quotation of Wavell's). Back in 1918, Colonel Arthur L. Conger had presided over the "Belfort ruse," fooling the Germans as to the direction of the Saint-Mihiel offensive with such devices as leaving carbon paper carrying details of a phony plan in a wastebasket at a hotel frequented by German agents. But the United States entered the war behind the times in tactical deception and wholly innocent in strategic deception. In peacetime maneuvers the navy had developed skill in deceptive radio signaling, but that was about as far as American expertise went. A few officers on the army General Staff, notably Bill Baumer, tried to encourage interest in strategic deception, but it was uphill work, and it was hard to separate deception from psychological warfare in their bosses' minds.

The real break came when American forces were established in the Mediterranean, and Eisenhower and his chief of staff, Walter Bedell Smith, got to know Dudley Clarke's work. Powerfully impressed, they saw to it that a number of American officers were assigned to "A" Force, or worked with it, to learn Clarke's methods. This move, while professionally successful, had mixed results on the human level. Clarke was a bit of a lion hunter and snob. "A" Force lived well and ate well, and he had staffed it with sprigs of the Establishment, male and female, preferably with something colorful about them, and with people of somewhat flashy accomplishments, such as a famous magician and a racing driver. Plain, straightforward midwestern Americans found themselves in an outer circle, while Americans from, say, Yale and Wall Street found a warm welcome. (So did Douglas Fairbanks Jr., whose navy "beach jumpers," or tactical-deception teams, fit in neatly with Clarke's work.) Nevertheless, such minor personal problems did not interfere with the work at hand.

✦

DECEPTION UNDERSTANDABLY attracted people who were out of the ordinary. In Bevan himself, as Baumer recalled in later years, "there was this diabolical mind operating. . . . He was playing a keyboard." Another deceiver recalled, "He was just having a lovely time." The rest of the LCS was cut from the same motley cloth, a collection of uniformed civilians ranging from Dennis Wheatley—bon viveur, man-about-town, gentleman vintner, and author of popular thrillers and tales of the occult—to "stockbrokers to manufacturers of soap to a small-part character actor," as one member described them.

JSC was almost as varied once it really got under steam. This took time. During its first year or so it was feeling its way, perhaps to some extent smothered under military bureaucracy. It devoted an inordinate amount of time and energy to a plan called Wadham, which was the American element of Cockade, one of the LCS's less-happy projects, designed to make the Germans think a cross-Channel attack would come in 1943. (The Germans barely took notice.) Along about late 1943 it began to find itself. The Special Section, or deception element, was put under Lieutenant Colonel (soon to be Colonel) Newman Smith. Under him were Lieutenant Colonel Carl Goldbranson for army matters and Lieutenant Commander Harold Burris-Meyer for navy matters, while a reserve navy lieutenant named E. P. Schrup monitored "special means."

Newman Smith was an urbane and cosmopolitan fifty-four-year-old Alabamian who had led a varied and adventurous life. At the age of eighteen he dropped out of college for a fling as an enlisted man fighting the Moros in the Philippines. Returning to Montgomery to read law and work in a bank, and commissioned in the National Guard, he took part in Pershing's Mexican expedition; fought in the American Expeditionary Forces from Champagne-Marne to the Meuse-Argonne, commanding a machine-gun battalion in the Rainbow Division; and served as aide-de-camp to Herbert Hoover in his postwar relief work. In the 1920s and early 1930s, Smith managed European affairs for major New York financial institutions, living first briefly in Constantinople and subsequently in Brussels, and then was a banker in New York and Atlanta. He was a notable fencer with the Royal Fencing Club of Belgium, and a player of polo. A dapper man of middle height with a trim mustache, he is described by one who knew him as a "miniature Pershing." His wife, née Rosalind Sayre, was daughter of a judge of the Supreme Court of Alabama. (Her sister Zelda married F. Scott Fitzgerald.) Newman Smith, classical Southern gentleman, and Johnny Bevan, classical English gentleman, were ideally paired as opposite numbers, with one surprising mismatch: Smith was solemn and humorless about his work—a rare characteristic for a deceiver.

Burris-Meyer, by contrast, was a fellow of infinite jest, who brought to his work a boundless energy and joie de vivre. A professor of theater and director of research in sound at Stevens Institute, he had pioneered in the development of stereophonic recording and had worked with Leopold Stokowski and Walt Disney in developing *Fantasia,* the first film to bring multitrack stereo to movie theaters. A hands-on pragmatist who was not above dropping Coca-Cola bottles out of airplanes to see if they would imitate the sound of falling bombs (they did not), Burris-Meyer was behind the development of much of the sonic-deception equipment used by Fairbanks's beach jumpers, and he had seen it in action in the Mediterranean.

Goldbranson, in turn, was JSC's direct link with "A" Force. In civilian life an executive with the Union Pacific Railroad and an Iowa National Guard officer from the "Red Bull" Division, he had been one of the first Americans assigned to Clarke and for a time had been joint commander of the Advanced Headquarters of "A" Force at Algiers. Schrup, in peacetime a lawyer with the Federal Trade Commission, worked with the FBI in preparing traffic to be sent through controlled German agents.

So by 1944, largely because of Dudley Clarke and ultimately because of Sir Archibald Wavell, the skills and the organizations were in place worldwide for Allied strategic deceptions to cover the final onslaught against the Axis.

✦

FOR 1944 in Europe and the Mediterranean, Bevan and his LCS formulated an overall deception plan called Bodyguard. Within its general provisions a number of theater plans were drawn up and implemented. Fortitude (divided into Fortitude North and Fortitude South) was designed to keep the Germans edgy over possible landings in Norway and the Pas de Calais. (It was originally called Mespot, but Churchill did not like that name, and it was soon changed.) Zeppelin was designed to continue Clarke's notional buildup in the Mediterranean; within Zeppelin, Turpitude was to worry the Germans over a move against the Balkans, and Vendetta to make them think southern France was to be invaded at the time of the Normandy landings. Ironside was to make them expect a landing in the Bordeaux region at the same time. The whole package was to be backed up by diplomatic moves collectively called Royal Flush, while specific diplomatic initiatives with Sweden, called Graffham, were to reinforce German concern over Scandinavia. Finally, Bevan and Baumer spent five memorable weeks in Moscow in February and March of 1944, to brief the Soviets on Bodyguard and seek their cooperation by mounting deceptive threats in the far north and in Bulgaria.

The key operations in support of the invasion of Europe were Fortitude South and Vendetta. Fortitude South with its successor, Fortitude South II, is by now the best-known—indeed, still the only well-known—deception operation of the war. Less well known, and deserving of lasting fame for his work, is its true designer, Lieutenant Colonel (later Colonel) David Strangeways. Strangeways was a Cambridge graduate and a regular officer in the Duke of Wellington's Regiment. He was no deskbound planner but a frontline soldier. At Dunkirk he had saved his men by wading and swimming through the surf to an abandoned barge, loading his troops on it, and, clad only in a doormat he found on board, sailing it to England with a compass and a school atlas. (Once again fully clothed, he dined that same evening at the Savoy with his wife, as he liked to recall). He had been the first Allied soldier into Tunis, dashing ahead to seize classified materials at German headquarters before they could be destroyed. On the small side, always immaculately turned out, handsome, brisk, and efficient in manner, with a very quick mind and an impish sense of humor, he was a master technician at his work, a perfectionist who did not hesitate to speak his mind to superiors and did not suffer fools gladly.

Strangeways had been in charge of deception for Alexander's Army Group in North Africa and Italy, as commander of Tactical HQ "A" Force. When in December 1943 Montgomery was appointed commander of the Twenty-first Army Group for Overlord (and Allied ground commander in the opening phase), he designated Strangeways his deception chief.

Strangeways arrived back in London at Christmastime 1943, carrying with him a full share of the bumptiously self-confident take-charge attitude that Montgomery and his people brought to Overlord preparations. At the same time, Colonel Noel Wild, who had been Clarke's deputy in Cairo, arrived to take over the deception section of Eisenhower's headquarters staff, called Ops (B). Waiting for them was a deception plan for Overlord, known originally as Torrent but now just called Appendix Y, designed to make the Germans believe that the main invasion would come not in Normandy but across the Strait of Dover and into the Pas de Calais region of France. To achieve this, it proposed to rely mainly on an extensive array of dummy installations and feigned troop movements in southeastern England, together with maximum camouflage of activities farther west, with the modest goal of making the Germans think a six-division force was poised in the southeast.

Neither Strangeways nor Wild thought this plan remotely adequate. Nobody did, not even the inexperienced Americans. Clarke himself had been fiercely critical of it. No one disagreed with the idea of focusing German attention on the Pas de Calais—that was the only possible choice—but the proposed implementation was utterly clumsy. It was like "putting a hooped skirt and ruffled pants on an elephant to make it look like a crinoline girl," said Major Ralph Ingersoll (in civilian life former general manager of Time Inc. and editor of the newspaper *PM,* who studied the plan for the Americans). Strangeways took charge; he seized Appendix Y and rewrote it, and it became the legendary Fortitude South.

The "story" for Fortitude South, in the words of the implementing directive drawn by Strangeways, was that "the main Allied assault is to be made against the Pas de Calais area" forty-five days after the Normandy landings, while "Neptune [the code name for the Normandy assault itself] is a preliminary and diversionary operation, designed to draw German reserves away from the Pas de Calais and Belgium. Once the main German reserves have been committed to the Neptune battle, the main Allied attack against the Pas de Calais will take place. . . . The enemy will be induced to believe for as long as possible after Neptune D day that the main threat to the Pas de Calais is still to be carried out."

Within Fortitude South, the code words Quicksilver I through Quicksilver

VI denoted the various operations to implement the threat. Quicksilver I, the crucial order of battle deception, was Strangeways's stroke of particular genius. It came about this way: There existed a skeleton headquarters for a future army group, designated First United States Army Group and usually called by the acronym FUSAG. It was intended as Lieutenant General Omar N. Bradley's command and, once fully activated, would comprise Lieutenant General Courtney H. Hodges's U.S. First Army and Patton's U.S. Third Army. During the initial phase of Neptune, however, FUSAG would still be inactive. During that phase, Montgomery, as commander of the British Twenty-first Army Group, would be in overall ground command, with the British Second Army under Lieutenant General Sir Miles Dempsey and the Canadian First Army under Lieutenant General H. D. G. Crerar on his left, and the U.S. First Army under Bradley on his right. Once the buildup in Normandy reached the point of activating the Third Army, Hodges would take over the First Army and Bradley would activate FUSAG, commanding both Hodges and Patton, while Montgomery's Twenty-first Army Group would become purely Anglo-Canadian. Strangeways conceived the audacious scheme of basing a notional order of battle on FUSAG, and implanting in the mind of the German command a detailed image not of a mere six divisions, as in Appendix Y, but of an entire army group, waiting in southeastern England to pounce across the Strait of Dover.

To quote again from Strangeways's implementing directive, the pre–D day "story" was that Eisenhower "has under command two Army Groups, the Twenty-first Army Group, and the First United States Army Group, which consists of the First Canadian Army with under command 2 Canadian and VIII U.S. Corps, and the Third United States Army with under command XX [U.S.] Corps and XII [U.S. Corps]." FUSAG was "located in the East and South East of England," with the Ninth U.S. air force associated with it. After D day the story would be that FUSAG "and a proportion of its associated air force [are] ready to attack the Pas de Calais. Once the forces under command 21 Army Group have enticed the enemy reserves in the Pas de Calais area toward the Neptune bridgehead, the supreme commander intends to assault the area Pas de Calais" with FUSAG. "Before the final assault a series of large-scale exercises will take place (of which the mounting of the assault on Neptune is one)." This scheme had the added advantage that at the outset only genuine, rather than notional, units needed to be included in the order of battle—though the Germans would be led to believe that they were in different locations from their real ones. In a touch inspired by Major Roger Fleetwood Hesketh and Major Christopher Harmer of "special means," the Germans were further to be led to believe that FUSAG was commanded by the redoubtable Patton.

Strangeways not only designed Fortitude South; he was in charge of implementing it by all methods other than "special means." Bogus radio traffic was by far the most important of these methods. Allied control of the air over England was so total that, with rare exceptions, German aerial reconnaissance had practically disappeared over coastal areas; and MI5, the British security service, was confident that there were no still-uncontrolled Axis agents in Britain. Accordingly, Strangeways made the bold decision to risk scrapping the whole concept of fake installations, except for some dummy landing craft and similar activity in coastal areas. (If Ken Follett's fictional *Needle* had existed, he would have found in East Anglia not canvas buildings and plywood airplanes, but rather—nothing at all, except the innumerable airfields already known to be there.) Three American officers worked under Strangeways's direction on the American aspects: Lieutenant Colonel (later Colonel) William A. ("Billy") Harris, a regular officer and West Point classmate of Bill Baumer; Major Ingersoll; and Lieutenant Colonel Clarence Beck, another regular.

"Special means" were controlled by Major Hesketh (in civilian life a barrister) of Colonel Wild's SHAEF Ops (B), in liaison with MI5 through Major Harmer, one of its case officers (in civilian life a solicitor); Hesketh's brother Cuthbert, a regular army captain who spoke German well, was also involved. Aided with respect to American matters by Captain Wentworth Eldredge, in peacetime a Dartmouth sociology professor, and operating from a detailed plan drawn up largely by Hesketh, they worked with Strangeways and with the case officers of the now-famous double agents known as Garbo, Brutus, Tricycle, and Tate (and some others on occasion) to feed the "story" to German intelligence.

Fortitude South was an unqualified success. Not only did the Normandy invasion catch the Germans completely by surprise, but they clung to the idea that it was merely a feint. Day after day, German (and Japanese) reports deciphered by Allied code breakers confirmed that the Germans had an exaggerated notion of Allied strength, and that divisions of the German Fifteenth Army in the Pas de Calais that might have driven the Allies into the sea in Normandy were instead being held back to meet Patton's expected assault.

As June wore on, the deceivers' very success presented a new problem: More and more real divisions supposedly part of FUSAG were joining the buildup in Normandy, and soon Patton would be unveiled as commander of the Third Army and Bradley as commander of FUSAG. Could the deception nevertheless be continued? It was again Strangeways who came up with the answer: Leave FUSAG as a notional headquarters and redesignate Bradley's real army group by some other number. (It became, of course, the Twelfth Army Group.) Feed the Germans the "story" that Eisenhower had had to strip divisions from FUSAG to reinforce Normandy, and had allowed Bradley to form a new army group there; that Patton had protested in insubordinate terms the denuding of his army group, and an angry Ike, fed up with Patton's behavior, had demoted him to army command under Bradley as a result; and that the troops sent to Normandy from FUSAG would be replaced by the British Fourth Army, transferred from Scotland, and by new American units grouped into the U.S. Fourteenth and Ninth armies. (Both the Fourth and Fourteenth armies and almost all their elements were bogus.)

All that was needed was a suitably prestigious commander for FUSAG to replace Patton. The SHAEF staff recommended to Eisenhower that he ask General George C. Marshall, the army chief of staff, to send him Lieutenant General Lesley J. McNair, commanding general, Army Ground Forces, or some similarly well-known senior general. Ike gladly complied. "I cannot overemphasize the importance of maintaining as long as humanly possible the Allied threat to the Pas de Calais area," he cabled to Marshall, "which has already paid enormous dividends and, with care, will continue to do so." McNair was an officer of immense prestige, certain to impress the Germans, and his job of training and organizing a great citizen army was now largely completed. Marshall sent him promptly.

Thus was born Fortitude South II. Its "story" was the one described above, with added details of FUSAG's notionally planned operations: training and concentration to be completed by July 26; thereafter an assault "by three infantry and three airborne divisions on the beaches exclusive River Somme to inclusive Boulogne," with the British 55th and 2nd airborne divisions on the right, the 59th and 17th divisions of the U.S. XXXVII Corps on the center and left, and support by the U.S. 9th and 21st airborne divisions, dropped inland; the immediate follow-up would be the British 58th and U.S. 25th armored divisions. Every single one of these units except the British 55th Division was a fake.

McNair's participation ended in tragedy, for he was killed on July 25 by American bombs while watching the Saint-Lô breakout. But Fortitude South II successfully continued the deception. To replace McNair, Marshall promptly dispatched another prestigious senior officer, Lieutenant General John L. DeWitt. Though less well known than McNair, DeWitt had a reputation for the type of toughness the Germans could be expected to understand, for it was he who had supervised the removal of Japanese Americans from the West Coast in 1942.

After the breakout from Normandy, of course, the strategic deception of Fortitude was no longer necessary. Strangeways and Billy Harris and their teams turned to smaller-scale deception, while the "special means" team, augmented by officers from the OSS, set up shop turning and running German stay-behind agents on the Continent. When Lieutenant General Jacob L. Devers's Sixth Army Group came under Eisenhower's command in September, Strangeways and Harris were joined by a third deception team under Lieutenant Colonel Eugene Sweeney and his intelligence officer, Captain Arne Ekstrom. (Bevan considered Sweeney and Ekstrom to be the ablest of all the American deceivers.) FUSAG itself was slowly phased out. The Germans were fed the "story" that the Allies finally had canceled the plan to land in the Pas de Calais because of the unexpected success of the breakout. More than a quarter of a century passed before surviving German officers learned it had all been a hoax.

✦

WHILE FORTITUDE SOUTH was keeping German troops in the Pas de Calais away from the Normandy beachhead, another operation to implement the overall scheme of Bodyguard sought to do the same with German troops in the south of France. Dudley Clarke gave the credit for this operation, called Vendetta, to an American officer, Lieutenant Colonel George Train, in civilian life a Wall Street financier, who at that time was head of "A" Force's Advanced Headquarters, West in Algiers. The background "story" was that because of political troubles among the Greek troops under his command (these were real, and the Germans were certain to know of them), Field Marshal Henry Maitland ("Jumbo") Wilson, Allied commander in chief in the Mediterranean, had abandoned earlier plans to invade Crete and the Peloponnese and had decided to focus on the western Mediterranean instead. Accordingly, he had directed Lieutenant General Alexander Patch, commander of the U.S. Seventh Army, headquartered in Algiers, to land in southern France in the area of Sète and Agde for a drive inland to seize the Carcassonne Gap and thence exploit toward Toulouse and Bordeaux. Supposedly, the Seventh Army was organized into three corps, the U.S. XXXI Corps and two French ones, comprising eleven divisions: the U.S. 91st Infantry and 6th Airborne, three British divisions, and six French ones. All were phony except for one French corps headquarters, three French divisions, and the U.S. 91st Division.

Implementation of Vendetta was somewhat hampered by this thinness of resources. Not only were nearly all its troops imaginary, but the U.S. 91st Division was called for in Italy, and one of the genuine French divisions, the 9th Colonial Infantry, was needed for the occupation of Elba. Most of the genuine landing craft were in England for Overlord. There were not even spare genuine antiaircraft guns with which to make a show of beefing up air defenses over the ports of embarkation.

Vendetta got going in early May with a whirlwind of activity in North Africa, especially in the ports of Bône, Ferryville, and Oran, the bases from which the expedition would notionally set out. Smoke screens were laid over the three ports, and increased antiaircraft protection was simulated. Ten thousand tons of supplies were bundled up and waterproofed. Dummy landing craft were set afloat at Ferryville and Bône. Maps and reconnaissance photographs of the notional target area were issued, instruction in basic French was offered to the troops, directives for civil-affairs authorities were drawn up, and Allied diplomats asked Spanish officials to make available at Barcelona facilities for landing nonmilitary supplies and evacuating wounded.

From June 9 to 11 a huge amphibious exercise was held involving sixty naval vessels (including the British carriers *Indomitable* and *Victorious,* which were passing through the Mediterranean on their way to the Pacific); 13,000 men and 2,000 vehicles of the 91st Division were actually put afloat in Oran and kept at sea for three days, while the ether was filled with appropriate wireless traffic, heavy bombers ranged far up the Rhone, and fighters struck targets in the Sète area. On June 11 the frontiers between Algeria and Spanish Morocco were closed, and the cipher and diplomatic-bag privileges of neutral diplomats were suspended. Activity was kept up for as long as possible, but with the 91st sailing away for Italy, the 9th French Colonial for Elba, and HMS *Indomitable* and *Victorious* for the Orient, the pretense could not be maintained indefinitely. So, beginning on June 24, Clarke began feeding through "special means" the "story" that because reconnaissance had determined that the Germans had kept their forces in southern France instead of moving them north to the Normandy bridgehead, Wilson had decided to postpone the attack. The border was reopened on July 6, and on July 14 the Spanish authorities were advised that owing to the progress of the campaign, it seemed unlikely that the Allies would need the requested humanitarian facilities.

Postwar investigation showed that although Vendetta did not take in the Germans as thoroughly as did Fortitude South, the bottom line came out right. The Germans noticed the heightened activity in North Africa, but to the extent they took it seriously—they suspected that a lot of it was indeed deceptive in nature—they thought that the target might be Italy or the French Riviera rather than the Sète region. Nevertheless, the goal of the operation was achieved: German forces in the south of France were not sent to reinforce Rommel in Normandy. During the whole crucial month of June, of the ten German divisions protecting the French Mediterranean coast, only one was sent to Normandy. (This was the 2nd SS Panzer Division Das Reich, in the course of whose march north there took place the notorious atrocities of Tulle and Oradour-sur-Glâne.)

An amusing footnote was added to Vendetta by a minor satellite operation to Fortitude, called Copperhead, in which an actor disguised as Montgomery paid a highly visible visit to Gibraltar and Algiers just before the Normandy landings. The purpose was to encourage a relaxed attitude on the part of the Germans along the Channel, since they must have known that Montgomery would have a major role in any cross-Channel attack. But Copperhead had no noticeable effect on the Channel front; it did, however, aid Vendetta by further attracting the attention of German intelligence to southern France and Italy.

Meanwhile, over on the Bay of Biscay, poor little Operation Ironside was not even noticed by the Germans. No harm done; it was put on only by a few "special means" efforts, and the attitude toward it from the first was simply that it didn't hurt to try.

✦

BODYGUARD WAS the LCS's show. Joint Security Control's only role was to contribute notional units and their commanders, and pass along "special means" items through the FBI's controlled agents. But at the same time, on the other side of the world JSC was supervising an operation that is still unknown to the general public: Wedlock, the first purely American strategic deception of the war.

Wedlock had its genesis in an Anglo-American conference—suggested by Wavell, once again—held in Washington in May 1943, to agree on machinery for deception of Japan, which in turn led in September 1943 to adoption by the Combined Chiefs of a general policy for such deception. No equivalent to Bodyguard was prepared for the Pacific that year, and this general policy received no code name; but in November it led to War Department instructions (inspired by JSC) to Lieutenant General Simon B. Buckner Jr., commander of the Alaska Department, to prepare a deception plan for the North Pacific for 1944. Buckner complied; his plan was reviewed by Admiral Nimitz's staff, who proposed various changes; the Joint Chiefs approved the final plan, called Wedlock, in February 1944, and details were worked out at a conference in San Francisco in March.

Wedlock never had a Clarke-style strategic "story." On the operational level it was based on a notional Ninth Amphibious Force composed of five American divisions, a Canadian force, and headquarters and corps troops (organized into the I Alaskan Corps), supported by a notionally augmented Ninth Fleet. The Ninth Amphibious Force would be portrayed to the Japanese as staging for an invasion of the Kuriles, the island chain that runs from Hokkaido, the northernmost of the four main Japanese home islands, up to Kamchatka. Specifically, the two key islands of Paramushiro and Shumushu were notionally to be assaulted from the Aleutians, with a target date of June 15—Nimitz's scheduled D day at Saipan. Shumushu was notionally to be hit by an American division and the Canadian force, Paramushiro by three American divisions; one American division would be held in reserve. The attack would be staged from bases on Adak, Attu, and Amchitka, and from Fort Means at Dutch Harbor and Fort Greeley on Kodiak. Meanwhile, the heightened activity in Hawaii in preparation for Operation Forager, Nimitz's invasion of the Marianas, would surely come to the attention of the Japanese; it was hoped that they would interpret it as preparation for follow-up in the Kuriles, or perhaps for a merely secondary operation in the central Pacific.

Given the limited capabilities of the Japanese for reconnaissance in the North Pacific, the chief means for putting this picture over was a program of fake radio traffic. This was well under way by April 15. The army poured out the traffic of American and Canadian formations arriving at their staging areas, setting up, and training. Air Corps radio traffic simulated an air buildup in the North Pacific. The almost entirely notional Ninth Fleet kept up steady back-and-forth communication with the genuine Third and Fifth fleets and with imaginary task forces of its own.

Meanwhile, JSC had been busy with "special means" as early as November 1943. Tidbits were given to the FBI to be passed to the Germans (and hopefully thence to Japan) through their controlled enemy agents, and to the British for passing through their own double-agent network. Advance information of the establishment of a new 17th Naval District covering Alaska, with headquarters in the Aleutians, was fed in March, and the secret establishment at Adak of the Ninth Fleet and Ninth Amphibious Force headquarters was fed in May. Rumors were floated, and seeming indiscretions committed, in neutral capitals. All American soldiers passing through Seattle that spring, even if they were in fact shipping out for the tropics, were issued Arctic equipment and clothing and required to sign a pledge to keep that fact secret. A Russian fishing boat put into Adak in late April; conspicuously visible for its benefit was a large building marked Adak Reserve Depot, and the captain was given an earful of gossip about all the activity in the Aleutians and the difficulty of keeping civilian employees in the islands. Thirty thousand shoulder patches for phantom divisions were shipped to Alaska Department headquarters. (They were never actually issued.) The press was encouraged to discuss the advantages of the short northern great-circle route to Tokyo and to speculate about what was going on in Alaska.

There was concrete activity as well. A dummy base was built on Attu, complete with fake airstrip and phony landing craft. The Kuriles were attacked by air every day, weather permitting; unfortunately, it did not permit often enough. Cruisers and destroyers bombarded Paramushiro and Shumushu in February, March, and June.

Finally, in early June, the Japanese radio-interception service was treated to the wireless traffic of more than five divisions boarding ships, forming two assault forces, and sailing for Paramushiro and Shumushu. But Wedlock, like Vendetta, did not succeed in persuading the enemy that the notional operation would take place on schedule. The Japanese regarded General Douglas MacArthur's drive up the New Guinea coast as the key Allied offensive, and they were caught off balance at Saipan and the Philippine Sea not because they had focused their attention on the Kuriles but because they had directed it southward. They regarded the northern threat as serious, but thought offensive operations unlikely to take place there till the central and southern operations were completed.

Nevertheless, again like Vendetta, Wedlock was a success at the bottom line, for it induced the Japanese to keep thousands of men in the Kuriles who might otherwise have been killing Americans in the Marianas and, later, the Philippines. Japanese intelligence estimated that American forces in Alaska rose from 100,000 men and 300 planes in January to 400,000 men and 700 planes in June. (In fact, American manpower in the theater declined from 100,000 men to 64,000 men during that period, though the number of airplanes did increase from 300 to 373.) Five American and two Canadian divisions, all bogus, entered the order-of-battle holdings of Japanese intelligence. To counter this perceived buildup, the Japanese increased their own forces in the Kuriles from 25,000 men and 38 planes to 70,000 men and 589 planes, strengthened fortifications on Paramushiro, and organized a new Twenty-seventh Army for the Kuriles defense.

These successes were evident to American intelligence from deciphered Japanese messages. Accordingly, although after June 15 a program of spurious radio traffic was instituted to suggest that the original invasion had been canceled and the Allied force brought back to its bases, the Kuriles threat was maintained. A conference called by JSC in Hawaii in July decreed a follow-on operation, code-named Husband. This consisted largely of radio traffic suggesting general sustained activity in the North Pacific, including augmentation of naval forces in the theater in the late summer and fall. Success continued. By November the Japanese had 80,000 men in the Kuriles who might otherwise have been helping General Tomoyuki Yamashita hold off MacArthur in the Philippines, and they stayed there till the spring of 1945. Two further deception operations, Bambino and Valentine, continued winding down the Wedlock deception into early 1945.

By that time JSC had come fully into its own. It had received enlarged authority over deception planning. In the autumn of 1944 it had conducted a major training program for deception officers and sent them out to the theaters as missionary teams. (This was largely Lieutenant Commander Burris-Meyer's doing. He called it the "Young Ladies' Seminary," and called the course book he prepared for it the *Young Ladies' Guide to Truth and Honour.*) The navy element of JSC was strengthened. Looking toward the fall of Germany and the consequent drying up of that channel to the Japanese, JSC opened new "related means" channels to Japan through neutral countries, especially Argentina. Lieutenant Colonel Goldbranson went out to Manila to take charge of MacArthur's deception planning for the final showdown in the Far East. The first comprehensive plan for deception against Japan comparable to Bodyguard in Europe, called Broadaxe, was adopted. The most extensive and sophisticated of all American deceptions in the Pacific, Bluebird, covered the invasion of Okinawa. In June 1945, Johnny Bevan came to Washington one last time, and he and Newman Smith worked out an agreed division of "special means" labor for Japanese deception. Plans called Pastel and Pastel II, plus a further, unnamed, deceptive operation, were devised to cover the invasion of Japan.

But all that is another story.

PUSAN, Korea, March 15,1946—Flushed with victory after the liberation of Shanghai, U.S. Marines and soldiers today landed in Korea to complete the encirclement of Japan, while Admiral William F. ("Bull") Halsey Jr.'s Third Fleet steamed through historic Tsushima Strait into the long-forbidden Sea of Japan itself. . . .

PEPPERMINT
AND ALSOS

FERENC M. SZASZ

Fear of a Nazi superweapon would not go away: "One of the mysteries of the Second World War," Richard Rhodes has written in his history of the atomic bomb, "was the lack of an early and dedicated American intelligence effort to discover the extent of German progress toward atomic bomb development." The obsession with secrecy—one might almost call it paranoia—of the head of the Manhattan Project (the code name for America's atomic bomb program), Leslie R. Groves, may be the answer. To instruct intelligence agents on what to look for, they would have had to be briefed on nuclear research—which would mean the risk of a captured spy being turned or giving up secrets under torture. (The Germans had the same fear, and the same lack of knowledge, of American efforts: By 1944 they were examining bomb craters in Berlin with Geiger counters.)

As D day approached, that fear of a superweapon took two forms for American military planners. The first was that the troops crossing the invasion beaches might be drenched with a nuclear "poison"—or have to pass through a lethal radioactive barrier. The second was even more frightening: an atomic bomb. In April 1944, George C. Marshall, the U.S. chief of staff, sent a special messenger to England to warn Dwight D. Eisenhower of possible nuclear dangers. So the top-secret Peppermint and Alsos missions were born. The first, and least known, was Peppermint, and Ferenc M. Szasz's article may be the first time it has been revealed to the general public. On D day Eisenhower sent a small group of men equipped with atomic detection devices onto the Normandy beaches. The second, ultimately more important, was Alsos. (Alsos is the Greek word for "grove," apparently a coy reference to the Manhattan chief.) Alsos operatives rushed ahead with the advancing Allied armies, searching first for German laboratories and then for the German scientists themselves. Behind a steel door in a cave in the Black Forest, they would come on the answer to their frantic search. More important for the next war, the Cold one, they would deny the Soviet Union the most important German atomic researchers as well as more than a thousand tons of high-grade uranium ore—some of which would be used for "Little Boy," the atomic bomb that the Americans would drop on Hiroshima.

Ferenc M. Szasz is a professor of history at the University of New Mexico and the author of two books on the atomic bomb: *The Day the Sun Rose Twice: The Story of the Trinity Site Nuclear Explosion, July 16, 1945,* and *The British Scientists and the Manhattan Project: The Los Alamos Years.*

ON THE EVENING OF JUNE 5, 1944, DWIGHT D. EISENHOWER, commanding general of the Supreme Force (SHAEF), walked quietly among the paratroopers standing in the marshaling area of England's Greenham Common airfield. "How are you, soldier?" he would say to one, flashing his famous grin. "Where are you from, soldier?" he would ask another.

Two hardly noticed units, code-named "Peppermint" and "Alsos," waited in the wings of the D-minus-one crowds. Although considered vital at the time, these units have faded almost completely from public memory. But in 1944, Peppermint and Alsos represented the Allies' greatest fears about the forthcoming invasion of the Continent: that the Germans had somehow created a nuclear "poison" or an atomic weapon. The D day planners concluded that it would most likely be in the form of nuclear poison—an isotope of cesium, strontium, iodine, or some other radioactive substance—that the Nazis could drop over the beaches and invading armies, creating a deadly radioactive barrier.

This fear was prominent in many military minds. During the interwar years, everyone acknowledged that German science, especially nuclear physics, ranked as the best in the world. Although attacks on "Jewish physics" during the early 1930s had driven numerous scientists to Britain or the United States, a significant number stayed loyal to the Fatherland, including Nobel Laureate physicist Werner Heisenberg, who remained because "Germany needs me," and physical chemist Otto Hahn, co-discoverer of the process of fission. Continental refugees voiced the opinion that "if anybody in the world could make the atomic bomb, Heisenberg could."

Rumor played on these fears. British enlisted man Vernon Scannell recalled that just before his battalion departed for Normandy, the soldiers worried aloud that "the Germans had a secret weapon that would destroy the entire invasion force." Behind the lines, British intelligence seriously debated whether the Nazis would utilize some type of "radioactive powder" in their V-1 or V-2 rockets.

Ever since Wilhelm Röntgen discovered the X ray in 1895 and Madame Marie Curie discovered radium in 1898, the public had been both charmed and mystified by the power of radioactivity. Here was a substance that one could not see, feel, smell, or taste, yet its potential seemed limitless.

During the first years of the century, various entrepreneurs and hucksters touted radium as a medical cure-all. They sold radium hearing aids, hair tonic, face cream, and toothpaste; one firm even marketed a radium-laced beverage, Radithor, that remained on the market well into the mid-1930s.

Simultaneously, however, the nation also confronted the dark side of this strange, invisible power. Madame Curie died of cancer and so, too, did Thomas Edison's top laboratory assistant, the man whose chief assignment had been to perfect an X-ray bulb. The cause célèbre of radiation-induced illness, however, emerged with the tale of the radium-dial painters. During World War I, the U.S. Radium Corporation of New Jersey had hired workers, usually young women, to paint radium dials on clock and watch faces. To make a finer point on their brushes, the women often licked them, ingesting small amounts of radium paint as they worked. Within a few years, many developed severe mouth and jaw cancers. Their celebrated postwar suit against the company—which steadfastly denied any responsibility—brought the lethality of radioactivity to the public's attention.

In December 1938, German physical chemists Otto Hahn and Fritz Strassmann unknowingly split the uranium atom in two, releasing additional neutrons in the process. But other scientists understood the implications. Danish physicist Niels Bohr conveyed the news of the splitting of uranium to a national gathering of physicists at George Washington University in Washington, D.C., in January 1939. As soon as he heard the news, another refugee from fascism, Italian physicist Enrico Fermi, began to speculate on the size of the crater that a kilogram of a uranium-based explosive might create.

On September 19, 1939, only two weeks after the German armies had invaded Poland, Chancellor Adolf Hitler drove to Danzig to deliver a major radio address in which he threatened France and England with "a weapon against which there is no defense." British intelligence officers puzzled over what the German chancellor meant by this phrase, and they suggested three possibilities: Hitler might have been bluffing. He might have been pointing to the power of the Luftwaffe (most likely). Or he might actually have some variety of chemical or nuclear terror weapon. In the fall of 1939, nothing could be disregarded. It was a time, after all, when pulp writers ground out so many stories involving an invisible "death ray" that the theme became something of a cliché.

American military planners soon became intrigued with the concept of a radioactive "poison," and the idea received considerable discussion during the initial stages of the Manhattan Project (the code name for America's atomic-bomb program). Producing an atomic bomb would demand enormous industrial effort and expense, but an atomic "poison" might be both easier and cheaper to manufacture. In 1941, a scientific advisory committee to the National Academy of Sciences recommended that the United States consider using radioactive-fission products as a potential military weapon. Manhattan Project scientists seriously discussed the possibility of dropping fission materials from a plane to contaminate the ground below. In May 1943, Fermi and physicist J. Robert Oppenheimer, the director of the secret wartime laboratory at Los Alamos, discussed the possibility of radioactive food poisoning. Oppenheimer demurred from Fermi's initial suggestions, however, arguing that the scheme would not be practical unless the scientists could discover a way to "poison food sufficient to kill a half a million men." The American radiation-poison plan never moved beyond the discussion stage.

But had the Germans reached the same conclusion? There was no guarantee. Consequently, Allied intelligence examined every scrap of data they could find on the state of the Nazi uranium program. The results were not encouraging. In June 1942, a Swedish scientist informed a London colleague that Heisenberg had begun overseeing nuclear-fission work at a number of laboratories in Germany and that "results must not be excluded." Simultaneously, Hungarian émigré Leo Szilard, a physicist, warned American officials that he had heard from a Swiss contact that the Germans had placed a "power machine" in operation, one from which they could easily derive fission products for military use.

That fall, Manhattan Project scientists inaugurated a secret civil-defense program to guard against a possible German atomic attack. The army ordered the metallurgical laboratory of the University of Chicago to develop sophisticated radiation-detection instruments. By the summer of 1943, the army had discreetly placed the detection devices at Manhattan Project district offices in Boston, Chicago, New York, San Francisco, and Washington, D.C.

A number of American scientists argued that since the Germans were about two years ahead of the Allies in uranium research, they had probably al-ready stockpiled large quantities of radioactive isotopes, and that it would not be difficult for them to use long-range bombers to shower major American cities with radioactive poisons. In late 1943, some Chicago scientists so feared this possibility that they sent their families into the Illinois countryside. A number of people urged General Leslie R. Groves, overall head of the Man-hattan Project, to warn the nation that the Germans might drop an atomic bomb, but this he steadfastly refused to do. (Ironically, only a year later, the Germans were using Geiger counters to test bomb craters in Berlin for evi-dence of an American atomic bomb.)

Within a few months, however, American officials began to relax. While scientists believed that German use of atomic weapons against the United States was still plausible, they also agreed that it was unlikely. All civilian de-fense measures against German radiological warfare were soon discontinued.

The proposed invasion of the Continent brought the matter back to life. Since intelligence had been unable to penetrate the German scientific com-munity, the Allies had virtually no knowledge of the extent of the German uranium project. Refugee rumors invariably placed the Nazis far ahead in the race for atomic weapons. Moreover, recent aerial photographs had revealed the location of a number of probable missile-launching sites. Although the V-1 and V-2 missiles were not launched until after D day, the Allies realized their potential from the outset. These missiles could carry conventional weapons, radiological weapons, or even crude atomic bombs. The Americans warned the British that if the Germans ever dropped radioactive-fission products on London, the city would have to be evacuated.

Navy Captain W. S. "Deke" Parsons wrote General Groves from Los Alamos to remind him of the dangers of radiation poison that might be dropped from rocket-propelled, unmanned German aircraft. Polish-born sci-entist Joseph Rotblat, who was stationed at Los Alamos as part of the British Mission, had also analyzed the matter in detail. Rotblat argued that a Nazi uranium pile could be "milked" every three days for radioactive materials, which could then be easily transported in lead casings to the various rocket-launching sites. From there they could be combined with ordinary explosives and detonated over beaches or advancing troops. "It is unnecessary to picture the destructive possibilities of such an arrangement," Parsons warned.

Groves sent a memorandum to George C. Marshall, the U.S. chief of staff, urging him to inform Eisenhower (who knew nothing of the Manhattan Pro-ject) of the potential danger from radiation poisoning. The Pentagon agreed, and Marshall immediately dispatched Major A. V. Peterson to England on this assignment. On April 8, 1944, Peterson briefed Eisenhower and his staff about the possibility. The Allied response to this threat took on the code name of Peppermint.

The small crew of Peppermint soldiers—their exact number and identities are unknown—formed a potentially vital part of the D day preparations. The Allies decided that both American and British forces should approach the radiation-poison problem on an independent basis, with coordination, if necessary, by SHAEF. The chemical-warfare service officer had charge of the centralized equipment, and he was instructed to work closely with the chief surgeon, Major General Paul R. Hawley. Hawley issued a deliberately vague cover order that alerted all D day medical personnel to a set of physical symptoms they might encounter among the invading troops. The report warned of a "mild disease of unknown etiology" that manifested the following symptoms: fatigue, nausea, leukopenia (an abnormally low white-cell count), and erythema (redness of the skin). Any medic who met soldiers with this "disease" was to contact the chief surgeon immediately.

The men of Peppermint also carried numerous packets of unexposed film when they landed, because ordinary film, when exposed to radiation, fogs or blackens. The cover memo regarding the film proved even more vague. It referred only to "rumors" about recent blackening of film and the desire to track down the source of these rumors. The vague tone of the memos suggests that the Peppermint soldiers were never informed of the true nature of their mission.

If anyone saw his film turn black or encountered any strange "diseases," he was to notify his superiors, who would immediately get word back to Groves in the States. Groves had laid contingency plans to dispatch both additional instruments and highly trained technical personnel to Normandy. In addition, British scientists at the Cavendish Laboratory at Cambridge University agreed to help identify the specific type of radiation. Everything, of course, remained top secret. Fearing a potential panic among the troops, Eisenhower decided to withhold this information on radiation poisoning from the Allied commanders participating in the actual assault.

On the morning of June 6, the Peppermint soldiers landed in Normandy with 1,500 film packets, 11 survey meters, a Geiger counter, a calibrating source, and a number of spare parts. The stateside instruments, which were ready to be shipped to the European theater with top air priority, consisted of 1,500 additional packets of film, about 225 survey meters, and 25 Geiger counters.

The activities of Peppermint units during the invasion must remain somewhat speculative. Those carrying the film packets, presumably the majority, surely carried out other assignments as well. The few with radiation meters or Geiger counters must have watched dials and listened for telltale clicks. When the first V-1 rocket landed in London on June 12, scientists tested the bomb fragments with Geiger counters to see if they contained any traces of radioactivity.

Since no member of Peppermint found any signs of radiation poisoning, either on the beaches or along the invasion routes, all contingency responses were quietly shelved. After the close of the war, both the detection equipment and documents were collected and placed in the Manhattan Project files. Not until 1952 did A. V. Peterson, then a lieutenant colonel, write up the history of Peppermint for the intelligence and security section of the proposed thirty-five–volume manuscript *Manhattan District History.* The documents were not declassified until 1976. They are still not widely known. The Peppermint soldiers faded quietly into obscurity.

✦

IF THE GERMANS *had* laced the beaches with dangerous radiation, the consequences would have been long-term rather than immediate. It is unlikely that a barrage of radioactive isotopes—spread on land, in the water, or in food—could have halted the Allied armies. The Germans would have had to spew forth these isotopes at intensities of about 100 roentgens per hour to produce any immediate effect. This would hardly have been possible. Even if the beaches had been "poisoned," the war would have ended as it did.

The consequences for the soldiers, however, would have emerged years later. In 1944, as today, there existed no real defense against massive radiation poisoning. Allied commanders would have had to instruct their men to shower and change clothes frequently—an absurd order under the circumstances. Moreover, since no one could see, feel, or taste radiation—except in the most severe doses—how was a soldier to know if he had been exposed? The results would have shown up much later as statistics—a vast increase of cancer rates among those who had taken part in the invasion. Moreover, these cancers would have differed according to both exposure levels and the type of isotope used. Even worse, the illnesses would have emerged in an entirely random pattern, for low-level exposures become statistically meaningful only on a large numerical basis. Two men, fighting side by side, would almost surely have developed very different problems. The negative evidence that Peppermint discovered in June 1944 removed the fear of this sort of slow death.

✦

WHILE THE PEPPERMINT soldiers worried about the immediate conse-
quences of radiation poisoning at Normandy, the Alsos team dealt with the
long-term, overall impact of the German nuclear effect. The term *Alsos*
(Greek for "grove") provided a somewhat coy cover name for their operation.
Some security officials, however, feared that the Germans knew about General
Groves and worried that "Alsos" came too close to giving the game away.

As historians David Irving, Thomas Powers, and Mark Walker have
shown, this was a tangled tale. The old adage, "The most important aspect of
history involves not what is actually true but what people *think* is true" was
never better illustrated than by the German and American perceptions of each
other's nuclear programs. Each nation viewed its opposite as moving in tan-
dem with its own scientists' research. Since the German program remained
largely theoretical and academic, German scientists assumed the Americans
were on roughly the same level. In turn, the Allies, who were marching
steadily toward the creation of an atomic weapon, believed the Germans were
doing at least as well. Each side was in total error.

Yet hindsight remains a poor substitute for contemporary realities, and Allied fears were eminently justifiable under the circumstances. From 1942 on,
the Allies *believed* the Germans were close to the creation of an atomic weapon.
Because they so believed, they staged perhaps the most dramatic and successful sabotage effort of the entire war: the assault at the end of February 1943
on the Norsk Hydro Hydrogen Electrolysis Plant, located in a deep valley in
Vemork, Norway.

Now it was left to the Alsos team to discover exactly how far the German
scientists had progressed. Originally formed in 1943, Alsos began as a small
team of scientific investigators during the Italian campaign. Alsos soldiers
helped capture and interrogate Italian scientists about the progress of the
German uranium program. But the results of this foray proved disappointing.
None of the initial Alsos men were scientists, and they simply didn't know
the proper questions to ask the captured Italians.

As D day approached, Alsos was reconstituted and refined. Their orders
now were expanded to include investigations into ten fields of German research, among which were aeronautical, missile, proximity-fuse, and chemical
research, as well as bacteriological warfare. The most important segment of
Alsos, however, remained the effort to investigate "the uranium problem." As
nuclear intelligence was treated separately from the rest of scientific intelligence, this wing of Alsos operated under the strictest security.

The army appointed Major Boris T. Pash, a Californian born of Russian parents, as military chief of the Alsos mission. Dutch-born Jewish physicist Samuel Goudsmit, hastily borrowed from the MIT Radiation Laboratory, became his chief scientist. Both were ideally suited to their tasks.

Pash possessed a natural arrogance that meshed perfectly with his assignment. Risking capture, he invariably insisted on traveling at the front of the advancing Allied troops. On August 25, 1944, Pash arrived in Paris, riding in an open jeep, directly behind the first five French tanks to enter the city; he accomplished this after being forced back four times by sniper fire. With considerable aplomb, he had telephoned a French scientist the day before to alert him that the Americans would soon arrive with a barrage of questions. His autobiography reads like an adventure tale. Later, Pash personally led the Alsos team into the three major German nuclear installations in southern Bavaria. On another occasion, Pash and a small group were crossing a mountain road in Bavaria at dusk when a German officer approached with an offer to surrender. Realizing that his band was greatly outnumbered, Pash tentatively accepted the surrender but told the Germans that he would return the next day to complete all the arrangements. When night arrived, he and his men retreated to Allied lines and then hurried on to the next mission.

Goudsmit was widely respected for both his knowledge of nuclear physics and his personal acquaintance with major German scientists; in addition, he spoke several European languages, including fluent German. He had never been involved with the Manhattan Project, something that was vital for this assignment—if the Germans had captured and tortured Goudsmit, he would have been unable to reveal any Allied atomic secrets.

Alsos operated in self-contained units of both military and civilian personnel. Their plan was to race to the major German university towns, capture the German nuclear physicists (who were all well known), collect their scientific documents, confiscate all stocks of uranium, and (perhaps) destroy any nuclear bomb–making capabilities. Pash carried a personal letter from Secretary of War Henry L. Stimson urging all military officials to give him "every facility and assistance."

Goudsmit arrived in London on D day and worked with his British counterparts for several weeks. Then, on August 9, 1944, he and other men from Alsos crossed the Channel to France. They then hurried across France into Germany, often leading the main body of the invading armies. Initially they went to Strasbourg on the French border, where Goudsmit pored over manuscripts of captured Nazi physicists. The documents Goudsmit uncovered convinced him that the German research was far behind the Allies', making him "virtually certain" that the Nazis did not have the bomb. Still, he admitted that he could never be completely certain.

Wherever the Alsos team went, they rounded up a number of key German scientists, men whom Goudsmit graciously termed his "enemy colleagues." Afterward, the Allies shipped ten of the scientists to England, including both the respected Otto Hahn and Werner Heisenberg, and subsequently sequestered them in an eighteenth-century English manor house, Farm Hall. (Later, Goudsmit was also spirited out of Germany; Allied authorities feared that the Russians might capture him.) Before he left the Continent, however, Goudsmit visited his hometown of The Hague, where, to his horror, he found his childhood home in ruins and learned that his parents had both been deported to a concentration camp and later executed.

As the captured German scientists began to adjust to life at Farm Hall during the winter of 1945, one jested with another about where the microphones had been installed. "Microphones installed?" replied Heisenberg. "No, they're not as cunning as all that. I don't think they know the real Gestapo methods. The English have always been a bit old-fashioned."

But the British had, indeed, installed microphones, and they listened carefully to the German scientists' conversations for several months. What they heard confirmed Goudsmit's initial suspicions. The German conversations revealed nothing about either an atomic bomb or a scheme of radiation poisoning. The ultimate meaning of these conversations (which were not declassified until February 1992) is still being disputed by historians.

Capture and imprisonment, however, had little impact on German scientific arrogance. The scientists seemed to assume that the Allies had sequestered them at Farm Hall primarily to learn from their uranium experiments. They suggested among themselves that even though the war had been lost, they might "win the peace" through their research on nuclear power plants. Only the announcement of Hiroshima and Nagasaki disabused them of this idea.

In the postwar years, Heisenberg and several other German scientists maintained that they had never intended to manufacture an atomic bomb. Instead, they said, they had chosen to work on a "uranium machine," a large power source that could be used only for peaceful purposes. "If we had all *wanted* Germany to win the war," one remarked, "we could have succeeded." Recently, American historian Thomas Powers has argued that Heisenberg was largely telling the truth. In *Heisenberg's War* (1993), Powers suggests that Heisenberg deliberately tried to retard Germany's progress toward atomic weapons and, virtually single-handedly, may have saved humanity from an incredible disaster.

This view, needless to say, is extremely controversial. Most American historians dismiss it out of hand. David Hollinger believes that Powers has fallen victim to the myth of the heroic "scientist-as-hero," the man who controls the destiny of the world from his private laboratory. Similarly, Mark Walker has argued that the German scientists turned away from the quest for a nuclear weapon or a nuclear "Poison" largely because they assumed the war would be over by 1942, and there would be no need for these weapons. The Nazi General Staff showed little interest in a weapon that seemed to have no immediate battlefield use. Hitler also failed to appreciate the military significance of atomic power. When Berlin finally realized that the war would be a long one, they could not muster the enormous industrial resources needed to produce an atomic bomb.

Although the Manhattan Project involved perhaps 250,000 people, fewer than 100 scientists were connected with German uranium research. The Allied atomic effort cost about $2 billion, while the German scientists had to survive on the equivalent of about $1 million. Moreover, the German scientists often quarreled among themselves over petty matters of rank and reputation. It appears as if many of them utilized the war chiefly to gain funding for their pet research projects. Most of the German scientists seemed to have considered atomic research as an academic exercise, not a major weapon of war.

Finally, the German scientists failed to produce an atomic weapon because they could never enlist the support of German industry. But the Germans certainly *could* have manufactured atomic weapons during World War II. The projects that the Reich supported with both men and money proved eminently successful. At the war's close, the Germans led the world with their V-1 and V-2 rockets. With the Messerschmitt 262, German scientists had developed the first operational jet plane. The chief reasons the Nazis did not produce a nuclear weapon had nothing to do with their technical or scientific skills. The absence of a German nuclear weapon can be traced solely to the political conditions and cultural context that enveloped their world.

All this meant that when the Alsos mission arrived at the various German nuclear installations, they found that the Nazi uranium project had barely emerged from the theoretical stage. Although the German physicists had completed some rather extensive work with uranium piles, their research remained preliminary. Because of heavy Allied bombing raids in the Berlin area, the Germans had been forced to move their uranium research to several small towns in the Black Forest region of southern Germany. This section was scheduled to become part of the French zone of occupation. Groves, who feared French left-wing political leanings, desperately wanted to keep both German uranium and German scientists out of French hands.

In mid-April 1945, Pash and his team bluffed their way through various French checkpoints to occupy the hamlet of Hechingen. On April 23, they discovered a heavy steel door that led into a cave dug into the base of an eighty-foot cliff that towered above the town. When they ordered an official to open the door, they stumbled upon the Nazi uranium "machine"—the chief German atomic pile. Pash remained nonplussed, but his scientific colleagues were overjoyed. After removing the equipment, they dynamited the cave.

Meanwhile, part of the team had begun to interrogate some captured German scientists, and one confessed that he had hidden valuable scientific documents in a drum that had been dropped into a nearby cesspool. Goudsmit oversaw the somewhat daunting task of recovering the container, but the results were well worth the effort: The hidden drum held the chief reports on the German uranium project.

Back in November 1944, Goudsmit had concluded from his perusal of the captured Strasbourg documents that the German atomic program could never have produced a weapon. The finds in the Hechingen region confirmed this beyond a doubt. Germany had established no Oak Ridge, Hanford, or Los Alamos. In fact, they had erected only a small number of modest laboratories that were hidden in an underground cave, a made-over wing of a textile factory, and a few rooms in an old brewery. The message radioed back to the Pentagon in Washington phrased it succinctly: "Boris Pash has hit the jackpot."

"Isn't it wonderful that the Germans have no atomic bomb?" Goudsmit had earlier remarked to army major Robert K. Furman. "Now we won't have to use ours."

"Of course, you understand, Sam," the major replied, "if we have such a weapon, we are going to use it."

V

THE END IN EUROPE

1944–1945

THE AIRBORNE'S WATERY TRIUMPH

T. MICHAEL BOOTH AND DUNCAN SPENCER

It is hard to overestimate the importance of June 6, 1944, D day, in the history of the West. D day brought democracy back to the European continent for good and, backed by American military and economic power, established it in the heart of Europe. What realistic chance did the Nazi army have of repelling the Normandy invasion? Very little, probably, once Eisenhower had recognized his weather advantage—and once Hitler had refused to listen to the pleas of the commander of German forces in the Low Countries and Northern France, Field Marshal Erwin Rommel, for an extra panzer division. A more likely prospect was the one that Rommel aimed for: to keep the Allies penned in a narrow bridgehead, creating an Anzio on the channel, as it were.

But what once might have been the realm of futuristic war fiction did provide a much-needed chance for fluidity early on. That was the airborne landing, which could be as devastatingly disruptive to the enemy as it was risky for the attackers. (In 1941, the slaughter of Nazi paratroops in Crete had led the Germans to suspend airborne operations.) Both British and American parachute and glider drops in the hours after midnight were, as T. Michael Booth and Duncan Spencer write, "part success, part disaster." Target zones were missed. Men fell into marshes or the sea and drowned—or dangled helplessly from trees and were shot. Disorganized groups blundered through a darkened countryside, trying to link up with their fellows. In the area behind Utah Beach where the Americans of the 82nd and 101st Airborne Divisions came down, units were never larger than a company. But these were crack troops and eventually they began to accomplish their mission, seizing key bridges, roads, and towns. For all that we focus on the long-term geopolitical results of the Normandy landings, we should not forget that they were originally the sum of countless isolated melees, many of which became the unexpected hinges of the battle, bitter small encounters that could have big consequences. Brigadier General James Gavin and the men of the 82nd proved just that in the confused series of actions that centered on the bridges at La Fière and Chef-du-Pont. Their success would keep the Wehrmacht from concentrating superior forces against the bridge-head at Utah Beach.

T. Michael Booth and *Duncan Spencer* are the authors of *Para-trooper,* a biography of General James M. Gavin, from which this article was adapted.

BILL WALTON WATCHED BRIGADIER GENERAL JAMES MAURICE Gavin gripping the doorframe of the C-47 as it flew low over Normandy, buffeting through the cold air. Behind Gavin, Walton stood amidst a "stick" of eighteen paratroopers, straining under the weight of weapons, hooked by a thin static line to a jump cable. For the hundredth time, Walton, a civilian journalist who had begged to get on the plane, cursed this stupid idea. Now he could clearly see his own death in a dozen different versions. The noise was a drug, overwhelming. Numbed by the roar of laboring engines, air sucking and screeching past the metal plane, Walton kept his eyes on the figure in the doorway and tried not to think.

Below, the land looked flat as cardboard, but Walton knew there were thousands of German soldiers down there, ready to kill him. There would be no support or protection. The clumsy transports had flown through the coast-line defenses, flak rocking the planes. Preflight briefings had shown the tall poles: "Rommel's asparagus," which the Germans had set up to smash landing gliders. The beaches were bristling with guns and metal obstacles. But the planes droned on, dropping lower. The final stage of the European war, the invasion of occupied France and the destruction of Germany's waning military machine, would begin at the door where Gavin stood.

Walton was glad to be close to Gavin. Before taking off he had hoped for a big story for *Time* magazine on the man rapidly becoming a legend, but the hopes had dissolved and been replaced by fear. This was Walton's first jump. He vowed then and there never to do such a thing again—if only God would spare him this time, if only the parachute worked! Walton felt himself pushed forward toward the wind-tortured doorframe of the rocking aircraft. At least, he thought, the Germans would not expect them. Then came the buffeting blows and the sound of metal spattering. Flak pinged and pattered, random jagged bits of metal meant to cut, wreck, and kill. There would be no surprise.

That night, all over Normandy, paratroopers jumped in a broad band beyond the beaches, bent on many different errands of war. By the end of the next day, more than 1,000 men of the 82nd Airborne would be dead, wounded, or missing. Many would fall into the marshes and sink, or hit trees, where they would dangle to be murdered later. Some of the missing would be disabled, many with broken bones, and quickly taken prisoner.

Most of the men of the 82nd knew they were jumping into something very big, into history, like Crécy or Waterloo or Cannae. But for days they would fight alone, almost out of touch with the seaborne invaders, not knowing the outcome of the invasion.

The Normandy drop was Gavin's doorway to fame in battle. It captured the attention of the entire world and made him seem larger than life. Looking for heroes, Americans found them in Gavin and his paratroopers. The unforgettable images of the Normandy beach, by *Life* magazine photographer Robert Capa, gave Americans the picture of their boys storming ashore past wreckage, past even the corpses of their friends, but irresistible. Gavin's black-faced troopers fulfilled another fantasy: the elite, tough warriors who fought by stealth and surprise, who put their lives at risk behind enemy lines. Gavin was their beau ideal.

Thirty-seven years of age on the night of the Normandy drop, Gavin looked about ten years younger. Throughout his life, until arthritis from a jump injury and, later, Parkinson's disease slowed and finally stopped him, youth was his trademark. But not only youth, a particular brand of it. Lean to an extreme, his strength was of the sinew-and-muscle kind, the strength of endurance. He lived a Spartan regimen, uninterrupted since early childhood, of heavy manual work, long-distance marches, simplicity of diet, and a belief in the virtue of physical toughness.

At the height of his powers the night he hurled himself out of the transport at the German enemy, Gavin had been preparing for this moment for twenty years. He had spent most of his waking moments thinking about his work and ways to improve it. He had read almost continuously about the great soldiers of history, and he had written out favorite aphorisms from their recorded statements for his own reference. Now the hoped-for opportunity had come.

Suddenly the green light came on, the signal to jump, and Gavin, soon to

be the youngest major general since George Armstrong Custer, left Walton
with a last flashing image—the wind plastering dark cloth against the paratrooper's wiry arms, his form outlined by the naked light, both hands tensed
on the alloy doorway. Gavin flung himself forward and disappeared into the
prop blast. Like a suicidal caterpillar, the rest of the stick, automatons now,
pushed forward, a sharp metallic sound marking each man's exit. "Don't
push," Walton heard himself saying, "I'll go quick." Then he, too, reached the
door and jumped into the black-and-white photo below. Twisted and tossed
by the turbulence of the prop blast, his mind went numb, and then with a
wonderful lurch it all stopped. Silently, the canopy blossomed above his head,
and he was swaying, masterfully, above the earth. The ground approached
fast; then Walton heard gunfire and saw tracers streaming across the ground,
and his fear returned.

✦

JIM GAVIN LANDED hard, in an apple orchard about two miles from where
he was supposed to be, though he didn't know that until an hour later. At first,
he had no idea exactly where he was. Checking that all his parts worked after
his collision with the ground, he got out of his harness. About him the tree
branches hung low, and among the fallen blossoms cows grazed in the moonlight. Gavin's aide, Captain Hugo V. Olson, had landed nearby. The two men
"rolled up" their stick, then moved out toward heavy firing in the distance.

It was a calm, damp, mysterious spring night that Gavin would always remember. The Cotentin Peninsula in Normandy is difficult enough to move
about at best; at night and with the danger of ambush, it was treacherous. The
land lay in a checkerboard of ancestral fields surrounded by steep fences and
walls, some overgrown, some neglected—the characteristic hedgerows of rural Normandy. These walls were fortresses: piled with dirt and brush, often
heaped in stout mounds up to twenty feet high, and covered with trees and
tangled undergrowth. The Germans had already fortified the hedgerows with
rifle and machine-gun pits, and Gavin had found several, unmanned, scattered about the edge of the orchard. He knew that nervous German troops,
alerted by antiaircraft fire and the racket of the low-flying transports, were a
hazard. Lost paratroopers crackling through the underbrush invited vicious
close contact, but Gavin had to risk it. He needed to find the rest of the 508th
Regiment.

Right off the orchard was a small, worn, tree-lined road. Gavin and his little group walked along both sides of it, moving in crouched position with
M-1s at the ready. Then, about 400 yards down, they encountered a watery
marsh where they could see equipment bundles floating. Gavin wanted the

bundles retrieved because they contained critical gear—machine guns, bazookas, and radios. While some of the men went after them, a red light began flashing across the marsh, then a blue one. The red was an assembly marker for the 507th Regiment, the blue for the 508th. Gavin sent Olson out to contact those groups. Meanwhile, more paratroopers joined their party, now up to about ninety men.

Olson soon returned with news. He had found a railroad embankment on the far side, which told Gavin where they were. Checking his map, he could see they had overflown their zone and were just west of the Merderet River, about two miles north of La Fière bridge, one of the 82nd's objectives. The Germans had flooded the Merderet, creating the marsh, which had been hidden from aerial reconnaissance because the high grass disguised it as solid ground. What should have been a small river was now a thousand-yard-wide lake. The men of the 508th had landed on both sides and in the middle of the lake. Those on the other side had told Olson that they were moving out to La Fière. It was the nearest objective they knew of.

Gavin's paratroopers had little success retrieving the equipment bundles. The water was too deep and the bundles too heavy. They were collecting more men every minute, but most of them were of the 507th and green to combat. Furthermore, their commanders had told them to black out all rank insignia, so no one knew who the officers and NCOs were. The men were confused, unsure of themselves, and—exhausted by the shock of the jump—some were falling asleep. As German fire built, they took cover in the hedgerows, where it was almost impossible to organize them. Gavin was frustrated. With dawn approaching, he still had no idea what had happened to the rest of his command, and he had accomplished virtually nothing. He roused his disoriented men and moved out across the marsh and then south to La Fière.

✦

IT WAS AS WELL Gavin could not see the whole picture of the early hours of invasion. The drop had been part success, part disaster. Paratroopers of the 82nd and 101st Airborne Divisions had landed in Normandy all right, but they were widely dispersed. Individuals and small groups wandered isolated, or fell into skirmishes with the Germans in those early hours; for two or three days, few met their objectives as standard military units.

A small force of pathfinders, whose job it was to help guide the mass of troops following close behind them, had taken off from England about 10:00 P.M. on the night of June 5. Their specially trained pilots took a circular route to the drop, first to avoid the possibility of "friendly fire" from the fleet below, then to approach their targets from an unexpected side, the southwest. Along the way, things went seriously wrong. The planes encountered little antiair-craft fire, but as soon as they reached the Cotentin, they found themselves in thick turbulent clouds. The clouds cleared just as they reached the drop area, but by then the pilots had grown disoriented and only two pathfinder teams hit their drop zones.

About a half hour behind the pathfinders came the 101st Airborne Divi-sion with 485 aircraft, 52 gliders for heavy equipment, and nearly 7,000 para-troopers. They, too, hit the clouds, and soon their formations became wildly dispersed. The 82nd, about 6,400 paratroopers in 377 aircraft and 52 gliders, followed at about 11:00 P.M. They formed in the air and headed for the Co-tentin efficiently enough.

The 82nd's lead C-47s, containing the 505th Regiment and Major General Matthew Ridgway, the division commander, fared best. Their mission was to drop between the Merderet River and Sainte-Mère-Eglise to secure that town and the bridges at the hamlets of La Fière and Chef-du-Pont, while forming blocking forces near the towns of Neuville-au-Plain and Beuzeville-au-Plain. They were ordered to link up with forces of the 101st, which should have been between Sainte-Mère-Eglise and Utah beach itself. Like all the planes before them, the 505th transports ran into the clouds and bucked and twisted their way through blindly. Like the others, they were dispersed, but not so badly. About half of the men landed within one mile of their drop zones. Another 350 landed within two miles of their zones, and the rest of them, around 600, came to earth scattered as much as fourteen miles from their targets.

The 508th, with assistant division commander Gavin's plane, followed the 505th. It was supposed to secure the west side of the Merderet, facing the 505th; however, its drop accuracy was even worse. Men were so scattered that the regiment never formed elements larger than company size—and most units remained platoon size. Some men landed as far as twenty miles from their drop zones. Some went into the sea and drowned. One company landed almost complete—but it hit Utah Beach.

Time and retelling have obscured how random was the emergence of the battle groups. Gavin's own recollections are of organized units and certain ac-tions, and historian after historian has followed his pattern. In fact, it was never that simple. Most groups were at half strength and had in their ranks men of other battalions and regiments.

For the next few days, the little bridges of the Merderet River were the fo-cus of several battles that raged between the outnumbered paratroopers and the defending Germans. Larger numbers of men from both sides gradually moved toward them, intensifying the fighting. Fate gave the fiercest of all these fights—at La Fière—to Gavin.

The bridge at La Fière was critical because it spanned a place in the stream that could make a formidable German defense line. Gavin wanted to make sure it was taken. There were other possible objectives as well, including another bridge near Chef-du-Pont, which was also critical. Squatting in the hedgerows, Gavin made his plan: If he could move his motley force to the opposite side of the river, he could help the imminent bridge action at La Fière and also attack the Chef-du-Pont bridge.

First, he dispatched Lieutenant Colonel Arthur Maloney to see if a better way could be found to cross the flooded river. Then, because Chef-du-Pont was not far, less than two miles, and a Frenchman had told Gavin that there were no Germans there, he took his remaining men, commanded by Lieutenant Colonel Edwin J. Ostberg of the 507th, and moved south to Chef-du-Pont. Perhaps from there they could double back to La Fière. Meanwhile, Maloney's patrols succeeded only in exhausting themselves, finding no boats and no path. The Germans had destroyed them all.

When Gavin's small force reached the small town of Chef-du-Pont, a train was moving from the railway station. Gavin ordered it assaulted. As soon as his troopers opened fire, Germans aboard scattered and sprinted for the bridge. The train contained nothing but empty bottles and Normandy cheese. Disappointed, Gavin ordered his troopers west to the riverbank, where they discovered that rising water had turned the bridge and approaches into a causeway almost a mile wide. An island in the middle bristled with Germans, who immediately fired on them. Gavin ordered Ostberg to take the bridge "whenever it would be feasible," intending the assault to take place that night. Ostberg, a determined man, had other ideas.

While Gavin footed back to La Fière, trying to unlock the tactical situation facing him, an unfortunate incident occurred at Chef-du-Pont. Impatient and bent on seizing the bridge, Ostberg moved troopers closer to the bank. Suddenly a nearby German rose to surrender. A tired trooper shot him. Another German stood up, and he too was shot before anyone could call a cease-fire. Now the Germans who might have surrendered all together found themselves unwilling to retreat down the causeway and unable to surrender. They would fight to the last.

Ostberg organized a charge even though the bridge and the island lay a little over a hundred yards from the closest cover. About fifty brave paratroopers rushed straight into German fire. As soon as they reached the arch of the bridge, the colonel and five of his men were cut down by a stream of machine-gun bullets. (Ostberg survived his wounds, only to be killed later in Holland.) By this time, Maloney, sent by Gavin to take command, had arrived and mounted a second charge. This one stopped at about the same point with roughly the same effect, though Maloney was not wounded. Next, he and his crew crawled onto the bridge approach and fought at close quarters from one foxhole to the next with grenades and rifle fire. This went on inconclusively all afternoon. In the midst of it, Gavin recalled Maloney to La Fière, and command at Chef-du-Pont passed to Captain Roy Creek.

The stalemate then took a bad turn. The stubborn Germans wheeled up a fieldpiece to the western end of the causeway, and now the crouching troopers—numbering just over thirty—endured direct artillery fire. Creek looked to the rear of his position to discover a German platoon deploying for an assault. But help came from an unexpected direction. An American glider carrying a 57mm antitank gun, lumbering in on schedule, landed amidst Creek's position. It seemed miraculous. The troopers quickly turned the 57mm on the field gun across the marsh and scored a direct hit. Next, they turned it on the German infantry to their rear, breaking their ranks with a few shots. As they did, a reinforcing American platoon arrived. The crisis had passed.

Just as the sun set, Creek discovered a position north along the riverbank that offered a perfect field of fire to hammer the remaining Germans on the island. Within ten minutes, the island fell. So instead of being wiped out, Creek now had half a bridge, thirteen dead, and twenty-three wounded. But the western side still loomed a distant 700 yards away, and from all appearances, the Germans held it strongly.

Trouble came elsewhere. Because of the hedgerows, the small crossroads town of La Fière did not fall easily or swiftly, though it was defended by only one German platoon. The Americans assaulted with more than a battalion, but the Germans held all morning. The separate parts of several forces were unaware of their comrades; the hedgerows and the lack of radio communication led many American paratroop elements to assault the town piecemeal. It finally fell in the early afternoon, and A Company of the 1st Battalion of the 505th took up positions on the riverbank, on the north side of the road overlooking a causeway similar to the one at Chef-du-Pont. Captain Robert D. Rae, with a mixed batch of 507th and 101st Airborne men, held the south side of the road. Other 507th men had already crossed to the west side of the river; but they seemed a long way off.

✦

MEANWHILE, VERY little had been happening as it should have on the west bank. The two regiments that should have landed there had not, and only three significant battle groups had formed. The first, commanded by Colonel George V. Millett, had been cut off and battered by the German 91st Division around Amfreville. The second was under the leadership of Lieutenant Colonel Charles J. Timmes, the commander of the 2nd Battalion of the 507th. After extricating himself from the marsh, where he had nearly drowned, Timmes had moved toward the sound of gunfire near Amfreville. Along his cross-country route, he picked up more men. At Amfreville, large detachments of the 91st Division waited entrenched, and as Timmes and his party got close, the Germans responded with heavy fire. But seeing that they were overmatched, the Americans began a fighting withdrawal, hedgerow to hedgerow, with the Germans in pursuit. Finally, they reached the same orchard Gavin had left the night before. There, with their backs to the marsh, they dug a defensive perimeter. They were soon surrounded by Germans moving into the area.

The third group of American troops had been assembled by Lieutenant Colonel Thomas J. B. Shanley about three miles southwest of the bridge at La Fière, well behind German lines. His battalion was the only one of the 508th that was dropped somewhat intact, though their assembly took time. When, at dawn, he had collected as many men as he could, Shanley found himself facing serious German pressure just holding his own position. Artillery soon found the range of his foxholes, and machine-gun fire raked his force. He and his men prepared for a siege.

On the morning of D day, Colonel Timmes, in the apple orchard, sent a ten-man patrol under the command of Lieutenant Louis Levy to fortify the La Fière bridge. As Levy and the patrol, without radio or further orders, kept anxious watch at the bridge, several other American paratrooper bands passed by, but none of them stayed. They all sought objectives elsewhere. When the 505th began to fortify the east side of the river, they sent up an orange smoke signal, signifying friendly invasion forces. A relieved Levy on the west side, at Cauquigny, responded with orange smoke. The 505th did not know that their signal had been answered by a ten-man platoon and assumed that the 507th or the 508th were across the river in force. Shortly, a German battalion with tank support attacked Levy's little group from the west. The platoon fought bravely—they succeeded in disabling three of the German tanks—but, without relief from the 505th, they were soon forced to retreat to the orchard. At the end of D day, the Americans found themselves blinking with fatigue, but holding only the eastern halves of the two critical bridgeways they had been dropped to capture.

✦

ELSEWHERE, THINGS were better. The critical town in the 82nd's area of operations was Sainte-Mère-Eglise, the transportation hub for the area, the intersection of all local roads. Holding it meant German reinforcements to the beaches would be severely disrupted. Early on the morning of D day, it fell easily to Lieutenant Colonel Edward ("Cannonball") Krause's 3rd Battalion of the 505th, becoming the first French town liberated in World War II. Krause had learned from a drunken Frenchman, who gaily offered to guide him, that only one enemy platoon remained there; the Germans had thought the fight over. Krause found an ugly sight. Pilots confused by a house fire had dropped their sticks right on Sainte-Mère-Eglise. The Germans had killed most of the unfortunate troopers as they hit the ground. Dead and wounded GIs lay on the streets; many were hanging from telephone poles and buildings. One man dangled from the church steeple for hours, saving his life by feigning death. Fortunately, because of Krause's timely arrival, by noon on D day Sainte-Mère-Eglise had become the center of 82nd Airborne operations—and a target of German wrath.

By the time Gavin returned to the La Fière bridge in midafternoon, the situation had deteriorated badly. As he approached, retreating 505th troopers rushed past with news that the Germans had broken through. Aghast, Gavin ordered them to turn back. He found Colonel Roy E. Lindquist, the ranking man, who had a small reserve of about eighty men, and double-timed for the causeway, meanwhile sending a runner for Maloney's men, still at Chef-du-Pont. Gavin arrived at the causeway ready for a fight.

That afternoon, the same German battalion that had scattered Levy's little band launched an armored attack across the causeway. A Company of the 505th, under the command of Captain John J. Dolan, dug in at the eastern end of the causeway and took the attack head-on. The Germans led with a powerful barrage of mortar and artillery fire, then came on with two French Renault tanks, infantry running in their wake. Opposing them, Dolan's men squatted in formerly German rifle pits, supported by two bazooka teams.

The bazookas did their work on the thinly armored French tanks; both stopped after a close-range duel of bazooka rounds and point-blank cannon fire. The foot soldiers, now without their shield, were exposed, cut down, or routed back across the causeway by accurate American fire. Dolan's men still controlled the approach to the causeway, their success bolstering their confidence. The Germans returned several more times, but troopers kept driving them back; however, the artillery barrage never ceased. By morning, it would cost Dolan six more men.

✦

GAVIN COULD DO nothing further at either Chef-du-Pont or La Fière, so he moved back toward Sainte-Mère-Eglise and established a command post between the two bridgeheads. His awkward position baffled him. As yet, he had no word from Utah Beach, so he did not know that the landing had gone smoothly and seaborne troops were bearing down on Sainte-Mère-Eglise. In fact, that night the vanguard would reach a point only about a mile east. He had no idea what fate had held for the paratroopers on the west side of the Merderet. He had no jeep or truck to shuttle between his two critical bridgeheads. However, he did have radio contact with division headquarters just outside Sainte-Mère-Eglise, where Ridgway had set up his command post, and he knew that the town was under siege from several points. At evening, headquarters finally sent him a jeep with a radio, and he succeeded in raising the embattled Colonel Shanley, dug in far to the west. Shanley had little good news to share, but at least Gavin knew he was still fighting.

As night fell on D day, Gavin lay down to rest. For a blanket, all he could find was a parachute laid across a dead trooper. He could not bring himself to use the man's shroud for a blanket, so he found a camouflage net, lay down against a hedgerow to give himself shelter from artillery fire, and fell asleep. A runner soon brought a summons from Ridgway's staff. Gavin walked with Olson through the full moonlight back to Sainte-Mère-Eglise, only to find that the message had been in error. Ridgway was asleep himself and annoyed at the visit. Frustrated and weary, Gavin trudged back to his command post and resumed his rest.

This trivial incident rankled in both men for years, even though both were no doubt blameless. Communications are the first thing to be lost in the chaos of combat. It marked the beginning of a coolness between Ridgway and Gavin. Years later, in his own writing, Gavin described the summons by Ridgway as related here. Ridgway, however, in his autobiography, describes the visit from Gavin as if he had been awakened by a panicked messenger bringing news of a counterattack on La Fière. Both of them made a point of mentioning it years after the war. It signaled a break in their friendship, or at least the end of reverence, the start of rivalry. Ridgway would maintain that a distraught Gavin had come to ask for permission to withdraw from La Fière that night, an implication Gavin resented.

Dawn of June 7 found the 82nd in a precarious triangle of French soil. Time was against them, for unless relieved, and unless the overall invasion plan was working, the 82nd had no chance. Ridgway had gathered only about one-quarter of his division. The Germans had tanks, superior numbers, and vastly superior firepower. The 82nd's position was anchored by corners resting on La Fière, Chef-du-Pont, and Sainte-Mère-Eglise. The division's lower echelons still had no assurance of an advance from the beachhead. Soldiers' rumors spread that the invasion had failed. Ridgway and Gavin, however, ignored the rumors. They were determined to hold what they had no matter what—especially Sainte-Mère-Eglise.

The Germans had not finished with La Fière. That morning, after a two-hour mortar barrage, they launched a final attack on the bridge with all they had. Four French tanks led the way. Once again the valiant bazooka men fought their duel, this time helped by a lone 57mm gun to their rear. The combination wrecked the first tank, and that stalled the others. But it gave the Germans a steel shield of wrecked tanks just thirty-five yards from Dolan's lead platoon, under the command of Lieutenant William A. Oakley. The Germans zeroed their mortars on the ground and kept up small-arms and tank fire. Oakley fell, badly hit, almost immediately and was dragged to the rear, where he died just a few hours later. Sergeant William D. Owens, leader of the first squad, replaced him. Owens found himself in a desperate situation. More than half his men had fallen already, and the survivors had little ammunition. His machine guns fired so fast they quit from the heat. The company first sergeant grabbed the wounded and threw them back into the fight.

Owens, a quiet Detroit punch-drill operator in peacetime, stood his ground and ran from man to man redistributing ammo from the dead and wounded. When his gunners died, he took over their machine guns. Later he said:

> The artillery shells and mortars were coming in like machine-gun fire. I don't know how it was possible to live through it. Then the infantry came again and we gave them everything we had. The machine gun I had was so hot it quit firing. I took Private McClatchy's BAR, he had been wounded earlier, and I fired it until I ran out of ammunition. I then took a machine gun that belonged to a couple of men who took a very near hit. They were killed. The gun had no tripod, so I rested it across a pile of dirt and used it. With this and one other machine gun and a 60mm mortar, we stopped them, but they had gotten to within twenty-five yards of us.

Then, abruptly, the Germans called a halt. Owens was down to fourteen men. He kept firing and yelling for them to hold on. He had no radio because his radio man had taken a direct hit from a German 88mm gun, so he sent a runner to Dolan describing the situation and asking for orders. His answer came back in writing: "I don't know of a better place than this to die." Owens passed along the message, and the survivors hung on. Suddenly, the Germans raised a flag with a red cross. Firing tapered off, then ceased. The Germans indicated they wanted to evacuate their wounded—and their other soldiers went with them. One platoon had broken the back of the last German attempt to secure the bridge at La Fière. The tide had risen to a height, and now Gavin could plan his own attack.

He had a small mobile reserve. As pressure came at the critical points, he kept moving Lindquist and a scratch bunch to the rescue. Both he and Ridgway wondered how long they could hold, for German infantry, armor, and artillery continued to threaten Sainte-Mère-Eglise. Unknown to the airborne commanders, help was coming: The armored task force under Colonel Edson D. Raff had landed on D day as planned, and Raff rushed them toward Sainte-Mère-Eglise with all the speed the armor could make. But two miles east of the town, the Germans had constructed a strongpoint of infantry and 88mm cannon. Not only did it stall Raff's column, it occupied a vantage point overlooking the landing zones designated for gliders. The 88s hit four of Raff's armored vehicles. Then, as the sun set, the gliders came winging in toward a double death trap. The field was too small for proper landings, so most crash-landed heavily. Then, those who survived the crash came under fire from the Germans. Shaken soldiers were unable to defend themselves as they fought to get out of the flimsy planes. In minutes, the landing zone was strewn with crashed gliders and dead and dying glidermen, while Raff could only look on helplessly.

Although at that time the 82nd had no radio link with the outside world, one patrol had gotten out word of the paratroopers' predicament, so the commanders on Utah Beach knew the situation. As soon as General J. Lawton "Lightning Joe" Collins landed on D-plus-one and heard, he ordered a reserve tank battalion, the 746th under Lieutenant Colonel D. G. Hupfer, forward to break through.

✦

ON THE MORNING of D-plus-one, German forces launched an assault on Sainte-Mère-Eglise. They opened with an artillery barrage, supported with self-propelled guns. Lieutenant Colonel Ben Vandervoort's 505th troopers resisted with verve. They had been holding well against the Germans, and their confidence ran high. They yielded no ground except to evacuate wounded and to readjust fields of fire. At noon, the 8th Infantry under Colonel James Van

Fleet arrived, along with Hupfer's and Raff's tanks, followed by General Collins himself. With the tanks and the help of the 8th Infantry, Vandervoort's paratroopers counterattacked immediately. German troops in the Sainte-Mère-Eglise area were decisively thrown back that afternoon. The liberation of the town was final.

After the 8th and the armor had arrived, the triangle of ground held by the 82nd no longer seemed so tenuous. But the bridges remained blocked, half held by strong German forces, and the Millett, Timmes, and Shanley units, isolated on the west side of the Merderet, remained stranded. Ridgway and Gavin evolved a plan. They would break the deadlock with fresh 325th glider infantry, who had just landed. On the morning of June 8, D-plus-two, the 505th, with elements of the 325th in support and assisted by the 8th Infantry, would attack north toward Montebourg to expand the area the division already held. Meanwhile, the 1st Battalion of the 325th would attack across the river, using a fortuitously discovered ford across the Merderet between the two causeways, to relieve Timmes in the orchard. They then intended to smash the Germans at Cauquigny from the rear. Simultaneously, Lindquist was to assault the Chef-du-Pont causeway with 507th and 508th troopers and relieve Shanley. Millett's force would attack toward the 325th men and in the process break out themselves.

The assault by the 505th proved difficult. The troopers and glidermen advanced rapidly against heavy, determined German resistance, hedgerow to hedgerow; however, the 8th Infantry assisting was not able to make such rapid progress, stalling the overall attack.

Lower-level commanders were allowed to make their own decisions on the assault across the Merderet. Trouble began with Lindquist's group at Chef-du-Pont, where Shanley was ordered by radio to clear out the opposite end of the causeway before an attack was attempted. Shanley sent a twenty-man scratch patrol forward, led by Lieutenant Woodrow W. Millsaps, which proceeded to fight one of the hardest engagements of the invasion. Everyone considered Millsaps an eccentric, but this night he proved pure warrior. As his men approached the head of the causeway, they struck machine gun after machine gun. At first his column buckled, and some of the men tried to run, but Millsaps steadied them. They kept moving forward, methodically destroying the German machine guns with grenades and accurate fire, hedgerow after hedgerow. Then they reached a road junction near the causeway where three machine gunners and riflemen waited. Again Millsaps urged his men forward, and again they destroyed the German positions. Millsaps himself was knocked down three times by German grenades, but neither he nor his men hesitated. They were in a killing frenzy; each man was alone, paying no attention to those who fell. They fought and killed until the Germans broke before their charge. Now Lindquist needed only to charge the causeway.

But Lindquist decided not to mount the attack. He had seen what the fixated Millsaps had not—that artillery was failing near the causeway—and he feared shells would hit the trucks he planned to send over the bridge, blocking it. After all his effort, Millsaps was mortified, and he begged Lindquist to go. But Lindquist would not be moved. Just before dawn, Shanley withdrew the survivors of Millsaps's charge, squandering a military advantage gained through horrible sacrifice. He did not send a relief force across for another full day. Meanwhile, Shanley's men—low on food, water, ammunition, and medical supplies—sweated in their foxholes.

North of La Fière, the 325th men led by 1st Battalion commander Lieutenant Colonel Terry Sanford, made their move across the ford. As they crossed, they drew not a shot, but as soon as they reached the first hedgerow, German machine gunners found their range. The men advanced, but the fight became confused in the hedgerows. Companies lost contact with one another, and the fight grew desperate at close quarters. Ridgway, watching from across the river, remembered it as one of the most intense combat actions he saw in the war. It proved fruitless, and Sanford and his men ended up in retreat, joining Timmes beneath the apple trees.

During the withdrawal of one platoon, Private First Class Charles N. DeGlopper stood defiantly with his Browning automatic rifle, acting as rear guard for his friends until he was killed. He was the largest man then in the 82nd, and those who were there remember the last sight of him, his six-foot-seven-inch, 240-pound frame illuminated by the flickering muzzle flashes of his weapon. When he finally fell dead of multiple wounds, his comrades were on safer ground. DeGlopper was awarded the Congressional Medal of Honor, but his action, too, had been in vain. The Germans still held Cauquigny, the causeway remained useless to the Allies, and a battalion of the 325th now sat bottled up with Shanley. As for Millett's men, they were unable to break through to Shanley or Timmes, and Millett himself was captured.

With the dawn of June 9, D-plus-three, Ridgway faced difficult decisions. His night assaults—which had not been Gavin's responsibility because of their command structure—had been humiliating failures. Now Collins suggested that his newly arrived 90th Division be used to force the La Fière causeway. Ridgway refused to consider it. He was far too proud and determined to let others do what had been assigned to him. He discussed it with Gavin, who agreed, and Ridgway gave the mission to him. Gavin was to force a crossing and drive the Germans back westward toward Amfreville. For the mission, Ridgway augmented his already stretched forces with the 3rd Battalion of the 325th, under the command of Lieutenant Colonel Charles A. Carrell, and one company of 507th paratroopers commanded by Captain Rae. This unit had been defending the La Fière side of the causeway since D day and had been severely punished by the Germans. In support, Gavin also had use of the 90th Division's artillery, what artillery the 82nd itself could assemble, and twelve Sherman tanks. They scheduled the attack for the morning of June 10, D-plus-four.

Psychologically, the 3rd Battalion was hardly ready for the task it had drawn. The objective looked daunting from the far shore. The Merderet was 500 yards across at that point, and the men would be silhouetted without cover on the causeway as they charged its length. To make matters worse, this battalion had been part of the 101st and was given to the 82nd at a preinvasion reorganization. Carrell thought Ridgway and Gavin were going to sacrifice the transferred battalion. His attitude was infectious, and the troops had little enthusiasm for their mission.

Gavin himself was uneasy with it on the morning of the attack. To get a closer look, he and the commander of 90th Division artillery, Brigadier General John M. Devine, crawled out onto the causeway as close as they dared. Gavin precisely pinpointed targets he wanted the artilleryman to hit. Meanwhile, Olson lined up the tanks to give direct fire support at any targets across the river they could find. By the time Gavin ran, crouching, back from the causeway, it was 9:00 A.M.

A spring-morning calm fell over the placid Merderet waters. It might have been a pretty, deep green landscape, with the hump of the bridge the focus, except for the German fire that raked the American positions. But Gavin saw no scenery; he worried about the glidermen. Their commander had made it clear that he thought the causeway charge stood little chance. To hedge his bets, Gavin called over Colonel Maloney and Captain Rae, both men he trusted. Maloney looked the part that day. He was a huge man, six feet four inches tall and about 240 pounds. The morning of the assault, a close artillery round had sent a large fragment his way, ripping his helmet and gouging a deep wound in the side of his head. Maloney, who could have honorably stood down from the action, had his head bandaged and found a new helmet. When Gavin summoned him that morning, he noticed how tough Maloney looked with his hulking form and blood-streaked stubble of red beard.

Gavin gave brief instructions. He told Maloney to have Rae ready to charge instantly if the 325th assault faltered. He wanted them to "yell their heads off" and attack through the 325th in order to carry along the faint-of-heart. Rae and Maloney walked back to brief the anxious troopers, who took the news hard, for a glance showed every man he would be under fire from three sides for 500 yards of hard running. Maloney told them they owed it to Timmes and his men. They would give it a try.

Gavin ordered the 325th glidermen to move into jump-off position using a walled road that afforded a covered approach to the causeway. At 10:30 A.M., artillery, small arms, and tanks cut loose at the Germans' positions on the west bank. It was vicious and accurate. Gavin thought it seemed the whole shore-line caught fire. Stunned Germans with bleeding ears jumped from their positions and dashed across the causeway to surrender. The barrage ceased, and a short lull followed. The Americans had planned to end the barrage with a smoke screen to shield the charging troopers. Everyone waited for its welcome sight, but it never happened—the artillery batteries had no smoke. Then the Germans recovered from the barrage and began firing. The wall shielding the glidermen vibrated with the impact of bullets, and German artillery and mortars pummeled the causeway and the shoreline. Gavin, crouching on a rise to the rear, expected the glidermen to come into view as they charged forward, but they didn't appear. Incensed, he ran to Carrell by the wall and shouted, "Go! Go! Go!"

Carrell yelled back, "I don't think I can do it!"

Gavin stopped in his tracks and asked, "Why not?"

"I'm sick," Carrell responded.

Gavin's voice fell almost to a whisper and he said, "Okay, you're through." In Carrell's place, Colonel Harry Lewis, the 325th's commander, appointed the regiment's S-3, Arthur W. Gardner, to command.

Gardner ordered his new command to move, and they did, but not as they should have. Most of the lead platoon took off, but as the next group moved up, a man fell dead in the gap in the wall, a bullet through his brain. The men behind him froze. As a result, the initial assault consisted of about three squads, thirty men. They charged into the combined weapons of the better part of a German regiment. Captain Al Ireland, Gavin's S-1 with the 505th and a longtime friend, remembered it as a "firestorm of shell and whining bullets." Yet that first bunch of glidermen did not waver. Arms pumping hard, they charged on and reached the other side, miraculously nearly intact. It was not until they had made it across that they realized no one had followed them. Still they pushed on, and they began rolling up German positions in relentlessly sharp actions at close quarters.

Soon, other glidermen overcame their shock and, with officers and NCOs kicking them, moved forward. Accurate German fire cut down many. Others simply lost nerve and lay in the road ditches. As Gavin watched, the causeway became strewn with the living and the dead. Many men withered into frozen immobility, as if by recoiling they could somehow avoid death. Gavin knew it was the moment between success and failure. He, Ridgway, and Maloney ran out onto the causeway and urged the men on—Maloney bellowing in his deep voice, Ridgway setting a calm example as he tried to move a disabled tank blocking the way. Troopers remember Gavin telling soldiers, "Son, you can do it." All three officers were without cover, yet none of them was hit. The forward observer for the artillery, crouching in his foxhole, was stunned when Ridgway appeared and thanked him for the good barrage that had preceded the first wave.

Gavin turned to Maloney and told him to bring on Rae. Maloney signaled, and Rae led about ninety troopers in a mad rush onto the causeway. Now the wrecked tank proved an obstacle. The dead, the wounded, and those seeking cover filled the space behind and beside it. The wreck offered respite to shocked soldiers who could find nothing to move them on. Rae's men charged the tank like a football line. Kicking, prying, and pushing, they manhandled men out of the way and broke the jam, and their charge rolled on. Troopers ran, fired, reloaded, and ran some more. The wave of olive drab carried forward until it swept into the German embankment. With them went many glidermen who had also been trying to get through, and now the causeway and the bridge—though bodies were already stacked in the gutters—filled with running, shouting Americans sweeping around the wreck and forward. When the wave hit the Germans, they withered and began surrendering in droves.

Many who were there, including Gavin, give Rae and his troopers credit for carrying the day, and they did break the attack loose; but they had help. The small contingent of glidermen had gone first and grappled in the teeth of the German defenses, so when Rae's assault came, German fire at the causeway had slackened somewhat. Rae's arrival consolidated a toehold at Cauquigny, but surviving Germans beyond that toehold fought on desperately to contain the breakthrough, and the glidermen and paratroopers trying to push beyond Cauquigny west toward Amfreville ran into stiffer and stiffer resistance.

Once the wreckage was cleared, Gavin returned to the causeway and continued pushing men forward. They needed every man possible to strengthen their assault. When, around noon, all available men and tanks were across, Gavin went to Cauquigny himself, where he found glidermen and paratroopers still routing the last resolute Germans out of firing positions. He learned that his forward troopers had expanded the bridgehead fast, relieving Timmes's and Shanley's positions. He headed for Shanley first, because he had to know what shape the men were in after hanging on alone. He needed them now to expand the bridgehead farther.

As he moved gingerly along the riverbank, Gavin found a dead paratrooper, still in harness, hanging from a tree. After the recent vicious action, the sight angered him deeply. The Germans had shot the helpless man, rather than capturing him as the professional code dictated. With his rage came the determination to push punishing offensive operations.

He found Shanley's unit battered but still game. After grouping two battalions of 325th men, Rae's troopers, and Timmes's and Shanley's, he set off to find Ridgway in order to make plans. Gavin wanted his troops pushing westward as relentlessly as possible to expand the bridgehead and to beat back the Germans from the counterattack that he knew must come.

Sure enough, even as Gavin conferred with Ridgway late that afternoon, the Germans hit back, hard. As evening fell, the Americans started to break. A radio message from Colonel Lewis, the 325th commander, told Gavin the new bridgehead was collapsing. He broke off his hurried conference with Ridgway and ran back across the river to the 325th command post. German guns were sending panicked men streaming rearward, and when Gavin reached the 325th, chaos ruled. Lewis had collapsed from shock. Medics gave him an injection and evacuated him to the rear. (No one knew it then, but he had cancer and died just months later.) In his place Lieutenant Colonel Herbert Sitter, the regimental executive officer, took command. Gavin found Sitter at Cauquigny, recently taken, preparing a withdrawal. Gavin asked what he was doing. Sitter responded, "I can't hold."

Gavin's eyes became icy gray slits, and he told the shaken colonel before him, "We are going to counterattack with every resource we have—including you, regimental clerks, headquarters people, and anyone else we can get our hands on with a weapon." Sitter blanched but did as he had been ordered. Then Gavin located Maloney. The giant, somehow unscathed in the charge, stood calm and ready for instructions. They ran back to the causeway, where, for the second time that day, Maloney stood on the road and forced men back into battle. Gavin remembered it as a magnificent sight—Maloney, this time holding a broken-off tree limb in his hands, bellowing that no one was going to get by him. Gavin's place was now with his forward elements, and he headed for the front lines, farther west of the bridgehead.

That night, the 90th Division arrived and relieved the 82nd. The roads to the beach were now clear of Germans, and American tanks and infantry plowed inland. The Wehrmacht had lost its chance to concentrate superior forces against the beach. Allied air pressure prevented them from reinforcing at the decisive moment, and every day thousands of British and American troops streamed across those beaches into Normandy. The initial crust of enemy behind Utah Beach, caught between strong forces on the beaches and the stubborn resistance of the paratroopers, had been ripped up badly. The Germans had yielded the beaches and the low Merderet country, principally because of the double blow dealt them from behind.

✦

AT THIS POINT the 82nd's involvement might well have been over, but it continued to play a vital role in cutting off the Cotentin Peninsula. Along the way, it mauled the better parts of four German divisions—including the hated 91st, which had shot defenseless paratroopers caught in trees. While Cherbourg was being taken, a new corps—the VIII, under Major General Troy Middleton—was created. Middleton was given the 82nd to use as needed to punch southward; by the end of June, Middleton had ordered the division to assist with the breakout from the hedgerow country: The 82nd was to provide the main punch in the center.

Ridgway was happy to oblige to please higher command, but Gavin voiced strong misgivings. The division was badly understrength. In many of the combat companies, actual strength totaled around 50 men or less (at least one mustered just 12); there should have been over 150. At least two of his regimental commanders protested the attack order. Gavin concurred, and he took the issue to Ridgway.

Ridgway was unbending, and the division jumped off as planned. Gavin's protests and Ridgway's insistence that they continue attacking fueled ill feelings between the two men. Gavin felt Ridgway was wrong, that he did not understand the limits of his own men. There were many other units available for the job, and it was long past time when the paratroops should have been withdrawn and the division rebuilt.

Yet the breakout attack went off well. The desperately understrengthed companies reached all their assigned objectives. Airborne was beginning to acquire a reputation for performance. Higher command was once again impressed by what those "crazy characters" could do. But Gavin's fears were also confirmed. The final attack, in heavy rain from a bridgehead at Pont-l'Abbé, carried them to the outskirts of La Haye-du-Puits with such speed that the other divisions were left lagging, and higher command had to halt the paratroops to protect their exposed flanks. The hedgerow fighting proved costly once again. Understrengthed regiments became more so, and several battalion commanders were wounded, including Maloney and Shanley. Other notables, such as Lieutenant Louis Levy, died. When the 82nd Airborne Division finally pulled out of the front lines to return to England, sixteen of its original twenty-one regimental and battalion commanders had been killed, captured, or wounded. In total, the division lost 46 percent in killed, wounded, and missing.

Losses like these have paralyzed most divisions; however, throughout the Normandy campaign, the 82nd never lost combat effectiveness in spite of it. And somewhere, during the desperate night actions and the bloody slog through the hedgerows, legend descended on the division. If their exploits had not been widely reported before, they were after Normandy. Though their dead lay strewn from Sainte-Mère-Eglise to Amfreville to La Haye-du-Puits, their deeds and rakish air captured the American imagination at a time of one of the nation's greatest successes. And above them rose the image of their lean, handsome, and articulate commander, Slim Jim Gavin. He had long been known to higher command. Now the press took him, and he became a public figure. He had achieved more from his war than he had ever planned, but now he wanted sole command of a division. And he was about to get it.

ROMMEL'S LAST BATTLE

SIR DAVID FRASER

Though Field Marshal Erwin Rommel gained immortality—and his nickname, "The Desert Fox"—in North Africa, his last campaign in Normandy may have been his most brilliant. The year 1944 found Rommel in command of Army Group B, responsible for the defense of much of Northwestern Europe. The man who was the master of mobile operations reasoned that the invasion had to be defeated at the water's edge, and he set about organizing a formidable defensive system. His hope, naive in the face of the implacable Allied hostility toward Nazi Germany, was to beat the Allies in the West and make a decent peace with them, while releasing reinforcements to hold off the Soviets in the East. The equation on the other side was simple. The farther inland the Allies penetrated, the greater was their chance of victory. Once they were ashore, Rommel recognized, the *Materialschlacht,* the material battle, was bound to prevail. Moreover, the complete Allied command of the air made maneuver difficult for the defenders, as well as reinforcement and supply. But at a time when decision making on the spot was at a premium, Hitler refused to relinquish control of even small details. It was Stalingrad all over again: Rommel never had the operational freedom—or the availability of panzer divisions near the invasion coast—that might have enabled him to change history.

At Normandy, he fought, as it were, with one hand tied behind his back. Even so, it was a battle that he conducted with his usual skill. Rommel was a master not just of the offense but of the bold defense—a distinction that gave him the edge of greatness over a man he just missed encountering, George S. Patton. By this time Rommel, who was a German patriot first, was convinced that Hitler had to go. He was one of the few people on either side who foresaw the prospect of another epic ideological conflict (one we would come to know as the Cold War) and he was prepared to do everything in his power to ensure that the Western Allies reached Berlin before the Soviets. What would have happened if Rommel had not sustained a near-mortal wound from a strafing British plane on July 17? Would he have been able to put together his inchoate scheme to let the Allies through? Or would Hitler's emissaries simply (as the Argentines later put it) have "suicided" him a month or so earlier than they actually did?

What, finally, were the attributes that made Erwin Rommel stand out in a war that was notable for its fine generals? As Sir David Fraser writes, his "especial flair was undoubtedly for the battle itself, for the cut and thrust of maneuver, for personal leadership at the point of decision, above all the speed and energy with which he decided and acted." Rommel, Fraser concludes, "was one who believed war seldom forgives hesitation or delay."

Sir David Fraser, once one of Britain's senior generals, has made a distinguished second career as a historian of World War II. This article was excerpted from *Knight's Cross: A Biography of Erwin Rommel.*

FIELD MARSHAL ERWIN ROMMEL WAS AT HIS HOME NEAR ULM, in Germany, visiting his wife on her birthday, when the call came early that morning: Allied paratroops had landed in Normandy. His last campaign was beginning, a campaign that claimed him as a casualty and ended in the total defeat of the German armed forces. Like Napoleon's, his last campaign, his last battle, ended in catastrophe.

Rommel conducted it with a good deal of internal torment. Throughout the weeks until he was carried wounded from the field, he was a man within whose mind and heart there were deep divisions, and he found it decreasingly possible to heal them. He was three different persons simultaneously. With part of himself he was simply the good, brave, disciplined soldier he had always been, fighting—and losing through no fault of his own—a battle against the odds, doing his intelligent best during that battle, reacting with skill and fortitude to depressing military circumstances, maintaining men's spirits as far as he could, never giving in. The operational dilemmas were comparatively straightforward, but they were appalling, and Rommel faced them with the mounting sense that his superiors were refusing to recognize the truth of the situation as it evolved.

With another part of himself he was the patriot with a perfectly clear strategic sense, who realized—as he had realized when first formulating his philosophy for the defense of France; as, indeed, in Africa and then in Italy— that Germany's only hope lay in peace, that the material balance of power was so hostile to Germany that the nation could be saved ultimate and total destruction only by reaching an arrangement with the Western powers. He believed that this arrangement could best be—perhaps could only be—secured when the Wehrmacht had won some sort of temporary success in the West, had eliminated for a little while the immediate threat of land war on two fronts; and the belief strengthened his efforts—unavailing efforts as it turned out—to win the defensive battle on the ground.

With the third part of himself, in those weeks, Rommel drew inevitable conclusions from the second, from the patriot who saw the strategic situation clear. These conclusions were, it may be contended, tardy. They were certainly unpalatable. The final obstacle to peace lay in the person and character of the führer himself. Hitler, clear-sighted in this at least, had said that nobody would make peace with him. The führer had, as Rommel had by now and unwillingly learned in part, placed himself beyond the international pale, was adjudged in much of the world not simply as an enemy statesman but as a criminal. With Hitler ruling, Germany could expect nothing but a continuance of war, of pounding to pieces by the Western air forces; could ultimately expect only the overrunning by the Red Army from the east. As June became July, Rommel struggled with all three parts of himself.

✦

THE ORDEAL BEGAN midmorning on June 6, when he became positive that an invasion was taking place. He drove back to France, stopping at Nancy to telephone his headquarters at La Roche-Guyon, along the Seine, to check that the 21st Panzer, the only tank division within reach of what appeared the enemy's main landing area, had been committed to counterattack. It had, at 7:30 A.M., five minutes after the easternmost (and nearest) enemy landings from the sea had touched down. The 21st Panzer, however, was considerably dispersed. Its four panzer grenadier battalions had been deployed on either side of the Orne River, around and north of Caen, to stiffen the static division (716th) responsible for that part of the coast. Panzer grenadiers possessed mobility and heavy weapons; they constituted a counterattack force, and their presence in that sector undoubtedly helped it, but the commander of the panzer division, Major General Edgar Feuchtinger, reasonably complained that the dispersion—ordered by Rommel—meant that his strength was everywhere dissipated. In the conditions of Normandy, and according to

Rommel's convictions, dissipated strength mattered less than the ability to respond instantly wherever the enemy's initial blows fell. But, as Rommel had forecast, movement was desperately difficult and traffic chaos considerable throughout that and the next day and throughout the area of operations.

When Rommel reached La Roche-Guyon at half past nine in the evening, he was briefed on the situation as far as it was known. The enemy was ashore; ashore in shallow beachheads, separated from each other, but ashore. He had not been dislodged or driven into the sea by immediate counterattack, but neither had he been able to establish himself at certain key points such as Caen.

In dealing with these events, commentators on both sides of the line have periodically criticized both Rommel's dispositions and his absence. His deployments have been blamed for reducing the impact of the 21st Panzer Division's counteraction, by dispersing the division; and for denying to the other sectors targeted by the Allied invasion any possibility of armored counterstroke at all, since no panzers were within reach. But Rommel had known perfectly well that not every mile of threatened coastline could be within easy reach of panzer reserves; "immediate" or "timely" counterattack must mean action when the enemy was still within the coastal defensive zone. Had he been given operational control of more of the OKW (German high command) reserve in Panzer Group West, he would have been able to deploy some tanks farther west, able to counterattack early toward Bayeux or Carentan; but his own resources had not run to that—that which alone might have tipped the scales.

As to his absence in Germany and the time lost before he reappeared, it is true that some on the German side have believed that Rommel, on June 6, might have somehow inspired earlier counteraction. Given the fact of Allied air power, however, given the delay imposed on every daylight German operational move, given the distant deployment areas of the panzer reserves, and given the fact that Rommel could not have sought a decision until he was *sure* that this was a major assault, it is difficult to believe that his presence, however persuasive, could have decisively affected the panzer counterattack on June 6.

It is surely also true that, given the weight of Allied assault, the weight of aerial bombardment and ship-to-shore bombardment (often stunning the Germans with its accuracy and lethality), the strength simultaneously at several points, together with the extremely successful airborne assault—even a heavier and earlier counterattack by the 21st Panzer Division would have affected only one local situation. The Allied invasion was named Overlord, and it was destined to overcome. Material superiority, ingenuity, practice, and planning—together with human courage and resourcefulness—triumphed. Only wholehearted acceptance by Hitler and the OKW of Rommel's "heretical" proposal, to deploy more panzer divisions under his own operational control and very near the coast, might have changed history.

By the end of what the enemy called D day, France had been invaded. What Rommel had hoped to forestall had happened. The battle, however, was still confined to the coastal zone or near it. The penetration toward Caen was only about four miles. The invaders might yet be driven into the sea; though he did not know it, Rommel's defending forces had checked the Allied advance many miles short of the objectives that General Bernard Montgomery, commanding all the Anglo-American invasion forces, had set. But unless wholly extraordinary successes could be achieved in the next few days, Germany, on June 7, was facing what Rommel had always regarded as certain to lead to ultimate disaster in the field: a protracted land war on two main fronts.

✦

THE TWO PRINCIPAL AREAS of concern to Rommel were the sector around Caen, in the east, and Cherbourg, on the Cotentin Peninsula, in the west. As long as the enemy could be denied any significant progress in these two directions, there was a chance of smashing him by counterattacks, necessarily local though these might be. Denied Caen, the invader's left flank had no firm hinge and was vulnerable; while without Cherbourg he had no major port. During June 7 and 8, there was heavy fighting both west and east of the Orne River, north of Caen. The 12th SS Panzer Division had now joined the battle and, on the night of June 8, attacked strongly, using its powerful Panther tanks, toward the sea. Rommel had visited the Caen front that day. He called on the redoubtable Obergruppenführer Sepp Dietrich, commander of the I SS Panzer Corps, a roughneck Nazi who, despite Rommel's aversion to the SS, gave his army-group commander total loyalty. Rommel remarked bitterly that had the panzer divisions—and in this instance he meant both the 21st and the 12th SS—been permitted actually to deploy their tanks nearer the coast as he had desired, there could have been a stronger attack two evenings previously. This was spilt milk. The essential now was to contest the ground around Caen and to prevent the enemy from cutting off the Cotentin Peninsula.

The next day, June 9, the Panzer Lehr Division arrived in the Caen sector from Chartres. Two more infantry divisions, the 346th and 711th, had sidestepped west from the Seine basin to strengthen the westward-facing German defenses east of the Orne; and there were now three Panzer divisions ringing

Caen. General Geyr von Schweppenburg, commander of Panzer Group West, planned a limited thrust northward from Caen astride the light-gauge railway, to drive a disruptive salient into the British front. In the west the enemy had cleared Isigny, but his progress was slow in the difficult *bocage* country south of the place as well as in the reclaimed marshland between the coast, Carentan, and Sainte-Mère-Eglise. The German front was holding.

But the enemy front was now nearly continuous, beachheads clearly soon to be linked and being reinforced all the time. By June 10, the Americans had reached a line only just short of the Merderet River, a few miles northwest of Carentan, while the next day a British division—identified as the 51st Highland, familiar to Rommel from El Alamein days—attacked southward in the sector east of the Orne, an attack that was smashed within hours by local counterattacks, short jabs that Rommel was sure the situation everywhere demanded and which were all that his resources—and the air situation—permitted. East of the Orne, nevertheless, panzer casualties were heavy.

On June 10, Rommel visited Geyr at Panzer Group West headquarters in an orchard at Le Caine, twenty miles south of Caen. They discussed the fuel and ammunition situation. Both were bad—replenishment convoys were having to make a round trip of 125 miles, so serious had been the enemy's attrition of dumps and communications. The Luftwaffe appeared totally absent. All movement—including, more often than not, Rommel's own movement—was hazardous and sometimes impossible. Rommel left Geyr, having planned to visit the 12th SS Panzer Division, and found the journey impracticable unless he were minded for suicide; and that afternoon Geyr's own headquarters was bombed—whether betrayed by civilians or detected by radio fix, Rommel wrote, was unclear (it was, of course, from Ultra, the vital Allied decoding operation). Most of Geyr's staff were killed, and any offensive planned by Panzer Group West was halted.

The battle was turning, once more, into a *Materialschlacht* (material battle); Rommel's forces were being pounded to pieces by the enemy's weight of fire from ground, sea, and air, and by the enemy's seemingly inexhaustible supplies of ammunition. Rommel remained as sure as he had been from before the beginning that this was not a situation that could be remedied by concentration, by an operational offensive—the air situation and much of the terrain made such concepts wholly impracticable. The only resource was to patch up a stretching front, to strike locally and hard whenever the enemy gave the opportunity, to keep him hemmed in as far as possible. Often the intensity of enemy fire made even local and limited countermoves impossible, and casualties in men and equipment were mounting alarmingly; but there were occasional rays of light. The enemy often seemed to be sluggish, slow to exploit tactical success, and to have been checked—indeed driven back with remarkable celerity—on those occasions when the Germans had been able to show fierce local strength. The Tiger tank with its 88mm gun—here, as in Africa, master of tank-versus-tank combat—had achieved some astonishing successes, even when committed singly or in tiny numbers; indeed, only tiny numbers were available, but they had undoubtedly spread alarm. During the first fortnight in July, they began to arrive in larger numbers.

On June 11, the British 7th Armored Division, another old desert ac- quaintance of Rommel's, began moving around the west of Caen. On June 13, it entered Villers-Bocage, fifteen miles southwest of Caen itself; but here one Tiger tank moved from the south into the town, shooting up everything in its path, and the British advance was checked and turned. Ringing Caen were now four panzer divisions. The Panzer Lehr and 12th SS had joined the 21st Panzer on the ground, all under the I SS Panzer Corps. On June 13, they were reinforced by the 2nd Panzer from Pas de Calais, after a most laborious jour- ney. Rommel's armor was nearly concentrated, and there was more to come.

That same day, the two western enemy beachheads linked up; on the pre- vious day Carentan had fallen. In that sector the defenders were being pushed westward, and it was clearly only a matter of days before the Cotentin Penin- sula was cut off. On June 14, Rommel made a difficult journey from the XLVII Panzer Corps (General Hans von Funck) in the west of the Cotentin, driving to meet the 2nd Panzer Division at Bremoy, near Villers-Bocage. He found that the Panzer Lehr Division had defeated a British tank attack and de- stroyed twenty-five of them in that sector.

In general, Rommel found the heart of the troops commendably sound. But they were being exposed to a terrible battering, and here Rommel ques- tioned his own orders. He had been wholly in sympathy with Hitler's initial determination not to give ground; that the battle must be won in the coastal defensive zone had been Rommel's own message to all from his first day. Now, however, the enemy had—tenuously but indubitably—won the first battle and established himself ashore. Every effort having been made and continuing to be made to eject that enemy, it was now essential therefore to redeploy troops where necessary to fight another day and to minimize the effect, in par- ticular, of naval gunfire. This implied some operational freedom; it implied certain local withdrawals; but there had been (as so often before in Rommel's experience) an order from Hitler himself: no withdrawals. This meant that virtually every movement of troops needed OKW approval. It was a ludicrous interference from on high in tactical detail.

The Normandy battlefield was comparatively small. Huge masses of men and steel were opposing each other in a restricted space. Decisions, when needed, were needed instantly; and it was Rommel's way, in any case, to inspect, decide, and express his wishes without delay. But in Rommel's visits at this time there is no particular sense of the commander, who on occasion usurped his subordinates' roles. Each side's team in Normandy was necessarily fighting in very close collusion with neighbors, and if the German chain of command had originally left a good deal to be desired, proximity, as far as Normandy went, now tended to correct the error; proximity left little scope for confusion or inappropriate interference; senior commanders were inevitably involved in the tactical battle on so confined a field.

On June 17, Rommel drove to a temporary headquarters Hitler had established at Margival near Soissons, in Champagne, in quarters originally prepared for the führer during the 1940 invasion of England that never happened. Rommel welcomed the summons.

The grimness of the situation, which he hoped to impress on Hitler, derived, in Rommel's view, from two self-evident factors, and although he had probably underestimated one, he had given fair weight to the other. It resulted from the enemy's total air superiority, which he had forecast; and from the enemy's huge matériel superiority, which had been deployed ashore with great energy and ingenuity. Normandy was rapidly turning into an El Alamein. It was as it had been in Africa, but considerably more so; and there was an added tactical factor—naval ship-to-shore gunnery—which was tipping the odds even further against troops remaining within range of it. All this led Rommel to renewed pessimism in strategic terms. Convinced as he was that the only hope for Germany would have lain in some sort of strategic stalemate in the West, providing a rational basis for negotiation and permitting reinforcement of the Eastern Front at least in the short term, he had pinned this strategic hope on the tactical defeat of the enemy invasion. That hope had almost died. An established western front—the phenomenon he had feared—was near reality; and he could not hold it long.

At the conference on June 17, Hitler made a surprisingly robust impression, and he was able for a tiny while to communicate something like optimism to his hearers. Rommel opened proceedings with a pretty accurate indication, on the map, of enemy and German positions and strengths. He drew the analogy with Africa—the enemy was using his huge matériel superiority to steamroll the way to success. The greatest German lack was air power and air defense—it was this deficiency that reduced movement and thus replenishment to pitiable proportions. The troops were fighting well against great odds, but the battle was being lost in the air. Field Marshal Gerd von Rundstedt made a few observations and produced the one detailed request he wanted to carry with Hitler—permission to withdraw troops in the northern part of the Cotentin Peninsula toward Cherbourg.

Then Hitler spoke. The Cotentin would now, inevitably, be cut in two, he accepted that; but Cherbourg itself must be strengthened and must for a while be held at all costs. An exceptionally able commander must be appointed—Cherbourg must certainly hold out until mid-July. Without Cherbourg the enemy's supply situation would remain difficult and could become critical. This, Hitler said, was the key to the whole situation; and he gave promises of a new mining program, undertaken by both the Luftwaffe and the Kriegsmarine between Le Havre and the east coast of the Cotentin, which would isolate Normandy from sea supply. As to the rest, Hitler contented himself with saying that the situation east of the Orne appeared particularly important to clear up.

As to Rundstedt's brief survey of possible enemy landings on other parts of the coast, Hitler observed that the British had now deployed in Normandy all their most experienced divisions, among others. This showed that the enemy was committed to exploitation of Normandy, to prime emphasis upon it, although a landing in the Pas de Calais area was still possible. Rundstedt suggested certain anodyne principles for agreement: that the enemy bridgehead must be contained; that "tactical adjustments should depend on the local situation" (surely an optimistically crafty formulation); that reserves should be held ready for commitment against attempts to break out of the bridgehead. Rommel, finally, warned against leaving the panzer divisions within range of naval gunfire; and emphasized that to use them in large-scale attacks would wear them down. As far as could be managed, infantry divisions should be deployed holding ground and the panzers be withdrawn to reserve, on the flanks of possible enemy breakout axes and out of range of enemy ships' guns.

Hitler, in concluding, again emphasized that the northern part of the Cotentin, and thus Cherbourg, must be held as long as possible. A purely defensive battle in the rest of the bridgehead—from Caen to Carentan—was an unacceptable long-term concept because the enemy could build up too great a matériel superiority. He must, therefore, be attacked, and the way to attack him was by interdicting his supplies through the air and sea measures that he, Hitler, had already spoken about. And with this his hearers had to be content.

By a bitter coincidence, the Margival conference was followed by a ferocious four-day storm, which disrupted Allied supply for a while (just as Hitler had promised would be accomplished by the Kriegsmarine, rather than divine intervention); but the German forces were in no condition to take the offensive and exploit this circumstance.

✦

THE SECOND PERIOD of Rommel's ordeal lasted from June 18 to 29, when he had another session with Hitler. During this time the situation in Normandy worsened remorselessly. On June 18, as it happened, the enemy command had itself judged that the bridgehead was firm and that the first phase of Overlord had been accomplished. In the west, American progress in the Cotentin was relentless. In the *bocage,* there was an unending sequence of enemy pushes, both small-scale and large-scale, each accompanied by intensive artillery and air attack; this was fighting of a particularly expensive kind, high in casualties, small advances purchased with a good deal of blood both of attackers and defenders. Tactically, the Germans of Army Group B still felt that they often had the best of it, but their strength was being sapped by attrition. The front was not long, and 2 million men were contesting it.

As the last ten days of June passed, Rommel felt ever more acutely the imminence of catastrophe, and sometimes spoke to intimates about it, about his feeling of déjà vu as he watched the advance of a calamity he could do nothing to avert but for which he felt responsible. When he had left Hitler on the afternoon of June 17, he had been initially almost buoyant. But as the days went by, and the enemy was known to be all the time reinforced, and the enemy aircraft flew sortie after sortie, and the bombs and shells fell, and men died and died, Rommel found that it was impossible to believe anymore in tactical successes, except occasional, purely defensive, and very local; and if that were all that could be hoped at the tactical level, what could be hoped strategically? And, that meant, what could be hoped politically? What could be hoped for Germany?

There were occasional shafts of light. When he visited Sepp Dietrich on June 21, Rommel heard that the I SS Panzer Corps commander was tolerably confident of holding any British push with his panzer divisions. The long-expected V-weapons had been launched against England on the night of June 12, and a ripple of optimism had run along the German front. Since manpower was failing, it was agreeable for Rommel to be told by Feuchtinger of the 21st Panzer Division that he could enlist 2,000 French volunteers, keen to fight against the British, if it were permitted. Such things gave temporary hope.

Rommel discussed the situation with Rundstedt on June 26 and telephoned him again the next evening—the same day that Cherbourg surrendered, although German efforts destroyed its function as a port for a further four weeks. Would Rundstedt agree to Rommel's making a special journey to Berchtesgaden to seek another interview with the führer and to lay before him the full seriousness of the situation? On June 17, they had been given promises of miraculous methods by which the enemy's supplies would be interdicted. It was perfectly plain that even if these measures came about, they would take time to be effective—and there was, anyway, no sign of them. Meanwhile, the situation on the ground was getting worse daily. Rommel did not believe Hitler was told the truth by the OKW, or at least some of its members.

Rundstedt agreed to Rommel's proposal and said he would accompany him. Both men set out on June 28, and met by arrangement near Paris on the main road to Germany, Rommel being accompanied on this occasion by Colonel Hans-Georg von Tempelhoff's assistant, Major Eberhard Wolfram, as well as Captain Helmuth Lang.

Rommel and Rundstedt spoke together for some time, and Wolfram could hear the conversation, or some of it. "Herr Rundstedt," Rommel said, "I agree with you. The war must be ended immediately. I shall tell the führer so, clearly and unequivocally." Rommel knew very well what that implied—had Hitler not said to him, "Nobody will make peace with me"? But the recent fighting and simple logic had persuaded him that this was not a matter that could be deferred. The stalemate from which—unrealistically—he had hoped negotiation might be developed was not going to happen. The fighting in the West had to be stopped. Every day would make matters worse. And as he drove on toward Germany, Rommel quietly said to Wolfram what was in his heart: "I feel myself responsible to the German people." He said his burden could not simply be regarded as that of a military commander. The whole world was in arms against Germany. Victory was out of the question. The enemy had now won his foothold in the West. The war must be ended.

Rommel spent that night at home and drove next morning to Berchtesgaden. There he found both Joseph Goebbels, the propaganda minister, and SS chief Heinrich Himmler and decided to try a word with them before reporting to Hitler. After a talk with the ever-friendly Goebbels, he supposed—and said to Wolfram—that he had gained an ally for his project: telling Hitler the unvarnished truth and asking that conclusions be drawn. Wolfram was unconvinced; nor was he convinced that Rommel had turned Himmler into an ally by dilating on the fighting performance of the Waffen SS. Himmler, according to Wolfram, remained "opaque."

At six o'clock the session with Hitler began. Besides Rundstedt, Field Marshal Wilhelm Keitel and Colonel General Alfred Jodl from the OKW were present; and after two and a half hours they were joined by Reichs-marschall Hermann Göring and Grand Admiral Karl Dönitz, commanders of the Luftwaffe and the Kriegsmarine respectively, as well as by the large and stertorously breathing Field Marshal Hugo Sperrle (commander of the Third Air Force in the West) and many others.

According to the official record, Hitler summed up with a number of points, a harangue—dignified by the term *directive*—of startling banality, fal-sity, and irrelevance to the real needs of the situation. The most important task, the führer said, was to halt the enemy offensive, preparatory to clearing up the whole Allied bridgehead. This would largely be accomplished by the Luft-waffe; in addition, mining at sea would decisively interrupt Anglo-American supplies. A variety of special weapons—and 1,000 new aircraft—were about to come into service. A large number of torpedo boats and submarines would soon be operating in the English Channel—in, at the most, four weeks. And fleets of new transport vehicles would soon be moving west from the Reich.

But off the record, at the start of the conference matters had gone as no staff officer or stenographer recorded. Hitler had asked Rommel to speak first; and Rommel had begun, as he had vowed, by saying he thought that day the last moment at which he would have the chance to lay the whole situation in the West before the führer. "The whole world stands arrayed against Germany," he continued, "and this disproportion of strength—"

Hitler interrupted him sharply. Would the *Herr Feldmarschall* please con-cern himself with the military, not the political, situation. Rommel rejoined that history demanded he deal with the whole situation. Hitler again rebuked him, telling him to deal only with the military situation.

Rommel did so, and the conference took its unrealistic course. Before it ended, however, he made a final attempt. Having castigated the Luftwaffe for its inadequacy, he said that he could not leave without having spoken to Hitler about Germany. "Field Marshal," Hitler responded icily, "I think you had better leave the room." Rommel left. He never saw Hitler again.

✦

HENCEFORTH, ROMMEL'S MIND was clear, and during the last two and a half weeks of his active service, the third period of his ordeal, he spoke it to a good many who, shattered by the course of events, asked him what was to happen to the army and to Germany. He did his duty assiduously, visiting, cheering, correcting errors, proposing tactical improvements with as much energy as ever. To do less would have been to betray his men. He was their commander, and Germany was still at war. As far as it lay with Rommel, the enemy's attacks would be defeated and the enemy's progress halted, and in these final weeks Rommel was everywhere. But Germany must have peace, and he could not believe that the supreme commander was minded to help bring that peace about—in which case it must fall to somebody else with power to act. He believed that it was obviously vital to seek peace while the Germans still held some territory. Time had nearly run out.

Rommel visited Geyr at Panzer Group West the day after returning from Germany and told him at least some of what had transpired. They discussed the Caen sector, on both sides of the Orne. The enemy was very likely to try a major breakout there; and during the next fortnight Rommel visited that area frequently. Geyr wished to hold the three divisions of the I SS Panzer Corps over twenty miles south of Caen, in woods near Saint-Laurent-de-Condé, poised to strike any massed enemy advance on advantageous ground. Rommel disagreed. True to the philosophy he had held throughout, he believed that at least part of the panzer force should remain immediately east and southeast of Caen, to stiffen the front. To withdraw most of the armor as far as Geyr proposed would be to leave the infantry, unsupported, to be rolled up by the enemy when it attacked—and he agreed that it was in this sector that the enemy would certainly attack, if only to race by the shortest route eastward toward the V-1 sites.

It was his last conversation with Geyr. Hitler had heard that the commander of Panzer Group West was as pessimistic as the commander of Army Group B—and even more anxious to withdraw to positions in depth—and had ordered his replacement. Succeeding Geyr in command of the panzer group was General Heinrich Eberbach. Visiting him on July 5, Rommel again discussed the Caen sector. The enemy, when it attacked southward east of the Orne, as it undoubtedly would, must be broken up by antitank artillery fire, *Nebelwerfer* (rocket launchers), and panzers. The defense must be organized in great depth.

All divisions, including the panzers, were now very short of men as well as equipment, and divisions from other areas—like the Fifteenth Army's—were arriving in Normandy without a full complement. Rommel returned to this sector, east of Caen, on two further occasions, July 12 and 15, suggesting adjustments, aiming to give maximum depth to the front, replacing panzer units committed to ground-holding with infantry as far as humanly possible. He heard frequent requests for withdrawal and refused them. In his orders he was entirely true to the *Führerbefehl*—the führer's decree.

But Rommel was under no illusions about what the troops were suffering. "Our soldiers," wrote one of his commanders, "enter the battle in low spirits at the thought of the enemy's enormous material superiority. They are always asking 'where is the Luftwaffe?' The feeling of helplessness against enemy air-craft operating without any hindrance has a paralyzing effect and during the barrage this effect on inexperienced troops is literally soul-shaking." Many a British veteran of Dunkirk would have agreed with him; and losses were ap-palling from artillery as well as air strikes. Even the smallest enemy attacks appeared to be preceded by saturation bombardment. On July 14, Rommel found one parachute regiment wherein, of a total of 1,000 reinforcements re-ceived since battle began, over 800 had already fallen. Sometimes Rommel talked of the possibility of suicide, but only to reject it. In these circumstances suicide was merely desertion.

Old acquaintances, officers who had long served Rommel and knew him well, put the matter to him plainly, and he to them. "Lattmann," Rommel had asked his artillery representative on July 10, as they drove together to visit the LXXXIV Corps, "what do you think about the end of the war?"

"Herr Feldmarschall, that we can't win is evident. I hope we can keep enough strength—" He meant to continue, "to reach a decent peace."

"I will try to use my reputation with the Allies," Rommel said frankly, "to make a truce, *against Hitler's wishes."* He still envisaged, quite unrealistically, a future in which the Anglo-Americans would agree to help hold the line against the Soviet Union, and he spoke of this to Colonel Hans Lattmann. A few days later he was talking to Lieutenant Colonel Elmar Warning of the 17th Luftwaffe Division. Warning had been on Rommel's staff in North Africa—had, indeed, been at El Alamein when Rommel had received Hitler's "no withdrawal" order. Now, out of earshot of others, Warning put the ques-tion frankly: "Field Marshal, what's really going to happen here? Twelve Ger-man divisions are trying to contain the whole front."

"I'll tell you something," Rommel replied. "Field Marshal von Kluge and I have sent the führer an ultimatum. Militarily the way can't be won, and he must make a political decision."

Warning looked at Rommel with astonished disbelief. "And what if the führer refuses?"

"Then," Rommel said, "I open the west front. There would be only one important matter left—that the Anglo-Americans reach Berlin before the Russians."

To his old subordinate Siegfried Westphal, also serving in Normandy, Rommel spoke in the same grim sense. Later he told his son, Manfred, that the time to "open the west front" would have been when the Anglo-Americans ultimately broke out. Then it should be possible unilaterally to abandon re-sistance and let the impetus of purely military events set the pace of history, since political initiatives had been neglected. But by the time of this conversation, all had moved on.

✦

ROMMEL'S "ULTIMATUM" WITH Field Marshal Hans Günther von Kluge was in fact signed on the following day, July 16. Geyr had not been the only casualty of the meeting with Hitler on June 29. After it the führer had decided that the elderly Rundstedt had also better be replaced, by an officer who could drive the defeatism—and the insubordination—out of the commander of Army Group B. Rundstedt had sent a pessimistic report to the OKW urging, like Geyr, withdrawal at least from the Caen bridgehead, and quoting Rommel—fairly—on the necessity for this degree at least of operational freedom; the report had not pleased Hitler. Asked by Keitel what he really proposed, Rundstedt had said shortly, "Make peace!"

Von Kluge was Hitler's choice to replace Rundstedt as OB West. A Prussian, he had been Rommel's army commander in 1940, driving the Fourth Army triumphantly through France. In the terrible winter of 1941, he had relieved Field Marshal Fedor von Bock in command of Army Group Center on the Eastern Front; and it was after visiting von Kluge's headquarters in 1943 that Hitler had narrowly escaped death at the hands of conspirators who had placed a bomb in his aircraft. Before taking over from Rundstedt, von Kluge had been briefed at the OKW; and he knew, of course, from his experiences in 1940, the headstrong nature of Rommel, now characterized as a pessimist.

Their first meeting was disagreeable. It took place on July 3, immediately after von Kluge assumed command at Rommel's headquarters at La Roche-Guyon. Von Kluge told Rommel bluntly that although he was a field marshal, he must get used to obeying orders. The rebuke, unequivocally, was for disobedience; and it could derive only from von Kluge's recent OKW briefing.

Rommel was angry. He had, he knew, faithfully obeyed orders. His crime was speaking bluntly about the facts of the situation. On July 5, he sent von Kluge a situation report. He set down the measures he had earlier—repeatedly—requested, and the results of not meeting them. All this—and the consequences for resupply of the air situation—Rommel reiterated to von Kluge; and he repeated his angry complaints about the early denial to Army Group B of control over the divisions of Panzer Group West. It was this that had produced the present appalling situation, not Rommel's disobedience. He sent the report under cover of a brief note in which he simply said that von Kluge's remarks, in the presence of Rommel's own staff officers, had hurt him deeply. He asked OB West what possible grounds there were for the accusation. And he sent the report (but not the covering letter) to Hitler.

Rommel's first encounter with von Kluge had been unpromising, but von Kluge was a shrewd, experienced commander, and it did not take him long to form his own impressions. They entirely confirmed the view of the situation that Rommel had presented to him. It was unimportant how it had happened and whether it could have happened less disastrously; the situation now was one of imminent catastrophe. The front could not possibly hold for more than a few weeks. The troops were being ground to pieces in a *Materialschlacht* of monstrous proportions. The enemy now had some forty divisions in the field, but a simple count of formations meant nothing—what mattered was that the Anglo-Americans could call on seemingly limitless reinforcements of men, equipment, and supplies while the Wehrmacht was wasting away. Kluge saw Rommel repeatedly during the first fortnight in July, discussing the situation and dining at La Roche-Guyon on July 12. And, on July 16, Rommel sent him what he had described to Warning as his ultimatum. He assumed that it would immediately be sent to Hitler. And, indeed, when it was forwarded, Kluge's covering letter said he had concluded that "the field marshal [Rommel] was unfortunately right." The Wehrmacht had lost 117,000 men, including 2,700 officers, since June 6, and had received only 10,000 replacements. It was time for truth.

In this brief and stark document, Rommel said the ultimate crisis in Normandy was now approaching. The troops were fighting heroically, but the strength of the enemy, above all in tanks and artillery, the paucity and slow arrival of replacements for the hideous losses, the inexperience now of many of the German formations, and the intensity of the air and ground bombardment to which they were incessantly exposed meant that the enemy must break through into the French hinterland in the near future. Rommel did not put an exact term on this, but the message was clear, and he knew that Kluge, from his own observations, endorsed it. Rommel had added to the two-and-a-half-page draft a sentence in his own hand: "It is necessary to draw the political conclusions from this situation."

Two of Rommel's staff, General Hans Speidel and Colonel Tempelhoff, no doubt mindful of Hitler's explosion when Rommel had tried to advert to the situation inevitably facing Germany as a consequence of the strategic position on the Western Front, persuaded Rommel to delete the word "political." He did so. And signed.

The next day, Rommel set out to visit the II Panzer Corps and two divisions near Villers-Bocage that had experienced heavy casualties. Thence he decided to drive to the I SS Panzer Corps, to Sepp Dietrich; once again to the threatened sector east of the Orne. He left Dietrich at 4:00 in the afternoon and took the road through Saint-Pierre, en route to La Roche-Guyon. Enemy aircraft were active everywhere; to reduce the risk, Rommel's driver, Ober-feldwebel Daniel, was told to take a minor road before Livarot. The intention was to rejoin the main road a few miles north of Vimoutiers, and thereafter to work eastward toward the Seine and home.

Rommel's car reached the main road, leading south toward Vimoutiers. An air sentry, Obergefreiter Holke, was riding in the back of the car. The accom-panying staff officers were Major Neuhaus and Captain Lang.

Suddenly Holke yelled that there were enemy aircraft heading in on the road they were taking; they were coming from behind, low and fast. There was a shout to the driver, Daniel, to speed up, to race 300 yards to where it looked possible to pull off the road and take cover. Before they got there, the leading enemy aircraft opened fire. The car went out of control and ended up in a ditch on the left of the road. Rommel had already been hard hit even be-fore the second attacking aircraft came in, strafing the wrecked car and the prone bodies of its occupants once again.

The nearest military hospital was at Bernay, on the road to Rouen, twenty-five miles away. Rommel was first attended by a French doctor in a French hos-pital—the property of a monastic order—in Livarot, near the scene of the wounding; but getting him even there had involved a wait of three-quarters of an hour before Lang could get a vehicle. Thence an unconscious Rommel, to-gether with Daniel, was borne to Bernay. Rommel's skull was severely fractured, and there were wounds to the temple and face. Daniel died of his injuries.

✦

NEXT DAY, July 18, the British Second Army attacked over the ground that Rommel had repeatedly visited and where he had consistently anticipated the next major operation—east of Caen, east of the Orne. The attack was preceded by one of the greatest air bombardments in support of ground forces that the war had seen. The bombardment went on for three hours, between 5:30 and 8:30 of a beautiful morning. The British VIII Corps, with three armored di-visions and an infantry division on the left flank, then moved southward. At the same time the II Canadian Corps attacked in the city of Caen itself.

By the end of the day, although their forward positions had been overrun with considerable casualties, the Germans were still in control of the high ground south of Caen and had destroyed a significant number of enemy tanks. This was no enemy breakout, no defeat. The German assemblage of antitank guns, supported by the panzer regiments lying back just behind the forward positions, had done great execution. The German line was holding. Perhaps, unlike Napoleon, Rommel did not lose his last battle after all.

✦

ON JULY 20, 1944, *even as Rommel was still lying unconscious, Count Claus von Stauffenberg placed a briefcase with a bomb under a conference table at Hitler's Rastenburg headquarters. The führer survived the explosion, and the conspirators were rounded up. Though Rommel—by now on his way to recovery—had played no part, and felt that a murdered Hitler would only have condemned Germany to civil war, the Gestapo did learn of his intention to make peace overtures to the Allies. As he convalesced at Herrlingen, his home near Ulm, he watched helplessly as friends and associates were executed or, like von Kluge, committed suicide. On October 14, two generals dispatched by Hitler showed up with an offer he believed he could not refuse: If he swallowed poison, his family would be spared. The alternative was to appear before a people's court on a charge of high treason. Rommel drove off with them, and not long afterward the field marshal's body was dropped off at an Ulm hospital. The public was told only that he had suffered a heart attack on the way to a meeting. Rommel was given a state funeral. Hitler's wreath and messages of condolence were conveyed by Rundstedt, who said, in the funeral oration, "His heart belonged to the führer."*

FALAISE: THE TRAP NOT SPRUNG

CARLO D'ESTE

Rommel did not leave the field a defeated general: The line he had tried to hold, with such desperate ingenuity, only began to give way at the end of July—by which time he was in the hospital. He knew that disintegration had to happen, but before it did, he had forced the Allied generals to confront the prospect of "a World War I–type stalemate" (as Omar Bradley wrote). Once the Allies did break loose from the hedgerows and marshlands of Normandy, their progress—particularly that of Patton's Third Army—was spectacular. By August 25, they had liberated Paris. *"Blitzkrieg,"* John Keegan writes, "was what the Third Army's breakthrough amounted to; it was the first—and, as it would turn out, the last—true exercise in that operational form achieved by a Western army in the Second World War. *Blitzkrieg* proper entailed not merely the sudden and brutal penetration of the enemy's front by concentrated armored force and the rapid exploitation of that success; it also required that the enemy forces lying beyond the point of break-in should be encircled and destroyed."

Encircled and destroyed. The *Kessel,* or cauldron, the Germans called the bag of envelopment. Therein lies the story of the greatest Allied victory of the summer campaign in France, as well as the most controversial: The Falaise Gap. The battle began with what Carlo D'Este, the biographer of Patton, has called "one of the most colossally stupid decisions of the war": Hitler's order to counterattack between the towns of Mortain and Avranches, even as the Allies were charging into open country. The German drive of August 6–7 was not just stopped; it left well over 100,000 men in danger of being trapped. Killing was not the question: a massacre did take place. But could the Allies have closed the gap, thus preventing the escape of twenty to forty thousand Germans—a hard core that they would eventually have to deal with on their own turf? Could a total victory have ended the war months sooner? Decisions made in the heat of battle—even those that result in wholesale annihilations—can return to haunt.

Carlo D'Este is a former army officer and the author of *Decision in Normandy, Bitter Victory, Fatal Decision: Anzio and the Battle for Rome,* and his biography, *Patton: A Genius for War.* He is at present completing *Eisenhower: A Soldier's Life, 1890–1945.*

AFTER THE EXTRAORDINARY SUCCESS OF THE D DAY LANDINGS on June 6, 1944, Allied forces quickly bogged down. Bad weather, the deadly hedgerows of the Normandy *bocage,* and the furious defense of Field Marshal Erwin Rommel's German Army Group B combined to prevent the Allies from advancing beyond the Caen bridgehead in the east or the Cotentin Peninsula in the west. As the commander of American ground forces in Normandy, Lieutenant General Omar N. Bradley, later wrote, "By July 10, we faced a real danger of a World War I–type stalemate." The British failure of General Bernard Montgomery's Operation Goodwood in mid-July to seize the vital Caen-Falaise plain, as well as several costly attempts by Bradley's First Army to escape the *bocage* and swamps of the Cotentin, only exacerbated the already mounting anxiety within the Allied high command.

With Patton and his Third Army awaiting official activation on August 1, Bradley devised an operation, code-named Cobra, that employed massive aerial carpet bombing to blast open a corridor through which it was hoped the U.S. VII Corps could finally break out from the confining hedgerow country west of Saint-Lô. Cobra began badly, when a calamitous error by Allied bombers killed 111 American soldiers and wounded 490, and initially it appeared to have failed. But when German resistance suddenly began to collapse, Bradley assigned Major General Troy Middleton's VIII Corps to the Third Army to spearhead a thrust toward Avranches, the last remaining obstacle to a full-scale breakout into Brittany and the plains of southern Normandy. There he could exploit the mobility of Patton's armored divisions.

Cobra immediately altered the entire Allied concept of what had been a battle of attrition to drive Army Group B from Normandy and east of the river Seine. The notion of a decisive breakout in the Cotentin and a pursuit across the plains of southern Normandy was not part of the Allied blueprint for the campaign; the plan for the Allied advance had been, in effect, a gigantic swinging door hinged on Caen and sweeping slowly and deliberately in an arc toward the Seine.

Although it took three days too long for the Allied leadership to scrap its abruptly outmoded master plan to take advantage of Cobra's success, Bradley finally acted to make official what Patton had already begun to orchestrate: a swing to the east by the Third Army. Patton was ordered to leave the VIII Corps to secure Brittany, while the other three corps of the Third Army turned eastward to drive toward the Seine through the least-defended region of Normandy, the Orléans gap.

Hitler believed the outcome of the Normandy campaign would decide the destiny of Germany. Without consulting Rommel's successor, Field Marshal Hans Günther von Kluge, he made one of the most colossally stupid decisions of the war: He directed an immediate, powerful armored counterattack between Mortain and Avranches. Its object was to recapture the neck of the Cotentin Peninsula and cut off all U.S. forces south of Avranches and in Brittany.

The German attack on August 6–7 was repulsed at Mortain by the heroic stand of the U.S. 30th Division at Hill 317, which the VII Corps commander, Major General J. Lawton Collins, called "one of the outstanding small-unit actions of World War II." Instead of splitting the U.S. First and Third armies, Hitler's blunder left the German Seventh Army and elements of the Fifth Panzer Army exposed and in danger of being encircled.

On August 7, Montgomery launched Totalize, a major offensive by Lieutenant General H. D. G. Crerar's Canadian First Army to capture Falaise, while Lieutenant General Miles Dempsey's British Second Army swept the *bocage* on their right flank. Together the two armies would pivot to their left and drive east. Meanwhile, the U.S. First and Third armies would thrust across the open southern flank and trap the Fifth Panzer Army and Seventh Army in a double envelopment along the Seine. This became the so-called long envelopment.

Mortain suddenly changed the thinking of General Dwight D. Eisenhower and Bradley. Wade Haislip's XV Corps was spearheading the Third Army drive east and was already outside Le Mans. Bradley reasoned that if he could quickly swing the XV Corps behind the Germans in the direction of Alençon and Argentan, in a "short [left] hook," the Allies might be able to annihilate the Seventh Army trapped in the pocket between the XV Corps and the Canadians advancing toward Falaise.

As an exultant Bradley told visiting U.S. Secretary of the Treasury Henry Morgenthau, it was "an opportunity that comes to a commander not more than once in a century. We're about to destroy an entire hostile army. . . . We'll go all the way from here to the German border." Eisenhower enthusiastically endorsed Bradley's change of plan, which would later spawn one of the great controversies of the war.

Bradley then phoned Montgomery to obtain his concurrence. Argentan, Haislip's objective, was some twelve miles inside the British boundary, but as Bradley later remarked, "Monty happily forgave us our trespasses and welcomed the penetration."

Even as he gave permission for Bradley to violate the interarmy group boundary, Montgomery was confident that the Canadians could close the pocket at Argentan before the Americans got there. Although the Canadians were nearly halfway to Falaise by August 9, German resistance was savage, and the offensive soon slowed to a crawl. Like the earlier protracted, bloody battle for Caen, renewed attacks to punch through to this key town were unsuccessful.

Time was critical if the trap were to be sprung successfully, and the Canadians were clearly in serious trouble; Montgomery's optimism was unfounded. He could have influenced the outcome of Totalize by immediately reinforcing the Canadians with a division from the Second Army, which was progressing through the *bocage* with relative ease in a series of secondary attacks between the Orne River and Vire. The British 7th Armored Division was the formation that he could have shifted to the Falaise front most easily. That Montgomery failed to do so likely stemmed from the fact that he deeply mistrusted his own "Desert Rats" because of their consistently poor performance in Normandy. Another option, dropping two British airborne divisions behind the German lines near Falaise to break the screen of deadly 88s holding up the Canadian advance, was proposed several days later by Bradley; Montgomery turned him down.

The Canadians remained stalled north of Falaise. By the evening of August 12, the XV Corps had taken Alençon and Sées and was prepared to drive north with four divisions to close the gap, now only eighteen miles wide. With the Germans holding their own at Falaise, Montgomery expected General Heinrich Eberbach's Fifth Panzer Army (called Panzer Group West until August 5) to react furiously to hold open the southern perimeter of the gap until the Germans could make good their escape. He continued to press the Canadians to capture Falaise and drive on to Argentan.

Montgomery's misjudgment resulted at least partly from the repeated failure of the British commanders, with their penchant for the set-piece battle, to perceive the ability of the U.S. Army to move rapidly and decisively under conditions of mobile warfare. The disastrous American baptism of fire in North Africa in early 1943 was still fresh in their memory. Although many American units had landed in Normandy untested in battle, two months of almost constant combat had changed that. The British leaders also disparaged Patton's ability, and even the Third Army's exploits in Normandy later failed to convince them that the strongest assets of the U.S. Army were a mastery of mobile warfare and the ability to improvise on the battlefield.

Montgomery's decision not to reinforce the Canadians was made August 11, even as von Kluge was pleading with Hitler that continuing the Mortain counteroffensive was hopeless. As British historian Max Hastings has observed, "As late as 8 or 9 August, von Kluge could readily have executed the only sane movement open to him, a withdrawal to the Seine covered by a sacrificial rear guard. Hitler, and Hitler alone, closed this option to him and presented the Allies with their extraordinary opportunity." Thus, although the Germans began to shorten their line around Mortain on this date, there was still no retreat eastward.

As the XV Corps drove north toward Argentan, Haislip reported to Patton that he was close to capturing his final assigned objective and that with additional forces he could effectively block the east-west roads in his sector north of Alençon. The Canadians remained well north of Falaise, making frustratingly slow progress. Patton foresaw that they could not close the gap quickly. On the night of August 12, he directed the XV Corps to capture Argentan and then carefully push north toward Falaise.

When Bradley learned of Patton's intentions, he made a crucial, and later much-criticized, decision: He countermanded Patton, ordering the XV Corps to halt at Argentan. Patton begged to be allowed to continue north, saying half in jest: "We now have elements in Argentan. Shall we continue and drive the British into the sea for another Dunkirk?" The British, who soon learned of Patton's flip remark, were not amused.

Bradley would not relent. He later defended his decision by arguing that he was fearful of a deadly collision with the Canadians, and "much preferred a solid shoulder at Argentan to the possibility of a broken neck at Falaise." He also insisted, "To have driven pell-mell into Montgomery's line of advance could easily have resulted in a disastrous error in recognition. In halting Patton at Argentan, however, I did not consult with Montgomery. The decision to stop Patton was mine alone. . . ."

On August 13, the Germans had at last begun to build up the shoulders of the pocket, but three more days elapsed before the Germans began organizing their withdrawal to the east in a desperate bid to escape the Allied trap. As they withdrew, they were pounded unmercifully from the air and by hundreds of Allied guns. The devastation was appalling. As Max Hastings has noted, the German army endured "one of the great nightmares of military history in the Falaise Gap."

The Canadians did not capture Falaise until late on August 16, which still left a fifteen-mile gap between the American and Canadian armies. The ferocity of the battles was typified by the experience of a small Canadian tank and infantry task force commanded by Major D. V. Currie that was sent to Saint-Lambert-sur-Dives to capture the three vital bridges over the Dives: By doing so, the Canadians would have blocked the retreat of the German Seventh Army. Currie's force arrived in Saint-Lambert the evening of August 18 and found German troops swarming through the village, fleeing the gap before it closed for good. The Canadians immediately became heavily embroiled with German armor and antitank guns. Despite mounting tank and antitank losses, 700 German POWs had been taken by the following day, but the Germans still held the vital bridges. At one point the Canadian tanks began firing their machine guns at one another to dislodge Germans attempting to affix explosive charges to their hulls and tracks.

Eventually the Canadians fell back to nearby Hill 117. Canadian artillery fired point-blank in support of Major Currie's rapidly dwindling force, which eventually lost every single officer except its commander. On the morning of the third day (Sunday, August 20); a wave of German infantry attempted to rush the Canadian positions on Hill 117, only to be mowed down by Canadian machine guns. In Saint-Lambert a Canadian patrol was suddenly ambushed and disarmed by 400 troops of the 12th SS Panzer Division, who disappeared into the gap, leaving the Canadians unharmed.

Throughout that Sunday, German infantry and armor descended upon Saint-Lambert and were relentlessly shelled by Allied artillery. However, as one of the few existing accounts of this action notes, "the fantastic traffic over the bridge could not be stopped that day. It was like a valve through which the whole pocket was deflated. "The battle raged into the fourth day, with the Canadians once again attacking the bridges. Saint-Lambert itself was a funeral pyre of burning wreckage and dead bodies. About 800 German troops surrendered to Currie's force. They included a convoy of ambulances whose medical commander demanded to be let through for humanitarian reasons. When Currie opened the doors he found German wounded "piled in like cordwood. I told the doctor that if he were really interested in saving lives, he had better go to our lines and to our hospital. He didn't have enough gas in the ambulances to go anywhere else . . . [and] finally decided that we were right."

Late Monday afternoon Major Currie was finally relieved by the Canadian 3rd Division. His little task force had lost nine Shermans and twelve self-propelled antitank guns but had destroyed seven German tanks, killed some 300 troops, wounded another 500, and taken 2,100 POWs. They had been unable to seize the bridges, but without the valiant stand of Currie's outgunned and outnumbered force, many more German troops would have escaped the Allied trap. The Canadians had managed to repel repeated counterattacks that included panzers and 88s and helped funnel a great many German troops into the only remaining exit at Chambois, the place that came to be known as the "Couloir de la Mort"—the Corridor of Death. For his exceptional leadership at Saint-Lambert, Major Currie became the first Canadian to win the Victoria Cross in Normandy.

The pocket was officially sealed on August 19, when the Polish 1st Armored Division and the U.S. 90th Division joined forces at Chambois. But heavy fighting continued for several more days. In one instance, a column of some 3,000 vehicles was destroyed. In all, of the nearly 80,000 German soldiers originally trapped in the Falaise pocket, some 10,000 perished and an estimated 50,000 were taken prisoner. Most German units simply disappeared, as troops fled individually and in small groups toward the Seine. Of the fifty divisions in action in June, only ten could now even be called fighting units.

The scope of the German defeat was starkly visible around the villages of Trun, Saint-Lambert, and Chambois, which were littered with unburied bodies, thousands of dead horses and cattle, and smashed and burning vehicles. It was one of the most appalling scenes of the war. The powerful stench reached hundreds of feet in the air to sicken the pilots of Allied spotter planes. A British account described it this way:

> In the hot August sun . . . there was no dignity of death. In the worst bombarded areas fragments of bodies festooned the trees. . . . Some roads were impassable due to the congestion caused by burnt-out trucks, dead horses, smashed tanks, and destruction on a scale which the Western Allies had never seen.

German disarray was typified by the example of the British XII Corps, which took prisoners from thirteen different divisions southeast of Falaise.

Eisenhower described it as unquestionably one of the worst "killing grounds" of the war. "Forty-eight hours after the closing of the gap I was conducted through it on foot, to encounter scenes that could be described only by

Dante. It was literally possible to walk for hundreds of yards at a time, stepping on nothing but dead and decaying flesh." Montgomery called the carnage in the Trun area "almost unbelievable."

The fate that befell the once proud 12th SS Panzer Division was typical. The division, or rather what was left of it, was a shambles. Its commander, Kurt Meyer, was alone, filthy, weary, and on foot when he escaped from the pocket. Meyer, who was renowned for his courage and fanaticism, later said he left with "my knees trembling, the sweat pouring down my face, my clothes soaked in perspiration." Others, like Lieutenant Walter Kruger, walked for days as part of a chaotic, seemingly endless line of survivors, many of whom dropped from exhaustion. In June the division had nearly 20,000 men and 139 tanks; after Normandy it had barely 300 men, 10 tanks, and no artillery. The survivors of the battle were a beaten, disconsolate army in complete disarray.

Allied investigating teams later found a staggering array of equipment on the battlefield: well over 500 tanks and self-propelled guns; more than 700 artillery pieces; almost 7,500 military vehicles, civilian cars, and staff vehicles; over 150 armored cars and personnel carriers—in all, over 9,000 items. It has been estimated that fewer than 120 armored fighting vehicles made it across the Seine.

Despite the earlier stalemate, the campaign in Normandy succeeded far beyond the expectations of its architects. But with success came a legacy of controversy and unanswered questions about the battle in the Argentan-Falaise pocket. Was it a great triumph or an enormous blunder?

Churchill was the first to question what he perceived as an excessively low number of German POWs. "I had, of course, rather hoped we should be in the region of hundreds of thousands when sixteen divisions were mentioned," he cabled Montgomery, who replied that, since July 25, Allied ground forces had taken 133,000 German POWs, killed 23,000, and wounded 100,000, making the total 256,000 enemy "written off." However, it was far too early to gain even an approximation of German losses in the Falaise pocket until Allied investigation teams could complete a rough count. Montgomery's extravagant estimate only fueled the controversy, especially his claim that the Allies had taken 133,000 prisoners since Cobra. Both the American and British official histories later concluded that the Allies had captured about 50,000 Germans in the battle of the Falaise pocket.

What Churchill and others failed to comprehend was that the sixteen German divisions had all been severely decimated in the grueling battles fought since D day, and few of their losses had been replaced. Each panzer division had entered Normandy averaging 160 tanks and 173 assault guns, antitank guns, and artillery pieces. By August 25, all the German divisions had been reduced to a combined total of 72 tanks and assault guns and only a handful of understrength infantry and panzer grenadier battalions. Six of the panzer divisions had no artillery at all.

There is little dispute over the figure of 10,000 German dead. The greatest uncertainty remains about how many German troops actually managed to escape the pocket. As the U.S official history records, even before the Germans began their retreat from the pocket some nonessential personnel and equipment had already been moved toward the Seine. According to the military historian Martin Blumenson, "Later estimates of the total number of Germans escaping varied between 20,000 and 40,000 men. . . . The average combat strength of divisions was no more than a few hundred men, even though the overall strength of some divisions came close to 3,000."

Whatever the figures, the aftermath left lingering doubts that despite their great victory the Allies had let slip from their grasp an even greater opportunity, not only of bagging the entire remnants of Army Group B, but the greater psychological victory of forcing a formal surrender and perhaps of ending the war sooner. The responsibility for the failure—if it was a failure—to close the pocket has been the subject of an endless postwar debate.

Though Bradley took full responsibility for halting Patton at Argentan, he nevertheless blamed Montgomery for failing to close the gap. As he complained in his 1951 memoirs, *A Soldier's Story:*

> Rather than close the trap by capping the leak at Falaise, Monty proceeded to squeeze the enemy out toward the Seine. If Monty's tactics mystified me, they dismayed Eisenhower even more. And at Lucky Forward [Third Army headquarters], where a shocked Third Army looked on helplessly as its quarry fled, Patton raged at Montgomery's blunder.

What is certain is that until at least August 14, both Montgomery and Bradley were committed to the plan to close the trap between Argentan and Falaise. Bradley's argument that U.S. and Canadian forces should not risk an accidental collision is illogical, as is his suggestion that the XV Corps had been halted because the Allied air forces had sown the highways in the area with time bombs, thus making movement northward risky. In fact, the bombs, dropped over a three-day period, had only twelve-hour delay fuses, a fact that the airmen could easily have confirmed. Equally suspect is Bradley's argument that he was reluctant to "chance a head-on meeting between two converging armies, as we might have done had Patton continued on to Falaise."

In addition to failing to reveal that extensive precautions had been taken to prevent such a tragic head-on meeting, Bradley also ignored the fact that if the pocket was ever to be closed, the U.S. Third Army and the Canadian First Army eventually had to meet. Where they met was irrelevant. The truth is that if Bradley had wanted to close the Argentan-Falaise gap he could have done so without opposition from Montgomery.

Bradley's contention that he lacked authority to send the XV Corps north of Argentan is absurd. Not only was it already well beyond the now rather meaningless interarmy group boundary, but Montgomery had already given permission to advance to Argentan. As Blumenson notes, "Bradley needed Montgomery's permission to go [any] farther to the north." And if "Montgomery did not sanction an American advance beyond Argentan, neither did Bradley propose it."

Although Montgomery's failure to reinforce Crerar's Canadians during the critical period of the battle for Falaise remains inexplicable, there is ample evidence that he was fully committed to closing the gap. Nevertheless, he clearly preferred the long envelopment to the Seine to ensure that a blocking force would prevent the mass escape of Army Group B from Normandy—especially if the pocket could not be closed. Bradley obviously shared the same concern. He never wavered in his assertion that Montgomery had nothing to do with his decision to halt Patton at Argentan. The decision "was mine and mine alone. . . . I was determined to hold Patton at Argentan and had no cause to ask Monty to shift the boundary." Bradley's decision was fully supported by Eisenhower.

Thus, by August 14, both commanders felt that a long envelopment still held promise. Bradley had three alternatives: He could move beyond Argentan toward Falaise (an option he firmly ruled out); he could sit tight where he was until reinforced by units of the Third and First armies moving east from the Avranches-Mortain sector (never seriously considered); or he could quickly strike east toward the Seine, while continuing to hold the Argentan shoulder temporarily with a smaller force. Bradley later related that the choice was not as simple as hindsight might suggest:

> Of all three [options], the dash to the Seine offered the greatest tactical promise. For if Patton were to secure a bridgehead there, he would have thwarted the enemy's last bright chance for defense of the Seine River line. But by the same token, we would also be taking a chance. For in striking out for the Seine in preference to the Chambois attack, we might make it easier for the enemy to escape that Falaise trap. Normally, destruction of the enemy's army is

the first objective of any force. Was a Seine River bridgehead important enough to warrant our rejecting that military tenet?

Bradley thought so, for he records, "George helped settle my doubts when on August 14 he called to ask that two of Haislip's four divisions on the Argentan shoulder be freed for a dash to the Seine. With that, I brushed aside the first two alternatives and sided with Patton on the third."

Bradley's decision plainly suited Montgomery, who observed after the war, "The battle of the Falaise pocket never should have taken place and was not meant to take place." Montgomery's point was that the short envelopment was not his idea, nor did it fit in with his concept of the battle. In September 1944, when a war correspondent asked Patton if the Falaise encirclement had been part of the original Overlord master plan or an improvisation, he replied: "Improvisation by General Bradley. I thought we were going east and he told me to move north."

By August 14, when it was clear that the Argentan-Falaise pocket would not be closed, Montgomery exhorted Crerar to seal the only remaining corridor of escape, a narrowing gap between Trun and Chambois. In so doing, he signaled his growing belief that the gap could still be plugged farther east while Patton was making his end run to the Seine.

That same day, Montgomery wrote optimistically to his friend Sir James Grigg, the secretary of state for war: "These are great days. . . . We have the great bulk of the German forces partially surrounded; some will of course escape, but I do not see how they can stand and fight seriously again this side of the Seine."

In this age of conspiracy theories and historical "what ifs," there is no better example than the seemingly endless discussion of who was "at fault" for the decisions made during a single, crucial week in August 1944. The expression "Falaise gap" is a postwar creation of the media. As Major Tom Bigland, Montgomery's liaison officer to Bradley, notes, "it was not called the battle of the 'Falaise Gap.' It was only one of the matters which were being considered . . . there was a great deal of the 'fog of battle' at that time."

The postwar controversy might well have died had not Bradley fueled the flames by publicly second-guessing his own decision to send the Third Army to the Seine. He blamed Montgomery and faulty intelligence. "To this day I am not yet certain that we should not have postponed our advance to the Seine and gone on to Chambois instead," he wrote in *A Soldier's Story.* "For although the bridgehead accelerated our advance, Chambois would have yielded more prisoners."

More recently, in *A General's Life,* Bradley candidly admitted this "was not only a poor decision but a distinctly dangerous one." It had been made on the basis of [Ultra] intelligence, which estimated that a full-scale German retreat to the east had already begun and that a number of German divisions had escaped. "Unknown to us, the major share of German forces were still inside the pocket, still vulnerable to encirclement. Had we known this—had we not been misled by intelligence—we would have held Haislip solidly in place on the Argentan shoulder and most likely would have sent [Walton] Walker directly north on Haislip's right flank toward Chambois, to help close the gap."

Bradley believes—with some justification—that Collins's VII Corps, Haislip's XV Corps, and Walker's XX Corps (totaling eleven divisions) would have formed a firm front on an east-west line to hold the southern edge of the sack. "We would probably have then requested that Monty pull the boundary back so that our forces could advance on Falaise to link up with Crerar and Dempsey, probably on August 16. Had this been done, we would have trapped most of the German force inside the pocket." Instead, Bradley notes, he left behind a gravely weakened southern shoulder at a moment when it was the most vulnerable. Fortunately, there was no further counterattack at this time.

✦

THE BATTLE of the Falaise gap was one of the most dramatic events of the war, and the fact that between 20,000 and 40,000 German troops eluded the trap has triggered the notion of a great Allied blunder. Yet the only troops who escaped across the Seine were the remnants of the shattered Seventh Army and the Fifth Panzer Army. They left on foot; most of their heavy weapons and armor remained behind. The survivors retreated eastward in disarray.

The most compelling evidence of Allied success consists of the assessments of many senior German officers. General Hans Speidel declared, "There were barely a hundred tanks left out of six panzer divisions." Von Kluge's successor, Field Marshal Walther Model, reported: "Five decimated divisions returned to Germany. The remains of eleven infantry divisions allowed us to regroup four units, each with a handful of field guns and other minor equipment. All that remained of eleven armored divisions when replenished with personnel and matériel amounted to eleven regiments, each with five or six tanks and a few artillery batteries." Moreover, as Blumenson notes, "What critics of Bradley's decision sometimes overlook is the fact that by escaping through the Argentan-Falaise gap, the Germans ran a gauntlet of fire that stretched virtually from Mortain to the Seine. Artillery and air attacks took a fearful toll of the withdrawing enemy troops."

Moreover, critics tend to overlook another crucial factor: Without major reinforcements, the ability of Haislip's XV Corps to keep the gap north of Argentan closed was at best suspect. Despite crushing Allied superiority, the Germans in the pocket were still a dangerous fighting force. The frenzied, suicidal German reaction at Mount Ormel, where the Poles blocked the only route of escape left open between Trun and Chambois (the Corridor of Death), offers stark affirmation of what the XV Corps would have faced.

Is there more to be learned about the Falaise gap? Certainly, the role and responsibility of the Allied air forces have yet to be seriously examined. The chief of staff of a panzer corps noted that the German retreat across the Seine was made easier by the absence of Allied air forces at a critical moment. "Only a few enemy fighter and reconnaissance planes were in the air. Crossing of the Seine would have been impossible if the enemy's air forces had kept the ferrying sites under constant observation."

It is illogical to expect that in the chaos of mid-August 1944 an entire army group of veteran German troops could have been bagged in toto. This was not Stalingrad, where the Red Army was able to surround and annihilate the German Sixth Army, but a series of desperate battles across a sizable, rugged region of Normandy, well suited to the German skill in defense. The Argentan-Falaise gap was simply never the great tactical blunder that some armchair strategists have claimed. What, in retrospect, seems self-evident was, at the time, part of the inevitable fog of battle. Moreover, as Max Hastings has observed, "Far too much of the controversy and criticism surrounding the Falaise gap and other Normandy battles has focused solely upon the generals, as if their making of a decision ensured its effective execution."

More than likely, the Allies would have been even more successful if Bradley had not tried to have his cake and eat it by carrying out both a long and short envelopment, and instead opted for only one. To what extent will never be more than conjecture. If Bradley had aggressively reinforced the XV Corps between Argentan and Falaise, the short hook would have promised greater success. However, had the long envelopment been initiated earlier and had more attention been paid to seizing the Seine crossings, the results might have been even more spectacular.

The Falaise gap was one of the few battles of military history where perfect success was theoretically possible; for this reason alone, it will continue to be debated. Basil Liddell Hart has taught us that no battle can be fully understood unless viewed from "the other side of the hill." The totality of the German defeat is evident in the photographs of the death and destruction wrought by the Allies, and in the tormented faces of the survivors. War may

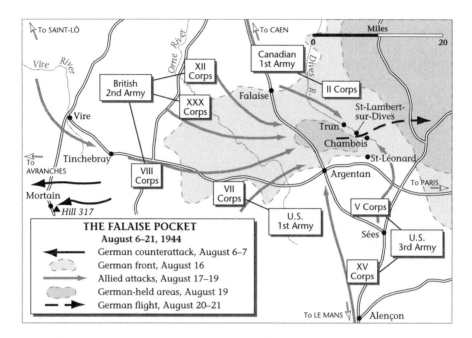

To SAINT-LÔ

Vire River

Ome River

To CAEN

Canadian
1st Army

Miles
0   20

XII
Corps

British
2nd Army

Falaise

Dives R.

II Corps

XXX
Corps

Vire

St-Lambert-
sur-Dives

Trun

Chambois

St-Léonard

To
AVRANCHES

Tinchebray

VIII
Corps

Argentan

To PARIS

VII
Corps

V Corps

Mortain

Hill 317

U.S.
1st Army

Sées

U.S.
3rd Army

THE FALAISE POCKET
August 6–21, 1944
German counterattack, August 6–7
German front, August 16
Allied attacks, August 17–19
German-held areas, August 19
German flight, August 20–21

XV
Corps

To LE MANS

Alençon

Bogged down by marshland, hedgerows, and determined German resistance, the Allies gained little in the first seven weeks after D day (the key city of Caen did not fall until July 10). But with the launching of Operation Cobra on July 25, they broke through, liberating Paris by the end of August. The Germans managed one brief counteroffensive in Normandy, against Mortain on August 6–7, but it quickly failed. Though the remnants of two German armies were nearly trapped in the shrinking Falaise pocket, the Canadians, slowly advancing south, and the Americans, moving north from Alençon, could not quite close the gap. In fierce fighting around St.-Lambert and Chambois, many Germans got away.

appear as neat and tidy lines on battle maps, but its reality is chaotic, and no battle fought in the West was more savage and untidy than the battle of the Falaise gap.

We must therefore return to the angry observations of the defeated German commanders who never forgot that the battles fought at Mortain, Falaise, Trun, Chambois, and Mount Ormel had brought about the dismemberment of Army Group B. Twenty years later, Kurt Meyer said, "It was all useless. What crass folly." And that most ardent of Nazis, Obergruppenführer Sepp Dietrich, declared: "There was only one person to blame for this stupid, impossible operation. That madman Adolf Hitler."

IN DEFENSE
OF MONTGOMERY

ALISTAIR HORNE

No Allied general in World War II has more detractors than Bernard
Law Montgomery, and most of them are American. George Patton hated
him. Omar Bradley never forgave him for his smug put-down of the Battle of the Bulge's importance. Dwight Eisenhower barely tolerated him
and turned against him after the appearance of Montgomery's war memoirs in the late 1950s. Military historians (again, mostly from the United
States) criticized his alleged lack of aggressiveness at Caen, Falaise, and
Antwerp and for his outright failure at Arnhem. The American public
joined the negative fan club of this tactless arrogant man when, in a
memorable 1957 weekend with Ike at Gettysburg, he said that both
Robert E. Lee and the Union leader George G. Meade should have been
"sacked" for their performance at the battle. Public relations were never
Montgomery's strong point. You take on American military icons at your
risk.

  Alistair Horne, a fellow Englishman and a distinguished military historian, feels that the time has come to make a case for Montgomery, and
a substantial one. Horne has no qualm about asserting—indeed, insisting—that he was Britain's greatest soldier since Wellington. The man
who gave the Allies their first land decision over Hitler at El Alamein—
Stalingrad was very much in the balance in October 1942—would go on
to become one of the chief architects of victory in Western Europe. It is
quite possible that without Montgomery the Allied return to the continent would have been far more perilous—if not disastrous: Perhaps
Rommel would have obtained the negotiated peace he sought. El
Alamein was a battle whose results were out of proportion to its size; but
it was Europe, Horne maintains, where Montgomery proved his true
worth, more perhaps before Normandy than after. He underlines three
points: Montgomery's insistence, in 1944, that the initial invasion forces

for Operation Overlord—the D day landings—be increased from three divisions to eight, including three airborne divisions; the training of those Allied forces into a winning army; and his drawing up of the strategic blueprint that achieved victory in Normandy, even though "it did not go"—to use a favorite Montgomery phrase—"according to plan."

The two-month hold-up of the British and Canadians at Caen is a major count against Montgomery's generalship. But as Horne points out, he was deprived of the extra division that might have given him needed elbow room for his armor—mainly because landing craft were being withheld for the invasion of Southern France later in the summer. (That invasion, he always believed, was unnecessary, and he was probably right.) Overcaution is another charge against Montgomery. Remember, though, that this was a man who had witnessed the Western Front slaughters of World War I and who refused to be a party to a similar expenditure of life. Horne finds Montgomery's operational plan in Normandy justified, insofar as the British pinned down seven of eight Panzer divisions, which made it possible for Patton to break out to the South. (Horne is also critical of Spielberg's *Saving Private Ryan,* where throwaway remarks about Montgomery are insulting to the British and Canadian forces in Normandy—who, in fact, formed the majority that landed on D day.) Finally, Montgomery broke with Eisenhower over the American's insistence on a broad-front strategy. At a time—the end of August 1944—when the Germans were reeling, Montgomery felt that a single "powerful and full-blooded thrust"—led by him, of course—would end the war. It would have been El Alamein all over, if on a vaster scale.

Alistair Horne was a captain with the Coldstream Guards in World War II and went on to write such notable books as *The Fall of Paris, 1870–71; The Price of Glory: Verdun 1916; To Lose a Battle: France 1940; A Savage War of Peace: Algeria 1954–1962;* and two books on Napoleon, *Napoleon: Master of Europe, 1805–1807* and *How Far from Austerlitz?* He has been awarded both the British CBE and the French Legion d'Honneur for his historical work, and is Doctor of Literature at Cambridge University.

IT IS DIFFICULT TO THINK OF ANY ALLIED MILITARY COM-
mander whose reputation, in the United States, has undergone such a reversal of fortunes as Field Marshal Viscount Montgomery of Alamein. After a half
century, it is time for a rehabilitation of Monty. This revisionism does not re-
quire knocking Ike. I give way to no one in my respect for Dwight D. Eisenhower—both as an Allied commander in war and as a president—or in my
high regard for the American forces in World War II.

I was a British teenager partially educated in the United States during
World War II, and George Patton, with his swift-moving get-up-and-go, was
my natural hero. It was probably more under his influence than Montgomery's
that I went into tanks with the British Coldstream Guards. At the end of the
war, I found myself a lowly lieutenant serving under Monty, who had become
Britain's chief of the Imperial General Staff.

I did not enormously like what I first saw—that terrible, overweening self-
confidence. He had just come out to the Middle East, where I was serving,
with the unpalatable task of telling us that exigencies of the world situation
demanded the postponement of our demobilization. The venue for this dis-
tressful encounter was a large, partially covered squash court. The moment
the great soldier began speaking, volleys of flapping pigeons took off, making
a mockery of his speech. The field marshal turned to the general with the
command, "Get those pigeons out of here!" In the best military fashion, the
general turned to the major general, who turned to the brigadier general, and
so on; the order passed all the way down the line to an embarrassed subaltern
who ineffectually endeavored to catch the pigeons with a butterfly net. The
birds were unmoved; nobody dared laugh. With mounting irritation, Monty
persisted against a backdrop of flapping; we all sat there stonily, our mirth
suppressed only by the grimness of the tidings he pronounced.

I remember reflecting long afterward on the Canute-like disbelief of this
small general that a flock of pigeons should possibly interrupt his delivery. It
all seemed appallingly arrogant. As Winston Churchill once said of him: "In
defeat, unbeatable; in victory, unbearable."

Patton, who hated his guts, dating back to the North Africa and Sicily
campaigns, once dismissed him (during the Battle of the Bulge) as "a tired little fart." His two great failings were his inability to get on with his contemporaries (not only with Americans) and his insistence that he was always right
and that "all had gone according to plan"—when it palpably had not. These

failings, alas, tended to conceal and blur—especially in American eyes—his very great contributions to victory in World War II.

He was predominantly a "soldier's general"; if the senior officers whom he brutally dispatched on physical-fitness courses hated him, the rank and file and the junior commanders venerated him. Sporting the famed black beret with its unorthodox twin cap badges, he exploited his popularity to inspire his men as did perhaps no other commander of the war. He promised them they would never go into battle with inferior air and artillery backup, and assured them that they would win. This often accounted for what American commanders criticized as his excessive caution; indeed, it helps explain his persistence with the theme, for reasons of morale, that operations had gone "according to plan." No one knew better than he what a fragile instrument the British army was, after such a long run of evacuations and defeats, before El Alamein.

Apart from his victory in that battle (which was, of course, only a small-scale engagement), if I were asked to select points that ensure his historic greatness as a commander, I would underline three: his insistence, in 1944, that the initial invasion forces for Operation Overlord—the D day landings—be increased from three divisions to eight, including three airborne divisions; the training of those Allied forces into a winning army; and his drawing up of the strategic blueprint that achieved victory in Normandy, even though it did not go "according to plan." All three factors were essential to the success of the campaign in northwestern Europe.

Twenty years after our first encounter, Monty, much mellowed in his old age, treated me with kindness—as a young military historian. His only son, David, had become a lifelong friend of mine from Cambridge days. It was under David's persuasion, to produce a truly objective view of his father (with whom his own relationship had never been comfortable), and with recourse to his own unpublished (and copious) papers, that I wrote *Monty: The Lonely Leader, 1944–45*. In it I concentrated on the Normandy campaign and the year 1944–45, and I intend to do the same here.

✦

MONTGOMERY'S FATHER, of old Protestant Irish extraction, was a bishop; his mother was a strong-willed woman with whom he never got on. It has been said that he joined the army only to annoy her. The Montgomerys, a large family, had little money, and in the affluent days of early-twentieth-century Britain, young Montgomery never had an easy time as an infantry officer. Probably it made him work all the harder to get ahead. A lieutenant at twenty-six years old, in October 1914 he was all but mortally wounded by a sniper's bullet through the lungs, in the grim First Battle of Ypres. But that bullet saved him for posterity; awarded the Distinguished Service Cross, a high decoration for a junior officer, he spent the rest of World War I on the General Staff—otherwise, by the law of averages, he would almost certainly have been killed.

He ended the war as a young lieutenant colonel, deeply affected by the wastage of life he had witnessed, the incompetence of the generals, and their total lack of contact with the front line. This was greatly to influence his own style of command a generation later.

In the interwar era, he made himself highly unpopular among pleasure-seeking army contemporaries with his urge for reform of the British army. Though he was by no means a revolutionary, or even an innovator of new prin-ciples, to him training, meticulous preparation, "balance," and—above all—morale were everything. (By "balance," one of his favorite expressions, he basically meant careful disposition of all arms and reserves, so that forces un-der his command could never be caught on the wrong foot by a sudden ri-poste, of the kind in which the German army excelled.) To the historian B. H. Liddell Hart, then a stern critic but in late life a close friend, by the 1920s "he was already one of the most thoroughly professional soldiers in the army."

After nearly a half century of NATO, we all tend to take for granted the close proximity of American and British officers' joint headquarters. But in the 1920s and 1930s, for a senior British officer ever to have met his Ameri-can counterpart was about as unlikely for either one as encountering a Mar-tian in Piccadilly. This lack of contact, and deficiency of mutual understanding, was to have a most important bearing on his relations (and those of his contemporary, and later chief, Alan Brooke) with the Ikes and Bradleys from 1942 onward.

✦

IN 1937, Montgomery lost his much-beloved wife, from the most absurd of causes: an infected insect bite. The deep loneliness caused by this tragic be-reavement made him even more dedicated to his profession—and even more incompatible with his contemporaries. Two years later, as war began, he was a major general commanding, in France, Britain's 3rd Infantry Division, which—by dint of hard training—he had made into one of the few truly crack units in the British army at that time. In the retreat at Dunkirk in May 1940, his division fell back in excellent fighting order.

But it was questionable, after the fall of France that June, whether British soldiers would ever again set foot in a Europe dominated by Hitler—except as prisoners of war. Between then and the end of 1942, Britain continued to experience one humiliating defeat after another: Norway and Dunkirk were followed by Greece, Crete, Singapore, Hong Kong, and Tobruk. Her losses in manpower, mostly in POWs, amounted to several times the size of her prewar army. In August 1942, a mainly Canadian attack on the northern French port of Dieppe—a trial run for a cross-Channel invasion—was easily repulsed by the German defenders, inflicting disastrous casualties. Montgomery, who as the area commander had been involved in the early planning stages but had left for Egypt before the attack took place, narrowly escaped responsibility. Dieppe raised the question of whether the Allies would ever be strong enough to regain a foothold in France, even supported by fresh American manpower and equipment.

Meanwhile, between 1940 and 1942, Montgomery, as a corps commander training new divisions in southern England, had consolidated his reputation. Those who fought in Normandy in 1944 owed much to him; however, being a martinet who ordered elderly colonels to go on forced marches, even if it killed them, did not enhance his popularity with his contemporaries. He never cared much about their opinion of him—which is one reason that, until the shooting down of the commander in chief–designate of the beleaguered Eighth Army in Egypt, Lieutenant General William ("Strafer") Gott, Montgomery was not a natural choice for army command, despite all his qualifications.

Then, when Churchill sent him in August 1942 to reverse catastrophe within sixty miles of Alexandria, his moment arrived. In October, the tide of war turned with his historic victory over Erwin Rommel at El Alamein. An Anglo-American force, under General Eisenhower, landed in North Africa, and by the following spring all the German and Italian forces had been cleared out of Tunisia. On the Eastern Front, meanwhile, the Soviets encircled and destroyed the German armies at Stalingrad in January.

At El Alamein, Montgomery—decisively reinforced by Sherman M4 tanks (which were then, for a brief period, the best on the field of battle)—left nothing to chance. Though Rommel was heavily outnumbered, El Alamein was nevertheless no easy victory. Montgomery was criticized for his failure to trap Rommel completely, and to follow up more swiftly. He made his name as the cautious commander—but he had reasons for caution. Nobody knew better than he how fragile a weapon the British Eighth Army was, after such a run of defeats. In terms of tactical battle handling, his armor was simply not up to the Germans'. He could not take risks.

In Sicily, in 1943, he first enraged Patton by getting bogged down around Mount Etna. (His critics remarked at the time that he seemed to mislay his

genius when he met a mountain.) Patton made a whirlwind digression to capture Palermo—and the headlines—but it was of no great strategic consequence to the main battle. In an evacuation most skillfully conducted by the
enemy commander in chief, Field Marshal Albert Kesselring, 60,000 Germans escaped across the Strait of Messina. The battle cost the British 12,000
casualties and Patton 7,500. It was not Montgomery's finest hour; nor was the
slow movement by his Eighth Army up through the rugged countryside of
Italy. After more than a year's solid campaigning, he was tired, and his heart
was elsewhere—hoping for a command in the coming invasion of Europe.

✦

A SMALL (five-foot-seven), wiry figure who reminded one of his junior officers
of a Jack Russell terrier, Monty was not Churchill's first choice to be the
ground commander of Operation Overlord, any more than he had been for
Egypt in 1942. Number one was General Sir Harold Alexander, Montgomery's nominal boss at El Alamein—nowhere near as outstanding a battlefield commander, but a far more emollient personality. Montgomery, in
contrast, was abrasive; though he had become beloved by his junior officers
and the rank and file, who appreciated him as a leader who would not sacrifice
their lives unnecessarily, he had few friends among his contemporaries—or in
high places.

As Britain's most dedicated professional soldier, Montgomery was instinc-
tively critical of the Americans' military prowess, largely on the basis of what
he had seen in the early battles of North Africa, such as the debacle at Kasserine Pass. Often he rated them, tactlessly and unfairly, as "amateurish." He
could forget that Eisenhower (and many of the generals under him) had had
no combat experience, and he deplored what he considered to be unnecessary
casualties resulting from poor training. As with the almost equally critical
Alan Brooke (though he was better at hiding his feelings), this patronizing attitude derived notably from the total lack of Anglo-American contacts in the
interwar period. And it should be remembered that almost up to the beginning of 1944, Britain—numerically—remained very much the senior partner,
at least in the European theater.

To Americans, there were many things about the wartime Montgomery
that were profoundly unpalatable (indeed, to his British contemporaries, too):
his smug boastfulness, his ex post facto insistence that all his operations had
gone precisely according to plan, his supercilious treatment of Eisenhower
and Americans in general. At times, one feels Eisenhower must have had a for-
bearance of heroic, if not saintly, proportions. Alexander might have got on
better with the Americans—but then Alexander would almost certainly never

have had the tactical skill to land a half-million men in Normandy, nor the in-spired touch to persuade men to slog on at Caen, nor the persistence to con-tinue, in the teeth of all opposition (from the Allied press as well as the enemy), with a strategy that would lead to the greatest Allied victory of the war to date.

Montgomery's first—and outstandingly important—contribution to the planning of D day was immediate, and reflexive. He told Churchill at once, on his appointment in December 1943, that the existing plan, Cossac (which stood for "chief of staff, supreme Allied commander"), was inadequate and could only lead to disaster—Dieppe on a larger scale. The beachheads would be "roped off" by the Germans and destroyed piecemeal. Instead of an initial landing force of three divisions, there would have to be five, backed by simul-taneous drops inland of three airborne divisions. Eisenhower at once con-curred.

This agreement symbolized the remarkable amity that came to surround all the Overlord planning. It represented the culminating triumph of the "special relationship"; never before, or after, would there be such close unison between GIs and Tommies as on June 6, 1944.

If there were disputes, they were not between Allies (thanks greatly to Eisenhower's outstanding diplomatic attributes), but between the ground forces and the "air barons"—the Spaatzes and the Harrises on both sides. Montgomery, one of the first British generals to place a premium on close air support, was bitterly opposed to their efforts to persist in their own strategic-bombing campaign of Germany, at what he felt could be the cost of the inva-sion forces. Getting a reluctant Churchill to place his weight behind the "transportation scheme," to smash the French rail and road system leading to Normandy, was one of the most important battles he won before D day.

He was not, however, able to win Eisenhower and the Americans round to canceling Operation Anvil (later renamed Dragoon), the diversionary attack planned for the south of France. Originally planned to take place during the Normandy landings, Dragoon was finally carried out, after much Anglo-American wrangling, by the U.S. Seventh Army (with some Free French forces) after the Battle of Normandy had been won. Montgomery fought in-cessantly against that operation as an unnecessary diversion of precious land-ing craft. In his memoirs, he called it "one of the great strategic mistakes of the war." It further persuaded him that Ike had no proper sense of strategic priorities.

The overall shortage of landing craft also reflected badly on President Roo-sevelt and some of his early decisions after Pearl Harbor. With the need to replace U.S. warship losses uppermost in his mind, in early 1942 FDR was on record as saying that he thought construction of landing craft was "a mistake." By November he had permitted it to slide down to twelfth place on the U.S. Navy's Shipbuilding Precedence List. In March 1943, the British warned the U.S. Joint Chiefs of Staff that invasion in 1944 was being jeopardized by a shortage of landing craft, and that British production could not make up the shortfall. This was greeted with suspicion that Britain was using deficiences as an excuse for shuffling its feet over invasion plans; in turn, the British believed, not without reason, that Admiral Ernest J. King was surreptitiously diverting landing craft to the Pacific for his own purposes.

It was altogether an unhappy story; in February 1944, forty-one of the precious landing craft were ordered diverted from Overlord to the Mediterranean and Anvil—even though only a few weeks earlier Ike himself had warned General George C. Marshall, army chief of staff, that Anvil could "cost us a month of good campaigning weather." At the same time, from Italy, Alexander was refusing to release thirteen landing craft for Overlord, on the grounds that they were essential for supplying the mismanaged Anzio bridgehead; nor was it easy to make any swift redisposition of these lighter vessels from the Mediterranean to the Channel.

The truth was that Monty was largely right about this: the failure of landing-craft construction left the Overlord planners with an uncomfortably slender margin in which to operate. He always held that one of the most critical factors governing the scale of the initial landings was this shortage of crucial landing craft. It was to make D day, I believe, a much closer-run thing than has generally been accepted. It *could* have failed, the landings repulsed, which would have meant no further attempt to invade France until the campaigning season of 1945—with all that that implied, such as the probable use of the atomic bomb against Germany, and a deeper push by Stalin into western Europe.

The shortage also probably impeded the British critically in their drive east of the river Orne, thereby delaying the capture of the key city of Caen by many weeks—a failure that was to come close to causing the dismissal of Montgomery by an impatient Churchill. No less than three separate attempts were to be made by Montgomery to seize Caen, and each one failed, largely because the confined space east of the Orne deprived him of necessary elbow room in which to deploy his massive superiority of armor properly. Another division, even a brigade, landed between the mouth of the Orne and the river Dives on D day might have made all the difference. But the landing craft were simply not available.

✦

WITHIN THE WAITING ARMIES of 1944, many of the British still had memories of Dunkirk, and there were still those (not all that old) who could recall with horror the slaughter of the Somme in the previous war. Most had a wariness, bred of so many defeats and setbacks, toward the German enemy. Among the Americans—fresh, untried troops piling into England in ever-increasing numbers, better paid and infinitely better fed than their British counterparts—morale was exuberant, but with the zest of inexperience.

Between January and May 1944, Montgomery set to visiting every unit in the British and Canadian invasion force, and many in the American, often personally addressing some 30,000 men in a day. His technique, eminently successful, would include buttonholing one individual infantryman and—head characteristically tilted to one side while fixing the man with a penetrating gaze—barking, "You. What's your most valuable possession?"

"My rifle, sir."

"No, it's not; it's your life, and I'm going to save it for you. Now listen to me."

He would then go on to explain how he would never make the infantry attack without full artillery and air support.

Monty never forgot the lessons he had learned from the terrible wastage of 1914–18. His reassurance that it would not be repeated was a boosting of morale ("bingeing up," he would call it) that was one of his outstanding contributions to the success of Overlord.

On April 7, Montgomery gave a full, grand presentation of his master blueprint, thoroughly endorsed by Eisenhower, at his headquarters at St. Paul's School in west London. The entire Anglo-American cadre of commanders—land, sea, and air—who would take part in D day were present. It was a remarkable performance, but he made one error in judgment that was to fuel a deadly historical controversy, unresolved to this day.

This was to show a map, with hastily sketched in "phase lines," showing where in northwestern France the Allied armies would be expected to reach, up to ninety days after the invasion. This last line, D+90, stopped along the Seine, just short of Paris. But where the storm burst, raising the ire of Montgomery's critics, was the D+17 line—which showed the British firmly in possession of Caen. Omar Bradley, commanding the U.S. First Army, was infuriated; he had not been consulted, and he refused to commit himself to the phase lines. Though Montgomery's staff stressed the intended flexibility of these lines, they stuck—and, therefore, so did the fact that it was well beyond D+40 before Caen was actually secured. Never allowed to be forgotten, this opened Montgomery to criticism that might have been avoided, but for his seemingly rigid commitment to those unfortunate phase lines. Nevertheless, in terms of overall, long-term strategy, it could equally be argued in defense of the controversial phase lines that it was Montgomery's blueprint that, in fact, did get the Allied forces under his command to the Seine, and to Paris, well ahead of D+90.

✦

THE FACTS of D day—the desperate, bloody struggle of the Americans on Omaha Beach, the relatively easy Canadian and British landings farther east—have been more than well aired. Yet Americans have a surprising unawareness of the extent of the British (and Canadian) participation—although they were, in fact, marginally in the majority on D day: in the first wave, some 83,000 Britons and Canadians arrived on the beaches, about 75,000 by sea and 7,900 by air; there were 73,000 Americans, 57,500 arriving by sea and 15,500 by air. Five out of eight assault brigades were British and Canadian; two out of the three airborne divisions were American. Of the planes deployed that day, 6,080 were American and 5,510 were from the RAF or other Allied contingents; but of the naval force, only 16.5 percent was American (because of the demands of the Pacific war). The landing craft were fairly evenly divided.

From D+1 onward, however, the proportions swiftly changed, until by V-E Day the U.S. predominance was to become along the order of three-to-one. This in itself was to lie in the background behind the first major breach between Montgomery and Eisenhower, as of September.

Montgomery landed in Normandy early on D+2, and he set up his forward tactical headquarters (TAC HQ) in the Château de Creullet—which for days lay only three miles from the forward German lines. General Bradley, then his subordinate, remained at sea aboard the cruiser USS *Augusta*. For the overall battle commander of a half-million Allied soldiers, this may have seemed an extraordinarily, almost rashly far-forward position for Montgomery to choose, and the chateau frequently came under enemy fire. But it was a symbol that D day had succeeded, the Allies were firmly established—and the war in fact was won.

It was also very much in tune with how he exercised his own unique style of command. From his forward TAC HQs (he moved no less than twenty-seven times in the eleven months between D day and VE Day) would radiate out daily his liaison officers, young men in their twenties who constituted his eyes and ears, and whom he aptly dubbed "a gallant band of knights." Several were killed or wounded in the ensuing months. Montgomery's TAC HQ system, which was at variance with the ways of Eisenhower and other senior U.S. commanders, had the great advantage of putting him supremely in touch with the fighting formations under him.

On the other hand, it also left him out of touch with senior staffs at SHAEF, then still back in England; and with the speed of the advance, that disadvantage increased. Thus, with every setback, the murmurings of Montgomery's many enemies at SHAEF—British as well as Americans—rose unchecked, and Montgomery was never there to make any effort to explain, and reexplain, his strategy to Eisenhower. Equally significant, in this context, was his almost continual separation from his own able and outstandingly diplomatic chief of staff, Major General Freddie de Guingand, who got on conspicuously well with Ike and his staff.

For Monty, the most serious setback on D day was his failure to capture the key center of Caen and its adjacent airfield—as he had promised that he would do at the phase-lines conference in April. Once the initial thrust on Caen had been checked, a skillful defense by dug-in German tanks and 88s (a high-velocity antitank gun) stopped every British attack dead. Heavy bombardments by massed strategic bombers destroyed the medieval gem that was Caen, but the rubble and craters they caused made it impossible for British armor to advance. When Monty tried to break through a third time with mass deployment of armor, in Operation Goodwood, his lack of elbow room—again, because a lack of landing craft significantly impeded attempts to outflank Caen east of the Orne—also led to failure.

For the next two months, the struggle to capture Caen was to prove costly, and it inflicted the first major dent on Montgomery's reputation in northwestern Europe. Worse than his inability to explain what he was up to was his habit of trying to rewrite history, claiming that "everything had gone according to plan," and that Caen had not been his prime objective.

In fact, given a little more of the humility that Montgomery so sadly lacked, long-term events should have vindicated him entirely in Normandy. His grand strategy, as he had expounded it with utmost clarity back in April and even earlier, was to draw the enemy panzers to the British front on the east end of the line and wear them down, preparatory for the American "end-run" breakout from the west. And he kept to it. The capture of Caen would have been a bonus, but it was certainly not essential to the success of the invasion—as American-captured Cherbourg was. (It should be noted here that the German success—under Hitler's no-surrender order—in warding off the American attack on Cherbourg for three weeks enabled the defenders to render the port unusable until autumn. This was to handicap greatly the final drive on Germany.)

Montgomery's great error was not his failure to take Caen but his prediction of its capture in the initial assault. The figures of German dispositions make it hard to deny the rightness of his strategy: by mid-July, eight out of nine of Rommel's panzer divisions—610 tanks compared with 190 facing Bradley, who was now reinforced by Patton's Third Army—were pinned down facing Lieutenant General Sir Miles Dempsey's British and Canadian armies in the Caen sector. The figure remained constant, right through to July 25 when Cobra, the breakout battle, began. If the Germans could have shifted even a single battered panzer division toward Bradley (who had already undergone an appallingly costly battle to secure Saint-Lô), it would have made his breakout infinitely more difficult and costly—perhaps even impossible before August.

For a while, in July, it seemed as there might be a stalemate reminiscent of the Western Front, and—under extreme pressure from both the U.S. and the British press—Churchill came close to sacking Montgomery. The general may have damaged his reputation by claiming infallibility, but in the end it was his strategy of drawing all the German panzers onto the British, eastern end of the front, while the faster-moving Americans broke out in the west, that paid off. At the end of July, an unleashed Patton swung out relentlessly toward Paris—and Germany.

After the breakout, the fleeing remnants of the German armies in Normandy were smashed in the trap at Falaise. As in his failure to destroy the Afrika Korps after El Alamein, Montgomery has been criticized for not closing the jaws of the trap, allowing a large number of the enemy to escape (though without most of their heavy equipment). With the experienced British armored divisions resting after their battering around Caen, possibly he erred in employing inexperienced Canadian and Polish armor to head the thrust southward. Their poorly armored Shermans were stopped, with heavy losses, by the dreaded 88s once again. But Patton's claim that, if permitted, he could have closed the gap from the south is not sustained by his chief, Bradley. As Bradley wrote in his memoirs, "I much preferred a solid shoulder at Argentan to the possibility of a broken neck at Falaise." Patton's greatly extended forces at hand were simply not strong enough to take such a risk.

Nevertheless, Falaise meant the end of the Normandy campaign. The Germans were reckoned to have lost as many as 450,000 men, including 210,000 POWs, as well as more than twenty generals (including Rommel, severely wounded by British fighter-bombers), 1,500 tanks, and 3,500 guns. Only a score of tanks were ferried east across the Seine, where all the bridges had been destroyed under the transportation plan for which Montgomery had fought so

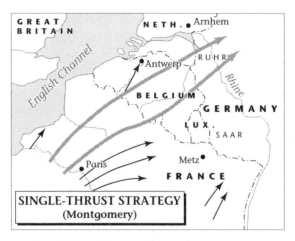

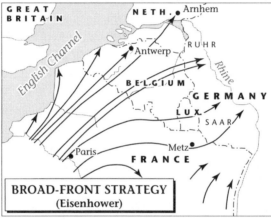

Montgomery and Eisenhower disagreed about the plan of attack the Allies should follow after the Normandy breakout. Monty favored a narrow thrust focusing on Antwerp and the Ruhr. Ike preferred a broad-front advance to the German frontier.

hard before D day. Allied casualties had by no means been light, testimony to how hard the Wehrmacht had fought, despite an almost total lack of air support: 209,672, of whom 36,976 had been killed (roughly in a ratio of two British and Canadian casualties to three American).

In strategic terms, it was a decisive victory that would rank with Stalingrad—though casualties inflicted in France were substantially higher. And no one can take away from Montgomery the key role he played in it. As one of his severest critics, Eisenhower's redoubtable chief of staff, Walter Bedell Smith, was to remark of D day in retrospect: "I don't know if we could have done it without Monty. It was his sort of battle. Whatever they say about him, he got us there."

✦

ON AUGUST 25, Paris was liberated. Abruptly, the whole tenor of the war changed. Now the falling-out between Eisenhower and Montgomery began in earnest. A sense of euphoria afflicted both American and British armies; there was a strong feeling—irrational, but based on history—that with one more big push the Germans would collapse, as they had done in 1918. But at a level above Montgomery and Eisenhower, that of the Combined Chiefs of Staff, there was no contingency plan for fighting the next stage of the war—if the Germans did *not* collapse.

Eisenhower's intentions were to advance with the whole of the Allied armies to the German frontier, then wait for an opportunity to present itself, "bulling ahead on all fronts," as he put it. Again, as with Anvil, Montgomery thought this broad-front strategy represented a dangerous dispersal of effort. From mid-August on, he began besieging Eisenhower with his own scheme of a narrow, single thrust toward the vital industrial area of the Ruhr, and then Berlin. But in the meantime, Eisenhower had been promoted to assume overall command of the Allied armies; Montgomery, though made a five-star field marshal on September 1, was in effect demoted and, as an army-group commander, placed on a par with his former subordinate, Omar Bradley.

Given the preponderance of U.S. forces now in the coalition, and the Americans' historical distaste for serving under foreign commanders, this was only to have been expected. Montgomery, however, was deeply angered: it was not just an affront to his pride, but also his unshakable conviction, based on a lifetime as Britain's most professional soldier, that Eisenhower's strategy was catastrophically wrongheaded. As he told Ike, repeatedly—never letting up, to the point where a lesser man than Eisenhower would have exploded (and he nearly did)—the only way to finish off the war was with his one "powerful and full-blooded thrust": The resources in men and matériel did not exist for anything more. The thrust would be spearheaded by the British armies in the north, under Montgomery himself—though at one point he did offer to place himself under Bradley's overall command to meet American wishes.

If Monty opposed the notion of a single thrust headed by Patton in the Saar area to the south, this was based less on personal grounds than on geographic ones. In the fall of 1944, Patton had gotten seriously bogged down around Metz, suffering heavy casualties, which Monty considered quite unnecessary. Ahead of Patton, across the Rhine, lay far more difficult country than presented to the north, and—in contrast to the Ruhr—it led to no immediate strategic objective. This was a view largely reinforced by the German generals interviewed by Liddell Hart after the war. Liddell Hart's own view was that, as of September 1944, Eisenhower's broad-front plan

> would have been a good way to strain and crack the resistance of a strong and still unbeaten enemy. But it was far less suited to the actual situation where the enemy had already collapsed, and the issue depended on exploiting their collapse so deeply and rapidly that they would have no chance to rally. That called for a pursuit without pause.

Recalling the pursuit after El Alamein, however, critics of Montgomery might well wonder whether he was ideally suited to conducting such an action, given also that the British forces were more battle-fatigued than some of the fresh American reserves who were then reaching the front. The case remains open.

At the same time, perhaps with more sound reason on his side, Monty criticized Eisenhower's intention to take over command of all land operations, in addition to his all-consuming role as supreme Allied commander—and from a forward headquarters then on the western side of the Cherbourg peninsula, far behind the front. Ike should not leave his "very lofty perch," Montgomery felt; to exert direct control over such a massive agglomeration of land forces as well would be altogether too much for one man.

History was to prove that both commanders were wrong—and both were right. Logistically, as well as politically, the odds were against a single thrust; it might possibly have worked at the beginning of September, when the Germans were still off balance—but after five years of war, the British forces (who would, inevitably, have led the spearhead) were beginning to show serious signs of exhaustion. Yet Eisenhower's broad-front strategy—combined with the attempt to "bounce the Rhine" at Arnhem to the north—was, through its overstretching of reserves, to lead (at least in Montgomery's not very tactful view) directly to the December catastrophe in the Bulge.

✦

THE ALLIED AIRBORNE disaster at Arnhem in mid-September—for which Montgomery was held largely responsible—has historically been regarded as the key to the disappointments at the end of 1944. Possibly Eisenhower was at fault in allowing him to go ahead, while at the same time allowing Patton to press on Metz and the Saar far to the south. Yet, strategically, of far greater consequence was the earlier neglect to clear the approaches to Antwerp in the estuary of the river Scheldt. I am convinced that this, and not Arnhem, was the biggest single error of the whole post-Normandy campaign.

Antwerp, the largest port in northwestern Europe (and, by the fall of 1944, still largely undamaged), straddles both sides of the Scheldt, the estuary of which extends some fifty miles to the open sea. The entrance to the estuary is no more than three miles wide. To utilize the port, the approaches on both the Belgian and the Dutch sides of the estuary, as well as Antwerp itself, would have to be cleared of the enemy. Had Montgomery and Eisenhower not been in dispute then, this critical failure to secure Antwerp in early September would probably not have occurred. British armor had actually captured most of Antwerp itself by September 4; then, running out of fuel, it went no farther. But with the Germans still reeling back in disorder, a determined move could easily have secured the approaches to the city on the Dutch side of the Scheldt in that first week of September.

Meanwhile, in the south, and out of Eisenhower's control, Patton's Third Army was consuming vast quantities of fuel that could have been allocated to the British thrust. As a result, for vital weeks—until well into November—the Allies were deprived of the large port, essential to carrying the war into Germany. Much of their vast tonnage of supplies was still arriving via the beaches of Normandy, hundreds of miles to the rear. (It is worth noting that by April 1945, one month before the end of the war, over 1.6 million tons of stores and fuel were unloaded at Antwerp, of which two-thirds went to the American armies. This compares with 450,000 tons via Le Havre and 630,000 tons from Marseilles and all the other southern French ports—combined—that had been liberated by Operation Dragoon.)

Moreover, 100,000 German troops—the whole Fifteenth Army, trapped in the Pas de Calais by the collapse in Normandy—were permitted to escape across the Scheldt into Holland. The evacuation of these troops across the three-mile-wide estuary, in the teeth of Allied air and sea supremacy, was a feat little less remarkable than Dunkirk. It was these troops who were in position on September 17 when Montgomery launched his airborne attack on Arnhem—and many of them, later, were available to take part in the Bulge.

Arnhem, the risky gamble so out of character with Montgomery's cautious character, had much to do with his single-minded determination to prove that *his* strategy of the narrow thrust into Germany from the north was right. As an undertaking, Arnhem had many planning defects; not least, it was a fundamental error to land the British 1st Airborne Division so far from the vital bridge, and the relieving armored column was not able to move fast enough to link up with it. But these defects could only indirectly be laid at Monty's door, insofar as he was overall commander. Yet had it not been for that earlier failure at Antwerp, Arnhem could well have succeeded; Montgomery's strategy, not Eisenhower's, would have been vindicated; and the field marshal would have been regarded as one of history's greatest commanders. At Antwerp, both Ike and Monty were to blame; but it cannot be forgotten that as of September 1, Ike was commander in chief of all Allied ground forces. Surely he should have *ordered* Monty, after the liberation of Paris, to go flat out for Antwerp.

Cornelius Ryan gave his book about Arnhem the title *A Bridge Too Far,* meaning that it was too far from the armored column that was supposed to link up with it. But it may also have been located strategically and geographically too far to the north, away from the main line of advance. Wesel, lower down the Rhine, would have been a better choice.

As it was, failure at Arnhem meant that the Allied line was left stretched still farther northward, inviting a German counterthrust. The British forces were now desperately short of replacements. The Pacific war was at its peak, and America's recruitment program had fallen down in its provision of infantry reserves, so that even with her huge manpower the U.S. Army was running short of trained riflemen. Eisenhower's strategy meant that there were simply not enough reserves available to meet an unexpected emergency. And Hitler obtained a breather to re-create the two new panzer armies that were to smash through the weakened American line in the Ardennes two months later.

✦

THE BULGE, that epic of American heroism in the bitter winter of 1944–45, wrestled victory out of defeat, but at an appalling cost—80,000 U.S. casualties against 120,000 German. It represented the shattering of any last, crazy hope that Hitler may have had of winning the war, and it opened the door to the invasion of Germany in March 1945. But should it ever have happened? Should General Troy Middleton's VIII Corps have been left spread out so thinly that a single regiment found itself attacked by an entire panzer corps? Could it all have been avoided through a better-conceived strategy back in September?

Certainly Montgomery always thought so, for the rest of his life; and, with his usual tact, he could not resist rubbing it in to his fellow American commanders when the battle was over. With communications between General Courtney Hodges's First Army and Bradley's command headquarters in Luxembourg severed by the German thrust of December 16, a reluctant but shaken Eisenhower placed all of the U.S. forces north of the Bulge back under

Montgomery's command four days later—temporarily. Bradley, in his memoirs, claimed that his consent to this shift in command was "one of my biggest mistakes of the war."

Montgomery's cool defensive dispositions to prevent any danger of the Germans' crossing the Meuse and seizing Liège or Antwerp—which would, in effect, have cut the Allied armies in two, much as Hitler had done in May 1940—was undoubtedly an important contribution to stabilizing and then winning the battle in the north. It is simply not true to say, as the historian Stephen E. Ambrose did recently on television, that Montgomery's role was "nil." Still, the actual victory was almost entirely American, with Patton's remarkable ninety-degree left wheel, which relieved Bastogne, and the Allied casualties were nine-to-one American.

So it was appallingly maladroit when, on January 7, 1945, to mark the halting of the German panzers, Montgomery rashly held a disastrous press conference, which even he later conceded was a mistake. At his very worst that day, he could not resist a note of "I told you so." Though he paid high tribute to both the American troops and Eisenhower, his reference to the Bulge as "a most interesting little battle" seemed insufferable to battered U.S. pride.

One of the most serious casualties of the press conference—which admittedly was most skillfully distorted and exaggerated by German propaganda minister Joseph Goebbels—was the "special relationship" within the Allied high command, which had held up so superbly from D day, and before. Bradley never forgave Montgomery, and Eisenhower was to claim it caused him "more distress and worry" than anything else in the entire war. For the remainder of the campaign, Eisenhower paid minimal attention to Montgomery's strategic pleas; the two armies largely did their own thing. Montgomery's British and Canadians headed northward to Hamburg and the Baltic, where Monty accepted the first German surrender, at Lüneburg on May 4. Bradley, under Ike's orders, directed his main axis toward Leipzig, Dresden, and southern Germany—where there were exaggerated intelligence reports of the establishment of a last-ditch Nazi "redoubt." Berlin, to Monty's chagrin, was left to the Soviets—as per the political accords agreed to with Stalin at Yalta in February.

The discord in the last months of the war provided a sad ending to the brilliant display of Anglo-American amity that had preceded Overlord—and it was compounded by the "battle of memoirs" that flooded both sides of the Atlantic for decades after 1945. If there is a lesson to the slide that followed the triumph in Normandy, it is what happens in coalition affairs when great allies fall out and go their own way. The lessons remain valid today. Perhaps it could have been different—if Montgomery had been less of the single-minded military commander and much more of a diplomat, and Eisenhower had been less of the great diplomat that he was, and marginally more of a commander. One fact, however, is undeniable: the combination of both men was absolutely essential to victory in the West.

Perhaps the last word should go to Winston Churchill, who appointed Montgomery in the first place, and who often found himself infuriated by Monty's arrogant intractability—yet recognized his surpassing qualities of generalship. When, after the war, members of his entourage were passing snide comments about Monty, Churchill bit back:

> I know why you all hate him. You are jealous: he is better than you are. Ask yourselves these questions. What is a general for? Answer: to win battles. Did he win them without much slaughter? Yes. So what are you grumbling about?

DID STRATEGIC BOMBING WORK?

WILLIAMSON MURRAY

"The most controversial aspect of the war . . ." That is how, in effect, most studies of the Combined Bomber Offensive against Nazi Germany begin. If one can't argue with the assessment, one usually can with the various conclusions. "Strategic" bombing—or carrying the war to the military and industrial heart of the enemy—was seen as a way of destroying his ability to wage war as well as his will to fight. It was not only immoral, its critics claim, but it didn't work; even for the Allies, the uncertain results were disproportionate to the high costs. Strategic bombing was immoral in the sense that it killed some 600,000 Germans (of whom more than a 100,000 were children) and maimed another 800,000. As much as it hurt German industry—the extent will always be debated—strategic bombing didn't shut it down until the end. Armament production, for example, never ceased—which is why, after the crisis of the late summer of 1944, the Nazis were able to re-equip their army for a last stand on the borders of the Reich. As for sapping the will to fight, German civilian morale remained steadfast. And the cost to the Allies was prohibitive. The American Eighth Air Force, operating out of England, lost 2,400 bombers in 1944 alone. The British Bomber Command could count 55,000 dead airmen for the entire war, more than the number of British army officers killed in World War I. Certainly in the grim early years of the war, strategic bombing was the one way that the British could take the war to Germany. Just the sight of Allied bombers overhead must have been a morale-lifter in occupied countries—though in 1941 more aircrew died in bombing raids than German civilians. But as the raids increased in size and strength, and the Americans joined in, the antiaircraft system in Germany was forced to drain as many as two million from combat elsewhere. That in itself was a justification for strategic bombing, especially in 1942 and 1943, when it kept men from being shipped out to Russia or North Africa, where they might have tipped balances. (It's worth noting that in this form of combat the Germans did not hesitate to use women as antiaircraft gunners. In England, meanwhile, women could aim the guns and pass the ammunition; but men were still required to fire them.)

Nothing, certainly, was more successful than the air campaign against the German transportation system: oil plants, rail lines and roads, bridges, switching yards, and locomotive repair shops. As much as anything, strategic bombing won the battle of Normandy. And as thousand-plane raids became the norm, the transportation campaign, even more than the destruction of factories, would in the end shut down the German war economy. Murray concludes that we can never judge, only speculate, how well Germany would have done if it had not been for the Combined Bomber Offensive.

Williamson Murray is a professor of history emeritus at Ohio State University and, with Allen R. Millett, the author of the recently published *A War to Be Won: Fighting the Second World War.*

THE MOST CONTROVERSIAL ASPECT OF THE WAR THAT THE United States and Great Britain waged against Nazi Germany was the Combined Bomber Offensive. The Harvard economist John Kenneth Galbraith, a member of the U.S. Strategic Bombing Survey, has articulated the arguments of those who dispute the contribution of strategic bombing to victory in the war. As he wrote in his memoirs:

> German war production had, indeed, expanded under the bombing. The greatly heralded efforts, those on the ball-bearing and aircraft plants for example, emerged as costly failures. Other operations, those against oil and the railroads, did have military effect. But strategic bombing had not won the war. At most, it had eased somewhat the task of the ground troops who did. The aircraft, manpower, and bombs used in the campaign had cost the American economy far more in output than they had cost Germany.

Galbraith's comment, that at most the Combined Bomber Offensive saved a few infantrymen's lives, suggests the pervasive view in much scholarly literature about World War II in Europe. That view contrasts the small savings with the wreckage of some of the world's most cultured and beautiful cities and the slaughter of innumerable civilians. Such criticisms reflect the fact that strategic bombing was not a pretty thing, and it laid waste to some of the great monuments of the Old World.

But World War II was a matter of national survival, a war waged against a tyranny that represented a hideous moral and strategic danger. Consequently, any judgment on the Combined Bomber Offensive must rest on the grounds of expediency rather than on those of morality. As Clausewitz suggests, "It would be futile—even wrong—to try and shut one's eyes to what war really is from sheer distress at its brutality."

We need first to examine the conduct of the British and American campaigns from their intellectual and doctrinal origins to their actual implementation. The countries' theories of air power had much in common. Both held that aircraft represented the decisive weapon of the next war; that their only proper role was as strategic bombers that would directly attack an enemy nation's centers of population and industrial production; that strategic bombing would lead to quick victories and avoid the prolonged attrition that had characterized trench warfare; that cooperation with other services represented a mistaken diversion of air resources; that enemy fighters could not interfere in any significant manner with the conduct of a bombing offensive; and that the experience of previous war—in short, military history—had nothing to teach airmen.

Nevertheless, considerable differences developed between the British and American strategic-bombing doctrines that evolved during the period before the outbreak of World War II. The British emphasized attacks on enemy population centers, which they believed would destroy enemy morale. The Americans, however, favored a conception of strategic bombing that sought to destroy specific targets within the enemy's industrial system, leading to widespread economic dislocation and collapse.

War soon contradicted the assumptions with which airmen began the war. By the time the Royal Air Force initiated strategic bombing in May 1940, in response to the German attack on western Europe, the British already understood that their bombers could not survive in daylight against German fighters. Initially, they attacked specific industrial targets such as refineries or rubber plants at night, an approach more like the American one than their own interwar doctrine.

But in the summer of 1941, a detailed study of bombing raids brought depressing news to the RAF. Less than one-third of its bombers were dropping their loads within five miles of the specific industrial targets they were attacking. A target with a radius of five miles would contain over seventy-five square miles—yet two-thirds of the crews could not even come close to them. The obvious conclusion was that the only targets suitable for attack under nighttime conditions were German cities. Thus began Bomber Command's "area bombing" campaign, an effort that aimed to "dehouse" Germany's urban population and break the Nazi morale—which had been the original rationale of British strategic bombing. This effort represented the only possibility in 1941 of carrying the war to Germany. But in the face of defeats in North Africa and the Far East, it was more the strain on British morale than German that made some such campaign a political necessity.

The initial German response to the British night attacks was halfhearted. Some investment in a night-fighter force did occur, and the Germans did create an extensive radar and communication system. But two things prevented them from making major investments in air defense at this early date. First, their own offensive proclivities drove them to a strategy that aimed at paying the British back with attacks on British cities. The "Baby Blitz" of 1942 is a good example of an approach that in the long term was to have such a negative impact on German defenses. Second, given the difficulties the British were having in the early days of their attacks, the Germans for the most part failed to catch the significance of the long-term threat from the British bombing offensive. In early 1941 the British launched nighttime raids against Karlsruhe and Stuttgart; German radio reported British bombers over "Aachen, Eupen, Malmédy, Koblenz, Neuwied, Kreuznach, Frankfurt am Main, Wiesbaden, Limburg, Darmstadt, Mainz, Worms, Trier, Offenburg, Saarfels, Nuremberg, Erlangen, Bamberg, Bayreuth, Coburg, Pegnitz, Aschaffenburg, Schweinfurt, Würzburg, Regensburg, Weiden, and Chemnitz." It is not hard to see why some Germans might have underestimated the threat in 1941.

In February 1942, Arthur Harris was appointed head of Bomber Command. His name soon became synonymous with the conduct of the RAF's bombing campaign. At the beginning, substantial changes in the weaponry of the command aided Harris: coming into service were new four-engine bombers, the Sterling and the Halifax, and soon the first Lancasters, the best heavy bomber of the European war (with a bombload averaging over seven tons versus barely four for the B-17). As important was the fact that the RAF also acquired navigational aids and tactics that revolutionized the conduct of nighttime strategic bombing.

Bomber Command achieved a number of notable successes in 1942. Harris understood two crucial factors in that year: first, the technological limitations of his command were such that only area bombing offered potential that could be realized; second, he had to achieve significant successes immediately or the resources allocated to his command would shift elsewhere (such as to the Battle of the Atlantic). Consequently, Harris picked cities for their vulnerability rather than their economic or military significance. He first went after Rostock and Lübeck, which were easy to find because of their location on the Baltic. Then, in late May, Bomber Command put everything it had into the air, including the operational training squadrons. It launched 1,000 aircraft against Cologne and plastered that city's downtown area. Adolf Hitler himself recognized the significance of the raid. He remarked to his Luftwaffe aides that the British were opening up a second front in the West in support of the Soviets, who were struggling in the East.

Bomber Command's efforts over the rest of 1942 were less successful, which in the long term proved an unanticipated piece of luck. Because the air defense of Germany's cities never received Hitler's undivided attention, the Germans lost crucial time preparing for the coming storm. In January 1943, British and American air leaders agreed to wage a nonstop day-and-night offensive to break Nazi Germany, and by now the production to support it was beginning to flow from the factories of both nations.

In late winter and spring 1943, Bomber Command, largely reequipped with four-engine bombers, battered the population centers of the Ruhr, Germany's industrial heartland. Although its aircraft never reached hoped-for levels of destruction, they were now punishing the Germans severely. In late July, Bomber Command attacked the Baltic port of Hamburg with four major raids: it hit the jackpot. By using strips of aluminum, code-named Window, the British blinded the German night air defenses: radar stations, antiaircraft guns, and night fighters simply ceased to operate effectively. Conditions over Hamburg were ideal. Not only was visibility for marking the target nearly perfect, but the weather was dry and hot. The first markers went down on the great lumberyard into which Baltic timber arrived in Germany; within a relatively few moments, Hamburg's center was a raging inferno. Succeeding crews dropped their bomb and incendiary loads over the fire, spreading it. A tower of superheated air reached up to and over the bombers. The resulting vacuum sucked in masses of air from the surrounding countryside. Winds reached 300 miles per hour; temperatures, upward of 1,000 degrees, in some cases incinerating those in shelters. Over 40,000 Germans died. The catastrophe came as a terrible shock to the German nation. The Nazi minister of armaments, Albert Speer, even warned Hitler that four or five more Hamburgs over the summer would lead to a general collapse of national morale.

But Bomber Command was not in a position to duplicate its success. In October it did create a second firestorm at Kassel, but a combination of bad weather and increasingly effective defenses, as the Luftwaffe countered the effects of Window, spelled increasing difficulty for the British.

As for the Americans, the first U.S. B-17s arrived in England in the summer of 1942 and immediately began attacking industrial targets in occupied France, such as the Renault factory outside Paris. Supported by British short-range fighters in their daylight raids, the American bombers suffered relatively low casualty rates. But the Americans never reached the level of 300 operational bombers that air leaders felt was necessary to strike beyond the range of fighter escorts. Moreover, the North African landings in November 1942 siphoned off U.S. bomber strength from England to the Mediterranean.

It was not until spring 1943 that Eighth Air Force in England reached sufficient strength to attempt deep-penetration, daylight raids into German airspace beyond the range of Allied escort fighters. From the first, the Americans discovered that this was going to be a nasty business. The Germans had built their air defenses in depth. And the Luftwaffe began to bring significant numbers of its best fighter squadrons back to the homeland to defend the daytime skies over the Reich as the American effort expanded.

Throughout the summer and fall of 1943, a terrible attrition of Eighth Air Force aircrews took place, as its leaders struggled to prove that unescorted daylight missions against precision targets deep in the Reich could work. For the command, crew losses averaged over 30 percent per month over the summer and fall. Of thirty-five aircrews that arrived in England with the 100th Bomb Group at the end of May, only 14 percent of the crew members made it through the twenty-five missions required for rotation. The rest were dead, wounded, missing, psychological cases, or prisoners of war. Things were no better for the Luftwaffe. Although extravagant claims by Eighth Air Force gunners had little relationship to reality, Luftwaffe fighters suffered heavy losses throughout the period. To put it into perspective, a young American had a better chance of surviving the war by fighting with the Marines in the Pacific than flying in bombers over Germany in 1943; similarly, a young German had more chance of surviving the war by fighting in the Waffen SS than in a fighter in the skies over the Reich.

In August, Eighth Air Force launched its most ambitious deep-penetration mission thus far. Two separate formations, supposedly mutually supporting, attacked the ball-bearing factories at Schweinfurt and aircraft-production facilities at Regensburg in an effort to take out both those facilities with precision bombing. Unfortunately, because of fog over English air bases, the missions entered German territory at widely different times. After savaging the first formation, Luftwaffe fighters had time to land, rearm, and refuel. They shot down sixty bombers from both missions. But damage to Schweinfurt and Regensburg was considerable. That night, a major Bomber Command raid wrecked the research-and-development station at Peenemünde, where the V-1 cruise missile and the V-2 ballistic missile were under development. Underlining the strain that the German defenders were under, the Luftwaffe's chief of staff, General Hans Jeschonnek, committed suicide the next day.

After a slowdown in September to recover from heavy losses in midsummer, the Americans attacked in force in October. Again losses were high. On "Black Thursday," October 14, B-17s attempted to complete the destruction of the ball-bearing factories at Schweinfurt; again the attackers lost sixty aircraft. These air battles over targets deep in Germany represented a significant short-term victory for the Luftwaffe. The message was clear: bombers could not survive beyond the range of fighter escort. There was another problem. By the time the B-17s recovered enough from their losses in August to return to Schweinfurt in October, the Germans had already dispersed much of the production of ball bearings. And the losses that Eighth Air Force suffered in the second attack ensured that the B-17s would not be able to go back to Schweinfurt until February 1944.

As the fortunes of the American strategic bombing were skidding toward a low point, Harris launched Bomber Command in an all-out effort to destroy Berlin. From November 1943 through March 1944, his bombers hammered the German capital in hopes that they could break the morale of the government and the people. They broke neither, but their losses came close to wrecking the command. Though poorly supported by Hitler and Reichsmarschall Hermann Göring, the commander in chief of the Luftwaffe, German night defenses nevertheless rose to the occasion; British losses reached staggering proportions. In addition, on the night of March 30–31, 1944, Bomber Command lost 108 bombers in an attack against Nuremberg. Bomber Command had reached the same point that the Americans had reached in October 1943: bombers could not survive at an acceptable rate of attrition without protection from escort fighters.

By this point, however, Eighth Air Force was on the way to recovery. General Jimmy Doolittle replaced General Ira Eaker as its commander at the end of 1943, while a new fighter, the P-51 Mustang, which few in either the RAF or the U.S. Army Air Forces had believed could be built, provided the sought-for capability—long-range fighter escort. Eighth Air Force returned to attack the German aircraft industry in February 1944. The attacks had considerable impact on German aircraft production. Although German production of fighters rose significantly over the course of the year, the Germans achieved that only by stopping production of virtually all other aircraft types.

More significantly, Eighth Air Force's attacks forced the Luftwaffe to concentrate on defending its industrial base from American blows. For the four months between February and May 1944, a terrible battle of attrition occurred between the Americans and the Germans. Each month the former lost the equivalent of 25 percent of the bombers and approximately 30 percent of the crews with which they had begun the month. But such was American production strength that the number of operational bombers available in the squadrons actually climbed. On the other hand, the Luftwaffe was losing over 20 percent of its fighter pilots every month. The Allies could afford their aircraft and crew losses; the Germans could not. In May the German resistance collapsed. No longer was the Luftwaffe capable of defending even the Reich; on the frontiers of the Nazi empire, the Wehrmacht would now fight without any protection from the blows launched by Allied air forces.

In April, British and American strategic bombers came under the control of General Dwight Eisenhower, supreme Allied commander in Europe, and his chief deputy, the British airman Sir Arthur Tedder. They found themselves involved in a campaign to shut down the logistical support that the German army required to fight the coming battle in Normandy. Given the defeat in the Battle of Berlin, Bomber Command had no choice but to comply. The commanders of Eighth Air Force were less willing, but in the end they also played. Over the course of April, May, and early June, Allied air attacks smashed up the road and rail networks of northern France and Belgium. In early June, just before D day, a German logistical report admitted their effectiveness:

> In Zone 1 [France and Belgium], the systematic destruction that has been carried out since March of all important junctions of the entire network—not only of the main rail lines—has most seriously crippled the whole transport system (railway installations, including rolling stock). Similarly, Paris has been systematically cut off from long-distance traffic, and the most important bridges over the lower Seine have been destroyed one after another. As a result . . . it is only by exerting the greatest efforts that purely military traffic and goods essential to the war effort . . . can be kept moving. . . . The [enemy] aim has so successfully been achieved—locally at any rate—that the *Reichsbahn* [the German railroad] authorities are seriously considering whether it is not useless to attempt further repair work.

In the end, the campaign against the logistical network played a crucial role in Allied victories in Normandy and eventually in the reconquest of France and Belgium. Thanks to Allied air power, the Germans had lost the battle that may have mattered most, the battle of the buildup.

So overwhelming had Allied air resources become by spring 1944 that General Carl Spaatz, overall commander of the U.S. strategic-bombing effort since the start of the year, persuaded Eisenhower to allow his bombers to attack the German oil industry. Since Fifteenth Air Force in Italy was already bombing the Romanian oil fields, it seemed likely that attacks on the German synthetic-oil industry in the Reich would cripple Nazi fuel production. On May 12, 1944, some 935 B-17s and B-24s attacked synthetic-oil plants at Zwickau, Merseburg-Leuna, Brüx, Lützkendorf, Böhlen, Zeitz, and Chemnitz. Almost immediately, the American air commanders received confirmation from Ultra decryptions of the enemy's high-level ciphers that the Germans were desperate about these attacks. From this point to the end of the war, the Americans made the oil industry the focus of their air campaign.

The collapse of the German position in the West in August and the Allied advance to the German frontier wrecked the Luftwaffe's early-warning network. Beginning in September, Bomber Command returned to its savaging of German cities. The emphasis of American attacks remained on oil targets. But both bombing forces cooperated in an additional effort to destroy Germany's transportation network. Tedder managed this campaign, as he had the one in France. By February 1945, these attacks had finally broken Germany's ability to move and distribute its industrial and war production; the inevitable result was the collapse in the West that began in March 1945.

✦

THUS FAR, we have concentrated on the conduct of operations during the war. What impact did the extraordinary efforts of the British and American strategic-bombing offensive actually have on winning the war?

Regarding the British effort, it must first be noted that the bombing of Germany in the early war years was essential to bolstering British morale. With the string of German successes through 1942 in the land war, and the U-boat successes that threatened the very survival of Britain, the bombing of German cities was the only means of striking back at the enemy.

In a direct sense, the effectiveness of Bomber Command's offensive was more limited than that of the Americans. In its attacks on French transportation targets in spring 1944, the tactics, techniques, and technological capabilities developed in 1942 and 1943 allowed it to play the crucial role in breaking the Wehrmacht's transportation network in northern France. With effective navigational aids, British pathfinder bombers—the aircraft that dropped target markers to help following aircraft—were able to identify the transportation targets, and then, with each bomber dropping its load independently, the British were able to achieve more accurate patterns than their American counterparts. Ironically, Harris had made a thoroughly disingenuous effort to persuade Winston Churchill that Bomber Command could not strike precision targets in France—thereby reinforcing Churchill's fears that tens of thousands of French civilians might die in such raids, with serious political consequences for postwar Anglo-French relations. But a series of test raids had shown that Harris was wrong. Bomber Command followed with a series of devastating raids against the marshaling yards on which the French railroad system—and German logistics—depended.

Bomber Command's greatest contribution to the winning of the war came in an indirect fashion. By 1943, area bombing had caused a dramatic decline in the morale of the German populace. These ferocious attacks also caused considerable dislocations in Germany's economic performance. A German economy unburdened by such attacks and drawing on all of central and western Europe might have reached production totals close to those of the United States or the Soviet Union.

The impact on German morale seriously worried the Nazi leadership, particularly since that leadership blamed Germany's defeat in 1918 on the collapse of morale at home rather than on military defeat at the battlefront. Thus, the British assault on German morale led Hitler and Göring to base their decisions on political rather than military factors. As a result, they made two serious military mistakes.

Because Germany's population drew considerable psychological support from the comforting sound of antiaircraft artillery blasting at RAF bombers, Hitler and Göring emphasized that in their response to the bombing—even though the Luftwaffe knew as early as 1942 that these weapons were not cost-effective: antiaircraft guns expended more resources in shooting down a bomber than it took the British to build it.

By the summer of 1943, no fewer than 89 flak batteries defended Berlin. From 791 batteries (88s, 105s, and 128s) defending the Reich in 1940, Germany's antiaircraft forces grew to 967 batteries in 1941, 1,148 in 1942, and 2,132 in 1943. All of these batteries used up ammunition in prodigious quantities and to little effect. For example, the 88mm flak 36 weapon required the expenditure of more than 16,000 shells to bring down a single aircraft, even when the enemy bombers attacked in a concentrated stream.

But intense pressure from Joseph Goebbels, the minister for propaganda, and the *Gauleiters,* Nazi Germany's political bosses, kept the emphasis on flak to meet the British bombing offensive. Obviously, the presence of somewhere around 10,000 antiaircraft guns, all of which were also highly capable as antitank weapons, and the half-million men to operate them would have had a significant impact on any of the battles in 1943 and 1944, whether one talks about Kursk, Salerno, or Normandy.

The second indirect impact of area bombing was in its influence on Nazi leaders who were making crucial choices about weapons production. To the end of the war, ironically, the Nazis remained firmly tied to the notion of air strategy that Giulio Douhet, the Italian air theorist, had articulated in the 1920s. As Douhet had argued, offense was the key, and except in the case of antiaircraft guns, the Nazis did not rely on defensive measures to try to ward off Allied air attacks.

Instead, the Nazis struck back with terror attacks of their own. Hitler set the tone. In the aftermath of Harris's 1,000-bomber raid on Cologne in May 1942, the führer warned that the only reply to such attacks was retaliation in kind. A year later, shortly after the Hamburg firestorm, he suggested that "terror can only be broken with terror. Attacks on German airfields made no impression on him [Hitler], but the smashing of the Reich's cities was another matter. It was the same with the enemy. . . . The German people demanded reprisals." In November 1943, believing that the V-1 and V-2 were close to operational use, Hitler proclaimed that "our hour of revenge is nigh! . . . Even if for the present we cannot reach America, thank God at least one country is close enough to tackle."

A number of senior Nazis, particularly Göring, echoed Hitler's comments. In October 1943, *Der Dicke* ("the fat one," as most of the Luftwaffe's flying crews referred to their commander in chief, with less than admiration) announced that the German people did not care a whit whether the Luftwaffe attacked British airfields. "All they [the German People] wished to hear when a hospital or children's home in Germany is destroyed is that we have destroyed the same in England; then they [are] satisfied." One month later, during a conversation with Fritz Sauckel, slave-labor procurer for the Third Reich, Göring emphasized that the Luftwaffe needed bombers as well as fighters to meet the Allied air offensive. "I cannot remain on the defensive," he snorted; "we must also have an offensive [capability]. That is most decisive." Sauckel immediately agreed: "The only argument that makes an impression on a racial cousin [the British] is that of retaliation."

Such attitudes reinforced the emphasis on bomber and fighter-bomber production into the early months of 1944. Despite desperate warnings from senior Luftwaffe officers, Hitler and Göring refused to restructure the German aircraft industry in 1942 or 1943 to provide the level of fighter production necessary to meet the threat. Their decision rested on the belief that Germany had to reply to Allied strategic bombing in kind—with bombing attacks on British cities, attacks that continued sporadically from the "Baby Blitz" of 1942 into the winter of 1944. When the Luftwaffe's chief of production and logistics, Field Marshal Erhard Milch, urged Hitler in 1943 to accept a production program of 5,000 fighters per month for 1944, he received a contemptuous no for an answer.

Meanwhile, senior Nazi leaders pushed Germany's industry toward the development of rocket and jet technologies, almost exclusively for offensive purposes. In 1943 the Luftwaffe and the army rushed into production two separate weapons whose nomenclature—V stands for revenge weapon—underlines their purpose. A pulse jet engine powered the Luftwaffe's weapon, the V-1, while the army's answer, the V-2, was the world's first true ballistic missile. The latter weapon excited enormous interest on the part of the German leadership. Speer in particular waxed enthusiastic over the potential of the new weapon to strike at Britain. Having seen a test firing of the A-4 (the preproduction name for the V-2), he told a crowd of receptive Ruhr workers that "German mills of retribution may often seem to grind too slowly, but do grind very fine. . . ."

But the V-2, for all of its impressive technological accomplishments, represented a weapon that possessed little military capability. Like artillery shells (the army's artillery branch developed the V-2), it operated on the principle that what goes up must eventually come down. However, no one was sure where it would land. The circular area of probability seems to have been an area not much smaller than all of southern England.

The V-2 also represented a weapon that demanded considerable investments of time, scientific expertise, production resources, skilled labor, and scarce raw materials, all to produce a weapon that had a difficult time in hitting London with a conventional warhead. And unlike a bomber, which if it survived could bomb again, the V-2 flew on a one-way trip. Developmental demands for the V-2 soaked up much of the limited capacity that German industry possessed in the electronics and instrument spheres. By 1944, work on the V-2 was having a serious impact on research and development for Germany's radar programs and for production of the electronic components required by night fighters and ground-based radars.

As if this situation was not serious enough, the V-1 and V-2 programs seriously affected production levels of fighter aircraft. Yet it took only a film clip from a single V-2 test firing to persuade Hitler to approve plans to put the rocket into high-quantity production. On July 7, 1943, he decreed that V-2 production was to receive the highest priority of any weapons system. The U.S. Strategic Bombing Survey suggests that the industrial effort and resources expended on the V-2 were enough to have produced 24,000 fighters. A more recent study of the V-2 program has suggested that the Germans expended the equivalent in resources of one-third of what the Americans expended on the Manhattan Project. The payoff for the Germans was, however, minuscule in comparison to the atomic bomb. The V-2s achieved a paltry level of damage in strikes on London and Antwerp, and because it was impossible to defend against their descent, the British never bothered to divert military assets.

✦

THE IMPACT of American precision bombing is easier to estimate. Since the Eighth and Fifteenth air forces were aiming at particular target sets—specific groups of targets that supported production in a single industry—it is possible to demonstrate their success or failure with some accuracy.

In 1943, the Americans targeted the German aircraft and ball-bearing industries. Given the resistance that the Luftwaffe mounted, the former was an obvious choice. American planners also selected ball bearings because the industry possessed a limited number of production facilities concentrated in a few areas, and ball bearings were essential to the production of virtually every weapons system. In the first case, the Americans hoped to destroy the Luftwaffe's industrial structure. They were not fully successful, but they did substantially reduce production of new fighter aircraft. In July 1943, monthly German fighter production reached a high for the year, 1,263; thereafter, there was a steady decline that reflected the sustained pressure of U.S. bombing. By December, German production of new fighters was down to 687 for the month.

In the second case, however, the two great and costly raids on Schweinfurt, the center of the ball-bearing industry, had less impact. There were a number of reasons for this. First, the bombs the Americans used did less damage than planners had expected. Second, the Germans had higher inventories of ball bearings throughout their industrial structure than even they had calculated. In addition, they discovered that some factories could substitute roller bearings for many of the ball bearings used in weapons production. Finally, the neutral Swedes and Swiss were delighted to step in and sell large amounts of ball bearings to the Germans for hard cash.

In 1944 the Americans again selected several discrete target sets. This time, with better intelligence, luck, and greater resources, they achieved significant results. As suggested above, attacks on the aircraft industry did not prevent the Germans from increasing the numbers of fighters produced in 1944. But American bombing attacks placed considerable limitations on how much the Germans could increase fighter production and resulted in a considerable drop in the quality of that production. But the crucial contribution was that these attacks on the Luftwaffe's production facilities from February to May 1944 forced the Luftwaffe to come up to fight, and in the end the American escort fighters accompanying the bomber formations broke the German fighter force. By the end of May, the Luftwaffe had only a few extraordinarily skilled fighter pilots, while the great majority—well over 90 percent—could barely take off or land their aircraft. Whereas the Americans lost nearly a quarter of their bombers every month through May 1944, from that point on losses dropped significantly. Few of the 177,000 Allied troops who came ashore on June 6, 1944, would see a German aircraft. The situation would not change for the remainder of the Normandy campaign.

In May, Eighth Air Force began attacking Germany's synthetic-oil production centers. Along with the attacks that Fifteenth Air Force was making on the oil industry in Romania, the U.S. strategic bombing threatened the Wehrmacht's entire basis of mobile warfare. Immediately after the first American attacks on May 12, Speer cautioned Hitler that "the enemy has struck us at one of our weakest points. If they persist at it this time, we will soon no longer have any fuel production worth mentioning. Our one hope is that the other side has an air general staff as scatterbrained as ours!"

However, the American emphasis remained on oil, as Speer feared. That focus largely resulted from Ultra intelligence available to senior American commanders. On June 5, just hours before the D day landings, an Ultra message revealed the following:

> Following according to OKL [Oberkommando der Luftwaffe, the air force high command] on fifth [of June]. As a result of renewed interference with the production of aircraft fuel by Allied [bombing] action, most essential requirements for training and carrying out production plans can scarcely be covered by quantities of aircraft fuel available. [Normal] allocations only possible to officer for bombers, fighters, and ground attack. . . . No other quota holders can be considered in June. To assume defense of Reich and to prevent gradual collapse of readiness for German air force in the east, it has been necessary to break into OKW [Oberkommando der Wehrmacht, the German high command] reserves [of fuel].

By mid-June, systematic attacks were having a devastating impact: American raids had knocked out 90 percent of aviation-fuel production. By mid-July, desperate efforts by the Germans quadrupled that production, but to a rate that still was 50 percent under normal levels. And when Ultra alerted Eighth Air Force's commanders about German efforts to rebuild, a new series of raids lowered production back to 2 percent of normal aviation-fuel output.

For the Germans, the situation regarding other petroleum derivatives was not so desperate; nevertheless, it hardly allowed for optimism. By July, American attacks had reduced the synthetic-oil complex at Leuna to 70 percent of normal production, while other major facilities dropped to between 43 and 58 percent of normal production. By October the Germans not only had lost their access to Romanian oil, because the Soviets had captured the fields, but were producing only 43 percent of their normal total production of synthetic fuel.

Fuel shortages severely impeded the Luftwaffe's air operations and forced it to reduce the number of flying hours in training schools, thus making new pilots even less capable of defending themselves. The impact of such shortages on ground operations was also dramatic. The Battle of the Bulge saw Hitler launch his panzer forces into the Ardennes with only enough fuel to get halfway to their objectives, hardly an enviable logistical situation. Elsewhere, the impact of fuel shortages prevented the Germans from conducting a mobile defense. On the Eastern Front, the Germans possessed 1,800 tanks to defend Silesia in January 1945, but a lack of fuel virtually immobilized them. With the panzers incapable of movement, Soviet forces overran Silesia in less than a week.

But the greatest contribution of strategic bombing to the Allied war effort came in preventing a last battle on the ruins of Germany's cities. Whatever the impact of attacks on the Reich's petroleum industry, we must not believe that the oil campaign exercised the only impact on the last year of the war. With the exception of August 1944 on the Western Front and July–September on the Eastern Front, the Germans were able to wage a tenacious defense that held their opponents to relatively small gains and blocked any breakthroughs.

As the Western Front settled down to stalemate in late 1944, Allied air forces launched a massive aerial assault on the transportation network within Germany. Advocates of this transportation campaign were Eisenhower's chief deputy, Tedder, and his chief scientist, Solly Zuckerman. The two argued that a campaign against this network similar to that in Normandy would have more than just direct military consequences; it would result in the collapse of the German war economy.

However, control of the strategic bombers had returned from Eisenhower and Tedder to Eighth Air Force and Bomber Command in early September 1944. Spaatz and the American commanders now wanted to put their whole emphasis on Germany's faltering petroleum industry. Not surprisingly, Harris, with his devotion to attacking German morale, wanted to place his command's focus on attacking Germany's cities.

In the end, Tedder, Spaatz, and Harris patched together a compromise. When the weather was not suitable for attacking petroleum facilities, Eighth Air Force would strike transportation targets. Similarly, Bomber Command would select as its aiming points such transportation targets as marshaling yards and the great railroad stations in the heart of major German cities. In addition, Tedder received support for the campaign from Allied tactical air forces, whose operating bases were now up on the German frontier.

Beginning in September, Allied air attacks fell with increasing severity on the structures of the German transportation network. Air planners divided the Reich into nine specific districts, five of which lay west of Kassel along the western frontier. The aim was to break the transportation system along these axes so that raw materials, finished goods, and parts could not move. The offensive hoped to block not only the Reichsbahn (the German railroad system) but also the canal and waterway systems.

The attacks had an immediate impact: loading of railroad cars in the Reich plummeted. For the week ending August 19, the Reichsbahn loaded and dispatched 899,091 carloads of material; by October 28 the figure for the preceding week had fallen to 703,580 cars; and by December 23 that number had fallen to 547,309, despite heavy demands from the Ardennes fighting. As early as October, Ultra indicated that "the Reich Minister for Equipment and War production reported that, on account of the destruction of traffic installations and lack of power, from 30 to 50 percent of all works factories in west Germany were at a standstill." By December 1944, marshaling capacity in railyards had declined to 40 percent of normal; by February it had dropped to 20 percent. In effect, the U.S. Strategic Bombing Survey reported, the attacks on transportation "reduced the available capacity for economic traffic in Germany [to a level] which could not hope to sustain, over any period of time, a high level of military production."

The breakdown of transportation meant that coal did not reach power stations, coke and iron-ore foundries, factories for tank turrets and engines, or plants for aircraft engines and aluminum subsections. Under such conditions, neither planning nor production could take place in an orderly fashion. The collapse of coal transportation suggests the extent of the damage. In January

1944, the Essen division of the Reichsbahn loaded an average of 21,400 cars daily. By September, that average had dropped to 12,000, of which only about 3,000 were long-haul shipments. By February, Allied air attacks had cut the Ruhr off from the rest of Germany. The Reichsbahn often had to confiscate what little coal was loaded and shipped just to keep its locomotives running.

Underlining the impact of transportation attacks was the state of coal production and stocks in the Ruhr between August 1944 and February 1945. Despite a dramatic decrease in coal production, stocks in the Ruhr collieries rose from 45,000 tons to 2,217,000 tons. Though the Ruhr was awash with its coal production, the transportation system could no longer move it to the industrial centers of the Reich.

The evidence thus points to a general destruction of the German war economy by midwinter 1945. Since the stoppage was not sudden and complete, it was difficult for even those conducting the bombing campaign to discern its full impact. In July and August 1944, German forces on both fronts had collapsed after suffering massive losses in equipment. Nevertheless, because armament production outside of aircraft factories remained largely untouched, the German army was able to reequip both surviving troops and new men (mostly boys) with excellent equipment. On the borders of the Reich, the Germans made a stand that brought the onrush of Allied forces to a halt and then even managed to launch an offensive into the Ardennes.

The resulting Battle of the Bulge, however, represented Germany's last shot. Beginning in the East in January 1945, followed within a month and a half in the West, the German armies gave way. Neither on the Rhine nor on the Oder were they able to pull themselves together for a last stand on the ruins of the Reich. There was no last-ditch *Götterdämmerung*. The cause of this collapse lay in the fact that the transportation campaign by Allied bombers had successfully shut down the German war economy; what little the economy produced could no longer move to the front. Without weapons and ammunition, even blind fanaticism could not maintain the struggle.

✦

HOW, THEN, is one to judge the effectiveness of the Allied strategic-bombing campaign in achieving the defeat of Nazi Germany? It is impossible to separate the individual contributions of British and American bomber forces into distinct contributions. In the end, they achieved synergistic effects: the sum of their efforts was greater than the parts. Together, there is no doubt that strategic bombing played a crucial role in Nazi Germany's defeat. Victory over Germany was simply inconceivable without the Combined Bomber Offensive, just as it required the success of Allied navies in the Battle of the Atlantic, the Red Army on the Eastern Front, and the Allied ground forces in the Mediterranean theater and the great invasion of western Europe in spring 1944.

Much of the problem in evaluating the contribution of strategic bombing to Allied victory is that by claiming so much for air power before the war, and afterward as well, airmen created perceptions that historical evidence indicates are false. Perhaps the best way to address the question is to ask what alternatives existed for the Anglo-American powers. The answer is nothing. A greater emphasis on ground forces would not have made possible an earlier landing on the coast of France. And without total Allied air superiority, which only the massive assault of the bombing offensive could give, such an invasion might have faced the same ignominious fate that the Dieppe landings suffered in August 1942.

Moreover, the capabilities developed by the earlier strategic bombing of Germany made possible the later transportation campaigns that in the first case wrecked the Wehrmacht's logistical support in France and in the second brought the German war economy to a grinding halt. One must also not forget that without strategic-bombing attacks in 1942 and 1943, the Germans would have had manpower and other resources available for use in North Africa and the Soviet Union that they instead devoted to the antiaircraft defenses of the Reich.

As for its impact on German war production, the evidence in the U.S. Strategic Bombing Survey suggests that it was considerable. What is hard to judge is how much better the Germans might have done with their war production had there been no bombing. It is well to remember that they could draw on the entire economy of continental Europe, with both its economic base and its industrial production. Certainly they could have rationalized production to a much greater degree than they did: instead of dispersing production, they could have concentrated it and used the same mass-production techniques that American industry was using to such effect.

The cost of the Combined Bombing Offensive was high indeed. In many ways the attrition that took place mirrored the terrible casualties of the Western Front in World War I. But now those charged with attacking Germany's population and economic structure measured progress by changes in the percentage of bombers lost per hundred sorties and in the number of tons of bombs dropped, rather than by the number of yards gained and artillery shells fired. The disastrous losses suffered by the two great raids in 1943 on the ball-bearing works in Schweinfurt and on Nuremberg in early 1944 have conditioned our historical memoirs. With hindsight, we can argue that airmen waged the Combined Bomber Offensive in an unimaginative fashion, that air forces often failed to adapt to changing tactical and technological conditions, and that the offensive often minimized rather than maximized the contributions that air power might have made. But could we not make these sorts of criticisms about military leadership in all wars?

What is certain is that strategic bombing was the only means with which the Western powers could strike at Germany in the dark early years of the war. And if such attacks did not achieve decisive results, the fact that they at least hit the Germans had a considerable impact on Allied morale. More important, the bombing offensive was crucial in military and operational terms in the winning of the war from 1943 on. An exact quantifiable measurement is impossible, but even the most cursory examination of the alternatives suggests the extent of the contribution.

THE BLACK KNIGHT

CALEB CARR

World War II saw many fine generals in Europe, a few of them probably exceptional, and we have already encountered most of the best. But we have overlooked the man who was, more than anyone else, responsible for prolonging the war in the West into the spring of 1945. He was Field Marshal Gerd von Rundstedt, "the very model of the Prussian old school," Caleb Carr writes, a man known throughout the German army as the "Black Knight." Rundstedt was not a fighting general like Rommel but a resourceful inspirer whose greatest gift was in recognizing talent, and then delegating authority to those parts of the front where sure-handed direction was most needed. At sixty-nine, he was the oldest serving officer in the German army, and when Hitler brought him back in September 1944 to cobble together a defense of what remained of the Third Reich in Western Europe, Rundstedt had already retired three times. The results of his "Indian Summer" (as Carr calls it) were "almost miraculous. But in the end that defense, like all Rundstedt's efforts, would prove not only in vain, but a terrible betrayal of both the troops he led and the Prussian military code of which he was an inheritor."

The Allies, Carr believes, unwittingly contributed to that miracle with the "broad front" strategy that emerged from Allied Supreme Headquarters in August—eschewing a single thrust into the German homeland that might well have finished the war in the West that fall, allowed the Western powers to reach Berlin while the Soviets were still in Poland, and saved hundreds of thousands of lives in the bargain. Rundstedt most feared the northern route that Montgomery advocated, though the army best equipped for the task was not Monty's but Patton's Third. Carr is squarely in the camp of the eminent military historian B. H. Liddell Hart, who maintained that "the best chance of a quick finish was probably lost when the 'gas' was turned off from Pattons' tanks in the last week of August, when they were a hundred miles nearer the

Rhine, and its bridges, than the British." But other military historians
are as quick to argue that logistics made victory in 1944 impossible. We
had the gas but not the means of transporting it. Coalition warfare did
not permit the freeing of one army at the logistical price of immobilizing
the rest.

The broad-front strategy played into Rundstedt's hands, but to an end
that Carr views as ignoble. Like Rommel, he was a German patriot who
disdained politics in general, and Nazi politics in particular. But unlike
Rommel, he never wavered in his loyalty to Hitler. Despite the fact that
he knew the war was lost, Rundstedt buried himself, and his conscience,
in the purely military struggle, "because it was my duty." As Carr writes,
"one culminating act of bravery and wisdom" would have ensured the
Black Knight's place in history. It never happened.

Caleb Carr is best known as the author of three best-selling novels,
The Alienist, The Angel of Darkness, and *Killing Time* (which appeared in
Time, in Dickens-like installments). He has also earned a considerable
reputation as a military historian, notably with *The Devil Soldier* and
America Invulnerable (with James Chace).

ON SEPTEMBER 5, 1944, BATTLE-WEARY OFFICERS AND MEN OF
the German army's Western Command watched a car pull up in front of their
headquarters in Arenberg, near the confluence of the Rhine and Moselle
rivers. Exhausted by more than a month of continuous retreat before the punishing advance of those American, British, and Canadian forces that had broken out of Normandy at the end of July, these soldiers of the Third Reich had
little reason for either optimism or enthusiasm—yet as they watched the car
outside headquarters deliver up its passenger, they found it in themselves to
cheer. Immediately and electrically, a new sense of confidence swept first
through the troops around headquarters and then, as word of the arrival
spread, through all units of Western Command's Army Group B to the north
and Army Group C to the south: Field Marshal Gerd von Rundstedt, known
throughout the German army as the "Black Knight," had returned.

Rundstedt had angrily relinquished command in the West earlier in the
summer, after arguments with the German high command over how to meet
the Allied invasion; and since his departure German fortunes had plummeted.

For the average German soldier, the field marshal's return marked the resurgence of hope, even in the face of overwhelming odds—an effect that no other general in the Reich could have produced.

Nor was that hope misplaced: In the weeks following his return to command, Rundstedt would use his ability to inspire his troops, along with an innate instinct for elastic defensive maneuver, to pull the badly mauled Western Front into a coherent line. Assisted by the strategic ineptitude of the Allied Supreme Headquarters (a debt that Rundstedt always acknowledged), the Black Knight gave his Reich a critical moment's breath during September and October of 1944, and thus played a vital role in prolonging the war through the winter and into the spring of 1945.

At sixty-nine (he was the oldest serving officer in the German army at the time of his arrival in Arenberg), Rundstedt hardly fit the model of youthful, fanatic heroism that the propagandists of National Socialism had spent years drilling into the collective German consciousness. Thin, ascetic, and self-deprecating, possessed of a wit that could be both entertaining and cutting, Rundstedt was to all appearances the very model of the Prussian old school, a man whose ancestors had been warriors since the thirteenth century. Few men were more professionally steeped in the philosophy of the Prussian and German Great General Staff that had been molded by Scharnhorst and Gneisenau in the early nineteenth century and then modernized by the elder von Moltke during the last decades of that century: Rundstedt was a military purist, a man who lived to serve his Reich and for whom politics was the basest and most distasteful of human affairs. He was also an adept operational leader who had played the key battlefield command roles in the invasions of Poland in 1939, France in 1940, and Russia in 1941. That background, combined with his gentlemanly air of quiet confidence, never failed to inspire in his men a kind of loyalty and determination that went beyond anything Hitler's Nazi officers—for whom Rundstedt always displayed disdain—could ever quite achieve. This was never more true than during the desperate late summer of 1944, when Rundstedt's brand of inspiration proved far more potent than all the vulgar posturing of the Nazis.

But as much as he typified the finest qualities of the German army at the time of World War II, Rundstedt also embodied that force's single greatest evil: its willingness to prostitute itself to the mad schemes of Adolf Hitler. For while Rundstedt always viewed the activities of the Nazi party (whom he dismissed as "brown dirt") with disgust, he nonetheless served the man he accepted as führer with notable loyalty. There were old-school Prussian officers who did not do so, of course: Ludwig Beck, Franz Halder, and Claus von

Stauffenberg were only a few of those who sacrificed their careers and in some cases their lives in an attempt first to battle and then to destroy Hitler. But such men were exceptional in the German army of the 1930s and 1940s. The vast majority of officers, following the lead of senior commanders like Rundstedt, swallowed their revulsion, swore allegiance to Hitler, and marched with him down a path they knew to be suicidal. For six years these men staved off that national self-destruction with brilliant battlefield displays—just as Rundstedt would, in September and October of 1944, cobble together a defense of Germany's western frontier that was almost miraculous. But in the end that defense, like all Rundstedt's efforts, would prove not only in vain, but a terrible betrayal of both the troops he led and the Prussian military code of which he was an inheritor.

How could such an apparent paragon of all that was best in Prussian and German history arrive at such an inglorious fate?

The answer lies both in the Black Knight's personal history and in the history of the German army between 1914 and 1939 (two histories that were, of course, nearly one). Born the eldest son of a Prussian hussar in 1875, Karl Rudolf Gerd von Rundstedt was the scion of a family whose male members had fought wars both at home and abroad for 700 years. One had campaigned for William of Orange against Spain, another for Charles Stuart against England in the 1740s; and Rundstedts had served in every Prussian war except that of independence in 1813, when there was no male of age. Thus, there was never any doubt that Gerd would enter the military. At his cadet college one instructor rather sourly noted that Gerd was *lebhaft,* a term implying both intellectual keenness and a certain willfulness: The first quality marked him as a likely candidate for the General Staff, the second for effective field leadership. Rundstedt excelled in all the examinations required to earn him enrollment at the Kriegsakademie, the General Staff's training center, and by 1914 he had so impressed his superiors that when World War I broke out he was made the chief of operations for a division, the most distinguished duty to which a staff major could aspire.

Rundstedt spent most of World War I—as did so many future leaders of Hitler's Wehrmacht—safely behind the front lines doing staff work. (General Staff officers, the brain trust of the German army, were considered too valuable to waste on battlefield service.) But several early wartime experiences did presage Rundstedt's World War II field service, and especially his defense of Germany in the late summer of 1944. Thirty years earlier, Major Rundstedt, assigned to the 22nd Reserve Division, became responsible for the organization and mobilization of large numbers of inexperienced soldiers. Having done so, he charted the division's advance through Aachen, into Belgium, and finally to the Marne. During the retreat from that fateful river, the commander of the 22nd was wounded, and Rundstedt stepped in. In a performance that was by all reports as cool, carefully planned, and daring as any of his World War II exploits (albeit on a smaller scale), Rundstedt got his division safely back to the Aisne, where they drew up a coherent, effective line of defense.

Such a peformance was not altogether surprising. Because of the country's location—in the center of Europe, between various enemies—the predominant military tenet of the Prussian and German general staffs had always been mobility, in defense as well as in offense. By 1915, Rundstedt had begun to fully absorb (and by the end of the war would openly espouse) the methods that supported this tenet: an aversion to fixed fortifications and a pronounced emphasis on mobile reserves, which could strike with overwhelming force at key spots rather than trying to fight along the entirety of a linear front. These methods brought dramatic results as the Germans struggled to defend themselves in 1918; it was a deeply confirming period for Rundstedt.

The victorious Allies, seeing in the German General Staff the embodiment of nearly every evil in German society, tried to eradicate that organization in 1918, as well as reduce the German army generally to what amounted to a constabulary force. They had not reckoned, however, on the resourcefulness and determination of the German officer corps, and of one officer in particular: General Hans von Seeckt, architect of Germany's interwar military forces. Known as "the Sphinx" because of both his impassivity and the shielded nature of his dealings, von Seeckt constructed an army in miniature during the Weimar years, one that was technologically advanced and capable of expanding dramatically at a moment's notice should the terms of the Versailles treaty ever be repudiated. Himself an old-school aristocrat who was nonetheless open to progressive military theories, von Seeckt relied for the successful completion of his scheme on similar men: Rundstedt fit the mold perfectly. Though an infantry officer, Rundstedt was, again, a confirmed disciple of mobility, in offense as well as in defense; and he therefore approached the work of the new prophets of mobile mechanized warfare—Fuller and Liddell Hart in England, de Gaulle in France, and Guderian in his own country—with an open and appreciative mind. And while he never became as radical in his opinions as any of these men, Rundstedt did favor the construction of a very new kind of army in Germany, whose purpose was a new kind of warfare: *Blitzkrieg.*

Lightning war, however, was not the only new philosophy that took hold of the German officer corps during the interwar years. Because of the political extremism that characterized Weimar Germany, von Seeckt and his followers came to believe that the ultimate fate of the nation rested not with any one of the volatile political parties of the left and right that were jockeying for power but with the army itself: Germany's safety could be secured only if the army chose to remain separate and aloof from politics. Thus was born the ethic of *Überparteilichkeit*—literally, the trait of being above political factionalism. This became the rule for German officers during the interwar era, though it conflicted resoundingly with Prussian tradition.

It had, after all, been the philosophical godfather of the Prussian army, Carl von Clausewitz, who had so forcefully declared a century earlier that war *is* policy, by different means; and certainly the elder Moltke had carefully trained his General Staff officers to take a keen interest in extramilitary affairs, particularly politics. Prussian officers were always highly professional, to be sure; but the greatness of the nineteenth-century Prussian system lay in the fact that this was not a narrow professionalism. The *Überparteilichkeit* of von Seeckt and his officers was therefore not a continuation but a profound per-version of Prussian tradition, in which lay not the salvation but the ultimate destruction of Germany—and the transformation of the officer corps into pawns, not masters.

No one saw the potential for such a transformation more clearly than Adolf Hitler. By appealing to the innate nationalism and traditionalism of the Ger-man military establishment, and by playing up the dangers posed by his Communist rivals, Hitler was able to convince the officer corps that his goals and theirs were the same: the restoration of a strong Germany according to the old imperial boundaries, along with the revival of the Great General Staff and the rapid expansion of the German armed forces along the most progressive lines. As the 1930s passed, the German officer corps buried its head ever more determinedly in the sand of military expansion, snidely dismissing the Nazis even as they ensured Hitler's ultimate success. They overlooked disturbing signs that Hitler was beginning to exceed even those limits of behavior that could be rationalized by *Überparteilichkeit*—that he was, in fact, beginning to consider himself less the army's partner than its master.

On November 1, 1938, Rundstedt left the army and what he called "that pigsty Berlin" for the first time, hoping to devote more time to his favorite extra-military pursuit—gardening. Hitler, however, was far from finished with the old soldier. The relationship between these two diametrically opposed characters is crucial to any understanding not only of the German prosecution of World War II but of Rundstedt's life and fate. Separated by an immense cultural, intellectual, and philosophical gulf, Rundstedt and Hitler were nonetheless strangely bound by the unusual deference that the führer always displayed toward the grand old man of the German army. Hitler's pathological envy and resentment of the Prussian military class—born out of his own bourgeois Austrian background—was infamous, as was the bullying, dismissive way in which he treated most senior German officers. But toward Rundstedt and Rundstedt alone Hitler consistently behaved with something of the respect that a corporal owes a field marshal. There were many possible reasons for this, not least Rundstedt's determined refusal to allow any of the army-Nazi tensions to develop into an open breach: He consistently honored his oath to the führer, even when he thought the younger man's military decisions foolish or even unbalanced. But on the most basic level, one gets the feeling that in Rundstedt Hitler encountered a persona that, though radically different in type and tone from his own, was equally powerful. And Rundstedt was not immune to such deference: He generally exempted Hitler from the scathing indictments he unleashed on other Nazi and high-command leaders. Whatever its genesis, the peculiar relationship between Hitler and Rundstedt ensured that the latter, despite his own misgivings, always offered his services to the Third Reich when called on to do so; and those services were crucial to Germany's successes early in the war.

Before planning the invasion of Poland, Hitler asked Rundstedt to come back from retirement, and the Black Knight—though aware that the invasion would likely precipitate a European war—answered the call. It was Rundstedt's army group that played the key role in that invasion in 1939, and Rundstedt's emphasis on improvisation and mobility that turned that campaign from a mere success into a rout. And again, it was Rundstedt's army group in the West that first planned the unexpected strike through the Ardennes and then achieved the most miraculous results in that campaign. Rundstedt himself was not responsible for the innovations behind these triumphs—the strategic plan was designed by his chief of staff at that time, General Erich von Manstein, while the tactics were General Heinz Guderian's—and during the campaign he was somewhat unnerved by the magnitude of their results. But the ability to defer to talented, revolutionary subordinates was one of Rundstedt's strongest talents, and while he did, like Hitler, urge a reorganizational pause in the armored sweep through France that angered the panzer purists, he never let any break in the momentum endanger ultimate success.

During the first part of the 1941 Barbarossa campaign, Rundstedt's army group again played the key role, and the peculiar relationship with Hitler remained harmonious. Rundstedt himself felt deeply pessimistic about the long-range prospects of a war with Russia, but again he adopted an attitude

that combined resigned compliance with Hitler's ambitions and brilliant execution of his own designated part in them. Though he found Hitler's ethnic
policies in Russia objectionable enough to warrant a letter of protest to the
chief of the General Staff, General Franz Halder, Rundstedt did not follow
Halder's lead by pursuing his disagreements with Hitler to the point of open
conflict. (Halder was destined to finish the war a prisoner at Dachau.) But by
the end of November, even Rundstedt's pronounced fatalism could not keep
him from tangling with the führer: With the Russian attack bogging down,
Rundstedt called for withdrawal to a defensible line, perhaps as far back as the
original jumping-off points. When Rundstedt in fact ordered a retreat in one
sector of his line, Hitler reprimanded him, to which Rundstedt acidly suggested that perhaps Hitler ought to find another commander in whom he
could place greater faith. Hitler agreed, though cordially, and for the second
time Rundstedt retired from active service.

Like the first, this second retirement was short-lived. As soon as the United
States entered the war in December 1941, Hitler realized that the possibility
of an Allied invasion of western Europe was dramatically magnified; he therefore recalled Rundstedt to service in March 1942 and appointed him commander in chief in the West. While he faithfully attempted to organize an
effective defense of his assigned area, Rundstedt concluded in early 1943 that
a German defeat was certain if the high command stayed on its overexpansive
course in Russia. Only at this point did the true extent of the field marshal's
underestimation of Adolf Hitler become clear: Rundstedt had always assumed
that the führer, whatever his eccentricities, would agree to negotiate peace
with the Allies once defeat was no longer the prophecy of pessimists but an
unavoidable eventuality. Instead, Rundstedt was informed through several
typically deranged harangues by Hitler that the only solution to the dangers
facing Germany was increased effort and heightened devotion.

There were at least a few German officers who, at this time, began to think
in terms of removing Hitler forcefully: Their efforts culminated in several
failed assassination attempts, and finally Stauffenberg's near miss with a bomb
on July 20, 1944. It would not have been unreasonable to expect Rundstedt,
as the oldest, most respected, and in many ways wisest soldier in Germany, at
least to heed the counsels of such officers. Yet there is no indication he ever
did—quite the contrary. Persistently citing his oath of loyalty to Hitler, he
stated at the time as well as after the war that to turn against the führer would
have marked him for all time as a traitor to his country. Certainly, as he continued throughout 1943 to try to prepare for an Allied invasion of Europe,
Rundstedt blocked out all thought of politics and concentrated on securing

men and supplies for the task at hand: *Überparteilichkeit,* having been the rationale by which he had attained military greatness, would not release its hold on the man even when defeat came into view.

Still, by the end of 1943 Hitler had become worried enough about Rundstedt's enthusiasm to send one of his favorites, Erwin Rommel, to oversee the construction of defenses along what the führer deludedly referred to as the "Atlantic Wall." Ever the innovator and iconoclast, Rommel—whom Rundstedt considered "a brave man, and a very capable commander in small operations, but not really qualified for high command"—quickly determined that the Allies, when they landed, should be met on the beaches and thrown back into the sea. In effect, he was proposing the enforcement of an enormous linear front, which naturally placed him in conflict with Rundstedt's instinctive philosophy of mobile defense. For his part, Rundstedt wished to keep as many forces as possible, and especially the bulk of his armor, in a mobile reserve that could meet the Allies wherever they landed and engage them in a decisive land battle after they had come ashore. The debate over the two strategies went on through the first five months of 1944, but it was ultimately made academic by Hitler's refusal to adopt either approach. By keeping some forces in reserve and allotting the rest to Rommel, Hitler satisfied neither commander and ensured an inadequate response to the Normandy invasion.

One of the many effects of that invasion was Rundstedt's third retirement from active command. Hitler's absurd order that no German forces give an inch of ground to the invading Allies continued to make a mockery of Rundstedt's ongoing efforts to establish a mobile strategic reserve; and on July 1 Rundstedt was forced to call the high command and say that the latest German efforts to stop the British and Americans from breaking out of Normandy were failing. In one of the most famous exchanges on the German side of the war, Field Marshal Wilhelm Keitel, one of Hitler's toadies at high command, frantically squealed at Rundstedt, "What shall we do, Field Marshal, what shall we do?" to which Rundstedt, exasperated beyond patience, snapped, "Make peace, you fools! What else can you do?" Of course, Keitel took the remark straight to Hitler, who in short order politely but firmly informed Rundstedt that it was time to make a change at Western Command.

The weeks that Rundstedt spent away from the front saw not only the Allied drive first to the Seine and then to the German frontier, but suicidal German counterattacks ordered by Hitler personally and, finally, the assassination plot of July 20. In the madness that followed this last event, Rundstedt once again made himself available to Hitler, by overseeing the military court that stripped implicated officers of their ranks and thus made them subject to the

merciless decrees of Nazi courts. According to his chief of staff, General Günther von Blumentritt, Rundstedt had great misgivings about this task—but
the fact that he performed it is significant. There is a hint in the affair that his
own mounting uncertainties about the wisdom of *Überparteilichkeit* caused
Rundstedt to react sternly to any officer who had the courage to throw off the
by now obviously mistaken doctrine. With his own ethical discomfort apparently growing, it is small wonder that Rundstedt agreed to return to the comparative simplicity of the front and the fighting in early September; his own
later explanation was that he came back "simply because it was my duty as a
soldier not to refuse at a moment of the greatest danger."

The immense joy with which the troops of the German Western Command
greeted the field marshal's return was thus simultaneously justified and terribly misplaced. Certainly they were right to hope that he would lead them ca-
pably in the final defense of their homeland; but none of them could have
known as well as Rundstedt how very much the führer to whom they had all
sworn loyalty had identified his own fate with that of the German nation.
Hitler was prepared to see every German soldier and citizen die before he
would accept the end of the Third Reich—Rundstedt surely suspected if not
knew as much, and by not using his great popularity, wisdom, and influence
to avert such an end (there is every indication that the Allies, though committed to total victory, would have opened a line of communication to Rundstedt had he requested it), and by focusing instead on the purely military
struggle, Rundstedt ensured for himself the hard judgment of history.

But in early September 1944, military considerations *were* the order of the
day at Western Command, and for at least a few weeks Rundstedt and his men
were able to show the Western Allies a little more of the brilliance that had
made German domination of Europe such a near thing. In his deceptively reserved fashion, Rundstedt undertook a review of the forces at his disposal, as
well as those arrayed against him, upon taking command; and we are able today to understand his reaction to this review because the ordinarily reticent
field marshal later wrote several memorandums concerning this period, revealing with unusual clarity his pride in his own performance as well as in
that of his men.

"The main task of Western Command at the beginning of September
1944," Rundstedt wrote with typical understatement, "was to stop the entire
withdrawal movement and stabilize the front." This represented no small
challenge: In the north, Rundstedt's Army Group B, commanded by Field
Marshal Walther Model, was faced by Bernard Montgomery's Twenty-first
Army Group; in the south, Army Group G, under General Johannes

Blaskowitz, was battling Omar Bradley's Twelfth Army Group. These four operational units, however, were similar in name only: The two German army groups were skeletons, in which entire divisions that had been lost to such battles of annihilation as the Falaise pocket existed almost solely on paper. German troops who had not been killed, caught, or overwhelmed by the urge to desert had been forced to leave most of their heavy equipment behind in France and Belgium as they approached Hitler's vaunted West Wall, the barrier along the Dutch and German western borders that the Allies knew as the Siegfried line. "I can pass lightly over the inadequacy of the 'West Wall,'" Rundstedt later recalled of Hitler's fantasy bulwark; for the most part it "was marked on the map, but never built. . . . Nothing had been done or prepared for the defense of the Rhine and the security of the crossings over the river." The Allied army groups, on the other hand, were fully equipped and supplied and well positioned to deliver a death thrust to the German homeland along any one of a number of routes, the most obvious being either the line from Aachen, through the Ruhr, to Berlin, or the "indirect approach" from the south, through the Saar and then northward to the German capital.

Rundstedt believed that the first of these options represented the Allies' best chance for success; yet nothing that he or any other German commander might have done early in September could have prevented such an operation from being crowned with success, had it been undertaken in a timely and forceful manner. "I had, of course," he later said, "always assumed that the Allies would do everything in their power to reach Berlin before the Russians out of regard for 'Western ideals' and to prevent the Russians from advancing too far to the west over the Oder. What machinations of a political nature stood in the way of such operations is beyond my knowledge."

The political machination responsible for the Allies' hesitancy was, of course, the "broad front" strategy worked out by the Allied Supreme Headquarters in August. In fact, Montgomery favored exactly the kind of decisive northern strike that Rundstedt was anticipating, and he wanted all other Allied operations subordinated to such a move. He was opposed, however, by Bradley and the American Third Army commander, George Patton, who pointed out that the American armies had moved more quickly and resolutely in their French campaign than had Montgomery, and they stood a better chance of crippling Germany through the indirect route farther to the south. Ultimately, Dwight D. Eisenhower decided that neither strategy would receive priority; all armies would advance simultaneously.

It was as disastrous a mistake as Hitler's preinvasion failure to choose between Rundstedt's and Rommel's ideas had been; for had the Allied Supreme

Headquarters pursued one bold thrust into Germany—along either the northern or the southern route—the Germans would have been incapable of resisting such a concentrated attack. It is hard to argue with the contention of such distinguished analysts as Basil Liddell Hart that the war could have ended in September 1944. When one tallies up the lives lost both at the front and inside Germany during the months that the war dragged on—not to mention the physical destruction characterizing the period—one is left with an all-too-vivid illustration of the costs of playing politics in the midst of a military campaign.

So far as the Black Knight was concerned, however, the Allied decision to forgo a decisive thrust provided the chance he needed to regroup and try to face the Allies coherently. Conflict with Hitler and the high command came quickly, for Rundstedt's first desire was to abandon Holland, which the führer typically demanded be held at all costs. But Rundstedt and his very able lieutenants (as usual, the field marshal was willing to give wide latitude to able army group and army commanders) at this point began to stray farther from the letter of their leader's instructions than they ever had before: Holland was not abandoned by the German Fifteenth Army outright, but Rundstedt did devise a clever plan by way of which most of that army—on the verge of being trapped in the Antwerp area by the British and Canadians—pulled back into the interior with a night crossing of the Schelde Estuary aboard small craft.

Even with the bulk of the Fifteenth Army now withdrawn toward the east, however, the Allies continued to enjoy an enormous numerical and material advantage; yet once again they failed to press it, a failure that the German commanders found almost unnerving. "Why did the Allies not make use of this favorable opportunity at the time?" General Blumentritt continued to ask after the war, never gaining a satisfactory answer. As it was, the continued pause in Allied operations in early September gave General Kurt Student time to consolidate the unbelievably resourceful assembly of his First Parachute Army to the south of the Fifteenth Army. These battle-tested troops began to offer tough resistance to Montgomery's forces, creating the impression that the German enemy was far stronger in the area than was the case; ever cautious, Montgomery bought the ruse and further slowed his advance.

Indeed, so impressive was the impromptu German defense in his area that Montgomery began to think in terms of a massive surprise airborne strike at the German rear, rather than a continued pressing at the front. This resulted in the infamous Operation Market Garden on September 17, a plan that failed not least because perceptive German commanders anticipated it. (As Blumentritt later wrote, on September 17, "The weather was fine and sunny, besides being a Sunday when, as war experience teaches, something often happens!") Market Garden's failure gave Rundstedt enough time to reorganize another critical defensive force, the Fifth Panzer Army, under another able subordinate, General Hasso von Manteuffel. Through skillful mobile counterattacks of the kind that Rundstedt had always advocated, Manteuffel eventually succeeded in stabilizing the front between Army Groups B and G.

But the area that remained of greatest concern to Rundstedt was the north, specifically the route to Berlin that began in the city of Aachen. Because of his determination to hold that city—through which his own 22nd Reserve Infantry Division had marched thirty years earlier—as long as possible, and because of the Allied Supreme Headquarters' refusal to allow Patton to make the decisive strike against Berlin from the south, the fall campaign began to show signs by the end of September of resulting in a stalemate: an unthinkable result just a month earlier. Throughout October the battle for Aachen raged, and at the end of the month the city fell; but by then more resourceful German commanders—notably Hermann Balck, a young panzer general who took over Army Group C from General Blaskowitz at the end of September—had made more and greater strides in patching together defensive forces west of the Rhine. Rundstedt wished to withdraw behind that river as quickly as possible, but Hitler continued to forbid any such move; the field marshal had to satisfy himself with making sure that all the river crossings were adequately laced with explosives, so that when a retreat finally became imperative even to Hitler, it could be adequately covered.

By the end of October, Rundstedt's Indian summer was coming to an end; he had reason to be proud of his own efforts, as well as those of his soldiers. Germany's Western Front had been salvaged by a combination of the genius of her Western commanders, the energy of their troops, and the dullness of their enemy leaders. But typically, Hitler stepped in at this point to ensure that all advantages gained by his generals in September and October would be negated by one last bid for domination. On October 26, the führer—perhaps afraid of the reaction he would receive from the two field marshals themselves—told Rundstedt and Model's chiefs of staff that he intended to launch a dramatic new offensive in the West. The location of the attack would be the Ardennes Forest; its objective would be Antwerp; and its purpose would be to separate the British armies from the American, thus buying time for the development of the new Nazi "wonder weapons"—jets, rockets, and supertanks—that would renew German hopes of victory.

The idea, which would have been audacious under other circumstances, was in the fall of 1944 merely deluded: Rundstedt himself stated at the time,

"The entire planning of this offensive strikes me as failing to meet the demands of reality." Yet the Black Knight made no more forceful protest. The most he would do, throughout November, was argue for a less ambitious objective than Antwerp. When the Ardennes offensive was finally launched in December, Rundstedt simply stood aside, turned over actual operational control to Model, and observed the spectacle—which, ironically, came to be called the "Rundstedt Offensive" by the Allies—with bemused, somewhat bitter interest.

Could Rundstedt have taken any more forceful action? Probably not, as regards Hitler and the high command (not, that is, without losing his position and possibly his life). But the idea of contacting the Allies and perhaps arranging a surrender was still not out of the question: As late as February 1945, in fact, the Allies were broadcasting messages to the German side saying that they would accept surrender from only one German—Rundstedt. Doubtless this was at heart a divisive tactic; but Rundstedt was as respected and as legendary among his Western enemies as he had always been, and one culminating act of bravery and wisdom would have ensured that such admiration had indeed been justified.

It never came. Rundstedt resigned once more before the end of the war, in March 1945, and was eventually taken prisoner and removed to Great Britain, where he would be placed in solitary confinement for several years before being allowed to return home. At Nuremberg he offered testimony (though he himself was never accused of war crimes) with the same courtly elegance that had marked his entire life; yet that style continued only to mask the deeper sense in which the Black Knight had, finally, betrayed the most fundamental principles of the class and the tradition that had produced him. As if aware of this somewhere deep in his soul, Rundstedt—almost alone among senior World War II commanders on both sides—wrote no personal account of his life and service in the quiet years that led up to his death in 1953. As a result, the Black Knight remains one of the great enigmas of the war, a man revered by his troops but, in the end, condemned by history for his betrayal of them. The richness of character that made him a superb wartime commander was not sufficient to elevate him into the ranks of great leaders of men; and the inspiration that he fueled in his soldiers only propelled them to acts that, while heroic in their immediate details, were in their essence futile at best and criminal at worst. As such, the resonance through time of those acts and sacrifices has proved a hollow one. Rundstedt had every way of knowing that this would be the case, yet he fought on; there is a blackness in that fact that is in no way chivalric.

THE LAST BARRIER

STEPHEN E. AMBROSE

By the end of the winter of 1945, Field Marshal Gerd von Rundstedt was running out of miracles, and now it was the turn of the Americans to pull off one of their own—a miracle that would send the Black Knight into his fourth, and final, retirement.

The Bulge had been flattened, and now the Germans were pulling back to the east bank of the Rhine. Hitler regarded the river as an impassable moat, to be held (as always) at all costs. This time German national pride and the difficulty of crossing made this stand, which was literally a last-ditch effort, more than an empty exhortation. The Rhine was wide, deep, and swift-flowing, and steep escarpments rose from much of that heavily defended right bank. As Hitler's battered but still-dangerous legions retreated, they began methodically to blow up the bridge crossings. The flatter north, where Montgomery's 21st Army Group was closing on the river, seemed the most promising area for the final assault, and his staff had begun planning an elaborate combination of amphibious and airborne crossings as early as October. Ever the soul of caution, Montgomery was determined to leave as little to chance as possible; he invited Churchill, Eisenhower, and other assorted dignitaries to watch his big show, which was scheduled for March 24. Meanwhile, to the south, Patton was racing toward the river in an effort to beat Montgomery across.

As it turned out, the honor would go to neither general. On March 7, the 9th Division of General Courtney H. Hodges's First Army approached the river town of Remagen, where a railroad bridge spanned the Rhine—the Ludendorff Bridge, built in World War I to facilitate the movement of supplies to the German armies on the Western Front. On the opposite side, tracks emerged from a tunnel through a nearly sheer 570-foot palisade called the Erpeler Ley. That morning a Piper Cub observation plane dipping under low clouds saw something unbelievable:

the bridge was intact. Suddenly it became, as Stephen E. Ambrose
writes, "the most critical strategic spot in Europe."

Stephen E. Ambrose has written more than twenty books, including
multivolume biographies of Dwight D. Eisenhower and Richard M.
Nixon, as well as the best-selling *Undaunted Courage,* the story of the
Lewis and Clark expedition, his two accounts of the end of World War II
in Western Europe, *D day* and *Citizen Soldiers*—from which "The Last
Barrier" was excerpted—and, most recently, *Nothing Like It in the
World: The Men Who Built the Transcontinental Railroad 1863–1869.* Professor Ambrose is the founder of the Eisenhower Center and president of
the National D day Museum, both in New Orleans.

IN THEIR MARCH ACROSS NORTHWESTERN EUROPE IN 1944–45,
the Rhine was by far the most formidable of the rivers the GIs had to cross.
It rises in the Alps and flows generally north to Arnhem in the Netherlands,
where it makes a sharp turn to the west. It was between 200 and 500 meters
wide, swift and turbulent, with great whirlpools and eddies, two to three meters deep. The Germans on the far bank were disorganized and demoralized,
dismayed by their losses in the insanity of trying to fight it out on the
Cologne Plain, as Hitler had ordered, but still determined and capable of uti-
lizing the natural advantages the Rhine gave them to defend their country.

Those advantages included the scarcity of suitable crossing sites. There
were only two or three places from Cologne south that were even possible.
Worse, along that stretch there were no major objectives on the east bank or
inland for some fifty kilometers, and the hinterland was unsuitable for offensive warfare. The terrain was heavily wooded, undulating and broken in many
places by narrow valleys, with roads that twisted and turned, rose and fell.

North of Cologne, Field Marshal Bernard L. Montgomery's Twenty-first
Army Group had many suitable crossing sites, good terrain for a mobile offensive, and major objectives just across the Rhine in the Ruhr valley. Beyond
the Ruhr, the north German plain led straight to Berlin. So while the heart of
the Allied commander, Dwight D. Eisenhower, was with his generals, Omar
N. Bradley, Courtney A. Hodges, and George S. Patton, his mind was up
north, with Monty. General Harold "Pinky" Bull, Supreme Headquarters'—
SHAEF's—G-3, and his planners had decided that up north was the right

place for the main crossing. Eisenhower agreed, but warned that "the possibility of failure cannot be overlooked. I am, therefore . . . making logistic preparations which will enable me to switch my main effort from the north to the south should this be forced upon me."

To the north, Montgomery's armies were closing to the river. As they did, he began to build his supply base for the assault crossing and exploitation that would follow. Altogether he required 250,000 tons of supplies, for the British and Canadian forces and the U.S. Ninth Army and 17th Airborne Division. Ninth Army had been part of Twenty-first Army Group since the preceding fall; the 17th Airborne Division had arrived in Europe in December and had been thrown immediately into the Battle of the Bulge. It had combat experience, but had not made a combat jump and was currently making practice jumps in Belgium.

Montgomery's staff had begun planning for the Rhine crossing back in October 1944, as soon as it was evident that the first attempt to get across the river, Operation Market Garden, had failed. The final plan was almost as elaborate as the one for the Overlord invasion of Normandy, the scope almost as big. Eighty thousand men, slightly less than half the number who went into France on June 6, 1944, would cross the Rhine by boat or transport airplane on the first day for Operations Plunder (the crossing by boat) and Varsity (the airborne phase), with an immediate follow-up force of 250,000 and an ultimate force of 1 million.

As usual, Montgomery proceeded with what one historian has characterized as the majestic deliberation of a pachyderm. He set D day for March 24. For the two weeks preceding the assault, he laid down a massive smoke screen that concealed the buildup—and gave the Germans ample warning about where he was going to cross. He gathered 600 rounds of ammunition per artillery piece. Beginning March 11, the air forces pounded the Germans on the east bank, hitting them with 50,000 tons of bombs. Monty invited Churchill and many other dignitaries to join him to watch the big show.

✦

ON FEBRUARY 28, Ninth Army was pushing east toward the Rhine. Progress was slow and costly. Company K, 333rd Regiment, received orders to advance on and take the village of Hardt, between the Roer and the Rhine. After an all-day march through mud and cold, followed by a few hours' rest, the company formed up an hour before dawn. More than half the company were replacements. Everyone was groggy, exhausted even before the day began. And wary, since they knew their flank was open, yet they were pressing on deeper into the German lines.

By the first spring week of 1945, four American armies had crossed the Rhine, as shown in this map. German resistance varied from stiff to nonexistent. The time for rapid exploitation, indicated by gray arrows, had arrived. The end of the war in Europe was little more than a month away.

Sergeant George Pope was delayed in getting his squad to jump off. "And here comes [Captain George] Gieszl and the battalion commander, right?" he said. "And the battalion CO says, 'For Christ's sakes, Pope, it's after eight and you haven't . . .' And I stopped the colonel right there and said, 'What's the big fucking rush? Where the fuck you think you are at, Louisiana on maneuvers? This ain't maneuvers, this is real shit, and I'm going out there, not you.' That's what I told the colonel, right? I didn't give a crap about nothing."

The company moved out, reached Hardt, attacked, and got stopped by machine-gun fire and a shower of 88s. Two men were killed. The others hit the ground. Private Mel Cline called on skills he'd not used since basic training. "We were flat, prone on our bellies. This German machine gunner was directly to our front. That was the only time in combat that I fired aimed shots like we did on the range in training. We could see this German come up from his hole, fire, and duck down again. I adjusted my sights, got the range, and squeezed off several clips before I finally hit his gun and put him out of action. When we reached his hole, I found the bullet had glanced off his machine gun and mangled his arm."

Private Leonard Bowditch was in a turnip patch when he was hit with shrapnel in the knee. "They were getting ready to evacuate me, and Lieutenant Leinbaugh was talking to several of us who had been wounded. I told him I wanted him to have my scarf as a good-luck piece, so I gave it to him and he wrapped it around his neck. He told me it couldn't have been too lucky, since I had just been hit. I said it worked just fine for me since I had a million-dollar wound and was going home."

Pope's squad got caught in the open. "We were all pinned down," he remembered, "and I see guys turning their heads, I felt like doing that myself. It was flat as a floor. There wasn't a blade of grass you could hide under."

Lieutenant Bill Masters took charge. He was in the edge of a wood with half of his platoon. The remainder of his men and the other platoons were getting pounded out in the open flat field. Masters recalled, "The fire was awfully heavy and the casualties were increasing. I decided I had to get these guys moving or a lot more were going to get killed." He ran forward, swearing at the men to get them going as he passed them. "I got up as far as a sugar-beet mound that gave some cover, close enough to toss a grenade at the German machine gunner right in front of me. But I couldn't get the grenade out of my pocket—it was stuck." A German tossed a potato masher at Masters. "It landed right next to me but didn't explode."

The enemies commenced firing at each other. Both missed. Both ran out of ammunition at precisely the same time. Masters knelt on one knee, reloaded, as did the German. Again the enemies looked up at the same time and fired simultaneously. Masters put a bullet between the machine gunner's eyes. When Masters took off his helmet to wipe his brow, he found a bullet hole through the top.

Masters ran to the first building on the outskirts of town, where he had some cover. "I had this dead-end kid from Chicago I'd made my bodyguard [Private Ray Bocarski]. He came in close behind me, and then a number of men pulled up and we went from building to building cleaning out the place and captured a sizable batch of German paratroopers in those houses." Lieutenant Paul Leimkuehler gave a more vivid description of Masters's action: "He killed a machine gunner and opened the way into that little town. He was leading, running down the main street like a madman, shooting up everything in his way."

The Germans had two 75s and two 88s presighted on the village. Armor-piercing shells crumbled the walls. Captain Gieszl and the forward observer called for a counterbarrage. Within minutes, the German guns were out of action. Over the next few days the company advanced toward the Rhine. Sometimes there was resistance, sometimes not. Just before the leading platoon got to the Rhine a German platoon barged into the middle of the company column. A point-blank exchange of rifle fire and grenades lasted several minutes. Four men were wounded, including Masters. Several Germans were killed; the rest surrendered.

By March 7, the company was in Krefeld, on the banks of the Rhine. By some miracle, the men found an undamaged high-rise apartment in which everything worked—electricity, hot water, flush toilets, and telephones with dial tones. They had their first hot baths in four months. They found cigars and bottles of cognac. Private Bocarski, fluent in German, lit up, sat down in an easy chair, got a befuddled German operator on the phone, and talked his way through to a military headquarters in Berlin. He told the German officer he could expect K Company within the week.

That was not to be. Having reached the river, K Company, along with the rest of Ninth Army, would stay in place until Montgomery had everything ready for Operation Plunder. The troops badly needed the rest. The night after taking Hardt, Private J. A. "Strawberry" Craft was so totally exhausted that after getting into his foxhole he told the sergeant he was going to sleep that night. The sergeant warned him, "You might wake up dead." Craft replied, "I'll just have to wake up dead." Decades later he still remembered the exchange and explained, "I needed the sleep, and I got it, too."

✦

ON MARCH 7, Patton's forces were still fighting west of the Rhine, trying to close the river from Koblenz south to Mainz and in the process trap further German forces facing Lieutenant General Alexander M. Patch's U.S. Seventh Army. Patton was having divisions stolen from him, to dispatch south to help Seventh Army get through the Siegfried Line east of Saarbrücken. That made him furious, but he calmed down when Bradley, commanding the 12th Army Group, agreed to move the boundary between Third and Seventh Armies some twenty kilometers south of Mainz. That put the best stretch of river for crossing south of Cologne in his sector. He was thinking of crossing on the run and hoping he could do it before Montgomery's elephantine operation even got started, and before Hodges, too, if possible.

But his men were exhausted. "Signs of the prolonged strain had begun to appear," one regimental history explained. "Slower reactions in the individual; a marked increase in cases of battle fatigue, and a lower standard of battle efficiency—all showed quite clearly that the limit was fast approaching." Company G, 328th Infantry Regiment, was typical. It consisted of veterans whose bone-weariness was so deep they were indifferent, or on the edge of battle fatigue, plus raw recruits. Still it had the necessary handful of leaders, and superb communications with the artillery, as demonstrated by Lieutenant Lee Otts in the second week in March, during Third Army's drive toward the Rhine. Private George Idelson described it in a 1988 letter to Otts: "My last memory of you—and it is a vivid one—is of you standing in a fierce mortar and artillery barrage, totally without protection, calling in enemy coordinates. I know what guts it took to do that. I can still hear those damn things exploding in the trees. I lost one foxhole buddy to shrapnel in that barrage, and then his replacement. I don't know who was looking after me."

Otts established a platoon command post, took off his equipment and both field jackets and began to dig a hole. "Mortar shells started falling almost as thick as rain drops and we all hit the ground fast," he remembered. "Instead of covering my head, I, like a fool, propped up on my right elbow with my chin resting on my hand, looking around to see what was going on. All of a sudden something hit me on the left side of my jaw that felt like a blow from Jack Dempsey's right. . . . I stuck my hand up to feel the wound and it felt as though half my face was missing." One of the men crawled over to try to put a bandage in place. He looked at Otts and cried, "Oh God, Lieutenant, this is all for me." He had to be evacuated. The company commander came limping over to Otts. He had been hit in the foot and intended to turn the company over to Otts, but he took one look at Otts's face and cried, "My God, no, not you, too," turned, and limped back to his foxhole.

Otts got up to start walking back to the aid station when a sniper got him in the shoulder, the bullet exiting from his back without hitting any bone. He was on his way home. For the others, the pounding continued. Lieutenant Jack Hargrove recalled, "All day men were cracking mentally and I kept dashing around to them but it didn't help. I had to send approximately fifteen back to the rear, crying. Then two squad leaders cracked, one of them badly."

First Army was moving east, all along its front. Hodges had divisions making ten miles per day, sometimes more. They were taking big bags of prisoners. His men were looking forward to getting to the river, where they anticipated good billets in warm, dry cellars and a few days to rest and refit. There was even a chance they could stay longer, as there were no plans for crossing in their sector, where all the bridges were down or soon would be. First Army was, in essence, SHAEF's reserve. Eisenhower counted on it to give him the flexibility to send a number of divisions either north to reinforce Monty or south to reinforce Patton, depending on developments. To free up those divisions, First Army had to close to the river along its whole sector. There would then be no danger of a German counterattack and large numbers of Americans could be pulled back and put in reserve.

The Germans, meanwhile, were in near full retreat. Although their orders were that no unit could cross to the east bank of the river without authorization from Hitler, individuals were taking matters into their own hands. At Bonn, Major Rolf Pauls, who had lost an arm in Russia but continued to serve (he later became West Germany's first ambassador to both Israel and China, and ambassador to the United States), found himself fighting with the river immediately at his back. He ordered his 88s and the few remaining tanks to retreat over the last standing bridge in his sector. The high command threatened to court-martial Pauls and called him a coward. He pointed out that he needed his artillery behind the front lines and that the tanks were almost out of fuel, and got away with it.

Eighteen-year-old Private Siegfried Kügler recalled hiding in a wood and watching the Americans marching toward the Rhine. "When we saw everything that was going past, all the artillery, tanks, and trucks, well, I've got to say I just flipped. I thought: How can you declare war on such a country?"

✦

ON THE MORNING of March 7, General John Millikin, commanding III Corps on First Army's right flank, sent his 9th Armored Division too close to the west bank of the Rhine. The mission of Combat Command B (CCB) of the 9th, commanded by General William Hoge, was to occupy the west bank town of Remagen, where a great railroad bridge spanned the Rhine. It had been built in the midst of World War I, to facilitate the movement of supplies to the Western Front, and named for General Erich Ludendorff. On the east bank, there was an escarpment, the Erpeler Ley. Virtually sheer, rising some 170 meters, it dominated the river valley. The train tracks followed a tunnel through the Erpeler Ley. (A touch of irony: In December 1918, III Corps, First Army, had crossed the Rhine at Remagen as part of the Allied occupation forces. My grandfather, Colonel Harry M. Trippe, U.S. Army Corps of Engineers, was one of the men to cross the Ludendorff Bridge.)

It was dank, cold, with clouds down almost to the treetops. That kept the American fighters and bombers on the ground, but not the little Piper Cubs. As CCB moved toward the Rhine, Lieutenant Harold Larsen of the 9th Division artillery flew ahead in a Piper Cub looking for targets of opportunity. At around 10:30 A.M. he was approaching Remagen, when to his astonishment he saw the Ludendorff Bridge, its massive superstructure looming out in the fog and mists of the river valley. Larsen radioed the news to General Hoge, who immediately sent orders to the units nearest Remagen to take the bridge. They were the 27th Armored Infantry Battalion and the 14th Tank Battalion. Hoge formed them into a task force under Lieutenant Colonel Leonard Engeman, who put Lieutenant Emmet "Jim" Burrows's infantry platoon of Company A in the lead. Brushing aside light opposition, Task Force Engeman reached a wood just west of Remagen a little before noon. Burrows emerged from the wood onto a cliff overlooking the Rhine. There was the Ludendorff Bridge, intact. German soldiers were retreating across it.

Burrows called back to 2d Lieutenant Karl Timmermann, twenty-two years old, who had just assumed command of Company A the previous day. Another irony: Timmermann had been born in Frankfurt am Main, less than 160 kilometers from Remagen. His father had been in the American occupation forces in 1919, married a German girl, and stayed in the country until 1923, when he returned to his native Nebraska with his wife and son. Timmermann had joined the Army in 1940 and earned his bars at OCS at Fort Benning.

Timmermann took one look and got on the radio to Colonel Engeman, who told him to get into the town with his infantry and tanks. As Timmermann set out, Engeman called Hoge, who set off cross-country in a jeep to get to the scene, weighing as he did the prospects of losing a battalion when the bridge blew up against the possibility of capturing it. In addition, he had just received an order to proceed south on the west bank until he linked up with the left flank of Third Army. To go for the bridge he would have to disobey direct orders, risking a court-martial and disgrace.

At three in the afternoon Hoge arrived, looked, and ordered Engeman to seize the bridge. He figured he would only lose one platoon if the Germans blew it when it came under assault. Timmermann, meanwhile, had fought through scattered resistance and by four o'clock was approaching the bridge. Germans on the east bank were firing machine guns and antiaircraft guns at his company. His battalion commander, Major Murray Deevers, joined Timmermann. "Do you think you can get your company across that bridge?" he asked.

"Well, we can try it, sir," Timmermann replied.

"Go ahead."

"What if the bridge blows up in my face?" Timmermann asked. Deevers turned and walked away without a word. Timmermann called to his squad leaders, "All right, we're going across."

He could see German engineers working with plungers. There was a huge explosion. It shook Remagen and sent a volcano of stone and earth erupting from the west end of the bridge. The Germans had detonated a cratering charge that gouged a deep hole in the earthen causeway joining the main road and the bridge platform. The crater that resulted made it impossible for vehicles to get onto the bridge—but not infantry.

Timmermann turned to a squad leader: "Now, we're going to cross this bridge before—" At that instant, there was another deafening rumble and roar. The Germans had set off an emergency demolition two thirds of the way across the bridge. Awestruck, the men of A Company watched as the huge structure lifted up, and steel, timbers, dust, and thick black smoke mixed in the air. Many of the men threw themselves on the ground.

Ken Hechier, in *The Bridge at Remagen,* one of the best of all accounts of the U.S. Army in action in World War II, and a model for all oral history, described what happened next:

> Everybody waited for Timmermann's reaction. "Thank God, now we won't have to cross that damned thing," Sgt. Mike Chinchar said fervently, trying to reassure himself.
>
> Pvt. Johnny Ayres fingered the two grenades hooked onto the rings of his pack suspenders and nodded his head: "We wouldn't have had a chance."
>
> But Timmermann, who had been trying to make out what was left of the bridge through the thick haze, yelled:
>
> "Look—she's still standing."
>
> Most of the smoke and dust had cleared away, and the men followed their commander's gaze. The sight of the bridge still spanning the Rhine brought no

cheers from the men. It was like an unwelcome specter. The suicide mission was on again.

At the east end of the bridge, Timmermann could see German engineers working frantically to try again to blow the bridge. He waved his arm overhead in the "Follow-me" gesture. Machine-gun fire from one of the bridge towers made him duck. One of A Company's tanks pulled up to the edge of the crater and blasted the tower. The German fire let up.

"Get going," Timmermann yelled. Major Deevers called out, "I'll see you on the other side and we'll all have a chicken dinner."

"Chicken dinner, my foot, I'm all chicken right now," one of the men of the first platoon protested. Deevers flushed. "Move on across," he ordered.

"I tell you, I'm not going out there and get blown up," the GI answered. "No sir, major, you can court-martial and shoot me, but I ain't going out there on that bridge."

Timmermann was shouting, "Get going, you guys, get going." He set the example, moving onto the bridge himself. That did it. The lead platoon followed, crouching, running, dodging, watching for holes in the bridge planking that covered the railroad tracks (put down by the Germans so their vehicles could retreat over the bridge) but always in the direction of the Germans on the far shore.

Sergeant Joe De Lisio led the first squad. Sergeants Joe Petrencsik and Alex Drabik led the second. In the face of more machine-gun and 20mm antiaircraft fire they dashed forward. "Get going," Timmermann yelled. The men took up the cry. "Get going," they shouted at one another. "Get going." Engineers were right behind them searching for demolitions and tearing out electrical wires. The names were Chinchar, Samele, Massie, Wegener, Jensen. They were Italian, Czech, Norwegian, German, Russian. They were children of European immigrants, come back to the old country to liberate and redeem it.

On the far side, at the entrance to the tunnel, they could see a German engineer pushing on a plunger. There was nothing for it but to keep going. And nothing happened—apparently a stray bullet or shell had cut the wire leading to the demolition charges. Halfway across the bridge, three men found four packages of TNT weighing thirty pounds each tied to I-beams under the decking. Using wire cutters, they worked on the demolitions until they splashed into the river. De Lisio got to the towers, ran up the circular staircase of the one to his right, where the firing was coming from, and on the fourth level found three German machine gunners firing at the bridge.

"Hände hoch!" De Lisio commanded. They gave up; he picked up the gun they had been using and hurled it out the aperture. Men on the bridge saw it and were greatly encouraged. Drabik came running on at top speed. He passed the towers—the north one proved to be empty—and got to the east bank. He was the first GI to cross the Rhine. Others were on his heels. They quickly made the German engineers in the tunnel prisoners. Timmermann sent Lieutenant Burrows and his platoon up the Erpeler Ley, saying, "You know, Jim, the old Fort Benning stuff; take the high ground and hold it." Burrows later said, "Taking Remagen and crossing the bridge were a breeze compared with climbing that hill." He took casualties, but he got to the top, where he saw far too many German men and vehicles spread out before him to even contemplate attacking them. He hung on at the edge of the summit. But he had the high ground, and the Americans were over the Rhine.

Sixteen-year-old Private Heinz Schwarz, who came from a village only a short distance upstream on the east bank of the Rhine from Remagen, was in the tunnel. "We were all still kids," he recalled. "The older soldiers in our unit stayed [in the tunnel], but the rest of us were curious and went up to the bridge tower to get a better look." He heard the order ring out: "Everybody down! We're blowing the bridge!" He heard the explosion and saw the bridge raise up. "We thought the bridge had been destroyed, and we were saved." But as the smoke cleared, he saw Timmermann and his men coming on. He ran down the circular stairs and got to the entrance to the tunnel just as De Lisio got to the tower. "I knew I had to somehow get myself out through the rear entrance of the tunnel and run home to my mother as fast as I could." He did. Fifteen years later he was a member of the Bundestag. At a ceremony on March 7, 1960, he met De Lisio. They swapped stories.

As the word of Timmermann's toehold spread up the chain of command, to regiment, division, corps, and army, each general responded by ordering men on the scene to get over the bridge, for engineers to repair it, for units in the area to change direction and head for Remagen. Bradley was the most enthusiastic of all. He had been fearful of a secondary role in the final campaign, but with Hodges over the river he decided immediately to get First Army so fully involved that Eisenhower would have to support the bridgehead.

First, however, Bradley had to get by General Bull. The SHAEF G-3—the head of operations—was with Bradley when the word arrived. When Bradley outlined his plan, he related, "Bull looked at me as though I were a heretic.

He scoffed: 'You're not going anywhere down there at Remagen. You've got a bridge, but it's in the wrong place. It just doesn't fit the plan.'"

"What in hell do you want us to do," Bradley replied, "pull back and blow it up?"

Bradley got on the phone to Eisenhower. When he heard the news, Eisenhower was ecstatic. He said, "Brad, that's wonderful." Bradley said he wanted to push everything across he could. "Sure," Eisenhower responded, "get right on across with everything you've got. It's the best break we've had." Bradley felt it necessary to point out that Bull disagreed. "To hell with the planners," Eisenhower snapped. "Sure, go on, Brad, and I'll give you everything we got to hold that bridgehead. We'll make good use of it even if the terrain isn't too good."

The Germans agreed with Eisenhower and Bradley that the Ludendorff Bridge was suddenly the most critical strategic spot in Europe. So, like the Americans, they began rushing troops and vehicles to the site, to constrict and then eliminate the bridgehead, and made the last great commitment of the Luftwaffe to destroy it. Major Rolf Pauls, who had almost been court-martialed for sending his tanks and artillery over the bridge at Bonn on the morning of March 7, in the afternoon heard praise from the high command "for having been alert enough to get across when you could." He was ordered to march south immediately to Remagen, that night, March 7–8.

The Luftwaffe attacked the next morning. Sergeant Waldemar Fuhring, one of Major Pauls's men, arrived in time to see the strike: "I lay a half mile from the bridge in some bushes. I could see how our Stukas tried to blow up the bridge. They were brave. They got close. But not a single bomb hit the bridge."

Two great masses of men and weapons were on the move, heading toward Remagen. For the Germans, it was a hellish march through mud, traffic jams, abandoned vehicles, dead horses, dead men. Piper Cubs would spot them and bring down a tremendous shelling from American artillery on the west bank.

✦

FOR THE AMERICANS, it was a similarly hellish march over the bridge. Captain Charles Roland of the 99th Division recalled the sign on one of the west bank towers: "Cross the Rhine with dry feet, compliments of the 9th Armored Division." As he crossed, the night of March 7–8, "my mind flickered back to the historic episode in which Caesar crossed the same stream at almost the same location to fight the same enemy two thousand years before. My reverie was cut short by the whistle and crash of hostile shells. How exposed and vulnerable I felt on that strip of metal high above the black, swirling waters. Walking forward became extremely difficult. I had the feeling that each projectile was headed directly at my chest. Actually, we who had gained the bridge were relatively safe. The shells were hitting in the approaches to the bridge amid the marching troops who suffered many casualties." On the bridge, one shell hit on or near it every five minutes.

Colonel William Westmoreland, chief of staff of the 9th Armored, crossed that night lying on his belly on the hood of a jeep, spotting ahead for the driver for holes in the planking. In the morning he set up an antiaircraft battery on top of the Erpeler Ley. He saw his first jet aircraft that day, a German Me-262.

Hitler ordered courts-martial for those responsible for failing to blow the bridge. The American crossing at Remagen cost Field Marshal von Rundstedt his job as commander in the West; on March 8, Hitler relieved him and put Field Marshal Albert Kesselring in his place. Hitler dismissed four other generals and ordered an all-out assault to destroy the bridge, including those jets Westmoreland saw, plus V-2s, plus frogmen to place explosives in the pilings, plus constant artillery bombardment. The Americans hurried antiaircraft into the area. One observer of a German air strike recalled that when the planes appeared "there was so much firing from our guys that the ground shuddered; it was awesome. The entire valley around Remagen became cloaked in smoke and dust before the Germans left—only three minutes after they first appeared."

The struggle for the bridgehead continued. The Americans poured in the artillery, depending on the Piper Cub FOs to direct the shells to a prime target. Sergeant Oswald Filla, a panzer commander, recalled "the impossible amount of artillery. Their artillery observers in the air were very good. Whenever we went anywhere around the bridgehead to see what could be done, we had, at most, a half hour before the first shells arrived." As the infantry and armor gradually forced the Germans back, hundreds of engineers worked to repair the bridge even as it was getting pounded, while thousands of other engineers labored to get pontoon bridges across into the bridgehead. The 291st Engineer Combat Battalion (ECB), commanded by Lieutenant Colonel David Pergrin, worked with grim resolve despite air and artillery assaults. The engineers also built a series of log and net booms upstream to intercept German explosives carried to the bridge by the current.

Major Jack Barnes of the 51st ECB was in charge of building a twenty-five-ton heavy pontoon bridge. His description of the way it was done illustrates how good the American engineers had become at this business. Construction began at four in the afternoon of March 10, with the building of approach ramps on both shores two kilometers upstream—that is, to the south—of the bridge. Smoke pots hid the engineers from German snipers, but, Barnes remembered, "unobserved enemy artillery fire harassed the bridge site. Several engineers were wounded and six were killed. The Germans even fired several V-2 rockets from launchers in Holland, the only time they ever fired on German soil." None hit the bridge.

Construction continued through the night. "The bridge was built in parts, with four groups working simultaneously on four-boat rafts, mostly by feel in the dark. By 0400 the next morning, fourteen four-boat rafts had been completed and were ready to be assembled together as a bridge. When the rafts were in place they were reinforced with pneumatic floats between the steel pontoons so the bridge could take the weight of thirty-six-ton Sherman tanks."

The engineers used triple anchors to hold the rafts in place, but as the bridge extended out to midstream the anchors couldn't hold, despite help from motorboats:

> At about this time we discovered that the Navy had some LCVPs [landing craft vehicle and personnel] in the area and we requested their assistance.
>
> Ten came to the rescue. They were able to hold the bridge against the current until we could install a 1" steel cable across the Rhine immediately upstream of the bridge, to which the anchors for each pontoon were attached. This solved the problem of holding the bridge against the current. The remaining four-boat rafts were connected to the anchor cable, eased into position and connected to the ever-extending bridge until the far shore was reached.
>
> Finally [sic!], at 1900 March 11, 27 hours after starting construction, the 969-ft heavy pontoon bridge was completed. It was the longest floating bridge ever constructed by the Corps of Engineers under fire. Traffic started at 2300, with one vehicle crossing every two minutes. During the first seven days, 2,500 vehicles, including tanks, crossed the bridge.

On March 15, the great structure of the Ludendorff finally sagged abruptly and then fell apart with a roar, killing twenty-eight and injuring ninety-three of the engineers working on it. But by then the Americans had six pontoon bridges over the river, and nine divisions on the far side. They were in a position to head east, then north to meet Ninth Army, which would be crossing the Rhine above Düsseldorf. When First and Ninth Armies met, they would have the German Fifteenth Army in the Ruhr valley encircled. It took First

Army ten days of fighting through deep gullies and dense woods against fierce opposition to reach the autobahn, only eleven kilometers east of Remagen. But once there, it had good roads leading north.

✦

UP NORTH, Montgomery's preparations continued. Down south, Patton's Third Army cleared the Saarland and the Palatinate in a spectacular campaign. As his divisions approached the Rhine, Patton had 500 assault boats, plus LCVPs and amphibious trucks, DUKWs, brought forward, along with 7,500 engineers, but with no fanfare, no fuss, no publicity, in deliberate contrast to Montgomery and so as to not alert the Germans. On the night of March 22–23, the 5th Division began to cross the river at Oppenheim, south of Mainz. The Germans were unprepared; by midnight the entire 11th Regiment had crossed by boat with only twenty casualties. At dawn, German artillery began to fire, and the Luftwaffe sent twelve planes to bomb and strafe. The Americans pushed east anyway. By the end of the afternoon these divisions—the 5th, the 90th, and the 4th armored—were on the far side. The Germans launched a counterattack against the 5th Division, using students from an officer candidate school at nearby Wiesbaden. They were good soldiers and managed to infiltrate the American positions, but after a busy night and part of the next morning they were dead or prisoners.

On the morning of March 23, Patton called Bradley: "Brad, don't tell anyone, but I'm across."

"Well, I'll be damned—you mean across the Rhine?"

"Sure am, I sneaked a division over last night."

A little later, at the Twelfth Army Group morning briefing, the Third Army reported: "Without benefit of aerial bombing, ground smoke, artillery preparation, and airborne assistance, the Third Army at 2200 hours, March 22 . . . crossed Rhine River."

Patton drove to Oppenheim on the twenty-fourth and walked across a pontoon bridge built by his engineers. He stopped in the middle. While every GI in the immediate area who had a camera took his picture, he urinated into the Rhine—a long, high, steady stream. As he buttoned up, Patton said, "I've waited a long time to do that. I didn't even piss this morning when I got up so I would have a really full load. Yes, sir, the pause that refreshes." When he reached the east bank, he faked a fall, rose with two hands of German soil and remarked, "Thus William the Conqueror."

That night, March 23–24, Montgomery put his operation in motion. Generals Eisenhower and Simpson climbed to a church tower to watch Ninth Army do its part. More than 2,000 American guns opened fire at 1:00 A.M.

For an hour, more than a thousand American shells a minute ranged across the Rhine, 65,261 rounds in all. Meanwhile 1,406 B-17s unloaded on Luftwaffe bases just east of the river. At two the assault boats, powered by fifty-five-horsepower motors and carrying seven men with a crew of two, pushed off. Not until the first boats were almost touching the far shore did the American artillery lift its fire and begin plastering targets farther to the east. The enemy was so battered that only a few mortar shells landed among the first wave. Things went so well that before daylight, the 79th and 30th Divisions were fully across the river, at a cost of only thirty-one casualties. They set off, headed east.

✦

AT AIRFIELDS in Britain, France, and Belgium, meanwhile, the paratroopers and glider-borne troops from the British 6th and the American 17th Airborne Divisions began to load up in their C-47s, C-46s, or gliders. This was an airborne operation on a scale comparable with D day; on June 6, 1944, 21,000 British and American airborne troops had gone in, while on March 24, 1945, it was 21,680 British and American. Altogether there were 1,696 transport planes and 1,348 gliders involved (British Horsa and Hamicar gliders, and American Wacos; all of them made of canvas and wood). They would be guarded on the way to the drop zone and landing zone (DZ and LZ) by more than 900 fighter escorts, with another 900 fighters providing cover and patrol over the DZ. To the east, 1,250 additional P-47s would guard against German movement to the DZ, while 240 B-24s would drop supplies to the men in the DZ. Counting the B-17s that saturated the DZ with bombs, there were some 9,503 Allied planes involved.

The airborne troopers' objectives were wooded high ground affording observation of the river crossing sites, exits from Wesel, and crossings of nearby streams. Churchill, Eisenhower, and many other dignitaries, plus the press, were present to watch. A couple of B-17s were loaded with cameramen and assigned to fly around the DZ to take pictures. What concerned the planners of the airborne attack was the flak; the Ruhr valley and environs, Germany's industrial heartland, was the most heavily defended area in the country. German artillery and antiaircraft gunners had years of experience in fighting off the air raids over the Ruhr, and the transports and gliders would be coming in low and slow (500 feet at 120 knots per hour), beginning just after 1000 hours. The tow planes had two gliders each, instead of one as on D day and in Market Garden, a hazardous undertaking even on an exercise.

The DZ was just north and east of Wesel. It took the air armada two and a half hours to cross the Rhine. Lieutenant Ellis Scripture was the navigator on the lead plane, a B-17. It was a new experience for him to fly in a B-17 at 500 feet and 120 knots—that was perilously close to stall-out speed. Still, he recalled, "it was a beautiful spring morning and it was a tremendous thrill for us as we led the C-47s to the middle of the Rhine. Hundreds and hundreds of aircraft came flying over. . . . The thrill was the climax of the entire war as we poured tens of thousands of troops across the final barrier to the Fatherland."

Reporter Richard C. Hottelet was on one of the B-17s carrying cameras to record the event. "The sky above was pale blue," he wrote. "Below us, golden soil and bright green meadows were cut by long morning shadows. Flying at a few hundred feet, banking steeply to let the cameramen get their shots, we saw the solid phalanxes of olive-green troop carriers and tow planes and gliders. . . . It was a mighty olive-green river that surged steadily and inevitably over Germany."

Once across the river, on the edge of the DZ where the big bombers and fighters had just dropped their bombs, the scene changed: "Here there was no sunlight; here in the center of green and fertile land was a clearly marked area of death. The smoke seemed a shroud." The German antiaircraft guns sprang to life. Hottelet's plane was hit; he had to bail out, but fortunately not until the plane had crossed back to the west bank of the river, where he landed safely among friends.

Earlier that morning, before the flights took off, over the radio "Axis Sally" had told the men of the 17th Airborne to leave their parachutes home, because they would be able to walk down on the flak. She had not lied. The flak and ground fire were the most intense of any airborne operation of the war. One American officer, a veteran from the Normandy drop, said there "was no comparison," while an equally experienced British officer said that "this drop made Arnhem look like a Sunday picnic."

Sergeant Valentin Klopsch, in command of a platoon of German engineers in a cow stable about ten kilometers north of Wesel, described the action from his point of view. First there was the air bombardment, then the artillery, all of which put the fifteen- and sixteen-year-olds in his platoon into panic. When the shooting stopped, they were amazed to find themselves still alive, even though badly shaken. They got up, began looking around, and started congratulating each other for surviving. Klopsch and a couple of other old hands told them to get down, because the enemy was coming.

"And now, listen," Klopsch said. "Coming from across the Rhine there was a roaring and booming in the air. In waves aircraft were approaching at different heights. And then the paratroopers were jumping, the chutes were opening like mushrooms. It looked like lines of pearls loosening from the planes." The Luftwaffe flak gunners, who had thought their day was over when the bombers passed by, went back to work. The flak was heavy, "but what a superiority of the enemy in weapons, in men, in equipment. The sky was full of paratroopers, and then new waves came in. And always the terrible roaring of the low-flying planes. All around us was turning like a whirl." The Americans formed into squads and platoons, set up their mortars, and went to work themselves. They attacked Klopsch's cowshed. His platoon fired until out of ammunition, when Klopsch put up a white flag. "And then the Americans approached, chewing gum, hair dressed like Cherokees, but Colts at the belt." He and the surviving members of his platoon were marched to a POW cage on a farm and ordered to sit and not move. Decades later, he recalled, "What a wonderful rest after all the bombardments and the terrible barrage."

The C-46s took a pounding from the flak. This was the first time they had been used to carry paratroopers. The plane had a door on each side of the fuselage, which permitted a faster exit for the troopers, a big advantage over the single door on the C-47s. But what was not known until too late was that the C-46's fuel system was highly vulnerable to enemy fire. Fourteen of the seventy-two C-46s burst into flames as soon as they were hit. Eight others went down; in each case the paratroopers got out, but the crews did not.

For the gliders, it was terrifying. The sky was full of air bursts and tracers. Machine-gun bullets ripped through the canvas. The pilots—all lieutenants, most of them not yet eligible to vote—could not take evasive action. They fixed their eyes on the spot they had chosen to land and tried to block out everything else. Over half the gliders were badly hit and nearly all made crash landings amid heavy small-arms fire.

Private Wallace Thompson, a medic in the paratroopers, was assigned a jeep and rode in the driver's seat behind the pilots of a Waco. He was very unhappy about this. Through the flight he kept telling the pilots, Lieutenants John Heffner and Bruce Merryman, that he would much prefer to jump into combat. They ignored his complaints. As they crossed the river, the pilots told Thompson to start his engine, so that as soon as they landed they could release the nose latches and he could drive out.

Over the target, just a few meters above the ground, an 88 shell burst just behind Thompson's jeep. The concussion broke the latches of the nose section, which flipped up and locked, throwing the pilots out. The blast cut the ropes that held the jeep, which leaped out ahead of the glider, engine running, flying through the air at high speed, Thompson gripping the steering wheel with all his might. He made a perfect four-wheel landing and beat the glider to the ground, thus becoming the first man in history to solo in a jeep.

The glider crashed and tipped, ending up in a vertical position, rear end up. Lieutenants Merryman and Heffner somehow survived their flying exit, but were immediately hit by machine-gun bullets, Heffner in the hand and Merryman in the leg. They crawled into a ditch. Thompson drove over to them.

"What the hell happened?" he demanded, but just then a bullet creased his helmet. He scrambled out of the jeep and into the ditch, where he berated the pilots and the entire glider program. "His last word," Merryman recalled, "was that he had just taken his last glider ride, they could shoot him and put him in one, but that would be the only way." Then Thompson treated their wounds and, after treating other wounded in the area, drove Merryman and Heffner to an aid station.

✦

OPERATION VARSITY, the airborne phase of Montgomery's Rhine crossing, featured not only a flying jeep; it also provided a unique event in U.S. Army Air Force history. The glider pilots bringing in the 194th Glider Infantry were told two weeks before the operation that one more infantry company was necessary to the 194th's mission, and that they would be it. There were nearly 200 of the Air Force officers. They had received a quick briefing in infantry tactics and weapons. They landed under heavy ground fire and took substantial casualties among the infantry and pilots, but despite continuing machine-gun fire and exploding mortars, they got organized and did their job. Later that day they were attacked by 200 German infantrymen, a tank, and two flak guns, but managed to drive them off. Lieutenant Elbert Jelia damaged the tank with his bazooka. The retreating tank ran over one of the flak guns; the other was captured by the glider pilots. Overall the air force officers fighting as an infantry company suffered thirty-one casualties. They got written up in *Stars and Stripes*.

At the aid station, Lieutenants Merryman and Heffner met the crew of a B-24 that had been shot down and successfully crash-landed. The Air Force men told their story: when they started to dash out of their burning plane, the first man was shot, so the rest came out with hands up. The Germans took them to the cellar of a farmhouse, gave them some cognac, and held them "while the Germans decided who was winning. A little later the Germans realized they were losing and surrendered their weapons and selves to the bomber crew. The Germans were turned over to the airborne and the bomber crew went to the aid station." This was perhaps the only time a bomber crew took German infantry prisoners.

The German gunners, all in the Luftwaffe, wanted no part of ground fighting. When the airborne troops began to form up and move to their objectives, the Germans tended to give up. It helped the men of the 17th Airborne considerably that they had just been issued the new 57mm recoilless rifle, which weighed only forty-five pounds, was fired from the shoulder, and was more deadly than the bazooka. Before the end of the day the airborne troops had all their objectives, and over the next couple of days the linkup with the infantry was complete. Twenty-first Army Group was over the Rhine and headed east.

By the first week of spring 1945, Eisenhower's armies had done what he had been planning for since the beginning of the year—close to the Rhine along its length, with a major crossing north of Düsseldorf—and what he had dared to hope for and was prepared to support, additional crossings by First Army in the center and Third Army to the south. The time for exploitation had arrived. Some of the Allied infantry and armored divisions faced stiff resistance, others only sporadic resistance, others none at all. Whatever was in front of them—rough terrain, enemy strongpoints, more rivers to cross—their generals were as one in taking up the phrase Lieutenant Timmermann had used at the Remagen bridge—"Get going!"

The 90th Division, on Patton's left flank, headed east toward Hanau on the Main River. It crossed in assault boats on the night of March 28. Major John Cochran's battalion ran into a battalion of Hitler Youth officer candidates, teenage Germans who were eager to fight. They set up a roadblock in a village. As Cochran's men advanced toward it, the German boys let go with their machine gun, killing one American. Cochran put some artillery fire on the roadblock and destroyed it, killing three. "One youth, perhaps aged sixteen, held up his hands," Cochran recalled. "I was very emotional over the loss of a good soldier and I grabbed the kid and took off my cartridge belt.

"I asked him if there were more like him in the town. He gave me a stare and said, 'I'd rather die than tell you anything.' I told him to pray, because he was going to die. I hit him across the face with my thick, heavy belt. I was about to strike him again, when I was grabbed from behind by Chaplain Kerns. He said, 'Don't!' Then he took that crying child away. The chaplain had intervened not only to save a life but to prevent me from committing a murder. Had it not been for the chaplain, I would have."

From the crossing of the Rhine to the end of the war, every man who died, died needlessly. It was that feeling that almost turned Major Cochran into a murderer. On the last day of March, Sergeant Schlemmer of the 82nd had a particularly gruesome experience that almost broke him. His squad was advancing, supported by a tank. Six troopers were riding on the tank, while he and five others were following in its tracks, which freed them from worry about mines. A hidden 88 fired. The shell hit the gun turret, blowing off the troopers, killing two and wounding the other four. "The force of the blast blew them to the rear of the tank near me," Schlemmer recalled. "They lay as they fell. A second round then came screaming in, this time to ricochet off the front of the tank. The tank reversed gears and backed up over three of our wounded, crushing them to death. I could only sit down and bawl, whether out of frustration of being unable to help them, whether from the futility of the whole damn war, or whether from hatred of the Germans for causing it all, I've never been able to understand."

That same day, Corporal James Pemberton, a 1942 high school graduate who was now serving in the 103rd Division as a replacement, was also following a tank. "My guys started wandering and drifting a bit, and I yelled at them to get in the tank tracks to avoid the mines. They did and we followed. The tank was rolling over Schu mines like crazy. I could see them popping left and right like popcorn." Pemberton had an eighteen-year-old replacement in the squad; he told him to hop up and ride on the tank, thinking he would be out of the way up there. An 88 fired. The replacement fell off. The tank went into reverse and backed over him, crushing him from the waist down. "There was one scream, and some mortars hit the Kraut 88 and our tank went forward again. To me, it was one of the worst things I went through. This poor bastard had graduated from high school in June, was drafted, took basic training, shipped overseas, had thirty seconds of combat, and was killed."

Pemberton's unit kept advancing. "The Krauts always shot up all their ammo and then surrendered," he remembered. Hoping to avoid such nonsense, in one village the CO sent a Jewish private who spoke German forward with a white flag, calling out to the German boys to surrender. "They shot him up so bad that after it was over the medics had to slide a blanket under his body to take him away." Then the Germans started waving their own white flag. Single file, eight of them emerged from a building, hands up. "They were very cocky. They were about twenty feet from me when I saw the leader suddenly realize he still had a pistol in his shoulder holster. He reached into his jacket with two fingers to pull it out and throw it away.

"One of our guys yelled, 'Watch it! He's got a gun!' and came running up shooting, and there were eight Krauts on the ground shot up but not dead. They wanted water but no one gave them any. I never felt bad about it although I'm sure civilians would be horrified. But these guys asked for it. If we had not been so tired and frustrated and keyed up and mad about our boys they shot up, it never would have happened. But a lot of things happen in war and both sides know the penalties."

Hitler and the Nazis had poisoned the minds of the boys Germany was throwing into the battle. Captain F. W. Norris of the 90th Division ran into a roadblock. His company took some casualties, then blasted away, wounding many. "The most seriously wounded was a young SS sergeant who looked just like one of Hitler's supermen. He had led the attack. He was bleeding copiously and badly needed some plasma." One of Norris's medics started giving him a transfusion. The wounded German, who spoke excellent English, demanded to know if there was any Jewish blood in the plasma. The medic said damned if he knew, in the United States people didn't make such a distinction. The German said if he couldn't have a guarantee that there was no Jewish blood he would refuse treatment.

"I had been listening and had heard enough," Norris remembered. "I turned to this SS guy and in very positive terms I told him I really didn't care whether he lived or not, but if he did not take the plasma he would certainly die. He looked at me calmly and said, 'I would rather die than have any Jewish blood in me.'

"So he died."

✦

BY MARCH 28, First Army had broken out of the Remagen bridgehead. Major General Maurice Rose's 3rd Armored Division led the way, headed for Paderborn and the linkup with Ninth Army to complete the encirclement of the German army in the Ruhr. That day, Rose raced ahead, covering ninety miles, the longest gain on any single day of the war for any American unit. By March 31, he was attacking a German tank training center outside Paderborn. Rose was at the head of a column in his jeep. Turning a corner, his driver ran smack into the rear of a Tiger tank. The German tank commander, about eighteen years old, opened his turret hatch and leveled his burp gun at Rose, yelling at him to surrender.

Rose, his driver, and his aide got out of the jeep and put their hands up. For some reason, the tank commander became extremely agitated—later, it was rumored in the American army that the German knew Rose was Jewish, but that almost certainly was not true—and kept pointing to Rose and hollering at him while gesturing toward Rose's pistol. Rose lowered his right arm to release his web belt and thus drop his hip holster to the ground. Apparently, the German boy thought he was going to draw his pistol; in a screaming rage, he fired his machine pistol straight into Rose's head, killing him instantly. The driver and the aide managed to flee and lived to tell the story. Maurice Rose was the first and only division commander killed in the European Theater of Operations.

The tank school at Paderborn had brand-new Tigers. They could be deadly. Ten of them caught a column of Shermans in the open. The Tigers destroyed seventeen Shermans and a dozen half-tracks, but they paid a price of their own. One advantage of the Sherman was that it could traverse its turret much faster than the Tiger. In the right circumstances, an American tank commander could get in the first shot. In this action, one 3rd Armored tanker used that advantage well. Knowing that the Sherman's 75mm cannon could not penetrate the Tiger's armor, he had his gunner load a white phosphorus round. As a Tiger turned on him, he fired. The shell struck the glaces plate of the Tiger right above the driver's compartment with a blazing crescendo of flames and smoke. Captain Cooper, who saw the fight, reported that "the whole face plate in front of the turret was covered with burning particles of white phosphorus which stuck to the sides of the Tiger. The smoke engulfed the tank and the fan in the engine compartment sucked the smoke inside the fighting compartment. The German crew thought the tank was on fire and immediately abandoned it even though the tank actually suffered very little damage."

The American tanker turned his turret and fired another white phosphorus shell at a second Tiger, again hitting the front glaces plate with similar results. Cooper commented, "Thus the brave, ingenious tank commander knocked out two Tigers without ever getting a penetration."

Such resistance was rare. In most cases the retreating Germans did not stop to fight. Generally they passed right through the villages, rather than use them as roadblocks or strongpoints. This was fortunate for the villages, because the American practice was to demolish any building that was defended, but if white flags were waving from the windows and no German troops were in sight, they let it be.

First and Third Armies were advancing in mostly rural areas, untouched by the war. The GIs were spending their nights in houses. They would give the inhabitants five minutes or so to clear out. The German families were indignant. The GIs were insistent. As Lieutenant Max Lale put it in a March 30 letter home, "None of us have any sympathy for them, because we all have been taught to accept the consequences of our actions—these people apparently feel they are the victims of something they had no hand in planning, and they seem to feel they are being mistreated." The stock joke had it that every German had a cousin in Milwaukee.

The rural German homes had creature comforts—electricity, hot water, flush toilets, soft white toilet paper—such as most people thought existed in 1945 only in America. On his first night in a house, Private Joe Burns spent five minutes in a hot shower. Fifty-one years later he declared it to be "the most exquisite five minutes in my life. Never before or since have I had such pure pleasure." Private David Webster recalled washing his hands at the sink and deciding, "This was where we belonged. A small, sociable group, a clean, well-lighted house [behind blackout curtains], a cup of coffee—paradise."

Things were looking up, even though there was still a lot of Germany to overrun.

THE LAST
PICTURE SHOW

GEORGE FEIFER

The story that follows has to be one of the strangest in this book. In September 1944, as Allied bombs were flattening Berlin and German armies retreating on every front, the end of the war seemed a foregone conclusion. Then Joseph Goebbels, the Nazi propaganda minister—the man many Germans referred to as the "Poison Pygmy"—had an inspiration. He would uplift the flagging spirits of the people with a movie, a Nazi version of one of his favorites, *Mrs. Miniver,* Hollywood's sentimentalized Academy Award–winning portrayal of an English family's fortitude during the Blitz. The autumn of 1944 was a period when everyone was trying to pull martial rabbits out of hats, and some of those efforts, like Rundstedt's, seemed to be having a brief success. Goebbels reasoned that the time had come to go beyond talk of the Master Race's need to purify Western civilization. For the moment new meaning had to be pumped into a struggle that, to the ordinary German, seemed increasingly doomed. Courage *could* produce miracles—and Goebbels's film project was to be a miracle weapon for the home front, one that would help to turn the tide as surely as the miracle weapons for which the high command and the armaments industry were searching. (The Germans had passed up the only miracle weapon that might have made a difference, the atom bomb, but that is a subject already discussed.) The movie, *Life Goes On,* would tell the story, *Grand Hotel*–style, of the occupants of a Berlin apartment house in a city under aerial siege. As one of the characters puts it: "The only important thing is that we meet the test, most of all in our own eyes."

No cost was spared. All other film projects at Babelsberg, the German Hollywood south of Berlin, were put on hold. The original shooting schedule, 121 days, was twice that of a normal movie. Technicians fashioned models of an intact Berlin—the movie was set in 1943—that could be bombed and burned: It would not do to show the mile after mile of actual destruction. Slave laborers were dragooned as extras. Bombing, power outages, and the advance of Allied armies forced the production to move elsewhere: It was the spring of 1945 by now. Luftwaffe crews, their aircraft largely grounded for lack of fuel, gaped as a night fighter took off and landed, again and again, until the director was satisfied that he had the right take. Art was not just imitating life; art was pre-empting it—and that was just part of the story of *Life Goes On*.

George Feifer is the author of eleven books, including the novel *Moscow Farewell*, based on the years he spent in Russia, *Tennozan: The Battle of Okinawa and the Atomic Bomb*, and most recently, *Red Files: Secrets from the Russian Archives*.

In the ruins and rubble of our bombarded cities, life goes on. Not as rich as before, it can no longer be ladled from a full pot. But we stand solidly on our feet and show not the smallest inclination to sink to our knees.

—JOSEPH GOEBBELS, APRIL 1944

ONCE UPON A TIME, AN APARTMENT HOUSE STOOD IN A FINE residential district of Berlin. Its occupants cooked, quipped, and went about their business as if their conditions were ordinary instead of catastrophic: this was 1943, when Allied bombing had begun leveling Berlin. Thereby hangs the tale of the Third Reich's last movie, which went into production in September 1944, and whose making mirrored the absurdities of the regime's death throes.

Life Goes On, the Reich's last word on film, provides sharp insight into the attempts of nonpolitical Germans—even some who once favored the Nazis—to survive privation and fear after there was no point in continuing the war except to achieve an "honorable" death—which was the film's point. As Germany's defenses crumbled, Hitlerite purposes became more and more mad. The dementia of priorities that sustained the extravagant, useless cinema project echoed Nazi use of precious rolling stock, at the same critical time, for shipping victims to murder camps instead of for transporting supplies to the disintegrating fronts.

Life Goes On followed six families that occupied the Berlin apartment house. The central character, Ewald Martens, was engaged in a secret effort to save the Reich, and his splendid wife's tender devotion to him and their children reflected German womanhood at its best. The other residents included Leonore, a lonely librarian; an elderly medical researcher named Professor Huebner; and the building's superintendent and air raid warden, who represented the proletariat. That fine fellow had a heart as big as his mouth, from which emerged lovably wise-guy quips in typical Berlin lingo.

One way or another, all were bewildered by their calamity. Why on earth were Germans being victimized in this grueling war? When Gundel Martens visits Professor Huebner one evening, she ventures that maybe the bombers, whose last raid was some time ago, will now leave them in peace. "Why should they destroy our houses, our everything?" "Why is man man's enemy?" Huebner replies. "Not even Socrates could answer that. War is a natural catastrophe, just like an earthquake. . . . It's only important that when we look into the mirror afterward, we don't have to feel ashamed."

In a later scene, the knowing professor similarly soothes the lonely librarian, who has confessed she finds it "really hard" not to lose courage.

"Yes, of course—but that's precisely the test we're facing," he replies. "Who sent it to us? God, Providence, Fate, Nature; there are so many names. The only important thing is that we meet the test, most of all in our own eyes."

✦

COME AGAIN? Was the sage professor suggesting that the war was a "natural catastrophe," not a consequence of Hitler's trumpeting that "right consists only in strength" and that the German *Volk* have a "moral right to acquire foreign soil"? Could it truly be that God or Nature caused it, and not the führer? Such strangely un-Nazi dialogue, with its acceptance of fate's triumph over will, was spoken in an equally extraordinary setting. After the disastrous Stalingrad defeat in January 1943, German moviegoers caught glimpses of the war only in carefully edited newsreels. The feature films—airy fantasies, merry musicals and romantic comedies, lavish costume spectacles and historical dramas—provided escape from daily pain and privation. Only one of the sixty German movies produced in 1942–43 was about the war that was squeezing everyone in its killing grip. (Helped by German immigrants, and safe from Axis bombers, Hollywood churned out more than a hundred anti-Nazi films during the war.)

No German movie soundtracks now blared "Heil Hitler!" The Nazi dream factory never hinted at German hardship, rubble, or death. In presenting screen images of that misery, the last Third Reich film was also a first. The great Durchhaltefilm—from the verb *durchhalten*: "to endure through thick and thin, stick it out together to the end"—was to be a miracle weapon for the home front while the German armaments industry and high command dreamed, not coincidentally, of miracle weapons for turning the battlefield tide.

The apartment house's occupants live in "movie reality." Professor Huebner, for one, refuses to take refuge in the basement shelter at the sound of the air raid alarm, but does deposit two suitcases there in hopes of saving his cancer research. During a savage bombing raid, a charismatic man enters the shelter. A Luftwaffe major named Hoesslin, he quietly comes and goes from the building—until late in the film, when he reveals that he flies night fighters against the enemy raiders.

Hoesslin: Death's my friend, you know. We've often met. And when he invites me to join him, I'll tell him that I've always been curious to see his place.

Leonore: I could never do that. Take death so easily.

Hoesslin: I never take it easily, it's life I take easily. Just think of luck. It gives such a sensation of happiness! Just when you think you've lost your life, it returns like a roaring river, swelling your heart.

Leonore {laughs}: A man who has death as a friend, and who loves life!

Perhaps to keep the little community from seeming too wholesome, a selfish couple schemes to profit from every opportunity, including even the brutal bombing raids. But good qualities overwhelm the bad. Many reside in the valiant Ewald Martens. His secret effort is designing a new radarlike device for detecting enemy planes at a distance: a wonder weapon that will lift the air siege by giving German night fighters an unsurpassable advantage over Allied bombers. The brilliant inventor predicts the progress for armament industry officials:

Scene 84. Martens's Office. Day.

Martens: Gentlemen! In six weeks, we'll have the data. In eight weeks, we'll complete the tests. In twelve weeks, we'll finish development. And in fourteen weeks, the first plane will take on the enemy with the device installed.

He opens his window to let in air.

Scene 85, Shift Change. Day.

Entering factory gates, a thick stream of workers breaks up into groups headed for various parts of the factory. Cut to Martens's hands as he stands near his window, then moves inside his office.

Martens: Gentlemen! Who are we really doing this for? If a military band were playing now, I'd say it was for the Fatherland. But as it is, I prefer saying it's for us. Because after all's said and done, we are the Fatherland.

Throughout the devastating raids that follow, Martens feverishly toils to perfect his invention while his lovely Gundel protects the family's wits and hearth from the flames and fear. While the other residents become entangled in soap-opera subplots, Martens manages to make the device operational—but too late; and bombs have taken his beloved Gundel.

How could that have happened to so exemplary a positive hero—and to Berlin? How to explain so startling a departure from the conviction that Nazi triumphs were preordained? Who authorized the talk of death instead of the "master race's" rewards for "purifying" Western civilization? The sanctioner of those previously blasphemous notions was none other than the German film industry's absolute ruler, whose name is synonymous with Nazi propaganda.

✦

JOSEPH GOEBBELS studied philology and history at eight German universities (where, as a biographer put it, the little scoundrel prepared to be a big one). But he yearned to be a writer. His early attempts, like Hitler's as an artist, failed ignominiously. Now, however, the inventive minister for the people's enlightenment and propaganda continued devising characters, plots, scenes—of movies, for they excited him more even than radio.

But what was his purpose in *Life Goes On,* with the first screen depiction of German corpses and ruins, after previous offerings that entertained with melodramatic and merry diversion (not unlike Hollywood's during the Depression)? Was he going soft?

Hardly. Dr. Goebbels still exulted in the elimination of "the bacillus" of European Jewry, using "the most brutal methods"—which, he rejoiced, were producing "a global solution" for which "no other government or regime would have the strength." His devotion to Hitler remained supremely slavish, even compared to his fellow satraps. After twenty years of intimate service to his führer, he still thrilled to the sight of him, approaching ecstasy when the beloved Hitler petted his dog and turning "almost benumbed," a subordinate recorded, when leaving his presence.

The new film did not signify the abandonment of Goebbels's monstrous ideals, but rather that this most educated, intelligent member of the upper Nazi crust had already accepted that the war was lost and now saw his duty as providing new meaning for the doomed struggle. He did that duty brilliantly. Like many of his colleagues, Goebbels was less the Nazi image of the strong, strapping Aryan than a deformed shrimp who dreamed of becoming one. (That didn't stop the "Poison Pygmy," as some Germans recklessly called him, from doggedly seducing "his" actresses while preaching family morality. Hollywood's anti-Nazi films included one about a crudely libidinous Joseph Goebbels.) But whatever he lacked physically, he was a master propagandist.

The first major bombing of Berlin in mid-1943 put Goebbels in a "catastrophic" frame of mind, as an underling described. No more National Destiny now; the deeply shaken maker of moods hungered to stiffen the losers' spirit. He must show the world what Germans—and his film industry—were made of, even under the hardest test.

Goebbels was a devoted fan of *Mrs. Miniver,* Hollywood's highly sentimental portrayal of civilian English fortitude during Great Britain's hard times earlier in the war. Vexed as he was that "cultureless" America could have made such a morally uplifting film, he especially admired its final scene: a vicar promising that the dead, just buried near a ruined church, will eternally inspire future generations. The desire to make *"my Mrs. Miniver"* grew in Goebbels as the shock of the first severe bombings changed to indignation at their relentlessness. The enemy's dreadful "terror-bombing" must become "our high school for communal spirit."

Thus did the German movie industry's best author, as the minister regarded himself, launch *Life Goes On.* To avoid the embarrassment of identifying that fiercest propagandist of total war as a mere movie hand, the treatment was credited to three other writers, with the help of an article by him: no doubt his April 1944 call for steadfastness under the bombing. "In the ruins and rubble of our bombarded cities, life goes on." The last three words comprised the headline of the article and became the film's title. The story's blend of kitsch and heroism was just as in his writings and speeches, now promising that courage could produce "genuine miracles." When the highly ambitious treatment was sent to the Nazi film bureaucracy in the summer of 1944, the ministry of propaganda's instructions were to label the extravaganza "of the highest importance," deserving "the greatest attention."

Goebbels felt that only one director could achieve the impact he craved. That man, thirty-nine-year-old Wolfgang Liebeneiner, accepted the daunting challenge of crafting an artistic miracle. Liebeneiner was chief producer of Germany's now monopolistic Universal Film Corporation (UFA in the German acronym). Although he had profited from the artistic vacuum after the elimination of Jews from German cultural life, the handsome, thoughtful-looking artist might have risen to the top without such help. He had acted in and directed extremely popular films, including two blockbusters about Bismarck that earned Goebbels's highest praise, especially for Liebeneiner's ability to translate scripts into huge celluloid canvases, full of character and action.

✦

WHEN THE "critical weapon" in the Geistige Kriegführung ("Morale War Effort") was announced in September 1944, Allied armies were approaching the Fatherland from east and west, and Liebeneiner's new cause appeared correspondingly hopeless. He rewrote the screenplay churned out by Nazi scriptwriters. Its full content became known to few because the shortage of paper severely limited distribution. The vast, complex sets posed graver problems. No fewer than six workshops would be needed to make them. The filming would take 121 days, almost double the average production schedule. Meanwhile, Paris had been liberated, and the Red Army, having freed all Russia of German troops, was 400 miles from Berlin and advancing relentlessly.

Even in peacetime, a mammoth undertaking like UFA Film 205 (the official designation for *Life Goes On*) would have strained Babelsberg, the German Hollywood located just southwest of Berlin's city limits. Now the capital was a day-and-night target, suffering constant fuel shortages and power outages. With fewer and fewer workers available, the elderly and partially disabled were recruited, all increasingly hungry and exhausted by the newly imposed seventy-two-hour workweek. Like a cinema version of the Egyptian pyramids, the project strained everyone and everything to the limit. Subject to intense propaganda ministry pressure to surmount its huge obstacles, it brought all other productions in Babelsberg to a virtual halt.

The costs struck the production managers as absurd. The technical director believed the stunt artists, crowd scenes, complicated special effects, and extensive use of models posed impossible problems. But Goebbels would put all his eggs in this one basket for most of the following year, and Liebeneiner's determination endured. Still rewriting during pre-production, he eliminated the worst clichés about German heroism, but without changing the basic message.

Casting had been easier. In such a production, so certifiably crucial to national morale, stars were mandatory. Liebeneiner quickly assembled a glittering collection, including his wife, the beautiful, talented Hilde Krahl, for Gundel Martens, the inventor's enviably competent wife; and Marianne Hoppe, one of Germany's greatest stage actresses, for the librarian. Neither they nor the luminaries playing the other major roles were typecast. The exception was the armaments chief, perhaps because it was hard to imagine that part not played by the jovial Heinrich George, one of Germany's most popular actors.

Günther Anders, among the country's best cameramen, led the equally talented behind-the-camera crew. Norbert Schultze, composer of "Lily Marlene," wrote the score.

Why did they sign on? Embers of faith in miraculous salvation still burned. SS investigation of civilian morale in 1944 had found that fear, chiefly of Anglo-American bombs and of the vengeful Red Army, alternated with hope for deliverance by a secret weapon. So too with the actors and crew, especially since the alternative—certain impressment into the armed forces or arms factories—was appallingly worse. However bizarre the torrent of energy and money spent on this movie behemoth, it provided a smidgen of security to those involved.

The ministry ordered all possible support and help, but seemed not to have noticed that much of 1943 Berlin was already destroyed. Because the destruction had to be shown as it happened, shots of smashed buildings and burning debris could only supplement the exterior scenes. Mountains of rubble wouldn't do as background when many streets contained nothing else. Thus arose an urgent need for models of the intact city, which would be "bombed" and "burned" to convey the previous year's disasters. Even the bomb shelters had to be replicated because Berlin's real ones had become too dangerous and awful.

By New Year's Day of 1945, British and American forces were flattening the Bulge, ready to cause Wehrmacht losses so great as to enfeeble all further defense in the west. In the east, nearly 4 million Red Army troops were poised for a massive attack that would strike for the Oder River, forty miles from Berlin. At home, shortages were so severe that reviews of unimportant films, to cite just one of a thousand frantic expedients, were banned. What to make of the frenzied effort to re-create Berlin's destruction while the real thing's smoke darkened the studios? How to explain the wantonly expensive crash drive for state-of-the-art effects to heighten the multiple action and crowd scenes—jammed bunkers, bomb shelters, railroad and S-Bahn stations— when piddling resources remained to oppose the approach of the Allied armies? Madness within madness! The lunacy of seeking a home-front "miracle weapon" was greater than that of trying to fashion and deploy the real thing for battle. Some of the latter efforts at least—such as the V-2 rocket— still promised conceivable success.

✦

NONETHELESS, LIEBENEINER kept his nerve, even as the bombing, hunger, and fear ballooned—and as some of his actors objected. The sharpest controversy was provoked by a scene at the Martenses' bedroom window, where

Gundel praises the beauty of the night, which peacetime traffic and lights had often obscured. For days, Liebeneiner's wife, supported by the distinguished actor playing Ewald, refused to say the utterly cynical line, as she saw it. How can nights that bring so much death be beautiful? Arguing that the line means darkness always makes the celestial stars more beautiful, the director eventually prevailed. Some of the cast suspected he saw bombing raids as aesthetic spectacles.

Although the enemy bombers largely spared Babelsberg, perhaps because the Allies intended to use UFA's facilities, its lights were literally going out. The production stopped in late January, on the eve of an American raid that killed 22,000 in Berlin. Hugely massed Soviet artillery was firing more heavily than ever in the east. Observers doubted Liebeneiner would be able to continue.

But work resumed on February 23, after a break of nearly a month. Since outages and blackouts rendered the sets virtually unusable during the day, the actors and crew—many exhausted from fighting fires to save their housing in Berlin—now started work at eleven in the evening. Leaving the studio's sets of bombed buildings before dawn, they made their freezing way back to devastated Berlin, hearing the crescendo of thunder from heavy Soviet guns, wondering whether a roof would still stand over their heads.

Despite everything, filming continued. One scene has the librarian and her Luftwaffe ace meeting in a train station. Many of its 250 extras had been chosen from the quarter-million foreigners living in Berlin, mostly Poles and Russians held in one or another form of slavery. Did they appreciate the irony? Not long after elaborate models of Berlin's Stettiner Bahnhof were destroyed to depict the city's frightful bombing, the real station was blown to bits.

On March 19, Hitler issued his notorious "scorched earth" order for Germans to deny their assets to the enemy by destroying them. Babelsberg accountants chose the following day to finally release their unprecedentedly huge budget for the film. But no meticulously prepared paper fortune nor ledger-book feat could sustain more shooting in the face of the advancing Allied armies. *Life Goes On* had to somehow pick up and move.

Knowing the way was unequivocally lost, summoning patriots to burn their property, the collapsing Reich nevertheless lavished the money and otherwise virtually unobtainable gasoline to truck the crippled "morale-builder" to a new location. It was an airfield in the town of Lüneburg, some 100 miles farther west from the surging, sacking Red Army. All organizations, including military ones, were requested to assist. Although that struck the airfield's commander as senseless, he accommodated the crew in the barracks and cleared the field for cinema shooting—as opposed to the real kind RAF fighters were un-leashing on it. But since those enemy planes failed to deliver their bombs and bullets conveniently on time or with sufficient style, the special effects team had to return to work, getting the pyrotechnics right for the cameras.

To the actors and crew, the shot-up airfield still represented less danger than the alternatives, including a tragic fate in uniform. Desperately clinging to the quaking production, all hoped it would never end. After completing their roles, some actors went underground in mountains and remote farms.

On April 10, units of the U.S. 9th Army occupied Hanover, less than sev-enty miles to the south. The British 2nd Army was even closer. Still, the im-possible production went on, with Liebeneiner appearing to take no notice of the enemy's approach. Calmly, professionally, the director ordered repeated takes of critical shots, until fully satisfied by his fine-tuning.

Liebeneiner's persistence is largely explained by his desire to stay alive. He had always harbored silent doubts about the project. Shortly before the future director's first reading of the treatment, the UFA's press chief, Richard Due-vell, had been charged with defeatist talk. "Get off my back with that brown sauce [Nazi propaganda], I'm already vomiting," Duevell had told a col-league. Trying to save him, Liebeneiner appealed to everyone he could think of, including Goebbels. But Roland Freisler, the vicious "hanging judge," prevailed. (Freisler would soon gleefully sentence many conspirators in the July 1944 attempt on Hitler's life.) Duevell was guillotined; Liebeneiner found *Life Goes On* all the more a macabre title.

Then Berlin suffered one of its worst air attacks, just before the start of shooting in September 1944. Touring the enlarged "desert of rubble" with its unburied corpses from previous bombings, Liebeneiner came across a clutch of shell-shocked women urging Goebbels to deploy Hitler's wonder weapons now. Dismayed by their faith in German victory, the director felt uneasy about committing himself to a deceiving film. That was his social qualm. His personal one, since every sane German knew defeat was inevitable, and immi-nent, was not to expose himself to the victors' retribution by waging a sense-less last propaganda battle.

✦

AN IDEA FOR RESCUE dawned. It was to write a substitute ending to the film, reversing, as Liebeneiner saw it, the official one. The director was con-vinced his secret final scenes—which would have enraged Goebbels—would appeal to the Allied authorities, saving his film and putting him in their favor. *Life Goes On* would become the first postwar film rather than the last Nazi one.

The approved ending was a scene between Martens and the librarian, Leonore. Although awarded an Iron Cross, First Class, for his invention, Martens is bitterly disillusioned because all defense is hopeless against the enemy's "all-mighty power," and his revered Gundel is dead. For her part, Leonore is dismayed that her Major Hoesslin nevertheless still risks his life every night, attacking the enemy bombers. Although both recognize that all such effort has become senseless, they remain convinced that the sacrifices couldn't have been in vain. "We let ourselves get into something that's so monstrously enormous," reflects Leonore. "It's life and death—and so much blood has already flowed that no one can say it was all for nothing."

Cut to cemetery gates. Passing through, Leonore and Martens walk down a long alley of poplar trees, looking long and hard at graves as the picture fades out and the movie . . . *ends*.

The mood of that final scene fit Liebeneiner's direction throughout. He, paradoxically, came as close to artistic freedom as any other director in Nazi Germany. Berlin's increasingly demolished telephone and postal service severely weakened the censorship and surveillance apparatus, depriving the propaganda ministry of tight control, all the more because the staff were preoccupied with their own survival. With the director's relative independence still greater in Lüneburg, he indulged himself in a vague fatalism, as if war's inferno had taken good, ordinary Germans with it when it swept over the land like some inexplicable *Götterdämmerung*. With no idea of what brought it on, let alone the power to stop it, those decent men and women could only do their best to cope.

Liebeneiner's never-found secret ending remains secret. The best guess is that his reversal would have been in the attitude of his good, ordinary Germans. Essentially, the official version suggests that the whole horror was worth it, despite everything. The opposite conclusion, in his new version, enabled Liebeneiner to hope, surely in delusion, that his daring double game would save himself, his great film, and his crew. Although less warped than the ministry's, his perception nonetheless provided another illustration of the almost universal myopia of people fighting total wars in a sinister and losing cause.

On March 22, 1945, Goebbels exulted that a strong wave of anti-Semitism was sweeping America, much of which supported Nazi treatment of the Jews. He also boasted that the Allies realized there would be no collapse in German military or civilian morale. For this, he credited his own war propaganda, "quite openly eulogized" in London as the best, and "primarily responsible" for the reduced but continuing German resistance.

Two weeks later, on April 5, Goebbels announced that if a single white flag was hoisted in Berlin, he would not hesitate "to have the whole street and all its inhabitants blown up. This has the Führer's full authority." Ten days later, in the penultimate issue of a Nazi rag called *Das Reich,* he summoned all to fight to the end rather than "bear the dishonor of surrender." Then, in burning Berlin, he gathered his subordinates for the last time. Confirming his enduring faith in the medium of film, he praised *Kolberg,* a 1944 paean about a town whose unity at home as on the front defeats Napoleon's awful siege. (At the height of the war, two full Wehrmacht divisions were used to film that huge melodrama.) Goebbels went on to promote another "fine, elevating" film that had evidently just occurred to him. This one would record "the terrible days we're [now] living through."

> Gentlemen! Don't you want to play a part in that film, to be returned to life after a hundred years? . . . Stick to your guns now, so that a hundred years hence, moviegoers won't hoot and whistle when you appear on the screen.

Even some admirers who had previously hung on his words now thought he had taken leave of his senses. But Goebbels suffered fewer delusions about saving his hide than Himmler, Göring, and others in the highest Nazi clique, many of whom were scheming to make a deal with the enemy. True believers seek no such indulgence. For this one in particular, nothing more was left than to do what he did best: inventing the notion of judgment by future film buffs, promising eternal glory from a senseless death, making meaning from none. Remaining his cleverly inventive self, the master propagandist prepared the poison he would administer, two weeks later, to his six children before shooting his wife and himself hours after his führer's suicide.

No known evidence suggests he had lost faith in *Life Goes On* as his last miracle weapon. In any case, its filming proceeded. On Saturday, April 14, Lüneburg's Luftwaffe crews, their planes largely grounded for lack of fuel, observed an old night fighter landing again and again, until Liebeneiner approved and ordered a print. In that scene, the respected actor playing the inventor Martens emerges, smiling, from the plane. He is met by the even more famous Heinrich George, playing the portly armaments chief. Although slightly breathless from running to the tarmac, the older man is ecstatic. "Fabulous, Martens. Congratulations—it worked!"

In real life, the Luftwaffe onlookers, the British forces almost upon them, were bewildered. None believed in miracle weapons any longer . . . but who knew? Who knew anything at that terrible time? One had to hope for some form of rescue from catastrophe.

When Lüneburg fell on April 18, three weeks before the final German surrender, Liebeneiner was among the spectators who watched the British tanks roll through. His crew had relocated again: attacks on the airfield kept them forever sprinting to adjacent woods. They camped out with a nearby village's farmers. On April 16—a year to the day after publication of Goebbels's "Life Goes On" article—Liebeneiner publicly abandoned the project. Privately, he prepared to tempt the Allies with its completed two-thirds. The cans containing the undeveloped film were hidden in a fifteenth-century cathedral, alongside mummified clergy reposing in zinc coffins—until a nearby mayor courted the new occupiers' favor by informing them about the cache. British soldiers opened the cans. The light of a spring day erased the fruit of the heroically deluded effort.

So goes one version. Shortly before dying, the cameraman reportedly revealed he'd actually hidden the cans in nearby, but otherwise unspecified, woods. Other versions had them stolen as souvenirs or offered by a pawnshop. Finding film cans in an abandoned coal depot in 1945, a local innkeeper and his friends ignited the contents for their brilliant blaze, and ran when English soldiers appeared. . . .

But all leads led nowhere when Hans-Christoph Blumenberg, a German film critic, tried to follow them in 1992. The script and storyboards were found, but never the cans; most of what is known about the undertaking comes from Blumenberg's 1993 account, entitled *Das Leben geht weiter (Life Goes On)*. The postwar German government prohibited a few of the participants, including composer Schultze, from working for a few years because their Nazi connections were considered too active. However, no star of UFA's pathetic last hurrah shared the company's 1945 demise. On the contrary, all advanced their careers even further during the postwar period. Wolfgang Liebeneiner did not need his deal with the Allies in order to work prolifically, sometimes in projects again starring his wife. Goebbels had something very different in mind than the couple's postwar life, fully blooming only after his death.

BERLIN

JOHN KEEGAN

"The siege of cities," the eminent military historian John Keegan begins his essay, "seems an operation that belongs to an earlier age"—the time of Maurice of Nassau and James Wolfe and Vauban. But, in fact, some of the key encounters of World War II centered on cities: Leningrad, Moscow, Stalingrad, Warsaw (twice), Budapest and Manila are a few that come to mind. And then there was Berlin, the battle that signaled the end of the war in Europe. Though the siege lasted little more than a week, at the end of April and the first two days of May 1945, it was as intense as Stalingrad, with total casualties on both sides approaching a half million. (General Vasily Chuikov, one of the heroes of Stalingrad, had the honor of leading the assault.) As Keegan writes, cities, and especially capital cities, "are military positions as strong as any an army can construct to defend frontiers, perhaps stronger indeed than the Maginot Line or the Westwall, which merely tried to replicate artificially the intrinsic features of capital cities." Because it was a relatively modern place, with wide avenues that acted as firebreaks, Berlin, though it had been battered from the air for two years, had never experienced the kind of firestorms that had swept densely packed old-world towns like Hamburg and Dresden. In the midst of rubble, buildings still intact made for notably difficult street fighting. Here, too, were the last fanatics of the National Socialist revolution. At the same time that Russians were raping and murdering behind what passed for front lines, SS teams hunted down real or imagined German deserters and strung them up from lampposts. One German survivor remembered "the acrid smell of smoke mingled with the stench of decomposing corpses. Dust from pulverized bricks and plaster rose over the city like a heavy fog. The streets, littered with rubble and pock-marked with huge craters, were deserted . . ." And yet it was worth your life to try to get across them. Three million Soviet troops ringed the Nazi capital: three hundred thousand would become casualties, or one out of ten.

This was death's city, and at its center was the *Führerbunker*. In an underground garage built beneath the Reich Chancellery—it still housed several Mercedes-Benzes that Hitler once used for parades and political rallies—an entrance led to the bunker system that had become a virtual underground city. Hundreds of people, including those wounded from the battle, inhabited the badly overcrowded upper chambers; three levels and fifty-five feet under the ground was the actual führer headquarters, from which Hitler still directed the war, even as radio and telephone communication with the outside world—and with it, all sense of reality—gradually disappeared. "I was shocked by his appearance," wrote a young German officer who was charged with delivering situation maps to Hitler. "He was stooped, and his left arm was bent and shaking. Half of his face drooped, as if he'd had a stroke, and his facial muscles on that side no longer worked. Both of his hands shook, and one was swollen. He looked like a very old man, at least twenty years older than his fifty-six years."

But let Keegan detail the end of Hitler and his Thousand-Year Reich. It may only have lasted twelve years, but they were twelve of the most violent years in the history of humankind.

John Keegan was for many years senior lecturer at the Royal Military Academy, Sandhurst, and has taught at Princeton University and Vassar College and is defense correspondent for the *Daily Telegraph* in London. He is the author of fourteen books, including *The Face of Battle, The Second World War* (from which this account of the Battle of Berlin was excerpted), and, most recently, the best-selling *The First World War*.

THE SIEGE OF CITIES SEEMS AN OPERATION THAT BELONGS TO an earlier age than that of the Second World War, whose campaigns appear to have been exclusively decided by the thrust of armored columns, the descent of amphibious landing forces, or the overflight of bomber armadas. But cities are as integral to the geography of war as great rivers or mountain ranges. An army, however well mechanized—indeed precisely because it is mechanized—can no more ignore a city than it can the Pripet Marshes or the defile of the Meuse.

On the eastern front the three "cities of bolshevism"—Leningrad, Moscow, and Stalingrad—which Hitler had marked out as the targets of his advance through Russia, each brought one of his decisive campaigns to grief. His own designation of cities as fortresses—Calais, Boulogne, and the Ruhr complex in the west; Königsberg, Posen, Memel, and Breslau in the east—had imposed severe checks on the progress of his enemies' armies toward the heartland of the Reich. And capital cities—with their maze of streets, dense complexes of stoutly constructed public buildings, storehouses of fuel and food, labyrinth of sewers, tunnels, and underground communications—are military positions as strong as any an army can construct to defend frontiers, perhaps stronger indeed than the Maginot line or the Westwall, which merely tried to replicate artificially the intrinsic features of capital cities.

Hitler's return to Berlin on January 16, 1945, and his decision by default not to leave it (the final moment when he might have done so, over which he deliberately prevaricated, was his birthday, April 20) ensured that the last great siege of the war—shorter than Leningrad's but even more intense than Stalingrad's—would be Berlin's. "I must force the decision here," he told his two remaining female secretaries on his birthday evening, "or go down fighting."

Berlin was a stout place for a last stand. It was unique among German cities in being large, modern, and planned. Hamburg, densely packed around its port on the Elbe, had burned as if by spontaneous combustion in July 1943; the fragile and historic streets of Dresden had gone up like tinder in February 1945. Berlin, though heavily bombed throughout the war, was a tougher target. A complex of nineteenth- and twentieth-century apartment blocks, standing on strong, deep cellars and disposed at regular intervals along wide boulevards and avenues that served as effective firebreaks, it had lost about 25 percent of its built-up area to the Allied Bomber Command during the Battle of Berlin in August 1943 and February 1944. But it had never suffered the effects of a firestorm, as Hamburg and Dresden had, nor had its essential services been overwhelmed. While the destruction of their dwellings had driven many Berliners into temporary accommodation or out of the city, the ruins left behind, through which new roadways had been driven, were military obstacles as formidable as the buildings left standing.

At the heart of the city, moreover, beat the pulse of Nazi resistance. Hitler's bunker had been constructed under the Reich Chancellery at the end of 1944, a larger and deeper extension of an air-raid shelter dug in 1936. Its twenty tiny rooms, fifty-five feet under the Chancellery garden, included a kitchen, living quarters, and copiously stocked storerooms, had an independent supply of water, electricity, and air-conditioning, and communicated with the outside world through a telephone switchboard and its own radio link. For those of troglodytic inclination, the bunker was completely self-sufficient.

Hitler, though he had spent extended periods of the war in Spartan and semisubterranean surroundings, was devoted to the fresh air; his after-dinner walks were favorite occasions for his monologues. On January 16, however, he descended from the Chancellery into the bunker and, apart from two excursions, on February 25 and March 15, and occasional prowls about his old accommodations upstairs, he did not leave it for the next 105 days. The last battles of the Reich were conducted from the bunker conference room. So was the final Battle of Berlin.

Berlin did not have its own garrison. Throughout the way, except for the brief, uneasy peace between the French armistice and Barbarossa, the German army had been at the front; units of the Home Army that remained within the Reich performed recruitment and training functions. In the capital, the only unit of operational value was the Berlin Guard Battalion, out of which had grown the Grossdeutschland Division. It had figured largely in the suppression of the July 1944 plot to kill Hitler and was to fight in the Battle of Berlin. But the bulk of Berlin's defenders were to be supplied by Army Group Vistula as it fell back from the Oder.

Its strength at the start of the siege was about 320,000, divided between the Third Panzer and Ninth armies, to oppose nearly 3 million in Generals Zhukov's, Konev's and Rokossovsky's fronts. The most substantial force was the LVI Panzer Corps, containing the Eighteenth Panzer and SS Nordland divisions, as well as fragments of the Twentieth Panzer Grenadier, Ninth Parachute, and recently raised Müncheberg; the latter belonged to a collection of "shadow" formations, based on military schools and inexperienced reinforcement units. To them could be added a motley of *Volkssturm,* Hitler Youth, police, antiaircraft, and SS units. Among the latter was a detachment of the SS Wallonien Division, formed from pro-Nazi French Belgians commanded by the fanatically fascist Léon Degrelle, the man Hitler allegedly said he would have liked for a son. Degrelle would lead his unit in a fight to the end over the ruins of the Reich Chancellery.

During the last weeks of March and the first weeks of April, Zhukov's and Konev's fronts assembled the forces and supplies they would need for the assault on the city. Zhukov accumulated 7 million shells to supply his artillery, which was to be massed at a density of 295 guns to each attack kilometer; Konev, who needed to capture assault positions across the river Neisse from which to launch his offensive, had concentrated 120 engineer and 13 bridging battalions to seize footholds, and 2,150 aircraft to cover the operation.

While Zhukov and Konev were preparing for the great assault, Generals Tolbukhin and Malinovsky opened the drive on Vienna out of central Hungary. Beginning on April 1, their tank columns raced northward across the wide Danubian plain, brushing aside German armored brigades that could put few tanks in the field. By April 6 Tolbukhin's spearheads had entered the western and southern suburbs, and on April 8 intense fighting for the city center developed. Local SS units fought fanatically, with total disregard for the safety of the monuments they made their strongpoints. Point-blank artillery duels broke out around the buildings of the Ring; there was fierce fighting in the Graben and the Kärntnerstrasse, in the heart of the old city, which had resisted the Turkish siege of 1683; and the Burgtheater and the Opera House were totally burned out.

Miraculously, the Hofburg, the Albertina, and the Kunsthistorisches Museum survived. But when the remnants of the German garrison eventually dragged themselves northward over the Danube across the Reichsbrücke on April 13, acres constituting one of the great treasure houses of European civilization lay burning and devastated behind them.

In the west, also, the great cities of the Reich were now falling to Allied attack. At the beginning of March, seven armies were aligned along the west bank of the Rhine from north to south: the Canadian First; British Second; American Ninth, First, Third, and Seventh; and French First, facing the Black Forest on the far bank of the river. George Patton's Third and Alexander Patch's Seventh armies were still separated from the Rhine by the difficult terrain of the Eifel and the Saar, but both succeeded in driving deep corridors to the river by March 10.

Eisenhower's plan for the Rhine crossing was for a deliberate assault on a wide front, but with the heaviest effort in the north—by the 21st Army Group: the Canadians, the British, and the American Ninth Army—aimed at encircling the great industrial region of the Ruhr. The operation, code-named Plunder, was a vast and spectacular offensive involving large numbers of amphibious craft, massive air and artillery preparations, and the dropping of two divisions of the Allied Airborne Army behind the German defenses on the east bank of the river. Plunder began on March 23 and was lightly opposed.

However, the evolution of Eisenhower's considered plan had already been altered by a chance event. On March 7, spearheads of the U.S. Ninth Armored Division, belonging to the First Army, had found an unguarded railway bridge at Remagen, across the Rhine below Cologne, and had rushed it to establish a bridgehead on the far side. It could not at first be exploited, but on March 22 Patton's Third Army drove the Germans back in a surprise assault near Oppenheim. New bridges had to be constructed, but by March 24, the German defenses of the Rhine had been broken at two widely separated places, in the Ruhr and at the confluence of the Mainz, thus threatening the whole Wehrmacht position in the west with envelopment on a large scale.

On March 10 Hitler had relieved General Field Marshal Gerd von Rundstedt of supreme command in the theater, the old warrior's third and last dismissal, and replaced him with Albert Kesselring, brought from Italy where he had so successfully contained the Anglo-American drive up the peninsula. But a change of commanders could not now deflect the inevitable penetration of Germany's western provinces by the seven Allied armies. While British and Canadian armies pressed on into northern Germany, aiming toward Hamburg, the U.S. Ninth and First armies proceeded with the encirclement of the Ruhr, which they completed on April 1, forcing the surrender on April 18 of 325,000 German soldiers and driving their commander, Walther Model, to suicide. At the same time Patton's Third Army was embarking on a headlong thrust into southern Germany, which would have carried it to within thirty miles of both Prague and Vienna by the beginning of May had he not received an order to stop.

On the evening of April 11, in a major leap forward, advance guards of the U.S. Ninth Army reached the Elbe, designated the previous year as the demarcation line between the Soviet and Western occupation zones in Germany. The Second Armored Division seized a bridgehead near Magdeburg, and the next day the Eighty-third Division established another at Barby. The soldiers believed they were going to Berlin, from which the Eighty-third Division, after enlarging its bridgehead on April 14, was only seventy miles distant. But word swiftly came down the line that they were misinformed. Eisenhower was bound by the inter-Allied agreement, which meant that his American forces in the central sector would stay where they were, while the British and Canadians continued to clear northern Germany and the southernmost American and French armies overran Bavaria and occupied the territory in which Allied intelligence had suggested the Germans might be organizing a "national redoubt." The capture of Berlin was to be left exclusively to the Red Army.

This was not, however, to be a simple operation of war, but a race between military rivals. In November 1944, Stalin had promised Zhukov—who, as his personal military adviser, senior staff officer, and operational commander, was the principal architect of the Red Army's victories—that he should have the privilege of taking Berlin. But on April 1, at a Stavka meeting in Moscow devoted to the question of how the Soviets could assure that they and not the Western powers would be the first into the Reich capital, General Antonov of the general staff had posed the question of how the demarcation line should be drawn between Zhukov's and Konev's fronts. To exclude Konev from the drive on Berlin would be to make the final operation more difficult than it need be. Stalin listened to the argument and then, drawing a pencil line on the situation map, designated their approach routes to within forty miles of the city. Thereafter, he said, "whoever breaks in first, let him take Berlin."

The two fronts jumped off across the Oder on April 16. On Zhukov's front the honor of leading the assault had gone to Vasily Chuikov's Eighth Guards Army (formerly the Sixty-second Army, which had defended Stalingrad). Its soldiers had sworn to fight the coming battle without thought of retreat, but German resistance was particularly strong in their sector, and at the end of the day it was Konev's front that had made greater progress. Konev continued to advance faster, closing on Zossen, the headquarters of OKW, the German high command, on April 17, and he persuaded Stalin by telephone that he was better placed to open the assault on the city from the south, rather than from the direct eastern route, where Zhukov's armored columns were laboring against fierce opposition by German antitank teams.

Zhukov now lost patience with his subordinate commanders and demanded that they lead their formations against the German defenses in person; officers who showed themselves "incapable of carrying out assignments" or displayed a "lack of resolution" were threatened with instant dismissal. This warning produced a sudden and notable increase in the pace of advance through the Seelow Heights, thirty miles east of Berlin. By the evening of April 19, Zhukov's men had cracked all three defense lines between the Oder and Berlin and stood ready to assault the city.

Rokossovsky's Second White Russian Front was now aiding Zhukov's advance by pressing the German defenders of the lower Oder, where their defenses still held from the north. Zhukov was more concerned with the urgent advance of Konev's front through Cottbus on the Spree, Berlin's river, to Zossen, which threatened to take the capital's fashionable suburbs from the south. By the evening of April 20, when Konev ordered his leading army "categorically to break into Berlin tonight," Zhukov had already brought up the guns of the Sixth Breakthrough Artillery Division and begun bombarding the streets.

April 20 was Hitler's birthday, celebrated with bizarre solemnity in the bunker, which he left briefly to inspect an SS unit and to decorate a squad of Hitler Youth, orphans of the Allied bombing raid on Dresden, who were defending the capital. This was to be his last public appearance, but his power over the Germans remained intact. On March 28 he had dismissed Heinz Guderian as chief of staff of the German army and replaced him with General Hans Krebs, once military attaché in Moscow and now installed in the bunker at his side. Soon the führer would dismiss others who managed to make their way to the bunker to offer their congratulations on his birthday, including Hermann Göring, as head of the Luftwaffe, and Heinrich Himmler, as head of the SS.

There would be no lack of Germans willing to carry out his final orders. More impressively, there was no lack of Germans—whether or not intimidated by the "flying courts-martial" that had begun to hang deserters from lampposts—ready to continue the fight for the Nazi regime. Wilhelm Keitel and Alfred Jodl, intimates of every one of Hitler's command conferences throughout the war, left the bunker on April 22 to take refuge at Fürstenberg, thirty miles north of Berlin and conveniently close to Ravensbrück concentration camp, where the group of so-called *Prominenten,* well-connected foreign prisoners, were held as hostages. Albert Speer, Hitler's favored chief of war industry, visited the bunker and left on April 23; others who left included Joachim von Ribbentrop, still his foreign minister; his adjutant, Julius Schaub; his naval representative, Admiral von Puttkamer; and his personal physician, Dr. Theodor Morell, who many in the inner circle believed had secured his privileged place by dosing Hitler with addictive drugs.

A few others overcame great danger to make their way to the bunker. One was Göring's successor as commander of the Luftwaffe, Ritter von Greim, and the celebrated female test pilot Hanna Reitsch. Outside the bunker the garrison of Berlin kept up a ferocious struggle against the encroaching Russian formations throughout the week between April 22, the day on which Hitler definitely announced his refusal to leave—"Any man who wants may go! I stay here"—and his suicide on April 30.

On the morning of April 21, Zhukov's tanks entered the northeastern suburbs, and the units following them were regrouped for siege warfare: Chuikov, who had fought the Battle of Stalingrad, knew what was necessary. Assault groups were formed of a company of infantry, supported by half a dozen anti-tank guns, a troop of tank or assault guns, a couple of engineer platoons, and a flamethrower platoon. The theory was to use the assault weapons to blast or burn down resistance in the city blocks, which the infantry would then attack. Overhead the heavy artillery and rocket launchers threw crushing salvos to prepare the way for the next stage—house-to-house fighting. Medical teams stood close in the rear; street fighting produces exceptionally heavy casualties, not only from gunshot at short range but also from severe falls in heavily damaged buildings and the collapse of debris.

On April 22, Zossen, twelve miles south of Berlin, with its elaborate telephone and teleprinter center still receiving messages from army units all over

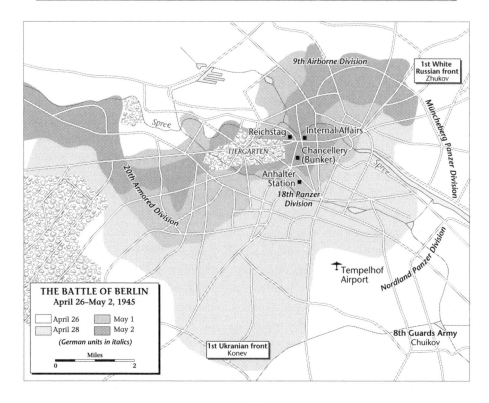

This map shows the siege of Berlin and the fast-diminishing areas held by the Germans during the week before the fall of the Nazis' capital. Once the Soviets captured Tempelhof Airport, they completely controlled supply lines into the city. The fighting continued, street by street, though the advance was often measured by buildings and pockets beyond the lines. Even after Hitler's suicide on April 30, the Germans held on until General Karl Weidling surrendered two days later.

what remained of unconquered Germany, fell into the hands of Konev's front. And the next day Stalin finally delineated the thrust lines for the advance into central Berlin. Konev's sector was aligned on the Anhalter railway station, a point assuring that his vanguard would be separated by 150 yards from the Reichstag and Hitler's bunker. Zhukov, whose troops were already dug deep into the city's streets, was to be the "conqueror of Berlin" after all, as Stalin had promised the previous November.

But German resistance was still stiffening. Hitler, entombed in the bunker, constantly demanded to know the whereabouts of the two surviving military formations nearest the city, General Walther Wenck's Twelfth and General

Theodore Busse's Ninth armies. Though he railed at their failure to come to his rescue, both were fighting hard from the west and southeast to check or throw back the Soviet advance. Nevertheless, by April 25, Konev and Zhukov had succeeded in circling the city from south and north and were assembling unprecedented force to reduce resistance within it. Konev, for the final stage of the assault on the center, massed artillery at a density of 650 guns to the kilometer, literally almost "wheel to wheel," and two Soviet air armies, the Sixteenth and the Eighteenth, had also been brought up to drive away the remnants of the Luftwaffe still trying to fly munitions into the perimeter.

On April 26, 464,000 Soviet troops, supported by 12,700 guns, 21,000 rocket launchers, and 1,500 tanks, ringed the inner city, ready to launch the final assault of the siege. The circumstances of the inhabitants were now frightful: Thousands had crowded into the huge concrete "flak towers" that dominated the center; the rest, almost without exception, had taken to the cellars, where living conditions rapidly became squalid. Food and water were running short, and the relentless bombardment interrupted electrical and gas supply and sewerage. Behind the fighting troops, moreover, ranged those of the second echelon, including many released prisoners of war who had bitter personal grievances against Germans of any age or sex and vented their hatred by rape, looting, and murder.

By April 27, when a pall of smoke from burning buildings and the heat of combat rose a thousand feet above Berlin, the area of the city still in German hands had been reduced to an east-west strip some ten miles long and three miles wide. Hitler was still alive—and still demanding the whereabouts of Wenck; but Wenck had failed to break through, as had Busse's Ninth Army, while the remnants of General Hasso von Manteuffel's Third Panzer Army were withdrawing to the west. Berlin was now defended by remnants, including shreds of foreign SS units—Balts, and Frenchmen from the Charlemagne Division, as well as Degrelle's Walloons, whom the chaos of fighting had tossed into the environs of the bunker.

On April 28 these last fanatics of the National Socialist Revolution found themselves fighting for its government buildings in the Wilhelmstrasse, the Bendlerstrasse, and near the Reich Chancellery itself. According to historian John Erickson,

> the Tiergarten, Berlin's famous zoo, was a nightmare of flapping, screeching birds and broken, battered animals. The "cellar tribes" who dominated the life of the city crept and crawled about, but adding to the horror of these tribalized communities clinging to life, sharing a little warmth and desperately improvised feeding, when the shelling stopped and the assault troops rolled through

the houses and across the squares there followed a brute, drunken, capricious mob of rapists and ignorant plunderers. . . . Where the Russians did not as yet rampage, the SS hunted down deserters and lynching commandos hanged simple soldiers on the orders of young, hawk-faced officers who brooked no resistance or excuse.

On the same day, the German defenders of the central area around the Reich Chancellery and the Reichstag (the Parliament building) tried to hold off the northern Russian thrust into this "citadel," as it had been designated, by blowing the Moltke Bridge over the river Spree. Damaged but not destroyed, the bridge was rushed shortly after midnight. A fierce battle then developed for the Internal Affairs building—"Himmler's house," the Russians dubbed it—and shortly afterward for the Reichstag.

By now, early morning, April 29, the fighting was a mere quarter of a mile from the Reich Chancellery, which was being demolished by heavy Russian shells, while beneath the surface of the cratered garden Hitler was enacting the last decisions of his life. He spent the first part of the day dictating his "political testament," enjoying the continuation of the struggle against bolshevism and Jewry. He entrusted copies to reliable subordinates to smuggle through the fighting lines to OKW headquarters, to Field Marshal Ferdinand Schörner, and to Grand Admiral Karl Dönitz. By separate acts he appointed Schörner to succeed him as commander in chief of the German army and Dönitz as head of state. He also dismissed Speer, for recently revealed acts of insubordination in carrying out a "scorched earth" policy, and expelled Göring and Himmler from the Nazi party, the former for daring to anticipate his promised succession to Hitler's place, the latter for having made unauthorized peace approaches to the Western Allies. He had already appointed Ritter von Greim (who made a last-minute escape with Hanna Reitsch in a light plane) commander of the Luftwaffe and specified eighteen other military and political appointments to Dönitz in the political testament. He also married his longtime mistress, Eva Braun, in a civil ceremony performed by a Berlin municipal official hastily recalled from his *Volkssturm* unit defending the "citadel."

Hitler had not slept on the night of April 28–29 and retired to his private quarters until the afternoon of April 29. He attended the evening conference, which began at ten o'clock, but the meeting was a formality, since the balloon that supported the bunker's radio transmitting aerial had been shot down that morning and the telephone switchboard no longer communicated with the outside world. The commandant of the Chancellery, SS Colonel Wilhelm

Mohnke, reported the progress of the fighting around the building. General Karl Weidling, battle commandant of Berlin, warned that the Russians would certainly break through to the Chancellery by April 30 at the latest, and urged that the troops remaining in action be ordered to break out of Berlin. Hitler dismissed the possibility. It was clear that he was committed to his own end.

During the night of April 29–30 he took his farewells, first from the women—secretaries, nurses, cooks—who had continued to attend him in the last weeks; then from the men—adjutants, party functionaries, and officials. He slept briefly on the morning of April 30 and then lunched with his two favorite secretaries, Gerda Christian and Trudi Junge, who had spent the long months with him at those earlier underground bunkers, Rastenburg and Vinnitsa. They ate noodles and salad and talked sporadically about dogs; Hitler had just had his cherished Alsatian bitch, Blondi, and her four pups destroyed with the poison he intended to use on himself, and inspected the corpses to make sure that it worked.

Eva Braun, now Frau Hitler, remained in her quarters. But at three o'clock she emerged to join Hitler in shaking hands with party functionary Martin Bormann, propaganda minister Joseph Goebbels, and the other senior members of the entourage who remained in the bunker. Hitler then retired with her into their private quarters—into which Frau Goebbels intruded briefly and hysterically to plead that he escape to Berchtesgaden. After a few minutes—measured by the funeral party waiting outside—he and Eva together took cyanide. Hitler simultaneously shot himself with a service pistol.

An hour earlier, soldiers of Zhukov's front, belonging to the First Battalion, 756th Regiment, 150th Rifle Division of the Third Shock Army, had planted one of the nine Red Victory Banners previously distributed to the army by its military Soviet. They hung it on the second floor of the Reichstag, the building chosen as the point whose capture would symbolize the end of the siege of Berlin. The Reichstag had just been brought under direct fire by eighty-nine heavy Russian guns, but its German garrison was still intact and fighting. Combat within the building would rage all afternoon and evening, until at a little after ten o'clock a final assault allowed two Red Army men of the I/756th Regiment, Sergeants Mikhail Yegorov and Meliton Kantariya, to hoist their Red Victory Banner on the Reichstag's dome.

The two Hitlers' bodies had by then been incinerated by the funeral party in a shell crater in the Chancellery garden. Once the flames, kindled with petrol stored in the Chancellery garage, had died down, the remains of the bodies were buried in another shell crater nearby (from which they were to be disinterred by the Russians on May 5). Shells were falling frequently in the garden and in the Chancellery area, and fighting was raging in all the government buildings in the "citadel." Goebbels, now officially Reich chancellor, nevertheless felt it important to make contact with the Russians to arrange a truce so that preparations could be made for peace talks, which, in the deluded atmosphere prevailing in the bunker, he believed were possible.

Late in the evening on April 30, a lieutenant colonel was sent as emissary to the nearest Russian headquarters and early in the morning on May 1 the new army chief of staff, General Hans Krebs, who spoke Russian, went forward through the burning ruins to treat with the senior Soviet officer present. It was Chuikov, the commander of the Eighth Guards Army, once the stalwart of the siege of Stalingrad.

A strange, four-sided conversation developed. Chuikov heard Krebs out and was connected by telephone to Zhukov, who in turn spoke to Stalin in Moscow. "Chuikov reporting," the general said. "General of Infantry Krebs is here. He has been authorized by the German authorities to hold talks with us. He states that Hitler ended his life by suicide. I ask you to inform General Stalin that power is now in the hands of Goebbels, Bormann, and Admiral Dönitz. . . . Krebs suggests a cessation of military operations during these talks."

Krebs, like Bormann and Goebbels, remained deluded by the belief that the Allies would be ready to treat with Hitler's successors as if they were legitimate inheritors of the authority of a sovereign government. Stalin, however, tired quickly of the conversation, declared abruptly that the only terms were unconditional surrender, and went to bed. Zhukov persisted a little longer but then announced that he was sending his deputy, General Vasily Sokolovsky, and broke off communication.

Sokolovsky and Chuikov between them engaged in interminable parleys with Krebs, who had difficulty establishing his credentials, so murky were recent developments in the bunker. Eventually Chuikov reached the end of his patience. He later recalled that on the afternoon of May 1, he told Krebs to tell Goebbels that the new government's powers were limited to "the opportunity of making a public announcement that Hitler is dead, that Himmler is guilty of treason; and of making a declaration of full surrender to the three governments of the USSR, the U.S.A., and Britain." To his own forces he sent the order "Pour on the '*fausts*,' and the shells. . . . And no more talks. Storm the place."

At 6:30 that evening every Soviet gun and rocket launcher in Berlin opened fire on the unsubdued area. The eruption was signal enough to those remaining in the bunker that hopes of arranging a succession were illusion.

About two hours later Goebbels and his wife—she had just killed her own six children by poison—committed suicide in the Chancellery garden, close to the Hitlers' grave. Their bodies were more perfunctorily cremated and buried nearby. The rest of the bunker party, including nonentities but also grandees, like Bormann, now organized themselves into escape parties and made their way through the burning ruins toward what they hoped was safety in the outer suburbs.

Meanwhile, the Soviet troops—understandably reluctant to take casualties in what were clearly the last minutes of the siege of Berlin—pressed inward behind continuous salvos of artillery fire. On the morning of May 2, the LVI Panzer Corps transmitted a request for a cease-fire. At 6 A.M., General Weidling, the commandant of the Berlin "fortress," surrendered to the Russians and was brought to Chuikov's headquarters at 2 Schulenbergring. There he dictated the capitulation signal:

> On April 30, 1945, the *Führer* took his own life and thus it is said that we who remain—having sworn him an oath of loyalty—are left alone. According to the *Führer's* orders, you, German soldiers, were to fight on for Berlin, in spite of the fact that ammunition has run out and in spite of the general situation, which makes further resistance on our part senseless.
>
> My orders are: to cease resistance forthwith.

Erickson records that at three o'clock

> on the afternoon of 2 May Soviet guns ceased to fire on Berlin. A great enveloping silence fell. Soviet troops cheered and shouted, breaking out the food and drink. Along what had once been Hitler's own parade route, columns of Soviet tanks were drawn up as if for inspection, the crews jumping from their machines to embrace all and sundry at this newfound cease-fire.

The peace that surrounded them was one of the tomb. About 125,000 civilian Berliners had died in the siege, 11,000 apparently by heart attack, 6,400 by suicide; the suicides included Krebs and a number of others in the bunker party. Probably tens of thousands of others died in the great migration of Germans from east to west in April, when 8 million left their homes in Prussia, Pomerania, and Silesia to seek refuge from the Red Army in the Anglo-American occupation zones. Through one of the most bizarre lapses of security in the entire war, the demarcation line agreed upon by Moscow, London, and Washington had become known to the Germans in 1944, and the last flight of the Wehrmacht to the west was motivated by the urge to hold the line of retreat across the Elbe open to the last possible moment. Civilians, too, seemed to have learned where safety lay and to have pressed on ahead of the Red Army to reach it—but at terrible cost.

For the Red Army, the cost of victory in the siege of Berlin had also been terrible. Between April 16 and May 8, Zhukov's, Konev's, and Rokossovsky's fronts had lost 304,887 men killed, wounded, or missing—10 percent of their strength. Apart from the captive toll of the great encirclement battles of 1941, these were the heaviest casualties suffered by the Red Army in any battle of the war. And the last sieges of the cities of the Reich were not yet over. Breslau held out until May 6, its siege costing the Russians 60,000 killed and wounded; Prague, capital of the "Reich Protectorate," staged an uprising in which the puppet German "Vlasov Army" changed sides and fought the SS garrison in the hope of delivering the city to the Americans—a vain hope for which A. A. Vlasov's men paid in blood when the Red Army entered it on May 9.

By then, however, the war in what remained of Hitler's empire was over almost everywhere. An unconditional surrender had been arranged in Italy, through SS General Karl Wolff, on April 29. On May 4, Admiral Hans von Friedburg surrendered the German forces in Denmark, Holland, and north Germany to Field Marshal Bernard Montgomery. On May 7, Jodl, dispatched by Dönitz from his makeshift seat of government at Flensburg in Schleswig-Holstein, signed a general surrender of German forces at General Dwight D. Eisenhower's headquarters at Reims. It was confirmed at an inter-Allied meeting in Berlin on May 9. Norway, into which the Russians had fractionally penetrated only at the very north of the country from Finland in October 1944, was surrendered by its intact German garrison on May 8. The Kurland pocket capitulated on May 9. Dunkirk, La Pallice, La Rochelle, and Rochefort, last of the "führer fortresses" in the west, surrendered on May 9, as did the Channel Islands, Lorient, and Saint-Nazaire on May 10. The final surrender of the war was at Helgoland on May 11.

Peace brought no rest to the human flotsam of the war, which swirled in hordes between and behind the victorious armies. Ten million Wehrmacht prisoners, 8 million German refugees, 3 million Balkan fugitives, 2 million Russian prisoners of war, slave and forced laborers by the millions also—the raw material of the displaced-person tragedy that was to haunt Europe for a decade after the war—washed about the battlefield. In Britain and America crowds thronged the streets on May 8 to celebrate "V E Day"; in the Europe to which their soldiers had brought victory, the vanquished and their victims scratched for food and shelter in the ruins the war had wrought.

VI

ARMAGEDDON IN THE PACIFIC, 1944–1945

THE MYTH OF
THE SAIPAN SUICIDES

HARUKO TAYA COOK

For the Americans, the capture of Saipan early in the summer of 1944 was more than just another stepping-stone in what was becoming an irresistible progress toward Japan itself. The island in the Marianas was only 1,500 miles from Tokyo, and there we could hack out of the coral the airfields that put the new B-29 bombers within range of the home islands. For the Japanese (and even today we know far too little about the Pacific war as they experienced it), the loss of Saipan marked a psychological turning point. For the first time a supposedly invincible outpost, part of the prewar empire, and one populated not just by soldiers but Japanese civilians, had fallen. (That a majority of those civilians came from the southernmost prefecture of Okinawa and were considered second-tier citizens was conveniently overlooked.) It was at last clear that the "American Devils" were closing in on Tokyo itself. The time had come, Japan's leaders decided, to prepare its people for a battle to the death, to be fought by all. They "were willing to steer the Japanese public toward self-destruction," Haruko Taya Cook writes, "rather than surrender control of the war and their grip on national and political leadership."

An incident that occurred at a place called Marpi Point at the end of the battle provided the mythmakers in Tokyo with the opening they sought—though it took a month, and a news article in, of all places, *Time* magazine, for them to recognize their propaganda coup. They learned that there had been civilian suicides at a scenic overlook tourist guides now like to call "Banzai Cliff." As many as a thousand died—though as Cook points out, an unseemly proportion of those were murdered by soldiers on their own side. (The Americans interned some 15,000 civilians, a fact that hardly fit the burgeoning myth and was ignored.) Horrible as those deaths may have been, the military leadership in Tokyo turned them into something unimaginable, directing the people of Japan to follow the example of Saipan. Their cynically manufactured exhortation, "One Hundred Million Die Together," would define the final year of the war, and in terrible ways.

Haruko Taya Cook is a professor of history at Marymount College, Tarrytown. She is co-author of *Japan at War: An Oral History.*

SAIPAN WAS THE BATTLE THAT DEFINED THE CHARACTER OF the Pacific war. In the course of nearly a month of bitter combat in June and July 1944, U.S. Marines and army troops seized from Japan an island that Prime Minister Hideki Tōjō had declared to be a "bastion of the Pacific." After the war, contemplating the 16,525 U.S. casualties, including 3,426 killed or missing, out of the 67,451 men of his command, Holland M. "Howlin' Mad" Smith, the Marine Corps general who commanded the assault that began on June 15, 1944, declared that Saipan's seizure had made Allied victory absolute. "I have always considered Saipan the decisive battle of the Pacific offensive," he wrote.

The importance of the battle for Saipan was measured not only in the considerable human costs paid by the Americans in conquering it and the Japanese in attempting to hold it, but also in the huge psychological impact the battle exercised on the subsequent course of the war. In particular, how the events on Saipan were reported, both in the United States and in Japan, had an extraordinary influence on how the people of each country came to view both their own will and resolution and that of their adversaries. Such perceptions, combined with deliberate manipulation of facts and events by the government and the press, particularly in Japan, affected the remainder of the war in the Pacific in profound and sometimes terrible ways. For those who made decisions about how the Japanese and their leaders would act, the deaths of some 1,000 civilians—exaggerated by propaganda, indifference to individual suffering, and desperation ultimately proved the most significant statistic of all.

The fall of Saipan had direct repercussions on Japan's war effort. First, an outpost that was supposed to be invincible and that was populated not only by soldiers but by Japanese civilian settlers had been lost. This made it clear to Japanese who had not already grasped it that the Americans were closing in on the home islands and that direct attacks from American bombers would only accelerate. The capture of Saipan and its neighbor, Tinian, made possible the large-scale bombardment of Japan from the Pacific by the new B-29 bombers, once airfields had been cut from the coral and laid out over what had been hills and gullies.

In the political arena, the announcement that Saipan had fallen was soon followed by the news that the Tōjō cabinet had been forced from office and replaced by one led by General Kuniaki Koiso as prime minister, with Admiral Mitsumasa Yonai as navy minister and virtual deputy prime minister. The collapse of the government that had led Japan from October 1941 was a sign that the war had entered a new phase. At the same time, the Japanese people were soon to be subjected to a new barrage of propaganda about the nature of the war, which eventually developed into a massive call for final mobilization and culminated in the notion that the Japanese must be prepared for a battle to the death, to be fought by all—perhaps even on the home islands.

✦

SAIPAN WAS THE JEWEL in the crown of the Japanese South Sea Mandated Territories at the start of the Pacific war. The Mariana Islands, former German colonies awarded to Japan after World War I as League of Nations mandates, were gradually developed by settlers from the Japanese Empire, until the civilian population on Saipan reached a prewar peak of about 29,000. Of these, 22,000 were Japanese, the vast majority from Japan's southernmost prefecture of Okinawa, themselves deemed second-tier citizens by Japanese from the home islands. Lower still on the social scale were the 1,300 Korean subjects of Japan and 5,000 Kanaka and Chamorros peoples, whose islands the Marianas were originally.

The largest town on the island was Garapan—"the Tokyo of Saipan" to the residents—located on the coast to the west of Mount Tapotchau, the principal geographic feature of the island, forming the main spine of a very rocky central and northern part of the island. Among Carapan's schools, churches, temples, and commercial enterprises were forty-seven houses of prostitution, employing as many as 277 women. The major industries were moderate-scale production of sugarcane and sugar, tuna fishing and the processing of dried bonito, and the mining of mineral phosphates for the fertilizer that Japan increasingly needed.

Saipan was not fortified before the war and had only a light garrison—no more than 2,000 men—until the first large-scale military force, an army billeting party, arrived there and on Tinian in February 1944. Vice Admiral Chūichi Nagumo—who led the Japanese Mobile Fleet of aircraft carriers that had struck Pearl Harbor and ranged across the Pacific until devastated at Midway—found himself the overall commander of a largely notional collection of land-based aircraft and naval-base troops rather grandiosely named the Central Pacific Area Fleet. It was scattered through the Marianas, north to the Bonin Islands, and south to the Carolines, from Truk to Palau. Theoretically, all army troops in the region were also under the fleet and Nagumo, whose headquarters were on Saipan; in practice, their commander was Lieutenant General Hideyoshi Obata, whose Thirty-first Army headquarters was on Guam, though his chief of staff, Major General Keiji Igeta, was on Saipan.

Approximately 40,000 naval and army forces defended Saipan. The largest group was Major General Yoshitsugu Saitō's 43rd Division, which had seen much of its combat strength decimated before any fighting began, during the voyage from Tokyo to Saipan through waters teeming with U.S. submarines. The 118th Regiment, for example, lost about 850 men en route; the remainder arrived less than two weeks before the invasion, without weapons or equipment.

The island itself seemed hardly ready in the late spring of 1944 to meet an invasion. "The impression I had when I landed," one survivor, Takeo Yamauchi, told me in an interview, "was that they had made no preparations for defense at all. Along the coastline there were only a few partially dug trenches, like earthworms laid out on the sand. I noticed no concrete gun emplacements. I did hear some noise coming from high above in the mountains and was told that they were constructing heavy-artillery positions."

Moreover, the squad Yamauchi led were all recent call-ups, most of them close to thirty years old. Yet the total number of men was large, and—though badly armed, inadequately trained, and very poorly integrated into a single command—the defenders of Saipan for the most part acquitted themselves in the tradition of the imperial armed forces: obeying orders that meant almost certain death and clinging for days to positions in the face of overwhelming American air, sea, and land strength.

The battle for Saipan began with several days of air and naval bombardment before a dawn assault on June 15 by a force that consisted primarily of the 2nd and 4th marine divisions, as well as other marines, soldiers, and artillery units. In the face of what Americans described as withering fire, U.S. forces poured onto the beach from what one Japanese defender said was "like a large city that had suddenly appeared offshore." By the end of D day on Saipan, despite the difficulties that the new tracked landing craft had in negotiating the beach, the Americans were firmly established on the beaches above the town of Charan Kanoa, had occupied the town itself, and were moving north toward now-deserted Carapan and southeast to Aslito Airfield. Their initial objectives had not yet been secured when General Saitō ordered a counteroffensive by the 43rd Division and other ground forces on the night of June 16. Japanese soldiers burst from their "spider holes," only to be mowed down by concentrated American fire.

But resistance did not collapse. The fighting continued for three weeks, with the Americans trying to force the Japanese from the caves where they had taken shelter, from their few prepared positions in the hills, and from the shell holes and pits where many simply cowered. For the Japanese, it was a struggle for mere survival, and it lasted until their commanders ordered a "final attack."

The true conditions on Saipan in early July were known to Imperial General Headquarters. General Igeta, whom many credit with operational command of army troops on Saipan, had been reporting to Tokyo since the invasion of what Tokyo was calling a "bastion" began. His assessments of the army were so negative that the General Staff (and many war historians since) have either downplayed his role or completely shifted the blame for Saipan's disastrous outcome to him. The records of the Imperial General Headquarters Confidential War Diary for June 23 incorporate most of Igeta's criticisms, in a report made only eight days after the landings; it was also only three days after the Battle of the Philippine Sea and the destruction of Japan's naval air forces, which doomed the now-isolated defenders of Saipan.

Igeta's cable of June 26 identified American control of the air and sea as decisive, rendering movement by day impossible, while "night attack using soldiers who have not received good training means increased losses or a simple scattering of our forces." He noted that communications had been severed by "aircraft flying arrogantly low" and severe naval gunfire from all directions, and that frontline and rear forces were losing any strength to fight.

Igeta reported to Tokyo the "unique points of the Saipan battle," especially that some 11,000 of the defenders had arrived only in late May and early June, many of them survivors of ships that had been sunk, so they were completely disorganized and had no clear chain of command. Further, American bombardments had destroyed all known sources of water, limiting possible defensive positions to wherever the Japanese could find ponds. This also produced "great pain at how to deal with Japanese [civilians] on the island numbering some 20,000."

Nagumo, Saitō, and Igeta met for the last time on July 5. Faced with the choice of either withdrawal to the northernmost part of the island and continued resistance or an all-out final attack, these commanders issued the order for a total assault, and then they took their lives before it began in the early morning of July 7. Before killing himself, Igeta sent a final radio message repeating many of the same criticisms he had noted earlier. He admonished Imperial General Headquarters, "There can be no victory without control of the air. I strongly hope [you] will increase aircraft production," and chastised them with these final words: "The success or failure of the forces depend on the commanding officers. Please pay great attention to the men above the rank of battalion commander. Before ending, I pray for the prosperity of the imperial forces and say banzai to the emperor."

The final "banzai charge," three weeks after the Americans first came ashore, soon began to take on mythic proportions. According to the *New York Times,* describing the battle nearly a year after the fact, Japanese poured through a gap in the lines of the 27th Division "like crowds swarming onto a field after a football game. Some were armed only with bayonets lashed to bamboo sticks, some were unarmed, but all were screaming *'Banzai!'* and *'Shichisei Hokoku!'* ["Seven Lives for the Fatherland!"]." Two artillery batteries of the 3rd Battalion, 10th Marine Regiment, were overrun near the village of Tanapag. One American said, "These Japs just kept coming and coming and didn't stop. It didn't make any difference if you shot one, five more would take his place." The 27th was a National Guard division whose commander, Major General Ralph Smith, had been dismissed on June 24 by Howlin' Mad Smith (no relation) and whose men the latter had virtually accused of cowardice. This only made the losses during the Japanese charge a more bitter experience in the years to come.

The "human storm" the Americans experienced that morning looked very different from the other side. The number of Japanese who took part has never been accurately determined, but it was probably about 3,000, a ragtag collection of units and remnants of units from the 43rd Division, as well as field hospital and headquarters sections, mountain artillery troops, supply men, and assorted naval-base and maintenance personnel. One man who survived to describe the event was Mitsuharu Noda, a navy enlisted man who was a paymaster for Admiral Nagumo's headquarters, in charge of cash for troops throughout the Central Pacific, and who was stranded on Saipan when the Americans landed.

Our last stand was at "Jigoku Dani," the Valley of Hell. Headquarters sent out its final message and then destroyed the radio. The telegram included those famous lines of Admiral Nagumo: "Whether we attack or whether we stay where we are there is only death. But realizing that in death there is life, let us

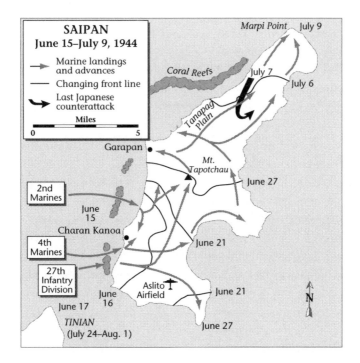

SAIPAN
June 15–July 9, 1944

→ Marine landings and advances

— Changing front line

⤷ Last Japanese counterattack

Miles

0   5

Marpi Point   July 9

Coral Reefs

July 7

July 6

Tanapag Plain

Garapan

Mt. Tapotchau

June 27

2nd Marines

June 15

Charan Kanoa

4th Marines

June 21

27th Infantry Division

June 17   June 16

Aslito Airfield

June 21

N

TINIAN (July 24–Aug. 1)

June 27

The U.S. 2nd and 4th Marine divisions and the army's 27th Infantry Division moved steadily across Saipan and northward, as shown by the gray arrows on this map. On July 7, remaining enemy forces launched a suicidal "banzai charge" (black arrow), overrunning American positions before being annihilated. Many of the civilian deaths later exaggerated by both sides took place at Marpi Point.

take this opportunity to exalt Japanese manhood. I shall advance upon the Americans to deliver still another blow and leave my bones upon Saipan as a bulwark of the Pacific. . . ."

About twenty members of the headquarters participated in the final battle. We drank the best Japanese whiskey—Suntory Square Bottle, we'd saved it to the last minute. We smoked our last tobacco—Hikari brand. We were even able to smile. Maybe because we were still together as a group. I even had feelings of superiority, for we were doing something we had to do.

On July 7 at 4 A.M., shouting all together we headed toward the enemy camp. Navy men were along the seaside. We may have advanced 500 meters [about a third of a mile]. We are not going to attack enemies. We were ordered to go there to be killed. Some probably may have gone drunk, just to overcome fear, but that last taste of Suntory whiskey was wonderful. It was a kind of suicide. We didn't crawl on the ground, though bullets were coming toward us. We advanced standing up.

We had hardly any arms. Some had only shovels, others had sticks. I had a pistol. I think I was shot at the second line of defense. Hit by a machine gun, two bullets in my stomach, one passing through, one lodging in me. I didn't suffer pain. None at all. But I couldn't stand, either. I was lying on my back. I could see the tracer and bullets passing over. This is it, I thought.

Then I saw a group of four or five men, Japanese, crawling toward each other on their hands and knees. Their heads were now all close together. One of them held a grenade upward in his right hand and called out an invitation to me: "Hey, sailor there! Won't you come with us?" I said, "I have a grenade. Please go ahead."

I heard "Long live the emperor!" and the explosion of a hand grenade at the same instant. Several men were blown away, dismembered at once into bits of flesh. I held my breath at this appalling sight. Their heads were all cracked open and smoke was coming out. It was a horrific way to die. Those were my thoughts as I lost consciousness.

American soldiers were there looking for their own wounded. But when a Japanese corpse turned out to be alive, they helped the man. I woke up when they kicked me and they took me to the field hospital. It was July 7. There had been about fifty men in naval headquarters; all died but me.

Postwar figures for Japanese casualties on Saipan vary considerably. U.S. sources speak of identifying 23,811 "enemy buried" and 1,780 captured, including 838 Koreans, along with some 14,560 civilians taken into custody. One Japanese source claims that out of a total of 43,682 defenders from all units on the island, 41,244 died between June 15 and July 9, when the Americans reached the northern end of the island; however, the actual figures are much closer to the American totals.

On July 19, bold headlines in the morning newspapers told the Japanese public of another major battle fought and lost: "All Members of Our Forces on Saipan Meet Heroic Death / Remaining Japanese Civilians Appear to Share Fate." The official announcement from Imperial General Headquarters, issued at five o'clock the previous afternoon, compressed the most recent news from Saipan into an "acknowledgment" that Japanese forces had made a "last attack" on July 7, and added that some troops had fought on until as late as July 16 before they finally "attained heroic death." A second paragraph described the fate of nonmilitary personnel: "It appears that the remaining civilian Japanese on

Saipan Island always cooperated with the military, and those who were able to fight participated bravely in combat and shared the fate of officers and soldiers."

Few of those reading the story at home, or hearing the news whispered between neighbors, could have appreciated fully the consequences that awaited them. But the fact that Japan had lost a key outpost in its Mandate territories, only 1,500 miles southeast of Tokyo itself, was confirmation for most Japanese that the war had entered a new stage. The home islands themselves were now exposed to attack.

The fall of Saipan had not come suddenly, however, but after a long series of reversals that followed the successes of the early stages of the war. For two years, since Midway, the Japanese people had heard little good news from the front. Increasingly, many greeted failure and defeat with resignation and even lassitude. This was an astounding change from the public attitude of even a year earlier, when Attu, a Japanese outpost in the Aleutians, had fallen and the whole country seemed galvanized by the tragedy.

One month after the official news of the fall of Saipan, the battle was suddenly in the news again—an unprecedented event. On August 19, the *Asahi Shimbun* ran large block-character newspaper headlines that were riveting: "The Heroic Last Moments of Our Fellow Countrymen on Saipan / Sublimely Women Too Commit Suicide on Rocks in Front of the Great Sun Flag / Patriotic Essence Astounds the World. The following day, the *Mainichi* proclaimed that Japanese women had "Changed into Their Best Apparel, Prayed to the Imperial Palace, Sublimely Commit Suicide in Front of the American Devils / Sacrifice Themselves for the National Exigency Together with the Brave Men."

Why were these stories appearing more than a month after the battle on Saipan had died down, Tōjō had been replaced, and the next battles in the Pacific were in the offing? Unlikely as it may seem, they stemmed from a one-page article by an American reporter, Robert Sherrod, published in *Time* magazine on August 7. "The Nature of the Enemy," though understandably partisan and at times maudlin, was one of the most stunning pieces of reportage of the entire Pacific war. Filled with graphic, unforgettable images, it raised powerful questions in its investigation of the extraordinary stories Sherrod said he had heard of suicides among some of Saipan's approximately 20,000 civilians—of whom the Americans had subsequently interned some 10,000.

Massaged and replayed by the government and editors, stories by Japanese overseas correspondents based on Sherrod's account now became the fuel for an unprecedented orgy of glorification of death splashed across the front pages of all the major dailies in Japan. The national spiritual mobilization campaigns they fostered established new levels of commitment among Japan's civilians despite the grim wartime conditions they confronted in the late summer of 1944.

"It has been reported that noncombatants, women, and children have chosen death rather than to be captured alive and shamed by the demonlike American forces," ran an August 17 story in the *Asahi Shimbun,* credited to a Japanese correspondent in neutral Stockholm. "The world has been astounded by the strength of the fighting spirit and patriotism of the entire people of Japan."

Most of the information in this story and the ones that followed was lifted from Sherrod's *Time* article—except for anything that might conflict with the notion that civilians would willingly die rather than surrender or submit to their enemies. The edited versions did not cite Sherrod's description of a schoolboy struggling in vain to stay afloat after the instinct for life overcame his resolve to drown, or of an officer who hacked at his men's necks to kill them, or of a sniper who mercilessly "drilled" a couple who had led their children to the edge of the sea, only to falter and begin to turn back.

Sherrod's article culminated in questions that are essential for any student of the Pacific war to confront in order to understand both the U.S. and Japanese visions of the orgy of death and destruction that was to follow in the year after Saipan. When we compare how Sherrod wrote them with how they were "translated" and used in Japan, we can better understand what an opportunity Saipan afforded Japan's "statesmen" in their efforts to use the battle to save themselves.

Under the heading "Death for 80,000,000?" his last paragraph begins:

> What did all this self-destruction mean? Did it mean that the Japanese on Saipan believed their own propaganda, which told them that Americans are beasts and would murder them all? Many a Jap civilian did beg our people to put him to death immediately rather than to suffer the torture which he expected. But many who chose suicide could see other civilians who had surrendered walking unmolested in the internment camps.

The paragraph ends:

> Saipan is the first invaded Jap territory populated with more than a handful of civilians. Do the suicides of Saipan mean that the whole Japanese race will

choose death before surrender? Perhaps that is what the Japanese and their strange propagandists would like us to believe.

Indeed, that was exactly what the Japanese high command not only wanted Americans to ask, but also wanted the Japanese people to believe. Naturally, the last section of Sherrod's article was not quoted in Japan exactly as written. Instead of Sherrod's heading, the *Asahi* substituted the large headline "Prefer Death to Surrender" over their version of the article, which covered more than half the front page of the August 19 issue. "Self-destruction" was translated as *gyokusai,* and "their own propaganda" was dropped. The third sentence was rendered, "Many Japanese civilians preferred death, rather than capture and torture, and resolutely killed themselves." The last two sentences of the above-quoted paragraph were completely excised, and the "translation" ended:

> Saipan is the first invaded Japanese territory populated with many civilians. Thus, the success of Japanese noncombatants on the islands shows that "Japanese, the whole race, choose death before surrender."

The readers of *Time* and of *Life* magazines—a version was published there later that month, accompanied by photographs "documenting" Sherrod's "eye-witness" statements—were being prepared for the actions American forces would "have to take" that could lead to the destruction of the Japanese people as a whole. By implication, Sherrod's questions force the reader to that conclusion. "If the Japanese do not distinguish between combatants and noncombatants, why should we?" he seemed to ask, even though he knew very well that the overwhelming majority of Japanese civilians and many in the military had surrendered and that large numbers of Japanese were killed by their own side.

Naturally, the Japanese accounts based on Sherrod's article omitted any suggestion that Japanese civilians had surrendered; in fact, at least 10,000 civilians were being held on Saipan. The official line in Japan, however, was the glory of self-sacrifice. The poet Ryū Saitō, for example, turned to history for parallels with the women on Saipan who chose to die. The *Nihongi,* an ancient Japanese chronicle, told of Obako, a woman whose husband and son were killed in Korea in A.D. 562 by an enemy of Yamato [the ancient name for Japan]. Taken captive, she took her own life. The women of Saipan stood on the cliffs above the Pacific and waved their sleeves, praying to the mother country before death, just as she had fourteen centuries earlier. Moreover, they "held their children firmly in their arms and died together." The poet concludes by urging all Japanese women to be prepared for "a beautiful death" as the enemy nears the main islands of Japan.

Commentators filled newspapers with praise of such acts as "the true nature of Japan," and they repeatedly emphasized that the women of Saipan were ordinary people, not members of samurai families. Moreover, in the *Mainichi,* a young woman poet declared:

> I swear to the sisters of Saipan that *we will fight to the end* [italics added] with the pride of the women who fought to the last in a sea of blood. With the encouragement of death, we will battle on beside the spirits of these women who fell beside soldiers.

Privately, of course, not all Japanese accepted these notions uncritically. "Japanese can neither objectively write articles nor read them," the critic and foreign policy expert Kiyoshi Kiyosawa wrote in his diary on August 20. He denounced the intellectuals' accounts of the deaths of women on Saipan as "feudalism—the influence of ancient warriors—in the time of the airplane, a great admiration for hara-kiri!" Yet neither Kiyosawa nor any other leading figures publicly questioned the message—implicit in the articles about the Saipan *gyokusai* (as the victims' putative heroism was now known)—that all Japanese civilians were henceforth expected to be ready for this kind of death.

✦

THE TERM *gyokusai*—made up from two ideograms literally meaning "jewel" and "smashed"—derived from a Chinese classic telling of the morally superior man who would rather destroy his most precious possession than compromise his principles. During the Pacific war, it was first used in May 1943, after U.S. forces retook Attu in the Aleutians, seized by Japan a year earlier. The final charge under Colonel Yasuyo Yamazaki was transformed from the meaningless obliteration of a garrison overwhelmed by superior numbers and firepower into an act of heroic self-sacrifice dignified by the name *Attu gyokusai*. The poetically resonant euphemism soon caught on.

The most important fact about the "Saipan *gyokusai*" is that it did not happen. Despite numerous horrible scenes of suicide and murder, fear and misery, desperation and despair on Saipan—especially at Marpi Point and what the tourist trade now calls "Banzai Cliff"—the stories of the mass death of the civilians, all supposedly ready to die rather than surrender, are distortions and exaggerations exploited for policy ends.

The fact is that the idea that Saipan's garrison—and, ultimately, the island's entire population—should destroy itself originated directly with military policy at the highest level. The Imperial General Headquarters Army Section Confidential War Diary for June 24, 1944, contains the following entry, along with the detailed discussion of why operations on Saipan had not gone as hoped: "The Saipan defense force should carry out *gyokusai*. It is not possible to conduct the hoped-for direction of the battle. The only thing left is to wait for the enemy to abandon their will to fight because of the '*Gyokusai* of the One Hundred Million.'"

✦

SOMEWHERE BETWEEN 16,000 and 20,000 civilians (including settlers, natives, and military employees) were on Saipan the day the U.S. V Amphibious Corps stormed ashore; the precise number is extremely difficult to determine accurately. Large-scale evacuation efforts had begun in March 1944, but three of the big transport ships were sunk during the five-day passage to Japan, deterring many others from attempting it. In addition, able-bodied males between elementary-school age and sixty years old were forbidden to leave.

Frightened out of Garapan by the early bombings, civilians found themselves exposed to firepower from both sides. Some surrendered on encountering American forces, then had to endure life in camps, which, at least at first, were little better than enclosed wastelands. Others, along with the remaining Japanese troops, were driven to the northern end, where nearly 4,000 civilians were eventually cornered. It was here, around Marpi Point, that most of the civilian suicides and killing by Japanese forces and American assaults took place. A third group of noncombatants wandered around the mountains scavenging for food and hiding anywhere they could.

In all, at least 15,000 civilians survived the battle. Despite the dramatic coverage in American and Japanese publications, only about 1,000 civilians killed themselves or were killed in the desperate final moments of the battle; several thousand more had died during the preceding month. Terrible as those numbers are, they do not amount to *gyokusai*. However, they gave the military leaders in Japan an excuse to glorify the destruction of many lives—while bestowing on it a sense of tragedy and encouraging righteous indignation among those at home.

Long after the capture of Saipan, wounded and starving soldiers still wandered through the mountains until they were killed or fell into American hands; thousands of noncombatants also remained in hiding for weeks—some until the end of the war. But back in Japan, everyone on the island was viewed as the "heroic dead." After the war was over, about 1,000 survivors were repatriated to the home islands and 10,000 more to Okinawa. On his return home, Mitsuharu Noda, the sailor who described being wounded and captured in the banzai charge on July 7, found that his parents in Japan had set up a grave marker for him and removed his name from the family registration. The survivors of the battle on Saipan became living ghosts; erased from public memory, they remain "missing" in most accounts to this day.

✦

THE STORY of Saipan *gyokusai* was much more than mere sensationalism. There is strong evidence many Japanese leaders—members of the so-called peace group as well as the military—were willing to steer the Japanese public toward self-destruction rather than surrender control of the war and their grip on national and political leadership.

At home, while the toll in human lives mounted on Saipan, political struggles triggered by military defeat intensified. Another battle, for political leadership in Japan, was fought behind the doors of the Imperial Palace and government chambers as Emperor Hirohito's senior statesmen and Tōjō's cabinet debated in secret who should take responsibility for defeat and how blame could be kept away from the emperor, in whose name the war was being fought.

In the view of many politicians, the easiest solution was to "blame Tōjō for everything." On July 2, even before the final charge on Saipan, Prince Fumimaro Konoe (who had been prime minister during much of the Sino-Japanese War of 1937–41) sized up the situation. "The army and navy have both concluded that defeat is unavoidable. But today they are at the stage where they don't have courage to say so publicly." He then argued that "the enemy was making Tōjō the ringleader of the war, parallel to Hitler, and were focusing their attacks on him. Thus, he should be kept in his position in order to avoid responsibility for the war being placed on the Imperial House." As early as June 25, he had shown a willingness to consider an interim cabinet, to pave the way for one that could actually seek peace. "The end is almost in sight," he wrote, "but it is still necessary for the people to resign themselves to the point where they will accept that as unavoidable."

Konoe's words reflect the true concerns of many of Japan's leaders in early July 1944. It is difficult to say whether the deaths of noncombatants on the islands of the Marianas had any impact on them. They seemed to view enemy bombings of Japan's cities and civilians—even an enemy invasion of the mainland—as a prerequisite for acceptance by the Japanese people of Japan's forthcoming defeat. When that happened, these leaders intended to come for-

ward as the peacemakers, thus saving Japan—and, more important, the Imperial House—from the consequences of their own earlier decisions.

Saipan was seized on as the ideal tool to mobilize the Japanese public in the
direction of the "peace process"—which could take more than a year to implement. If the people's minds could be directed toward death, they might be
prepared for several months of struggle. In turn, a willingness to fight to the
last would be the bargaining chip the "statesmen" hoped to use to convince
the Allies to abandon their demand for unconditional surrender, which
threatened the position of the Imperial House.

It is vital to remember that the vast majority of the million Japanese civilian casualties of the war, and perhaps over half of the more than 2 million military deaths, occurred in the last year. Between July 1944 and August 1945,
as Japan's leaders sought to protect themselves and the institutions they
claimed to serve, the people of Japan were sacrificed under a national slogan
that was eventually refined into "One Hundred Million Die Together"—an
extension of the cynically exaggerated image of Saipan's civilians and soldiers
embracing death together in service to their emperor.

In the year after Saipan's fall in July 1944, and in the subsequent half century, portrayals and interpretations of the battle for Saipan have helped define
the ways in which history described and justified American strategy and victory, Japanese resistance and defeat, and the horrors of the last year of the Pacific war. For both sides, Saipan—the battle and the myth—helped forge an
unholy alliance of national stereotypes and self-justification. The conviction
that took root in the United States—that demanding unconditional surrender
and exacting the highest possible toll in enemy lives, military or civilian, provided the only guarantee of final victory—guided American policy through
the firebombing of Japanese cities, the invasion of Okinawa, and the atomic
devastation wrought on two Japanese cities that averted an invasion of the
home islands. The strategy in Japan that exploited the image of Saipan
amounted to a threat of national self-destruction, embraced by Japan's leadership to stave off abject surrender and acceptance of American demands at any
cost.

THE UNCOMMON COMMONER

ERIC MORRIS

The greatest generals, as we've remarked before, excel in retreat as well as in offensive, and the experience of one can bulwark the other. But they also share the ability—an instinct, almost—to adapt to the environment and make it work for them, and to inspire their men to do likewise. Robert E. Lee's defense in the piedmont scrubwoods of northern Virginia in 1864; Ferdinand Foch's maneuvers in the marshes of Gond in 1914; Yamashita's Malayan jungle campaign in 1942; and Rommel's stand in the hedgerows of Normandy in 1944 come to mind. To this select list must be added both William J. Slim's thousand-mile retreat through the jungles of Burma in 1942—the longest in British history—and his triumphant return through the same area three years later, in what was the most notable land victory over the Japanese in World War II. Slim, who had molded an army that was part Indian, part British into a fighting force that perhaps only the best German troops could match, was faced with a problem that would have daunted lesser commanders: not just how to fight in the jungle but how to supply large forces (his Fourteenth was the biggest single army in the whole war) in a place not suited for motorized transport. Slim's answer was to perfect the logistical art of supply by air. He not only met the Japanese, who were heretofore unequaled as jungle fighters, on equal terms but, in nine months of incessant fighting, from August 1944 until May 1945, dismembered three of their armies.

Slim, in his war memoirs (which Williamson Murray ranks with those of U. S. Grant), set forth four principles for a plan of campaign, and they are worth considering:

1. The ultimate intention must be an offensive one.
2. The main idea on which the plan was based must be simple.

3. The idea must be held in view throughout and everything must give way to it.

4. The plan must have an element of surprise.

That was Burma in a nutshell.

But beyond the jungle, Slim had to cope with the fact that he came from a lower-middle-class background, normally the career kiss of death for an officer in the British army. So, after the First World War (he was badly wounded at Gallipoli), he joined the Indian army, which offered a respectable alternative for someone who could not depend on family wealth. Even so, he would find himself passed over and higher commands handed to lesser men. This happened even after his brilliant Burma campaign—though the slight was soon righted—and again, when he was chosen as chief of the Imperial General Staff over the protests of the man he succeeded, a formidable commander but by no means a greater one, Bernard Montgomery.

It is time for readers to get better acquainted with one of the handful of truly fine World War II generals—the man his admiring troops knew as "Uncle Bill."

Eric Morris is chairman of a Geopolitical Analysis Company which advises government and business in the United Kingdom and elsewhere. The author of numerous books, including *Circles of Hell,* an account of the Italian campaign in World War II, he is working on a biography of Field Marshal Viscount Slim. Morris lives in Wales.

ON A COLD, MISERABLE WEDNESDAY AFTERNOON IN DECEMBER 1935, Major General A. P. "Archie" Wavell, then in command of a division based in Aldershot, in the south of England, addressed a distinguished military audience at the Royal United Services Institution in London. Wavell delivered a paper on generalship entitled "The Higher Commander," and his delivery was typically bold and controversial. He described two quite different types of commanders. One is a competent executive officer always at his best in a subordinate position, and even excellent at handling and administering troops, providing he is acting on the orders of a superior. The French called such a man *le bon général ordinaire.* Place him in sole command

and he will likely fail. Then, said Wavell, there is the officer fitted for independent command: a man confident in his knowledge and at ease with his
professional skills and abilities, a general who indeed delights in responsibility. There are far fewer of these, and they are the men military historians
call "the great captains."

William Slim—"Uncle Bill"—was such a man. Some historians maintain
that Slim was the only true "great captain" that the British produced in
World War II, for unlike Field Marshal Bernard L. Montgomery, he experienced high command across the spectrum, in retreats and in defensive as well
as offensive set-piece battles. Burma was a far-off land where Slim commanded the largest Allied army in World War II. Despite being last on the
list for everything, his men, who dubbed themselves "the Forgotten Army,"
advanced a thousand miles over hostile terrain, in the worst climate imaginable, and still inflicted the single biggest defeat on the ever-formidable Imperial Japanese Army in its history.

Slim's accolades are impressive. He is the only Indian Army officer to become chief of the Imperial General Staff (CIGS), and one of only two officers
to begin his career as a private soldier and rise to field marshal and CIGS, the
other being Sir William Robertson during and soon after World War I. After
leaving the army, Slim became governor-general of Australia, one of the most
popular and successful in the nation's history.

Born in 1891, William Joseph Slim came from an ordinary family; his father had a small hardware business, which did not allow his son to aspire to
the status of army officer. After a short spell as a teacher, Bill clerked in a steelworks and then joined his brother's university cadet corps as a private soldier.
He passed all his cadet courses and on August 22, 1914, became a temporary
second lieutenant in the 9th Battalion, Royal Warwickshire Regiment.

Slim's experience as a junior infantry officer in the Great War was unusual
in a number of respects. First, and distinctly against the odds, he survived. He
was badly wounded at Gallipoli in 1915 and did not return to his battalion
until late 1916, when he fought in Mesopotamia. Second, Slim realized that
he was professionally fulfilled as a soldier and decided to become a regular officer. As a company commander, he was wounded for a second time during the
march on Baghdad and won the Military Cross.

The war caused an enormous upheaval in Britain's hitherto rigid class
structure. Many less affluent but able officers like Slim found a niche in the
Indian Army: He was commissioned as a captain in the 1st Battalion, 6th
Gurkha Rifles, and fought along the frontiers in those campaigns so typical of
the interwar years. In 1934 Slim, now a brevet lieutenant colonel, was sent to

England. He spent two years as an instructor at the Army Staff College and a further year as a student at the Imperial Defence College.

Slim then returned to India. He was forty-seven years of age and by convention too old to lead a battalion, essential for an officer destined for higher things. An exception was made, however, and Slim was given command of the 2/7th Gurkhas. In September 1939 he took command of the 10th Indian Infantry Brigade. Now began a run of military reverses, retreats, and defeats, which for Slim was to last until 1943. But he was learning all the while; when the time came, he would make the best use possible of those often-painful lessons. During the early years of the war, Slim fought the Italians in East Africa and the Vichy French in Syria, and he encountered the Russians in Iran when they deployed troops there to prevent a German occupation. At Gallabat in August 1940, during the Abyssinian campaign, he had the dubious distinction of leading his brigade into the first serious offensive by the British army in World War II; it failed. As a result of his error in deployment, a regular battalion of the Essex Regiment broke under fire. Slim sacked the commanding officer, for which the regiment never forgave him.

Things looked bleak. In mid-January 1941, Slim was wounded in an Italian air raid and evacuated to India. Subsequently he was given a staff assignment at Indian Army headquarters, where it seemed likely he would remain for the duration. Then, in May, a coup in Iraq produced a pro-Nazi government, threatening Britain's oil interests. A hastily assembled expeditionary force was dispatched from India under the command of Lieutenant General Sir Edward Quinan. Slim was selected by General Sir Claude Auchinleck (then commander in chief of the Indian Army) to be chief of staff. Within days of his arrival, the commander of one of Quinan's divisions fell ill and Slim took over. Early on, he had a string of small successes, achieved under trying circumstances and with considerable skill. Auchinleck thought him competent enough but not promotable beyond a division command.

Then fate intervened for a second time. In March 1942, Slim was promoted to acting lieutenant general and sent to command the two divisions constituting the recently formed I Burma Corps. General Harold Alexander had already been appointed under General Wavell—the Allied commander in chief in the Far East—to lead the British and imperial forces in Burma (Burcorps), and he needed a corps commander. Slim's name came up, though exactly who recommended him is still a matter of dispute.

✦

AFTER THE FALL of Singapore and Malaya, some 35,000 troops of the Japanese Fifteenth Army invaded Burma. The British were outfought; on

March 7, 1942, they abandoned the capital, Rangoon, and fell back north-ward in some disarray. By the time Slim arrived to assume command a week later, the remains of Burcorps were regrouping on a line anchored at Prome, about 150 miles north of Rangoon. The left flank was held by the 6,500 men of Lieutenant General Joseph Stilwell's Chinese Fifth Army, about seventy miles to the east at Toungoo.

The immediate priority was to prevent panic spreading as the troops de-ployed into the arid plains of central Burma. Slim traveled constantly, visiting the frontline units and instilling them with the quiet but infectious confi-dence for which he was to become renowned. Alexander ordered Slim to hold central Burma and thereby protect the precious Yenangyaung oil fields. It was a hopeless task. The Japanese enjoyed mastery of the skies and the confidence of the local population, as well as a superiority in morale over the shaken British and Indian troops. Despite Slim's best efforts, the retreat continued. It was a savage affair. The oil fields were torched. The Japanese tactics were to outflank the road and track-bound Allied troops, block their retreat, and in-duce panic. By the end of April, Burcorps's 1st Burma Division had lost half of its strength and all of its transport. Rear guards were at times forced to abandon their wounded, whom the Japanese butchered.

On April 25, Alexander put in one of his rare appearances at the front, meeting with Slim and Stilwell at Kyaukse, near Mandalay. He informed them the retreat would continue into India. Since the Japanese were also threatening the Chinese line of retreat toward the northeast, the decision left those troops in the lurch. Stilwell felt vindicated in his prejudices against the British generals, Alexander in particular, though he had established a rapport with Slim.

The Ava Bridge over the Irrawaddy River, southwest of Mandalay, was dy-namited on April 30; trains hauled the rear echelons of Burcorps and hun-dreds of refugees through Monywa north to the Chindwin River while an ever-diminishing rear guard sought to keep the Japanese at bay. Once again Slim was everywhere, invariably in the right spot at the right time. It was a close-run thing at Shwegyin, where the bulk of the transport had to be aban-doned; harried by Japanese artillery, the last troops took a river steamer to Kalewa. The rear guard crossed the Chindwin—where the Japanese halted their pursuit—and trekked overland. Hurrying to beat the coming monsoons, everybody walked through the malarial Kabaw Valley to Tamu and then across the border to India.

Slim's qualities can be measured by his reception at the Indian hill town of Imphal at the end of the thousand-mile retreat, the longest in the British army's history. He stood awhile at the side of the track as the shattered and exhausted remnants passed by. There was a bracing of shoulders and straightening of backs: Men picked up the step, sloped arms, and marched past their commander. Slim later visited the inadequate reception centers around Imphal, where the soldiers suffered further; yet they cheered him. He later wrote, "To be cheered by the gaunt remains who you have led only in defeat, withdrawal, and disaster, is infinitely moving—and humbling."

Meanwhile, the bulk of the Chinese had dispersed into small groups; some made it back into China. No longer able to reach Myitkyina, by then in Japanese hands, Stilwell turned west, and his group was one of the last to come out at Imphal, now in the throes of a monsoon. There he told American correspondents: "I claim we got a hell of a beating. We got run out of Burma and it is as humiliating as hell. I think we ought to find what caused it, and go back and retake it."

It was Slim who extricated the corps from Burma. By rights, his achievement over those two harrowing months of retreat should have been acknowledged. But in the BBC's documentary about it, *A Million Died,* Alexander was the hero. Stilwell dismissed the film as "crap." He knew "good old Slim" was the real hero, not Alexander, "who had the wind up."

Slim also came in for a lot of criticism from Lieutenant General Noel Irwin, commander of the India-Burma border area, who took over command of the remnants of Burcorps. Irwin had witnessed the arrival of the rear-echelon units out of Burma, some of whom had disintegrated into a rabble. He held Slim responsible, and told him so in no uncertain terms. But then, Irwin had served in the Essex Regiment.

✦

THERE FOLLOWED fifteen months of consolidation. The British had two weak corps—on paper, some 90,000 men—to protect the frontier of India. The Chinese continued to tie down whole Japanese armies; but with the enemy holding the end of the Burma Road, their supply route was reduced to a perilous air bridge, "the Hump," over the Himalayas. The reconquest of northern Burma was essential to restore land routes to China and retake the vital airfield at Myitkyina. A staff-college solution would have been an amphibious operation to retake Rangoon and open the road northward. But landing ships were at a premium elsewhere, and Burma had lowest priority; the only option was a land campaign.

Slim was given XV Corps, which he deployed almost immediately to put down an insurrection in Bengal. He needed more than sixty British and Indian army battalions, some 100,000 men, to police the troubled region. By this time, Irwin was commanding the Eastern Army and was therefore Slim's superior. He did everything to keep Slim away from a battle command.

In December, Wavell ordered the Eastern Army to make an advance in the Arakan, the coastal sector of Burma, and recapture the port of Akyab. The campaign required a corps at the very least, but Irwin dispatched only the reinforced 14th Indian Division, under Major General W. L. Lloyd. He also attempted to oversee the advance from his headquarters near Calcutta, some 500 miles away.

Lloyd wasn't very good, a not especially capable "général ordinaire," and the units under his command were wary of the Japanese. Irwin thought the answer was just to throw more and more men at the problem. By January 1943, Lloyd was in charge of nine brigades but had lost control. In March, Irwin ordered Slim to the Arakan—not to take command, but simply to report on the situation. This placed Slim in the intolerable position of being sent to spy on another officer. The solution was for a corps headquarters to direct the battle, but since the only one available was Slim's, Irwin demurred. On March 24, 1943, the Japanese counterattacked, infiltrating behind the British front and encircling the leading brigades. Lloyd ordered a retreat northward. Irwin sacked Lloyd and brought in Major General C. E. N. Lomax to run the tactical battle while he himself took command of the campaign. On April 5, with disaster looming, Irwin reluctantly called in Slim—but only to assume administrative control. The order was absurd, but by the time Irwin put Slim in command a week later, the situation was beyond saving. Slim extricated battalions and brigades cut off by the Japanese, salvaging what he could and stabilizing the front.

The blame for this disaster rested squarely with Irwin, who nonetheless informed Wavell that the fault lay with Lloyd and Slim. The vendetta was pursued to the bitter end. On May 26, Irwin wrote to Slim (then on leave pending reassignment), castigating him for his part in the disaster and indicating that he would be relieved of command. Had matters stood, this would have been the end of the road. There could be no second chance for a fifty-three-year-old temporary general.

Wavell, along with Winston Churchill and General Auchinleck, was in Washington conferring with the Americans. Even from that distance he had his own ideas of who was to blame. He dismissed Irwin. With great aplomb, Irwin immediately cabled Slim: "You're not sacked. I am." He was succeeded by Lieutenant General George Giffard.

Brigadier Orde Wingate was also in Washington. Between February and May 1943, Wingate had led a 3,000-strong force of infantry on a 1,500-mile raid behind Japanese lines. As a guerrilla raid it achieved little, at very high cost. Some damage was inflicted, but enemy troop deployments were hardly affected. The wounded were left to die, and 2,180 walking scarecrows marched out of Burma at the end of the raid; fewer than 600 ever saw battle again. But the first Chindit campaign (the raiders were named after a mythical Burmese beast) was an unqualified political victory. The positive aspects of the raid's exploits were given maximum publicity and undoubtedly lifted the morale of dispirited troops stationed on India's frontiers.

To this day, Wingate arouses more heated argument than any other British military leader of the war. Few would argue that he was erratic, abrasive, and unpredictable, or that he displayed bizarre personal habits. To some, his achievements were magnified out of all proportion by the media of the day. To others, notably his brigade commanders, men like Bernard Fergusson and "Mad Mike" Calvert, he was simply "military genius of a grandeur and stature seen not more than once or twice in a century."

Churchill paraded Wingate in front of the Americans, and they too succumbed to his appeal. As a result, Wingate returned to India promoted to major general, with Churchill's remit to plunder the Indian Army and create a new force of Chindits three times the original size. The Americans gave him their wholehearted support and his own air force; they also created their own counterpart, the 5307th Composite Unit (Provisional), better known as Merrill's Marauders after its commander, Brigadier General Frank Merrill, a West Point graduate. This regiment was composed of American volunteers largely drawn from units in India who were imbued with Wingate's doctrine on long-range penetration.

Wingate was followed in October 1943 by Lord Mountbatten, the new supreme Allied commander of Southeast Asia Command (SEAC). Stilwell was appointed deputy commander. Mountbatten made Giffard commander in chief of the Eleventh Army Group, and Slim assumed command of the Eastern Army, later renamed the Fourteenth Army. The scene was set for one of the truly remarkable turnarounds—a military metamorphosis—not just of World War II but in the annals of military history.

✦

SLIM HAD LONG since begun the task of creating an army capable of defeating the Japanese. He would not forget the lessons he had learned during the awful retreat in Burma and the battering in the Arakan. The troops were embittered, distrustful of their officers, and utterly demoralized. Wingate gave them hope, but the root of the problem was confidence—the soldiers' confidence in the quality of their training and in the leadership of their officers. In future, Slim would dispense with rear areas and lines of communication; if a unit was cut off by the usual enemy tactic, it was to form a ring defense and wait to be supplied by air.

Morale also meant improved health and hygiene. In 1943, for every man evacuated with wounds, 120 went down with malaria, typhus, or any of a dozen other tropical diseases; the malaria rate alone was a staggering 84 percent. The enforced introduction of the drug mepacrine, hospital treatment at the front, and new standards of hygiene reduced it to under 12 percent by the time Rangoon fell in May 1945.

Slim commanded a front of 700 miles from the Chinese border to the Bay of Bengal. A narrow-gauge railway stretched 600 miles from Calcutta to Dimapur, in the northeast Indian state of Assam, and beyond to Ledo. The main base at Imphal was ninety miles to the south, and Slim had three all-weather roads and dozens of airstrips constructed. The use of bitumenized burlap, called *bithness,* as a temporary surface made this possible. Throughout this period of reconstruction, Slim's role was vital. He was here, there, and everywhere, addressing his soldiers in English, Gurkhali, Urdu, even Swahili. His pep talks were no-nonsense affairs about things that mattered, such as pay, living conditions, and when his men could hope to go home. The men loved him for his style and dubbed him "Uncle Bill."

Both sides planned an offensive. Lieutenant General Masakazu Kawabe, commander in chief of the Japanese Burma Area Army, was less than happy with a front line anchored on the Chindwin. His few supply bases lay at the end of a tenuous line of communication. He was convinced the Allies were likely to return to the offensive. The Imphal plain, with its bases across the Indian border, offered a better front line, and there was always the chance that another successful offensive would promote panic among the Allies and political unrest in Bengal. The Indian National Army (INA), made up of turncoat Indian troops, was not a dependable fighting force, but it might help him exploit opportunities for mischief.

In June 1943, Tokyo approved Kawabe's plans and ordered the march on Delhi. However, organizing the campaign took time, and the Allies struck first. Mountbatten planned a three-pronged advance to break the blockade of China by opening the Ledo Road in northern Burma. A new thrust into the Arakan would guard the seaward flank. In the main effort, Slim, in the central front, would push the Japanese southward. On the left flank, Stilwell's Northern Combat Area Command (NCAC), consisting of two Chinese divisions and Merrill's Marauders, was to push down the Ledo Road to Myitkyina. Stilwell, now sixty years old and nearly blind, was his own corps commander. He refused to serve under Giffard, whom he despised, but agreed to work with Slim while his forces advanced to Kamaing, west of Myitkyina. Wingate's Chindits were to support Stilwell by cutting the enemy's lines of communication in the area around Myitkyina.

In December 1943, at the end of the monsoon season, three divisions of XV Corps—the 5th and 7th Indian and the 81st West African— attacked in the Arakan. The Allied forces met only light opposition until the Japanese launched a counterattack in February 1944, with the intention of drawing Fourteenth Army troops from the central front and securing their own seaward flank. The Allies met the onslaught, formed their defensive boxes, and, secured by air supply, shattered the enemy. The Japanese suffered 5,000 dead, and the legend of Japanese invincibility was broken.

✦

SLIM'S PLAN for the reconquest of central Burma was both simple and brilliantly conceived. He intended to defeat the enemy prior to an invasion and on a killing ground of his choosing: a plain in Assam centered on Imphal and measuring twenty by forty miles. The plan involved first an advance to the Chindwin, to provoke the enemy into a counterattack, and then a withdrawal to the killing ground—where the Japanese could be confronted by Allied air superiority and the full weight of armor and firepower. Not only did the timing have to be precise, but if the withdrawal degenerated into retreat or rout, the effect could be contagious and the whole front might collapse. The implications for India, for the war in China, and for the Allied cause in general were clear.

The Japanese attack on Imphal, code-named operation U Go, involved 100,000 enemy troops: the 15th, 31st, and 33rd divisions of Lieutenant General Renya Mutaguchi's Fifteenth Army and a division of the Indian National Army. They had no intention of advancing beyond Assam, farther into India; however, if the British were humiliated, every opportunity was to be made to exploit the Indian rebel forces. Mutaguchi was unimpressed with the Allies' fighting qualities so far, but knew that Imphal had to be taken quickly. The troops crossing the Chindwin on March 6, 1944, carried supplies for just three weeks. Waiting for them, Slim had mustered a force roughly equivalent in numbers: IV Corps under Lieutenant General Geoffrey Scoones, with the 17th Indian Division at the front and the 20th Indian in reserve. Farther back in Assam were the 2nd British Infantry and 11th East African divisions. As the battle developed, Slim moved up considerable reinforcements.

Major General "Punch" Cowan's 17th Indian Division was dispatched down the Tiddim Road but with orders to fall back when the enemy put in an

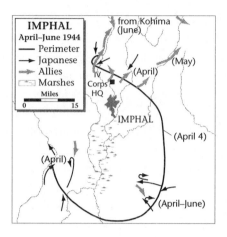

IMPHAL
April–June 1944
—— Perimeter
➤ Japanese
➤ Allies
▭ Marshes
Miles
0   15

from Kohima (June)

(May)

(April)

IV Corps HQ

IMPHAL

(April 4)

(April)

(April–June)

In the spring of 1942, the Japanese drove the British and Chinese from Rangoon all the way out of Burma, to border areas of India and China; that the Burma Corps came out at all was largely thanks to Slim's efforts. After fifteen months of consolidation, marred by a failed campaign in the coastal Arakan region, the Allies were ready to move again—with Slim finally at the helm of the Eastern (later 14th) Army. His tactical masterpiece was Imphal (detail above), where he drew the aggressive but poorly supplied Japanese into surrounding his men—who were supplied and reinforced by air. With the long siege broken in mid-June, Slim's forces pursued the Japanese—no longer seen as an invincible foe—into the heart of Burma. As Stilwell's troops moved south toward the Burma Road, Slim's raced for Rangoon; after it fell, only mopping up was left.

appearance. This was a blunder; Slim misread the first signs of main enemy advance, monitored by outposts along the Chindwin, and delayed for a nearly fatal twenty-four hours before giving Cowan the order. The Japanese 33rd Division outflanked the Indian troops and, before the Allies realized it, were across the line of communications. Cowan and his division were cut off and had to be rescued. It took the 17th three weeks and cost 1,200 casualties to get back to the Imphal plain. Scoones was forced to denude his reserves to save the day, while Slim persuaded Mountbatten to divert large numbers of U.S. aircraft to airlift the 5th Indian Division from the Arakan into Imphal.

The Battle of Imphal and Kohima falls into two phases. The first was the Japanese offensive, from March 8 until April 5, when they cut off TV Corps at Imphal and smaller garrisons at nearby Kohima and Jotsoma. It then took

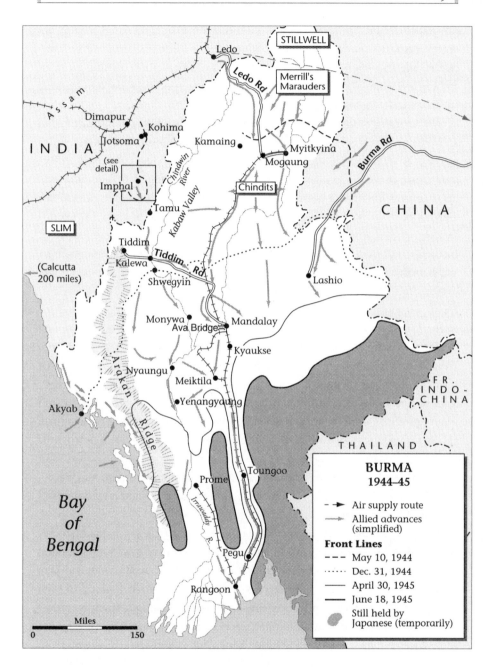

STILLWELL

Ledo

Ledo Rd

Merrill's
Marauders

Assam

Dimapur

Kohima

Jotsoma

INDIA

Kamaing

Myitkyina

Mogaung

Burma Rd

(see
detail)

Chindwin River

Imphal

Chindits

CHINA

Tamu

Kabaw Valley

SLIM

Tiddim

Tiddim Rd

Kalewa

(Calcutta
200 miles)

Shwegyin

Lashio

Monywa

Mandalay

Ava Bridge

Kyaukse

Arakan Ridge

Nyaungu

Meiktila

Akyab

Yenangyaung

FR.
INDO-
CHINA

THAILAND

Bay
of
Bengal

Irrawaddy R.

Toungoo

Prome

BURMA
1944–45

- → Air supply route

Allied advances
(simplified)

Front Lines

- - - May 10, 1944

.... Dec. 31, 1944

——— April 30, 1945

——— June 18, 1945

Still held by
Japanese (temporarily)

Pegu

Rangoon

Miles

0   150

the defenders until June 22 to break the encirclement. Imphal has sometimes been mistakenly portrayed as two, or even three, battles. In fact, Slim conducted the operation as a single coherent engagement, never losing sight of his original objective: to inflict a crippling defeat on the enemy as a prelude to the invasion of Burma.

The opening rounds went to the Japanese. By the end of March, the 15th and 33rd Japanese divisions had cut the Imphal-Kohima road thirty miles north of Imphal and placed IV Corps under siege. Slim had anticipated a second thrust at the all-important railhead at Dimapur, where he had deployed units from XXXIII Corps. Instead, the Japanese 31st Division under Major General Kotoku Sato descended on the hillside settlement of Kohima. The local garrison, from the Assam Rifles, was sacrificed in a delaying action while the 161st Infantry Brigade of the 2nd British Division sent 500 men of the 4th Royal West Kents into Kohima. The rest of the brigade dug in at Jotsoma, a hill village two miles to the west. By the end of the first week in April, there were three sieges in progress. It took the British nearly three weeks to fight their way from Dimapur and raise the sieges at Jotsoma and Kohima, by which time 300 of the Royal West Kents had become casualties. Even then the road to Imphal was still blocked.

Meanwhile, on April 18, Slim launched Stamina, the greatest air-supply operation of the war, to support the forces besieged at Imphal. Some 19,000 tons of supplies were flown in and 13,000 wounded and 43,000 noncombatants flown out (mostly Indian labor battalions working on the lines of communication through Assam to Imphal). Giffard and Auchinleck backed Slim to the hilt and ensured that he had the resources to win the battle. The besieged IV Corps was heavily reinforced, including the 7th Indian Division and a brigade of commandos flown in from the Arakan.

The strain on Allied air assets was considerable. As recently as March 5, the largest airborne operation of the war had gotten under way, supporting Wingate's second Chindit campaign, which was code-named Thursday. One brigade column marched south from Ledo, but two others and their pack mules were landed by Dakota transports and gliders behind enemy lines; thereafter the full force, some 30,000 strong, was sustained by air. The bravery and endurance displayed by the Marauders and Chindits in the ensuing months defy description. The Japanese poured fresh troops into Burma from Thailand to meet this new threat. The Chindits fought and marched across hundreds of miles without respite.

Their role changed after Wingate's B-25 Mitchell flew into a hillside near

Imphal in late March, killing him. One of the column commanders, Joe Lentaigne, succeeded to the command, but the Chindits now came under Stilwell's authority. He misused, if not abused, the Chindits and the Marauders, superb light infantry, by throwing them in as assault troops against the garrison at Mogaung, bleeding them white. It was only Mountbatten's belated intercession that finally got the Chindits relieved. By that time, more than 5,000 were dead, wounded, or missing. The last brigade out, the 111th (under the writer John Masters) was by then the size of a company. The Marauders had endured even worse privations; when their morale collapsed in early June, they had 50 percent casualties. Merrill, their commander, had suffered a serious heart attack and had to be replaced. Doubtless Stilwell had sterling qualities, especially when leading Chinese troops, but his fellow commanders breathed a sigh of relief when Roosevelt recalled him in October 1944. At any rate, the critical battle was Imphal, and the contribution the guerrillas made to that was negligible.

The monsoons began on April 27, and the shared miseries of the battlefield at Imphal increased a hundredfold. It was mostly infantry fighting, often hand-to-hand, with no quarter asked or given on either side. Japanese gun crews were frequently shot or bayoneted while firing their pieces at point-blank range. For the Japanese soldier, death on the battlefield was an honor and surrender meant shame. He was a formidable opponent, and nothing but death could stop him from carrying out his orders. The Indian divisions made use of tanks to blast the Japanese out of their positions. But the jungle was so dense that young officers and noncommissioned officers commanding tanks often had to walk in front to guide the vehicles, certain in the knowledge that they were risking death. The casualties among British officers was especially high, for they were easy to distinguish from the Indian troops.

The Japanese attempted to hold the line against relentless pressure much longer than common sense dictated, and they paid the price. In May the enemy, by then starving and desperate, launched suicide attacks in a last effort to achieve its original objectives. Such tactics played into Slim's hands, and the Japanese 33rd Division was almost entirely destroyed in situ. On May 31, Sato ordered the remnants of his 31st Division to break off contact at Kohima and fall back on Imphal; however, their arrival could do little to affect the outcome. On June 22, British tanks from the 2nd Division met the leading infantry from the 5th Division at Milestone 109; the road was open, and a convoy immediately passed through to provide IV Corps with its first overland supplies since March. After yet more suicide attacks, Mutaguchi ordered his starving columns on July 8 to retreat across the Chindwin. By that stage, the enemy had suffered over 60,000 casualties. It was the biggest defeat in the history of the Japanese army. Slim had completely outgeneraled Mutaguchi.

When it was over, some Gurkhas were engaged in collecting Japanese corpses for burial. One Japanese who was picked up proved to be not as dead as expected. One Gurkha had drawn his kukri to finish him off when a passing British officer intervened. "You mustn't do that, Johnny." (The British called all Gurkhas "Johnny.") "Don't kill him."

"But sahib," said the Gurkha in pained surprise, "we can't bury him alive."

In all, there were 17,587 British and Indian casualties. Many of the dead lie at Kohima beneath a monument that bears this epitaph:

When you go home, tell them of us, and say: "For your tomorrow, we gave our today."

After his victory at Imphal, Slim set about the reconquest of Burma. This was possible because the political and strategic imperatives had changed. Churchill now saw the retaking of Burma as an important instrument in securing some British say in the conduct of the war against the Japanese.

Burma must rate as one of the worst places in which to wage war. Slim described it as "an undeveloped labyrinth of mountains, rivers and jungle— without roads, railways or airfields." For at least half the year it is home to the world's worst climate and the breeding ground for the world's worst diseases. Into this tropical hell, the Fourteenth Army, now the single largest army of the war, pursued the Japanese. There was no respite. The advance began in the monsoon season, and the troops were supplied by air. Many regarded such tactics as the height of folly. Slim proved them wrong.

The campaign involved nine months of incessant fighting, from August 1944 to May 1945, a thousand miles south to Rangoon. In terms of time, this compares with Montgomery's advance from the beaches of Normandy to the banks of the Elbe. In each campaign, logistics and lines of communication were key issues and the battle was fought against a stubborn and resolute opponent. The difference was that in Europe the Germans surrendered when confronted by inevitable defeat; very few Japanese surrendered in Burma. All armies talk of fighting to the last man and the last round of ammunition. The Japanese actually did it. Incapacitated only by death, and always at his most dangerous when doomed, the Japanese soldier's combination of fanaticism, obedience, and ferocity made him an extraordinarily tough opponent.

Burma was preponderantly an Indian Army campaign. This was even more true after the summer of 1944. British infantry divisions and the long-service British battalions in the Indian divisions—men who had been overseas for four years or more—were repatriated; there were few replacements from home. But Slim had complete faith in the fighting qualities of his troops. "My Indian divisions there would go anywhere, do anything," he wrote later. By 1944, the Indian Army numbered over 2 million, every man a volunteer, making it the greatest volunteer army in history. Of the twenty-seven Victoria Crosses awarded in Burma, twenty were won by Indian troops.

The Fourteenth Army evolved the war's most sophisticated techniques in air supply, cleared the Arakan coast with a series of amphibious hooks, and conducted two opposed river crossings on the central front. The Chindwin was breached in December 1944, and in February 1945, Fourteenth Army engineers spanned the Irrawaddy, three times as wide as the Rhine, with the longest Bailey bridge ever built.

The crossing of the Irrawaddy was the supreme example of Slim's generalship. Not content with simple bridgeheads, he used the 19th Indian Division to battle for Mandalay while the coup de grace developed almost 100 miles downstream. At Nyaungu, Cowan's 17th Indian Division secretly redeployed to join XXXIII Corps, outflanked the Japanese defenses, and drove hard for Meiktila, the main enemy supply base in central Burma. There, XXXIII Corps slugged it out with General Masaki Honda's Thirty-third Army. The Japanese garrison, aided by wide lakes that constrained the attackers, fought with great ferocity. But after four days, during which the Japanese lost most of their artillery and suffered appalling casualties, the town fell to the Allies.

Thereafter, Slim changed the complexion of the Fourteenth Army from a jungle fighting force to armored cavalry as it plowed through the plains and rice paddies of lower Burma in a two-pronged advance, with XXXIII Corps moving down the Irrawaddy valley and IV Corps streaking along the railway to Toungoo and Pegu. It was the last charge of the Indian Army (accompanied by American pacifists serving as ambulance drivers), and 200 years almost to the day since the first Sepoy had donned East India Company uniform. And what a charge: 300 miles in thirty days, and into Rangoon before the monsoon season made further campaigning impossible. Slim, as was his wont, was everywhere, usually shuttling in a light aircraft between the advanced headquarters of his spearhead formations as he urged them on to even greater efforts.

The fall of Rangoon—to an amphibious force from the Arakan, while Slim's infantry was at Pegu, forty-five miles away—was anticlimactic, because the Japanese had already retreated northward and toward Thailand. By then, three of their armies had been dismembered, and they had suffered 250,000 casualties.

After Rangoon, at the moment of victory, Slim felt obliged to resign his command and his commission. Lieutenant General Sir Oliver Leese had been sent earlier to replace Giffard as army group commander. The next operation for the Fourteenth Army was to be the invasion of Malaya—but not, the high command decreed, under Slim. It was a messy business, and the full story has yet to be told, although there is enough evidence to suggest that replacing Slim was not Leese's idea. At SEAC, the official line was that Slim was tired and needed a break; the Fourteenth Army was needed, but under a new man with fresh ideas. Leese offered Slim command of the hitherto rear-area Twelfth Army to mop up enemy resistance in Burma. The sounds of outrage echoed in the corridors of Whitehall. Mountbatten moved quickly to restore the situation: Leese was sacked and Slim made army group commander. There must have been a certain sense of satisfying déjà vu, but Slim took it all in stride.

He did go home to England for a brief rest. During that time, the atomic bombs removed the need to invade Malaya. Now a full general, Slim was back as land-forces commander for the Japanese surrender at Singapore. He returned to England in December and soon became commandant of the Imperial Defence College. By then, Montgomery was chief of the Imperial General Staff (CIGS).

Later, Slim was offered senior appointments in the armed forces of the new states of India and Pakistan. He refused and decided to retire from the army in 1948. He had already "donned his bowler hat" to be deputy chairman of the newly nationalized British railway system when he was recalled to become Montgomery's successor as CIGS in November. Two months later he was promoted to field marshal. Governor-general of Australia from 1952–60, Slim died in 1970 at the age of seventy-nine.

✦

SLIM NEVER MADE a secret over which was his favorite infantry regiment: After his beloved Gurkhas, it was the West Yorkshires. The two regular battalions of the 14th Foot fought throughout the Burma campaign and suffered over 2,000 dead in battle. The Fourteenth Army was never able to maintain accurate casualty figures, but it can safely be assumed that the wounded would have outnumbered the dead by a factor of ten.

On one occasion as Slim traveled the front line during the advance on Rangoon, he was able to watch these two regiments in action. In February 1945, the 1st Battalion, West Yorkshire Regiment, spearheaded the assault by the 17th Indian Division on Meiktila. Alongside them were the 2/7th Gurkhas, which Slim had commanded before the war. He and a retinue of senior officers stood a couple of hundred yards away and watched the assault on a Japanese bunker. Slim suddenly realized that his group was in the direct line of fire as a Sherman tank opened up and slammed shell after shell with unnerving accuracy into the enemy strongpoint. Slim wrote in his memoirs: "Promptly one army commander, one corps commander, an American general, and several less distinguished individuals adopted the prone position with remarkable unanimity." In four hours of savage fighting, the West Yorks won their second Victoria Cross of the campaign and suffered seventy-three casualties.

Slim's admiration of these fine regiments was rewarded after the war when he became Colonel of the Regiment of both the 14th Foot and the 7th Duke of Edinburgh's Own Gurkha Rifles. As with other successful Allied generals, honors and awards came thick and fast after the war. But those that Bill Slim cherished most were the colonelcies of regiments that had fought with him in Burma.

A KAMIKAZE'S STORY

KANJI SUZUKI,
AS TOLD TO TADAO MORIMOTO;
TRANSLATED BY KAN SUGAHARA

The personal account that follows is a matchless document. It is by a former kamikaze flier, Kanji Suzuki. He belongs to that small number of young men who, through no fault of their own, survived their suicide attacks on U.S. ships. When Suzuki's account appeared in *MHQ* in 1995, it was the first description published in the West of what one of these young men experienced during moments that he expected to be his last.

Significantly, the notion of crash-dive attacks on American ships was first proposed after the fall of Saipan. As the call, "One Hundred Million Die Together," was broadcast, the first kamikaze ("divine wind") units were being organized. ("Divine Wind" referred to those famous moments in Japanese history when Mongol fleets approached the Home Islands and were twice wrecked by storms, in 1274 and 1281.) During the battles for the Philippines, Iwo Jima, and Okinawa, the Japanese dispatched 2,257 aircraft, which sunk twenty-six combat ships and damaged 300 others, killing some 3,000 men. Admiral William F. Halsey, commander of the U.S. Third Fleet, called the kamikazes "the only weapon I feared in the war."

At the time of the Okinawa campaign, which began on April 1, 1945, Flight Petty Officer 2nd Class Suzuki was attached to Japan's 406th Attack Bomber Squadron and stationed at Izumi Naval Air Station in Kagoshima Prefecture, near the southern tip of the Home Island of Kyushu. Suzuki, eighteen years old and fresh out of flight training, volunteered for *tokko,* the "special attack missions" whose operatives were not supposed to return. Suzuki—who did return, but only after the war—wrote his own story in an account that was the source of a portion of *Tokko,* a 1992 book by Tadao Morimoto, from which this article was translated and adapted (the original was written in the third person).

Tadao Morimoto, who was a naval aviator during World War II, is a former professor at Ryukoko University in Kyoto and senior adviser for Toroy Corporate Business Research, Inc., in Tokyo. Kan Sugahara, the translator, is an airlines-operations specialist who attended the Japanese naval academy during World War II.

IN MID-MARCH 1945, SHORTLY AFTER THE ABORTIVE *TOKKO* operation to Ulithi Atoll in the western Caroline Islands [a U.S. naval base— seized in September 1944—being readied for the assault on Okinawa], I was transferred, along with a number of other pilots and crewmen, to Izumi Naval Air Station. The early spring air was filled with the scent of plum blossoms. We were billeted in private homes in the village near the station and told to be on standby. I was a reconnaissance man—navigator, assistant bombardier, and sometimes forward gunner—in Ginga No. 8 Special Attack Squad, named for our plane, the three-man Yokosuka P1Y1 Ginga (code-named Frances by the Allies). By the time I arrived at Izumi, many of my classmates were already dead.

When I had first volunteered for the *tokko,* I did not seriously contemplate my own mortality. I was young, sensitive, full of hope, and curious even about death; I considered myself to be on a battlefield. However, as the standby period dragged on, I became increasingly anxious and depressed. Only death awaited. I was proceeding to an awesome destination, and there was no turning back.

Tokko operations during the Okinawa campaign were quite different from those conducted during the Philippines campaign. Launching sorties from bases in the occupied Philippines presented special problems, chiefly because the Filipinos were hostile to us. This had its rewards, however: It helped in- still and sustain a stronger fighting spirit and the sense of antagonism essen- tial for those on kamikaze missions. Most *tokko* operations to Okinawa, on the other hand, were launched from bases on Kyushu, in Japan itself. (Some of the Okinawa sorties originated on Formosa.) And in the Philippines there had still been a possibility that we would prevail. Better aircraft were used, more seasoned pilots were generally at the controls, and more often than not they were protected by fighter escorts. These differences had a considerable impact on our emotional state and, ultimately, on our view of life and death.

When their time came, crewmen on *tokko* missions were relieved of their standby duties; in the certainty that their mission would soon be over, they sometimes became cheerful, almost completely different people. But these feelings of well-being, sometimes bordering on euphoria, could be fleeting and transitory.

On March 19, Fumio Hirosawa, a classmate of mine from air training school who was also attached to the 406th as a member of the Ginga squad of the Kikusui Unit, was ordered to attack an enemy task force off the southeast coast of Kyushu. Those of us who were left went to see Hirosawa and his crew depart. We were soon hoarse from shouting encouragement. I noticed that Hirosawa had lost considerable weight; he climbed into his Frances with seeming casualness, although his face looked gloomy and sad. In an attempt to inject a cheerful and colorful note, someone had placed a branch of cherry blossom in full bloom inside the cockpit. I assumed that, as he confronted his forthcoming self-destruction, my classmate was ensuring that his behavior for the momentous occasion was perfect.

It was a cloudy day, but as the Frances taxied out, a ray of sunshine seemed to spotlight the aircraft. Hirosawa and his crew looked as if they had been placed in an airplane-shaped coffin.

The *tokko* squad, four Frances attack bombers, took off without a fighter escort—since the decimation of our forces in the Philippines, the empire was being pushed into an increasingly desperate corner as far as resources and matériel were concerned. As the aircraft began its takeoff roll, the onlookers stiffened for a moment; the next second, as if in an afterthought, we waved our caps vigorously. But our mouths were tightly closed.

After the formation disappeared in the clouds, we returned to our billets. We went to sleep with the laughter of the maintenance personnel in our ears. It was unbearable to listen to the thoughtless banter of outsiders. The contrast between them, who could enjoy being alive, and us, who were burdened with our standby for death, was particularly painful. The *tokko* squads had long since lost any momentum for living; we seldom laughed anymore.

✦

THE CREEK near the naval station began to warm up; catfish were waking from their hibernation. More of my friends died in action. One afternoon, yet another *tokko* unit vanished toward Okinawa. On this occasion, as previously, I was left behind. I was always anxious about the ground officers' intense observation of *tokko* crews. When the night came I was afraid. I disliked the brief period of sunset more than any other part of the day. After the sun set, the sky and my attitude grew darker and darker.

At night, some slept with their eyes open. During the dark hours, delirious utterances and groans could be heard at intervals through the billet, as if we were living in an asylum. Almost every day crews left the asylum for sorties. They boarded their aircraft with forced smiles on their faces. There was an air of lunatic melancholy in their expressions, in their eye. Each night, after they had departed on their one-way missions, I was again depressed, as though I had been deprived of both heart and soul.

Then, finally, for me—and others—the long standby period came to an end. Our sortie was scheduled for April 17.

The day before, Ginga No. 7 Squad left Izumi. I watched as Isao Yoshikawa, the pilot and bombardier on my crew, ran to one of the four Franceses, which was crewed by two classmates of his, Kensuke Eto and Shigeaki Enokida. They were in the cockpit, smiling. Yoshikawa knelt on the wing and poked his head inside to say good-bye. Just before the planes took off, he got down slowly from the wing. I stared at his face and was horrified. I would remember that desperate, terribly aged look forever.

On that day, Ginga No. 7 Squad, like many before it, disappeared into the sky south of us without a fighter escort, on its certain-death mission. The crewmen sacrificed their lives for their country at a point some fifty nautical miles from Kikaiga-shima, northeast of Okinawa.

"Tomorrow it is going to be my turn," I reflected. I pictured the faces of my fallen classmates. The end was near. It was surprising that I had lasted this long since volunteering, I thought. Then I found myself recalling the fun I had enjoyed in the past and felt depressed.

At last April 17, our death day, arrived. I went with Yoshikawa and Shigeyuki Tanaka, my plane's radioman and rear gunner, to the airfield command post to receive our orders. On the way, Tanaka stopped suddenly. He turned to me, his face as expressionless as a Noh mask, and began to talk in a rambling way. He was sorry; he praised me for coping with all the hardships that had brought us to this day. "I'm a coward, aren't I?" he said. I told him that wasn't true and, as the last moment of our lives was approaching, thanked him for the pleasures and sorrows we had shared as comrades.

Other crews were already assembled in front of the command post. Their faces were unfamiliar; by now most of my classmates had been killed in action. We officially received our orders. The mechanism for our destruction had been set when we volunteered and were put on standby, but the orders sealed our fate. I considered the orders sublime; I felt awed. Now I knew precisely what I had to do. It took no more than a few moments for my warrior's heart to overcome the ordinary human instinct to deny the possibility of mortality. And yet, underneath this newly acquired sense of dedication and excitement, I was still aware of a strong attachment to life. This worried and confused me. My bond to life was my karma, my fate, but still I felt like a hypocrite behind the brave facade.

As commander of our unit, I delivered the orders to Tanaka and Yoshikawa. "Location: east of Kikaiga-shima. Target: a carrier. Let's get going."

Tanaka, Yoshikawa, and I began the walk to our munitions-laden Frances, parked at the end of the airfield near the runway. The plane seemed to quiver in the spring heat. I was grateful the aircraft had been left so far from the command post—the farther I was obliged to walk, the longer I stayed on the ground. Behind me, Tanaka and Yoshikawa were running to catch up. "Why hurry?" I thought. "Walk. Take your time." That morning my crew had looked pale and vacant, as if lost in thought. Now their faces beamed joyfully; it seemed they had completely forgotten what was about to happen.

I, too, now had a sense of liberation from all the mortal ties that bound me and the rest of the world. We were utterly free. No one could give us orders anymore, much less criticize or discipline us. Even if death was just around the corner, there was joy in being released from the overwhelming pressure and restrictions of the vise that we called the navy. And it was glorious to be freed from the mental torture of our protracted standby. I found myself nonetheless bothered by trifling and incongruous thoughts: "What will happen to my laundry? Whom did I leave instructions with about my money and personal things?"

There was always a large crowd around a Frances that was being prepared for a sortie. I approached the aircraft with a conqueror's stride, outwardly arrogant and proud. I could hear the cheers and exclamations of admiration even above the din of the powerful radial engines. I would feel guilty if I did not smile. I forced one, but it was difficult.

Four Frances aircraft were scheduled for *tokko* sorties that day. I was getting impatient and began to feel agitated when I realized that the engines of some of the other aircraft had not been started.

"What time is it?" Tanaka kept saying nervously.

"Almost zero nine-thirty," Yoshikawa replied.

"What the hell's going on there?" Tanaka said.

"Maybe—" Yoshikawa began.

"Called off?" Tanaka interrupted.

Yoshikawa and I remained silent while Tanaka continued his irritated tirade. "Son of a bitch! I don't give a goddamn what happens."

At 10:10 A.M., the command post signaled the sortie. At that moment, I involuntarily turned and looked back. Only our Frances had taken off, and without a fighter escort. (The others might have experienced mechanical difficulties; their Nakajima engines were notoriously unreliable on the low-octane aviation fuel available toward the end of the war.) One solitary aircraft. I was struck with horror. One lone Frances could not possibly reach the target area— where, even if we did, powerful enemy fighters would undoubtedly be patrolling. Our superiors couldn't possibly expect successful results by sending out a single Frances armed with a 1,700-pound bomb; yet they dared to send the three of us on our mission anyway. It didn't matter to them. By this time, the deaths of the *tokko* fliers had become an end in itself, the primary aim of the cold-blooded operations planners. Is this why innocent young men were sacrificing their lives? Even now, a half century later, one is struck by the callous decisions that led to this slaughter. The tactics defied logic.

Isolated and prey to our uneasiness as we were, we all fell completely silent during the flight toward the target area. Our senses seemed paralyzed; even while we were still over land, the beautiful scenery below gradually blended into mere layers of colors. This was, in fact, the onset of the so-called fainting phenomenon.

To break the uncomfortable silence, I began singing, but Tanaka and Yoshikawa refused to join in the chorus, increasing the awkwardness and tension. My heart was now so constricted with the reality of approaching death and the resultant fear that I started to display visible physiological changes: faster, shallower respiration; cardiac palpitations; abnormal perspiration; micturition. My temples ached. When my voice began to sound hollow, I would stop singing for a time.

I glanced at the altimeter. When we took off, the aircraft had been headed south-southwest, cruising first at about 13,000 feet and later at about 16,000. Now the altimeter indicated we were at almost 30,000 feet. Had this happened because Yoshikawa, the pilot, was trying to evade the enemy fighters? In fact, he had unconsciously been applying gradual backward pressure to the control column. I had never flown so high before. A higher altitude might postpone the engagement—and by getting closer to the stars, perhaps we would find ourselves elevated to perennial youth and immortality! Somewhere far away in the depths of my consciousness, I realized that our unscheduled climb was both a result and a contributing cause of the fainting phenomenon, which would never have occurred during flight in formation with other aircraft.

Our symptoms were not unique. I am told that crew members of *tokko* aircraft often became so aware of their forthcoming extinction that they experienced this kind of reaction.

Predictably, just before we reached our target area we were spotted by fifteen Grumman F6F Hellcats on routine patrol. One against fifteen was hopeless odds. Some enemy aircraft began to climb and turn to get into firing position at our rear; others were already there on the starboard side.

In the midst of this chaos, as our plane dodged enemy fire, a small but significant mishap occurred. "The machine gun! I can't fire it! There's a cartridge jammed in the magazine!" Tanaka screamed through the speaking tube.

At this point enemy fighters occupied my entire field of vision, and I was frozen with terror. As an F6F approached head-on, I unconsciously closed my eyes an instant before the impact that seemed certain to come. When there was no crash, I felt tremendously confused and disoriented and found myself thinking, "Isn't there any emergency procedure to avoid this?"

My desperation alternated between feeling as though I was failing, because my knees were so weak from fright, and somehow trying to find a way to run from the attacking aircraft. But there was nowhere to run. I groped for some divine ray of hope that might extricate me from our catastrophe.

The Frances gradually lost altitude, yawing violently. We were still locked in a mortal struggle with the enemy fighters. "Haven't you sighted the target yet, Suzuki?" Tanaka kept asking. The fact that the F6Fs were attempting to block us probably meant that the carrier wasn't far away. Suddenly the Frances shook violently. The starboard engine had been hit and was trailing smoke. With the increased drag of the dying engine, our airspeed dropped sharply. I began to wonder if we would reach the target at all.

We were descending rapidly. An enemy round struck me in the face. I felt a sharp pain as though I had been whipped. Warm blood spurted out of the wound, streaming down my neck and soaking into my silk muffler. I lost consciousness for a moment, but the freezing air blowing into the fuselage through the cracks in the damaged nose canopy revived me. I felt very cold. A piece of the lenses of my goggles had stuck in the fur trim of my glove. I was vomiting reflexively and starting to lose consciousness again. I felt I was at the end of my rope. By now I was so disoriented I had become completely detached and decided that the enemy assault must be someone else's problem.

Despite this, somehow the realization clicked that the F6Fs had disappeared. Simultaneously I saw streams of red, green, and yellow tracer fire, apparently aimed straight at me. It was as though I was taking an inverted shower in Technicolor. The surreal image had come from a fusillade of anti-aircraft fire out of the task force below. "There they are!" I shouted in my mind. The badly damaged Frances was still trailing ominous black smoke.

At last I caught sight of the target carrier. "Here we go!" I shouted through the speaking tube to Yoshikawa and Tanaka. No one answered. The altimeter was pointing to zero.

I kept track of the target despite my restricted vision. "Turn starboard three degrees," I told Yoshikawa. I was bleeding profusely but felt no pain. Then I got very drowsy and almost lost consciousness again. "Am I going to pass out or am I going to die?" I thought. As I concentrated on our attack onto the target, I felt a strangling fear grip my entire body. From the other crew positions—I couldn't tell whether it was Yoshikawa or Tanaka—I heard meaningless sounds, more like groans mixed with shouts than words.

The large target loomed vaguely in my dimming vision. I think that I shouted, "Target, starboard, enemy carrier," but I couldn't be sure my words were clear or even audible. However, Yoshikawa was apparently alive and responsive to my instructions, because the Frances began a slow right turn. I could see a large shadow of the target, but it was almost obscured by the heavy barrage of AA fire. "Is this an illusion?" I wondered.

I watched as the bull's-eye of the target got bigger by the second, and, after the one-against-fifteen air battle of a few minutes ago, I was rather relieved and pleased. I felt proud that my hard training was about to be rewarded. As our distance from the carrier became shorter and shorter, I could no longer distinguish among the furious fireworks of the AA barrage, my fear of death, and my duties and responsibilities. As I was about to lose consciousness, I saw that a portion of the carrier's hull had been burned, and it appeared red. It was very striking.

Steady. At last the target was within reach. We had come an extremely long way, and a hard one. At that moment, just seconds before impact, I felt neither excitement nor animosity. The outline of the enemy target seemed merely a floating object on the water. I did not feel nearly as much fear as I had expected. I was finally relieved of my burden, and I did not want it any longer. "This will do it," I thought. "A perfect angle of approach on the target." It was the beginning of a solemn ceremony.

I felt cold again, as if shrouded in a pale veil. "I've done my duty. My war is over. I'm exhausted." With a sense of relief, I saw an out-of-focus, inexpressible death awaiting me in a space I had previously occupied. At that last moment, I felt relieved of duty. "Steady as you go—body impact. I've won!"

✦

Suzuki's Frances was shot down at that moment. A U.S. Navy destroyer picked him up; the other two crewmen died. He spent the remainder of the war as a prisoner. In his book, Suzuki chose not to describe the end of his military career. He certainly had not been afraid to die. Was he ashamed to have survived? Perhaps.

Little is known about Suzuki's later life. After his repatriation, he married, went to work for a local government fishery, and then became a fireman. He is now retired.

"Steady as you go—body impact. I've won!" When Suzuki wrote those final

words, years after the war, he was describing his feelings in what he believed were his last moments. After the long standby period as a tokko *volunteer, in which he suffered the agony of alternating between dedication to supreme sacrifice and attachment to life, he thought he had accomplished his ambition of a glorious death in battle. He probably felt more of a victory over himself than over the enemy. At the final moment he was, at least to himself, both a great warrior and a great human being. Did he feel cheated by his miraculous reprieve?*

What power inside these men enabled them to proceed? There was certainly nothing in the teachings of the various Japanese religions, all of which deplore human destruction and celebrate life. And what was tokko, *really?*

In his book on the Battle of Leyte, where kamikazes first became a force to be reckoned with, the writer Shohei Ohoka writes that "there were some people in our generation who overcame inconceivable mental agony and vacillation between life and death, and who reached their goals. This has nothing whatever to do with the stupidity and corruption of the Japanese war leaders of those times." The number of young men who sacrificed their lives in the tokko *operation is said to be between 3,000 and 4,000.*

OKINAWA

BRUCE I. GUDMUNDSSON

Okinawa, which began as a practically unopposed landing on April Fool's Day 1945, soon turned into a relentless close-contact slugging match. The battle lasted for two and a half months, and for uninterrupted nastiness its name joins the unenviable company in American military history of the Mule Shoe at Spottsylvania Courthouse, Blanc Mont, Tarawa, the hedgerows of Normandy, and Iwo Jima. Okinawa was a World War I–like struggle fought for an island just eighty miles long, and most of the killing took place in the southernmost fifteen. Bruce I. Gudmundsson makes the comparison, and it is an apt one, to Verdun. The aim of the Japanese at Okinawa was that of Erich von Falkenhayn, the chief of the German General Staff in 1916: to lure the Americans onto the beaches—as he had proposed to lure the French army into his Meuse River meatgrinder—and then to bleed them so white that they would hesitate before pushing on to the Home Islands. The name for Falkenhayn's operation was *Gericht*—a tribunal, or sometimes, and more pointedly, an execution place. That is what the Japanese wanted to make of Okinawa, and it is, along with Verdun, one of the few battles in military history where killing was the principal end.

In terms of death and destruction, not even the Hiroshima atomic bomb could equal Okinawa. The battle was notable not just for its hecatombs but for the relatively high number of Japanese who surrendered—7,400—a figure that was unheard of until then. (Surrender in the Japanese army was a court-martial offense, punishable by death.) The morale of the ordinary soldier had clearly begun to approach a breaking point. But a breaking point of another kind had manifested itself on the American side—the 25,000 casualties due to combat fatigue, or shellshock, as it had been known in the earlier World War.

Okinawa was a battle that, in itself, decided nothing and yet it may have decided Japan's fate. Would the United States allow another such bloodletting? On July 16, two weeks after the island was officially declared to be "secured," scientists at the New Mexico site code-named Trinity detonated the first atomic bomb.

Bruce I. Gudmundsson is a former Marine who currently makes his living advising the Armed Forces on matters of tactics, policy, and structure. A frequent contributor to both the *Marine Corps Gazette* and *MHQ,* he is the author of several books, including *Storm Troop Tactics, On Artillery,* and *On Armor.* He is affiliated with the Center for War Studies at the University of Glasgow.

WHILE A PRISONER ON ST. HELENA, NAPOLEON BONAPARTE WAS shocked to hear a British sea captain's description of the island kingdom of Okinawa, a place where people strove to live in harmony with one another and war was unknown. "No army. No soldiers. No war," the deposed emperor exclaimed. "What sort of barbarians are these?" A century and a half later, the island kingdom was peaceful no more. On Easter Sunday 1945, as if to atone for offending the man whom Carl von Clausewitz called the "god of war," Okinawa became the scene of the last great battle of the greatest war in human history.

Fought at the very dawn of the Atomic Age, the Battle of Okinawa was far more destructive than either of the nuclear explosions that compelled Japan to sue for peace. Yet despite this unprecedented firepower, the mechanism that brought American victory was as old as organized warfare itself. For while the "steel typhoon" of bombs and shells released more explosive power, killed or maimed more people (mostly civilians), and reduced more buildings to rubble and ash than the bombs dropped on Hiroshima and Nagasaki, it failed to destroy most, or even many, of the Japanese defenders. What it did do—in the course of a three-month campaign—was break up the Japanese forces on Okinawa into little pieces that could be eliminated one by one.

The means of this great destruction were largely provided by what Franklin D. Roosevelt had called the "Arsenal of Democracy." Okinawa was, among other things, a showcase for both Allied technology and American industrial might. One-ton shells fired by sixteen-inch guns cast in Bethlehem, Pennsylvania; electronically fused artillery shells perfected in Aberdeen, Maryland; tanks built in Detroit, Michigan; and napalm dropped by aircraft built in Los Angeles, California, were all tributes to what was then still called

"Yankee ingenuity." Neither the fruit of the laboratory nor the fruit of the assembly line, however, spared American fighting men the kind of combat associated with names like Verdun and Passchendaele. As in those earlier episodes of position warfare, long-range weapons of mass destruction demolished the works of man, churned the earth, and inflicted scars that remain to this day—but did not do away with close-in fighting, for which soldiers had to rely on the traditional weapons of trench warfare: the flamethrower, the satchel charge, and, above all, the hand grenade.

By the end of 1944, it was clear that Japan had lost the Pacific war. Its high-seas fleet had been destroyed, contact between the home islands and the rest of the empire was all but cut off, its population was on the verge of starvation, and American bombers rained death on its cities almost daily. The best Japan could hope for was a tolerable, negotiated peace. And the only way it was likely to get that was by convincing its enemies that dealing the death-blow to the Japanese Empire would take too much of the one resource the Western Allies were loath to spend—human lives.

As the United States was the linchpin of the anti-Japanese alliance, the key to Japanese success therefore lay in killing large numbers of American troops. The classic goals of battle—the rapid annihilation of a particular part of the enemy force or the control of a specific piece of ground—were subordinated to this consideration. It no longer mattered where an American was killed or what unit he belonged to. The important thing was that the butcher's bill grow to the point where the U.S. government would decide that the final humiliation of Japan was not worth the loss of one more American life.

An army usually employs the strategy of attrition because it thinks the other side will run out of manpower first. But the Japanese knew they were greatly outnumbered by their enemies. What supported them was the belief that their higher level of culture—their "spiritual strength," as they called it—rendered them far more capable of suffering loss than their "decadent" enemies. In particular, their warriors' famous willingness to accept certain death was seen as a means of killing large numbers of Americans.

The best-known embodiment of this belief in the spiritual superiority of the Japanese fighting man was the notorious kamikaze, an aircraft loaded with only enough fuel for a one-way trip to the deck of an Allied warship and enough explosives to do considerable damage once it got there. Less well known, but nearly as numerous, were the similarly rigged one-man motorboats and the entirely muscle-powered human bombs—swimmers trained to attack small craft, and men on land whose preferred targets were American tanks.

With the bulk of its navy in Davy Jones's locker, Japan could not force the United States into a situation where this great bloodletting could take place. Allied strategy in the Pacific was sufficiently transparent, however, to give the Japanese a good sense of where the Americans would mount their next major operation. One possible target was Formosa (now Taiwan), the large island off the coast of China whose capture would enable large American forces to come to the aid of the hard-pressed Chinese. The other was Okinawa, ideally suited to serve as both a stepping-stone to China and an air and naval base for an invasion of the home islands of Japan.

From the point of view of Japan's strategists, Okinawa was the preferred place for the shedding of American blood. At about 450 square miles, it was large enough to attract a sizable U.S. force. At the same time, the peculiar shape of the island allowed the Japanese to set up situations where they could sell their lives as dearly as possible. A long, thin jumble of peninsulas that the Americans compared to a silhouette of Mickey Mouse's pet dog Pluto, Okinawa was a mountain range in miniature. Cut by ravines that followed no pattern, the mountains broke the island into hundreds of tiny compartments, each of which provided its Japanese defenders with the opportunity for a first-class ambush. Better yet was the same factor that made Okinawa important to the Allies: its nearness—a mere 325 miles—to Kyushu, the southernmost of the home islands and where the majority of the remaining kamikaze squadrons were based.

Like the overall Japanese strategy in the Pacific, the plan for killing Americans on Okinawa depended heavily on these aircraft. It called for the Japanese ground troops (nearly 100,000 of them) to allow the largest possible number of Americans to land. Once the Americans were firmly ashore, the suicide planes and boats would attack Allied ships in the waters around the island. Once the ships were either destroyed or driven off, the American landing force would be significantly weakened. With no fighters overhead, no bombers on call from nearby carriers, and no gunfire coming from ships offshore, the Americans stranded on Okinawa would be deprived of the weapons the Japanese feared the most. Cut off from supplies and reinforcements and forced to rely on themselves, the invaders could then be eliminated in close combat.

As far as the Japanese were concerned, the best place for the Americans to land was just south of the narrow waist of the island, on a piece of relatively flat land that separated the jungle-covered mountains of northern Okinawa from the densely inhabited hills of the south, where the bulk of the island's 475,000 civilians lived. The bait that would draw the Americans to this spot was hard to resist. The west coast of this waist was formed by eight more or less continuous miles of the best landing beaches on Okinawa—the only place where four American divisions could land abreast. As a bonus, two of the island's four airfields were within rifle shot of these beaches.

In order to permit as many Americans as possible to walk into the trap, the Japanese all but evacuated the waist of the island. The only troops remaining there were air-force ground crews and other service personnel, formed into a provisional regiment whose chief purpose was to put up token resistance. The Japanese deployed the bulk of their forces—twenty-nine of thirty-one infantry battalions, all of the ninety or so tanks, and most of the artillery and heavy weapons—in the southern third of the island. The remainder of the troops—two infantry battalions reinforced with artillery and antitank guns— were assigned the defense of the northern two-thirds of the island and the airfield at Ie Shima, a small island just three miles off Okinawa's northwest coast. Northern Okinawa, heavily forested and thinly populated, was otherwise undefended.

Before they could fulfill their mission of wiping out the American landing force, the Japanese ground troops would have to survive the steady rain of bombs and shells that invariably preceded an American amphibious attack. To this end, the Japanese—or, more precisely, Okinawans pressed into Japanese service—built a system of tunnels deeper and more elaborate than any ever dug for a purely military purpose. They were aided by the irregular pattern of the Okinawan terrain, which provided an immense number of natural "back alleys," almost impossible to reach with naval gunfire and difficult to hit with air-dropped bombs. Further help came from the consistency of the Okinawan rock. Like the chalk of the Champagne region of France, the rock was sufficiently soft to yield to the laborers' hand tools and yet solid enough to bear up under the disruption of extensive digging. In addition to hundreds of tunnels designed to shelter single squads, machine guns, mortars, or antitank guns, the system included galleries large enough to contain headquarters, hospitals, heavy artillery pieces, and whole companies of infantry.

Privy to reports from the defenders of Iwo Jima, which the Americans took in heavy fighting from February 19 to March 26, the Japanese leaders on Okinawa were firmly convinced that burrowing into the earth offered their only hope of surviving the steel typhoon. When it came to the tactics for defeating the American landing forces, however, the consensus broke down. Lieutenant General Isamu Cho, a veteran of the long war against China, was chief of staff of the Thirty-second Army, the headquarters that united the efforts of all Japanese soldiers on the island. He advocated an all-out attack in the style

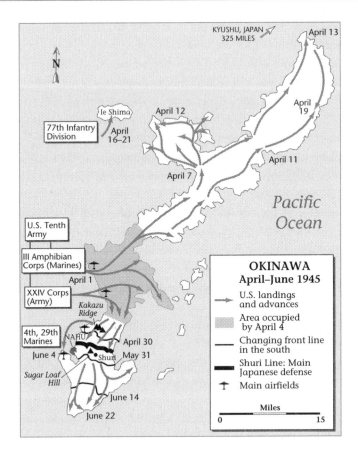

Most of Okinawa and neighboring Ie Shima—where the famous war correspondent Ernie Pyle was killed by a sniper—were captured within three weeks of the initial landing. Pacifying the remainder—heavily fortified places south of the landing beaches such as Kakazu Ridge, Sugar Loaf Hill, and Shuri Castle—required nearly three months of intense combat.

that had served the Japanese army so well over the previous half century. The traditional mixture of small-group infiltration, concentrated artillery fire, and timely banzai charge, Cho argued, would suffice to overwhelm the stranded Americans. Taking the opposite view, Colonel Hiromichi Yahara, operations officer of the Thirty-second, proposed that the Japanese remain on the defensive throughout the battle. Many more Americans would die trying to root each Japanese soldier out of his fighting hole, Yahara argued, than in an all-or-nothing attack.

The plans reflected the personalities of their advocates. General Cho was a firebrand who, in the course of the early 1930s coup that replaced Japan's constitutional government with a military dictatorship, had personally wielded the assassin's knife. On subsequent assignments in Manchuria, Malaya, and Burma, Cho had frequently displayed his love of aggressive action and relentless pursuit. Colonel Yahara was, by comparison, cold-blooded and shrewd. Closer to the ideal of a Prussian General Staff officer than a stereotypical samurai, he was a brilliant tactician who had served as an instructor at the Japanese Staff Academy, a secret agent in Burma and Thailand, and an intelligence officer specializing in Southeast Asia.

Both men were among the handful of Japanese officers who served exchange tours with the U.S. Army in the 1930s. Though Cho had spent more time in America, it was Yahara's plan that aimed at exploiting specific American weaknesses. In particular, Yahara was well aware that, for most American officers, tactics boiled down to a game of "king of the hill." A successful attack was one that left the attackers in possession of the hill, or, more precisely, the top of the hill. As a result, Yahara's plan took great pains to ensure that once they got to the top of the hill, the American attackers would find themselves subjected to fire from all directions.

The task of choosing between the two approaches fell to the Thirty-second Army's commanding general, Lieutenant General Mitsuru Ushijima. On the surface, Ushijima was well suited to his job. He had a commanding presence and a gift for inspiring genuine loyalty. Once, during the long wait for the American invasion, the Thirty-second suffered an epidemic of brawling between mainland Japanese and native Okinawans. In an army where minor infractions were often punished by brutal beatings, the normal response to such indiscipline would have been savage. Ushijima, however, responded by visiting a small group of imprisoned brawlers, telling them that their behavior had disgraced the emperor, and returning them to their units. Within hours, the brawling had stopped. Unfortunately for the Japanese war effort, such first-class leadership was not matched by what a German soldier would call "character." Though outwardly serene, Ushijima vacillated, refusing to commit himself entirely to one plan or another until the point in the battle when he no longer had a choice.

At first, Ushijima's indecision tended to favor the painstaking Yahara. Charged with such details as the disposition of troops, the location of shelters, and the organization of units, Yahara naturally made provisions that fit in with his vision of the upcoming battle. In particular, he converted the southern third of the island into an extensive fortified zone. The citadel of this fortress was Shuri Castle, a medieval stronghold that permitted unhindered observation of the surrounding waters. The curtains and bastions were created by digging shelters for men and weapons into the reverse slopes of ridges and hills. In accordance with the classic precepts of fortress design, these outworks were not so much barriers as traps. The job of the Japanese defenders, after all, was not to keep the Americans at arm's length but to kill them.

✦

THE INITIAL EVENTS of the American invasion of Okinawa proved that Yahara's judgment was sound. The great bombardment before the landing by four American divisions on April 1 was on an unprecedented scale. Over the course of seven days, planes from 40 aircraft carriers dropped their bombs in 3,000 sorties; the big guns of 10 battleships and 9 cruisers launched over 13,000 shells, and millions of more modest projectiles were fired by 23 destroyers and 177 landing craft converted into floating batteries. Thanks to Yahara's preparations, the bombardment—powerful enough to destroy every building but one in the island's capital city of Naha—did little immediate damage to the men and weapons of the Thirty-second Army. Even in areas where the bombardment wiped out all life—including birds, snakes, and insects—Japanese soldiers emerged from their shelters ready to fight.

But being right is no guarantee of favor. Soon after the Americans landed on the wide beaches just south of the island's narrow waist, as Yahara had predicted, Ushijima fell under the influence of General Cho. On the night of April 3–4, Cho pushed for a full-scale counterattack. With the Americans lulled into false confidence by the weak opposition to the landings and spread thinly between the western landing beaches and the eastern shore, Cho claimed, there was no need to whittle away at their strength in hundreds of little traps; by rushing inland, the Americans had walked into a much larger trap. The retail fighting Yahara advocated could therefore give way to wholesale slaughter.

Yahara was Cho's subordinate—indeed, his primary assistant—but he protested that the Japanese attack would fall apart in the face of superior American firepower. The colonel had no doubt that the best of the Japanese infantrymen had the skill to make their way through the American lines and wreak much destruction among artillery batteries and rear-area installations, even aviation units on the recently captured airfields. Once recovered from the initial shock, however, the Americans would respond with another steel typhoon—and this time the Japanese soldiers would be out of the shelter of caves and tunnels that had preserved their lives during the first great bombardment. To make matters worse, while the bulk of Japanese forces was fighting to the north, their southern flank would be vulnerable to a second American landing.

On the morning of April 4, while the Japanese were preparing their counterattack, U.S. ships appeared off the south coast. As if taking their cue from Yahara himself, they gave birth to a great number and variety of landing craft, each with its full load of marines and each playing its part in the almost ritualistic war dance of circles and lines that always heralded an American landing. It was not until the end of the day that the Japanese realized the pageant was just that, a demonstration designed to keep masses of Japanese soldiers tied to the southern beaches. But even before the landing craft turned away from the shore and the undoubtedly grateful marines climbed back aboard their ships, Ushijima rescinded his orders for the counterattack. The demonstration may have been pure Hollywood, but the marines and sailors in the boats were as real as any other fighting men at Okinawa.

On the same day, the main American landing force, having crossed the island and reached the east coast, turned south—and ran into the outer ring of the Japanese defensive system. Up to this point, almost all of the handful of Japanese units in the path of the rapidly advancing Americans had had orders to delay rather than defend. Indeed, resistance had been so slight that many Americans—including a number of generals—had begun to think the battle was over. Then, as tanks suddenly fell prey to hidden guns, officers were hit by snipers, and whole squads found themselves caught in cross fire at the bottom of ravines, the wishful belief that the battle was over gave way to a grim realization that it had just begun.

For three days, as the Americans pushed through outposts and into the heart of the first defensive belt surrounding the Japanese fortress, the fighting grew fiercer and the invaders' progress slower. While each little battle featured a slightly different mix of weapons, men, skill, and terrain, a general pattern emerged. Those who tried to fight "by the book," with whole platoons or even companies moving as units in order to seize hilltops, ended up with failure and heavy losses. Those who fought in small groups, with each man making the most of the irregular ground, enjoyed both greater success and a better chance of survival.

This was not a new insight. The lesson had been teamed time and again in both world wars. A lesson learned by one, unfortunately, was not a lesson learned by all. Up to the very end of the battle for Okinawa, there were officers who attempted to fight in ways that had been obsolete for years. A few times the old methods worked, as in the case of the 96th Division platoon that used the "walking fire" technique so beloved by General Patton—advancing

while continuously firing together—to kill the crew of a Japanese light mortar. Most of the time, they didn't. "To be avoided, and if necessary, ignored,"
said marine sergeant (and later noted writer) William Manchester, "were gung
ho platoon leaders who drew enemy fire by ordering spectacular charges.
Ground wasn't gained that way; it was won by small groups of men, five or six
in a cluster, who moved warily forward in a kind of autohypnosis, advancing
in mysterious concert with similar groups on their flanks."

"Gung ho" lieutenants were not, needless to say, peculiar to the American
forces. Despite the emphasis that Japanese doctrine placed on stealth, infiltration, and the independent action of small units and individuals, American
troops on Okinawa were often treated to the spectacle of an old-fashioned banzai charge. The larger ones were part of the multi-battalion counteroffensives
that General Ushijima ordered after he later fell under the influence of General Cho; the smaller ones seem to have had more local inspiration. At times,
these charges made a certain amount of sense. American troops who had just
captured a position, for example, tended to be vulnerable to a swift counterattack. In most cases, however, including the well-supported attacks ordered
by General Cho, the banzai charges were a gift to the Americans.

As long as the Japanese fought from their well-designed fighting positions,
the Americans were at a disadvantage. In order to attack the mouth of a single cave, they had to expose themselves to fire from all directions. On Okinawa, this was as true for antitank weapons as it was for machine guns and
mortars. Just as the U.S. infantrymen who went after a single Japanese fighting position often found themselves caught in a cross fire, the American tank
that turned to engage a particular target was often destroyed by a strategically
placed antitank gun. Indeed, for the Japanese of World War II as much as for
Vauban, the seventeenth-century French master of siegecraft, the essence of
the art of fortification was mutual protection. Instead of being preoccupied
with their own survival, the operators of a Japanese mortar or machine gun
were concerned with covering the approaches to other hidden emplacements.
In other words, the Japanese defense was a social act, with each small group
acting in "mysterious concert" with its fellows to create a whole that was far
stronger than the sum of the parts.

If, however, one squad abandoned its post for the sweet release of a banzai
charge, a tear appeared in the seamless garment. One side of a cave was left without cover. Once the Americans discovered this, they were free to start unravel-
ing the defense, one cave at a time. The process, which involved flamethrowers,
satchel charges, hand grenades, and, in some cases, bulldozers, was grim but
predictable. Once the glue of mutual support was gone, the task of reducing a

particular portion of the Japanese defensive network was no longer a matter of tactics but of engineering. The work was still dangerous—many Americans were killed or wounded dropping explosives or firing flamethrowers into the mouths of caves—but there was little doubt about the outcome.

What was true for smaller weapons was also true for the Japanese artillery. As long ago as the Russo-Japanese War, Japanese gunners had displayed a knack for concentrating the fire of widely dispersed batteries. While other armies managed this by radio and telephone, the Japanese relied, once again, on the "mysterious concert" that William Manchester thought necessary to marine small-unit tactics. On Okinawa, Colonel Yahara ordered the dispersed deployment of individual guns, not just of batteries as a whole. This presented considerable problems for the Americans. The U.S. weapons that were accurate enough to hit the caves where the Japanese guns were hidden were not powerful enough to do much damage. Conversely, the weapons that had the power to put the Japanese guns out of action (the larger American battleships' 16-inch guns, for instance) were not nearly accurate enough. When, however, the Japanese artillery emerged from its shelters to mass in support of General Cho's offensives, they made wonderful targets for the vastly superior American field artillery, supported as it was by the big guns of the fleet and aerial observers in Piper Cubs.

The last of the big Japanese attacks was launched on May 4, a little more than a month after the American landing. For General Ushijima, its failure served to confirm the wisdom of Colonel Yahara's approach. In the weeks that followed, Ushijima ordered units either to retire to more defensible ground or hold out to the end, and he refrained from ordering any more attacks. This change of heart, however, was far from a triumph for Yahara. The assumption on which all the Japanese planning was based—the rapid defeat of the American fleet by the kamikaze aircraft and suicide boats—had proved false. The suicide campaign was inflicting horrible losses on the Allied fleet off the coast of Okinawa—according to the U.S. Navy, 33 ships were sunk and more than 350 damaged during the campaign, mostly by kamikaze—but there were no indications that the fleet was going away. On the contrary, the American divisions that were supposed to have been stranded were constantly reinforced and resupplied; in some cases, they were even rotated out of the front lines for a few days of rest. The Japanese, on the other hand, got no reinforcements during the entire campaign (apart from a few hardy souls who had escaped from outlying islands in canoes and infiltrated through American lines to join their comrades in the caves). Supplies were limited to what had been stockpiled, and the only rest available to Japanese soldiers was of the eternal sort.

American participants in the battle for Okinawa often compared it, with some justification, to the long fight around Verdun during World War I. In both battles, thousands of men lived and died within yards of their largely unseen enemies. Huge shells gouged craters in sharply rising ridges and irregular ravines to create an inhuman wilderness devoid of both vegetation and water. The proliferation of automatic weapons in this moonscape often made it as difficult to retire as it was to advance, forcing the living to share their tiny shelters with the dead and the near-dead. The horrors of Verdun, however, were more evenly balanced; the Germans and French were both able to bring in fresh troops and evacuate the shattered remnants of broken units, so the battle could, and did, continue for nearly half a year. On Okinawa, only the Americans had this capability. The hope of many Americans on the front lines at Okinawa was the "million-dollar wound"—an injury bad enough to get you evacuated but not so bad as to interfere with enjoyment of postwar life. The Japanese lacked this escape mechanism. A light wound earned a man a recycled bandage and a quick return to duty. A serious wound meant a one-way trip to one of the hopelessly overcrowded underground hospitals, where conditions were deadlier than at the front lines. For the Japanese, the closest equivalent to the "million-dollar wound" was a quick and relatively painless death. As the battle wore on, more and more Japanese soldiers found their existence reduced to an agonizing wait, plagued with constant hunger and thirst, in the heat, darkness, stench, and filth of a tiny cave. Knowing it was just a matter of time before American grenades came tumbling through the mouth of that cave, or a ball of jellied gasoline turned their refuge into an inferno, or the entrances were sealed and the cave's inhabitants buried alive, many Japanese chose to expedite their own deaths.

In a few cases, this took the form of proper, if undermanned and futile, banzai charges. In others, all pretense of military purpose was abandoned. Some men simply left the caves and wandered about, zombielike, until dispatched by American rifles. Others chose more direct forms of suicide—a pistol to the head or a grenade to the belly. A few, like Generals Ushijima and Cho, died according to the prescribed rituals of *seppuku,* whereby a self-inflicted slash across the belly is followed by decapitation. (It is interesting to note that Colonel Yahara avoided death by disguising himself as a civilian and letting himself be taken into American custody. Eventually discovered, he ended the battle as a prisoner of war.) In a sense, the Japanese army's Spartan discipline was beginning to be carried to its logical extreme. The emperor could ask a man to fight without rations or water, without proper support, without even a glimmer of hope of eventual victory. What he could not deny was the right of every Japanese to escape misery and dishonor by taking his own life.

For a relatively few Japanese soldiers, release from the agonies of war came in a form hitherto unthinkable. As the Americans made their slow but steady progress through the island's defenses, and as the Japanese counterattacks failed one after the other, more and more Japanese raised their hands in surrender. How many attempted to give themselves up will never be known. Many who tried were killed by their comrades, as the reports of Japanese survivors attest. Others were killed by Americans who, out of fear of being tricked or sheer hatred of the enemy, were disinclined to take prisoners. Nonetheless, in the first month of the Battle of Okinawa, nearly 600 Japanese soldiers found their way into American POW cages. By the end of the campaign, the number had reached 7,400.

As in other campaigns, Koreans and Taiwanese who had been pressed into Japanese service as laborers were well represented among the prisoners. For the first time in this war, however, fighting men from the Japanese home islands, including officers and NCOs, were also giving themselves up. In some cases—like that of a certain Lieutenant Kimada, who surrendered on condition that he be allowed to marry his Okinawan girlfriend—the reasons were unusual. (Japanese prejudice against Okinawans, combined with the custom of arranged marriages, made defection Kimada's only hope of marital bliss.) Most of the Japanese soldiers who voluntarily laid down their arms, however, did so for the usual reason: They had suffered enough and simply wished, whatever the psychic cost, to survive the battle.

Less drastic than surrender, but still very helpful to the Americans, was the increasing tendency of Japanese soldiers to look out for number one. Imprisoned in their caves by day and reduced to foraging (in some cases, marauding) at night, small groups lost contact with the rest of the Japanese force and, as a result, the sense that they were part of a larger enterprise. The most telling symptom of this malaise was the increasing reluctance by a cave's defenders to expose themselves in order to protect the inhabitants of another. In the language of the social scientist, the Japanese were losing "social cohesion." For the American crawling up a hill to drop a satchel charge into the mouth of a cave, loss of social cohesion meant a greatly reduced chance of being shot in the back.

In the interests of encouraging surrender, American leaders on Okinawa took considerable pains to exploit the war-weariness of the Japanese. Hundreds of thousands of leaflets were dropped; Americans of Japanese ancestry, as well as prisoners of war, were provided with loudspeakers and sent out to encourage both soldiers and civilians to give themselves up. The captors of the lovelorn Lieutenant Kimada went so far as to provide a marriage ceremony and, in the form of a pyramidal tent, a honeymoon suite.

These efforts notwithstanding, the overall American approach to the battle, with its slow but steady pressure on the whole of the forward edge of the Japanese defenses, allowed the Japanese to make the most of their dwindling social cohesion. Until the very end, the Japanese could always respond to an American attack by reestablishing their defenses on the next ridgeline. At no point did the Americans do what Colonel Yahara feared the most—find a weakness in the Japanese line, rupture the line at that weak point, and break through to the Japanese rear. (In August 1945, similar attacks by Soviet forces caused the rapid collapse of Japanese resistance in Manchuria.) Indeed, the chief means by which the Americans could have effected such a blitzkrieg attack—six tank battalions, five amphibious tank battalions, and ten amphibious tractor battalions—were distributed piecemeal among the infantry divisions throughout the course of the battle.

✦

THE BATTLE for Okinawa—from the landings on April 1, 1945, to the U.S. declaration that the island was secure on July 2, 1945, ten days after the American flag was raised at the southern tip of the island—lasted three full months, largely because of the Americans' methodical pace. The losses were enormous. More people—about 150,000 Okinawan civilians, 75,000 Japanese soldiers, 10,000 enslaved Koreans, and 13,000 Americans—died at Okinawa than were killed as a result of the atomic explosions at Hiroshima and Nagasaki combined.

The devastation visited on Okinawa and its ancient culture, moreover, was far greater than even these numbing figures reveal. Nearly every house on the southern third of Okinawa was destroyed. Whole villages were wiped from the map, towns reduced to rubble, and nearly every artifact of an ancient culture—including the masonry walls of Shuri Castle—lost to future generations. Like the cost in human lives, the physical and cultural damage done by the roughly 25 million tons of conventional explosives dropped, fired, or tossed on the island was far greater than that resulting from the atomic detonations that ended the war.

THE RIGHT MAN

VICTOR DAVIS HANSON

In a century of near-continuous war, there has been no shortage of extraordinary campaigns—or of memorable operational artists. But what are the criteria for the greatest? Innovation, imagination, and an inspired ruthlessness are all involved, with the combination leading to a genuine decision. But more than that, the campaign must not just ratify the course of history; it must actually change it. One can make a convincing argument that no campaign in the twentieth century was more effective, or its consequences more far-reaching, than the air offensive of Major General Curtis LeMay's Twenty-first Bomber Command against the Japanese Home Islands in 1945.

LeMay has long been the object of antiwar sport—his reputation may never recover from the late Stanley Kubrick's dissection of a cigar-chomping nuclear loose cannon, General Jack D. Ripper, in the movie *Dr. Strangelove*. LeMay, however, was in fact one of history's outstanding military leaders. In Europe, he developed new formations and tactics that dramatically increased the potency of the Allies' strategic bombing campaign and reduced its losses. (Even later, in Europe at the beginning of the Cold War, it was LeMay who was the principal designer—and implementer—of the Berlin Air Lift.) In the Pacific, he soon recognized that high-altitude bombing of Japan was not working. He stripped down his B-29s and sent them in low, making them in effect giant dive bombers. He dumped incendiary bombs on Japan's major cities, which were largely built of wood. The atomic bombs dropped in August were merely the strategic offensive taken to an extreme—and they worked. As the Japanese Emperor Hirohito said, he did not want to see his nation "reduced to ashes." Until Kosovo (and the returns are still out on that), LeMay's campaign against Japan is the only instance in which a sustained air offensive ended a war.

The cost in lives was terrible, but LeMay's air campaign over Japan ul-

timately saved lives. We had to use the Bomb. We were running out of
time. The projected American-led invasion of Japan would have been
unimaginably costly, and the attempt to prove otherwise is, quite simply,
dishonest. We were not forced to transfer hundreds of thousands of reluctant and war-weary troops from Europe to the Pacific. The abrupt
end of the war kept the Soviets out of the home islands and allowed the
United States to rebuild Japan, unhindered by the stultifying mischief of
Moscow. Above all, LeMay's campaign terminated the most destructive
war in history—a war that might have gone on for months more, a year
perhaps, with consequences that are not pleasant to contemplate. We
are, as Victor Davis Hanson tells us, in Curtis LeMay's debt.

Victor Davis Hanson, who teaches classics at California State University in Fresno, is best known for his writings on classical military history. But that singular expertise has by no means limited his subject
matter. Among his many books are *The Western Way of War, Who Killed
Homer?* (with John Heath), *Fields without Dreams, The Soul of Battle,*
and, most recently, *The Land Was Everything: Letters from an American
Farmer.* His late father, William F. Hanson, flew thirty-four combat missions as a sergeant in LeMay's 504th Bomber Group.

IN *DR. STRANGELOVE,* STANLEY KUBRICK'S 1963 BLACK SATIRE
about a nuclear Armageddon, George C. Scott portrays the chairman of the
Joint Chiefs of Staff, gum-chewing, jingoistic, right-wing nut General Buck
Turgidson. Along with his wing commander, General Jack D. Ripper (the
cigar-chomping Sterling Hayden), Turgidson welcomes the chance to unleash
the nuclear firepower of America's bombers in the final showdown against the
"Russkies." Both Turgidson and Ripper, of course, bear some uncanny resem-
blances to General Curtis E. LeMay, who at the time was serving on the Joint
Chiefs in his role as chief of staff of the U.S. Air Force.

LeMay had clashed continually with Secretary of Defense Robert S. Mc-
Namara and the chairman of the Joint Chiefs of Staff, General Maxwell Taylor,
over the so-called missile gap and limitations on the use of American strate-
gic power during the Cold War—especially during the Cuban Missile Crisis
(October 1962) and early in the Vietnam War (1961–65). The unpredictable
LeMay was supposedly quoted at one Pentagon strategy session on Cuba as

saying, "Now we've got him [the Russian Bear] in a trap, let's take his leg off right up to his testicles. On second thought, let's take off his testicles too." Buck Turgidson likewise brags about catching "the Commies with their pants down" in a war that General Ripper says is "too important to be left to the politicians."

Nor has more recent history been kind to LeMay, the air force general most readily identified with the American strategic arsenal during the first two decades of the Cold War. For example, in Richard Rhodes's *Dark Sun: The Making of the Hydrogen Bomb,* LeMay is depicted as a hothead who tried his best to provoke a nuclear conflagration during the Cuban Missile Crisis. In Rhodes's opinion, LeMay felt that our nuclear forces (otherwise a "wasting asset") ideally should be used in a preemptive attack on the Soviet Union, a move that Rhodes believes would have resulted in "historic omnicide."

Once described as "a rogue elephant barging out of a forest," LeMay spoke too candidly and wrote too much. His method of argumentation and counsel was both undiplomatic and often theatrical; Maxwell Taylor remarked that LeMay "would jam that damn cigar in his mouth and place a chip on his shoulder and parade through the halls of the Pentagon looking for a fight." So, despite his substantial experience and proven record of success, LeMay is now remembered too often for his outrageous one-liners ("Well, maybe if we do this overflight right, we can get World War III started"), which seemed to confirm that for years a scary dinosaur from World War II had America's atomic weapons under his operational command. No wonder he ended up a near recluse, reluctant to appear publicly or grant interviews, still bitter over the crude and simplistic portrayal of him in the popular media during the 1960s.

LeMay was an obvious and easy target for caricature. After President Lyndon Johnson successfully portrayed Republican candidate Barry Goldwater as a trigger-happy nuclear warmonger in the 1964 campaign, and with disenchantment growing over the stalemate in Vietnam, the American public began to grow leery of the power—and intentions—of the country's Cold Warriors. In addition, in 1965 LeMay had at last published his memoirs (*Mission with LeMay*), which confirmed the hearsay and innuendo that had circulated about him for years. For once, in fact, the official record was far more inflammatory than the rumor and gossip of any liberal journalist. Of the existing "no-win" policy against the North Vietnamese, LeMay scoffed, "My solution to the problem would be to tell them frankly that they've got to draw in their horns and stop their aggression, or we're going to bomb them back into the Stone Age. And we would shove them back into the Stone Age with Air Power or Naval Power—not with ground forces." LeMay's "Back into the

Stone Age" became an often repeated, and soon embarrassing, part of the discourse about the war. Further, LeMay's experience in dealing with Japanese kamikazes in World War II, and his later concern over the human-wave attacks by North Korean and Chinese Communists, now appeared in print as racist advice on how to win another Asian war:

> Human attrition means nothing to such people. Their lives were so miserable here on earth that there can't help but be a better life for them and all their relatives in a future world. They look forward to that future world with delight. They're going to have everything from tea parties with long-dead grandfathers down to their pick of all the golden little dancing girls in Paradise.

Because of LeMay's theatrics and often uncouth pronouncements, most critics missed the fact that his advocacy of a strategic air campaign against military targets in North Vietnam—dockyards, ports, power plants, railroads, factories, and irrigation facilities—might have been more successful, as well as less devastating to civilians in the long run, than the actual policy of carpet-bombing the south. Because LeMay was his own public-relations nightmare, most forgot that he had, in fact, deplored the use of tactical fighter-bombers in occasional haphazard strategic roles, while—against his wishes—his beloved strategic B-52 bomber fleet was used tactically, resulting in slaughter without harming the enemy's infrastructure.

As for the fictional General Buck Turgidson's eagerness to push the nuclear button ("only 10 to 20 million killed, tops"), LeMay himself had written nearly as much in his 1965 autobiography:

> There was, definitely, a time when we could have destroyed all of Russia (I mean by that, all of Russia's capability to wage war) without losing a man to their defense. . . . It would have been possible, I believe, for America to say to the Soviets, "Here's a blueprint for your immediate future. We'll give you a deadline of five or six months"—something like that—"to pull out of the satellite countries and effect a complete change of conduct. You will behave your damn selves from this moment forth."

LeMay's nuclear fascination was in evidence as late as a 1984 interview, in which the seventy-eight-year-old retired general still lamented his inability as commander of America's strategic air forces to gain unquestioned access to nuclear weapons "and to take some action on my own" if—as Buck Turgidson puts it in *Dr. Strangelove*—"the normal chain of command has been disrupted."

In 1968, when he ran for vice president on George Wallace's third-party ticket, LeMay published the polemical *America Is in Danger*, which in part outlined a strategic air campaign against Red China. On occasion, he quoted Dr. Edward Teller—the model for Dr. Strangelove himself!—about the advantages of nuclear proliferation. "One could also question the basic premise," LeMay added, "that stability itself is always desirable."

LeMay's physical appearance only enhanced his hard-nosed reputation: a burly physique, thick hair combed straight back, bushy black eyebrows, a barrel chest bedecked with air medals, binoculars slung around his neck, a huge cigar perennially stuck out of one side of his mouth, occasional sunglasses—a cartoonist's dream, which ever since has provided the stereotype of the Pentagon's top brass. An avid big-game hunter and sports-car enthusiast, he was frequently photographed with elephant, buffalo, and bear trophies as well as souped-up racing cars. This was no technocrat, no West Point academician controlling our nation's nuclear bomber fleet, but a general more comfortable behind the wheel of a fully loaded bomber. Indeed, LeMay ended his autobiography with his favorite last order as he boarded his bomber: "Crank her up, let's go."

All this has made it difficult for the historian to separate LeMay's public bluster from his actual record as an air force general. Like many others, I accepted without question Kubrick's caricature of LeMay and considered him a reckless and one-dimensional military mind with little concern for human lives, civilian or military, the enemy's or those of his own men.

I also had some personal, anecdotal information about General LeMay—and it generally confirmed the image of a no-holds-barred, bombs-away hyperpatriot. During World War II, my father had flown on thirty-four missions (and was credited with two destroyed Japanese fighters) in a B-29 attached to the 504th Bomb Group, stationed with the 313th Bombardment Wing on the island of Tinian as part of LeMay's XXI Bomber Command. My father's stories of the fire-bombing of Japanese cities seemed to tell of indiscriminate attacks on the civilian population, and a reckless use of American aviators as well. By taking their magnificent precision bombers (which were theretofore targeting strictly military and industrial targets) from the near safety of 30,000 to 35,000 feet to fly as little more than huge dive bombers at 5,000 to 7,000 feet and occasionally lower, LeMay seemed bent on a deliberate sacrifice of aviators' lives simply to deliver more ordnance. That Hiroshima and Nagasaki were both nuked under LeMay's command with his support rounded out the crude stereotype.

Still, I have been intrigued these last thirty years by my father's failure to criticize LeMay directly, when it would have been so easy for him to do so. Despite his horrific stories of B-29s overloaded with napalm and blowing up on takeoff, of low-flying bombers shredded by flak and their eleven-man crews sent spiraling into their self-generated inferno over Tokyo, of the smell of burning Japanese flesh wafting through the bomb-bay doors, he never equated that barbarity with LeMay himself. On the contrary, he seemed to think that the carnage below his plane and the sacrifice of his friends in the air—twelve of sixteen B-29s in his 398th Squadron crashed, were shot down, or were never heard from again—had been necessary to win the war and save, not expend, lives. And despite his lifelong Democratic Party credentials, my father spoke highly of LeMay even in the midst of the general's entry into controversial right-wing politics. Increasingly I have wondered why he bore affection for such a seemingly unaffectionate personality.

To review the career of Curtis E. LeMay is to chronicle the growth of the U.S. strategic air force. To review his behavior and conduct in the military is to understand the American character itself, its mettle in wartime and its naïveté and impudence during the peace. No other American bore more responsibility for the development of strategic air power from 1944 to 1965, a twenty-year period that saw the strategic fleet develop from a force of often ineffectual propeller-driven bombers into the most powerful airborne arm the world had seen. LeMay's role was decisive at all levels—operational, tactical, and strategic—and characterized throughout by decisive judgment, aggressive leadership, and unquestioned personal courage. Anywhere American bombers were deployed, LeMay was not far away. Often he was in the cockpit itself. (By the end of his career, LeMay was certified to fly—and flew—seventy-five types of military aircraft, ranging from strategic and tactical bombers to tankers, cargo planes, fighters, civilian transports, and helicopters.)

✦

IN 1937, after nine years in the U.S. Army Air Corps, First Lieutenant LeMay was attached to the 2nd Bombardment Group, which was the first unit to fly the new B-17 bomber. LeMay's crews trained on it for the next four and a half years, until the United States entered World War II. In April 1942, Colonel LeMay was assigned to the Eighth Air Force, and he took command of the 305th Bombardment Group, comprising thirty-five B-17s. Although he was only thirty-five years old, no other American had more experience with the B-17: In fact, LeMay was the only pilot in his entire group to have flown the bomber at all. "I gave them a ride in a B-17 before we went overseas so they could shoot at a target as we flew across the desert at a hundred feet," he later recounted in his autobiography. "That's what we went to war with. They were not only a rabble, but I didn't have any confidence in their commander—me! I had never commanded anything."

But in little over a year, after leading many of the daylight missions over Europe himself, LeMay was made brigadier general. By March 1944, as a major general, he had taken command of an entire air division (266 B-17s and B-24s) and flown on some of the most dangerous air battles of the war, including the Schweinfurt-Regensburg raids. Although not yet forty, he had developed a reputation for organizational skill in creating professional, effective forces *ex nihilo.*

In August 1944, he was ordered to the Pacific theater to take over the XX Bomber Command, as part of the army's new strategic air campaign against Japan. This force, based in China and India, was understaffed and its novel B-29s still unproved: LeMay was largely frustrated in his attempt to destroy strategic Japanese industries on a wide scale. But in January 1945 he went to the newly conquered Mariana Islands and assumed command of the consolidated strategic forces of the XXI Bomber Command, a force far different from the B-29 squadrons he had commanded the year before in Asia. The new bases on Guam, Tinian, and Saipan were easily supplied by the navy, relatively safe from enemy attack, completely autonomous, and not surrounded by hostile native populations, while the B-29s themselves were gradually being freed from engineering flaws and early mechanical problems. Both crews and planes were arriving in increasing levels, and fighter squadrons of P-47s and P-51s were being assembled to escort the planes over Japan. In addition, the capture of Iwo Jima in February created a safe base for damaged B-29s on their return trip from Tokyo. Finally, LeMay's predecessor, Brigadier General Haywood S. Hansell Jr., had devised the foundation—infrastructure, command organization, tactical approach—of an effective bombing command during his three-month tenure. Unfortunately for Hansell, the inclement weather over Japan—the jet stream and thunderclouds that tossed planes wildly in random directions—and the enormous distances involved for the new planes and crews had meant a failure to achieve the dramatic results increasingly demanded by Washington from the corps's orthodox reliance on high-altitude, precision bombing.

It was here, with a radical change in tactics, that LeMay gained fame as he methodically engineered the destruction of most of the urban areas of Japan.

For six weeks after he arrived on Guam, however, LeMay did little to change his predecessor's tactical and strategic practices. The huge bombers, after all, had been created to fly well above Japanese fighters at 30,000 to 35,000 feet. From there, equipped with radar and protected by twelve .50-caliber guns whose turrets could be synchronized, the bombers' well-trained eleven-man crews could supposedly attack industrial targets accurately and with impunity.

In reality, that was rarely true. The bombers' unreliable engines overheated during the strenuous effort to reach high altitudes while overloaded with enormous bomb loads of 20,000 pounds. Mechanical difficulties and adverse weather reduced the number of bombers that could reach the target. Often less than 5 percent of the bombs dropped on Japan were landing within 1,000 feet of the designated target. Further, until Iwo Jima was captured, bombers were crashing into the ocean in increasing numbers on their long way back to the Marianas.

LeMay knew that if aircraft losses continued to rise and Japan's infrastructure remained largely viable, he, too, would be relieved of command. But he also was aware of some preliminary and successful trials with low-level incendiary attacks at night. The E. I. du Pont company had produced a new substance known as napalm that ignited and engulfed with flame anything it came in contact with. And in December 1944, B-29s had burned out more than 40 percent of the Japanese supply facility at Hankow, China. The challenge, then, for LeMay was to expand on that early, promising, and harrowing evidence—in the process, refuting the entire tradition of precision bombing, dismissing much of his own experience gained in the daylight air war over Germany, contradicting the previous training of his own bomber crews, ignoring the original design intent of the B-29 itself, and committing a democratic United States to a policy that would guarantee the incineration of thousands of noncombatants.

By early March, LeMay had finalized his plan for low-level, nighttime firebombing; planes would fly in low, below 10,000 feet—sometimes, if need be, down to 5,000, even if "flesh and blood can't stand it." At that level a number of advantages immediately accrued. The B-29s could fly singly beneath the cloud cover and not be subject to the jet stream. Strain on the engines would be minimized, as planes would not have to labor to reach 30,000 feet and fly in tight formation. Reduced fuel consumption meant no auxiliary gas tanks, permitting increased bomb loads. Japanese antiaircraft battalions were accustomed to high-level attacks, so there were few forty- and twenty-millimeter rapid-firing smaller batteries that were so effective below 10,000 feet. Although the Japanese could send up formidable fighters during day raids, they possessed few planes that were effective at night. And by flying over Japan under the cover of darkness, the returning bombers would be in the vicinity of Iwo Jima in daylight, easing the challenge of forced landings and ditchings.

LeMay also ordered most guns and ammunition removed, to save weight and reduce accidental firing on friendly planes in the night. He felt that initial losses to enemy fighters would be more than offset by the destruction of factories and refineries, which would ensure an end to most fighter and flak resistance in the near future. And so, for the inaugural fire raids, the bombers essentially flew in unarmed—until crew morale and increasing fighter resistance mandated a return to defensive capability. Still, by war's end, LeMay's missions were becoming progressively safer for his crews. By July 1945, the loss per mission was 0.03 percent, and LeMay could boast that the final incendiary raids over Japan had become the safest air assignment of the war.

Most important, LeMay realized that the Japanese cities were far more densely populated than European urban centers and largely built of wood. And because industrial production was often decentralized in smaller, family-run factories, the idea of simply torching the entire urban core not only was practicable, but also made strategic sense. Even if thousands of civilians were killed in the processor—"I suppose if I had lost the war, I would have been tried as a war criminal," LeMay said later—the general felt his plan would shorten the war and avert an American invasion of Japan, thus saving lives on both sides in the end. Besides, he reasoned, Japan had started the war and had a proven record of atrocity, including routinely torturing and beheading downed American fliers—of the roughly 5,000 B-29 crewmen of the Twentieth Air Force shot down during the war, little more than 200 were found alive in Japanese camps after the war.

The decision to go in low was entirely LeMay's. In a preview of LeMay's later operational style, he did not notify his immediate superior, General Henry "Hap" Arnold, of his radical redeployment of the B-29s. He reasoned, "If it's all a failure, and I don't produce any results, then he can fire me." He also ignored the fierce opposition of subordinates, some of whom called it suicidal.

On March 9, 1945, a trail of 334 B-29s, 400 miles long, left the Marianas. Preliminary pathfinders had seeded napalm over Tokyo in the shape of an enormous fiery X to mark the locus of the target. Planes flew over in small groups of three, a minute apart, most at not much over 5,000 feet. Five-hundred-pound incendiary clusters fell every 50 feet. Within thirty minutes, a twenty-eight-mile-per-hour ground wind sent the flames roaring out of control, as temperatures approached 1,800 degrees. The fire lasted four days.

No single air attack in the history of conflict had been so devastating. We will never know the exact number of people incinerated; officially, 83,793 Japanese died outright and 40,918 were injured. Nearly sixteen square miles were obliterated, 267,171 buildings destroyed, and 1 million Japanese left homeless; one-fifth of Tokyo's industrial sector and nearly two-thirds of its commercial center no longer existed.

The planes returned with their undercarriages seared and the smell of human flesh among the crews. Yet only fourteen bombers were lost and forty-two damaged. And the March 9 raid was only the beginning of LeMay's incendiary campaign. Suddenly all of Japan lay defenseless before LeMay's unforeseen plan of attack. Quickly he increased the frequency of missions, at one point sending his airmen out at the unheard-of rate of 120 hours per month each—the Eighth Air Force in England had flown a maximum of 30 hours per month—as they methodically burned down Tokyo, Nagoya, Kobe, and Osaka within ten days before turning to smaller cities. LeMay's supply of incendiaries posed the only real obstacle to his plan of attack: his ground crews now simply unloaded the bombs at the dock and drove them right over to the bombers, without storing them in arms depots.

In between fire raids, his B-29s dropped high explosives on industrial targets and aerial mines into harbors and ports, which eventually helped to shut down nearly all the maritime commerce of Japan. By war's end, LeMay's forces had wiped out 175 square miles of Japan's urban area in sixty-six cities. A million Japanese had died, over 10 million were left homeless, and the country ceased to exist as a modern industrial nation. Although it is often stated that the two atomic bombs prompted the Japanese to sue for peace, their own leadership cited LeMay's far more lethal fire attacks as the real incentive. As Prince Fumimaro Konoe put it, "The determination to make peace was the prolonged bombing by the B-29s." LeMay, who strongly supported dropping the atomic bombs, concluded, "The war would have been over in time without dropping the atomic bombs, but every day it went on we were suffering casualties, the Japanese were suffering casualties, and the war bill was going up."

By August 1945, LeMay had destroyed urban Japan; yet he had *more* planes and men under his command than ever. By November, he would have had 2,500 operational B-29s, with 5,000 more on order. Together with the 3,692 B-17s that were to be based on Okinawa as part of the redeployed Eighth

Army Air Force, and the 4,986 B-24s that were already in the process of being transferred from Europe, the Americans were planning the systematic destruction of Japanese society through the weekly use of over 12,000 bombers.
With the additional transference of Britain's Royal Air Force, including four-
engine Lancaster VII heavy bombers, more than 15,000 heavy aircraft would
soon have been operational. A force of that magnitude conceivably might have
dropped over 500,000 tons of bombs each month, far above the 34,402
monthly average dropped by B-29s on Japan between May 1 and August 15,
1945. Surely, dropping the two atomic bombs was, in fact, the correct decision—not so much because it circumvented an American invasion of Japan,
but because it abruptly ended LeMay's bomber crusade, which would have
eventually slaughtered millions of Japanese—a campaign he himself had
warned the recalcitrant Japanese about through preliminary leaflet droppings.
Had LeMay been given another year of bombing, the American assault would
have found Japan a vast crematorium.

✦

LeMay's subsequent career in the 1950s and 1960s is essentially the
history of America's venture into the potential for nuclear-equipped strategic
bombing and the general use of tactical air power in the hot spots of the Cold
War. A string of commands and crises followed his victories in the Pacific. From
1945 to 1947, he headed the U.S. Army Air Forces research-and-development
program and facilitated the transition to jet bombers and in-flight refueling.
In 1947 he took command of all American air forces in Europe and directed
the Berlin Airlift. (At one point, the highest-ranking U.S. Air Force commander in Europe flew in a load of coal himself. He explained, "In those early
days I had to make several runs to see how things were going.") When American strategic forces were considered inadequate to meet a potential Soviet response, LeMay was sent back to Washington in late 1948 to reorganize the
Strategic Air Command (SAC). Shocked by the poorly trained crews and absence of regulation, he concluded of his forces' first practice mission under his
command, "Just about the darkest night in American military aviation history. Not one airplane finished that mission as briefed. *Not one.*"

Quickly he brought in his trusted generals from the Pacific bombing campaign over Japan, and by the outbreak of the Korean War in 1950, the United
States had developed a formidable striking force under LeMay's command.
Accident rates plummeted from sixty-five per 100,000 hours flown to a mere
three. LeMay's forces dropped nearly as many bombs on Korea as on Japan. It
is too often forgotten that thousands of North Korean civilians were killed directly or indirectly as a result of these missions; in three months during the

first summer of the war, *all* assigned targets in North Korea were considered eliminated, the B-29 campaign was therefore called off as essentially completed, and the bombers were used only haphazardly thereafter against strategic sites. "We killed off—what—20 percent of the population," LeMay wrote of all bombing between 1950 and 1953, arguing that strategic bombing over China and restricted portions of North Korea would have made that carpet attack on civilians unnecessary. But after the winter of 1950–51, with the entry of China, the American restriction on targets near the Chinese border, and the appearance of Soviet MiG-15 jets, the B-29 strategic campaign over Korea became marginal: their targets were now off-limits and the planes too vulnerable. The protocols of unlimited bombing against the enemy, which had brought America success in World War II, no longer applied in a world of nuclear weapons. LeMay's worst postwar nightmare had materialized: America's strategic assets were either prevented from actively engaging the enemy or given the unheroic, dangerous, unpopular, and inevitably inconclusive role of tactical bombing of ground troops. LeMay realized that 169,676 tons dropped on Japan in 1944 and 1945 had destroyed the enemy's ability to resist; 167,000 tons dropped on North Korea between 1950 and 1953 had not. Worse still, when bombers were used wrongly, it discredited the entire doctrine of victory through strategic air power.

LeMay, forever the absolutist, believed in unchanging rules of military doctrine and felt that new geopolitical conditions did not alter the need to destroy utterly the enemy's infrastructure from the air, whatever the threat of Soviet intervention. The Pentagon's stricture on strategic bombing of North Korea and China ensured that LeMay's bombers, unlike their use against Japan, would not be able to resume their proper mission and thus win the war outright. LeMay later wrote:

> That wasn't what the B-29s were trained for, nor was it how they were intended to perform. The B-29s were trained to go up there to Manchuria and destroy the enemy's potential to wage war. They were trained to bomb Peking and Hankow if necessary. They could have done so. The threat of this impending bombardment would, I am confident, have kept the Communist Chinese from revitalizing and protracting the Korean War.

Although LeMay was never allowed "to turn SAC loose with incendiaries" over the major industrial arm of China and Korea, he continued to expand the Strategic Air Command during the increased tensions of the Cold War. When he arrived, the air force did not even have systematic reconnaissance, much less a list of strategic targets in the Soviet Union and China. LeMay soon acquired huge fleets of B-47, B-58, and B-52 jets, and in these early days of air superiority he developed a disturbing pattern of sending his planes over the territory of the Soviet Union to gain firsthand knowledge of both their air defenses and their strategic assets. By 1957, when he left SAC to become vice chief of staff of the U.S. Air Force, he had created an enormous organization that was capable of reaching every industrial center in the Soviet Union. In all, 224,014 people and 2,711 aircraft had been under his direct control at SAC, and he was eyeing command of the navy's intercontinental-missile program. (He supposedly had a model of a Polaris submarine *with an SAC insignia* displayed in his command hallway.) "There are only two things in the world," LeMay purportedly boasted at the time, "SAC bases and SAC targets."

While LeMay has often been condemned as trigger-happy and bellicose during his tenure at SAC, the command was perhaps a paradoxical one to begin with. LeMay—who inaugurated the command's motto, "Peace Is Our Profession"—was ordered to create a strategic air force of nuclear bombers formidable enough to deter Soviet aggression; yet, should he ever use one of his nuclear bombers in an actual attack, his entire command would be considered a failure, and its leader little more than a butcher who had sent millions to a nuclear crematorium. LeMay saw the paradox, quite unabashedly referring to his bombing command as enforcing a Pax Americana through a "Pax Atomica." To entrust to the most aggressive and successful bomber commander in our nation's history the task of creating an offensive bomber force that should never be used was fraught with irony from the beginning, and but a glimpse of LeMay's growing dilemma to come.

Between 1957 and 1965 he was vice chief and then chief of staff of the U.S. Air Force, overseeing the creation of America's nuclear ballistic-missile force and the modernization of its manned-bomber fleet. At this point, according to most critics, LeMay's previous energy and eccentric bellicosity for the first time posed grave risks for the nation and the world at large. While acknowledging the general's record in deterring Soviet air power in crises involving Berlin, China, and the Middle East, they have pointed out that such aggressiveness was precisely the wrong temperament for someone who was now to oversee America's nuclear arsenal. There is much in the LeMay record to bear this criticism out. "We must RACE!" he wrote in advocating enormous increases in nuclear weaponry and advances in new bomber technology, oblivious that "the arms race" was becoming a catchphrase for the danger and expense of a seemingly endless, pointless strategic competition with the Soviets. Throughout the Kennedy and Johnson administrations, as air force chief of staff, LeMay battled repeatedly over the restrictions placed on his command during the Cuban Missile Crisis and the war in Vietnam:

> Always I felt that a more forceful policy would have been the correct one for us to embrace with the Russians, and in our confrontation of their program for world Communism. In the days of the Berlin Air Lift I felt the same way. . . . I can't get over the notion that when you stand up and act like a man, you win respect . . . though perhaps it is only a fearful respect which leads eventually to compliance with your wishes. It's when you fall back, shaking with apprehension, that you're apt to get into trouble. We observed Soviet reaction during the Lebanon incident and during the Cuban incident. Each time when we faced the Russians sternly we've come out all right. It's only when we haven't stood up to these challenges that things went sour.

During the tense days of October 1962, LeMay repeatedly demanded offensive action ("city-busting") against the Soviet Union itself. "If there is to be war, there's no better time than the present and 'the bear' is not." Of Cuba itself ("a sideshow"), he remarked simply, "Fry it." Throughout the Cuban Missile Crisis, he specifically urged a comprehensive plan of open reconnaissance flights over Cuba, guarded armed fighter escorts; around-the-clock readiness of SAC nuclear bombers targeted at the Soviet Union; and the eventual use of nuclear weapons against Cuba itself. To LeMay, the thought of a small Caribbean state only ninety miles off the coast of Florida threatening the security of the United States, when the latter possessed overwhelming military superiority over both Cuba and its patron, was both unthinkable and dangerous for the future. As American officials hesitated, LeMay worried that even a blockade of Soviet armaments to Cuba was an admission of weakness, especially if monitored by United Nations inspectors. Far better, he urged, would be to send the fleet to Havana, circle the skies overhead with SAC bombers, and then order Fidel Castro to allow U.S. military officers to inspect the Soviet-installed nuclear-missile sites. LeMay shocked Attorney General Robert Kennedy, who wanted to know the capability of SAC bombers in a possible conventional strike against Cuban installations; when the president's brother asked how many of LeMay's planes carried nuclear weapons, the general said, "All of them." In disbelief, Kennedy asked, "How many of them could carry conventional weapons?" LeMay answered, "None of them."

To LeMay, incrementalism encouraged provocation, and only the ability and clear intent to face off the Soviets would ensure a cessation of their presence near the Americas. Of the peaceful final resolution to the Cuban crisis,

LeMay scoffed that it was "the greatest defeat in our history." He thought the secret trade-off of American Jupiter missiles in Turkey for Soviet weapons in Cuba, and the clear impression that the United States would not, when pushed, use its strategic assets against a Soviet Union inferior in nuclear power, meant that the Soviets would be free to continue to aid Cuba and meddle in Latin America. In short, he felt the United States had now gained the international reputation of an enormously powerful state that could not or would not act. Central to LeMay's brinkmanship was the belief that the Soviet Union either would not attack American interests or would be annihilated before its bomber fleet could reach the United States and its allies. LeMay was mostly correct on both counts: the Soviets probably would have backed off, and had they not, he probably could have caught their bombers and missiles on the ground. But "mostly" and "probably" were not guarantee enough in a new world in which a single surviving warhead might mean the loss of hundreds of thousands of Americans. Whatever LeMay's astute reading of human nature and his confidence in his superb bombers, he could not ensure the absolute safety of the American citizenry in the ensuing inferno—and it is not clear that he always understood this.

What, then, are we to make of this strange Curtis E. LeMay, this trigger-happy Buck Turgidson in the flesh? We can begin by realizing that LeMay's military success and public-relations catastrophes both evolved from a frank, often brutal, but ultimately realistic assessment of human and hence national behavior. LeMay's bleak summation of human character was entirely Thucydidean, nearly echoing the historian's famous dialogue between the Athenians and their doomed foes on the island of Melos in 415 B.C., in which he lays out the bleak, timeless realities anytime the strong confront the weak. LeMay wrote:

> In all candor the strong and the rich are seldom popular. They are sometimes feared and sometimes resented. But they are usually respected. Anyone who seeks an absolute end to the possibility of war might as well resign from the human race. Pacifists with their perennial utopian quests can harm the human race as much as conquerors. . . . There can be no doubt that the believed strength of an enemy's defenses and his counterattack capability have always been a deterrent to war. Unless we start to win the wars we get into, we may find ourselves overextended around the world on several frontiers, fighting equivocal wars. To maintain such vast military forces America would become an armed camp with all our sons being drafted for these endless foreign wars. God forbid!

For all his hyperbole and failure to grasp the dilemma of nuclear warfare, in which America demanded absolute, rather than near, invulnerability, LeMay's assessment of Soviet intentions and the need to achieve overwhelming strategic superiority seems, after the collapse of the Cold War, more rather than less correct. His distrust of the numbers crunchers in Robert McNamara's Pentagon ("so-called thinkers") was often based on the premise that it was amoral for bureaucrats to send Americans into a war they could not win—and that those and their associates who did so had not tasted fire themselves. Given McNamara's own recent confessional, LeMay's program for ending the war may have even been the more humane one, political issues aside, in the sense that an early and comprehensive campaign against all strategic targets in Hanoi and Haiphong would have saved more lives on both sides in the long run. LeMay's idea that guerrilla fighters and irregular armies could not be stopped with piecemeal use of American ground troops, but only through massive air attack on their ultimate sources of supply, seems in hindsight more logical than lunatic. LeMay, remember, thought entirely in a military sense: air power could be successful only when the enemy's entire infrastructure was strategically targeted. If politicians worried about subsequent escalation of hostilities, LeMay would again counter that any overwhelming military deterrence precluded enemy options and hence made all-out war less rather than more likely. Current American defense doctrine of the need for overwhelming force in cases of intervention is beginning to appear more rather than less in line with LeMay's earlier advice.

Nor does LeMay's innate skepticism about idealistic but inexperienced technocrats without battle experience seem shallow. For example, he worried about the young Harold Brown—who in 1980, as secretary of defense in the Carter administration, was to oversee the flawed and undermanned raid into Iran to try to free the American hostages in Tehran. In 1968, LeMay concluded that Brown was naïve and utopian, and could be dangerous in his misguided view of the nature of war. In anger, LeMay correctly ridiculed Brown's dictum that the air force was to use "the minimum force available to attain those ends. We are trying to minimize our own casualties, the casualties of our allies. We are even trying to minimize the casualties of our adversaries." In LeMay's eyes, minimizing "the casualties of our adversaries" inevitably meant prolonging war—and increasing our losses in the process.

While it is easy to quote the garrulous LeMay to his detriment and to find examples in which he may have exceeded authority, his subservience to civilian control was never really in doubt. Much of his rhetoric now seems to have been intended for in-house bickering over budgetary appropriations, designed to advance the extreme position in hopes that the eventual compromise might satisfy his insatiable need for more bombers. Moreover, his public lectures and writings echo a common theme: decisive, massive use of force—especially air power—can shorten, even circumvent war, and thus save more lives than it costs. Despite the limitations put on targets inside Iraq, the recent devastating American air campaign in the Persian Gulf War would seem to bear LeMay out; we can only imagine what he would say of our recent reluctance to use air power in Bosnia, of our implicit policy of allowing thousands to be butchered there so that a few professional airmen might not be lost, of a militarily inferior state issuing threats to the armed forces of the United States. His dismissal of the U.N. and Red Cross monitors in their proposed verification roles in the Cuban Missile Crisis ("Jesus Christ, what in the hell do a bunch of gray ladies know about missiles?") seems warranted from what we have seen in the dilatory ongoing audit of the Iraqi chemical and biological weapons of mass destruction. LeMay had no faith in the United Nations as a preventive force, and he urged the United States to act alone or with its NATO allies according to its own interests and military capability.

If, like Sophocles's Ajax, who finds his heroic code outmoded and unappreciated in a more complex and nuanced world, we find the LeMays of our country at times dangerous, surely uncouth, and always embarrassing, we must realize that theirs is the baggage that often comes with unsurpassed courage and a willingness to step forward to take on the burden of defense in war's darkest hours. Men of that temperament organize massive armadas, create air forces *ex nihilo,* and so cannot and should not be caged within established bureaucracies where the necessary business is maintenance, not construction; peace, not war; conciliation, not assault. In peace, of course, we wish men of education, prudence, and manners guiding our military. But in times of war, as we have learned from both the fire raids over Japan and the standoff with the Soviets, we have often been served far better by the improbable emergence of warriors like Curtis E. LeMay, who somehow can find, organize, and lead men into the inferno. In the darkest hours of the Cuban Missile Crisis, President Kennedy acknowledged this: "It's good to have men like Curt LeMay and Arleigh Burke commanding troops when you decide to go in. But these men aren't the only ones you should listen to when you decide whether to go in or not." By his careful use of "only," Kennedy acknowledged the value even of LeMay's blunt and often extreme advice.

Like Grant and Patton, the LeMays alone in a democracy can do what Lincoln called "the terrible arithmetic," and so understand that the American way of war is to quickly throw vast amounts of men and matériel into the fire in order to end, not prolong, the killing. They know battle for what it is, and so have no illusions that even a democracy must sometimes go to war whole-heartedly and therefore kill—thousands of the enemy if need be—to survive. Their legacy is that while being branded bellicose, they have saved more lives than they have taken. Their tragedy is that their brutal success in war produces a peace uneasy with their very continued presence, and that their continued ardor asks us to make sacrifices we cannot and should not make. Just as they have come out of nowhere, so too, when their foul business is done, it is better for us all that they disappear into the dark recesses that they inhabit. LeMay himself seemed to concede this: "I had blood upon my hands as I did this, but not because I preferred to bathe in blood. It was because I was part of a primitive world where men still had to kill in order to avoid being killed, or in order to avoid having their loved Nation stricken and emasculated."

Again, embattled and caricatured in his later years, LeMay understood his own Sophoclean dilemma. Many of his reckless pronouncements, as chilling as they sound today, were more likely the final proud bluster of an epic figure on stage who would rather perish in his absolute code of good and evil than change to meet the necessities of a far more nuanced and complex world for which he was so poorly suited both in comportment and speech. That he was not secretary of defense during the Cold War was wise; that he was even chief of staff of the U.S. Air Force with nuclear weapons under his command was cause for legitimate concern; that he commanded our bombers against Japan was a stroke of fortune for us all. And so now I tend to agree with my father that he had survived the war largely because of the daring and genius of the loudmouthed, cigar-chewing General Curtis E. LeMay.

PREVIEWS OF HELL

EDWARD J. DREA

One of the few mercies of the late century is that the invasion of Japan never happened.

The first stage, designated Olympic, was scheduled to hit beaches on Kyushu, the southernmost of the Home Islands, on November 1, 1945. With 400,000 men landing, it would have been a bigger operation than the Normandy D day. According to estimates made in June, when President Harry S. Truman gave the final go-ahead, the number of troops opposing those landings would be under 300,000, a forecast that was favorable to success. Then something happened that no one had predicted—and this is the frightening story that Edward J. Drea has to tell. As he writes, "Intelligence obtained mainly from reading Japanese military and naval codes uncovered a Japanese buildup on Kyushu of mindboggling proportions." Their high command recognized that Kyushu was the island most likely to be struck first and targeted the very beaches where the Americans intended to come ashore. Divisions poured into Kyushu. By August 6, the day the *Enola Gay* dropped the atomic bomb on Hiroshima, intelligence identified 600,000 troops in place, more than twice the original, and quite acceptable, estimates on which the invasion plans had been predicated. But that was just a part of it. New Japanese doctrine called for the fighting to begin, Tarawa-like, at the water's edge. Secret airfields for suicide planes were built and manned flying bombs and human torpedoes stockpiled. Caves were readied for the kind of mutual defense that had proved so devastating at Okinawa. Women drilled with sharpened spears. Kyushu was turning into nothing less than a kamikaze island.

"To a professional soldier," Drea writes, "the combination of suicide tactics and enemy troops stacked on the landing beaches—all directed at the overall Japanese objective of inflicting as many Allied casualties as possible—was indeed a preview of hell." The remedies suggested became increasingly desperate, including poison gas and the use of atomic bombs as beach-clearing tactical weapons. The decision to drop the two atomic bombs, the second of which fell on a Kyushu city, Nagasaki, has to be seen against this darkening background. Would Japan have surrendered that summer if we had refrained from that decision? The chances are against it.

Edward J. Drea is the former chief of the Research and Analysis Division at the U.S. Army Center of Military History in Washington, D.C., and the author of *MacArthur's ULTRA: Codebreaking and the War against Japan, 1942–1945* and *In the Service of the Emperor: Essays on the Imperial Japanese Army.*

OLYMPIC WAS A FITTING CODE NAME FOR THE AMERICAN INVAsion of the "land of the gods." A massive amphibious assault by nine divisions (six had stormed the Normandy beaches in 1944, plus three airborne divisions dropping farther inland) would seize three widely separate landing areas on Kyushu, southernmost of the main Japanese islands and a necessary advanced air and staging base for the later planned invasion of the Tokyo plain. A tenth division would assault offshore islands. More than 400,000 troops were slated for the assault forces, and by spring 1945 preparations for the invasion were under way. At the same time, the Japanese were struggling around the clock to turn Kyushu's beaches into massive killing grounds. The showdown was set for November 1, 1945.

Earlier intelligence forecasts had predicted that the landing forces would encounter ten Japanese divisions at most on Kyushu, and the planners confidently expected American attackers to outnumber Japanese defenders by two or three to one in the southern half of the island. But from early spring to mid-summer 1945, the forecast changed dramatically. Intelligence obtained mainly from reading Japanese military and naval codes uncovered a Japanese buildup on Kyushu of mind-boggling proportions. By August, more than ten Japanese divisions defended southern Kyushu alone. Standard tactics were to include widespread suicide attacks on the invasion fleet by everything from kamikazes to human-guided torpedoes.

Countless messages intercepted from the high command in Tokyo underlined Japanese determination to fight to the death against the invaders. Japanese designs for the defense of Kyushu forecast beachheads running red with American blood. Concern about estimated U.S. losses for the operation loomed large in the minds of the American decision makers. As more and more Japanese troops crowded onto Kyushu, there were even suggestions about switching the landing to another of the Japanese home islands. The intelligence forecasts ultimately led planners to think seriously about the tactical use of atomic bombs to clear Japanese defenders from the landing beaches.

Early in April 1945, the Joint Chiefs of Staff (JCS) instructed General Douglas MacArthur to plan and prepare for the invasion of Japan. The same directive named him commander in chief of U.S. Army forces in the Pacific, in addition to commander in chief of the Southwest Pacific Area. Now he controlled almost all U.S. Army and Air Force units and resources in the Pacific. In late May the JCS set the date for the invasion, code-named Olympic, for November 1.

American assessment of potential Japanese resistance to an invasion began calmly. On April 25, Major General Charles A. Willoughby, MacArthur's intelligence chief, submitted his initial estimate of the enemy defenses on Kyushu, based on intelligence—code-named Ultra—gleaned from reading Japanese military codes. Throughout April, Ultra revealed Japanese anxiety about an imminent invasion of the home islands. Navy messages ordered mining of several Kyushu bays "as soon as possible" and told of the evacuation of civilians from coastal areas, both of which were clearly counterinvasion measures. The Japanese vice chief of staff predicted an American invasion of Kyushu sometime after the middle of the year, and General Yoshijiro Umezu, the army chief of staff, sent out an urgent directive to all army commands to discover the time, place, and scale of the Allied invasion of Japan.

Ultra also identified two combat divisions on Kyushu, the 57th in the north and the 86th in the south. Adding in two other training divisions plus air force, fortress, and support units, the total number of troops on the island was estimated at about 230,000 and was expected to rise. Messages from army harbormasters at Pusan were reporting another 30,000 to 60,000 troops embarking from Korean ports and heading for Kyushu. Willoughby, who was expecting anywhere from six to ten combat divisions to be defending the island, was not alarmed by these reinforcements. Besides, the Japanese, who could not know exactly which beaches the invaders would pick, would have to protect the island's entire coastline, and that meant dispersing their combat divisions equally between northern and southern Kyushu. The Americans would still enjoy overwhelming superiority on the beachheads.

Willoughby predicted that three enemy combat divisions—perhaps

100,000 troops—would be deployed in southern Kyushu by D day, along with about 2,000 or 2,500 Japanese aircraft. Even if half the planes were obsolete or training aircraft, they could still be a serious threat, especially if used in kamikaze fashion. The remnants of the once formidable imperial battle fleet were not considered a significant danger.

In May, Ultra reports continued to indicate a steady but unspectacular buildup on Kyushu. As predicted, the 25th Division had arrived from Manchuria and was settling into central Kyushu. An amphibious brigade had been redeployed from the Kurile Islands to the island's southern end. And an unidentified but important headquarters began broadcasting messages from Takarabe, in southeast Kyushu, to major army command posts throughout Japan. By month's end, three divisions were definitely identified on Kyushu, with between three and five more either present or expected. The Japanese were working feverishly, but the numbers still fell within the forecast—to Willoughby, a tolerable eight or ten divisions.

The mystery of the headquarters at Takarabe was solved in June, when the Fifty-seventh Army was definitely located in southern Kyushu. Shortly afterward, the Fifty-sixth Army was identified in the northern half of the island. Two armies fit Willoughby's original model of Japanese forces on Kyushu divided between northern and southern commands. As of June 7, some 280,000 Japanese soldiers were estimated to be on Kyushu. Coded addresses on intercepted messages, though, suggested the existence of another major headquarters somewhere in southern Kyushu. Radio messages broadcast from the same region soon betrayed the 77th Division's move from northern Japan to Kyushu. It was the fourth division that U.S. intelligence knew to be on the island.

Decryptions of Japanese naval and air force messages suggested a renewal of the mass suicide attacks that had wreaked such havoc off the Philippines and Okinawa. The officer commanding the 12th Naval Flotilla, based on Kyushu, intended to hurl all of his 900 planes as kamikazes against an Allied landing. Naval air depots throughout Japan were converting more than 400 biplane trainers into kamikazes, and staging bases were being readied to repel any invasion. Workers at Sasebo Naval Base in northwestern Kyushu were on double shifts building suicide boats, and the command was deploying kaiten, the naval version of a piloted torpedo, to bases on the southern Kyushu coast. By mid-June the messages were voicing fears of an Allied landing in southern Kyushu. Japan's high command did not know the invasion was still months away, but they knew the Allies were coming. Kyushu's beaches were clearly the most likely landing areas, and the Japanese were doing everything possible to convert them into graveyards for American troops.

Interceptions of Japanese army air force communications showed them concentrating all available aircraft at fields on an arc stretching from Shanghai through Korea to Honshu. From bases inside this arc, the aircraft—even those not on one-way missions—were well within range of Kyushu's beaches. Army construction battalions were working on underground aircraft hangars and concealing dispersal airfields throughout Kyushu. With 1,400 suicide training planes in the homeland augmented by 4,000 other aircraft of varying quality, the prospect loomed of a bitter and protracted air war over the home islands. Allied air attacks would, of course, destroy hundreds of Japanese planes before the scheduled invasion. Even so, MacArthur's current intelligence estimates were forecasting serious damage to invasion shipping from enemy air attacks. Ultra was really telling two stories. One was a straightforward rendition of Tokyo's hurried efforts to transform Kyushu into a mighty bastion. The other was even more frightening: Nowhere in the enemy's mindset could Ultra detect pessimism or defeatism. Japan's military leaders seemed determined to go down fighting and take as many Americans with them as possible.

U.S. Army Chief of Staff George C. Marshall's preview of invasion beaches laced with mines, barbed wire, pillboxes, and thousands of Japanese defenders stiffened by massive numbers of kamikazes indeed troubled him. Before discussing Olympic with the rest of the Joint Chiefs of Staff and President Truman on June 18, he cabled MacArthur, asking for his estimate of American casualties in the invasion. The response shocked Marshall: 105,050 battle casualties in the first ninety days of fighting, plus 12,600 more noncombat losses. In his reply, Marshall implied that he found these numbers unacceptable but added, "President is very much concerned as to the number of casualties we will receive in the Olympic operation." MacArthur hastened to reassure Marshall, scaling back the estimate in a second cable. It had the desired effect. His message, Marshall later wrote, "arrived with 30 minutes to spare and had a determining influence in obtaining formal presidential approval for Olympic." Indeed, at the crucial June 18 meeting with Truman and the JCS, Marshall quoted verbatim an entire section of MacArthur's estimate supporting an invasion.

The invasion was on, but within weeks the changing intelligence picture of Japanese defenses on Kyushu rendered casualties even more of an obsession. Japanese army and navy codebooks captured on Luzon and Okinawa enabled Allied cryptanalysts to read the enemy's most important codes, and the forecast turned increasingly ominous. It became apparent that new Japanese divisions were mobilizing on Kyushu. Every day, enemy radio operators tapped out a steady flow of messages coordinating redeployments, issuing orders, and administering all the other things involved in preparing a new unit for operations.

As far as Marshall knew when he met the president on June 18, all the Japanese reinforcements earmarked for Kyushu were already there. That meant a maximum of eight defending enemy divisions. Ultra had, of course, alerted the chief of staff to the possibility that additional divisions were being raised in Japan. Still, American air and naval attacks, he told Truman, made further reinforcement of Kyushu suicidal. The Japanese would lose so many men and so much equipment that the attempt was just not worth it. But as July wore on, the Ultra reports made a mockery of Marshall's estimate.

The Japanese navy was busy converting 2,000 training biplanes, plus assorted fighters and floatplanes, into kamikaze aircraft. The biplanes were not as ridiculous as they sounded, since American radar did not register their flimsy wood-and-fabric construction. And pilots were practicing for night attacks. Under cover of darkness, determined kamikazes were deadly: Suicide biplanes sank one U.S. destroyer and damaged another in a moonlight attack in late July. Staging bases on Kyushu were being assigned for kamikaze units. Ultra's discoveries included secret airfields and underground storage dumps being built, as well as aircraft camouflaging and dispersal. The airfield construction battalions available weren't enough for all the military construction under way; appeals for thousands more men to fill labor battalions were sent as far away as central China.

One reason for the labor shortage was that so many men had been mobilized into new divisions. During 1945, Japanese strength in the homeland doubled—from 980,000 on January 1 to 1,865,000 on July 10. Early in July two more divisions, the 206th and the 212th, were identified on Kyushu. A week later, the 154th was positively located on the south-central coast. Within a few days Ultra exposed two tank regiments and three independent mixed brigades there. In the second half of July, the 156th Division, overheard broadcasting orders to its subordinate regiments, was added to the latest estimate of 380,000 troops garrisoned on Kyushu. On July 21, the troop estimate ballooned to 455,000. During the final days of July, a ninth confirmed division, the 146th, was pinpointed in southernmost Kyushu, along with three tank brigades. By the end of the month, Japanese strength was estimated at 525,000.

The most important Ultra find was a newly organized Fortieth Army headquarters, in southwestern Kyushu. The Japanese high command no longer regarded northern and southern Kyushu as equally liable to invasion. Two army headquarters in the south meant the Japanese had decided that the invaders would hit the southern beaches. The Allies had counted on Japanese defenders being dispersed throughout Kyushu, and that was no longer true. The Kyushu reinforcements were swarming into the very areas designated for the Olympic landings.

What the high command expected from its soldiers was also chillingly explicit. In early July the general staff completely reversed Japanese defensive doctrine. The instructions from Imperial Headquarters were that air and sea forces had to annihilate the invaders at sea. If the Allies were bold enough to risk a landing on Japan proper, a full-scale counteroffensive would be launched. Fighting at the water's edge was a return to the abandoned defensive doctrine of 1943–44. Ground forces would expose Allied weaknesses at the shoreline, then destroy him on the coast. If the invaders managed to establish a lodgment, mobile troops would counterattack and smash it in repeated attacks. Coastal troops would cover the concentration of mobile units into attack assembly areas. No matter what tactically important points the Allies took, divisions deployed along the coast could not retreat. Continual counterattacks were the order of the day, and Japanese soldiers could not depend on passive defensive tactics. From the high command to the lowest private, everyone must act boldly, aggressively, and decisively. Japanese soldiers were given a Hobson's choice: to die in the pillboxes and foxholes that dotted Kyushu's beaches or to die attacking the invaders.

The number one target on the beaches during an invasion of the sacred homeland was enemy tanks. Armor was the backbone of Allied ground units, and without it they would falter. Japanese units would build antitank defenses in depth from the water's edge inland. Engineers would demolish all coast roads, forcing tanks into rugged terrain where they would be vulnerable to attack by small suicide units. But Tokyo ordered all officers and men, regardless of branch of service, to carry out such suicide attacks.

Navy pilots, too, would join the fighting at the shore. For them, success depended on crashing into Allied attack and landing craft while the transports were still loaded with troops. The floatplane kamikaze pilots, previously identified by Ultra, were known to be practicing shoreline attacks. Their one-way mission was to smash into landing craft headed for shore. Of the 2,700 navy suicide training planes, 775 were already somewhere on Kyushu; naval authorities claimed that air and sea suicides could sink 30 or 40 percent of an invading convoy—more if the invasion came after August, because there would be more ships and thus more targets. Japanese army staff officers were more conservative, but still expected Allied losses of 10 to 20 percent.

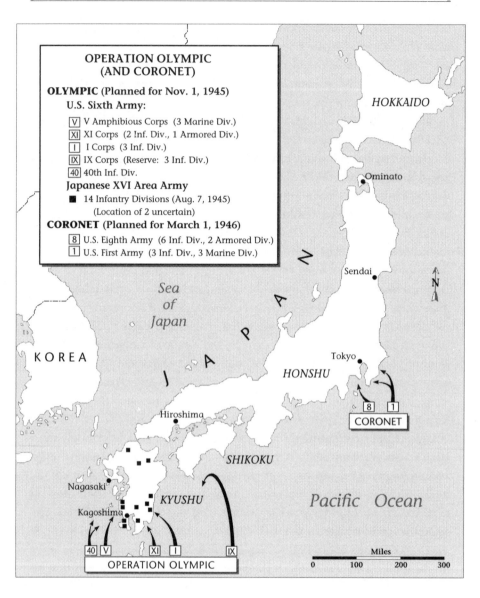

The Allied invasion of Japan would have begun November 1, 1945, with an as-
sault on the beaches of southern Kyushu. Increasingly worrisome were intercepted
reports of more and more Japanese divisions already moving to those very beaches.
Once seized, Kyushu would have been the launching pad for an invasion of the
Tokyo plain in March 1946, if necessary.

The intention behind all this was simply to inflict severe losses on the Allies, a tactic that the Japanese expected would prolong the war and thereby convince the Allies of the futility of further fighting. The stark military objectives paralleled the efforts by leaders—both at court and in the Foreign Ministry—to obtain a negotiated peace for Japan.

Ultra even let the Allies peer over the Japanese commanders' shoulders as they conducted a war game on the defense of the homeland. With an Allied landing in southern Kyushu correctly predicted, Tokyo was forecasting D day for August 20. By D+15 the tabletop maneuvers had ten U.S. divisions ashore, but heavy fighting on the beaches still contained the invaders' lodgment. In this scenario, two American airborne divisions had dropped behind Japanese lines, only to be checked by a fast counterattack. Tokyo concluded that a third of the assault troops could be destroyed at sea and another 15 to 20 percent of the first assault wave by artillery or beach defenses.

From the U.S. point of view, the odds were swinging against them; the defenders would soon equal or outnumber the attackers. This was, as Willoughby candidly put it, "hardly a recipe for success." On August 1, in an effort to counteract the Kyushu buildup, MacArthur's headquarters ordered an immediate air campaign to destroy the island's bridges, railroads, barges, and ports, as well as anything moving on the roads. It came too late even to slow down the movement of troops. Although U.S. submarines were now active in the Sea of Japan, the Japanese divisions redeployed from the Asian mainland had already arrived on Kyushu. Other new divisions were mobilized on Kyushu or arrived from nearby Honshu via the restricted waters of a narrow strait.

During the first week of August, Ultra identified four new divisions on Kyushu, for a total of thirteen confirmed out of the fourteen actually deployed: the 312th, from central Japan, plus the 216th, the 303rd, and a 351st, which was mentioned in messages passed from Imperial Headquarters to the Sixteenth Area Army, in charge of the overall defense of Kyushu. Besides the infantry divisions, the 4th Artillery Command arrived in southwestern Kyushu, complementing the 1st Artillery Command on the southeastern half of the island. These controlled at least six medium-artillery regiments as well as two heavy-artillery battalions. Rocket-gun units assigned to regiments in the newly organized infantry divisions increased their firepower to what seemed a quite formidable degree. By August 6, Washington's estimate of Japanese troops on Kyushu was 560,000.

These numbers were far beyond the original estimates—about 265,000 to 285,000 troops—used to plan the invasion. More troubling than the mere number of divisions was the fact that they were flowing steadily into southern Kyushu and, in particular, toward the beaches selected for the Olympic landings. Following electronic footprints left by routine radio transmissions from mobile headquarters, Allied intelligence experts tracked the Japanese 86th Division from central Kyushu to Ariake Bay at the southeastern end of the island, where the American XI Corps would land. The 146th and 206th divisions had moved to the beaches of the southwest coast where V Amphibious Corps would invade. As a mobile reserve, Japan's 77th Division would have to contend with rugged terrain but might move against either landing area. In any case, it sat perched in the city of Kagoshima, the objective of V Amphibious Corps. And the 212th was preparing to move farther south into the I Corps landing zone. To a professional soldier, the combination of suicide tactics and enemy troops stacked on the landing beaches—all directed at the overall Japanese objective of inflicting as many Allied casualties as possible— was indeed a preview of hell. It was all too easy to visualize the impending carnage along the beachheads. Our assault troops would need every weapon the United States could muster to get them inland with the fewest possible losses. By now those weapons included the atomic bomb.

Sometime earlier, Marshall had asked Major General Leslie Groves, director of America's atomic bomb program, about using the new explosives as tactical weapons. Groves's report on this reached Marshall on July 30. Each bomb (the same size as would be used at Hiroshima), Groves wrote, could wipe out enemy resistance over an area 2,000 feet in diameter, paralyze it over an area a mile in diameter, and seriously hinder it over an area five miles in diameter. Blast effect would kill soldiers in slit trenches within 800 feet of the explosion, but troops sheltering in deep caves a mile or so from ground zero would survive to fight. Eleven or twelve bombs might be ready by the invasion date. In the meantime the bomb would be used as a strategic weapon against Japan's cities. Many thought the evidence of its awesome destructiveness would be enough to force Japan's surrender.

On August 6 the first atomic bomb exploded on Hiroshima, but without the results Marshall hoped for. The weapon did not shock Japan's leaders into surrender. Dispassionate Japanese eyewitness accounts made plain the enormous destruction. One vivid description to the minister of the navy and the supreme naval commander, decrypted through Ultra but available only after the Nagasaki bombing, seems to have affected Truman more than Japan's warlords:

(1) Today 3 B-29s flew over Hiroshima at a high altitude at about 0825 and dropped several bombs—. A terrific explosion accompanied by flame and

smoke occurred at an altitude of 500 to 600 metres. The concussion was beyond imagination and demolished practically every house in the city.

(2) Present estimate of damage.

About 80% of the city was wiped out, destroyed, or burnt. Only a portion of the western section escaped the disaster. Casualties have been estimated at 100,000 persons.

The president secretly ordered that no more bombs be used without his express approval. Marshall now saw Hiroshima against a larger backdrop of strategic bombing. According to a deciphered message, an earlier air raid on Tokyo had killed nearly 100,000 Japanese people in the capital in a single night, but seemingly had had no effect whatever on Japan's determination to fight on. The even worse destruction at Hiroshima also yielded no surrender. Japan seemed determined to fight, and an invasion was still likely. Indeed, Ultra had confirmed three Japanese divisions on Kyushu, for a total of thirteen, the day the Hiroshima bomb was dropped. The Sixteenth Area Army now had 600,000 troops on the island, and more were expected.

Of course, the quality of the Kyushu divisions varied enormously. Some, like the 25th and 57th divisions, were first-class outfits, but many of the newer ones were desperately short of equipment, even uniforms. Training often consisted of drill and slogans, because weapons were lacking. Certainly soldiers in line units knew little about the grand operational plans at Imperial Headquarters. One young lieutenant had the vague notion that three days after the enemy landing his company would be thrown against the beachhead. It would be, their division commander assured them, a most splendid death. A conscript in another newly raised formation saw corruption undermining discipline as soldiers openly traded gasoline for food on the black market. Another example was the arrival of a division commander, to inspect his brand-new unit, in a staff car (a luxury in itself) crammed with fresh meat, poultry, and vegetables. A veteran of the China front who had been recalled wondered aloud if the general had come to inspect the officers' wives. Other recruits, many previously graded the equivalent of 4-F, resorted to black humor, referring to themselves as victim units. But it was one thing to be sullen and insubordinate, quite another to be openly defeatist. No ordinary Japanese soldier had any inkling of Japan's efforts to end the war. Besides, for a front-line soldier or sailor to surrender was a court-martial offense punishable by death.

At any rate, this mixed bag of reinforcements was already digging in along the very beaches where the Americans intended to land. The Japanese would be fighting from prepared positions. They would be fighting for their homes, their families. They had nothing to gain by surrender, everything to lose by defeat. And bitter experience—gained on the road from Guadalcanal to Okinawa—made it plain they could be expected to fight to the death.

Seen—or, more accurately, listened to—from afar, the deficiencies of the new divisions were less glaring. A special War Department analysis of the new Japanese divisions reached Marshall around August 6. From 1937 to 1943, it said, the Japanese army had mobilized an average of eight divisions a year. In 1944, thirty were formed. But in the first seven months of 1945, at least forty-two had been activated, twenty-three in Japan itself. And Japan had the potential manpower to create even more: as many as sixty-five infantry and five armored divisions by the time of the invasion. Equipment, especially artillery, was deficient, but the Japanese use of rocket units made up for their lack of artillery. According to decrypted messages, a single twenty-four-round volley from a rocket gun produced the equivalent in weight of 120 155mm U.S. projectiles. A bored naval watch officer in Hawaii noted in his log with malicious delight that all the "experts" on the Japanese army were quietly burning their estimates on enemy ground strength for late 1945 or early 1946. To Marshall it was no laughing matter. The Japanese army was still expanding, and it would continue to do so right up to the invasion.

The day after the Hiroshima bombing, Marshall sent an "eyes only" message to MacArthur. He admitted he was frankly worried by intelligence reports about the large enemy buildup of ground and air strength on Kyushu and southern Honshu, and he expected it to provoke discussions in Washington, too. Did it make sense to attack into the teeth of the Japanese defenses? Maybe it was better to shift Olympic to less well fortified places on Honshu such as Tokyo, Sendai (on the east coast), or Ominato (at the island's northeast tip). Imagine Marshall cabling Eisenhower three months before D day and asking him to consider switching the Normandy invasion to Norway. In his reply, received two days later, MacArthur dismissed reports of reinforcements as "greatly exaggerated." Besides, he said, Olympic would work because overwhelming logistical difficulties, exacerbated by his air campaign, would isolate and weaken Japanese forces on Kyushu before the invasion had started.

MacArthur's determination to lead the greatest amphibious operation in history—which would have been reduced in scope for an invasion of the more distant beaches on Honshu—blinded him to Ultra's disclosure of the growing risks of invasion. Indeed, throughout the war MacArthur had paid scant attention to any intelligence forecast that suggested the wisdom of caution or delay. He once remarked that there were only three great intelligence officers in the history of warfare—"and mine is not one of them." Up to now, talent, generalship, and good luck had allowed him to treat intelligence in this cavalier fashion.

Even after Hiroshima, the Soviet declaration of war on Japan (August 8), and the second bomb, on the Kyushu port city of Nagasaki (August 9), the Japanese were still proposing only a conditional surrender (August 10). A rapid series of shock actions—each considered by many to be capable of forcing immediate capitulation by itself—had failed to produce unconditional surrender. Grave doubts had replaced the certainties of only a week earlier. Thirteen divisions, not the anticipated maximum of ten, now protected Kyushu. More were thought to be en route to the island fortress. The Imperial Army was mobilizing new divisions at a record pace. What other surprises could the Japanese be saving for the Americans? None, as it turned out, but we didn't know that then.

As far as Marshall (or anyone else) knew, it would still take an invasion to subdue Japan. MacArthur told him that postponing the invasion, or altering its conduct, was unacceptable. Ultra told him that the Japanese defenders were still massing on the proposed landing beaches. Groves told him the atomic bomb could be used as a tactical weapon. What was needed was a way to avoid the likely slaughter on Japan's beaches. If the bombs could not shock the Japanese government into surrender—and, judging from Ultra reports and Japanese public braggadocio, they could not—then the bombs might at least be used to soften up invasion beaches before the American landings.

On August 10, Marshall instructed Groves that the third atomic bomb, which would be ready by August 16, would not be dropped without the express authority of the president. Truman was appalled at the thought of "wiping out" another "100,000 people" by bombing another city. The next day, Marshall told Groves not to ship more fissionable material to the Pacific. Then the head of army intelligence told Marshall not to expect a decisive effect from the atomic bombs in the next thirty days. When three days passed with no sign of an unconditional surrender, Marshall again considered the bomb's possibilities as a tactical weapon. On August 13, Lieutenant General John E. Hull, assistant chief of staff for operations and plans, told Groves's aide, Colonel L. E. Seeman, about Marshall's idea for using atomic bombs in direct support of operations.

Seeman said that they might have seven atomic bombs by the Olympic invasion date, and he confirmed that the blast effect of the bombs would clear the beaches while U.S. soldiers and marines stayed about six miles offshore. The invaders would land two or three days later. Hull doubted that another atomic attack against a city would convince the Japanese to surrender. For Marshall, the tactical use of atomic bombs to support the Kyushu invasion now seemed a realistic alternative to the continued pounding of Japanese cities.

Japan's apparent unwillingness to surrender unconditionally did shape Marshall's thinking. But the driving force behind his emerging plan to use atomic bombs on Japan's beaches was the sneak preview, courtesy of military intelligence in general and Ultra in particular, of thousands and thousands of Japanese infantrymen awaiting American GIs and marines on the landing beaches. "We had to visualize very heavy casualties," Marshall said later, "unless we had enough atomic bombs at the time to supplement the troop action, if the bomb proved satisfactory for that purpose." Of course, Japan's surrender on August 15 made such decisions unnecessary. But what if the militarists had insisted on a fight to the bitter end?

An atomic attack on such a scale along Kyushu's shores would have rendered Hiroshima and Nagasaki mere footnotes to history. But unlike the damage done in those cities, on the beaches the atomic inferno would have devastated both sides. Thousands of Japanese troops, not to mention numerous impressed Japanese civilians, would have immediately died on or near the beaches. But for those who survived the blast—including the American GIs and marines who would have landed on radioactive beaches—another hell, that of radiation poisoning, might have been in store. In 1945 no one really grasped the implications of radioactive fallout, and the hellish effects (for veterans of both sides) would undoubtedly have persisted for decades after the explosions themselves. With that scenario for Olympic, the land of the gods would have become the world of the dead.

THE SOVIET
INVASION OF JAPAN

DAVID M. GLANTZ

At the Yalta conference in February 1945, the Western Allies importuned Stalin to invade Manchuria, thus squeezing the Japanese empire from a fresh direction. They did not bargain on the consequences, which would make the Communists major players (and troublemakers) in the Far East. Fresh from the conquest of Germany, battle-hardened Soviet troops bulled across Manchuria in less than two weeks, and swept through what is now North Korea and down the Japanese half of Sakhalin Island. They were posed to gobble up even more, as David M. Glantz tells us. His article on Soviet plans to invade Hokkaido, the northernmost of the Japanese home islands, should come as a revelation. That invasion, a cobbled-together affair to be sure, would have taken place in the last week of August, more than two months before our D day on Kyushu. If the war had gone on for even a week or two longer, the entire East-West geopolitical situation might have changed irrevocably. In retrospect, it now seems clear that when Harry S. Truman warned Stalin to stay away from the Japanese home islands—and the Soviet dictator called off his invasion at the eleventh hour—our accidental president made one of his most important decisions, one that ranks with his decision to drop the Bomb.

Colonel David M. Glantz, U.S. Army (ret.), is editor of the *Journal of Slavic Military Studies* and one of the world's foremost authorities on the Eastern Front in World War II.

ON AUGUST 9, 1945, SOVIET RECONNAISSANCE DETACHMENTS deployed along a front of more than 600 miles crossed the border into Manchuria. Well before dawn, this vanguard of a force of more than 1.5 million men commenced the final Soviet campaign in World War II.

Most aspects of Soviet planning for the Far East campaign are well known and well documented, including the Soviet objectives that came out of Potsdam. Attendees had agreed on a demarcation line for U.S. and Soviet interests along the 38th parallel in Korea and north of Hokkaido, the northernmost of the Japanese home islands. But newly released Soviet documents now clearly indicate that Hokkaido was also among the Soviet targets in late August 1945, more than two months before the Americans' Operation Olympic was scheduled to begin at Kyushu, the southernmost home island. The Hokkaido invasion did not, of course, occur. Why did the Soviets decide—apparently at the last moment—to abort it? And had it occurred what would have been its consequences?

Soviet planning for the Far Eastern campaign began early in 1945. Almost immediately, the Soviets began moving manpower and matériel into the region. Detailed operational planning, which began after May, envisioned the conduct of four distinct operations beginning in mid-August. These included the three-front Manchurian strategic offensive against the Japanese Kwantung Army, the invasion of southern Sakhalin Island, an operation in the Kurile Islands, and, finally, landings on Hokkaido. In early August, however, the Soviets abandoned their original offensive timetable. On August 7 the Soviet High Command (known as the Stavka) apparently prompted by the dropping of the atomic bomb on Hiroshima, ordered the Far Eastern Command to begin operations in Manchuria two days later, even though the forces had not yet completed their regrouping. Operations against southern Sakhalin, the Kuriles, and Hokkaido were to begin on August 11, 18, and 22, respectively.

The Hokkaido invasion, which the Far Eastern Command planned as an amphibious operation, seems to have been an element of the original Soviet Far Eastern campaign plan. In outline, the plan called for initial Soviet seizure and occupation of all territory on the island north of a line extending from the port of Rumoi on the west coast to Kushiro on the east—roughly, the northern half. In the event that Japanese forces put up a stiff resistance, the invaders would subsequently conquer the southern half after reinforcements arrived. The Soviets timed the operation to commence simultaneously with the defeat of Japanese forces on southern Sakhalin and the Soviet occupation of northern Korea.

Like other amphibious operations in the Far East, the Hokkaido operation was to be hastily mounted and carried out. The Soviets presumed that the Japanese will to resist had been seriously weakened by the American use of the atomic bomb and by the spectacular initial success of the Manchurian invasion. According to Soviet intelligence assessments, three Japanese infantry divisions and one infantry brigade—about 50,000 men—were stationed on Hokkaido, in addition to the Fifth Area Army headquarters, which controlled all Japanese forces operating in southern Sakhalin, the Kuriles, and Hokkaido proper. Given the island's large size and mountainous nature, the Soviets were confident that their forces would initially engage elements of only one Japanese infantry division. They planned to land just enough troops to secure a beachhead; reinforcements would then secure the northern half of the island. These limited objectives would satisfy the Soviets' ends: The United States would have to give them a role in subsequent invasion operations and a larger voice in whatever political negotiations ensued.

The Soviet 1st Far Eastern Front's 87th Rifle Corps was assigned to conduct the operation in three stages. During the first stage, a single rifle regiment from the corps' lead division would land at Rumoi, their six assault craft escorted by four destroyers and torpedo cutters in all. Two hours later, six transports escorted by four frigates, four trawlers, and four large craft called hunters would land the remainder of the lead rifle division to secure the Rumoi region. During the second stage, when more shipping became available, a second rifle division would land to expand the initial beachhead into the northern valley of Hokkaido. During the final stage, a third rifle division would follow the assault divisions, cross the island, and then occupy the southernmost islands in the Kurile chain in conjunction with the main Kurile operation unfolding to the north.

At this point, all landing and supporting ships were to be ready at noon on August 19 to execute the mission. Ships would depart the port of Maoka (now called Kholmsk) on southern Sakhalin at 8:00 P.M. on August 21 and would now land initial elements of the force at dawn on the twenty-fourth. How long the operation would last depended on the availability of ship transport and, of course, Japanese resistance. The invasion would be an improvised affair, but that was beside the point.

On August 18, after Soviet forces had finally completed penetration of the forward Japanese fortified zone on Sakhalin, Marshal Aleksandr M. Vasilevsky, supreme high commander in the Far East, requested authorization from the Stavka to proceed with the Hokkaido operation. At the same time, he ordered the 1st Far Eastern Front to prepare to occupy the northern half of Hokkaido and "the southern half of the Kurile Islands to Shimushir Island," starting sometime between August 19 and September 1.

On August 20, having received no reply from the Stavka, Vasilevsky sent another message reviewing the progress of operations and the preparations for the Hokkaido landings. In part it read:

> We are now conducting naval reconnaissance and preparing aviation, artillery, infantry, and transport means. With your approval, the naval operation will begin shortly after the occupation of the southern portion of Sakhalin, on approximately 8.22.45.

A return message from Joseph Stalin late the same day approved continued preparations for the offensive. Early the next morning, Vasilevsky ordered his subordinate forces to accelerate their preparations and be ready to launch the assault, on his personal order, no later than the end of August 23. He also ordered the 87th Rifle Corps, held in reserve, to concentrate at Maoka. Preparations were virtually complete by midday on August 22 when Stalin suddenly instructed Vasilevsky to hold off. Just before 3:00 P.M., Vasilevsky dutifully ordered that the Hokkaido operation begin only "on the special orders of the Stavka."

In all likelihood, even if Stalin had not intervened to halt the operation, it could not have been launched earlier than August 24 or 25. As a report Vasilevsky sent to the Stavka in the late afternoon of August 23 indicated, Soviet operations on Sakhalin had proved more difficult than anticipated. The Japanese fanatically resisted the advance of the Soviet 56th Rifle Corps, and the Soviet 113th Rifle Corps did not seize Maoka until August 20. This delayed the arrival of advanced units of the 87th Rifle Corps until August 22, preventing the corps from fully satisfying Vasilevsky's ambitious timetable for operations against Hokkaido. Nevertheless, the operation could have begun late on August 24 or the following day.

Soviet forces finally crushed resistance on Sakhalin late on August 25. Two days later, Semen P. Ivanov, chief of staff of the Far Eastern Command, sent out an order that, in part, explained why the operation was canceled: "To avoid the creation of conflicts and misunderstandings in relation to the Allies, I categorically forbid the dispatch of any ship or aircraft near Hokkaido."

No doubt diplomatic factors as much as military realities influenced Stalin's fateful decision to abort the invasion. Partial review of fragmentary diplomatic correspondence permits certain judgments to be made about the cancellation. Clearly Stalin considered operations against Hokkaido, where the Japanese Fifth Area Army was headquartered, to have both military and political significance and to be an integral part of operations against southern

Sakhalin. Despite the Potsdam demarcation line that ran north of Hokkaido, Stalin had approved planning for the operation; Potsdam did, after all, permit contingency planning, which Allied commands could later approve.

On August 15, President Harry S. Truman had sent Stalin General Order No. 1, setting forth procedures for Japanese surrender. The next day Stalin proposed that the Soviets receive the surrender of Japanese forces on northern Hokkaido, regarding it as appropriate considering Japanese occupation of the Far East in 1919–21; he also referred to the demands of Soviet public opinion. On August 18, Truman responded with a terse message rejecting any such changes to the Potsdam agreement. Stalin's August 20 message to Vasilevsky to continue offensive preparations probably responded to existing military conditions and the real possibility for further Soviet gains: Despite the Japanese emperor's August 15 surrender declaration, Stalin obviously felt that continued heavy Japanese resistance in many regions justified further Soviet belligerence. Even after August 20, when it became clear that the official surrender would occur no later than September 2 or 3, Japanese forces on southern Sakhalin and in the Kuriles continued to resist, and they would do so until August 29. Until the cancellation of the Hokkaido operation, the Soviets could rationalize it as a means of outflanking the strong resistance in the Kuriles.

In light of this resistance, the Soviet dilemma was whether to ignore Allied wishes concerning Hokkaido. Russian historians have recently claimed that Stalin's motives for aborting the invasion were to prevent further loss of life and to avoid further dispute with the Allies. In reality, it was probably a combination of intense Allied pressure, the impending and by now certain Japanese surrender, and operational difficulties on Sakhalin and with transport. Only full revelation of the diplomatic exchanges between Stalin and Truman and release of all of Stalin's internal private correspondence will answer this question with finality.

What is certain is that the Soviets planned for a Hokkaido invasion, and, up to August 22, they were intent on carrying it out. Moreover, they timed it to occur long before planned Allied landings on the home islands farther south. If successful, it would have given the Soviets an even more advantageous position for subsequent military operations in Japan, had they become necessary, and an even greater role in surrender negotiations. The Soviets would have certainly occupied all of the island and probably, had Japanese resistance continued, participated in an invasion of the main island of Honshu. In light of what subsequently occurred in Korea and China, the implications for future regional and international tension, if not open conflict, were immense. Soviet control of all or part of Hokkaido would have created a situation in the Far East analogous to that which came to exist in postwar central Europe. A two- (or even three-) power—the United States, Soviet Union, and Great Britain—division of Japan would have forestalled postwar Japanese reconstruction, prolonged the military occupation of the country, compounded future difficulties in Korea, and placed Japan at the focal point of a more intense Cold War in northeastern Asia for decades to come.

THE VOICE
OF THE CRANE

THOMAS B. ALLEN AND
NORMAN POLMAR

World War II could not end without a final convulsion, this time an intensely private one that few were aware of and fewer witnessed. Its outcome could have prolonged the struggle indefinitely and brought death to millions.

With a war cabinet hopelessly divided over which direction to follow—to surrender or continue the war—Emperor Hirohito was asked for an imperial command, the so-called voice of the crane. ("According to an old saying," Thomas B. Allen and Norman Polmar write, "the crane, a bird revered in Japanese tradition, can be heard even when he flies unseen.") At a meeting in a palace bomb shelter, Hirohito answered that the moment had come to agree to Allied demands. The hour was 2 A.M. on the morning of August 10, and although that acceptance was passed on to the American, British, and Soviet governments through neutral channels, the matter was not yet ended. Four days passed. A military coup began to take shape. Then, on the morning of August 14, B-29 superfortress bombers appeared over Tokyo and dropped leaflets announcing the surrender offer; the secret of the capitulation, kept from the Japanese people, was out. Hirohito, who had never spoken in public, decided to record his proclamation of surrender on 78-rpm records, which would be broadcast to the nation the following noon. Almost from the moment when he stepped away from the microphone, army diehards set about trying to lay hands on those records and destroy them before the emperor's announcement put the war beyond their reach. Allen and Polmar describe their murderous efforts to silence the voice of the crane and prevent the final curtain from going down.

Thomas B. Allen and *Norman Polmar* collaborated on seven books, among them the Random House encyclopedias *World War II: America at War, 1941–1945,* and *Spy Book: The Encyclopedia of Espionage* as well as *Code-Name Downfall,* from which this article was adapted. Mr. Polmar, a defense analyst, is the author or co-author of more than thirty books, and Mr. Allen, formerly senior book editor of the National Geographic Society, has more than a score of books to his credit.

TOKYO, 11:30 ON THE NIGHT OF THURSDAY, AUGUST 9, 1945. Eleven government officials filed down a narrow stairway into the hot, humid bomb shelter of the emperor of Japan. It was sixty feet below the Imperial Library, a one-story structure standing amid the fountains and gardens of the emperor's palace. The shelter's conference room, eighteen by thirty feet, was poorly ventilated. Its arched ceiling, supported by steel beams, and its dark, wood-paneled walls added to the gloom enveloping the men. They took their seats at two long, cloth-covered tables, five on one side, six on the other. They were awaiting a rare event: a *gozen kaigin*—a meeting "in the imperial presence."

The emperor was the living god who ruled Japan through a mystic connection between him and his worshipful subjects. But half a dozen of the men sitting in the underground chamber had an iron grip on the country. Members of the Supreme Council for the Direction of the War, they were known as the "Big Six": Prime Minister Kantar? Suzuki, a seventy-eight-year-old retired admiral; Foreign Minister Shigenori Tōgō; the minister of war, General Korechika Anami; the minister of the navy, Admiral Mitsumasa Yonai; the army chief of staff, General Yoshijiro Umezu; and the navy chief of staff, Admiral Soemu Toyoda. The other five men were three senior aides, the chief cabinet secretary, and eighty-year-old Baron Kiichiro Hiranuma, president of the Privy Council and a former prime minister. The military's status in Japan's ruling body was apparent in the dress of the officials: Seven of the eleven were in uniform.

At 6 A.M. on July 27, Japan had received by radio the text of the Potsdam proclamation—an "ultimatum," as President Harry S. Truman called it. (Tokyo time was thirteen hours ahead of Washington, so when the text was received, it was 5 P.M. on July 26 in Washington.) The proclamation got its name from the Berlin suburb where Truman had been meeting with Soviet dictator Joseph Stalin and Clement Attlee, who had just replaced Winston

Churchill as British prime minister. It warned that unless Japan's armed forces surrendered unconditionally, Allied military forces were "poised to strike the final blows upon Japan."

Ever since, for an agonizing thirteen days, the Big Six had been debating a response during inconclusive formal meetings, punctuated with furtive huddles by advocates of surrender or diehards urging fanatic resistance. Now, deadlocked, they had brought the matter before the emperor.

✦

THE LONG DAY had started at about ten o'clock that morning, with Suzuki presiding over a meeting of the Big Six in his air-raid shelter near the Imperial Palace. He began the session by reminding his colleagues what was happening to Japan. An atomic bomb had wiped out Hiroshima on August 6. The Soviet Union had just declared war and was beginning to sweep through Japanese-held Manchuria. Warships of Admiral William F. Halsey's Third Fleet were bombarding the east coast of the northernmost home island, Hokkaido, and his carrier planes were smashing airfields north of Tokyo. "I believe," Suzuki said, "that we have no alternative but to accept the Potsdam proclamation."

The prime minister asked for comments from the others. A long silence was finally broken by Admiral Yonai, who said, "We're not going to accomplish anything unless we speak out. Do we accept the enemy ultimatum unconditionally? Do we propose conditions? If so, we had better discuss them here and now." Yonai had briefly served as prime minister in 1940 but had been forced to resign because he opposed alliance with Germany and Italy. Like many senior naval officers, he was more flexible about peace talks in the latter stages of the war.

Foreign Minister Tōgō favored immediate acceptance of the Allied ultimatum. General Anami, Admiral Toyoda, and General Umezu, on the other hand, all wanted to continue the war. They preferred waiting for a U.S. invasion and a "decisive battle" on the beaches. They knew that ultimately they could not win the war. But they believed Japan could inflict a bloody defeat on the United States in a beachhead battle that would drive the invaders into the sea, a Gallipoli-scale disaster that would turn American public opinion against the war and force a negotiated peace. To preserve military honor and the government structure supporting the military, they wanted to demand at the negotiating table the retention of the emperor; disarming of Japanese troops by their own officers; consideration of war crimes only by Japanese courts; and a short, token occupation of Japan.

Around noon, after two hours of debate, the Big Six received word that a second atomic bomb had hit Nagasaki. Toyoda had previously believed that the United States had used its only atomic bomb on Hiroshima; there could be no more, because critical materials were scarce. Toyoda may have based his comments on knowledge of the Japanese navy's atomic-fission program, which B-29s had bombed out of existence during the Tokyo raid of April 13. But now a second atomic bomb had devastated another city.

Still, the news seemed to have little influence on the council debate. It was hopelessly divided. Suzuki called a full cabinet meeting at his official residence at 2:30 P.M. There, Anami again demanded a decisive battle. "That we will inflict severe losses on the enemy when he invades Japan is certain," he said, "and it is by no means impossible that we may be able to reverse the situation in our favor, pulling victory out of defeat. . . . Our men simply will not lay down their arms."

Ominously, Geni Abe, the home minister, recalled the 1936 army mutiny, in which Suzuki, then grand chamberlain to Hirohito, had been shot and severely wounded; it had been put down only after the emperor—making a rare intervention in civil affairs—personally declared it to be an unlawful rebellion. Abe said he could not guarantee civil obedience if Japan surrendered, and he called for continued fighting.

The debate droned on. At 5:30, Suzuki called a one-hour recess, hoping perhaps that antagonists could get together informally and produce a solution in face-to-face talks. But when he reconvened, they were still at an impasse. The talking went on until 10 P.M., when Suzuki made a formal request for a consensus, got none, and adjourned the meeting.

By long tradition, a cabinet decision had to be unanimous; if that was impossible, the cabinet must fall. But in this supreme crisis, Suzuki could not allow that to happen. He and Tōgō went to the palace and asked the emperor to sanction an immediate *gozen kaigin* of the Big Six. Hirohito had been kept apprised of the day's crisis by his principal civilian adviser, Marquis Kōichi Kido, lord keeper of the privy seal. Without hesitation, the emperor agreed to the meeting. Prudently, he suggested the air-raid shelter under the Imperial Library. And so, as that fateful Thursday was ending, the Big Six and the others filed down the damp stairway.

✦

SHORTLY BEFORE MIDNIGHT, Emperor Hirohito entered the cramped underground room, accompanied by an aide. The officials stood and bowed, their eyes turned away from him as he sat in a straight-backed chair before a large gilded screen. The emperor wore his usual field marshal's uniform, ill-fitting because no tailor's hands were permitted to touch his imperial person. His hair tousled, the uniform rumpled, he looked tired but resolute. A sad-eyed man of forty-four, he was more comfortable as an amateur ichthyologist than as the divine ruler of a nation at war with most of the world.

He knew that this was more a rite than a meeting, a *gozen kaigin* on peace or war. What he did not know was that at least one man in the underground room had already decided what he and others would do if ordered to lay down their arms: They would rise in rebellion and then take part in another cere-mony—*seppuku,* or ritualized suicide. That man was the minister of war, Gen-eral Anami.

One by one, the ministers respectfully reiterated their arguments before the emperor. Anami again passionately vowed a glorious defense of the home-land in the Decisive Battle. At 2 A.M. Friday, August 10, after everyone had spoken, Suzuki stood and did something no prime minister had ever done: He requested a decision from the emperor. Suzuki was asking for an imperial command—the Voice of the Crane. According to an old saying, the crane, a bird revered in Japanese tradition, can be heard even when he flies unseen.

Hirohito stood, and all rose and bowed. Continuation of the war, he said, "is unbearable to me. . . . I give my sanction to the proposal to accept the Al-lied proclamation." He then left the room.

Suzuki, hoping to maintain the momentum of this epochal event, called an immediate cabinet meeting back at his official residence to legalize the action of the emperor and draft a response to the Allies. At 7 A.M., the foreign min-istry transmitted to the American, British, and Soviet governments—through Sweden and Switzerland—Japan's acceptance of the Potsdam proclamation, "with the understanding that the said declaration does not compromise any demand which prejudices the prerogatives of His Majesty as a sovereign ruler."

In their reply, sent on August 11, the Allies agreed to preserve the emperor but made him "subject to the Supreme Commander of the Allied Powers." In Washington, London, and Moscow, the war appeared to be nearly over. In Tokyo, however, a new war between military and civil power had begun.

✦

GENERAL ANAMI had heard grumbling among officers soon after the Pots-dam proclamation was received. He had even asked the Kempei-tai, the army's dreaded secret police, to investigate the reports. He remained uncom-mitted to the officers and their talk of rebellion. But his words, carried by Tokyo radio stations and newspapers, rang with defiance:

> We have but one choice: We must fight on until we win the sacred war to
> preserve our national polity. We must fight on, even if we have to chew grass
> and eat earth and live in fields—for in our death there is a chance of our coun-
> try's survival.

Supposedly, Anami had not authorized the statement. But he seems to have
made no move to correct it, for hours after it was broadcast on August 10, it
was published in the morning papers. Accompanying Anami's statement was
one from the cabinet that said the nation was "facing a situation that is as bad
as it can be." It was clear to any reader that the government was in a crisis it
had chosen not to describe.

In the United States, most people believed that peace had come. A *New
York Times* headline on August 12 summed up the mood: "GI's in Pacific Go
Wild with Joy; Let 'Em Keep Emperor, They Say." Lieutenant General Carl
Spaatz, head of U.S. Strategic Air Forces in the Pacific, ordered a halt to urban
bombing by B-29s, fearing it might complicate negotiations—which in turn
led American journalists in the Marianas to assume a cease-fire had gone into
effect. The next day, Truman, believing that any B-29 strikes would suggest
moves toward peace were faltering, halted all strategic bombing.

Although most Americans now believed the way was coming to an end, it
was not officially over. The president spent all of Sunday, August 12, in his office, awaiting Japan's acceptance of the Allied conditions about the emperor's
role. Press and radio reporters besieged the White House, as did crowds gathered across Pennsylvania Avenue in Lafayette Park. By Monday, the wait was
getting on Truman's nerves. Wits were asking, "Do you think Japan's surrender will shorten the war?" With no further moves toward peace by the Japanese
that day, all U.S. air commanders were told to resume bombing operations.

But when the B-29s appeared over Tokyo on the morning of August 14
(Tokyo time), they dropped pieces of paper that said in Japanese, "American
planes are dropping these leaflets . . . because the Japanese government has offered to surrender and every Japanese has a right to know the terms of the offer." The leaflets included the full texts of the Japanese acceptance of surrender
and the American reply. The secret of the capitulation, which the government
had kept from the Japanese public, was out.

An imperial chamberlain picked up a leaflet that fluttered to earth on the
palace grounds and brought it to Marquis Kido. "One look," Kido later said,
"caused me to be stricken with consternation. . . . If the leaflets should fall
into the hands of the troops and enrage them, a military coup d'état would become inevitable."

In fact, a coup was under way, and General Anami knew about it. Anami, a hard-drinking man and a fearless leader in combat, lived by the samurai code. He had probably been happier fighting the Americans in New Guinea than he was sitting behind a desk in Tokyo. An expert archer, he had also attained the fifth degree in kendo, Japanese swordsmanship.

If Anami were to give his support to the plot, much of the Japanese army—an army of millions, scattered across the empire—would almost certainly rise against the cabinet, claiming allegiance to an emperor duped by cowardly civilians. If Anami resigned from the cabinet, it would fall. Without a cabinet, Japan would be ruled in her death throes by a fanatic military, and he would get his wish for the Decisive Battle.

Kido showed the leaflet to the emperor and urged him to hold another *gozen kaigin.* Hirohito agreed, and Suzuki called a cabinet meeting at 10:30 A.M., again in the air-raid shelter. The situation was changing so fast that Kido ruled the usual court attire of frock coat or cutaway unnecessary. Men showed up in whatever they could hastily find to wear.

After listening to virtually the same words he had heard four days before, Hirohito said of the Allied response, "I consider the reply to be acceptable." He was weeping, as were many others in the room. He ended his speech with an imperial order: "I desire the cabinet to prepare as soon as possible an imperial rescript announcing the termination of the war." He would read the rescript—a proclamation of the gravest import—on the radio. For the first time in history, the emperor's subjects would hear the Voice of the Crane. Sobbing men slipped to the floor and knelt as Hirohito left the room.

The cabinet immediately convened to ratify the emperor's wishes (officially and traditionally not a "decision") and draft the rescript. Late that night, the Foreign Ministry asked the Swiss government to relay Japan's statement of surrender to the United States.

During a break in the cabinet session, Anami slipped into an anteroom for a prearranged meeting with Lieutenant Colonel Masahiko Takeshita, his brother-in-law and a leader of the planned coup. Takeshita had with him a blueprint for the plot, a document headed "Employment of Troops—Second Plan." Takeshita had thought he had the support of Anami and Chief of Staff Umezu. Now he asked Anami straight out to give his passive support to the coup by resigning and thus bringing down the cabinet. Anami refused. Takeshita stalked out. Anami's code of honor would not permit him to report Takeshita's mutiny.

In the headquarters of the 1st Imperial Guards Division at the north end of the palace grounds, Major Hidemasa Koga, a staff officer and son-in-law of former prime minister Hideki Tōjō , met with several other officers. He had just asked his wife whether she had preserved the fingernail clippings and lock of hair he had given her earlier when he went off to war. This was the traditional question of a Japanese soldier going into battle.

By late afternoon, far more soldiers than usual patrolled the grounds. Instead of a single battalion of guards there were two; one was led by the regimental commander himself, Colonel Toyojiro Haga.

Prince Fumimaro Konoe, a former prime minister, called on Kido. "I am afraid of what may be happening at the Imperial Guards Division," he said, telling of murmurs of a coup. Kido shrugged off the report, insisting that the rumors were unfounded. He went on with his arrangements for the emperor's speech.

The emperor was not an accomplished speaker, so Kido proposed that Hirohito record his speech rather than give it live. He arranged for a team of radio technicians from the Japan National Broadcasting Corporation (NHK) to bring in equipment for making a record and set up a temporary studio in the Household Ministry building. NHK told its listeners that an important announcement would be made at noon the next day. The source of the announcement was not revealed.

The cabinet, haggling over language for the rescript, kept the recording team waiting in a room near Kido's office. Around 8 P.M., the heavily edited rescript finally reached the copyists, who began transcribing it into classic calligraphy. Changes continued to come in, however, and the copyists, much against their aesthetic principles, had to make corrections on tiny pieces of paper and paste them in. Shamefaced, they presented two smudged and patched rescripts to Suzuki, who took them to the emperor for his signature.

The prime minister's office mimeographed copies of the final text and sent them to the morning newspapers, with orders that the text could not be published until after the noon broadcast by the emperor. At about the same time, Imperial Japanese Army headquarters sent statements to the newspapers that the army would fight on. One editor made up two front pages, one with the surrender story, the other with the army statement, and waited to see which side would win.

At 10 P.M., air-raid alarms in Tokyo warned of the last U.S. bombing of the war. (The surrender message had not yet been sent.) About an hour later, Hirohito, wearing his uniform, left his living quarters in the Imperial Library and was driven a short distance through the gardens of the sprawling, blacked-out Household Ministry. Around him were the ruins of buildings destroyed in March when fires from a B-29 incendiary raid spread to the palace grounds.

In the audience hall on the second floor, the NHK technicians bowed to the emperor. Looking perplexed and uncomfortable, Hirohito stepped before the microphone. "How loudly should I speak?" he asked. Hesitatingly, an engineer respectfully suggested that he speak in an ordinary voice. He began:

> To our good and loyal subjects: After pondering deeply the general trends of the world and the actual conditions obtaining in our empire today, we have decided to effect a settlement of the present situation. . . .

When he finished, the emperor asked, "Was it all right?"

The chief engineer stuttered, "There were no technical errors, but a few words were not entirely clear."

The emperor read the rescript again, his eyes and those of his audience filling with tears. "I am quite willing to make a third," he said. He was told another was not needed. Everyone bowed as he left.

Each reading took two 78-rpm records to complete. In the end, the technicians picked the first recording for the noon broadcast, but they kept all four disks, putting them in metal cases inside khaki bags. Like everyone else in the palace, the technicians had heard the rumors of a coup. Rather than take the chance of carrying the records to the NHK building, they decided to keep them in the palace and spend the night there themselves. A chamberlain placed the records in the safe of a small office used by a member of the empress's retinue, a room normally off-limits to men. Then he piled papers in front of the safe to hide it.

✦

AROUND THIS TIME, Captain Shigetaro Uehara of the army air force and Kenji Hatanaka, a zealous major attached to the Ministry of War, burst into the office of Lieutenant General Takeshi Mori, commander of the 1st Imperial Guards Division. Mori knew about the plot but had not supported it. Hatanaka pulled out a pistol, mortally wounded Mori, then slashed him with a sword. Uehara, wielding his own sword, beheaded another officer who happened to be in Mori's office. Hatanaka affixed Mori's private seal to a false order directing the Imperial Guards to occupy the palace and grounds, sever all communications out of the Imperial Palace except through division headquarters, occupy the NHK building, and prevent all broadcasts. Meanwhile, Major Koga, former prime minister Tōjō's son-in-law, tried in vain to recruit other officers, hoping to involve the Eastern District Army, deployed to defend the Tokyo region, in the plot.

At the palace, soldiers carrying bayonet-tipped rifles and wearing white bands across their chests to distinguish themselves from loyalists, rounded up the radio technicians and several officials, imprisoning them in a barracks. They stormed into palace buildings and began cutting telephone wires with fire hatchets, then disarmed and stripped the palace police and set up machine guns near the library.

Major Koga, hoping to destroy the emperor's recording, ordered a radio technician to find it. The technician, unfamiliar with the palace, led a group of soldiers into the labyrinth. They roamed the buildings, kicking in doors, flinging contents of chests onto the polished floors, and threatening aged chamberlains.

The lord keeper of the privy seal, fearing that the marauders would get their hands on important documents, gathered as many as he could, tore them into scraps, and flushed them down the toilet. Then he and several other palace aides locked themselves in a steel vault where other documents were kept.

Machine-gun fire was heard, but no casualties were reported on the palace grounds. In the library, the emperor, informed of the coup by chamberlains, remained in his quarters with the empress. Heavy iron shutters were closed to protect the royal couple.

A separate plot was unfolding in Yokohama, about twenty-five miles southwest of Tokyo. Captain Takeo Sasaki, commander of the Yokohama Guards, tried to mobilize a battalion and lead it to the capital to kill Prime Minister Suzuki. When his company commanders demanded a higher authority for his order, Sasaki instead rounded up twenty-nine soldiers, five students, and two members of the Yokohama Youth Corps. Armed with swords, rifles, pistols, and two machine guns, the group, calling itself the National Kamikaze Corps, climbed into cars and trucks and headed for Tokyo. When they got there, Sasaki and his men drove to the prime minister's official residence and raked it with machine-gun fire. But Suzuki was not there. Later, they set fire to his private home.

That same night, seven uniformed members of the army's secret police, apparently acting independently, swooped down on Marquis Kido's home. One of his own guards was wounded, but the raiders retreated and were never heard of again.

Elsewhere in Tokyo, soldiers swarmed into the NHK building, rounded up sixty employees, locked them in a studio, and demanded help to go on the air with an appeal to the nation to fight on. An executive slipped out of the building and tried to get word to the palace. With the soldiers holding the building, there would be no broadcast of the Voice of the Crane.

Shortly before 5 A.M. on August 15, Major Hatanaka walked into NHK's Studio 2, put a pistol to the head of Morio Tateno, an announcer, and said he was taking over the five o'clock news broadcast. Tateno refused to let him near the microphone. Hatanaka, who had just killed two army officers, cocked his pistol but then lowered it, impressed by Tateno's courage. In the meantime, an engineer had disconnected the building from the radio tower. If Hatanaka had spoken into a microphone, his words would have gone nowhere.

Lieutenant Colonel Takeshita tried once more to get General Anami to join the plot. But the minister of war again declined, saying he intended to commit *seppuku*. This he did some hours later in his home, in front of Takeshita. Kneeling on a mat and facing toward the palace, he drove an heirloom dagger into his stomach and drew it across his waist and upward. He then removed the knife and thrust it into his neck. As he lingered, Takeshita pushed the knife in deeper, until Anami finally died. Had Anami decided to join the plotters, it is possible that the war would have dragged on much longer—perhaps until he fought the Decisive Battle on the beaches.

✦

AT DAWN in Tokyo on August 15, loyal troops rounded up the mutineers they could find and liberated the palace without gunfire or incident. In the days that followed, nearly 500 more military men, including at least eight generals, followed Anami's example, choosing to kill themselves rather than see their country surrender. Among them was General Shizuichi Tanaka, the commander of the Eastern District Army, who waited until he was convinced there would be no further rebellion. Admiral Takajiro Ohnishi, the man who conceived the kamikaze air force, killed himself, as did Admiral Matome Ugaki, commander of the Fifth Air Fleet on Kyushu. Late in the afternoon of August 15, Ugaki led eleven Suisei dive-bombers, each with a crew of two, to Okinawa, hoping to die in the act of sinking American ships there. None reached their target; all perished at sea.

Major Hatanaka ended his mutiny outside the palace gates on August 15, trying to hand out leaflets that called on civilians to "join with us to fight for the preservation of our country and the elimination of the traitors around the emperor." No one took them. Hatanaka then shot himself in the head. A fellow conspirator stabbed himself in the stomach with his sword, then shot himself in the head. Around the same time, alone in an army office, Major Koga drew his sword and committed *seppuku*. Captain Uehara, who had joined Hatanaka in the murder of General Mori, fatally shot himself.

In separate cars using different routes, the NHK engineers took the records to the radio station and hid one set in an underground studio. At 7:21 A.M., Morio Tateno went on the air. Without recounting the adventures of the night, he announced, "His Majesty the emperor has issued a rescript. It will be broadcast at noon today. Let us all respectfully listen to the voice of the emperor. . . . Power will be specially transmitted to those districts where it is not usually available during daylight hours. Receivers should be prepared and ready at all railroad stations, postal departments, and offices both government and private."

(At the same time—6:21 P.M. on August 14 in Washington—President Truman was preparing to make his own announcement to the press some forty minutes later: Japan had surrendered. The war was over. Truman almost certainly did not know about the abortive coup.)

At noon throughout Japan, groups gathered to listen to the emperor. As his voice was heard, "the response of listeners was practically uniform throughout the whole nation," Kazuo Kawai, editor of the *Nippon Times,* later wrote. "In virtually every group, someone—generally a woman—broke out in a gasping sob. Then the men, who with contorted features had been trying to stay their tears, also quickly broke down. Within a few minutes almost everyone was weeping unabashedly as a wave of emotion engulfed the populace. It was sudden mass hysteria on a national scale."

The Voice of the Crane had an original view of the war. "We declared war on America and Britain," the emperor said, "out of our sincere desire to ensure Japan's self-preservation and the stabilization of East Asia, it being far from our thought either to infringe upon the sovereignty of other nations or to embark upon territorial aggrandizement."

The "war situation," he went on, "has developed not necessarily to Japan's advantage, while the general trends of the world have turned against her interest. Moreover, the enemy has begun to employ a new and most cruel bomb, the power of which to do damage is indeed incalculable, taking the toll of many innocent lives. . . . However, it is according to the dictate of time and fate that we have resolved to pave the way for a grand peace for all the generations to come by enduring the unendurable and suffering what is insufferable."

In his long and solemn speech, the emperor never used the words "defeat" or "surrender." But the message was clear. The Voice of the Crane had told his country what no other voice could have dared to say: The war was over, and Japan was a defeated nation.